The Cinema of Naruse Mikio

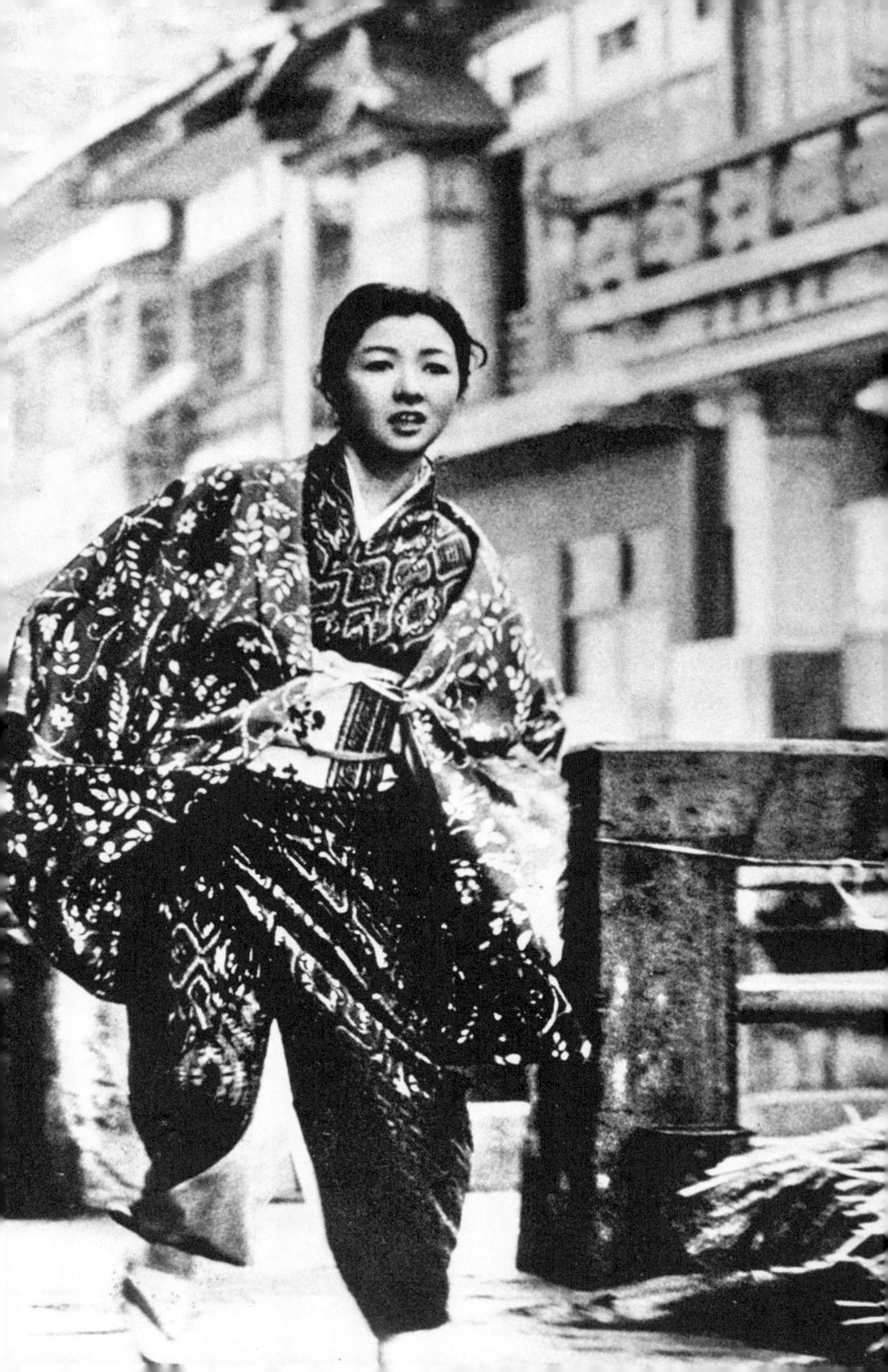

CATHERINE RUSSELL

The Cinema of Naruse Mikio

WOMEN AND JAPANESE MODERNITY

Duke University Press   Durham and London   2008

© 2008 Duke University Press
All rights reserved
Printed in the United States of America
on acid-free paper ∞
Designed by C. H. Westmoreland
Typeset in Adobe Jenson by
Tseng Information Systems, Inc.
Library of Congress Cataloging-in-Publication
Data appear on the last printed page
of this book.

Duke University Press gratefully acknowledges the support of the Japan Foundation, which provided funds toward the production of this book.

FOR MY PARENTS
SUE AND PETER RUSSELL

CONTENTS

ACKNOWLEDGMENTS   ix

PREFACE   xi

INTRODUCTION: The Auteur as Salaryman   1

1   The Silent Films: Women in the City, 1930–1934   39

2   Naruse at P.C.L.: Toward a Japanese Classical Cinema, 1935–1937   81

3   Not a Monumental Cinema: Wartime Vernacular, 1938–1945   131

4   The Occupation Years: Cinema, Democracy, and Japanese Kitsch, 1945–1952   167

5   The Japanese Woman's Film of the 1950s, 1952–1958   226

6   Naruse in the 1960s: Stranded in Modernity, 1958–1967   315

CONCLUSION   398

NOTES   405

FILMOGRAPHY   431

BIBLIOGRAPHY   435

INDEX   447

1. Naruse Mikio in 1933. Courtesy Kawakita Institute.

ACKNOWLEDGMENTS

Writing this book has been a collaboration with a great number of people over a long period. Such a project would not have been possible without the support and encouragement, language, and research skills of dozens of friends, colleagues, and students. A few individuals have been particularly important collaborators. Chika Kinoshita did a huge amount of research in Japanese archives, providing an excellent annotated bibliography and translation of many of the reviews of Naruse's cinema published in Japanese. This research became a vital part of my study. Guy Yasko translated over a dozen film transcripts and countless articles, and provided me with an extremely high level of expertise in Japanese language and culture at a critical point in the project. Kiyoaki Ohkubo was instrumental in providing Japanese language sources and enabled me to make this study far more comprehensive than I had ever dreamed. Adam Rosadiuk worked with me very closely in developing the frame grabs to illustrate the book, combining technical skills with an appreciation for Naruse's visual style. All four of these individuals contributed insights into this cinema that inevitably made their way into the book on all kinds of different levels.

Among the many students and assistants who helped me with translation, I would like to especially thank Yuko Yamade for her dedication to the project. Other translators include Adrienne Gibb, Kumi Hishikawa, D. R. Lindberg, David Lewis, Akiko Mizoguchi, Rumi Motohashi, Zen Nakamura, Ayano Nishikai, Tomoko Okabe, Daichi Saito, Akira Takahashi, and Ichiro Takayoshi. For their administrative assistance I would like to thank Gilda Boffa, Randolph Jordan, Hong Nguyen, Jodi Ramer, and anyone else whose name might have been accidentally left off this list.

For her invaluable assistance, advice, and support, I am especially indebted to Joanne Bernardi. Markus Nornes has also followed this project for quite some time and his support has been absolutely invaluable. Other individuals from the larger community who have helped me include Daisuke Miyao, David Desser, Dennis Doros, Iwamoto Kenji, Thomas Lamarre, Livia Monnet, James Quant, Michael Raine, Peter Rist, Susanne Schermann, Trond Trondsen, and Mitsuyo Wada-Marciano.

Various parts of the book have been published in earlier forms in a number of places, including *Camera Obscura*, no. 60 (2005): 57–89; *CineAction!* 60 (2003): 34–44; *Asian Journal of Communications* 11, no. 2 (2001): 101–20; *Asian Cinema* 10 (1998): 120–25; *Japanese Cinema: Texts and Contexts*, ed. Julian Springer and Alastair Phillips (London: Routledge, 2007), 124–36; *Global Cities: Cinema, Architecture, and Urbanism in a Digital Age*, ed. Linda Krause and Patrice Petro (New Brunswick, N.J.: Rutgers University Press, 2003), 87–114. I am grateful to all the editors of these books and journals for their help and support of the project. Sections have also appeared in liner notes for DVD publications by Masters of Cinema (*Meshi*, *Sound of the Mountain*, and *Flowing*) and the Criterion Collection (*When a Woman Ascends the Stairs*). Financial support of the project was provided by the Social Sciences and Humanities Research Council of Canada, the Faculty of Fine Arts at Concordia University, and by the Japan Foundation. At Duke University Press, Ken Wissoker has once again proven himself to be a supportive and enthusiastic editor.

At home, I would like to thank all the women of Choeur Maha for their fabulous company and uplifting voices. And last but not least, I must thank my partner, Marco Leyton, for—among many, many other things—watching so many Naruse films with me and loving them equally.

PREFACE

Over the years in which I've been working on this project, those who know Naruse's cinema invariably ask me which film is my favorite. I have no answer to this question. I like all the films, to different degrees perhaps, and for different reasons, and the process of discovering this cinema has been one of continual surprise and unexpected pleasure. Naruse seems not to have been able to make a truly bad film; but equally important is that my approach throughout has been to develop a methodology that would highlight the aesthetic values of his cinema without resorting to hierarchical or competitive models of ranking. For some cinephiles this might be a disappointment, and the study might appear to be disordered, but I hope that by replacing evaluative classification with historical analysis, another kind of knowledge might be produced about this director of women's films.

My fascination with this cinema led me to treat it comprehensively, without leaving out a single one of the extant films. Of Naruse's twenty-four silent films, nineteen have been lost, and of the sixty-five sound films, two have been lost, and one is available only in incomplete form.[1] However, I have been fortunate to view all the remaining sixty-seven of the eighty-nine titles in Naruse's filmography, including two short films that were produced as part of omnibus features.[2] The bulk of this book consists of close readings of these films. When I began working on this project, I thought I would have twenty to thirty titles to work with and that my analyses would be based on hastily scribbled notes in the dark.

But when the films gradually became available on VHS, and then on DVD, and broadcast on NHK television in Japan, I became a collector of Naruse's films. In this form, they became fragments of one much longer film, with recurring characters and motifs, plot twists and car accidents.

As many of the analyses in this book are based on electronic copies, the book can be located at the intersection of two forms of cinephilia as described by Thomas Elsaesser. The first "love of cinema" that has sustained an art cinema since the 1920s, fetishizing the big-screen indulgence in the image, has arguably given way to a second form of cinephilia fed by the "infinite archive" of DVD and video, but both forms, Elsaesser argues, are about memory.[3] Naruse's cinema was produced within the framework of a commercial film industry in which it was somewhat marginalized, but it has had a second life within the international cinephiliac culture of retrospectives and cinematheques. The scarcity of his films has endowed them with a certain cult value. One feels lucky to attend a screening of a film and luckier still, once in its grasp, to be caught in its flow, in a familiar "Narusian" world.

If my experience has been one of pleasure and discovery, the "memory" inscribed in Narusian cinephilia is not mine. In fact, by shifting the terms from evaluative ranking to cultural history, the nostalgia embedded in this cinema might be reconfigured as a historical awakening. For Elsaesser, it is our "mediated" relation to memory that is enacted in the cinephilia of the collector and the festivalgoer. It is precisely this media memory that is embodied in Naruse's largely forgotten cinema, cast aside in the Japanese headlong rush into modernity and the flight from the anxious memory of the Pacific war and its aftermath, a history in which Naruse was deeply implicated as a producer of mass culture.

Indeed, many other Japanese filmmakers and films from the studio era covered by this book (1930–67) have been forgotten, lost to critical study. If one of the methodological troubles of this book is the lack of comparison with Naruse's contemporaries over the thirty-seven years of his career, it is partially due to the relative lack of material available in translation. This said, many crucial and critical comparisons might be made with Naruse's more well-known contemporaries—Mizoguchi, Ozu, and Kurosawa—only a few of which are followed up on. A more comprehensive comparative study would require several volumes more than this already overstretched study. Therefore, I leave it to the reader and to other critics to fill in those crucial points of contact between Naruse and his contemporary auteurs.

Unlike conventional auteurist studies, I cannot really testify to the distinctiveness of Naruse's cinema, the degree to which it departs from the industry norms of his career, or the degree to which it is representative and typical of other studio products. My aim instead is to indicate how this cinema participates in and contributes to Japanese modernity as a cultural movement. The distinctiveness is something that can be accounted for only in the continuity and recognition of the director's name. By working through the films of Naruse, I hope to show in more detail the advantages of a critical methodology that shifts the focus from a discourse of "masterpieces" and "artworks" to one that is more culturally embedded. It furthermore enables us to avoid the pitfalls of national-cinema essentialism; it allows us to account for Naruse's weaker films alongside the outstanding ones; and it offers a means of tracing the construction of female subjectivity within Japanese cinema of the studio era. I hope that the book can provide a methodological model applicable to other collections of films.

Despite my claim not to be ranking the films, it will become apparent that there is an evaluative methodology at work, based on the extent to which the films expose the contradictions of everyday life, their representation of women's roles in family and society, and the narrative construction of women's agency and subjectivity. Formal analysis is balanced throughout with narrative analysis, as I am interested in what the films are about as well as how they are made. For this reason, plot descriptions have not been annexed or appended, but are integrated into the discussion of each film. Naruse's storytelling is very much immersed in the materialism of everyday life, in which every piece of clothing and item of food plays a crucial role. His editing patterns are governed by eye movements, architecture, weather patterns, and figure movement; his camera movements are governed by emotional expression and technologies of transportation. Naruse's aesthetics, in other words, cannot be separated from narrative event and detail.

In assessing the internal contradictions of Naruse's films, I am looking for ways that they enact a critique of Japanese society and point to the potential for social change and transformation. I will argue that Naruse's cinema details the ideological contradictions of the lost promises of the Meiji Reformation, followed by the false promise of the "democratic revolution" of the American occupation. Despite the many changes in the material culture of everyday life, social relations in Japan at the end of Naruse's career in the mid-1960s remained entrenched in outdated paradigms, as they arguably continue to do so even today. Inequities of class and gender, urban alienation and despair, and loss of faith in modernity are evident throughout the prewar and postwar films. In the twenty-six films that he made during the war and occupation, films that were ostensibly "politically correct" in order to pass the two very different sets of ideological regulations, contradictions are rampant. These contradictions suggest that popular culture and official policies were not always in sync. In his ability to work without pause throughout the thirty-seven years of his career, Naruse represents a continuity within a rapidly changing social and cultural formation. Analyzing the heterogeneity of the films and the career in terms of contradictions enables a reading of the ideological pressures and fissures within popular culture.

Especially looking back at these films from the historical and cultural distance that my readings articulate, Naruse's forward-looking characters, survivors of a dysfunctional class-bound society, seem to be stranded historically, as their "promise" is in many ways yet to be met. Especially with the benefit of historical and cultural distance, the films tend to take on an anthropological aspect and come to constitute an ethnography of modern Japanese culture. What distinguishes Naruse's ethnography is the way that he enables us to observe the desires and disappointments within women's lives over the middle decades of twentieth-century Japan.

In challenging the art cinema/popular culture divide as thoroughly as he does, Naruse invites a new critical methodology. Miriam Hansen has introduced the term *vernacular modernism* to refer to the way that, in the interwar years at least, Hollywood cinema constituted a modern democratizing influence on global metropolitan culture.[4] In Tokyo, as in Shanghai and other capitals of the world in the early 1930s, cinema was at the apex of a modern mode of experience, an experience that Ben Singer has further linked to the sensationalism of melodrama in silent cinema.[5] In the early years of his career, Naruse's cinema was at the center of Japanese modernity, featuring new women doing new things in the context of a new technology of representation. In tracing his depiction of women and their stories through the difficult Fifteen Years' War and seven years of occupation, we can see how the mass culture of the era functioned within the interstices of ideology and humanism. The perpetuation of modernity within its ostensible overcoming gave way to the abrupt shift in cultural imperatives dictated by the occupation authorities. In the continuity of Naruse's cinema, the vernacular modernism of the early 1930s becomes the foundation of the modernism of the 1950s.

Naruse's best-known films, such as *Sound of the Mountain* (*Yama no* oto, 1954), *Late Chrysanthemums* (*Bangiku*, 1954), and *Floating Clouds* (*Ukigumo*, 1955), have been recognized as part of the golden age of Japan's postwar cinema. Japanese modernity and modernism converge in Naruse's poetics, particularly in his ongoing use and revision of the "home drama" or *shoshimin-eiga* genre (films about "ordinary people"). The later years of his career feature a more spectacular mode of melodrama as Naruse's modernism converges with the discourses of excess in the 1960s. Even up to his last film, *Scattered Clouds* (aka *Two in the Shadow* [*Midaregumo*], 1967), Naruse's modernity remains vernacular, and his cinema is emblematic of Hansen's category in that it offers a "sensory-reflexive horizon for the contradictory experience of modernity."[6]

Moreover, we may be able to see more clearly, in the great stylistic variations within this body of work, how melodrama, vernacular modernism, and the historical-cultural analysis of mass culture converge as a critical methodology. The shifting of critical emphasis is furthermore articulated within what Walter Benjamin describes as a rescuing critique. My feminist analysis of a director and a body of work that engaged with neither the politics nor the vocabulary of feminism is explicitly made from outside the cultural framework of the films' production and reception. As Benjamin puts it in "On the Concept of History": "Articulating the past historically does not mean recognizing it 'the way it really was.' It means appropriating a memory as it flashes up in a moment of danger."[7] From the retrospective historical vantage point of transnational feminism, the utopian potential of Naruse's cinema and its implicit longing for social change might be recognized within the work.

Another question frequently posed to me is how I can complete this study without any comprehension of the Japanese language. Although this has not prevented many other scholars from writing about Japanese cinema, it is an important and valid concern. I have viewed many of the films with transcripts of the dialogue translated into English. Likewise, I have had a selection of Japanese-language criticism translated in an effort to gauge the reception of the films at the time of their release, as well as more recent criticism and interviews published by Japanese scholars. However, it is inevitable that fundamental aspects of both the dialogue in the films and the published criticism remain inaccessible to me. No translation can perfectly capture the idiosyncrasies of dialect, intonation, language use and—especially important in Japanese—the levels and effects of politesse and gender that are embodied in language.

With these reservations in mind, it is also true that cinema communicates on many levels besides spoken and written language. Analyses based on effects of lighting, camera, music, performance, costume, architecture, and set design can be productive, but this method too can miss key significations that are culturally specific. Yet, because Naruse's cinema has begun to circulate outside Japan, it remains open, in my view, to a plurality of readings. This is not to say that film is a universal language. Indeed, the notion of vernacular modernism implies a complex play of hybridization between the influences of the "global" culture of narrative cinema and the modification and continual reinvention of "local" Japanese culture and tradition.

Naruse's cinema was overlooked by Western scholars and critics for so many years in part because it was not seen to be formally radical enough. It was perceived to be "too close" to the Hollywood norm, despite its distinctive poetics based in Japanese architecture, literature, and design. Especially after 1935, through to the end of his career, Naruse's editing is more or less "invisible," and the films are stylish only to the degree that the characters and sets are stylish—which they often are. One of the arguments of this book is that Naruse's cinema is exemplary of a Japanese classical cinema. In keeping with Hansen's notion of vernacular modernism, it brings together the codes of classical narration with the modernity of new modes of experience and subjectivity and does so within the parameters of mass culture.

Naruse's cinema constitutes a language that is neither strictly Japanese nor strictly "Hollywood," but is that of Japanese modernity, understood as an urban, industrialized, mass-media-saturated society. Japanese modernity can in fact be dated back to the Meiji Restoration of the mid-nineteenth century, when Japanese institutions and social practices began to accommodate Western principles of "enlightenment" social organization. Modern Japan has gone through many phases since then; thus the term *Japanese modernity* is necessarily a flexible and open-ended notion. Postwar modernism, and its slow fade into Japanese postmodernism, are further semantic variations on the theme of Japan's anxious relation with the West, in which the unevenness of modernity continues to be a key feature.[8] For the purposes of this study, however, Japanese modernity denotes an era, roughly contiguous with Naruse's career, in which Japanese mass culture took on a primary role in the representation and fantasizing of everyday life.

Following Harry Harootunian, Japanese modernity needs to be recognized as exemplary of the process by which "modernity was always a doubling that imprinted the difference between the demands of capitalism and the force of received forms of history and culture ... in the space of everyday life."⁹ From the interwar period to the early 1960s, the Japanese studio system was the third largest in the world. Along with his contemporaries in the industry, Naruse produced a cinema that bears the traces of the foreign—including American-style individualism and female agency—and the traces of the Japanese—in the form of architecture, costume, gesture, language, and so on. These elements are combined within an industrial mode of storytelling, again hybridizing Western and Japanese narrative modes, and within a genre of everydayness, the shoshimin-eiga, making this cinema particularly emblematic of Harootunian's definition of Japanese modernity.

The category of Japanese modernity, although necessarily imprecise, is an important means of avoiding an essentialization of Naruse's cinema within categories of Orientalism or cultural nationalism. As a cultural economy of desire, fantasy, materialism, and everyday life, Japanese modernity is rife with contradictions and unevenness. It is precisely within this decidedly anxious social formation that the discourse of female subjectivity in Naruse's cinema is produced. By recognizing the contradictions within Japanese modernity, I am proposing that Japanese film studies might be able to move beyond the paradigms of modernism, nationalism, and otherness that, as Mitsuhiro Yoshimoto has pointed out, have seriously hindered the study of Japanese cinema.[10]

In film studies, Japanese cinema has had a longstanding place in the canon of film history, mainly because it presented an "alternative" to the Hollywood norm, which is how I first encountered it myself. I first became interested in Japanese culture at the tail end of the Western countercultural embrace of Zen Buddhism in the 1960s and 1970s. My Japanophilia was, however, quickly corrected by the translation and publication of Oshima Nagisa's writings in 1992, and through his writing and filmmaking, I came to understand that the beauty of Japanese aesthetics cannot be separated from the repressive and authoritarian cultural formation in which it originated. The critical theory associated with the Frankfurt school has always seemed eminently relevant to the contradictions of Japanese culture, and when I began to explore the question of gender in Japanese cinema, I quickly learned of the cinema of Naruse Mikio.

Although Naruse is not a radical filmmaker in any sense of the term, his cinema challenges much of the received wisdom and most critical conventions of Japanese film studies. The blossoming of critical cultural theory by Japanese studies scholars in English over the past fifteen years has shaped a new interdisciplinary space for the study of Japanese film. My approach to Naruse's cinema is indebted to this burgeoning body of work, along with the stimulating body of Japanese literary theory and criticism that has been published in recent years. Japanese film studies as a field of study has itself been greatly enhanced by the work of bilingual film scholars with access to primary sources in Japanese. This book relies greatly on this new interdisciplinary, intercultural, transnational disciplinary formation.

Because of Naruse's own modesty, and his willingness and ability to move with the fashion of the times, his oeuvre provides us with a collection of texts by which we can trace the vernacular modernism of mid-twentieth-century Japan. A detailed overview of Naruse's career will be followed in the introduction by an elaboration of the role of gender in the changing social formation during the thirty-seven years in which he worked, and the implications for the methodology of this study. Following that, the films are divided into six chronological chapters, each of which will offer an introductory discussion of how Naruse's modernity intersects with the history of the film industry and the national culture.

In selecting illustrations for this study, the new technology of DVD frame grabs provided a fantastic opportunity to slow down Naruse's editing patterns. The so-called invisibility of his editing is partially due to its pace. Although it certainly slowed down somewhat when he turned to wide-screen compositions toward the end of his career, he never actually thoroughly adopted the "rules" of continuity editing. Nor did he ever stop moving the camera, and the complex choreographies of figures, facial expressions, camera movement, and montage are clearly impossible to "capture" with frame grabs. Nevertheless, I have attempted to indicate, through the reproduction of sequences from many of the films, how they are constructed and how their movement is generated. Access to these films in English is presently extremely limited, but I hope that this situation will change soon and that English-language viewers will soon discover this remarkable filmmaker for themselves.

A note on Japanese names: Throughout the book, all Japanese names are given in Japanese order with the family name preceding the given name. When the person has published in English using conventional English name order, that order has been retained.

INTRODUCTION

The Auteur as Salaryman

Mr. Naruse was more than merely reticent: he was a person whose refusal to talk was downright malicious. —TAKAMINE HIDEKO

This is now the time for Naruse to reveal all the qualities and aspects of his cinema to the world.... the urgent need is to find a theory of film that suits this Age of Discovery. —HASUMI SHIGEHIKO

Almost all the writing in English on Naruse Mikio begins with a lament about the critical neglect he has suffered, a neglect closely linked to the relative unavailability of his films. Except for infrequent and largely incomplete retrospectives in North America and Europe since the 1980s, most of Naruse's eighty-nine films remain unknown to contemporary cinephiles. Although a substantial amount has been written in Japanese on Naruse, little has been translated, and in popular cultural history his name remains a virtual secret.[1] Within the tendency to rank directors in Japan, Naruse is frequently listed as the "number four" auteur, following Kurosawa, Mizoguchi, and Ozu in international—and Japanese—recognition. However, as Hasumi Shigehiko and Yamane Sadao point out, Naruse was not a "number one" sort of person, and he may partially have his own modesty to blame for his underappreciation.[2] Equally true, though, is the fact that Japanese producers did not see the need to promote films made for female audiences beyond their initial theatrical runs, and they did not see the export value in them either.[3]

Naruse was, above all else, a studio director, a company man who was notorious for bringing films in on time, on or under budget. He was not always pleased with his results but moved on quickly to the next production. His name became linked to women's pictures, and that was what he did best. Even his distinctive emphasis on female protagonists can be attributed to the industry practice of enhancing images of actresses associated with the studio, and in the 1960s especially, at the end of his career, his films were recognized as Toho films first and Naruse films second.[4] When the films of his contemporaries were first embraced by film critics outside Japan in the 1950s, Naruse was more or less overlooked.

One film, *Mother* (*Okaasan*, 1952), was screened in Paris in 1954, catching the attention of *Cahiers du cinéma* critics,[5] and remained in repertory circulation for the next few decades, but it wasn't until a retrospective of twenty-four films in Locarno, Italy, in 1983 that the larger body of work began to circulate outside Japan. Another, larger retrospective in San Sebastian in 1998 initiated a new round of screenings, including a comprehensive selection of thirty-seven films in Paris in 2001, followed by a touring show originating in Toronto in 2005. While the critical attention has significantly increased in the last decade, it is astonishing that a director with such a remarkable and distinctive oeuvre could be so overlooked. The delay in recognition points to the ways that the critical frameworks of orientalism, formalism, and auteurism that have governed the discipline of film studies are woefully inadequate for a director such as Naruse.

To compound the problem of critical appreciation, Naruse himself was an enigmatic and noncommunicative figure, notably lacking self-expression.[6] His humility and dedication to Toho, where he made more than half of his films, may partially explain his self-effacing manner, so that despite the visceral emotional impact of his films, there remains a curious emptiness at the center of his work. He came from a poor family, trained briefly as a mechanic, and began working as a prop man at Shochiku studio at the age of fifteen in 1920 when his father died.[7] He was briefly married to the actress Chiba Sachiko in 1930s and remarried after the war. His wife Naruse Tsumeko describes him in a 1993 interview as a very "serious" person, almost like an "old-time samurai" who had "no cracks in his character." She claims that he did not like to be called *sensei* by his assistant directors, or to ride in the back seat of his chauffeur-driven cars. She also describes him as "scary," perhaps because he did not express his anger directly and was more interested in emotions than in things—or, one suspects, people.[8] Although they had children, there is no evidence of Naruse as a family man. He seemed to be entirely devoted to his work, and relaxed only when drinking with colleagues such as his longtime director of photography Tamai Masao, who also claimed not to know anything about Naruse's private life.[9] Takamine Hideko, who made seventeen films with Naruse, says that she never once had a drink with him.[10] Naruse passed away in 1969, at the age of sixty-four, two years after making his last film, *Scattered Clouds* (*Midaregumo*, 1967).

It is difficult to attribute a particular worldview or social politics to Naruse. The American critic Audie Bock attributes Naruse's "gloomy outlook" to his own poor origins, yet after 1935 he was a well-paid salaryman. He gave very few interviews and provided only the most cursory and enigmatic comments on his films, which are notoriously open-ended and inconclusive. The beauty of his cinema lies partly in its passivity and restraint, so while the openness of the films brings them into the realm of modernist art and literature, they are sociological without being didactic or moralizing. The "darkness" often attributed to Naruse refers to the way the films evade the conventions of the happy ending, yet the spirit of "life goes on" never entails a simple resignation to fate or destiny. The most often cited words of Naruse may be his bleak claim, "From the youngest age, I have thought that the world we live in betrays us; this thought remains with me."[11] His films, however, are also full of the promise and possibility within social change, and his characters are rich and dynamic and often full of humor. It would be a mistake to let this view of life dominate the image of the director, whose films speak far more eloquently than does he.

Naruse's assistant director Okamoto Kihachi reports that in the late 1950s Naruse gave him the following advice: "You should stick to your own ideas. If you run from left to right and back again to suit the changing times, the results will be hollow. Look at me. I've been the same from before the war, up till now. What has changed has been fashion: sometimes it has coincided with my ideas, and sometimes it hasn't."[12]

As Naruse was neither an intellectual nor a diarist, his "ideas" as such were never clearly articulated. His preoccupation with women's stories, social justice, material hardship, and emotional turbulence give us some clues to his thoughts, and his intuitive sense of rhythm and visual composition indicate further thoughts about form. But equally importantly, Naruse had a profound sense of "fashion," which is to say that his own "ideas" are expressed in the regime of a visual culture that is in constant flux. This, I would argue, is the only way that a film director could possibly have such a long and prolific career. Most of the critical work on

Naruse focuses on his production during the two golden ages of the 1930s and 1950s. But if we look at the complete body of Naruse's work, including the two so-called slumps of the 1940s and 1960s, we can get a much better picture of the director himself, and of his times.

A consistency of tone, style, and thematics can most definitely be traced across this huge oeuvre, but there is also a stunning variety within the films, as Naruse continued throughout his career to explore new technologies and genres. The unevenness of his career challenges some longstanding auteurist principles. We shall see how he continued working under two radically different censorship regimes through the 1930s and 1940s, easily adapting to the ideology of the day. He allegedly never said "no" to any project,[13] but fortunately, given his reliability, he was frequently offered excellent literary sources to adapt. Japanese critics have long recognized him as a master of literary adaptation.

Naruse's 1935 film *Wife! Be Like a Rose!* (*Tsuma yo bara no yo ni*) was the first Japanese feature to get a commercial run in the United States, and it also won the prestigious *Kinema Junpo* first prize. *Wife! Be Like a Rose!* has been singled out by Western film critics as one of the great films of the period, although it has also been misunderstood as a formally radical example of avant-garde practice. In his orientalist method of praising antirealist effects of alterity in Japanese film, Noel Burch celebrates Naruse's prewar films for their formal innovations.[14] For Burch, his single masterpiece is *Wife! Be Like a Rose!*, in which the director developed a "system of matching on foreground movement" and demonstrated "a budding sense of formalization based, in the Western manner, on the transgression of norms" (191). The rest of Naruse's career is summarily dismissed by Burch as lacking a "specifically Japanese mode of filmic representation" (192).

Burch's analysis is emblematic of the orientalism deeply embedded in formalist film studies searching for alternatives to the Hollywood norm. As many critics have subsequently pointed out, the attribution of a radical Brechtian modernism to Japanese cinema of the 1930s reflects a profound lack of understanding of Japanese modernity.[15] To Japanese audiences, the modernity of a film like *Wife! Be Like a Rose!* was unquestionably the character played by Chiba Sachiko: an independent, adventurous, and forceful young woman. Her character, Kimiko, is a modern woman who nevertheless exhibits the family values and responsibilities that were said to be lacking in the new, independent, Western-influenced women who began appearing on the streets of Tokyo in the late 1920s. A *Kinema Junpo* reviewer of the time praised the film's detailed psychological portraits of women,[16] and the film is in many ways a clever hybridization of American and Japanese styles of representation—and styles of being in the modern world.

Naruse's films of the 1930s were at the apex of Japanese modernity, not for their formal innovations, but because of their depiction of an "everyday life" thoroughly permeated with modern characters, fashions, and consumer culture. Film itself was emblematic of modernity, and Naruse's cinema performs a constant process of negotiation between modern and traditional values, between a new visual landscape of urban modernity and an older one of Japaneseness. Women's social roles and expectations were caught precisely between the newer and the older social formations, and the ambivalence of Naruse's cinema is endemic to the cultural landscape of its production. Thus, a formalist analysis such as Burch's is wholly inadequate to the innovations Naruse made within Japanese visual culture of the twentieth century. Burch's ideal of a "specifically Japanese cinema" is itself an impossibility given the profound influence of American and European cinema on all the directors and studios engaged in developing a mass culture in Japan.

Audie Bock has been most responsible for keeping Naruse's name alive in the canon of Japanese cinema and for providing a biographical history of the director's career. Her catalog essays for the Chicago retrospective in 1984 and the Locarno film festival in 1983, along with the inclusion of Naruse in her book *Japanese Film Directors*, have been the key non-Japanese texts on the director.[17] She also subtitled and distributed a number of Naruse titles in the 1980s. For Bock, Naruse is above all a realist, although she also notes his fundamental reliance on melodrama as a narrative mode. His characters tend to reside at the "edges of respectability," where the detail of everyday life is part and parcel of the difficulties they face. His female characters—wives, widows, geisha, waitresses, businesswomen, and mothers—complain relentlessly about their circumstances. The hazards of modern life, including traffic accidents, straying husbands, and errant lovers and children, debt, and illness, constitute the social forces stacked up against Naruse's characters.

Bock's observations on Naruse's outlook indicate how his cinema evades both idealism and sentimentality: "There is no humanism in this cinema, because Naruse does not believe in the perfectibility of Man; no naturalism, because Naruse does not blame human suffering on outside causes; and neither is there idealism. His work evinces a harsh realism, demanding and without compensations. Naruse has sketched a portrait of that incurable wound that is called Life."[18] Despite her claim to the contrary, Bock nevertheless tends to situate Naruse within a humanist frame of reference. As Mitsuhiro Yoshimoto has pointed out, "the axiomatic characteristics of the humanist scholarship on Japanese cinema basically preclude possibilities of political intervention."[19] Because Naruse's career is so closely tied to shifts within the film industry, and to Japanese history on a larger scale, it is deeply inscribed within a cultural fabric of social difference, economic constraints, and geopolitical pressures. A humanist orientation focused on the "universal" principles of character, morality, and human relations is ultimately ill equipped to assess the contribution of this cinema to the construction of Japanese modernity.

Naruse's extensive body of work tends to force the critical opposition between art and popular culture into precarious alignment. As Phillip Lopate notes, "Naruse seems to lack an immediately identifiable 'arty' trademark."[20] One of the reasons Naruse's cinema has eluded critical attention is that, unlike many art-cinema auteurs, his is not a "long take" aesthetic. Nor is his style as rigorous or as systematic as Ozu's or other directors such as Bresson or Eisenstein who are known for montage-based styles.

Naruse's editing is quick paced, and after 1935, more or less invisible, even if he continues to break many conventions of continuity editing throughout his career. His editing is also rhythmic—the timing of scenes and the flow of the narrative are the most distinctive elements of his filmmaking across four decades of stylistic variation. Moreover, the rhythm of seasons and the weather, overlaid with the regular routines of everyday life, constitutes a kind of pulse that is frequently taken up by itinerant musicians (or extradiegetic clacking sticks) and gives each and every film a kind of inner energy. Some of the recurring motifs, such as two characters walking and talking, or a house lit from inside through soft paper screens, make this pulsing rhythm almost visible. Then the flow of everyday life is repeatedly interrupted—by sudden changes in the weather, or by illness, or by a car accident.

The most comprehensive effort to characterize Naruse's stylistics has been offered by Jean Narboni, whose study of thirty-four films emphasizes the musicality of this cinema, again within a humanist frame of reference.[21] For Narboni, Naruse is perhaps closer to Schubert than to any other cineaste. His title, *Les temps incertains*, registers the role of timing, and also the weather in the films. He points out that Naruse concentrates on the effects of unseen causes, and indeed the big things, like weddings, death, and the war, take place offscreen. Yet human suffering is caused not only by external forces, but often comes from within the characters themselves, who are implicitly imperfect. The recurring theme of illness is a means by which emotional states are somatized, affecting the body itself.[22] Narboni describes Naruse's realism as a form of naturalism in which reality is not "captured" but is a quality of the form itself: "In the spatio-temporal framework of fiction, the real is in infinite flight, existing before and without the fiction; and destined to continue after the end."[23]

In Susanne Schermann's study of Naruse, originally published in German and recently translated into Japanese, she argues that his fifteen years working in silent film provide the key to his subsequent career. His emphasis on editing and montage, his tendency to reduce dialogue to the minimum, and his ability to integrate the effects of new technologies all point to his formation in the silent period. Moreover, his straightforward approach to storytelling might also be attributed to the methods of silent film.[24] Schermann says that he never shot over a 2.5:1 ratio throughout his career, and he usually made a ninety-minute film in thirty days. Moreover, he insisted that the best films were those that made money, and that his work was more or less disposable—made literally for immediate consumption.

Schermann quotes him as saying, "Movies are ephemeral. They disappear in one or two weeks. A complete library of a director's works cannot be made."[25] From the silent period through to the 1960s, Naruse remained attached to the commodity form of the film text, always staying within his budget, planning the production down to the last yen, the last hour, and the last foot of film. Bock describes Naruse as a *katsudoya*, a term that refers to a craftsman of the old school of filmmaking, when filmmakers churned out up to ten films a year.[26] By the end of his career, the nostalgia associated with the shoshimin-eiga was infused with the nostalgia for the production method itself.

Given Naruse's attitude toward his own work, it is no wonder that it has taken this long for the films to be fully appreciated. At the same time, his casual approach to his "art" flies in the face of auteurist studies that strive to find a unity and coherence within the work that might be attached to some kind of personal vision. It is clearly an oeuvre highly contingent on history and embedded in the ever-changing public sphere to which the films are addressed. Naruse was a stalwart part of an industrial mode of production, a salaryman who never missed a paycheck through four decades of cultural change (with the exception of the Toho strikes of 1948). Moreover, as a key contributor to the mass culture of modern Japan, he arguably helped to shape this cultural transformation—not on the level of ideology, but on the level of the sensual experience of everyday life.

A Short History
EIGHTY-NINE FILMS IN THIRTY-SEVEN YEARS

Most of the twenty-three films Naruse made between 1930 and 1934 at Shochiku's Kamata studio were *nansensu* comedies, which evolved into *shinpa*-style melodramas of failed romances and broken families, culminating in two successful features in 1933: *Apart from You* (*Kimi to wakarete*) and *Every Night Dreams* (*Yogoto no yume*). Although only five of these silent films have survived, those five display an astonishing technical prowess, with some of the most dynamic editing and camera movement to be found in the silent period. Despite their virtuosity, Kido Shiro, the influential Shochiku producer, disliked Naruse's bleak vision and found his style to be too similar to Ozu's, the studio's top director. Naruse had begun to specialize in the shoshimin-eiga that Ozu also specialized in, making films about "ordinary people" (or petite bourgeoisie) in contemporary settings,[27] and Kido reportedly announced, "We don't need another Ozu."[28]

Naruse did not move with Shochiku to Ofuna but went instead to P.C.L., which became Toho in 1937. There he began making sound films and adapting scripts from literary sources, beginning with Kawabata's *Three Sisters with Maiden Hearts* (*Otome-gokoro sannin shimai*, 1935) and the prizewinning *Wife! Be Like a Rose!*, which was adapted from a shinpa play. In his years at P.C.L., Naruse became entrenched in an industrial system of production that found him working on weak scripts with weak actors, and the dynamic pace of his silent films gradually slowed down. Nevertheless, the films provide insight into the consolidation of the industry and the ways it shifted toward the mise-en-scène of the bourgeoisie. Naruse's films of the mid- to late 1930s, such as *The Road I Travel with You* (*Kimi to yuku michi*, 1936), *Feminine Melancholy* (aka *A Woman's Sorrows*; *Nyonin aishu*, 1937), and *Avalanche* (*Nadare*, 1937), constitute a subtle critique of the class character of the scripts he was given to work with.

The 1930s may have been a golden age of Japanese cinema, but they also saw an increasing cultural imperialism develop over the course of the decade, culminating in the China and Pacific wars, known in Japan as the Fifteen Years' War. The intellectual discourse of the interwar period culminated in a 1942 symposium on "Overcoming Modernity" as a means of

2. Naruse Mikio circa 1957. Courtesy Kawakita Institute.

overcoming Japan's dependence on the West. But insofar as the impulse behind the vision of Japan as imperialist power constituted a "utopian aspiration to mark out a zone not yet infected by the commodity," it was in many ways a modernist movement in itself. Harry Harootunian agues that "fascism provided a kind of inner lining to modernism."[29] Produced within the sphere of industrial mass culture that adapted to the war and to its critical aftermath, Naruse's cinema provides a unique insight into how the experience of modernity shifted and was sustained through the war and occupation.

From 1938 to 1945, Naruse, like most Japanese directors, retreated to "safe" topics that would not attract the censors' attention. Some of his wartime films, such as *The Whole Family Works* (*Hataraku ikka*, 1939) and *The Way of Drama* (*Shibaido*, 1944), might be said to contain veiled cautions against jumping headlong into imperialist propaganda, but in my view, it is impossible to position Naruse as an opponent of the war. His films make it possible, however, to see how Japanese modernity was not ruptured during the war but continued within popular culture, in modified but not unrecognizable form.

Naruse's output during the seven years of American occupation is not his best effort, but the films are interesting precisely because of what they can tell us about Japanese culture during this contradictory and confusing era. He took on many challenges, including didacticism, comedy, melodrama, "social problem films," pulp fiction, and modernist literature, in settings and communities as diverse as Aomori farmers, Edo samurai, small towns, and urban Tokyo and Osaka. The occupation films feature women in professional capacities, including reporters, doctors, teachers, and businesswomen, in keeping with the occupation policy of recognizing women's rights. From 1949 to 1953, Naruse made seven films at Toho and seven films at other studios—Shochiku, Toyoko, Shin-Toho, and Daiei—before returning to Toho for the rest of his career.

The films of the 1950s are the ones that really brought Naruse into the canon of international art cinema with titles such as *Repast* (*Meshi*, 1951), *Mother*, *Lightning* (*Inazuma*, 1952), *Older Brother, Younger Sister* (*Ani imoto*, 1953), *Sound of the Mountain* (*Yama no oto*, 1954), *Late Chrysanthemums* (*Bangiku*, 1954), *Floating Clouds* (*Ukigumo*, 1955) and *Flowing* (*Nagareru*, 1956), all of which placed in the *Kinema Junpo* top ten lists. These films combine dramatic intensity with a documentary-like attention to the detail of everyday life, akin to Rossellini's postwar realism—and the affinities with Italian neorealism were certainly noted by Japanese critics.[30] Naruse's realist style articulated a Japanese modernity that could retain a national integrity on the world stage of self-representation, although it took over thirty years for that to happen. Indeed, Naruse's films of the 1950s are exceptional not only in their realist style, but also in their deflated and episodic narratives that tend toward open and ambivalent endings. The two films that were exported before the 1980s, *Wife! Be Like a Rose!* and *Mother*, tended to be read as representative of Japanese cinema—and Japanese everyday life—rather than the work of an auteur.

Jean Douchet notes that Naruse's cinema lacks Rossellini's faith in the future. "Only the present happens. And there is no past. It exists only to the extent that it is borne by the present. Consequently there is no escape."[31] The difficulty of remembering the past is an essential feature of Naruse's postwar cinema, as it was for much of Japanese culture, unable to memorialize the catastrophe of the Pacific War. For Mitsuhiro Yoshimoto, the disavowal of the war is the defining feature of the postwar cinema and its melodramatic strategies that helped to produce a national victim consciousness.[32] He singles out Naruse's film *Floating Clouds* (*Ukigumo*, 1955) as one of the few films of the period to engage directly with the responsibilities of ordinary people during the war. Indeed, this is the title that is best known in Japan and widely recognized as one of the more thoughtful treatments of the immediate postwar period. Although Yoshimoto's theorization of postwar cinema may help to explain why *Floating Clouds* remains Naruse's most well-known film in Japan, in my view the tragic figure of Yukiko in that film is an anomaly in his cinema. It is the only film in Naruse's entire body of work in which the central character dies at the end; almost all his other female protagonists are survivors.

The 1950s have generated the most extensive discussion of Naruse's style, particularly his editing technique. Kurosawa Akira's description of Naruse's editing is especially provocative:

> Naruse's method consists of building one very brief shot on top of another, but when you look at them all spliced together in the final film, they give the impression of a single long take. The flow is so magnificent that the splices are invisible. This flow of short shots looks calm and ordinary at first glance then reveals itself to be like a deep river with a quiet surface disguising a fast-raging current underneath. The sureness of his hand in this was without comparison.[33]

Naruse, a master of depicting unspoken emotions, was notorious for eliminating dialogue from the scripts that were prepared for him. The restrained acting style and relative lack of action mean that the emotional weight and drama of the films is accomplished mainly through editing. By exploiting the possibilities of 360-degree space and mismatched eye lines, a wide range of effects could be created. That the editing itself remained somewhat invisible accounts for the realist style that made his filmmaking not "Japanese" enough for Western critics looking for an aesthetic signature they could associate with the director's cultural heritage. Kurosawa's image of surface and depth also invokes a familiar model of melodrama as it has been theorized by Peter Brooks and adapted to film studies.[34] The undercurrent of emotion "raging" beneath the quotidian detail of everyday life is, in Naruse's films, an incarnation of what Brooks calls "the moral occult"—"the domain of operative spiritual values"—which in the modern world is not metaphysical but melodramatic.

The parallels and contrasts between Naruse and Ozu, who also had a long studio career, are too extensive—and too variable over the length of their careers—to adequately deal with in this study. Generally speaking, Ozu's editing and shot compositions are more rigorously designed, especially in the latter part of his career. The "presentationalism" of his style has a far more reflexive dimension that led critics in the 1970s to align it with Brechtian modernism.[35] Naruse edits more often than Ozu on character movements, and his camera moves more often with the movements in the frame, creating a more seamless visual text. His cutaways to objects and landscapes are far less intrusive than Ozu's "pillow shots," because they are linked more closely to narrative space and because he doesn't pause on them, as Ozu does, or multiply them into small sequences. Thus, while both directors worked almost exclusively within the shoshimin-eiga genre, with dedramatized narratives about family relationships, Naruse's films seem to move faster. Where Ozu tends to use straight cuts between scenes, Naruse favors dissolves and fade-outs, creating that "flow" noted by Kurosawa. Naruse's films are relatively more dramatic, with weather and music complementing the emotional highs and lows, and his stories deal, far more often than Ozu's do, with the romantic relations between men and women.

In his comparison of the two directors, Yoshida Yoshishige suggests that Naruse was the "great shadow" of Ozu.[36] The commonalities between the two were certainly recognized by the latter, who was only two years older than Naruse. They were friends, but although Naruse said next to nothing about Ozu, Ozu was eloquent about his colleague's similar "voice."[37] He was particularly impressed with *Floating Clouds*, about which he said: "You can't tell a tofu maker to make meat sausage. It simply won't work. A tofu maker can only make tofu. The only question is how tasty he can make tofu."[38] This was significant praise from a man who also compared himself to a tofu-maker.[39] Jean Narboni suggests that Ozu's enthusiasm for *Floating Clouds* influenced his 1957 film *Tokyo Twilight (Tokyo boshoku)*. He points out that in this film Ozu departed from his familiar terrain of the aging family to incorporate such Narusian elements as suicide, abortion, marital separation, and resentful children.[40] The atmosphere of "distress and abandonment" that Narboni recognizes in *Tokyo Twilight* is otherwise described by David Bordwell as "melodramatic materials" that "clash with the Ozuian penchant for suggestion and abstract structure."[41] Under the "shadow" of Naruse, Ozu's tofu takes on a markedly different texture, but we should keep in mind that, especially in Japan, tofu has many different flavors.

Sato Tadao, who describes Naruse as "a poor man's Ozu," notes that both directors avoided matching eye lines in shot–reverse shot editing patterns because direct eye contact is impolite in Japan. For Sato, Naruse's own shyness led him to adopt a style in which eye behavior was emphasized over other dramaturgical elements: "Naruse fills his scenes with glances of affection or revulsion, scorn and malice, forgiveness and resignation; his characters look away unexpectedly, eyes seem to make contact and then look away."[42] Another recurring figure is the dropped eyes, often used as a woman's response to some new difficulty or scenario. It is a sign of a character's interiority and subjectivity, while also enabling the director to hold the actor's image on screen, pausing momentarily without necessarily idealizing their beauty within an aesthetic of *feminisuto*.

Sato defines *feminisuto* as a "special brand of Japanese feminism" and associates it especially with Mizoguchi. The "worship of womanhood" in which a woman's suffering "can imbue us with admiration for a virtuous existence almost beyond our reach"[43] is patently absent from Naruse's cinema, even if he frequently draws on the cultural heritage in which this aesthetic is inscribed. Naruse's heroines, in my reading of the films, are thinking, active women. Tsuneishi Fumiko's reading of the eye movements in Naruse's cinema is somewhat more helpful than Sato's.[44] She says that the failure of characters to meet each other's gazes is symptomatic of the "ever present veil between men and women," which Tsuneishi claims is made literal in the 1937 film *Avalanche (Nadare)*. The veil is occasionally lifted, creating moments of insight and recognition, fleeting moments of understanding, complicity, and love.

The veil is largely absent from relations between women, and Naruse's cinema is full of films about houses of women, usually living and working together through their association with the "water trade," or *mizu-shobai*. This term covers a number of different social practices and institutions that change greatly over the thirty-seven years of Naruse's career but are nevertheless seen to be integral components of the social fabric, providing women with professional careers outside the home. It includes the geisha business, but also the more mundane activities of café waitresses, hostesses, and various forms of women entertaining men. The lure and threat of sexuality is always in the offing, although Naruse's women rarely succumb.

Throughout his career Naruse remained extraordinarily chaste, refraining even from indulging in the sexual explicitness of the 1960s, by which time he and his characters seemed to become more and more out of sync with the times. Nevertheless, the emotional drive of romance sustains his melodramatic modality with an extraordinary consistency. Unrequited love, failed marriages, adulterous liaisons, and missed opportunities are rampant. Widows, single mothers, and families without fathers predominate, and in the later years of his career, women are left behind by salarymen transferred to different cities and even different countries.

The dropped eyes, the averted gaze, and the proud bearing of women who survive one setback after another point to the fact that Naruse solicited extraordinarily strong performances from both men and women. As early as 1934, actresses felt privileged to work with him, and he continued to earn their respect up until his very last film with Tsukasa Yoko. The great actresses Hara Setsuko, Sugimura Haruko, Yamada Isuzu, Tanaka Kinuyo, Sugi Yoko, Irie Takako, and Awashima Chikage are just some of the stars who give outstanding performances in Naruse's films. Yet all the evidence shows that he was a notoriously reticent and uncommunicative director. Takamine Hideko claims that he never gave her any acting instructions: "Even during the shooting of a picture, he would never say if something was good or bad, interesting or trite. He was a completely unresponsive director."[45]

By all accounts, it seems as if Naruse was extremely difficult to work for, and yet he commanded a high level of respect from his actors and crew members. Most frustrating for them was his refusal to show them the continuity script, making every day on the set a surprise. It is difficult to understand how Naruse accomplished so much working in these conditions, and yet it may be simply a matter of the results so consistently impressing the team that the hierarchical system of direction sustained itself. One wonders especially how Naruse obtained the exceptional performances that he got from his actors, given his reputation as a "mean old man."[46] According to Okamoto Kihachi, Naruse shot dialogue scenes by first filming one actor, and then repositioning the camera to shoot the other actor, so that all those reactions and eye movements described by Sato would have been largely unmotivated in performance.[47]

In a 2005 interview, Nakadai Tatsuya describes the challenge this technique presented for the actor, but he also indicates that he gained enormous respect for Naruse working this way.[48] By shooting the actors each separately, Naruse often gained the curious "talking to the camera" effect, and slightly mismatched eye lines that have also been noticed in Ozu's films.[49] The rationale for Naruse was not aesthetic but typically prosaic. Nakadai and Okamoto both indicate that it was a method of rationalization and efficiency in which the lighting had to be set up only once for each character. Dialogue scenes were thus essentially constructed at the editing stage, although they are typically book-ended and interrupted by two-shots that link the characters through compositional techniques, so they rarely seem as disconnected as this method might imply. Nakadai, who acted in five films with Naruse after 1957, says that he learned the fundamental difference between stage and screen acting from the director, primarily by remaining silent and using the smallest of eye movements and gestures for expression.

In the interviews collected in the San Sebastian catalog, a repeated theme is that the first time anyone received any praise or thanks from Naruse was after the completion of *Floating Clouds*. It is ironic that this is the film that brought Naruse the greatest recognition, because it is in many ways a departure from his usual model of shoshimin-eiga. It was the largest budget he had worked with—his first "big" film[50]—and it is much more of an epic, meandering, and historically based work than any of his other features up to that point. Naruse was notorious for disliking location shooting,[51] although he consistently used locations very well, and *Floating Clouds* is perhaps the most itinerant of any of his films. Indeed, in almost every film, street scenes or scenes set in parks or along rivers provide important contrasts to the tight framings of domestic space that predominate. From the testimony of those who worked with him, Naruse emerges as a director who liked to control things very closely, and the unpredictability of location shooting may have disturbed him, giving rise to this legendary detail that is so blatantly at odds with the films.

If there is a modernist aesthetic to Naruse's cinema, it is not, I would argue, a transgression of norms or a reflexive antirealism. It is more akin to what Hasumi Shigehiko has described as a "double signature" that he reads in the way that Naruse works with generic scenes and situations. Hasumi comments on the lighting that in a number of instances creates the sense of actors' expressions apparently floating out of the background, isolating their emotions as virtual forms. The relationships between what Hasumi refers to as "a man and a woman" in *Sound of the Mountain* and *Floating Clouds* are indeed extraordinary. Hasumi suggests that Naruse extracts certain cinematic effects of performance, editing, and lighting that constitute the filmmaker's signature "engraved on top of the movie."[52] As provocative an analysis as this is, we also need to bear in mind that this auteurist "double signature" is always laid over another cinema that is deeply embedded in the lives of very specific men and women: salarymen and their wives, mothers and their children, aging women of the water trade and their disillusioned patrons. Underscoring the technical and aesthetic achievements of these films are narratives that are firmly based in the popular culture of postwar Japan.

Starting with *Meshi* in 1951, Naruse began adapting the writing of Hayashi Fumiko. Hayashi was a popular woman writer, and the six films that Naruse adapted from her work—including *Floating Clouds*—

are among his most successful. Hayashi wrote about women struggling against the harsh social and economic conditions on the margins of the modern urban culture of Tokyo, precisely the milieu that Naruse had started to explore in the 1930s. Naruse claimed that he "learned a great deal from Hayashi," although he doesn't specify exactly what that was.[53] Audie Bock claims that Naruse's Toho films were originally released as the bottom halves of double bills that often followed Kurosawa's headline features.[54] If Kurosawa developed the heroic persona of the postwar male subject, in Naruse we find the inscription of a fairly well-defined female subjectivity in Japanese modernity. This is not a heroic or transgressive femininity but a subject of agency and desire, which, in the context of twentieth-century Japan, is a key figure of modernity.

Naruse, like other Japanese directors, worked with a consistent crew of scriptwriters, technicians, and actors, who may have evolved and changed over the decades, but who nevertheless helped to create a certain style associated with the director's name. Among Naruse's most important collaborators were two women screenwriters: Mizuki Yoko (who worked on seven films from 1952 to 1957) and Tanaka Sumie (who worked on six films between 1951 and 1962). Other than that, his production team consisted only of men, including scriptwriter Ide Toshiro, with whom he worked on twelve pictures, from 1951 to 1966. Often these writers are cocredited, which suggests the degree of collaboration and/or rewriting that went on in a given production. Takamine Hideko claims that starting with *Lightning* (*Inazuma*, 1952), she worked on the scripts herself with Naruse, mainly cutting out lines of dialogue that she "didn't want to say,"[55] presumably replacing them with performance elements of gesture, posture, and eye movement. Other significant collaborators include cinematographer Suzuki Hiroshi, who shot thirteen films from 1935 to 1952, from *Three Sisters with Maiden Hearts* (*Otome-gokoro sannin shimai*, 1935) to *Mother*; and Tamai Masao, who shot sixteen films, from 1949 to 1960, including all the 1950s masterpieces. Composer Saito Ichiro worked on all the 1950s films as well and continued through to *Yearning* (*Midareru*, 1964). Art director Chuko Satoshi worked with Naruse on twenty-five films, from 1939 to 1967, including the big films of the 1950s.

None of Naruse's filmographies credit any editor for any of his films, and it is generally assumed that he did all his own editing. However, in a 2001 interview with *Cahiers du cinéma*, actress Tsukasa Yoko picked up her mobile phone and called Takeda Ume, the woman who says she edited "about forty" of Naruse's films at Toho after the war.[56] Takeda claims that she simply assembled the shots as the director measured them out against the length of his arms. He knew each shot by heart already, and it was only a question of determining the final length, and very occasionally inserting a shot of a landscape or object as punctuation—often, she says, to compensate for a flaw in the performances. It seems there was no question of retakes. Although Takeda is predictably unassuming, she and Naruse evidently established an extraordinarily intuitive working relationship, through which she was able to execute his predetermined idea of each film. The fact that she is not credited for her contribution is testimony to the gendered landscape of film production during Naruse's career.

In 1958, Naruse made his first color widescreen film, *Summer Clouds* (aka *Herringbone Clouds*; *Iwashigumo*), set in the pastoral landscape of a farming community in Atsugi. The widescreen frame forced a real shift in his editing and framing strategies, so while the tempo is much slower, the pictoral elements become more complex. Although he continued to feature female protagonists and narratives about family and romance—the thematics of the woman's film—these films are not as well known as the 1950s films. In the context of the emergent youth culture and new wave directors, the support from the studio for films such as his began to wane. Even so, Naruse moved into the new decade with new characters, settings, and narrative material, borrowing stylistic and narrative ideas from American film noir and Hitchcock in films such as *The Stranger within a Woman* (*Onna no naka ni iru tanin*, 1966) and *Hit and Run* (*Hikinige*, 1966).

He also made a number of woman's films in the 1960s that explored and criticized more explicitly the social norms and institutions that remained entrenched in Japanese society, despite the apparent postwar recovery. Indeed, with only a few exceptions, the 1960s films tend to be set among the bourgeois upper middle class, including the high-stakes world of corporate culture and the hostess business attached to it, as exemplified in one of his best-known films of the period, *When a Woman Ascends the Stairs* (*Onna ga kaidan o agaru toki*, 1960). All but one of the films after *Summer Clouds* are in Tohoscope, and five are in color. Many of his late films exploit the aesthetics of black and white widescreen for remarkable effects of lighting and space. His final film, *Scattered Clouds*, uses a stunning palette of pastels that belies his ostensible dislike of color film.[57]

In his early films Naruse was at the cutting edge of Japanese modernity, applying new and exciting techniques of representation to tired shinpa stories, but by the end of his career, modernity might seem to have passed him by. The new wave manifestos of the 1960s proclaimed a new modern aesthetic of speed, sex, and political critique, in the face of which Naruse's ongoing preoccupation with his familiar themes of women and families was anything but avant-garde. He seems to be stranded in modernity at this point, desperate for a rescuing critique that can awaken the unrequited desires of his women wronged, still, by men and institutions. Indeed, in the 1960s his heroines do yearn, allowing themselves to fall in love, only to be all the more badly bruised. Some of the films attain a kind of campy excess that might allow them to be treated as postmodern texts in which the ongoing construction—and deconstruction—of Japanese modernity can be read.

Not all Naruse's films feature female protagonists; neither are they all *gendai-geki* (films with contemporary settings). During the 1940s he made several films set in the Meiji period, about male musicians, actors, and even warriors. None of these films can be described as "action films"; they almost always involve romantic entanglements with virtuous women and are set in the milieu of the middle class. The male characters developed in Naruse's cinema are anything but heroic. Defeated salarymen and worn-out, irresponsible lovers and husbands are variations on the classical *nimaime* role of classical Japanese theater[58] and are key elements of his construction of Japanese modernity. In the 1960s films, both men and women characters are psychologically scarred, as the ravages of industrial modernity take their toll. We could even point to his fatherless families and flawed male characters as a sustained challenge to the authoritarian institutions of family and state.

Those films that fall outside the generic mode of the woman's film still have important affinities with the styles and themes that Naruse developed within that genre. Moreover, I will also be concerned in what follows with the way that the woman's film changed over the course of his career. The 1950s films tend to figure as the dominant model, because of their unqualified success, their relation to Hayashi Fumiko, their casting of top stars, their stylistic maturity, and the context of the postwar social history, yet it is equally important to work backward and forward from those films to better understand the construction of gender and effects of subjectivity in the Japanese studio era. The span of Naruse's career encompasses a number of expressions of Japanese modernity, and in my view, he remained "relevant" up to and including his very last film. Through the diversity and continuity of his career, the two very different modernities of the 1930s and the 1960s are linked; and the turbulent years of war and occupation likewise brought into perspective. Indeed, there are so many commonalities across this oeuvre, in terms of themes, characters, actors, images, and compositions, as well as effects of performance, lighting, editing, and the details of everyday life, that the body of work seems to tell a story, which I am calling "women and Japanese modernity."

Auteurism and Rescuing Critique

As an auteur, Naruse remains an elusive figure. He is at once too closely tied to the vicissitudes of the volatile history of twentieth-century Japan and too removed from his own work. He produced a remarkable body of films dedicated to women's passions, disappointments, routines, and living conditions, but he made remarkably few comments about his interest in women characters or women's culture. One of the few indications of his interest in women's issues is his comment on *Untamed* (*Arakure*, 1957), a film in which Takamine plays an incredibly headstrong woman who goes through five men over the course of the film and has frequent eruptions of violent anger against her wayward husbands and their mistresses. Naruse said, "It was my original intention to tell a story about a strong-willed, independent female lead character. However, I discovered that this theme wasn't too popular at the box office."[59]

The study of Japanese cinema has tended to be governed by auteurist paradigms, with a persistence that seems impervious to the poststructuralist critique of authorship. To some extent this tendency is guided by Japanese industry practices that placed directors at the top of hierarchical production and marketing strategies that were even more rigid than the contemporaneous American studio practices. However, Naruse's career challenges many assumptions behind auteurist criticism. One can ignore two-thirds of his overall output, as Jean Narboni does, and analyze the poetic vocabulary of the masterpieces. While there is no question that his cinema warrants such an approach, there is something odd about "ranking" Naruse alongside Chekhov and Schubert, Dreyer and Rossellini. He may belong in their company aesthetically, but the circumstances of the productions, the literary sources, and the delayed reception are so different that he clearly begs another mode of analysis, one that might be better equipped to recognize his contribution to a popular cinema in a commercial industry. During the thirty-seven years of his career, women's social roles underwent great change, and so did the cinema itself, in terms of technologies and stylistics, and its inscription in the modern world.

The question posed by this body of work is not simply about authorship but more specifically about the study of auteur cinema, or what Dana Polan has described as "auteurism." Polan makes a key distinction between the desire, or personal stamp, of the auteur, and that of the auteurist, who "wants to create meaning by an imposition of will."[60] The model that Polan sets up to better understand the relationship between auteur and auteurist is especially appropriate to a cross-cultural study like this one because he appeals to the anthropological methodology of collecting. Like the anthropologist, the auteurist removes objects from their original context and gives them new meanings within a new system of classification: "The creativity of auteurism bases itself in strategies that construct its objects in value-laden ways" (13). As a collector, the auteurist can certainly be charged with assuming that "cultural workers don't always understand the meanings of their own creations" (16), and can be accused of replacing the intentional fallacy with equally "fanciful" interpretations. But auteurism can also be a means of moving beyond interpretation to a more historically based method of analysis.

Polan is critical of auteurist practices that fail to recognize their own imposition of meaning, and he appeals to James Clifford's model of reflexive collecting practices. The danger of auteurist desire lies in the potential for the subjectivity of the auteurist critic to displace "the sweep of history itself and its modes of production" (18), but done carefully, a revitalized auteurism can be "fully and finally historical" (20). To the extent that my interest in Naruse Mikio is guided in an interest in the construction of female subjectivity in twentieth-century Japan, it is admittedly a view from the very specific perspective of early-twenty-first-century global feminism. This perspective comes with a set of methodological tools that does not simply constitute a feminist approach but is better described as a form of "rescuing critique."

The quotidian detail with which Naruse's films are preoccupied constitutes a panorama of Japanese cultural history, which calls for a methodology closer to "dream analysis" than formalism. If the auteurist searching for origins and for vision can be described as "mythic," my approach is historical in Walter Benjamin's sense of the term. He suggests that "historical 'understanding' is to be grasped, in principle, as an afterlife of that which is understood."[61] It is an approach that is furthermore bolstered by the dialectical relation between the present and the past, if my present refers to my historical and cultural positioning: "In order for a part of the past to be touched by the present instant <Actualität>, there must be no continuity between them" (470).

In his study of the nineteenth-century Paris Arcades, Walter Benjamin describes the collector as an allegorist: "Collecting is a form of practical memory, and of all the profane manifestations of 'nearness' it is the most binding. Thus, in a certain sense, the smallest act of political reflection makes for an epoch in the antiques business. We construct here an alarm clock that rouses the kitsch of the previous century to 'assembly'" (205). In Benjamin's cryptic philosophy, collecting is aligned with the surrealist practice of displacement, its historical potential embodied precisely in its interminable incompleteness. The collector's practices of classification can never completely hide the productive disorder that is the collector's true canon. "As far as the collector is concerned, his collection is never complete; for let him discover just a single piece missing, and everything he's collected remains a patchwork, which is what things are for allegory from the beginning" (211). I find this to be a particularly provocative formulation for my own approach to Naruse. In my collection I have notes on films watched in archives and film festivals over the last few years, videotapes and DVDs with English subtitles, French subtitles, and no subtitles at all, transcripts of dialogue and catalog descriptions of lost films. In all of this, I do not in fact have "the cinema of Naruse," but traces of a cinema that is doomed to incompletion. This incompletion is also the sign of my access to Japanese language and culture, which is equally mediated and incomplete.

As an auteurist, I do have an interest that sustains this collection, which may be described as an attempt to make meaning out of a somewhat random array of material. It is a desire also guided by Benjamin's historiography of modernity, insofar as it is an attempt to conceptualize Japanese film history, or at least one small aspect of that history, in terms of modernity. Going back to the *Arcades Project*, we need to bear in mind that Benjamin's practice of collecting in that unfinished book was a redemptive one, dedicated to "the death of the Paris Arcades, the decay of a type of architecture. The book's atmosphere is saturated with the poisons of this process; its people drop like flies" (204). In the Paris Arcades and the discourse surrounding them, Benjamin wanted to extract the various deleterious effects of the modern phantasmagoria and also to see how these coterminal effects coincided within cultural modernity. "The century was incapable of responding to the new technological possibilities with a new social order.... The world dominated by its phantasmagorias—this, to make use of Baudelaire's term, is 'modernity'" (206). A failure of equal proportions may be observed in the twentieth century in the many ways that social relations in Japan have not progressed at the same pace as technological innovation.[62]

David Bordwell has situated Ozu's poetics in conjunction with the "broken promises of Meiji," rereading a director who is often labeled a reactionary as a liberal protestor "against the failure of the state's social responsibility."[63] Like Naruse, Ozu specialized in the genre of the shoshimin-eiga, deeply embedded in the detail of everyday life in the contemporary urban milieu. In their early films, both directors display what Bordwell describes as a "contemporary impulse toward documentation."[64] By the 1960s this contemporaneity is somewhat reified into the two filmmakers' mature styles, but both remain bound to the domestic spaces, urban architecture, and narrative conflicts of petit-bourgeois family life. In comparison to Ozu, Naruse's films are somewhat less nostalgic and, for me, somewhat more future-oriented, with less sense of resignation. The shoshimin-eiga form was nostalgic even in its original instantiation,[65] but in Naruse's films we can say quite literally that there is "movement at their interior," which, according to Benjamin, is necessary for images to "attain to legibility." This movement, on the cinematic level, is articulated in eye movements and camera movements, body movement and traveling shots. Ozu, as the more well-known director, often serves as the foil for Naruse's closely related oeuvre, and a comparison of the inner movement of Naruse's cinema with the stasis of Ozu's opens a space for a recognition within this movement of the terms of female subjectivity that is produced—otherwise known as desire.

It is misleading to describe either Ozu or Naruse as articulating a social critique, because in both cases, "the broken promise" of democracy tends to be taken as historical necessity, and one rarely finds a character in either body of work who really attempts to make a difference. The attitude of resignation, or *mono no aware* ("sympathetic sadness"), that is so prominent in Ozu's shoshimin-eiga[66] is also characteristic of Naruse's use of the genre. Yet a certain tension or instability often tends to complicate this sense of resignation in Naruse's films. Instead of "loss," expressions of hope and disappointment are more strongly felt in the depiction of social change. Naruse creates characters, often played by Takamine Hideko, in films such as *Lightning* and *Flowing*, who strive to break out of the social roles imposed upon them. If one of the main promises of the Meiji period was the emancipation of women, it was a promise that was renewed even more strongly in the postwar period, and Naruse's films provide a means of tracing the contours of a modern

Japanese female subjectivity, as well as the failure of Japanese society to fully realize the potential of gender equity.

In citing Benjamin's comments on collecting, I have implied that Naruse's cinema might be identified as "kitsch." Instead of the pejorative connotations of that term, I would like to consider Naruse's woman's films as elements of a popular culture that has largely been dismissed and forgotten by film historians. While for Benjamin, *kitsch* referred to "the overproduction of commodities; the bad conscience of producers,"[67] here it refers to the Japanese film industry's production of a mass culture that was very much informed and influenced by the American cinema. In Benjamin's notion of the dream world of commodity culture, kitsch is also the key to the awakening from the dream state of consumer capitalism in its baroque qualities of overabundance and excess. We could certainly note the sheer volume of Naruse's assembly-line productions as evidence of his participation in the mass production of popular culture. But in keeping with the utopian potential that Benjamin assigns to kitsch, we also need to emphasize the sensuous aesthetic qualities of Naruse's films.

Recognition of the kitsch elements of Naruse's cinema, which are especially prominent during the war and occupation years in films such as *Learn from Experience* (*Kafuku* I, II, 1937), *A Descendant of Taro Urashima* (*Urashima Taro no koei*, 1946) and *The Battle of Roses* (*Bara gassen*, 1950), is also a means of acknowledging the ways in which this cinema captures the experience of modernity. This includes the sensationalism of new pleasures and technologies, and the dangers they inevitably entail. The materialism of the constant preoccupation with money remains balanced with a keen eye for fashion, which Benjamin recognized as a "dialectical theatre" of modernity.[68] One of the chief methodological means of dealing with a cinema that is at once so stylized and so down-to-earth, so self-conscious and so realist, is through melodrama. If some of the later films seem positively Sirkian in their "double signature," it does not therefore follow that Naruse was a "progressive auteur," but it does speak to his inscription within popular culture and his ability to transform everyday life into affective (sensuous, aesthetic) discourse.

The notion of "rescuing critique" in Benjamin's writing was teased out by Jürgen Habermas in 1972. Habermas distinguishes Benjamin's methodology from the dominant trend at that time of "ideology critique" associated with Frankfurt school theorists and embraced by the Left.[69] While he is critical of the ways that in his view, "the theologian" in Benjamin "could not bring himself to make the messianic theory of experience serviceable for historical materialism" (114), he recognizes that Benjamin's theory of experience could nevertheless be made useful for cultural criticism, particularly on "the verge of *posthistoire*, where symbolic structures are exhausted, worn thin, and stripped of their imperative functions" (121). While his relevance "does not lie in a theory of revolution," Habermas concedes that Benjamin's approach, "which deciphers the history of culture with a view to rescuing for the upheaval," may be an important means of reconfiguring "a new subjectivity" for a dialectical theory of progress. He argues that Benjamin's criticism "was concerned with doing justice to the collective fantasy images deposited in the expressive qualities of daily life as well as in literature and art" (117).

It may be precisely the theologian in Benjamin that makes his cultural theory particularly relevant to the contradictions of Japanese modernity, in which traces of the past continue to persist within the ever-changing present. As Harootunian points out, the expansion of the Japanese empire at the height of the modern movement appealed to the priority of "a culture of depth that has left its traces in the present."[70] The search for a woman's happiness in Japanese modernity that persists throughout Naruse's cinema invites a critical methodology that can rescue and redeem these desires and impulses from within a tradition in which "progress" and "catastrophe" are deeply intertwined. As Habermas puts it, "Benjamin aims . . . at rescuing a past charged with *Jetztzeit*. It ascertains the moments in which the artistic sensibility puts a stop to fate draped as progress and enciphers the utopian experience in a dialectical image—the new within the always-the-same" (101).

An elaboration of Benjamin's cultural theory will be developed throughout this study, in an attempt to indicate its relevance to Naruse's filmmaking and its usefulness as a critical methodology in film studies. In both objectives, my approach is largely guided by Miriam Hansen's notion of "vernacular modernism," which is grounded in the cultural theory of Benjamin and his contemporary Siegfried Kracauer. Hansen argues for a "wider notion of the aesthetic" than has hitherto governed film studies methods. She focuses on the "nexus between modernism and modernity" as a means of recognizing the role of cinema in the global public sphere.[71] Vernacular modernism incorporates the various cultural practices by which the experience of modernity has been articulated and modified, placing cinema alongside the "everyday" discourses and practices that it also mediates: fashion, architecture, advertising, and so on. In this, Hansen endorses and follows up on Benjamin's key insight that "artistic practices" need to be situated within "a larger history and economy of sense perception . . . the decisive battle-ground for the meaning and fate of modernity."[72]

In Hansen's discussion of the Hollywood cinema as a vernacular modernism, she points to the way that the international distribution of classical cinema might have "advanced new possibilities of social identity and cultural styles."[73] What Hansen is suggesting, and I would like to follow up on in the context of Naruse's cinema, is that Hollywood "constituted, or tried to constitute new subjectivities and subjects" (344). Where we once thought of these subjectivities as bourgeois, Hansen argues that we should start to think of them as modern. My approach to Naruse is a methodological intervention into the paradigms of orientalism that have tended to emphasize the Japaneseness of Japanese cinema at the expense of its modernity. The framework of vernacular modernism enables us to recognize the modernity of Naruse's cinema as well as its role as a discourse of mass culture, without neglecting the aesthetic and sensual qualities that make it an auteur cinema, or its class character.

The Japanese Woman's Film

Naruse was a director who was very much bound to box office figures, and his audiences had very conservative ideas about gender roles and behavior. The only critic to have seriously attended to Naruse's feminist perspective, Joan Mellen, unfortunately holds him up to standards that are quite inappropriate to the cultural framework of the films' production. She describes "two Naruses": one who is sympathetic to the trials of the Japanese woman, and one who "could almost obscenely idealize the Japanese woman as housewife." She concludes by saying, "no revolutionary, Naruse neither predicts nor welcomes the kind of upheaval that would make possible true equality for women in Japan. But he is too honest not to admit its dire necessity."[74] While Mellen is correct in noting the deep ambivalence within Naruse's representation of women, to describe the idealization of the mother and housewife as "obscene" betrays a serious misunderstanding of the Japanese context.

Mellen's feminist perspective is grounded in a 1970s model of liberationist politics, and the revolution she alludes to is precisely what feminism still implies for many Japanese who are consequently extremely cautious about it. In fact, the kind of social change Mellen is looking for in Naruse's cinema could not be further from the point. He may chronicle the trials and tribulations of women in Japanese society, but they are often willing participants in their own entrapment within a network of social customs and historical forces. It is thus a cinema that demands a very different method of analysis than that deployed by Mellen to understand the dynamics of gender underscoring its dramatic effects and social significance. Japan cannot be simply accused of being a "feudal society" trying to be modern, as Mellen suggests. Over the course of the thirty-seven years of Naruse's career, one can trace the emergence of a modern Japanese female subjectivity, which is to say, a mode of being in the world that is female, modern, and Japanese.

From the late 1920s to the 1960s, the woman's film, or *josei-eiga*, was a mainstay of the Japanese film industry. The producer Kido Shiro, under whom Naruse began his career at Shochiku, recognized the commercial importance of the genre and effectively solidified the studio's production system by giving it priority.[75] Peter High has pointed out that the *gendai geki* dramas of the Taisho period, both stage and screen, consisted primarily of the "ever-victimized heroine of the *shinpa* tragedy," while *jidai geki* was dominated by male characters. Keeping in mind that until the late teens female characters were played by male *onnagata*, High's rather schematic assessment sketches the genesis of the woman's film genre: "While intellectuals and other nonsentimentalists scoffed at such fare as 'three hanky tear-jerkers,' the largely female audiences were enthralled. Many or most of them could readily identify with the heroines and their desperate struggles against the invisible powers of oppression in their male-dominated world. As the 1930s advanced, however, portrayals of women in Japanese cinema teemed with vitality."[76]

Naruse began his career precisely at the point where the genre began to incorporate more male characters—in the form of the notorious salaryman—and more dynamic, outspoken, female characters. Although the term *josei-eiga* was rarely used by either the industry or the critics, by the 1950s and 1960s Naruse's films were frequently discussed by female critics, and "round table discussions" among women celebrities appeared in the pages of *Kinema Junpo* and *Eiga Hyoron*. Certainly Naruse, his scriptwriters, actors, and audiences, would have been familiar with the Hollywood woman's films of the 1930s and 1940s. During the occupation, Japanese screens were flooded with Hollywood films in the interests of promoting American democracy, and the woman's film from the 1930s through to the 1950s was emblematic of modernity in Japan.

The confusing affinity of Western modernism and traditional Japanese aesthetics has tended to efface the discourse of Japanese modernity as the emergence of an urban image-culture. The development of an industrial consumer culture in Japan and the construction of Japanese modernity are much more complex than a process of "Westernization." Masao Miyoshi has pointed out that modernity is a disynchronous process, occurring in different cultures and social formations at different times.[77] Enrique Dussel has argued that "modernity is not a phenomenon of Europe as an independent system, but of Europe as center."[78] The influence of Japanese arts on Western modernism is a good example of how modernity is coincident with the establishment of Europe as the center of a world-system. The limits of modernity are therefore coincident with the decentralization of the world-system in a (potentially) globalizing cultural economy that is more self-conscious about its exteriorizing and othering effect on the non-European center.

Film studies scholarship has tended to miss the important point that, in the Japanese context, "modernity" involved the emergence of the bourgeois individual and the coextensive adoption of realist modes of representation.[79] In literature this meant the development of the I-novel, or *shishosetsu*, in the early twentieth century. While debates and discussions of this genre were intense throughout the 1920s and 1930s, there were few parallel intellectual debates concerning the cinema. Questions of gender and women's literature, which began to proliferate in the 1920s, tended to be ghettoized and cut off from the main arena of debate over the constitution of the Japanese subject, a situation that continues to persist in Japanese studies. Given the context of Naruse's cinema, it should be evident that without neglecting the persona of the auteur, auteurism can become a method of historical research that takes the author's work as a case study or sample of a complex historical-cultural formation. This study of Naruse's films is a method of investigating the articulation of female subjectivity in the Japanese cinema, as a discourse not of agency but of representation, and one that necessarily intersects with many other aspects of Japanese modernity.

The 1950s, when Naruse made his most popular films, is also a period in which the issue of women's rights and social roles became a matter of public debate. With the democratic reforms of the postwar period came a recognition of women's rights and a nascent women's movement, along with economic development that created more room for women in the workforce. But as Sandra Buckley points out, "a discourse of motherhood and the family was quick to surface through the 1950s in opposition to the emerging women's labor movement."[80]

The reforms included in the constitutional revisions during the occupation were arguably among the most progressive legislations of women's rights that the world had ever seen.[81] Women's rights and the reform of the family system of Japanese society were seen by SCAP as key elements of democratization, and they were supported by Japanese women's organizations in their efforts to this end. Susan Pharr argues that the experiment was a huge success, and obstacles such as an entrenched history of discrimination were overcome through the humanist agenda of the SCAP policy makers.[82] Others would disagree. While women achieved suffrage in 1945, many forms of discrimination remained deeply entrenched in social life, language, career expectations, and public policy. In this sense, we can look at Naruse's postwar films as a complex response to the "failed promise of democracy." Japanese feminism has developed its own goals, methods, and priorities, but it shares with Western feminism a commitment to the recognition of female subjectivity, even if it tends toward an essentialism that is not widely accepted in North American feminism.[83]

While there is no question that Naruse's films were produced with female audiences in mind, and frequently featured major stars playing female protagonists, there has been surprisingly little analysis of the generic characteristics of the Japanese woman's film. In Joseph Anderson and Donald Richie's seminal book on the Japanese film industry, they mention both the *haha-mono* and the *tsuma-mono* (mother and wife films) as important postwar genres that they are quick to dismiss as "trivial emotionalism."[84] However, the term *josei-eiga*, "woman's film," is used in Japanese film criticism as early as the 1930s to refer to films about women and addressed to female audiences. Naruse's cinema may exercise a certain restraint that distinguishes itself from the mainstream of *o-namida chodai eiga* or "tears-please films," but his films are nevertheless related in their privileging of female characters.

The "woman's film" in the Hollywood context refers to texts with very specific effects of subjectivity that have been analyzed extensively by North American film scholars. So-called emotionalism has come to be understood as a dramatization of the desires, struggles, and conflicts that are specific to women's experience. Insofar as the woman's film is a variant of melodrama, it "allows the return of repressed psychic conflict" and a playing out of the social pressures of a gendered society.[85] While I am not proposing that one could simply apply the lessons learned about the Hollywood woman's film to the Japanese context, the idea of the woman's film is a means of emphasizing the sociohistorical significance of Naruse's cinema and identifying the effects of subjectivity that it produces.

Naruse's films were very popular among female audiences; and he was

3. Women at the movies. Nakakita Chieko and Kyoko Kagawa in *Mother* (*Okaasan*, 1952), Shin Toho.

closely identified with women's subjects by his contemporary critics. For some, this devalued his work. One group of critics, for example, expressed relief when during the war his films featured more male protagonists and relegated women to secondary characters.[86] Female critics, on the other hand, tended to comment on Naruse's female characters, judging their behavior and decisions according to moral standards that are in themselves of critical interest. One female reviewer of *Mother* reported crying along with everyone else in the theater, although Naruse generally avoided the extreme sentimentality of many of his contemporaries.[87] In postwar Japan, half the cinemagoing public was female, most of them "office ladies" or single unmarried women who went to the movies in groups. Twelve women's magazines were published in the 1950s, many of them containing film reviews and stories about actors and actresses, indicating that Naruse's cinema was part of a much larger phenomenon. Suzanne Audrey observed in 1953 that in postwar Japan women were flocking to the movies to see a wide variety of films, including the many imported American films that displayed the lives of women in the United States.[88]

As a genre, the Hollywood woman's film is an inherently contradictory mode of practice, and Naruse's films are often equally unresolved.

THE AUTEUR AS SALARYMAN

Naruse's cinema, like Hayashi Fumiko's writing, is grounded in the quotidian lives of the lower middle classes, people living on a perpetual edge of poverty. An important effect of combining narrative analysis with anthropological or cultural-studies methods may be a complication of the structures of desire that inform the readings of texts. In the context of the woman's film, anthropology enables us to gain some distance from the films' original spectators and thus to circumvent Mary Ann Doane's critique of the genre. She argues that "the tropes of female spectatorship are not empowering," and that the American films consistently undermine their own address to the female spectator by "denying her a space of reading."[89] Rather than deciding whether Naruse's films are empowering or not, I want to try to regain that space of reading by shifting the viewing position slightly. Susan Stanford Friedman has suggested that in shifting the terms of feminist critical practice from psychoanalysis to anthropology, one is also moving from an emphasis on temporal structures to spatial ones.[90]

The spatial structures that are most prominent in Naruse's cinema are the architectural settings of the home drama and the urban setting of metropolitan Tokyo. Japanese film genres tend to be named for their semantic content, and thus there is a great deal of overlap between such genres as wife films, mother films, husband-and-wife films, salaryman films, home dramas, and shoshimin-eiga. In light of the lack of clear distinctions between genres, and the shared roles of family and domestic architecture in all of them, they can be heuristically grouped together under the umbrella of the home drama (*homu dorama*), a term often used interchangeably with *shoshimin-eiga*. This term specifies the important conjunction between family and architecture in this cinema. An affinity for the minimally furnished geometrical interiors of the Japanese home was very much part of Naruse's dramaturgy. The home drama is defined by Sato as being organized around the family,[91] and its origins can be found in the *katei shosetsu* or "domestic novels" that were serialized in the late nineteenth century and became staple source material for shinpa drama.[92] In Naruse's cinema we can see how the generic form of the home drama begins to show cracks and fissures in the postwar period, as he introduces strong and stubborn female characters into the form.

The maternal role is a cornerstone of the emperor system in its implicit link to the family system, a structure heavily reinforced in the imperialist home-front propaganda of the Fifteen Years' War. In the family-emperor system, which was codified in the Meiji period as the backbone of the "modern" nation, women were categorized, according to Aoki Yayoi, "as intellectually incompetent and unaccountable under the law. In this way, women were effectively excluded from public life." She adds that "these contradictory 'traditions' still cast their shadow over contemporary Japan."[93] As Masao Miyoshi has pointed out, many Japanese perceived democratic reforms such as women's rights as punishment for losing the war, and the ideology of male supremacy remained for many a cornerstone of the mythological "Japanese race."[94] Miyoshi notes that "these sexist-and-racist opinions are still voiced with impunity by high government officials and cultural leaders."[95] Thus, if modernity means different things in different cultural and national settings, in Japan it encompasses the threat of inverted gender relations—evoked most sensationally by the "modern girls" or *moga* of the interwar years that are featured in a number of Naruse's films of the early 1930s. Miyoshi notes further that even "postmodern" Japan remains inconsistent with other postmodernisms that have embraced feminism as an epistemological precept—precisely the orientation of this study, which cannot pretend to capture the Japanese perspective but can propose a parallel view from "nearby."[96]

In Naruse's cinema the veil between man and woman is rarely penetrated, as the gulf between the sexes often seems formidable. A deep-seated essentialism is conveyed in frequent platitudes about women's woes and the irresponsibility of men. No amount of romance, marriage, or coupling can truly bridge the divide between men and women, although the occasional spark of understanding and communication becomes all the more brilliant in this context. Yet Naruse himself, in his cinema if not in his personal life, seems to understand the emotional terrain that is ostensibly the province of women. This also is where his modernity lies, in his implicit understanding of women's desires and disappointments. Through his films these emotions are given tangible aesthetic and sensual form in the public sphere under the signature of a male auteur.

Because patriarchal and national structures are so closely bound in Japanese culture, it is necessary to step outside a national-cinema frame of reference to attain a critical perspective on the discourse of gender. The theory of vernacular modernism provides a useful method with which to assess the influence of Western humanism and liberalism within the sphere of popular culture. At the same time, it opens the possibility for other modernisms to be recognized alongside the formalist and orientalist models that have tended to dominate the study of Japanese art cinema. Naruse's aesthetics partake of both formal inventiveness and Japanese traditions—yet they are so thoroughly hybridized with realist film technique and with the fashions of everyday life that it remains, throughout, a vernacular aesthetic.

Subjectivity and Spectatorship

By referring to Naruse's films as "woman's films," we can begin to understand their contribution to the construction of Japanese modernity that has hitherto gone unrecognized. He was, after all, one of the most well-respected and prolific directors within the industry. Because Japanese modernity includes the recognition of women's rights and potential changes to the family system, the question of female subjectivity seems to me to be a particularly crucial, if neglected, discourse. As Rey Chow has argued in the context of Chinese cinema, the question of woman's sexuality and social function is central to the cultural production of modernity, precisely because it systematically challenges the norms of the premodern social formation.[97] In the Japanese context, female sexuality remains "contained" in the burlesque and striptease shows that first appeared in Asakusa in the 1920s (and in Naruse's first sound film *Three Sisters with Maiden Hearts*), reappearing in the postwar years (and in Naruse's film *Conduct Report on Professor Ishinaka* [*Ishinaka sensei gyojoki*, 1950]). For female subjectivity we must look to the home drama and the shoshimin-eiga.

As Friedman suggests, spatial indices of locale and setting are appropriate to a more culturally based reading of a given narrative, whereas a "time-centered model" gives priority to plot and character development.[98] In other words, the auteurist methodology that Naruse's cinema seems to call for is one that displaces psychoanalysis with anthropology. The role of desire in narrative is so different in this cinema than the Hollywood model that it seems to me more appropriate to set aside the question of psychoanalysis and its applicability to the Japanese context, without forgetting that these films are very much family dramas, in every sense of the term.

The discourse of subjectivity in narrative space is typically theorized in psychoanalytic terms by film scholars,[99] but the psychoanalytic paradigm does not seem to be particularly pertinent to the subject-effects of these films.[100] There is no question that many of the women in shoshimin-eiga films have deep-seated, unrequited desires, but they are embedded not so much in family romance as in their home, which is at once the site of their repression and their only token of identity. Thus the home, as the framework of domestic space, is a complex site of femininity. The architecture of the home is constitutive of the architecture of the gaze in these films, but it is pictorial space, rather than a space of desire, that governs the dynamics of looking. The female spectator of the Hollywood woman's film is brought "too close" to the image in Doane's analysis; their glasses are ripped off and their eyes are clouded with tears.[101] In contrast, the use of domestic architecture in the Japanese home drama, which inscribes frames within frames, maintains a sense of distance for the spectator, despite the pathos of the narrative events.

The form and structure of the traditional Japanese house plays an important role in constructing the visual field of Naruse's films about women's plight in a changing social formation. Insofar as the houses are often located in the heart of the urban metropolis, they constitute a visual form of the contradictions embedded in Japanese modernity. Like Hayashi's stories, Naruse's films are often set in the *shitamachi*, or "low city" of Tokyo, rebuilt in studio sets that, after the war, preserved a sense of the prewar city. Within these spaces, Naruse uses a 360-degree shooting space, like Ozu, frequently cutting right on the 180-degree axis. In the 1950s he refined his camera positions, so that he often frames the rooms at 90-degree angles, respecting the architectural forms of the home (although he was never as rigorous as Ozu in this regard, incorporating more variations in shot scale, more oblique angles, and more camera movements).

The city streets are often framed like corridors, inhabited by a dense network of neighborly communities. Many families in Naruse's films operate small businesses from the front or lower floors of their homes. Within this blurring of private and public space, parades of street musicians appear in almost every film, becoming one of Naruse's signature motifs. Thus the streets are as important as the interior rooms of the homes, as he uses the urban space as a site of community and ritual, and often as a softly lit scene of quiet beauty. Key scenes between lovers or potential lovers are set in parks or along rivers in Tokyo. The banal settings of urban life are often photographed in such a way as to bring out their sensuous qualities, while remaining within a realist aesthetic. Naruse's female characters are often able to articulate themselves much better outside the home, and there is a sense that these public spaces enable the production of female subjectivity.

Without losing sight of the historical-temporal aspects of cultural specificity, this turn to a spatial model seems to be particularly appropriate to the analysis of Naruse's cinema. For one thing, many of his films, especially those based on Hayashi's writing, tend not to be plot-driven narratives at all, but unwind slowly and episodically, often without satisfactorily resolving the conflicts that have been generated. In fact, this is a feature of Japanese writing that pervades much of the cinema of the 1950s. Masao Miyoshi has described the narrative style of *shosetsu* (the modern Japanese novel), as "paratactic rather than syntactic, arithmetic rather than algebraic, . . . the expression not of order and suppression, as the novel is, but of space, decentralization, and dispersal."[102]

Naruse's cinema may be a species of melodrama, but it is definitely not characterized by Manichean forces of good and evil. Although in his films of the 1930s one does find dramatic structures of coincidence, misunderstandings, and stylistic excesses that are associated with the Western melodrama and classical Japanese theater, these are greatly reduced in the postwar films.[103] Joseph Murphy has suggested that notions of melodrama that have been developed in the context of Hollywood are appropriate to Japanese cinema, especially the effects of gender, but the different relation of Japan to modernity must be taken into account.[104] While the early films partake of the "sensational melodrama" that Ben Singer has identified as a product of modernity in the first three decades of American cinema,[105] the later films evoke the more "modernist" theories of melodrama advanced by Peter Brooks and Thomas Elsaesser.[106] Naruse's particular aesthetics belong to a somewhat underappreciated aspect of melodramatic narrative: its affinities with realism. Women's writing and women's culture in Japan in the prewar period was closely associated with diary and confessional genres[107] and, like Naruse's cinema, immersed in the detail of everyday life. More recent theories of melodrama advanced by Linda Williams and Christine Gledhill take into account this crucial realist dimension of the genre, or as Gledhill describes it, this "mode" of melodrama.[108]

In discussions of spectatorship, we need to be able to distinguish between original historical spectators, and those who watch the films at growing cultural and historical distances. For most contemporary Japanese, the cinema of the studio era is embarrassingly old, bearing the traces of a culture still coming to terms with modernity. However, recent retrospectives have been tremendously popular in Europe, North America, and Tokyo, suggesting that Naruse's audience has become the international community of cinephiles who attend festivals and frequent cinematheques.

We need to think more carefully about the new modes of spectatorship that this international circuit of art cinema has engendered. To the extent that it is an intercultural "contact zone," we should be employing anthropological models of spectatorship, if not to displace psychoanalytic ones, at least to supplement them. This is particularly true for historical work, insofar as Japanese culture of the 1950s is regarded as other not only to my own culture but equally to contemporary Japanese spectators and scholars. I hesitate to call the original spectators of these films the "authentic spectators," because I believe that there are a variety of valid spectator positions for any given film, including those that incorporate cultural and ideological distances from the texts. While much is lost through the mediation of subtitles, Naruse's cinema opens up a world — a phantasmagoria — that is profoundly moving to a new, global community of spectators. Is there not a language of forms, a discourse of architecture and urban geography — not to mention music and costume — by which these films communicate to a global viewing audience?

In particular, a feminist frame of reference enables a viewing that is at once distanced historically and culturally, yet invested in the films' empathetic discourse of social struggle. Part of the address to contemporary international audiences may still be bound up in the "exotic" setting of the Japanese architecture that Naruse has closely integrated into his style of filmmaking; at the same time, the pathos of the narratives takes place on the most banal, everyday level of disappointment and regret, so that the urban and domestic spaces become uncannily familiar. The home drama is so deeply inscribed in the particularity of Japanese history that it cannot be contained in the universalizing discourse of humanism. Yet if Japanese patriarchy is to be challenged at all, as Miyoshi argues, "so-called cultural aspects of social life need to be scrutinized in the context of the history of Japan in the world, not in its transcendental essence."[109]

I'd like to conclude by situating this reading of gendered modernity within a theory of the subject because, as should be evident, Naruse's own subjectivity as auteur is important mainly as a term of classification. That is, he cannot be regarded as a "feminist" director, or an auteurist "visionary" with a personal worldview implied by his films, even if he is responsible for the subject-effects produced by the specific conjunction of performance, narrative, and visual style in those films. If the everydayness of Naruse's cinema seems to call for an anthropological spectator, I still need to locate my spectatorship (my auteurism, in Polan's sense of this word) in relation to the articulation of female subjectivity that is legible in the films. It may be only within a global sphere of cinematic spectatorship that the historical articulation of female subjectivity becomes legible, yet Japanese modernity needs to be recognized on its own terms.

The modernity of Japanese cinema is very much bound up with the production of Japanese subjectivities. Modern Japanese literature has developed around the I-novel or *shishosetsu*, a form in which subjectivity is deeply embedded in realist representation, which for Miyoshi, constitutes a "complex negotiation between the formal insistence on the 'I' and the ideological suppression of the self."[110] While Ozu's cinema, in my view, might be said to sustain this suppression of the self,[111] in Naruse's cinema, the tensions between form and subjectivity are produced through the discourse of bodies in space.

Of all the various discussions and debates on the Japanese subject, I've found the most useful and provocative to be that offered by Naoki Sakai. He points out that the process of translation by which the term *subject* has gone from English to the two Japanese terms *shukan* and *shutai* and back again creates an inevitable surplus that cannot be contained in either language. He proposes a hybrid conception of the Japanese subject that would incorporate both "the epistemic subject," *shukan*, derived from Western philosophy, and the subject "as a practical agent": *shutai*. These heterogeneous regimes of the subject coincide in the realm of theory, a discourse that, he argues, has no insiders and no outsiders but will always be under the sign of cultural difference.[112]

Sakai argues that what is at stake in the theorization of Japanese subjectivity is "how we envision the articulation of different social relations [and] the different articulation of cultural difference" (125). While Sakai does not address the issue of gender, he does suggest that the shutai, or the subject of agency and practice, is constituted in time, whereas the epistemic subject (shukan) is constituted in space. In the phenomenological relationship between these two regimes of the subject, the temporality of the former is specifically an "ecstatic temporality," or "time as duration," which seems to correspond well to the plotless temporality of the shoshimin-eiga. The epistemic subject, on the other hand, enables us to locate the anthropological, critical gaze of the non-Japanese feminist within a hybrid notion of the Japanese subject. Insofar as the spatial tropes of Naruse's home drama films are so strongly embedded within the architecture of Japanese culture, precisely where aesthetics meet social forms, they are equally attuned to this second, epistemic regime of the subject. That is to say, if the epistemic subject is spatially constructed, the cultural difference of my viewing is founded on the visual field of the films, a spatial arrangement in which the historical relation is a form of address. In articulating a visual mode of Japaneseness through the formalized use of domestic architecture, the films also (ironically) invite an anthropological/epistemic gaze.

As Sakai notes, the relationship between the two forms of the subject is unstable, but by inquiring into the tension that subsists between *shukan* and *shutai*, we may be able to "disclose the sites of political intervention as well as . . . the 'enunciative displacements' which inscribe and reinscribe various identities in the space of cultural representation" (125). If Japanese cinema can be understood as a discourse of Japanese modernity, its hybridity will necessarily comprise a certain tension. If new subjectivities are produced within the collision of forms and the discursive contradictions of cultural transformation, Naruse's cinema offers an emblematic site. Working within the terms of popular culture, his "woman's films" challenge the closures that are metaphorically and graphically imposed by domestic space. The modern subjectivity of his female characters is articulated in spatial terms, as a movement, as a desire to move beyond the container of the domestic role; and it is this mobility that Giuliana Bruno evokes in her rethinking of spectatorship as a mode of travel and dwelling.

Bruno claims that the parallels between cities and architecture entail a total overhaul of how we once conceived of film viewing. No longer "fixed" as a voyeur, the spectator is now a "voyageur" who moves through a film as someone walking through a building or a city, assembling views according to who and where she is and what she wants to see.[113] For Bruno, this mobile spectator is female, or at least—insofar as she is not the voyeur of classical film theory—she is of indeterminate gender. Furthermore, Bruno's emphasis on the body of the spectator who experiences the film aligns her approach to spectating with Jonathan Crary's notion of modern visual culture as a "deterritorialization of vision."[114] This theorization of urban space, spectatorship, and filmic space offers a valuable set of critical tools with which we can return to moments in film history that have been inadequately understood and analyzed, or that have been dropped out of the canon altogether because they did not fit the dominant critical paradigms governing film studies.

Along with the many other directors of the studio era of Japanese cinema, Naruse was developing the visual language of Japanese modernity. Clearly this is a language heavily informed by gender, although it may only be a "transnational feminist cultural studies" that can find the tools to read the split femininity that constitutes itself in its own disavowal, as Sakai would put it.[115] Transnational feminism is a term introduced by Gayatri Spivak and developed by Caren Kaplan and Inderpal Grewal to refer to feminist critical practices that create alliances across differences and contexts, and which eschew the unified subject for subjectivities that are contingent on historically specific conditions.[116]

Japanese feminism tends to be at once ghettoized and fragmented into a diversity of feminisms mobilized around different social issues,[117] and feminist film scholarship has not yet gained a foothold in the academic or publishing worlds. However, Japanese-speaking film scholars in North America, such as Chika Kinoshita and Mitsuyo Wada-Marciano—whose work has been very valuable to this study—are beginning to make important contributions to feminist scholarship of Japanese cinema. In the popular imagination, feminism in Japan refers to the Women's Lib of the 1970s and cannot seem to get beyond the threat of total social inversion contained within an ideology of emancipation. As Markus Nornes has argued, the 1970s feminist intervention into film theory did not take hold in Japan, and women filmmakers have had great difficulty in breaking into a male-dominated industry.[118] Neither has there been much interest in a politics of representation within the Japanese film studies community, a situation that is beginning to change as more Japanese-speaking scholars attend postgraduate programs in critical theory in North America and Europe. Thus, the relative neglect of Naruse's cinema within the study of Japanese film is deeply implicated in the methodological and metacritical debates that have characterized Japanese film studies since Noel Burch's groundbreaking study of 1979. The issue of gender is, I would argue, inseparable from issues of melodrama, modernity, and cinematic aesthetics and needs to be addressed from within those ongoing discussions.

1

The Silent Films

WOMEN IN THE CITY, 1930–1934

> As the global system reconfigures and the contradiction between the national and the transnational comes into greater relief, connections between Japanese film and the world will appear less as esoteric deviations than as the passkeys that allow entrance to a whole new series of productive questions and problems.
> —ERIC CAZDYN

Naruse's silent films were produced at the end of a period known as the *modan* years in which modern men and women, known as *moba* and *moga* (for "modern boys" and "modern girls"), commodity culture, and mass culture flourished on the streets of Japan's cities. The "flamboyant," rapidly paced style of these films is emblematic of the dynamic modernity of the times, capturing its spirit of excess, fragmentation, and mobility. Yet the narrative material remained embedded in the sentimental melodramatic mode of shinpa tragedy. The director's women-centered films are thus very much a hybrid of the new and the old, the foreign and the familiar, and they therefore embody the contradictions of Japanese modernity as it was constructed during these crucial years.

Shochiku was the only major studio operating in Tokyo from 1923 to 1934, a period in which the city underwent significant reconstruction and expansion following the 1923 earthquake. Modern transportation systems of streetcars, trains, roadways, and bridges were installed; department stores and hotels were erected; and old neighborhoods were completely transformed. At its Kamata studio, Shochiku specialized in *gendai geki*, or films with contemporary settings, leaving the Kyoto-based studios to concentrate on *jidai geki* or period films. The specific style associated with Shochiku-Kamata, sometimes abbreviated as SKS, tends to be identified with Ozu Yasujiro, who began directing there three years before Naruse. However, in addition to these two directors, the SKS style was developed within an industrial mode of production and included several other directors, including Shimizu Hiroshi, Gosho Heinosuke, Shimazu Yasujiro, and Ushihara Kiyohiko. Studio head Kido Shiro is also generally recognized as playing a major role in the development of SKS, as it developed into the dominant mode of gendai geki in Japanese cinema. Kido in fact scripted Naruse's first film, *Mr. and Mrs. Swordplay* (*Chanbara Fufu*, 1930), a twenty-one-minute domestic comedy that was shot in thirty-six hours straight.[1] It concludes with the husband going out to see another Shochiku feature at a movie theater.

Filmgoing is a favorite occupation of the characters in the Shochiku-Kamata movies, reflexively situating the cinema among the many everyday rituals and customs depicted in the films. In her analysis of SKS, Mitsuyo Wada-Marciano argues that the studio's extensive output during the formative years of the late 1920s and early 1930s constitutes a cornerstone of modern Japanese mass culture.[2] Not only did the studio exploit the locations of the burgeoning metropolis, it bridged the transition from silent to sound cinema and established the stylistic ingredients for a national cinema. It was responsible for providing the dominant imagery of metropolitan life for a nation that was still in fact largely rural and unevenly modernized. SKS combined the novelties of modern urban experience, heavily influenced by Western customs, iconography, and technologies, with a nostalgic portrayal of community. The dynamic configuration of everyday life in the city was counterbalanced by an image of the family, neighborhood, and "hometown" that was increasingly threatened by the fragmenting effects of urban life.

The audiences of these films were primarily the new urban middle class of salaried office workers and their families.[3] Women were especially targeted as potential audiences, and it was an important venue for both wives and "office ladies," or unmarried women holding clerical jobs, to go out in public. Kido Shiro understood that women did not go to movies alone but would always be accompanied by friends or relatives and were therefore a doubly lucrative market. He also perceptively claimed that "the fact that the old moralistic ideas have a repressive stranglehold on women presents opportunities for us to create various theatrical stories for our films."[4] The woman's film thus "solidified the studio's production system" and, as Wada-Marciano argues, "served both to configure a female identity as consuming subject and to provide material for her consumption."[5]

Shochiku-Kamata style involved a hybridization of Hollywood-inspired film techniques with the aesthetics of shinpa theater. Conventional film histories suggest that in the 1920s the "pure cinema" movement dispensed with the accoutrements of Japanese theater in order to hone a more modern and "realist" aesthetic based on the Hollywood model. The realism of SKS was, however, largely indebted to shinpa aesthetics, which were an early and important feature of Japanese modernity. Wada-Marciano argues that shinpa "formed the narrative core of the SKS film," particularly in its emphasis on the woman's film. Although by the late 1920s the notion of shinpa had fossilized into an aesthetic that is considered to be highly static, formal, and antirealist, in the 1900s it corresponded to a variety of styles.[6] Shinpa theater, or "new school drama," emerged as a theatrical movement after 1888 and originated as an oppositional form. Utilizing contemporary settings and costumes and addressing issues of modern life, shinpa represented an important antidote to the archaic language of kabuki and the formalism of no theater in Meiji Japan. As a theatrical movement, it reached its height during the Russo-Japanese War, when current sociopolitical issues of the day were staged.[7] As early as the 1890s, shinpa theater used actresses rather than *oyama* and developed stories from serialized novels with female protagonists. Above all, the plays addressed contemporary issues of morality and ethics emerging in a changing society—precisely the melodramatic material that Kido recognized as being of interest to women.

Although the construction of realism in modern Japanese theater, cinema, and literature is subject to some debate, it is somewhat simplistic to attribute all realist discourse to Western influence, especially given the forty years of Japanese cultural production preceding Naruse's first films. In Wada-Marciano's analysis of the role of shinpa in SKS, she points out that as the I-novel became the dominant mode of realism in the construction of Japanese cultural history, the romanticism of shinpa, along with its realist aesthetics, was undervalued.[8] The shinpa elements of SKS were also played down in Shochiku's own promotional discourse, which emphasized the modern cinematic qualities of the style. However, Wada-Marciano convincingly argues that it is only in its hybridization of shinpa and Hollywood technique that SKS was able to forge an aesthetic that would come to construct a "modern national Japanese identity." She points out that Shochiku's 1920s shinpa films were a calculated departure from Nikkatsu's version, so they dropped the terminology. However, they maintained a division devoted to shinpa-style film alongside their "new Kamata style film," and there continued to be a great deal of interaction between the two groups within the studio.[9]

Naruse's SKS films exemplify the fusion of traditional shinpa narrative elements with up-to-date filmic technique in a style that was known at the time as "Kamata modernism."[10] Ironically, it is the former that provides the films' realist elements, while the latter is used for expressive and disjunctive effects of space and time. The exuberant, dynamic, and "flamboyant" method of these films is anchored in the melodramatic milieu of everyday life in the city. Two of Naruse's early films, *Not Blood Relations* (*Nasanu naka*, 1932; aka *The Stepchild*) and *Wife! Be Like a Rose!* were adapted from shinpa plays, and in both instances, critics were impressed at how he enhanced them with cinematic technique. Naruse would continue to rely on shinpa-style narratives throughout the 1930s and during the war, gradually reducing the flamboyant effects and working more with performance elements to achieve emotional effects. Naruse was not alone in his revision of the typical shinpa melodrama. Kido Shiro's conception of the woman's film was one in which the old-fashioned, conventional morality of shinpa melodrama would be replaced by women with more modern attitudes.[11]

Naruse's distinctive style in his silent films corresponds to two of the tendencies that David Bordwell identifies in Japanese silent film. On one hand, he uses the "piecemeal style" that Bordwell associates primarily with the Shochiku-Kamata studio, and with Ozu, who eventually recast it into a more idiosyncratic poetics. This style "dissects each scene into neat static shots . . . having an average shot length of three to five seconds."[12] Bordwell attributes the origins of this style to the "one-bit-of-information-per-shot approach of Fairbanks, Lloyd, Lubitsch and William de Mille" and adds, "there is also a certain playfulness about the style, as unexpected cuts and sudden screen entrances disturb the limpid flow of information." While this certainly serves as a good description of Naruse's basic approach, the director also clearly combined the piecemeal style with what Bordwell calls the "calligraphic style," which was ostensibly used mainly for *chanbara*, or swordplay films. Bordwell describes the calligraphic style as a "flamboyant, frantic style, bristling with energetic figure movement . . . rapid and discontinuous editing, tight telephoto framings, and above all bravura camera movements (whip pans, fast dollies, bumpy handheld shots)."[13] Although he admits that these two styles, along with a third—the pictorialist—are often found in combination, Bordwell describes them as various "decorative" devices, used to "embroider" or "elaborate" the narrative point. Insofar as they are add-ons to the Hollywood model of narrative realism, in his opinion they constitute the "Japaneseness" of this period of Japanese cinema.[14]

A close analysis of Naruse's surviving work from this period challenges Bordwell's account on a number of levels. In the first place, the flamboyant effects were perceived at the time as add-ons to shinpa-style narrative, rather than to Hollywood style. Whereas Bordwell suggests that "the norms of the West provided a framework within which more distinctively 'Japanese' elements could be situated,"[15] in fact the reverse is more to the point—that the techniques of Western modernity were added to a framework derived from traditional Japanese theater, to construct a mode of "vernacular modernism." The dynamic use of camera movements, figure movement, and disjunctive editing in Naruse's silent films is emblematic of the "modern techniques" of cinematic representation. Given the urban settings of the films, they are frequently associated with the fragmentation of urban space and disjunctive temporalities of trains and automobiles. Second, the "flamboyant" techniques, including camera movements as well as montage effects, are always related to extreme emotional states. Naruse uses these techniques to explore the resources of cinematic language for their expressive potential, linking that expressivity to character psychology. There is no reason to attribute any particular Japaneseness to the special effects of his flamboyant style, and to dismiss them as merely decorative is to overlook their crucial role in the construction of subjective effects. Instead, I would link them to the discourse of modernity being developed during this period. The flamboyant style represents an intention on the part of the filmmaker to directly represent experience.

In each of Naruse's surviving silent films, he employed a particular distinctive variation on the flamboyant style: a rapid track-in to a character's face at a moment of great emotion. He uses this technique most spectacularly in scenes of heightened dramatic intensity in his most well-regarded films of this period, the three singled out by the critics in a 1934 *Kinema Junpo* roundtable discussion with Naruse: *Apart from You* (*Kimi to wakarete*, 1933), *Every Night Dreams* (*Yogoto no yume*, 1933), and *Street without End* (*Kagiri naki hodo*, 1934).[16] (It may not be sheer coincidence that these three films endorsed by the critics have been preserved while so many others have been lost.) All three films are about women working as geisha or café waitresses. Although the dramatic camera movements are used to convey the expressions of both male and female characters, one can see in these films, along with the fourth surviving feature, *Not Blood Relations*, how Naruse begins to articulate a discourse of female subjectivity in a melodramatic modality.

The stylistic excesses of Naruse's silent films carried over into his early sound films at P.C.L., and it really wasn't until the late 1930s that they were finally excised. In this respect we should also recognize the influences of "Taisho democracy" and the avant-garde movements of the late 1920s on his early style. Even though he was working within the context of mass industrial culture, the influences of Western modernity included both the modernist avant-garde alongside the productions of American mass culture. For example, many of his early films show the influence of the new "modern" culture of Asakusa urban entertainments and cultural practices. Many films feature women associated with the rebuilt district and its dance halls and geisha houses. Asakusa was the hot spot during this period for movie theaters, alongside dance halls and musical revues. His first sound film, *Three Sisters with Maiden Hearts*, was adapted from one of Kawabata Yasunari's many Asakusa stories, and two of its principal actresses, Tsutsumi Masako and Umezono Ryuko, were scouted by P.C.L. from dance reviews and dance teams.[17] Naruse's treatment of urban space is similar to Kawabata's, and the domestic melodramas are frequently interwoven with gangster narratives, a popular genre of the time that dominates Kawabata's stories of Asakusa.

Like Kawabata's serialized newspaper stories, Naruse's silent cinema represents an unusual confluence of popular entertainment and techniques that are associated in the West with the avant-garde. As Donald Richie notes of Kawabata, "This was possible because in Japan, then as now, the avant-garde is at once incorporated into the taste of the masses, so strong is the lure of the new."[18] Kawabata himself was strongly influenced by the movies, and the interaction and interpenetration of literature, newsreels, newspapers, and film was extensive during this period. While the Western modernism of Eisenstein and Brecht was itself heavily influenced by Asian styles of representation, in the late 1920s we see this modernism returning as the sign of the new. However, it is equally important to recognize that for Kawabata, as with Naruse, the new was always combined with more "local" aesthetics and traditional forms, to the extent that distinctions between "high" and "low" culture that are pervasive in Western modernism simply did not apply. Class distinctions are, however, embedded in the visual culture of the era, as many of the accoutrements of Western material culture were available only to the very wealthy.

From 1920 to 1936, Shochiku-Kamata produced 1,249 films, of which only 50 remain. Wada-Marciano notes that such a small sample makes it difficult to really understand the full extent of the relationship between cinema and modernity that was constructed during this period.[19] Yet it is a valuable starting point for theorizing the cultural components of Japanese cinema. Of Naruse's twenty-four SKS films, only five have survived the contingencies of institutional neglect and wartime destruction. Nevertheless, those films are consistent with many of the themes of Japanese modernity that were developed by Japanese intellectuals of the period. Moreover, the use of expressive cinematic technique for the elaboration of melodramatic emotion in Naruse's silent woman's films indicate the complex and contradictory configuration of gender that needs to be recognized as an important feature of Japanese modernity that has hitherto been overlooked.

Because of the few films surviving from this period, it is especially hard to gauge the extent to which Naruse's cinema distinguished itself from the SKS norm. Many directors made various types of women's films, and many of them employed novel techniques of cinematic representation. Bordwell notes that Ozu's silent films exhibit "far purer instances of the piecemeal approach" than those of other directors,[20] and certainly Naruse's silent films are far more "calligraphic" than Ozu's. His dynamic camera movements and fast-paced editing create psychological and melodramatic effects that are rare in Ozu's silent films, and the critical discourse of the period suggests that they were indeed unusual. While Naruse's cinema was very typical of the period's preoccupation with class difference, there is insufficient evidence to know how much the excesses of commodity culture were also depicted in other films.

Despite the avant-gardism of these remarkable films, we also need to bear in mind that, far from being a critic of capitalism, Naruse was deeply enmeshed in the excesses of commodity culture. With respect to *Chocolate Girl* (*Chokoreto garu*, 1932), for example, about a woman working in a candy shop, Naruse admitted that there may have been a little bit too much chocolate in that film, and it was not really intended to be an advertisement for the Meiji Candy Company.[21] Meiji chocolate actually appears in a number of Naruse's silent films, as a kind of product placement. In *Apart from You*, in a scene on a train, a character unwraps a chocolate bar and the camera frames it in close-up on her lap with the label clearly legible. Although many of his twenty-four Kamata films have a comic aspect that might classify them as *nansensu* films ("nonsense films"), Audie Bock claims that with *Now Don't Get Excited* (*Nee kofun shicha iya yo*, 1931), Naruse began inserting gags at necessary intervals to be able to "do what he wanted" with the rest of the film. Bock suggests that with his subsequent films that year, Naruse began writing from his own life experience living over a sushi shop.[22]

On the level of ideology, it is true that SKS was in many ways a "smoothing out" of the political agendas of the more radical "tendency films" of the 1920s that incorporated overt forms of social criticism endorsed by Prokino, or "Japan Proletarian Motion Picture League."[23] By the 1930s, SKS films were content to illustrate social tendencies of social inequity. Anderson and Richie suggest that the softening of the political discourse reflects a Japanese aversion to doctrinaire politics;[24] however, the more oblique illustration of irrevocable class differences is also more consistent with melodramatic modernism and with shinpa narrativity.[25] Moreover, nationalist impulses and government censorship intensified with the Manchurian incident of 1931 that gradually stifled the progressive impulses of "Taisho democracy." Even though all of Naruse's Kamata films deal with the working and lower classes, and their struggle for survival in a class-based society, none could be described as didactic. A few titles, such as *Hard Times* (*Fukeiki jidai*, 1930), are about *lumpenproletariat* (called *rumpen-mono*), but most deal with salarymen and their families and would thus be classified as shoshimin-eiga, or films about "common people." Others are set in the milieu of the water trade, or feature young people living independently in the city, films that depict the everyday life of a new urban class who socialize outside the home.

With the exponential development of mass media in the 1920s, the modern girl, or moga, became the iconic figure of Western values and consumer culture. Circulating within the pages of women's magazines, department store floor models, posters, advertising, and popular music, the moga typically sported a cloche hat, bobbed hair, and stylish Western dress. Needless to say, she was a controversial figure, and was as much a media construction as a real personage. In Barbara Sato's view, one of the biggest threats that the moga posed was the inability of intellectuals to "control" the moga image, and she came to represent the power of the media to influence cultural values. Sato suggests that the new images of women that emerged during the interwar period offered possibilities of a refashioning of culture, through the commodification of the everyday, "socially and psychologically" initiating "the fight for changes that would alter women's lives in the wake of post WW II reforms."[26]

While the moga was indeed a prominent figure in the cinema in her narrative contextualization and characterization, she was by no means embraced as a progressive figure. She was undoubtedly an important element of the visual spectacle, but as Wada-Marciano concludes from her analysis of SKS, "as modern signifiers they [the moga] are often contained within alternately patriarchal and national discourses." She argues, "There was no distinct break between Japanese modernity and nationalism in the transition of historical periods, but, rather, a nested box structure in which Japanese modernity occurred concurrently with nationalism, as is the case of the woman's film genre."[27]

Moga figures appear in a number of Naruse's silent and early sound films, including *Not Blood Relations*, *Three Sisters with Maiden Hearts*, *The Girl in the Rumor* (*Uwasa no musume*, 1935), and *Wife! Be Like a Rose!*. In each case, the modern girl is compared and contrasted with another woman or a sister and found wanting. In each case she is either reformed, marginalized, or domesticated, in keeping with the dominant ideology of the period. If the intellectuals could not "control" the moga, narrative cinema certainly tried, although in the excesses of the medium, the contradictions surrounding the image are nevertheless legible. In her very presence as a spectacle, and in her challenge to the norms of social convention, the moga constitutes a significant feature of the vernacular modernism of interwar Japanese cinema, underscoring, among other things, the crucial role of fashion in the construction of Japanese modernity.

In addition to the moga, new women in Japanese cinema of the interwar period included the young working professional, or "office lady," and the café waitress. While the figure of the office lady remains a constant in Naruse's films through the next two decades, the café waitress is somewhat more specific to the 1930s. Later in his career we find bar hostesses and retail workers, but the most fully developed café waitress is Takamine Hideko's impersonation of Hayashi Fumiko in the 1962 film based on Hayashi's autobiographical *Horoki* (*A Wanderer's Notebook*). Set in the early 1930s, Hayashi's narrative depicts the working conditions and lifestyle of the café waitress in terms of gender and economic relations. Her account is one of the only ones that offers a perspective from the woman's point of view, but there are many other accounts that indicate the central role of the café and the women employees in the changing landscape of everyday life in modern Japan. Miriam Silverberg has described the café waitress or *jokyu* as a figure who was undoubtedly eroticized within the gendered relations of café life, but who also engaged in a playful game in which her sexuality gave her an important leverage in the public sphere. Unlike the bar hostess who supplanted her in postwar Japan, and the geisha who preceded her, the café waitress was far more exposed in the openness of street life, available to anyone who could afford the price of a drink.[28]

Silverberg also notes that the café waitress tended to wear kimono and apron, which distinguished her from the moga, who filled the more sensational feminine role of the period: "The 'modern girl' was largely a media construct, but the café waitress, free in her highly restricted way to 'move up to Ginza' in response to want ads or to descend down into back alleys where prostitutes hid behind false store-fronts, embodied capitalist tensions through the commodification of her services in ways that the geisha who was both owned and trained could never do."[29]

Naruse's film *Street without End* depicts the trials and tribulations of two café waitresses, illustrating Silverberg's point about their social mobility in the public sphere. The heroine of *Every Night Dreams* also works in a bar, but the Yokohama setting is much more low-rent than the cosmopolitan venue of the Ginza café in *Street without End*. In each of his extant silent films, except perhaps for *Apart from You*, we find some variation on the new Japanese woman, but as Wada-Marciano indicates, the nationalist project was deeply embedded within the construction of modernity at Shochiku-Kamata. Even if Naruse's women repeatedly fall back into their places within a closed social system, they do so as changed subjects. Within the technological display of Naruse's "flamboyant style," they have become modern subjects, fully part of the future promised by new ways of seeing and being in the world.

Shochiku-Kamata Style and Japanese Modernity Theory

The only extant print from the director's first two years at Kamata is *Flunky, Work Hard* (*Koshiben ganbare*, aka *Little Man, Do Your Best*, 1931). This twenty-eight-minute film, the second that Naruse scripted himself, combines aspects of nansensu comedy, tendency film, and shoshimin-eiga with a particularly flamboyant method of decoupage. Although the penultimate scene is the most spectacular, it is full of unusual editing, special effects, and surprising camera movements. It is about an insurance salesman called Okabe (Yamaguchi Isamu) who competes with another salesman to sell a policy to a rich housewife named Mrs. Toda. He and the other salesman bully each other and compete for the attention of the woman's five children. The comparison between the men's competition and the competitive bullying of little boys is very much like the similar analogy depicted in Ozu's well-known silent film *I Was Born But . . .* (*Umarete wa mita karedo*, 1932). Okabe has a young son who is bullied by the son of the Toda family and fights back, jeopardizing his father's potential sale. Okabe strikes his son, who runs off, only to be hit by a train.

The dramatization of the accident, which Okabe himself does not witness but is told about, is extraordinarily kinetic, involving a fragmentation of space and time in a spectacular montage of imagery, combining flashbacks of previous scenes involving Okabe and his son, Okabe and Mrs. Toda, and Okabe and Toda's son with shots of a train, tracks, and the boy, Susumu, in negative, looking somewhat ghostly. The sequence is extremely fast, squeezing twenty-five shots into twenty seconds, so most of these images are merely glimpsed. Moreover, in addition to the speed and multiplicity of images, the sequence also employs a plethora of special effects, including kaleidoscopic divisions of the frame with both hard- and soft-edged seams. Okabe's close-up is fragmented horizontally and diagonally, while Susumu's eyes are multiplied and swirled. Vertical wipes introduce and separate the flashback images and two shots of train tracks converge in superimposition. Many of these effects of visual instability and dynamic movement can be found in Dziga Vertov's *Man with a Movie Camera* (1929), and the train shots, combined with the images of eyes, are particularly reminiscent of the Soviet film. Naruse's film departs from this influential city film in associating the crisis of perception—or what Vertov calls the "kino eye" of enhanced perception[30]—with the subjective experience of a fictional character. As the viewer learns about the accident only when Okada does, the special effects are clearly intended to represent the accident and at the same time indicate the father's shock.

The film ends with a rather solemn scene in the hospital as Okada joins his wife at their son's bedside. The "nonsense" aspect includes some lovely scenes of children playing in abandoned industrial lots, and the happy ending (the boy survives) is enhanced with imagery of laundry hanging and grass waving in the wind, indicative of the "life must go on" resolution of the typical SKS narrative. Despite its ostensible happy ending, *Flunky, Work Hard* depicts a world in chaos. Domestic unease is depicted from the outset by Okabe's wife, disgusted at his inability to pay the rent, sweeping madly. Transportation accidents will recur throughout Naruse's oeuvre as key narrative events, and it is already evident in 1931 that the cataclysmic accident is closely linked to the experience of

4. Okabe imagines his son's accident. Yamaguchi Isamu in *Flunky, Work Hard* (*Koshiben ganbare*, 1931), Shochiku.

everyday life in the city. The relationship of the accident to the father's struggle is left oblique, as a form of dramatic irony perhaps, because the story has no moral lesson to offer. The fact that Okada's own son is uninsured while he has just sold a policy to the boy's friend's wealthy family is a social "tendency" over which the characters have no control. The motif of the accident links the destiny of class difference to the irrevocable speed of modernity.

Flunky, Work Hard introduces many key themes of Naruse's work at Shochiku-Kamata and suggests the parameters of his vernacular modernism. In addition to the dynamic formalism typically linked to the modernist avant-garde, these films display an ethnographic focus on the everyday lives of the lower middle class. The role of the city in Naruse's visual style and narrative material is deeply evocative of the theorization of modernity developed by European intellectuals in the early decades of the century, especially Walter Benjamin, Siegfried Kracauer, and George Simmel. In fact, contemporaneous with Naruse's early career, Japanese intellectuals were thinking about Japanese modernity in strikingly similar terms. During the 1920s, the prevalence of new media, including the cinema, along with the visual culture of commodity capitalism (fashion and advertising) and women's new public roles as consumers and participants in café culture, spawned an extensive discourse around the phenomenology of everyday life.

Harry Harootunian has summarized many of the key ideas and thinkers of the interwar years, pointing out that in Japan, as in other peripheral sites, modernity was perceived as a perpetually incomplete process. It was necessarily characterized by an unevenness, not only between city and country life, but also within the private realm of the family and in the public life of the street, where different forms of everyday life coexisted. The contradictions within the theorization of Japanese modernity were eventually dissolved into the nationalist ideology that emerged in the late 1930s. Harootunian claims that in the postwar period "only the films of Ozu Yasujiro recall for us both the temporality of that moment when everyday life promised new possibilities and its customary materiality that granted it autonomy."[31] The presence of foreign films was an important feature of Japanese modernity of the 1920s and 1930s, but Japanese film production was equally implicated in the discourse of everyday life that Harootunian describes in terms of "dialectical optics."

That only one of Naruse's first sixteen films survives is testimony to the ephemeral status that the medium enjoyed at the time. The firebombing of Tokyo in 1945 is a major factor in the disappearance of so many films of this period (one estimate is that only 4 percent of Japanese silent films have survived),[32] but it was particularly catastrophic because there were so few prints made of each film negative in the first three decades of film production.[33] This fleeting aspect of everyday life in modern Tokyo—the sense of constant change and impermanence—is one of the major themes in Harootunian's analysis of the cultural politics of interwar Japan. A number of themes from Harootunian's work can be extracted to help situate Naruse's early films within the context of *bunka seikatsu* (cultural life) and the discourse of everydayness of the era. Harootunian's project is to translate and summarize the ideas of some of the intellectuals of interwar Japan and to correlate them to parallel studies of modern European culture. This method has the advantage of providing a valuable insight into the discourse of modernity specific to Japan, and comparing it to more familiar analyses produced within the cultures that the Japanese thinkers held up as emblematic of modernity and its discontents.

In the work of Tosaka Jun, the historiography of the present, the contemporary (*gendai*), took on the radical potential of actualization that we also find in Benjamin's writing of approximately the same period.[34] For Tosaka, the materiality of everyday life and the customs of social practice—including fashion and the sex industry or water trade—were valorized over the abstract moral principles of idealist philosophy. By developing the everyday as a philosophical concept, immediate experience was invested with the potential of actualization. The spatial properties of lived experience took priority over historical temporality in Tosaka's notion of the present as the locus of social change.[35] Harootunian suggests that Tosaka refrained from identifying the possibilities that he envisaged for Japanese modernity due to censorship.[36] He was evidently engaged in a social philosophy that was inspired by Marxist thought but, like Benjamin, he was equally engaged in the utopian aspects of cultural life in the modern city, even as he saw them threatened by the homogenizing forces of national imperialism.

The terminology of gendai and its role in Tosaka's theory alerts us most directly to the relationship between everyday life and the dual genre system that governed Japanese cinema during this period. Dating back to the distinction between the kabuki and shinpa styles of Meiji theater, the division between the jidai geki and gendai geki corresponds to an absolute divide between the past and the present. Tosaka's theorization of contemporary life is consistent with this distinction between a mythic historical past and a present tense that is in constant flux. All of Naruse's first twenty-nine films are gendai geki, and they exemplify the coexistence of a variety of cultural customs. The fashions and costumes are illustrations of Tosaka's observation that fashion constitutes the "physiognomy" or observable form of social structures.[37] Like Benjamin, Tosaka's philosophy was grounded in the phenomenological detail of everyday life. In this sense, it is significant that the Kamata shoshimin-eiga, with their extensive use of location shooting, incorporated the everyday life of the Tokyo suburbs into the fictional dramatization of the various anxieties of the period. In a film like *Flunky, Work Hard*, the discourse of insurance—as a form of gambling on the risks of everyday life—situates this short nansensu film within a network of social customs. The theme of toys, as the allegorical form of commodity capitalism, is yet another level on which this film, along with many other Naruse films, evokes the discourse of material culture that Tosaka and others recognized as the content of Japanese modernity.

The protagonist in *Flunky, Work Hard*, who has no control over the events of everyday life, represents another popular discourse of the period—the salaryman. Aono Suekichi was a theorist of the period whose book *Salaryman's Panic Time* (1930) detailed the contradictions of the petit-bourgeois householder at the mercy of the contradictions of capitalism.[38] The salaryman was the subject of many films and cartoons in prewar Japan, usually as a comic figure. In Naruse's film, the ironic and tragic conclusion points up those contradictions noted by Aono: that the psychological despair and depression of the lower-middle-class white-collar worker is symptomatic of the feudal structures still in place within corporate Japan. The *koshiben* of the title, translated as "flunky," refers to a low-paid employee who brings his own lunch to work.[39] In the unevenness of Japanese modernity, the salaryman is pressured into participating in commodity fetishism (thus the father needs to buy his child a toy), but because of the irrevocable class difference between him and his clients, his family is more vulnerable to the contingencies of everyday life. The accident, followed by the final scene in the hospital, constitutes an unusual addendum to what might otherwise have been a typical nansensu comedy. Naruse's ending is evocative of Aono's understanding of the modern forms of panic and grief experienced by the salaryman.

Although Marxist critics advocated a proletarian realism as being most appropriate to the everydayness of modern life, Kobayashi Hideo insisted on emotion and memory as a means of investing the everyday with meaning.[40] According to Harootunian, Kobayashi eventually remystified his conception of the everyday in keeping with the "Overcoming Modernity" ideology of the late 1930s.[41] However, we can also see evidence of the subjective mode in the bourgeoning genre of women's writing that was published in Japan during the interwar period, a genre that is overlooked by both Harootunian and the theorists who he associates with the discourse of everyday life. Hayashi Fumiko's *Diary of a Vagabond* (*Horoki*) was serialized in the journal *Nyonin geijutsu* (Women's Arts) from October 1928 to October 1930 and published as a book in 1930. Although women writers of the 1920s favored a confessional style, and their work was not unlike the I-novel, it tended to be labeled as *jiden shosetsu* (autobiographical fiction). The category of "women's writing" applied not to the style or content of the work, but to the gender of the author.[42] Both men's and women's fiction of the period evolved from *genbun itchi*, a Meiji-era movement that brought literary language more in line with spoken language.[43] As many commentators have pointed out, this development was inspired by women's classical confessional diaries such as Sei Shonagon's *Pillow Book*. Thus modern Japanese literature was influenced by a "feminine tradition" while at the same time modern women's writing was relegated to the inferior status of *joryu bungaku*.[44]

One of the principal themes of Japanese modernity, as it was discussed in the interwar period, was the "feminization of culture."[45] While the moga, the prevalence of women in the workplace and on the street, and the many new roles assumed by women in the metropolis threatened established gender roles, women's culture was embraced by at least one intellectual of the period. In Kobayashi Hideo's theorization of everyday life, women's culture is inscribed as a discourse of melodrama. As an example of the new meanings attached to experience in modernity, Kobayashi cites the instance of a mother mourning the loss of a child. According to Harootunian, he used the example "to emphasize his conviction that historical reality was always incomplete because it recorded only the existence of the event. The mother knows this lesson, he remarked, and she knows that the death of the child will fail to qualify as historical reality unless it is also invested with genuine feeling."[46] The mother thus becomes emblematic of the structures of subjectivity, memory, and knowledge specific to the sense of time and place in Japanese modernity.

Silverberg describes the intellectual project of Japanese modernity as an "ongoing construction of a new culture shared by all but at the same time differentiated by gender and class."[47] She notes the influence of the Soviet avant-garde on Japanese graphics and stresses the aspect of "construction" in the Japanese meaning of modernity. One of the principal ethnographic projects of early Showa was Kon Wajiro's phenomenology of everyday life, in which he attempted to identify the elements that went into the construction of Japanese modernity, including the gender codes associated with modern Japanese men and women. In elaborately illustrated essays published in magazines such as *Fujin koron* and *Modernologio*, Kon detailed the items of dress, food, work, and play favored by people in different social sites, including the street, the home, and the workplace.[48] Kon's practice may have been devoted to "recording and composing continuously the manifestation of Tokyo as it is being made anew," but as Harootunian notes, there is some irony in his commitment to drawing as his favored form of illustration.[49] Kon's neglect of photographic methods of documentation are symptomatic, Harootunian argues, of his own ambivalence toward modernity.

Thus we are directed back once again to the concurrent practices of the Japanese cinema, particularly the Kamata films that tended to incorporate so much location shooting, and, like Kon's project, also incorporated details of fashion and commodity culture on an ethnographic level of representation. The cinema in this sense needs to be recognized as a vital component of what Silverberg describes as "the construction of a complex identity informed by a type of cultural code-switching whereby elements of Western material culture were integrated into everyday practice."[50] In conjunction with Kon's contemporary project, the cinema constituted a form of ethnography that was more fully immersed in the constructivist project, especially once we take into account the montage aesthetics that dominated the visual style of the cinema of the late 1920s and early 1930s. In Naruse's silent films, a flamboyant visual style becomes directly linked to a gendered discourse of everyday life.

As Naruse's cinema began to focus on the everydayness of women's lives in modern Japan, it was in a sense caught up within the contradictions emerging from an intellectual discourse that seemed by and large unable and unwilling to embrace the role of the feminine in Japanese modernity. At the same time, through the discourse of melodrama and the technology of motion pictures, his cinema brings those contradictions to the fore, situating familiar iconography within a detailed depiction of life in the modern metropolis.

Not Blood Relations
THE OTHER MOTHER

Nasanu naka (*Not Blood Relations*, 1932) is Naruse's second feature-length film, and with the exception of the short *Flunky, Work Hard*, the earliest surviving print. Like many of Naruse's films of the period, and indeed, like many Shochiku-Kamata films, it deals with a contrast between a moga and a more traditional wife. In this instance, the moga figure, Tamae (Okada Yoshiko), is a famous actress who returns to Japan after a six-year absence in America. The plot hinges on Tamae's desire to reclaim her abandoned daughter Shigeko from the family she left her with. The daughter, however, has become attached to her adoptive mother, Masako (Tsukuba Yukiko), and refuses the attentions of her real movie-star mother. Assisted by her gangster brother, Tamae kidnaps the child but finally relents and gives her up.

The contrast between the two women constitutes the film's melodramatic tension. Tamae dresses in fancy Western clothes and jewels, although she wears a fancy kimono when she arrives from America to meet the press, underlining her authentic Japaneseness—which after a trip abroad an actress would be at pains to confirm.[51] As Tsuneishi Fumiko notes, the film is remarkable in the way that the emotional emphasis shifts away from Masako, "the good wife," toward Tamae.[52] However, in keeping with the dominant ideology of the period, the moga is eventually excluded from the family system and literally sent back to America.

Based on a popular shinpa play that was first adapted to film in 1909 by the Japanese production company M. Pathé (and undoubtedly by other companies as well in the interim), the story was declared to be "outdated" by the time Naruse was assigned to it. Nevertheless, the same critics who made this pronouncement also recognized Naruse's use of cinematic techniques to breathe new life into the story, even if, as Tokata Sachio claimed, the novelty is only on the surface.[53] It is in fact a completely wild film, employing more camera movements within a fast-paced edit than any of the director's other surviving silents, and perhaps outstripping any known silent films from anywhere. Fast dollies punctuate virtually every confrontation between characters, accentuating moments of emotional tension. These are frequently combined with horizontal pans, which are used in interior sets, and the film is also full of both traveling shots of chase scenes and swish pans in close quarters. The tracking shots move forward and backward, and in some instances end with the character moving out of frame, or a door closing in front of the camera, or even, in at least one instance, the camera swinging to the right, away from the close-up into which it has tracked.

The dynamic energy of the film is announced in the opening scene, which starts with a swish pan over a city scene, followed by an intertitle declaiming "Thief!" A boy has stolen a purse. This young ruffian is the film's principal comic character, who may have only a minor role but brings in an important *nansensu* element to an otherwise sentimental story. The boy turns out to be the cohort of Tamae's brother, a gangster who helps her kidnap the child, Shigeko. The kidnapping plot is aided by Shigeko's grandmother, who is devastated by her son's bankruptcy and easily tempted by the luxurious home of Tamae. The fishery business owned by Shigeko's father, Atsumi (Nara Shinyo), collapses early in the narrative, and because he cannot pay off his employees or his creditors, Atsumi is jailed. One of the film's most remarkable scenes is one in which Atsumi meets with his staff (salaried white-collar workers) who all stand in a line across from his desk. The camera pans left and right along their faces, stopping at individuals who speak for the group. Cut back to Atsumi alone on the other side of the desk, responding to their outrage and promising to find money for them. The rhythm of camera movements and 180-degree reversal cutting is a powerful means of underlining the drama of financial collapse. Atsumi has failed not only his family, but his employees as well.

The film may be principally a domestic melodrama, but it makes a significant nod to Depression-era labor unrest, and Naruse has evidently updated the original play to include contemporary issues. If the original play predates 1909, when there were very few actresses, let alone famous actresses, in Japan, Naruse's version has also changed the profession of one of the main characters. When Atsumi discovers that it is Tamae who has offered to bail out his company—in exchange for her daughter—he exclaims, "that ended six years ago." Although the paternity of the child is never discussed directly in the film, it is entirely possible that he is the natural father of Shigeko. Yet the central issue is one of maternity; it is Masako who is "not blood relations," despite the child's passionate attachment to her as an adoptive mother. Masako's brother Kusakabe, played by the striking actor Oka Joji, arrives from Manchuria and helps her negotiate with Tamae and the gangsters.

In the kidnapping scene itself, Tamae confronts the terrified child on the street, in an extraordinary sequence of reverse-cut rocket dollies intercut with screaming intertitles, but the ultimate capture of the girl is barely glimpsed. Likewise, the final confrontation involving all the key players, including the grandmother, the gangsters, Kusakabe, the two women, and the child, is a cataclysmic sequence, so rapidly edited that it is hard to know exactly what happens. The scene ends with a shot of Tamae alone, everyone else having suddenly disappeared. A slow track into her profile is matched with a shot of a streetlight, prolonging the moment in which she comes to the realization that she has made a mistake. Cut to Shigeko playing with her friends in her humble home. In a brief epilogue, Atsumi is released from prison and the family plans to visit Tamae, but she has already boarded a ship to return to America.

The ending restores order to the happy Japanese family, and its sentimentality confirms the critical denunciation of shinpa drama as being "cheap" and "tacky." If the tragedy consists in the famous actress's inability to get her child to love her, it is outweighed by the moral virtue of the adoptive mother. The film is, however, redeemed by its stylish excess. Naruse's adaptation of the drama renders it resolutely modern, not only in its technical flourishes, but also in the way the story is embedded in commodity culture and the dramatic discontinuities of everyday life in the city. *Not Blood Relations* features two accidents, both of which involve the little girl and a toy. In the first instance, Masako dives in front of a car and is hit trying to save the girl. In the second instance, Shigeko attempts to escape from Tamae's home and is hit by a bicycle. Both scenes are constructed from a rapid series of discrete shots of the different elements of the accident—bodies, toys, vehicles, pavement—without any real sense of causal connection between shots. The feel of the accidents is prioritized over the maintenance of continuous diegetic space. Naruse came to excel in melodramatic narrative precisely through this ability to create emotional effects from the minimal components of narrative information.

In another scene of *Not Blood Relations*, Tamae takes Shigeko to a department store, where they gaze at an overwhelming array of dolls. Tamae and the grandmother urge the girl to pick one out, but Shigeko simply asks repeatedly for her mother. Masako has in fact followed them to the department store and when she spots them a great chase ensues, with the women separated at first by a crowd of shoppers and then by an elevator door closing. As Tamae, the grandmother, and Shigeko descend in the elevator, Masako takes the stairs, only to catch up to them just as their car is leaving. Mother and (adoptive) daughter glimpse each other through the rear window of the car. It may be the ultimate in tear-jerking melodrama, but at the same time, the scene fully exploits the dynamic potential of urban space, conjoined with the full array of cinematic techniques to suggest the speed and discontinuities of the experience of modernity.

In keeping with the Depression-era sensibility, the film contains a critique of commodity culture, articulated through the grandmother's

5. Two mothers confront each other. Tsukuba Yukiko and Okada Yoshiko in *Not Blood Relations* (*Nasanu naka*, 1932), Shochiku.

"embarrassment" at being poor, and the failure of Tamae's money to buy her love. It may be a fairly clichéd politic of liberal humanism, but more important than these narrative conceits is the discourse of excess implicit in the array of toys surrounding the child. Shigeko is introduced playing with a toy kitchen, serving pretend tea, and it is this alternate reality of the toy to which Naruse's elaborate decoupage points. Already in this early feature, he constructs a movie world of fragmentation and speed from a somewhat tired story. It is from this "superficial" world that the moment of truth and authenticity is extracted. Everything turns, in the end, on a single close-up shot of the actress thinking. A psychological space is effectively carved out of the surrounding chaos of everyday life; the "bad" woman makes good and restores order to the family through the achievement of insight.

Apart from You
STYLE AND SENTIMENT

Apart from You (*Kimi to wakarete*, 1933) was described by Kitagawa Fuyuhiko in *Kinema Junpo* as being a typical Shochiku-Kamata film, but with a certain freshness that he attributes to Naruse's ability to "gaze at truth." In particular, he points to the urban setting that departs from the usual "Ginza-esque or Shinbashi-esque" neon signs. Instead, Naruse features "an apartment with the laundry hanging in the porch, and a forest of smoking chimneys and gas tanks."[54] This is the setting in which the two geisha, one "in training," the other facing the professional crisis of age, ply their trade. Like many of Naruse's films from this period, and from later years, *Apart from You* is about a constellation of characters, with a consequently bifurcated narrative focalization.

In contrast to the bourgeois setting of *Not Blood Relations*, this film is set among the working poor on the peripheries of the metropolis. It takes up the themes of Kawabata's Asakusa stories about women in the water trade and the violent activities of petty criminals, but far from being exoticized, the denizens of this world are linked to the cycles of perpetual poverty. The two geisha protagonists are anxious that their loved ones not be drawn into a world of which they are deeply ashamed. Kikue (Yoshikawa Mitsuko), the older geisha, has a son, Yoshio (Isono Akio) who is being drawn into a local gang of young hoodlums. He has stopped going to school because he is ashamed to be the son of a geisha. Kikue's younger geisha friend Terukiku (Mizukubo Sumiko) has a younger sister who is destined to be sold to a brothel.

Naruse scripted this film himself, and the parallelism of the two stories strengthens its articulation of a "social problem," while the plot is rather understated and somewhat contrived. Terukiku invites Yoshio to visit her family so that he will better appreciate his mother's love and not be ashamed of her profession. Terukiku's family is dominated by a drunk father who hits her and everyone else, although the harbor setting gives the hometown scenes a sense of pastoral beauty, while her clownish little brother lends the film a touch of nansensu good humor. Terukiku and Yoshio are just developing their relationship when, back in Tokyo, Terukiku is accidentally stabbed by Yoshio's "friends," and after she recovers in the hospital, she leaves him to travel to an unnamed destination. The unstated but strongly implied reason for her departure is that she must resort to prostitution in order to support her family, so that her younger sister will "stay pure" and not have to follow in her footsteps. Yoshio, meanwhile, reconciles with his mother and stays with her. Duty-bound to their families, the two confess their love for each other in a final scene at the train station.

Apart from You sustains the stylistic flamboyance of Naruse's version of SKS. In this film he further develops the rhythmic approach to cutting on movement that would eventually underpin his "invisible" editing technique at P.C.L. and later at Toho. Here it is not so invisible, and includes a great number of close-ups of objects and things: mundane articles of everyday life such as food, sake, baskets, beer, and washbasins; and more exotic things like pastries, a phonograph record, and a magic lantern apparatus. These items are often linked to a character's point of view, and some details, such as a hole in Yoshio's sock, or the little brother's yo-yo or close-ups of hands clasped together — or knees touching — provide narrative links between scenes. The shot of the chocolate bar on Terukiku's lap mentioned above is only one example of a technique that is exaggerated throughout the film. It follows a "phantom ride" shot of the train tracks, and begins the next scene, in which Terukiku offers a piece of chocolate to Yoshio as they sit side by side on the train. The two characters meet accidentally on the street shortly before this, through a series of shots in which Yoshio kicks a discarded can that rolls to Terukiku's feet.

While these shots of objects are certainly related to what Noël Burch described as Ozu's "pillow shots," they are far less detached from the narrative. They are crucial to the sense of the characters being linked through the exchange of material goods, including objects, food, and of course, money. They lack the careful composition that Ozu so often reserves for such close-ups, and in the silent films, they frequently point to the impoverished status of the characters. In an early scene of *Apart from You*, Terukiku fantasizes about a bowl of noodles, which is shown in superimposition, only to vanish as quickly as it appeared. Special effects, like the magnifying power of the cinematic close-up, are means by which Naruse underscores the desires and disappointments of characters. The damaged sock and shoe is a recurring detail throughout his films of the 1930s and 1940s.

Two particular scenes stand out in *Apart from You* as exemplary of Naruse's highly stylized editing. The first, which occurs shortly before Terukiku is stabbed—an incredible quick-paced scene in itself—is a series of crosscut shots inside the inn where the two geisha are working. In one room, Kikue is alone with her patron, an elderly man, who she is sure no longer wants to see her because she is a "hag." The two of them drink sake despondently until she suddenly grabs a razor, saying that she is prepared for him to leave her. He tries to wrestle the blade away from her before she can kill herself and perhaps him as well.

Meanwhile, in the room next door, Terukiku is with another geisha and two clients who drunkenly prance around and behave like idiots. They have both the phonograph and the magic lantern going, and a third girl comes in performing some kind of exotic Spanish dance. Close-up shots indicate that Terukiku's customer wants more from her than having his drinks poured. He smacks his lips and fumbles for money from a purse, but suddenly a beer bottle is spilled, and at the same time, the struggle in the next room appears in silhouette on the screen separating the two rooms. Kikue's patron yells for help and Terukiku is next seen nursing her friend—but this scene is in turn interrupted by Yoshio's gangster friends knocking at the door. While the crosscutting illustrates the different activities of the older and the younger geisha, their climactic convergence provides a narrative arc leading to the penultimate hospital scene.

After she is stabbed, Terukiku lies in a hospital bed with Kikue (who has returned to health) and Yoshio by her side. In this remarkable scene, in which Terukiku tells Yoshio that she has to leave, Naruse orchestrates a complex series of camera movements, framings through window frames and the bedstead, flashbacks and intertitles. It opens with a shot of a nurse hanging laundry and pulls back to Yoshio in the hospital room at the window, before cutting (and tracking forward) to Terukiku in bed. The ensuing scene lasts three minutes and fifteen seconds, with an average shot length of three seconds, including eleven intertitles and ten flashback images. The three characters are framed in different compositions, from different angles, and the cutting and camera pans and dollies are cued to their movements as Kikue and her son move around the bed. Terukiku lies in bed and does most of the talking. The scene includes a montage of images superimposed on one another drawn from the previous scene in which she and Yoshio visited her family. After this she says she would be happy if she could "die like this" and closes her eyes, rolling her head to the side. But then she opens her eyes and announces that she "won't be defeated by any hardships." The scene ends with an intertitle saying, "And when Terukiku's injury has been healed," before cutting to the final scene at the station.

This hospital scene is remarkable in the way it depicts a geometry of emotions. It is not only rhythmical, punctuated by intertitles, but spatial, amplifying the melodrama with a heightened sense of the bodies in space. By cutting on the figures as they turn their heads and move up and down to kneel by the bed, the characters appear as puppets or cogs in a kind of machine. In this way the emotional excess of the shinpa-style narrative is transposed into a very "modern" discourse of technology. This in turn gives the story a kind of utopian, or at least uplifting aspect, in counterpoint to the depiction of suffering and sacrifice. In the end, the parting of the lovers is less melancholy than the sense of change that their actions are directed toward. Thomas Elsaesser describes melodrama as a genre in which "the world is closed and the characters are acted upon,"[55] while at the same time, "the conscious use of style-as-meaning [is] a mark of what I would consider to be the very condition of a modernist sensibility working in popular culture."[56] In this scene from *Apart from You*, and in Naruse's silent cinema more generally, melodramatic narratives of social oppression are transformed into modernist texts that tend to direct the characters' destinies toward the "new" possibilities of a democratized, industrialized modern Japanese culture. The world is not closed, after all, but offers a plurality of views and possible subject-positions.

While Terukiku is a prototypical Narusian heroine, surviving and confronting the many obstacles in her life, references to sexuality are rare in Naruse's oeuvre until the late 1950s, and even in the 1960s it is typical that sex is obliquely suggested rather than directly spoken about. Geisha and prostitutes are nominally very different women, and only in the lower end of the geisha business would the role of prostitution be so lewdly implied. *Apart from You* is remarkable in its pragmatic view of the geisha world and sets the tone for Naruse's subsequent treatment

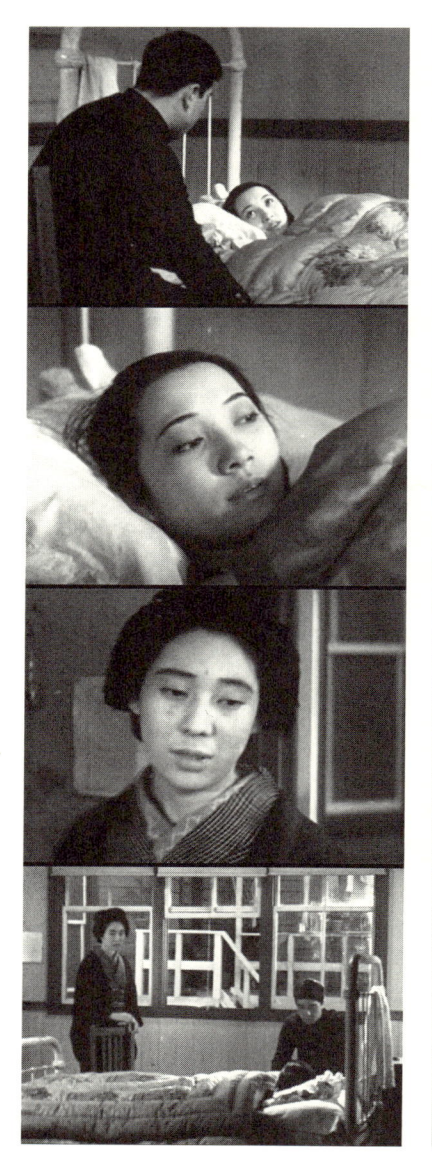

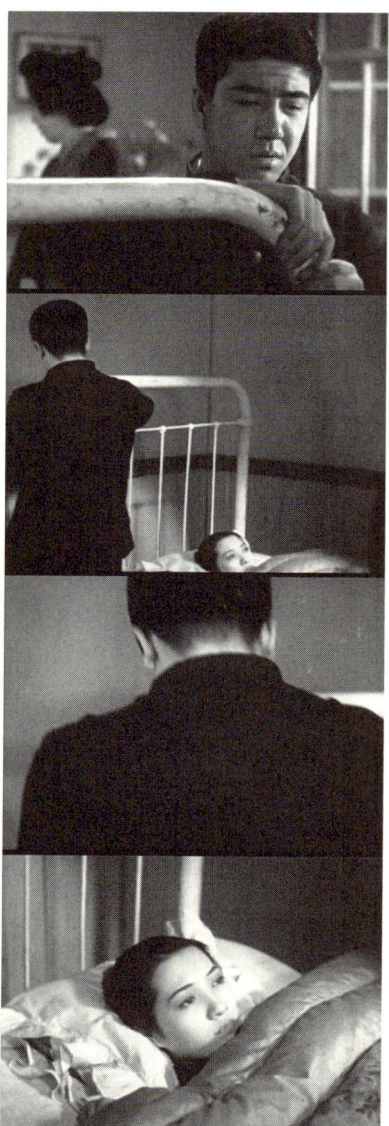

6. Issono Akio, Mizukubo Sumiko, and Yoshikawa Mitsuko in *Apart from You* (*Kimi to wakarete*, 1933), Shochiku.

of this milieu. While the (fully dressed) exotic dancer is a brief erotic touch, the coextensive representation of the male gaze is contextualized by the comic performances of the drunk salarymen clients. The film is very much geared toward the tastes of middle-class women (or women aspiring to be middle class) who would sympathize with the shame attached to the geisha profession. In fact it may be only by casting it in such a light that the film would appeal to Kido Shiro's ideal audience.

Kitagawa notes in his review that the story of *Apart from You* is a very familiar Shochiku-Kamata tale.[57] He encourages Naruse to work with more original material that might be more appropriate to his extraordinary technique. He also remarks on the influence of Ozu on the film's style, and he compares it favorably to the work of the more established director. The story of geisha as suffering heroines was evidently a Shochiku staple that Naruse invested with his own modern technique, amplifying the emotional and psychic tensions and isolating the details of material culture in the women's everyday life. The sweetness and sentimentality of the story is effectively counterposed by the stylistic excess, making *Apart from You* a virtually dialogic text.

Every Night Dreams
THE WORKING MOTHER

Naruse's 1933 film *Every Night Dreams* (*Yogoto no yume*, 1933) is about a bar hostess named Omitsu, played by Kurishima Sumiko, and constitutes one of the first sustained and developed female characterizations in his extant oeuvre. Kurishima Sumiko, known as the "Queen of Kamata" at the time, was one of the first big Japanese film stars, having started working at Shochiku as early as 1921.[58] That Naruse was assigned to work with her shows his rise through the ranks in the studio, and indeed the film placed third in the annual *Kinema Junpo* top ten list, followed by *Apart from You* at number four. Omitsu is trying to raise a son with the occasional help of a delinquent husband, who has trouble finding work. When the son is injured in a car accident, the husband attempts a burglary to pay the medical bills, but he is caught and commits suicide in humiliation.

As Wada-Marciano has noted about this film, the public space of the bar and the criminal spaces of the city are juxtaposed with the private domestic space of the family home. The mirror in front of which Omitsu prepares herself for her work, arranging her hair, acts as a conduit between the two spaces, framing the image of the eroticized woman within the domestic space. Wada-Marciano also points out that the Yokohama harbor setting of the film constitutes a kind of peripheral or marginal space; even if no foreigners are encountered, Omitsu's customers are mainly sailors.[59] The film opens with her meeting a few such men outside by the water. Like the café waitress, Omitsu has a certain autonomy and independence in this harbor space, but her desire for domesticity is inevitably compromised. Wada-Marciano argues that the film "reinforces middle-class domestic values" insofar as it operates as a "cautionary narrative" regarding Omitsu's role in the public sphere.[60] I would add that it does so only by foregrounding the contradictions implicit in her double role as mother and wage earner. Omitsu is at once "the most popular girl" at the bar and a more responsible and loving parent than her good-for-nothing husband.

The juxtaposition of domestic and public space, the Yokohama harbor setting and the empty semi-industrial spaces where children play, constituted for critics of the time a stunning new realist aesthetic. Perhaps because of the film's emphasis on the lumpenproletariat aspiring to the status of the petite bourgeoisie, the critics were drawn to the realist depiction of urban space that frames the class-based drama. Kitagawa Fuyuhiko wrote in *Kinema Junpo*: "The bright and dark sides of the emotions of these people who struggle for day-to-day survival in poverty unfold within everyday events such as those found in the daily newspapers."[61] The film journal also published a letter from a reader praising the film as a shoshimin-eiga that surpassed Ozu's examples of the genre.[62]

While Kitagawa declared the film a masterpiece, another critic, Matsui Hiro, writing in *Eiga Hyoron*, was more critical, complaining that the film was too dark with no "brightness" at all. He acknowledges that Naruse's observational style is a form of "sharp criticism" but believes his criticism is compromised by his petit-bourgeois romanticism that prevents him from going beyond the individualistic portrait to a more profound class analysis. The Marxian flavor of this critique implies that Naruse had adopted a more psychological treatment of social inequities, leaving himself open to the criticism that he failed to assume strong moral positions. However, Matsui also notes that the film may have been subject to censorship, and that some of the more detailed scenes of Omitsu's activities in the sex industry may have been cut.[63] This is entirely possible, given the state's increasing intolerance in the early 1930s for films set in the lower echelons of Japanese society, although other evidence suggests that this film was not censored at all.[64]

Every Night Dreams contains many instances of dramatic tracking into close-ups at moments of heightened emotion. These camera movements are often combined with, or followed by cuts to feet or hands or close-ups from new angles, cutting on movement, or cutting to an empty frame that is then filled by a character's movement. Camera pans, rack focusing, and the use of architecture for framing further add to the stylistic excess of the film. The fragmentation of space and of bodies often creates a spatial disorientation, but the sequences themselves are well marked off and the narrative information is clearly presented, despite the playfulness of the decoupage. Intertitles and performance elements help move the story along. The scene in which Omitsu finds that her husband has returned home is a particularly flamboyant example that nevertheless conveys a complex narrative situation. It begins with a neighbor trying to reconcile the family, but Omitsu calls her husband "the enemy." He admits that he will only cause trouble. After tracking into Omitsu's face from a long shot with the neighbor couple and the child flanking her, we cut to the husband's feet walking away. The tracking shot is repeated, followed by a shot of the husband's feet descending the stairs. Then we cut back to the close-up of Omitsu, and as the camera tracks back, she runs out of the frame. In a series of five quick shots, she follows her husband, and the sequence ends with him on the street turning with a smile and open arms. Cut to a new day, flowers on the table, and it is evident that the couple has reconciled.

With an average shot length of four seconds, this fifty-one-second sequence demonstrates an amazing narrative economy, using visual style rather than dialogue to convey a complex narrative event. The rapid cutting of this sequence, in conjunction with the camera movements, gives the scene an emotional impact that is otherwise missing from the performances and dialogue. It suggests how Naruse engaged in a process of filmic construction in which space and spatial relationships are foregrounded. As an intruder, the husband is banished from the domestic space and sent out to the street; the process of his rejection is a temporal form of the fragmented urban space of the film's setting. The abrupt change from rejection to reconciliation may be unmotivated, but it is nevertheless convincing. As a silent film, it may well have been projected with *benshi* narration, although this is not mentioned in the published criticism. Even though it is by no means dependent on narration for narrative comprehension, the benshi's presence may account for the priority that Naruse appears to have placed on stylistic effect, as if he were illustrating a narrative event rather than showing it happen. On the other hand, by 1933, by most accounts, benshi were not necessarily involved in all screenings of all films.

Another dynamic passage in *Every Night Dreams* occurs with the boy's accident, echoing the similar narrative event in *Flunky, Work Hard*. In this scene, the father accidentally knocks a toy car off a table when three children suddenly arrive to tell the parents that their son has been run over. Just before this, Omitsu is preparing to go to work in front of the mirror. Her husband asks her to quit, saying that he will find a job. Omitsu says she has to keep working at the bar for the sake of their son. This lead-up sequence is made up of thirty shots averaging 3.7 seconds each, including several track-ins to Omitsu, several abrupt 180-degree spatial reversals, and several close-up inserts of the toy car that the father picks up as if it symbolized the boy. Many of the cuts are on eye movements or glances. The domestic setting, introduced at the scene's opening with a kettle on a brazier, is disturbed by a certain restlessness of decoupage that punctuates the couple's argument. The car accident seems to erupt out of this destabilized and fragmented depiction of domestic space. The sequence of twenty shots in ten seconds once again mimics the "feel" of the violent event as a means of conveying the parents' shock at the news of their son's accident.

The direct connection between the toy car and the real car that hits the boy is one of the most striking incidences of Naruse's iconic use of the children's toy. In *Every Night Dreams*, the toy becomes the emblem of the family, linking domestic stability to consumption, a configuration that underlines the role of capitalism in the formation of the modern Japanese family. Children demand toys, and parents struggle to meet these needs, which is essentially the need to become bourgeois. This is the catalyst for the insurance salesman's ambitions in *Flunky*, while in another title from 1932, *Crying to the Blue Sky* (*Aozora ni naku*), a toy plane is a coveted object that leads to tragedy. In *Every Night Dreams*, despite the ostensible poverty of the characters, there is a certain excess of toys in the film. Shelves and closets filled with dolls and sports equipment are singled out by inserted close-ups in the family apartment. At one point the boy can be seen playing golf with a miniature set of clubs behind the adults, and the next-door neighbors also indulge him with a plethora of toys and games. The child's first line of the film is to ask his mother whether she has brought him anything back after her extended absence from home. Thus, the role of the toy car in the accident scene seems precipitous, as if the film were breaking apart from its own internal contradictions.

7. Car accident sequence from *Every Night Dreams* (*Yogoto no yume*, 1933), Shochiku.

The shock of the car accident itself, like the many accidents that run through Naruse's Kamata films, is consistent with the theorization of modernity as a network of perceptual and experiential shocks and stimuli that overwhelmed urban dwellers in the late nineteenth and early twentieth centuries. In Tokyo, no less than in Paris and New York, the cinema was a sensational new experience that took place alongside the new technologies and energetic pace of the city. Discussing this "modernity thesis" and its origins in the writing of George Simmel and Walter Benjamin, Ben Singer notes that, although the precise relationship between urban experience and the cinema remains imprecise, "we must acknowledge, and take seriously, the frequency with which early moviegoers described cinema as a medium of powerful fleeting impressions, kinetic speed, novel sights, superabundant juxtapositions, and visceral stimulation, and therefore as a medium in which people perceived a striking resemblance to modern urban experience."[65] In Japan, the parallels between film and urban experience converged most dynamically in the late 1920s, as the reconstructed city of Tokyo grew rapidly after the 1923 earthquake into a metropolis built around the car and the streetcar. In addition, there was the added aspect of commodity consumption in the discourse of film marketing and the spectacle of modern goods. As Harootunian points out, American films constituted "text book lessons" in "cultural living" because of their display of "a commodity culture produced by American capitalism and its main subjects, modern women and men and their customs and experience of everyday life."[66]

In a film such as *Every Night Dreams*, we can see how the desire for commodities is mapped onto the ideal of domestic stability through the allegorical status of children's toys. Through the depiction of the car accident, Naruse makes an oblique link between commodity culture and family tragedy. Whether these associations and the implicit social critique that they point to were legible to audiences of the 1930s—or even to Naruse himself—is difficult to say. However, in becoming legible with the perspective of historical distance, they enable us to situate the film within the contradictions of Japanese modernity. The "accident" that is at once a narrative device and a function of the technological urban space of the film's setting also becomes, in Naruse's cinema, a perceptual motif and a commentary on vision.

In Wada-Marciano's discussion of *Every Night Dreams*, she points out that the empty lot in which the son watches the father play baseball with some neighboring children is a "signature space" of the shoshimin-eiga, but is articulated slightly differently in this film. The Yokohama harbor that can be glimpsed at the edges of the open lot distinguishes it from the suburban playground familiar from films such as Ozu's *I Was Born But . . .* (1932). Like those desolate spaces crossed by train tracks and telephone lines in Ozu's films, the empty lot in this film signifies the incomplete modernization of urban renewal. In *Every Night Dreams*, the game ends when the father and son see a "real" family playing together, and the father receives news that a hoped-for job did not come through.[67] Thus the film evokes the generic expectations of the shoshimin-eiga and its "cozy domesticity" but also subverts them. Children in Naruse's cinema are often getting hit by cars and trains in this semideveloped terrain. The empty lot as playground is yet another aspect of the "everyday life" that the Japanese cinema of the 1930s incorporated into its discourse on class, nation, and modernity. Urban space played a key role in establishing the generic conventions that underscored Naruse's earliest films.

The final sequence of *Every Night Dreams* is one of the most striking of Naruse's career. In a series of forty-two shots lasting a little over two minutes (average shot length three seconds, including intertitles), Omitsu runs from the harbor, where she has been handed her husband's suicide note, to her home, where her son lies with a bandaged head. She reads the note, tears it with her teeth, and throws it on the tatami. Track in to a title saying "You coward," and then "you loser." Phrases such as "running away from reality," and "is this what a man does?" are intercut with track-ins to Omitsu in close-up and multiple images of her moving into frame in right and left profile. Finally she drops down out of the frame and kneels beside the child, to whom she says, "You have to be strong." The camera tracks in twice to a two-shot of mother and son in extreme close-up, and the sequence ends with a long shot of them from a new angle. The film ends with a series of nine shots averaging less than two seconds each of laundry, women gossiping, bridges, warehouses, and boats. In the last shot of the harbor with boats in the distant background, the camera pans slowly over the waves.

Despite the extreme fragmentation of actions and the stylization of expression, one critic in 1933 described the final sequence of *Every Night Dreams* as "extremely natural,"[68] by which I can only assume he is referring to the character's reactions and not to the visual style. In other words, the flamboyance may have been read at the time as an accurate means of depicting a character's emotional state of mind. For example, the intertitles are shot with dramatic camera movements that make their exclamatory punch that much more visceral. Indeed, it constitutes an ex-

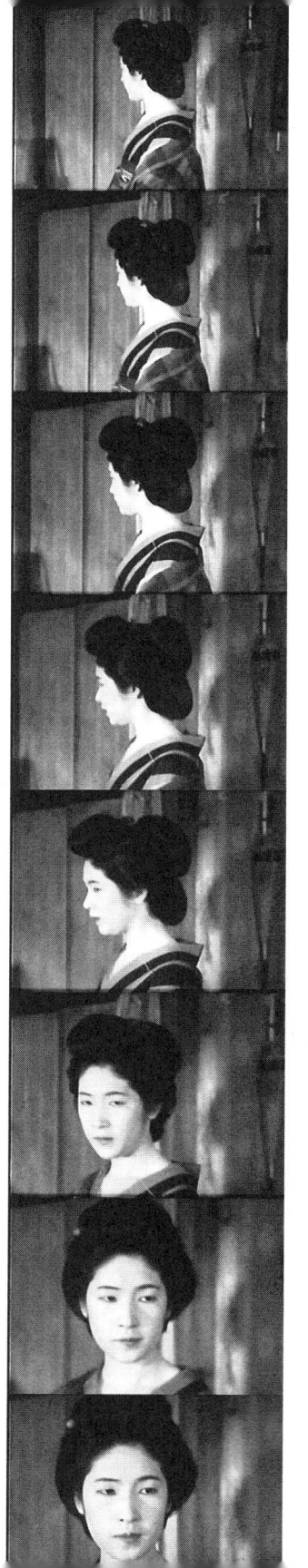

8. Kurishima Sumiko in *Every Night Dreams* (*Yogoto no yume*, 1933), Shochiku.

perimental technique of conveying the complicated emotional reaction of a woman whose grief takes the form of anger at her irresponsible husband.

Ironically, the film ends with Omitsu assuming the maternal role of the haha-mono ("mother film"), but the sentimentality of that genre is undermined by her angry and unsympathetic attitude toward her husband's suicide. The tenacity, endurance, and struggle that she offers as hope to her son will become characteristic of many of Naruse's heroines in the 1950s. However, the dynamic visual style of this sequence conveys a certain emotional excess that does not recur on this scale in Naruse's oeuvre. Especially the rapid track-ins to Omitsu's face, followed by the graphic statements of the intertitles, suggest a level of hysteria that is very rare in the shoshimin-eiga and very transgressive of the norms of polite femininity. It is also significant that the episode is followed by a montage sequence that moves away from Omitsu, through the urban sprawl, to the harbor setting. This sequence situates the drama within a sociological setting, suggesting that Omitsu's troubles are not hers alone, and that they might be in some way symptomatic of her station in life. The evocation of a social tendency is then reinforced by a final image of the water, which adds a poetic note of closure to the domestic drama.

As played by Kurishima, Omitsu's character is developed as a virtual and visceral collaboration between actress and director. Although she is rarely given more than a few seconds at a time, Kurishima is able to convey the tenacity of the character through facial expressions timed to coincide with the abrupt camera movements and editing. Her character may not be a café waitress per se, but like the women described by Silverberg, she circulates in public spaces where she is able to trade in on her eroticization, even while she is also able to dictate her own terms. Several scenes set in the bar indicate her vulnerability but also her ability to negotiate her own terms with the bar owner and the bar patrons. There may be no mogas in this film, but Omitsu's behavior and attitude are very modern. Likewise, the terms of her everyday life are clearly set by the pressures of commodity culture and new technologies, such as the automobile and the assembly line, that define and threaten the family. Her failed husband is symptomatic of the socioeconomic forces that have established impenetrable class divisions within modern life. While these are not social tendencies to be challenged, Omitsu depicts an unusual attitude of resistance to the otherwise aestheticized "tendency" of oppressive social ills.

Street without End
TRAFFICKING IN IMAGES

Naruse's last silent film is based on a popular newspaper serial by Kitamura Komatsu and bears some of the scars of collapsing a long narrative of many installments into a ten-reel, eighty-seven-minute feature. Despite the multicharacter narrative and multiple subplots with surprising twists and turns, *Street without End* (*Kagiri naki hodo*, 1934) constitutes a remarkable study of life in Ginza in 1934. In addition to scenes set in the teahouse or café where the film's two protagonists work as waitresses (the café is called "The Ginza Compal" and it serves "Tea and Meals"), the film includes many shots of the surrounding streets and the people to be seen there. It is a film about seeing and being seen in public, and not only because both protagonists are approached by talent agents from a movie studio. Shots of anonymous passersby and café patrons are inserted in the narrative to fill out the contours of a documentary-like study of the city. The opening montage of shots of the Ginza and its denizens include none of the story's main characters. The neon-lit cityscape is also featured, along with many inserts of streetlights. Coincidental meetings and sightings of characters speeding by in cars, along with the use of the telephone and the wall clock in the café, further implicate the city into the network of intersecting narrative plotlines. Compared to Asakusa, Ginza was far more cosmopolitan and "futuristic," lacking the nostalgic aspects of Asakusa,[69] and *Street without End* might be read as an attempt to find the "real people" (the "ordinary people" of the shoshimin-eiga) beneath the glitzy surface of the famous district.

Cars feature prominently, and *Street without End* predictably includes two car accidents. In the first one, one of the waitresses, Sugiko (Shinobu Setsuko), is hit on the streets of Ginza by a wealthy man named Hiroshi (Yamanouchi Ko), who falls in love with her when he visits her in the hospital. When she has recovered from her injuries, he drives her to her home in a humble neighborhood, passing a surprisingly banal series of cityscapes on the way, as Naruse seems to indulge in the traveling shots made possible by moving cars. Later, they drive to the country, where Hiroshi proposes to Sugiko in front of a view of Mt. Fuji. Their marriage is, however, doomed to failure, as Hiroshi's mother and sister strongly disapprove of Sugiko's lowly status as a waitress. While they abuse her at home, Hiroshi turns to drink and loose women, eventually driving his car off a cliff with a woman at his side (the woman is not identified, and her fate after the accident never revealed). The violence of this incident

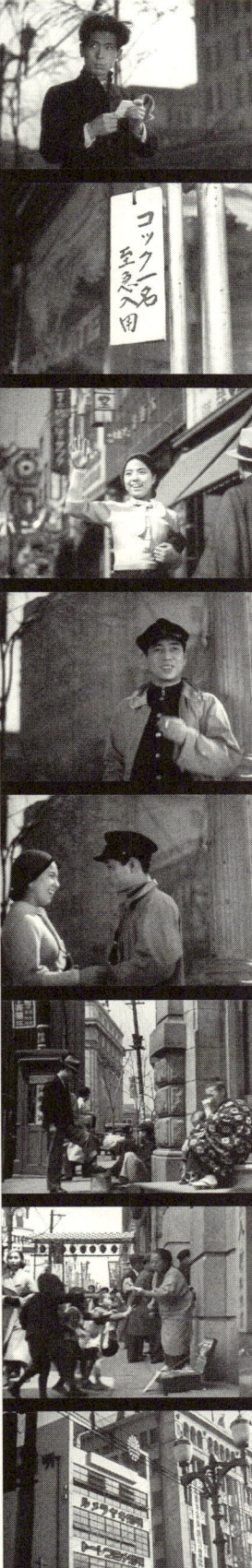

9. Opening montage of *Street without End* (*Kagiri naki hodo*, 1934), Shochiku.

is depicted in a series of quick shots of the car, the passengers and the winding mountain road, followed by close-up shots of a hat, a woman's purse, and a flask slowly sliding down a steep embankment.

Even before the accident, Sugiko has actually left her husband's home to live with her brother Koichi, who is studying to become an auto mechanic. In 1934, this would have been a bold move. Even if the trials and tribulations of the daughter-in-law were a shinpa staple, the act of leaving the family would have been quite radical. Sugiko goes to the hospital, where Hiroshi is wrapped in bandages, to say her farewells to the nasty family. She accuses Hiroshi of being weak and his family of loving their family name more than they loved her. Her husband reaches for her from his sickbed, but she turns her back on him; he drops his hand to his chest and dies shortly thereafter.

Sugiko's actions are those of a strong-willed woman who refuses to bow to social convention. A title is inserted shortly after she is first seen with her married woman's hairstyle, saying "In Japan today, the feudal ideal of the household [*ie*] is still tearing apart the pure feelings of the young," indicating, on one hand, that Sugiko's troubles are not hers alone, but those of a whole generation, and on the other, that this is not an original observation. Naruse takes up this generic narrative with enthusiasm, and although this film is stylistically a bit more restrained than his other surviving silents, he reserves the occasional dolly-in to close-up for moments when Sugiko is resolved to do what is right for herself. The confrontation in the hospital, and an earlier family fight in the dining room of the lavishly decorated, Western-furnished family home incorporate the dynamic configurations of camera and figure movements, fast-paced cutting, and intertitles that Naruse relies on for moments of high dramatic intensity.

Street without End has a subplot concerning Sugiko's friend Kesako, who also works at the café. Although Sugiko is first approached by the film talent scouts, it is Kesako who becomes a movie star, returning to visit her girlfriends in the café wearing fancy new moga clothes. Her rise and fall in the film industry comes fairly rapidly, and with the help of newspaper headlines and photos, the film points to the way that actresses are infinitely replaceable and their fates are tied to the random inclinations of the men who run the business. Kesako's performance is more comic than Sugiko's, and she ends up marrying her friend Yamamura, who is first introduced drawing caricatures on the streets of Ginza. Kesako gets him a job painting scenery at the film studio, and in one comic scene he plays at being director, which of course gets him fired. Yamamura and

Sugiko both end up back where they started, working in Ginza, while Kesako becomes a wife, bringing her husband his lunch. At the end of the film, Sugiko's brother Koichi appears at the café driving a new car. He can't stop, he says, because he "has to keep moving all the time." He drives off, leaving Sugiko standing on the street outside the café. She glimpses her original beau Harada (Yuki Ichiro), who she left for Hiroshi, pass by in a bus. A shot of him inside the bus as it passes is followed by the final shot of the film: Sugiko looking melancholy beside a tree and a streetlamp, with the Hattori building visible in the background.

The fascination and significance of *Street without End* lies in its transformation of urban space into a kind of abstract system where people's paths continually cross, or in this last scene, fail to cross. The impulse to keep moving extends to the energy of modernity, the new products glimpsed in shop windows, and the new foods (pancakes with butter) served in the café. In this sense, the film provides a popular-culture version of the kind of ethnography concurrently designed by Kon Wajiro as *kogengaku* or "modernologio." As Harootunian describes it, Kon's project meant "describing modern custom and its relationship to new subjectivities." He quotes Kon: "'Our research object . . . avoids the abnormal. In general, it's about the everyday life of society and its people.' Kon saw the buying of 'commodities' as an integral part of understanding daily life, one of its main constituents and not just a whim of curiosity. Research showed that there was a regular imitation in patterns of consumption, a transaction marked by a 'wave of custom in which the upper class is imitated.' . . . What interested him was the constant flow of goods and people and their endless circulation."[70] Naruse's cinematic version of this project adds the important ingredients of movement and narrativity, giving the panorama of everyday life the aspect of a networked system. The film further implicates the cinema itself as a commodification of the desires and customs noted by Kon.

Tom Gunning has written about the American film *Traffic in Souls* (1913) that the editing "sketches an urban entity that is more a system than a spectacle," introducing a perception of the city that would be subsequently developed into the aesthetics of the thriller by directors such as Louis Feuillade, Fritz Lang, and Alfred Hitchcock.[71] The Naruse film may be about neither prostitution nor detective work (as *Traffic in Souls* is), but it nevertheless conveys a similar sense of the urban milieu as a vast network, linked by the power structures that are maintained by the corporate capital of the film industry, aristocratic families, and mass media. The two women may escape the entrapment of these institutions, but everyday life in the city itself is no less predicated on the circulation of images of women, including the original story which was itself serialized in a newspaper. Gunning's remarks on *Traffic in Souls* ring true also for *Street without End*: "A traffic pulses beneath the city's surface, determining the direction and circulation beyond our will or even our knowledge, a system which has its origin in the contradictory relation of the figure of the prostitute with the categories of visuality and urban space."[72]

In all three of Naruse's surviving silent features, prostitution is merely hinted at as a possibility inevitably available with the circulation of single women in the public sphere. The female protagonists are always aware that their main currency in this sphere is their good looks, and they need to spend this currency wisely. To his credit, Naruse refuses to exploit this currency himself but integrates it into the "system" of visual culture which is the city of Tokyo. He uses his flamboyant techniques to represent the women's experience and self-determination to survive in this brave new world where men leer at women hungrily from café booths.

One further subplot needs to be mentioned in this respect. Before he accidentally hits Sugiko in his car and falls in love with her, Hiroshi was supposed to marry another woman favored by his mother and sister. This woman, who is unnamed, wears elegant Western fashions, including furs and high heels, but Hiroshi dismisses her as "boyish" and prefers the feminine (read: Japanese) traits of Sugiko. This moga, however, appears regularly in the streets, cafés, and theaters of Ginza, accompanied by a similarly decked-out girlfriend. They seem to be constantly running into Sugiko and Hiroshi, snobbishly dismissing the waitress as "not from the upper class." These women are an important element of the phantasmagoria of modernity, as it is crystallized around the Ginza district circa 1934.

One of the coincidental encounters between the two moga and Hiroshi and Sugimura takes place at a movie theater. Naruse actually includes a short clip from the movie they are watching, titled *White Woman*, a precode (1933) Paramount potboiler starring Carole Lombard and Charles Laughton. The scene features Lombard in an evening dress and Laughton in a dress uniform, arguing over a chessboard. The glamour and spectacular excess of the American film is exotic and risqué in the Japanese context; and yet the two snobby moga seem to have translated the flair of the movie into their appearance in the lobby of the Ginza cinema. In contrast, Sugiko in her kimono appears modest and chaste, although the narrative also demonstrates that the movies offer women like Sugiko and Kesako an easy route to the high life of the movie star.

The cinema as a cosmopolitan site of vernacular modernism is thus deeply implicated in the circuits and networks of metropolitan life. The female viewers of this Shochiku drama would have been invited to be *voyageurs* within a shifting panoply of identities, including the uniformed waitresses, and the same women off-duty in everyday kimono; Hiroshi's coldhearted mother and sister in high-end kimono; and the fashionable moga, alongside the image of Lombard.[73] Their gaze would effectively be "mobilized" within the various architectural spaces of shops, cafés, theaters, homes (in which class is rigorously marked by furnishings), and of course the street, which as the title suggests, is the key locus of transit and sightseeing.[74] For viewers looking back from the next century, the film is no less powerful in its display of the kaleidoscopic cultural dynamics of Japanese modernity in the interwar period.

Japanese Modernity and Interwar Cinema

Each of Naruse's five surviving silent films features a hospital scene or a sickbed. In *Every Night Dreams*, the boy is at home being nursed by his mother, while in the other three films the hospital becomes a site of heightened dramatic confrontation, conflict, and truth-telling. Not only are the shocks of the modern city registered on the fragile bodies of its inhabitants, these scenes are also moments of recognition and resignation, as they come at critical moments of closure. Karatani Kojin has described the meaning of sickness—or the articulation of sickness as meaning—in Japanese literature as more than metaphor, but as "an effect of a certain typological schema, a semiological system" institutionalized in the medical practices of the modern state.[75] In Naruse's cinema of the early 1930s, we can see how the transportation accident is metonymically linked to modern medicine and its promise of a healthy society. Within this particular articulation of everyday life, the hospital and the sickbed are at once emblematic and ambiguous, conjoining the dangers of modern life with the techniques of recovery.

Cultural historians Miriam Silverberg and Harry Harootunian have discussed the interwar period—which really refers to the postearthquake reconstruction of Tokyo in 1923 to the "overcoming modernity" conference of 1942—in terms of the construction of Japanese modernity as a discourse of everyday life. Naruse's cinema demonstrates how this discourse was articulated in filmic form, and how the dynamics of *modan* culture gave way in the latter part of the decade to a very different national culture. Although both Silverberg and Harootunian insist that film was instrumental in the construction of Japanese modernity of the "interwar years," they refer primarily to the popularity and subsequent disappearance of foreign films from Japanese screens, rather than to Japanese films themselves. Silverman points out that while in the 1940s both gender and national identities were firmly fixed, in the 1920s and 1930s a certain ambiguity and fluidity were permitted within these categories in popular culture, which raises the question: "How did they get from the *modan* years, celebrating the consumption of a multiplicity of images (and identities) into the Pacific War years of mobilization for the war effort and acknowledgement of material scarcity and an essentialized, rigidly gendered national identity?"[76]

Close analysis of Naruse's surviving silent films indicates that even during the modan years, categories of gendered identity were being negotiated. The moga, café-waitresses, and geisha in the films of the early 1930s were caught up within a series of competing styles of representation and narrative forms. The hybridity of Naruse's system enables us to see how female subjectivity was being constructed from the melodramatic emotionalism of shinpa drama and the exciting new possibilities heralded by modern life and its attendant mobility. These films also underline the fact that during this era, the cinema not only "displayed the commodity culture produced by American capitalism" and "the modern men and women who lived and experienced" that cultural life, as Harootunian notes,[77] but it was also invested in a nationalist project, seeking to contain the various threats posed by Americanization and the new gendered identities produced in modernity. In Naruse's melodramatic modality, the "new women's consciousness that the new system . . . sought to repress as the calamitous sign of social contradiction and uneven development"[78] is, in my view, contained, but not repressed. Female subjectivity is integrated into a new system of representation in which the aesthetics of emotion, experience, sensation, and insight belong precisely to the new Japanese woman.

2

Naruse at P.C.L.

TOWARD A JAPANESE CLASSICAL CINEMA, 1935–1937

Embedded in the seductive imaging of the modern girl was the formation of a new women's consciousness that the prevailing system of authority had not anticipated and which cultural ideology would seek to efface, displace, and even repress as the calamitous sign of social contradiction and uneven development.
—HARRY HAROOTUNIAN

In September 1934, *Kinema Junpo* published a roundtable discussion with Naruse and five critics, with the additional presence of Kojima Hiroshi, a representative of P.C.L. Strategically timed to coincide with Naruse's imminent move and embarkation on his first sound film, the roundtable marks Naruse's arrival as a prestige director.[1] While he comes across as extraordinarily humble and open to a variety of opportunities that the future might hold for him, the critics are primed to slot him into a modernist role. They are excited about the prospect of him adapting a Kawabata novel for his next project, and they discourage him from working with the popular comedian Enoken. Throughout the interview there is an implicit discrepancy between Naruse the auteur, who works from literary material and from his original screenplays, and Naruse the company man, who tries to do his best with the generic scripts that he is given. They also discuss the potential of "popular novels" as film projects, as opposed to literary works such as Kawabata's as they try to place Naruse within the cultural landscape of the period.

Kido Shiro had refused to let Naruse shoot a film that he had already scripted based on a Hayashi Fumiko novel, *Darakusuru Onna (Fallen Woman)*, which was one of the catalysts for his departure from Shochiku.[2] Other factors contributing to Naruse's move to P.C.L., besides Kido's famous dictum that he didn't need "two Ozus," were the fact that he was not allowed to make sound films and his very poor pay, despite the increasing popularity and critical endorsement of his filmmaking. It appears from the roundtable discussion that Naruse had already become identified with an aesthetic that he describes as "feeble," a taste associated with woman's magazines. Naruse agrees with them that he could be "tougher" and "deeper." Throughout his career, Naruse was often taken to task by critics for not taking a strong position regarding the social issues depicted in his films. His passive, observational stance is a technique that can be linked not only with gender, but also with the discourse of everyday life in modern Japan. Despite his flamboyant, fluid editing and psychological effects, his films tended to foreground systemic social issues without making large statements about them, as Mizoguchi was inclined to do, for example in the critique of the institution of the geisha at the end of *Sisters of the Gion (Gion no shimai*, 1936).

Producer Kojima Hiroshi says that at P.C.L. Naruse would not be asked to make the kind of compromises he had to make at Shochiku. In fact, they were bringing him in precisely to spearhead a new production policy, the implication being that he would be given the status and privileges of a top-flight director. Even though Naruse insisted that he wanted to continue to move between different genres and reach different audiences, and that he did not want to become stuck in one style, by this point he was becoming strongly associated with a certain mode of film practice that the P.C.L. producers saw as potentially lucrative. Although it is not named in the critical discourse of the period, Naruse's filmmaking was becoming deeply immersed in the cultural life of modern Japan, as it came to accommodate the trappings of Western modernity. He was clearly developing the means of expression, the characters, and the narrative voice appropriate to the complex and contradictory fabric of urban life. Subjective expression, particularly of women, became linked in his cinema to the dynamic energy of everyday life. At P.C.L. he could look forward to working conditions that would themselves be modernized, albeit in a more utopian direction than his own rather bleak films. To the roundtable critics, Naruse said that he liked a number of things about

P.C.L., including "the bright and clean ambiance of their buildings, in which I can expect to work in a cheerful and youthful mood; the work is from 8 a.m. to 5 p.m., and we have a day off every Sunday. The production schedule is relatively relaxed; we can watch rushes half way through the production."[3]

In 1937, Naruse Mikio's film *Wife! Be Like a Rose! (Tsuma yo bara no yo ni,* 1935) was exhibited at New York's Filmarte Theatre.[4] Although it was not the first Japanese film to be shown in the United States, it was the first to receive critical attention. Kinugasa's *Crossroads* was shown in 1932, but it was billed as an exploitation picture,[5] whereas Naruse's film, titled *Kimiko* for the American release, caught the attention of many journalists. While some reviewers dismissed it as "no competition" for the American industry, and others mistakenly described Naruse as the leader of a radical theater company challenging the status quo, many viewed it as a revealing glimpse into contemporary Japanese life.[6] For many Americans it constituted a real revelation that helped to counter prejudices against an unknown culture. Several reviewers, including Mark van Doren in the *Nation*, noted that the human emotions aroused by *Kimiko* were common to Japanese and North American cultures, initiating a longstanding critical framework of universal humanism for the reception of Japanese cinema outside its borders.

The exhibition of *Kimiko* in New York in 1937 was sponsored by Herbert Green at the University of Chicago as part of his Educational Film Cooperative. Green apparently asked a Japanese student named Kano Riho, the son of judo expert Kano Jigoro, to select a film. Kano probably chose Naruse's film because it had won the *Kinema Junpo* prize in 1935, and not because he was a film expert himself. In any event, the film was reedited from seventy-five to seventy minutes and renamed for the American release, but despite the good intentions of the Japanese tourism bureau and Professor Green, the run was cut short due to poor reviews.[7] The Filmarte, where it was screened, was an upmarket theater specializing in foreign films, but it is apparent from the reviews (which were in fact mixed), that the screening was radically decontextualized and neither critics nor audience had the appropriate framework for appreciating the merits of the film.

According to Okubo Kiyo, the film's relative "failure" as a commercial export is said to have stifled the distribution of Japanese cinema outside the country until the 1950 success of *Rashomon*.[8] Given the isolationism of imperialist Japan in the intervening years, this story is not particularly credible. However, the fact that Naruse's film was endorsed by Green and by the tourism bureau is significant. The 1930s saw Japan undergo a transition from a rapidly modernizing society with a full spectrum of political movements, to a militarized Imperial culture that privileged the Japanese past over Western modernity. As we shall see, *Wife! Be Like a Rose!* exemplifies the unevenness of Japanese modernity, even while it carefully negotiates a compromise of the new and the old, the metropolitan and the rural. Naruse's move from Shochiku-Kamata to P.C.L. studio in 1935 did not entail an abrupt change of style, but his filmmaking certainly did undergo a dramatic change during this first decade of his career, particularly as he began to explore the realm of the upper middle classes in 1936 and 1937. P.C.L. was arguably a key site for the emergence of a Japanese mass culture that would be at once "Japanese" and "modern," and it is important to recognize that even with *Wife!*, Naruse's modernity strayed from the modest milieus of the shoshimin-eiga's working poor.

P.C.L. (Photo Chemical Laboratories) was founded in 1929 and ceased being used as a company name in 1937, but in its brief existence, the small production studio arguably played a key role in the consolidation of the Japanese film industry. The studio initiated a number of innovations that helped to industrialize film production, including a "producer system" that made the director answerable to producers as the stewards of productions. P.C.L. employed personnel on a contractual basis, rather than following the "family system" of lifetime employment favored by other studios. P.C.L.'s first forays into film production were musical advertisements for beer and candy companies, followed by musical entertainments designed to exploit the technology of sound film.[9] Naruse, along with a number of other key figures, such as director Yamamato Kajiro and silent film star Irie Takako, came to P.C.L. from rival companies, attracted in part by the modern production methods. In lending his name and prestige to the new company, he was also participating in the construction of a new form of Japanese mass media: the modern sound film.

While the term *classical cinema* tends to be reserved for Hollywood in most film studies discourse, Miriam Hansen has recently proposed a slightly different understanding of the term that may help to identify the structure of a "classical Japanese cinema." If such a thing can be said to exist, its roots may well be in the brief existence of P.C.L., with its streamlined production methods designed to meet the demands of a mass urban audience. When Naruse came to P.C.L., it had already been bought by impresario Kobayashi Ichizo, who had taken over the company along with J.O., another small studio, to produce pictures for his Toho Distribution Corporation in 1935.[10] By 1937, Toho had absorbed P.C.L. to become a full-fledged production house, rivaling Shochiku and Nikkatsu, and by the end of the decade it dominated the Japanese industry. Kobayashi, who had formed the Takarazuka all-girls opera troupe and theater, had a knack for promoting popular entertainment. According to Anderson and Richie, "his formula for success, he said, was family entertainment, low admissions, and theatres convenient to public transportation."[11] His purchase of P.C.L. and consolidation of Toho was an important step in establishing a commercial film industry modeled on the American studio system.

For Hansen, *classical cinema* is a "technical term that has played a crucial part in the formation of cinema studies as an academic discipline."[12] While it has tended to be opposed to "modernism," Hansen points out that cinema has played a fundamental role in the historical formation of modernity. The hegemony of Hollywood in the global marketplace, in this reading, becomes a key component of the emerging mass publics in the "modernizing capitals of the world." She uses the term *vernacular modernism* to refer to the cultural practice of classical cinema—its reproduction of the experience of modernity, its industrialized means of production, and its vital links to the public sphere. She argues that in rethinking classical cinema as vernacular modernism, we can identify "alternative modernisms," other than hegemonic or high modernism.[13]

The hegemony of "classical cinema" has been bolstered by keeping other cinemas out of the running, as the "others" to Hollywood's dominance. The study of Japanese cinema has been perpetually confounded by the complex relation of modernism to Asian modernity, such that Japanese film could be understood as nothing other than an art cinema. The urge to position Naruse as a radical artist by critics such as Noël Burch and some of the American critics of *Kimiko*, is exemplary of the misunderstanding of the modernity of Japanese classical cinema. It leads Burch to dismiss Naruse's entire career after *Wife! Be Like a Rose!* as a capitulation to a Western mode of representation, or to the Hollywood "system" of narrative realism,[14] which is not borne out by a close look at the films. Moreover, despite Naruse's ongoing formal idiosyncrasies in the 1930s, he also demonstrates a continued preoccupation with gender, subjectivity, melodrama, and architectural space that were in many ways closely aligned with the American cinema, and which are, in the Japanese context, closely aligned with the modern. Hansen's reconsideration of Hollywood as an "international modernist idiom" is informed by an understanding of modernity as having "liberatory impulses," including "new possibilities of social identity and cultural styles" and "its glimpses of collectivity and gender equality."[15]

While his flamboyant style may indeed be increasingly toned down over the course of the 1930s, Naruse's films are nevertheless important indicators of how the modernity of Japanese cinema was sustained throughout the decade. In Harootunian's analysis of the role of the mass media in the construction of Japanese modernity, the focus is on the 1920s and early 1930s.[16] We can see, through Naruse's cinema, how that consciousness entered into the domain of mass culture on a profound level. The threat of the New Woman was negotiated through narrative strategies of containment that frequently failed to repress the desires and dynamics that she represented. While the moga herself had disappeared entirely by 1937, she had left traces in the formation of an industrialized mass media designed to exploit an explicitly gendered public sphere.

To describe the Japanese cinema of the 1930s, 1940s, and 1950s as a "classical cinema" is also a means of recognizing its integrity as a mode of production that is unlike the cinema that preceded it and unlike that which followed. Without designating any precise beginning and end, we can say that this classical studio-era cinema evolved in Japan from the experimental phase of the late 1920s in which the scriptwriting advocates of "pure cinema" wrestled it away from those who had more theatrical stakes in the medium.[17] In the 1960s, with the emergence of a new generation of directors and the incursions of television, Japanese cinema diversified and fragmented. By 1967, when Naruse made his last film, he was arguably out of step with the times, and not well supported by Toho.[18] If classical Hollywood cinema can be described as a national cinema,[19] it is not unreasonable to identify other national examples of industrial-based commercial cinemas in countries such as China, Japan, and India as classical cinemas that built on the American system to develop indigenous modern mass cultures.

It would require another kind of study to more adequately describe and theorize this classical cinema, although Anderson and Richie's *Japanese Cinema* goes a long way toward doing so. In comparison to the "unbiased sample" on which Bordwell, Staiger, and Thompson base their study of classical Hollywood cinema, the "sample" covered in this book is obviously heavily biased in that I am looking closely at only one director. Yet Bordwell himself suggests, quoting the *Cahiers du Cinéma* critic Pierre Kast, that it is the *cinema de salarie* [sic] that best represents Hollywood's classicism.[20] In this respect, Naruse is uniquely situated as

Japan's "number four" director, having close affinities with more prestigious directors such as Ozu (in terms of aesthetics) and Mizoguchi (in terms of women's stories), and with the host of lesser-known directors whose work has disappeared more quickly from view. The model of classical cinema that I am proposing is not aligned with the Bordwell-Staiger-Thompson model, although it is certainly influenced by many of the stylistic norms that they identify. A degree of stylistic consistency persists in the Japanese classical cinema, but like the American cinema, it was also characterized by contradiction, inconsistency, and unevenness—tendencies that the Bordwell-Thompson-Staiger model cannot account for.[21] The prewar and postwar golden ages of Japanese cinema were produced within historical eras of deep ideological tensions that were only cursorily smoothed over during the Fifteen Years' War and were openly debated in public discourse before and after the war and the occupation.

In his introduction to a reissue of Burch's treatise on Japanese cinema, Harootunian notes that the "contradictions" that Burch notes between the perpetuation of traditional elements of Japanese culture and the Hollywood system in the cinema of the 1930s must be situated within a framework marked by unevenness, which Japanese during the interwar period were living and experiencing intensely at the most fundamental levels of an everyday life constantly crisscrossed by different temporalities and political, economic, social, and cultural intensities."[22] Indeed, against the attractions of American cinema and the mass consumer culture that it embodied and displayed came increasing pressure from a centralized wartime government. Over the course of the 1930s, from the Manchurian Incident in 1931, the February 1936 Incident, and the China Incident of July 1937, government agencies stepped up their control of the industry. At the same time, though, filmmakers managed to produce some of the most enduring works of this "classical" cinema.

Peter High has offered a two-part explanation for this anomaly. On the one hand, film company executives, who were engaged in "swirling intercompany warfare" through the mid-1930s, tended to align themselves with government policy without hesitation. Meanwhile, many filmmakers were "ultimately inspired *by* state ideology to create works of quite superior quality."[23] While we will see shortly how this claim is borne out by Naruse's output during this period, High's observations indicate how Japanese cinema of the 1930s was integrated into a national cultural mandate. The title sequences of most of Naruse's P.C.L. films open with a shot of the monumental P.C.L. building in front of which a

10. P.C.L. logo and title sequence, 1935.

huge movie camera slowly rises to the accompaniment of a brass band playing a marching tune. While the films themselves make no mention of life beyond the local communities in which they are set, the studio clearly saw itself as part of a larger cultural mission.

Producers and directors were consciously attending to a national image, in which self-censorship played an important role. Between 1935 and 1937, while Naruse was at P.C.L., it is significant that the mounting escalation of military activities remains entirely unacknowledged in his film practice. Instead, the tensions of everyday life are played out in terms of an idiom of modernity—the cinema—and in terms of rituals and practices that are neither strictly modern nor "traditional." The older customs that persist in this cinema are not the theatrical and literary arts identified by Burch, but those of popular song, itinerant actors, and the conventions of middlebrow shinpa theater.

Naruse made ten films in his three years at P.C.L., testimony to the assembly-line mode of production. Although *Wife! Be Like a Rose!* is unquestionably the strongest of his P.C.L. films, the other titles represent the vocabulary of vernacular modernism in the middle years of the 1930s. This is not to suggest that they have merit only as cultural artifacts. Naruse's accommodation of the conventions of continuity editing is accompanied by an ongoing expansion and exploration of the visual field—and of the film's soundtrack. Even if he had to resign himself to projects that may have been ill conceived from the outset, and although he did not always have access to the top talent—the real drawbacks of the studio system of production—he continued to experiment with the technical resources and dramatic possibilities of film language.

Naruse's P.C.L. films cannot be described as replicas of the Hollywood style. He continues to use camera movements to express dynamic states of mind and to reframe the action within small spaces. One can find sweeping pans of theaters and audiences, and swish pans following character movements and glances in all these films. Editing patterns are frequently disjunctive, including mismatched eye lines and temporal leaps; but Naruse was also developing a style of cutting on movements and glances in such a way that he exploited the principles of the continuity system for dramatic effect. Flashbacks and scenes of parallel action are often inserted with minimal cueing, creating complex narrative temporalities and nonlinear storylines. One of the merits of *Wife! Be Like a Rose!* is its energy and kineticism, and indeed, many of the P.C.L. films—especially those released in 1935 and 1936—display similar techniques of action and movement. In some of the later films released in 1937, the pacing is distinctly slower. Naruse admitted to being dissatisfied with many of these pictures,[24] as the optimism of 1934 faded into the realities of industrial film production, yet they continue to show a kind of open visual style that had long since disappeared from Hollywood.

Among the signs of a classical cinema is Naruse's use of and implication within a well-developed star system. Besides the key actresses Umezono Ryuko and Chiba Sachiko, he also cast Fujiwara Kamatari in six of his ten P.C.L. films. This actor, who would become a mainstay of Kurosawa's stable of actors, almost always appears as a secondary character (his most memorable career role may be as one of the two thieves in Kurosawa's *The Hidden Fortress* [1958]). He is a superb comic actor, or what in the Hollywood context is described as a character actor, lending each of the films he made with Naruse a certain stability and familiarity. Okawa Heihachiro appears in five of the P.C.L. films, frequently as the love interest of either Umezono or Chiba. The continuities between the various roles taken by actors who reappear in film after film contribute to the development of what Hansen describes as an "idiom of its own kind, a locally and culturally specific aesthetics." In the context of Shanghai cinema of the 1930s, she describes the vernacular modernism of the cinema as a response to modernity that is not always consistent with the "ideals of national culture formulated in political discourse of the time."[25] Although Naruse was one of many filmmakers working in Japan at this time, a close look at the films he made at P.C.L. provides some insight into the nature of the idiom of vernacular modernism as a discourse that was sustained alongside and somewhat below the purview of intellectual discourse of the period.

From the critical discourse surrounding *Wife! Be Like a Rose!*, it appears that Naruse was forging a new genre that combined elements of shinpa theater and elements of the home novel, or *katei-geki*.²⁶ While some American critics appreciated his anthropological representation of everyday life, Japanese critics praised his psychological character portraits.²⁷ In the films that followed at P.C.L., including *The Girl in the Rumor* (aka *The Girl on Everyone's Lips* [*Uwasa no musume*, 1935]), he continued to work with the ingredients of popular culture to develop a "vernacular language" of modernity that would not be without a sense of poetry. The New Woman may be relegated to the sidelines after 1935, but films such as *Morning's Tree-Lined Street* (*Asa no namiki michi*, 1936) and *Feminine Melancholy* (*Nyonin aishu*, 1937) feature women pitted against very different social pressures. As in *Wife! Be Like a Rose!*, the trajectories of these two films are toward the emergence of women who have, by the end of the films, found their identity and sense of self after surviving various melodramatic crises and conflicts of modern life.

In the following discussion of the ten films that Naruse made at P.C.L., it should become evident that, although his cinema was "uneven" from an aesthetic point of view, it was deeply immersed in the contradictions and conflicts of everyday life. Male as well as female protagonists in a variety of genres act out the drama of modernity. Recurring figures of entertainers and actors of various types, as well as reflexive gestures pointing to cinema itself as a discursive operation, suggest that Naruse was engaged in a very specific form of vernacular modernism. The realism of his Kamata films became a mode of comedy as well as melodrama, a comic mode predicated on the detailed representation of ordinary people for whom every item of food, and every article of clothing has a price.

At P.C.L. the nansensu comedy elements of Naruse's silent films become more self-conscious, more ironic, and in some instances, in 1937, more mannered, as the bourgeois settings and lifestyles come under scrutiny. In films such as *The Road I Travel with You* (*Kimi to yuku michi*, 1936), *Feminine Melancholy*, *Avalanche* (*Nadare*, 1937), and *Learn from Experience* (*Kafuku*, 1937), the world of the nouveau riche, cluttered with the material effects of Western culture, indicates how the "newness" of modernity had already become fossilized. In these melodramas, this world is further revealed to be empty of moral values. As Naruse's melodramatic modality at the brink of full-out war with China takes on a new modernist idiom of vacancy, it begs to be read as a form of cultural critique. His classicism reveals its fissures and contradictions in ways that film scholars have come to associate with Douglas Sirk in the 1950s. In other words, while Japanese classical cinema evidently cohered around a bourgeois sensibility at P.C.L., Naruse had far less sympathy for these characters, producing inherently contradictory texts.

Three Sisters with Maiden Hearts
LIFE IN ASAKUSA

Three Sisters with Maiden Hearts (*Otome-gokoro sannin shimai*, 1935), based on a Kawabata novel, was Naruse's first sound film and first P.C.L. film. It opens with a panoramic display of Asakusa, including a plethora of banners and signage advertising dance reviews and movies, and an itemized menu with prices, quickly moving from the large scale to the more intimate level of everyday life in the infamous locale. The film promises an "inside look" at a district that was notoriously erotic, dangerous, and exciting. Much like his silent films, Naruse's first sound film constructs a distinctive "atmosphere" of the city through sets, lighting, and music, as well as extensive location shooting. With shots of the city lit at night, and a labyrinth of café-lined streets, *Three Sisters*, in keeping with the Kawabata original, is as much about Asakusa as it is about the three women. *Sisters of Asakusa* (*Asakusa no shimai*) was one of a series of novels that Kawabata wrote about the district, and it was serialized in a popular weekly magazine. In scripting the film, Naruse used "a few Kawabata stories," and the author apparently gave the director permission to freely adapt his work.[28]

The three sisters of the title includes a moga character named Chieko (Umezono Ryuko), the youngest; a middle sister named Osome (Tsutsumi Masako) who is the epitome of goodness and self-sacrifice; and an older sister, O-Ren (Hosokawa Chikako), who has left home, and whose story is filled in through flashbacks. The girls' mother is a samisen teacher who trains and boards girls from the country to play and sing for customers in the Asakusa bars. Osome manages the girls on the street, trying to protect them from her mother's meanness and from customer complaints and lasciviousness. The family business is a variation on a geisha house, in which once again, the opportunities for and temptations of prostitution are always in the offing. The girls are expected to hand over their earnings to the mother, to whom they are beholden for room and board.

Naruse uses a number of innovative technical devices in this film, including voice-over narration for both the present (spoken by Chieko) and for the flashbacks. O-Ren's story is filled in through a complex pattern of flashbacks narrated by Osome and by O-Ren herself when she unexpectedly returns to Asakusa. We learn that she went from samisen playing to more dubious and shady dealings with low-life characters. She started dressing in fashionable Western clothes but then cast in her lot with a man called Kosugi and had to escape from her gangster friends. However, when Kosugi contracts tuberculosis and can no longer work, he persuades O-Ren to raise money by going back to her old ways. The plot of the film coheres around O-Ren's complicity in extorting money from her younger sister Chieko's rich boyfriend. After O-Ren sets up the meeting of the gangsters with Chieko's boyfriend—a moba ("modern boy") named Aoyama played by Okawa Heihachiro—the good sister Osome intervenes and is accidentally stabbed in the confrontation.

While Osome is too good to survive in the debased milieu of the entertainment district, O-Ren, the middle sister, finally escapes with the TB-stricken Kosugi. In the closing scenes of the film, Osome sits alone in the rain at the train station dying, as O-Ren and Kosugi leave for Kosugi's hometown. Chieko arrives with Aoyama in a taxi at the last moment, too late to see O-Ren depart. The city is theirs after all, and even if the romance between the moga and the moba is treated somewhat cursorily, they are the survivors of a story of corruption, deception, and innocence destroyed.

Naruse's decoupage in *Three Sisters* remains as flamboyant as it was in his silent films. The pacing is very quick, and the scenes are often broken into a fragmented assemblage of close-ups and medium shots. He does not use architectural detail to frame interior shots in this film but chooses oblique angles. In several instances, Osome walks directly into the camera, fading out at the end of a scene, a technique that helps to emphasize her character as the emotional fulcrum of the film. Chieko's flirtation with Aoyama (Okawa Heihachiro) includes a scene of the couple boating in the Sumida River, filmed from a traveling camera on the shore with a railing in the foreground. They are a very "modern" couple, playfully discussing what people would think if they were to commit suicide together—a popular fad of the time.[29]

Among the details of everyday life in Asakusa are two scenes set in a burlesque theater. Chieko is on stage among a flock of dancers wearing chiffon skirts over leotards performing for rows of men sitting silently in suits. The girls' dancing is oddly low energy, out of sync with the music, and their performance is like a slow-motion version of the Folies Bergère. Clearly it is a sexual display, but one that is very specific to this time and place, and the exposed legs, arms, and necks constituted a scandalous "nudie" show—as such reviews were often advertised at the time. While the first dance scene establishes the relationship between Chieko on stage and Aoyama in the audience, in the second one, she scans the audience from the stage, looking for him—but he has been summoned by O-Ren to the ill-fated rendezvous with the gangsters. Chieko's job as a dancer is not a major plot point but helps to fill out the portrait of the city and its culture. However, the main reason for these scenes is to showcase Umezono Ryuko.

Working at P.C.L., Naruse found himself with a new stable of actors, many of whom had very little training. Of the three female leads in *Three Sisters*, only Hosokawa Chikako had theatrical training—in Shingeki theater. (She appears nineteen years later as Tamae in *Late Chrysanthemums* [*Bangiku*, 1954] looking virtually identical to her younger self.) Tsutsumi Masako (Osome) was scouted by P.C.L. from dance reviews in Asakusa,[30] and Umezono was a popular Casino Folies dancer. She appears as herself in Kawabata's *Scarlet Gang of Asakusa* when two characters identify her on the stage as a fifteen-year-old dancer in a performance of "Modern Ginza Song."[31] It is said that Kawabata befriended her, helping her to study dance with a Russian teacher,[32] although in the story itself the characters say that her mother had studied Russian dance. At one point in *The Scarlet Gang*, a theater review is advertised with the following headlines: "Eroticism Flowing From their Beautiful Pearl-White Naked Bodies, the Russian Dancer Miss Verenna Radosenko and her Troupe,"[33] clearly indicating the links between the foreign, the erotic, and the notion of the Russian dancer. Umezono was a prominent figure within the erotic display of Asakusa entertainments, and in her three films with Naruse, P.C.L. was clearly capitalizing on her star image, even though her high-pitched voice did not lend itself well to sound film.

At one point in *Three Sisters*, some little boys taunt Chieko, calling her a monster and a moga, in the most derogatory terms. She is unfazed, but their taunts are an important reminder that Umezono's image would have been highly controversial by this point in the mid-1930s. Umezono reprises her moga character in her starring role in Naruse's *The Girl in the Rumor* later in 1935. Her casting in Naruse's first P.C.L. films give them a tone of sensationalism, but also of ethnographic fidelity to the modern city. Compared to the Ginza setting of *Street without End*, Asakusa is more rough and more sexy, dense as it is with men and women selling food, entertainment, and, in many ways, themselves.

In *Three Sisters*, Naruse actually invokes the old style of silent film as

11. Umezono Ryuko and Heihachiro Okawa in *Three Sisters with Maiden Hearts* (*Otome-gokoro sannin shimai*, 1935), P.C.L.

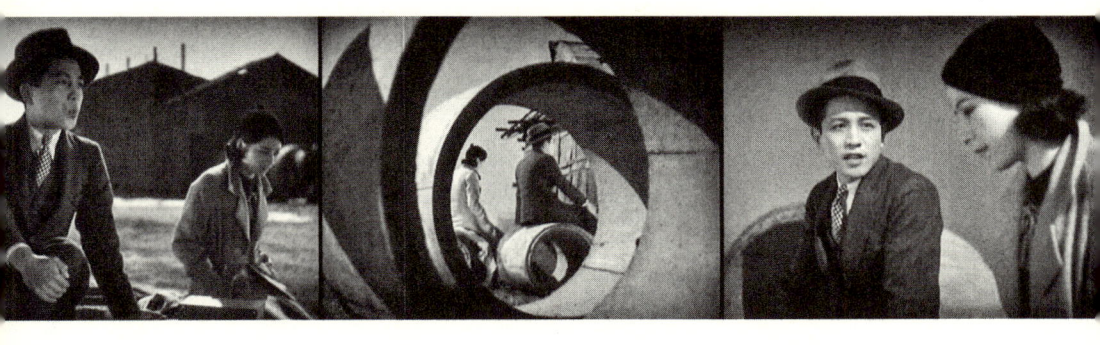

12. Umezono Ryuko and Heihachiro Okawa in *Three Sisters with Maiden Hearts* (*Otome-gokoro sannin shimai*, 1935), P.C.L.

a kind of narrative interruption. Osome, played by Tsutsumi Masako, sits beside the river eating an *anpan* (a bun) while a photographer takes her picture. The scene has no narrative function besides the development of Osome's character, or the fixing of her character as an allegory of passing times. She is the "good sister" who tries to help her mother's struggling samisen students. She tries to hide the hole in her sock while the photographer sets up the picture. In her wig and kimono, she is the image of the decline of the Asakusa water trade. The scene is completely silent, without background music or dialogue. After the photographer leaves, she takes out a pocket mirror and wipes a crumb from her cheek, dismayed that her image was flawed. This scene, rich in pathos, suggests how Naruse's modernism incorporates a deployment of visual culture as a discourse of identity, nationhood, and history. Osome belongs to a past that already includes the medium of silent film; her image is a construct that even (or especially) with its tiny flaw—the stray crumb—signifies a culture in decay.

In a "collective critique" of *Three Sisters* in *Kinema Junpo*, the critics note that at least two scenes were cut after Naruse had edited the film. In both instances it seems that references to prostitution were removed, although the scenes provided important narrative information. One of the scenes also featured a stunning mise-en-scène of Chieko and Aoyama on a beach framed by a foreground spiral of earthenware pipes, a few shots of which do remain in the film. According to Kishi Matsuo, Naruse was very disappointed that this key moment "in which everything fell into place" was cut from the film.[34]

Naruse adapted so easily to sound film that the critics enthused about his nonchalance. He claimed to be "relaxed" about using the new technology, and *Three Sisters* features a fairly sophisticated use of sound, including the brief passages of voice-off narration, which caught the critics' attention. Although it is not developed into any kind of subjective expression, as it is in Naruse's films in the 1950s, the new technique allows the characters to speak directly to the audience. The choice of subjects for this film—*kadozuke* girls, itinerant street musicians in the Asakusa district of Tokyo—is a means of foregrounding the role of sound. The critics' fear that Naruse might be drawn to "cine-operetta" is assuaged by a scene in which Osome singing with her samisen is interrupted by a phonograph in a bar.

The collective critique of *Three Sisters* is an interesting attempt to find the critical vocabulary most appropriate for Naruse. Some critics describe him as both a realist and a stylist; he is sober and humble, refusing to impose himself on his subject matter. The episode with Osome and the photographer is cited as an instance of Naruse allowing the form to be drawn from realist details. His depiction of Asakusa is praised for its elegance, yet the four critics—Iida Shinbi, Tomoda Junichiro, Kitagawa Fuyuhiko, and Kishi Matsuo—agree that he is not a realist. They describe him as being *sumato*, or sophisticated, and his achievement is to ground sweetness in realism. He is not a neorealist like Shimazu, but a lyricist, because although he is concerned with everyday life, it is ultimately on the level of detail that his films are strongest.[35] These are astute observations, and very appropriate to *Three Sisters*, which the critics finally decide is the best Japanese talkie they have seen to date.[36]

The Actress and the Poet
A NEW KIND OF WIFE

Chiba Sachiko was Naruse's second significant star at P.C.L., appearing in three titles of 1935: *The Actress and the Poet* (*Joyu to shijin*) and *The Girl in the Rumor*, and of course, most notably, in *Wife! Be Like a Rose!*. She also starred in *Morning's Tree-Lined Street*, and she had a minor role in *Kumoemon Tochuken*. She and Naruse married in 1937 and divorced in 1942.[37] By all accounts, these brief years constituted the director's only flirtation with public celebrity, as Chiba was a "vivacious" and popular star, and *Wife!* brought Naruse unprecedented recognition.[38] According to Bock, the couple had a child, but after the divorce, Naruse resumed his "second floor rented-room life" until he quietly remarried years later.[39]

Released in March 1935, three weeks after *Three Sisters with Maiden Hearts* (*Otome-gokoro sannin shimai*, 1935) and five months before *Wife!*

Be Like a Rose!, *The Actress and the Poet* represents the inversion or refutation of the emergence of the New Woman and more clearly indicates Naruse's implication within the increasingly repressive politics of the 1930s. Chiba plays Chieko, a successful stage actress, whose husband, Geppu, wears an apron, writes children's songs, and makes far less money than she does. But by the end of the film, she has learned to accept his status as master of his own house and cheerfully makes him breakfast in bed, apparently restored to her wifely role. As a light domestic comedy, *The Actress and the Poet* serves as a kind of morality tale or comedy of manners for modern Japan. Like *Wife! Be Like a Rose!*, it is adapted from a play by Nakano Minoru and is equally well written and structured. It's a clever film, with a reflexive play on Chieko's theatrical profession; and despite the ideological implications of the film's final scenes, the story demonstrates the threat to domestic stability that the New Woman posed in the mid-1930s. Chiba's inspired performance gives the lie to any attempt at ideological containment, as she can hardly be said to have become a submissive wife by the end of the film.

The characters, including Chieko and her husband, are caricatures of social types. She goes out with her theater friends wearing a fur stole and fancy kimono, despite the fact that they live in a modest suburban neighborhood. Geppu's friend Nose (Fujiwara Kamatari) is a frustrated bohemian writer deeply in debt, and the neighborhood gossip next door lives with her husband, an insurance agent, Geppu's drinking buddy. Thus, the story of the henpecked husband and glamorous wife is set among a constellation of characters subsisting in the "everyday life" of suburban Tokyo. The frequent cutaways to trains running across telephone pole–studded lots are similar to the desolate, treeless suburban landscape of *Every Night Dreams* and *Flunky, Work Hard*. A subplot involves a young couple who move into the neighborhood, buy life insurance, and attempt a double suicide—apparently a typical scam of the period in which the new wife is expected to die and the man to survive and collect the money—a scenario that Naruse will revisit in *Morning's Tree-Lined Street*. While Geppu considers submitting an advertising jingle for a ¥100 prize, his friend Nose is aiming for a ¥5,000 prize for a popular novel, further elaborating the cultural setting of the film as one thoroughly saturated with mass culture and its promise of infinite reward.

The Actress and the Poet opens with a dramatic knife-wielding scene that is quickly revealed to be a rehearsal Chieko is holding at home with her actor friends (sending Geppu out to fetch cigarettes and snacks for them all). Although it sets up a comparison between the theatricality of the scripted drama and the everydayness of the suburban neighborhood, that difference is eventually broken down as a means of staging Geppu's confrontation with his wife. She asks him to help her with her lines, but he is uncomfortable when they hit too close to home. When she says, "Who do you think pays the rent around here?" he asks her to please keep her voice down, for fear the neighbors will hear. But of course his friend Nose does overhear them, thinks they are really fighting, and tries to break up the "staged" violence. Nose has come to rent the couple's second floor, having been evicted from his own place, echoing the events of Chieko's script, in which the husband invites his delinquent friend to move in. Life imitates art in this film almost line for line, until the domestic violence escalates once again, this time unstaged. Nose and the gossipy neighbor show up, think it's a rehearsal, and sit down to watch, enthusiastically thinking they have front row seats to a play they can't afford.

The resolution comes when Chieko realizes that thanks to Geppu and Nose, she has finally learned how to be angry with her husband and will be able to play the part better on the stage. She thanks Nose for recognizing her husband as master of the house and invites him to move into the second floor. It's a terribly contrived ending that does little to fully restore the characters to their proper domestic roles. Nose is given a little closing monologue in which he reaffirms his bachelorhood by saying he can't put up with women's emotions. "A woman's heart is like the autumn sky," he says.

Because actresses like Matsui Sumako presented the most public face of the Japanese New Woman in the first decades of the twentieth century, they also bore the brunt of the backlash against women. Strongly identified with new theatrical forms such as *shingeki* and productions of Ibsen, they challenged many of the social norms of polite, submissive femininity. Their offstage, private lives were subject to public scrutiny as the differences between actress and character were typically jettisoned in public discourse.[40] By 1935, women had been on the Japanese stage and screen for over twenty-five years, so Chiba Sachiko's character Chieko in *The Actress and the Poet* is clearly a comic type, a parody of the rich and glamorous public figures that Chiba herself would have been. She may be brought down to size by a humble, talentless husband, yet the film ends with a covert suggestion of sexual play as the couple disappear behind closed doors, leaving their new boarder alone without breakfast.

Thus, Naruse's heroine may be turned back into a wife, but she is not without desire and may have become, in some respects, a "new wife."

Wife! Be Like a Rose!
THE CITY AND THE COUNTRY

Noël Burch's endorsement of *Wife! Be Like a Rose!* (*Tsuma yo bara no yo ni*, 1935) as a classic has helped to keep this title in circulation as a canonical example of Japanese cinema of the 1930s. Although there is no evidence to support Burch's claim that Naruse "refused certain norms of Western cinema,"[41] *Wife!* is indeed among his most well-executed films. Despite Burch's analysis, Naruse was not engaged in any kind of "transgressive" practice; and while his films of the 1930s are certainly stylistically and formally idiosyncratic, his experiments were motivated more by a need to find an appropriate means of expression for modern Japanese life, than to challenge established patterns of representation. *Wife!* features one of his most startling female protagonists, a suit-wearing professional woman, and earned accolades such as Mark van Doren's in the *Nation* as being "one of the most moving films I know."[42] Certainly part of the film's success must be credited to Chiba Sachiko, who plays the central character Kimiko. Her performance is at once bold and understated, as she is able to carry off both the Western-dressed office lady striding down the streets of Tokyo, and the kimono-clad daughter who tries to reconcile her estranged parents.

The success of *Wife!* at home and abroad solidified Naruse's reputation as a premier director. Burch is not alone in picking it out as a masterpiece, and he is quite right to identify certain formal editing traits that distinguish the film. He specifies the use of foreground elements, "movements which occur perceptibly just before or after the shot-change proper," and cutaways that are more "disruptive" than Ozu's pillow shots. He also notes the use of camera movement, which is not as "grossly expressive" as in the silent films but is used for a "sophisticated organization of profilmic movement."[43] To these observations I would add that in several scenes, elements of architecture are foregrounded to create a certain distance from the characters. In two instances, the camera tracks along a vine-covered lattice outside Kimiko's house, looking in as the characters move from one room to the next. In another instance, while Kimiko's uncle Shingo plays the samisen and recites *gidayu* (a scene that was cut from the American release),[44] the scene is framed through the rails of a chair, with Kimiko in the foreground and the uncle chanting in the background. Finally, in Oyuki's country home, the upstairs room is framed with the clay roof tiles in the foreground, and the characters observed through the window. Like the shots of lit homes seen from outside—a motif that by 1935 had already become a signature Naruse shot—these compositions constitute a kind of pulling back from the narrative events, and a movement toward a more passive observational stance.

The American critics of *Kimiko* were for the most part unimpressed by the film's technique, describing it either as "below Hollywood standards," or simply "aping" the American style. One reviewer noted influences of Russian and French cinematic techniques, which were indeed popular in Japan, along with German Expressionism, in the interwar period.[45] Those critics who wanted to position Naruse as a vanguard director concocted a story about him leading an experimental theater troupe that broke with "the ironclad restrictions of the classical *kabuki* drama."[46] This was either the work of a creative PR department at P.C.L., or a mistaken identification of Naruse with Nakano Minoru, who wrote the shinpa play *Futari zuma* (*Two Wives*), on which *Wife!* was based. However, Nakano did not run an avant-garde theater troupe, and while shinpa did originate in Meiji as a challenge to kabuki's archaic sensibility, by the 1930s it was anything but avant-garde.

By 1935 shinpa had acquired a poor reputation as a tacky and cheap form of entertainment, although Nakano's *Futari zuma* was hugely popular and had spawned several sequels. As critic Kishi Matsuo indicates in his short review of *Wife!*, the crux of the play was the difficulty of endowing a mistress with the qualities of motherhood, as the two roles are conventionally antithetical in traditional Japanese morality.[47] The achievement of the play, and in Naruse's adaptation of it, is its challenge to such formulaic and predictable stereotypes. Kishi's review is also interesting in that he takes the rural setting of Oyuki's home to be Manchuria, inferring a colonial context where in fact there is no mention of it in the film (it is clearly the Nagano region to which Kimiko travels). He also notes Naruse's "superb sense of timing" in his editing, and his creation of "real" characters that are so unlike shinpa figures.

The success of the film was very much due to its contemporaneity; both Japanese and American audiences appreciated its depiction of modern Japanese society. The techniques of cutting, framing, camera movement, and lighting that Naruse uses so deftly contribute to the sociological perspective and emotional tone, but the film's most significant innovation may have been the articulation of Kimiko's point of view as the narrative focalization. This point was not lost on Tokata Sachio. In his review in *Eiga Hyoron* in 1935, he observes that Naruse completely transformed the original shinpa play by aligning his authorial gaze with that of Kimiko. The use of voice-over, furthermore, frees the film from the affectation of theater and makes Kimiko herself the conveyor of the narrative, creating a "vivid interiority." He also recognizes the way that Naruse deploys the "exchange of glances" at key narrative moments for heightened dramatic effect. Tokata implies that the film distances itself from the sentimentality of shinpa through these techniques, without compromising the intensity of the "human feelings," or *ninjo*. He suggests that the melodramatic tension between *giri* (obligation) and ninjo are effectively relegated to the background, while Kimiko's modernity—at once practical and energetic—is foregrounded.[48]

Kimiko's character also undergoes an important transformation over the course of the narrative. Her main motive for reconciling her parents is her own marriage; also, her mother has been asked to be a go-between for another marriage, which has placed her in an awkward position. For these social institutions to function, the family must be whole. Kimiko decides to visit her father in the country where he lives with his mistress Oyuki and their two children. When she gets to Nagano, she discovers that her father, Shunsaku, is a failed gold prospector, and the money that she and her mother have been living off has come from Oyuki, who runs a successful tailoring business out of her home. She also realizes that her father is much happier with his new family. She brings him back to Tokyo, but sees that he and her mother, Etsuko, cannot be happy together, so she lets him go back to Oyuki. He gives his blessing to Kimiko's marriage and asks her to take good care of her mother. Kimiko's final words are "It's mother who has lost," over a climactic series of shots that track out from the mother's face and in to Kimiko's several times in a rhythmic pattern that is superimposed over a traveling shot of the Nagano landscape.

While *Wife!* is in some respects structured around a city-country dichotomy, it does not simplify the values attached to either setting. The film opens with a montage of shots of metropolitan Tokyo, introducing Kimiko as she leaves her office and meets her fiancé, Seichi, on the street. They are very much the modern couple, as they constantly compete with each other. They argue over who makes more money and refuse to make each other tea, and Seichi has a comic proclivity to be constantly hungry. Indeed, many of the characters, including the poetry-writing matron Etsuko, are depicted as comic characters. As Bock points out, Etsuko "constantly interrupts herself to compose poems, but the fact remains that her romantic odes are all addressed to a husband with whom she cannot stand to live."[49] Uncle Shingo's recitation of gidayu is likewise parodied by cutaways to a pair of caged birds who are visibly upset by his whining performance.

The parody of aristocratic arts would hardly be possible a few years later, as traditional cultural practices became a cornerstone of the imperial propaganda of the late 1930s. *Wife!* is situated on the cusp of the 1930s' ideological shift away from Western-influenced "modernity" and toward a more conservative nationalist agenda. At the same time, the film carefully negotiates the cultural setting of a new middle class, a salaried class that could not be identified with the nobility of previous eras. In this sense, Kimiko's failure to reconcile her parents is also her own emergence as a self-sufficient wage earner, who, with her salaryman fiancé, is free of the burden of the past. Although Kimiko's profession is unstated in the film, even if she is merely an "office lady," she is indubitably a professional working woman. As Barbara Sato explains, "The professional working woman's arrival . . . paralleled the first stage in the growth of the so-called new middle class, to which they largely belonged and for whom upward advancement beckoned."[50]

Perhaps the most visible evidence of Kimiko's social and cultural positioning can be found in her costumes. How is it that in Burch's analysis of *Wife!* he discusses "imperceptible cuts" in detail but fails to mention Kimiko's suit and tie? In the opening scene on the street her outfit is almost identical to Seichi's, although the jaunty tilt of her hat adds a touch of feminine style. When she travels to Nagano, she walks along the country roads in skirt, pumps, hat, and tie, and a trench coat over her arm, an obvious anomaly in the rural setting. At home with her mother, she keeps the tie on with her apron and headscarf to prepare the evening meal, in a kind of hybrid outfit for the domestic city girl. One way of reading the gender codes of this film is in terms of a softening of Kimiko's "masculine" traits. Kimiko wears kimono in some of the early scenes, as well as most of the later scenes, including the final closing shots, but the change she undergoes is much deeper than a change of clothes. Costume and fashion are key components of the film and of her characterization, but her real transformation occurs with her understanding of Oyuki's feelings, and in this respect the film deploys a trait of classical Japanese theater—the deep sympathies that exist among women who are ill served by social conventions.

The emotional climax of the film occurs with Oyuki's confession to

13. Chiba Sachiko in *Wife! Be Like a Rose!* (*Tsuma yo bara no yo ni*, 1935), P.C.L.

Kimiko that it is she who she has been sending the money to Tokyo, and she is worried that Kimiko might be taking Shunsaku away. (Kimiko wears a sweater and skirt in this scene—a Western outfit that is neither as stylish nor as masculine as her other Western outfits.) During this scene, in which Kimiko realizes she might have made a mistake, her stepsister Shizue is listening outside the door. When these two women of the same age first meet, they hold each other's gazes in a prolonged exchange. Although they speak very little to each other, they go to the public bath together, where they are briefly seen silently soaking in the soft steamy evening light—a scene far more sensual than anything with Kimiko and her fiancé in the city. Shizue bursts into tears when she hears the conversation between Kimiko and her mother, after which Naruse abruptly cuts away to an exterior view of the house with the lights shining through the paper windows. This is an excellent example of how he avoids a tear-jerking scene by shifting the point of view to a more oblique, aestheticized, and poetic perspective. Shizue's role also cements Kimiko's bond with the women in her father's second family, and it is this recognition around which the film pivots. Her own mother, Etsuko, is preoccupied with her poetry and her selfishness in contrast to the altruistic values of these working women who have sacrificed Shizue's education for Kimiko's. The city girl is thus endowed with the values of the country life, the land, and the community of women, ready to resume her career and her marriage.

Kimiko has a relapse on the train returning to Tokyo with Shunsaku, when she says in voice-over that she is reluctant to let him go. On the train and in the city, Shunsaku is mainly interested in drinking sake. Kimiko shows off to her parents when they go sightseeing by hailing a taxi—a gesture she has learned from the movies. Naruse shoots the city

14. Chiba Sachiko and Orikoshi Setsuko in *Wife! Be Like a Rose!* (*Tsuma yo bara no yo ni*, 1935), P.C.L.

in traveling shots from the perspective of moving vehicles, low angle shots of towering office buildings, and vertical pans up neon signs. (He also uses swish pans to emulate Kimiko's point of view in an early scene in which she searches for her father, whom she has glimpsed on a crowded street.) The outing with her parents ends badly as Shunsaku falls asleep at a kabuki performance, greatly embarrassing Etsuko. Kimiko realizes that he cannot live in her mother's world and agrees that he should return to Oyuki, despite Uncle Shingo's insistence that Shunsaku fulfill his responsibilities to his Tokyo family.

When Elsie Weil, writing in the American journal *Asia*, noted of Kimiko that "it is a revealing presentation of the middle class of Japanese today . . . not cherry blossom or *samurai* Japan,"[51] she did not appreciate that the film is also about the emergence of a middle class in Japan. Few working women appeared in Japanese films again until after the war; and few women of Kimiko's professional confidence appeared in films before 1935. The achievement of the film is not only the articulation of a subjective space for Kimiko's character, but also in the way that it mobilizes the materiality of everyday life in the city and the country—including costume, architecture, domestic objects, and taxis—for the characters' moral education. For example, the transitional sequence that opens the day in which Kimiko takes her father back to Tokyo moves from the landscape to the roof of the house, to shots of her suitcase and her father's, to Shunsaku putting on his tie. The details of architecture and objects ground the story in the material culture of everyday life, and it is a good example of how Naruse uses montage to create chains of objects that advance the narrative. In the scene that follows, the handful of bills that Oyuki gives to Shunsaku for his trip to the city is the hard currency of the film, as it registers the economic reality underlying the aesthetic differences between the two worlds of the film. In the city, Kimiko and Seichi go on a shopping spree, but no money is seen to change hands in their commodity culture.

Kimiko's costumes and her movie-influenced behavior situate her within a consumer culture of images in which a "fluidity of identity" is, as Silverberg argues, very much available.[52] In this respect, her abandonment of the hat, tie, and suit jacket in the last "act" of the film—after her return to Tokyo—might be read as a capitulation to a traditional feminine identity. In other words, we need to ask whether the "softening" of Kimiko's character is a capitulation to more conservative values. I would argue that while the film parallels and enacts much of the discourse on modernity that was carried on in intellectual circles in Japan at the time, and to some extent does overcome its own modernity, it does not entail a critique of modernity. Insofar as it is firmly grounded in popular culture, it articulates something closer to vernacular modernism.

Harootunian has pointed out that everyday modern life produced an anxiety over the loss of experience tied to memory and tradition, a phenomenon that was accentuated in Japan due to the uneven development of urban and rural life: "In response to the spectacle of modern everyday life in the cities . . . writers and thinkers often remained content with simply emphasizing what remained as the 'mysterious side of the mysterious' taking them no further. Yet the appeal to mystery exempted them from thinking about either history or the conditions of modern life, as such, without, as Benjamin has reminded us, the 'profane illumination of reading about . . . phenomena.'"[53] In this context, a film such as *Wife!* might be understood as specifically engaging with the phenomena of everyday life while attempting to restore an aspect of "experience" or, in melodramatic terms, *ninjo*, to it. To some extent, it can be seen as participating in what Harootunian describes as the "discourse on the social" that was produced during the interwar years: "This discourse on the social, culminating in the symposium on modernity in 1942, tried to overcome the spectacle of social division and observable unevenness between city and countryside, metropole and colony, and class and gender, manifest in dangerous 'internal competition,' by employing a folding operation that aimed to transform the negativity of unevenness produced in history into the positivity of cultural evenness, with its attending associations of authenticity and inauthenticity, respectively, marked by different spaces."[54]

Certainly the final superimposition of the Nagano landscape over the montage of Kimiko and her mother's faces suggests a kind of folding in of oppositions and a collapse of spatial and temporal categories. Yet this scene, with its rhythmic tracking shots, is also very stylized and expressive. Tokata describes it as "contrapuntal" in conjunction with the reprise of a musical theme associated with Kenichi, Oyuki's school-age son.[55] Indeed, it would seem as if the discourse on the social in *Wife!* is inconclusive. The overlapping of the tracking shots with their psychological connotations and the traveling shots suggesting train travel fail to harmonize time and space but harness both to the effects of technology. The children's song evokes the future and the virtues of education, but insofar as Etsuko is rendered anachronistic and "out of time," she and the aristocratic values that she represents will be excluded from this future. Moreover, the cultural memory that is preserved in the countryside is neither monumental nor spatial but is the memory of women's suffering in patriarchy. Kimiko finally overrules her uncle, and it is she and Oyuki who point the way to the future. Kimiko may cut a stylish figure, but she also represents the abstractions of capitalism; Oyuki, who works with her hands, engages in cash transactions. In this sense the film not only parallels the discourse on the social, it may be said to enact it and to offer a feminine solution to the loss of experience brought about by modernity. At the same time, Naruse has recovered some of the impact that shinpa had in the Meiji period, when it first emerged as a challenge to kabuki's institutional rigidity, suggesting that perhaps in the scrambled story in the American press there was in fact a kernel of truth.

Five Men in the Circus
ITINERANCY

In October 1935, P.C.L. released Naruse's light comedy *Five Men in the Circus* (*Saakasu gonin-gumi*) about an itinerant five-member brass band (bass and snare drums, trombone, trumpet, and clarinet). One member is played by Fujiwara, and another by Okawa. They are hired by a circus owner to replace his regular male performers, who are all striking to support one of their colleagues who has been refused the hand of the circus-owner's daughter, Sumiko. The film is set in a rural community, and the characters all miss Tokyo, where they feel their aspirations to be real artists would more likely be realized. The joke of the film lies mainly in the musicians' lack of talent, for which they compensate with clownish personalities. Like many Naruse films of the 1930s, popular music plays a key role, alongside popular entertainments. The theme of the itinerant musicians is one that recurs throughout his films of the 1930s and 1940s, and itinerancy becomes a dominant theme in some of his postwar romantic melodramas. In *Five Men in the Circus*, the *jinta*, or brass band, is extraordinarily quotidian; the players are bored and lazy. When they attempt to sing and play the violin, they are excruciatingly bad, and while the circus audience doesn't boo them off the stage, their silence is a consummate rejection.

The narrative climax comes with the fall of the owner's daughter Sumiko from the flying trapeze. Sumiko is played by Umezono Ryuko in a role far more conventionally docile than those in her other films with Naruse, although she once again does a dance routine. The accident is depicted in a series of superimposed shots of the girl on the trapeze, a close-up of her sister's shocked face, and a confrontation on the circus floor between the striking workers and the circus owner. Sumiko and her sister Chiyoko also perform a pseudo-ballet dance in the circus, which is really more of a catch-all vaudeville show than a conventional circus and serves as another showcase for Umezono's talents and body. Sumiko's fall from the trapeze resolves the narrative insofar as it is an attempted suicide, by which she successfully persuades her father to let her marry the performer, thus ending the strike. Meanwhile, the five musicians continue on their way, one of them having been so inspired by Sumiko's actions that he reconciles with his mistress, who has been tagging along after the band. Chiyoko, however, lets her favorite musician go, leaving the narrative slightly open; instead of the expected romantic closure, her final words are "life is a journey."

None of the characters are well developed in *Five Men in the Circus*, partly because of the role of the group of men as a central motif of the film. Although they are depicted as somewhat brutish and disrespectful of women at first, the narrative insistence on romantic themes has the effect of improving their manners. It is significant that the film treats labor relations in the form of melodrama. The musicians continue on their journey with a woman in their midst, the unnamed mistress, who has admittedly curried their favor by stealing goods from the local establishment where she worked as a hostess. The dramatic structure of this film becomes a familiar pattern for Naruse; a dramatic crisis resolves a key narrative conflict, but it often leads to an ending that opens onto a new beginning for the characters. Closure is rarely synonymous with romantic resolution or tragic death; nor is the narrative conflict always completely resolved. Naruse's films are journeys without final destinations.

The Girl in the Rumor
THE LAST MODERN GIRL

The fifth film that Naruse made in this busy year, *The Girl in the Rumor* (aka *The Girl on Everyone's Lips* [*Uwasa no musume*], 1935), released December 21, 1935, features Umezono once more, as the notorious moga of the title, named Kimiko. Chiba Sachiko plays her more conservative sister Kunie. Although the moga character is not to blame for the family's downfall, her presence is very much a visual inscription of the changing times. As in *Three Sisters*, the love interest for Umezono is played by Okawa Heihachiro, who once again plays a rich boy completely devoid of personality. In these two films about sisters and the relations between women, the rich preppy boyfriend is little more than an object of desire.

The Girl in the Rumor was based on Naruse's own script, and according to Bock, its success ensured that he would be given creative freedom at P.C.L.[56] (It ranked number eight in *Kinema Junpo* for 1935.) Kunie is promised to a suitor named Sato (Okawa), but Sato prefers her sister Kimiko, who is far less refined and is outspoken and playful, in keeping with her moga image. Kimiko's main interest in Sato is that "he is rich, and so comes in handy." The girls' father doesn't consider Kimiko to be "marriageable" and disapproves of her unauthorized relationship with Sato, although his moral authority is somewhat in question, as his own wife has died, and now he wants his mistress to move in with the family. In a conversation set on a bridge overlooking the river, the two sisters discuss the proposition, along with their differing views on women. Kimiko says that for her, the mistress "epitomizes the fact that woman is an ignorant slave to man." She gets her comeuppance for this progressive view when it is revealed that the woman in question is actually her real mother. The question of the mistress's status is one that will recur throughout Naruse's ouevre and is treated more thoroughly and with great sensitivity in *Wife! Be Like a Rose!*. These films are often concerned with the bonds and relations between women confronted with a social practice that is silently condoned by social convention but rarely publicly addressed.

Critic Shinojima Makoto describes *The Girl in the Rumor* as a film about a declining social class in which the melodramatic elements concerning marriage and mistresses border on shinpa tragedy.[57] He suggests that Kimiko is a "villain" rather than a representative of a certain ideology, although it is hard to see how she can be responsible for the ruin of their father's sake shop. It turns out that the father has been diluting the sake to make ends meet, and the film ends with his arrest. The film juxtaposes the moga, with her modern attitudes and behavior, with the plight of a small family-run business in downtown Tokyo. One might say that both tendencies are "symptomatic" of urban modernity in the thirties, and while critics of the time may have been tempted to see a causal relation between them, from a more distanced perspective, they are more objectively presented.

Although Kimiko's brashness is depicted as superficial and empty, her style and energy as she and her girlfriends dance to jazz music is adopted by Naruse in the decoupage of the film. At one point, the girls' music in Kimiko's room overwhelms the grandfather's studious plucking of a samisen in an overt contrast between the old and the new. This is followed by a shot of rain on a tiled roof, a kind of pause that poetically suggests the transience of history and the impermanence of tradition. The narrative moves quickly through many public and private spaces, often opening new scenes with close-ups of feet or some other detail. Not even Kunie, sitting quietly by her mirror, is given the full allegorical treatment that Osome is given in *Three Sisters*, as the spatial composition is fragmented and disjointed. The family home becomes a labyrinthine space of interconnected rooms, stairways, and passages. Unlike Naruse's canonical films of the 1950s, the domestic interiors are surprisingly cluttered, and the director here eschews formal spatial composition for a kind of disorienting implosion of narrative space. Yet from within this chaotic pattern emerge several scenes in which the exchange of glances, conveyed through point-of-view editing, is imbued with significance. In one instance, Kunie is in a boat on the river, and she looks up to see Kimiko with Sato on a bridge. The editing of this sequence makes it difficult to tell whether Kimiko sees Kunie seeing her. Although both women drop their eyes, Naruse cuts to each of their point-of-view shots of the other in the distance, so that an accidental encounter is inscribed within the architectonics of urban space.

The climactic scene in which Kimiko meets the mistress Oya, who has come to visit, features several dramatic track-in close-up shots as the two women realize their true relationship. Kimiko attempts to run away from home, but the police interrupt to arrest the father, and the camera tracks in to his stunned expression, followed by the grandfather's equally surprised and angry look. Oya then looks at Kimiko, who drops her valise, indicating a change of heart. Although the melodrama verges on extremes of coincidence and the clichés of recognition of filial re-

15. Chiba Sachiko, Umezono Ryuko, and Heihachiro Okawa in *The Girl in the Rumor* (*Uwasa no musume*, 1935), P.C.L.

lations (perhaps what Makoto means by lapsing into shinpa tragedy), it is significant that Naruse uses the flamboyant cinematic techniques that he developed in the silent period to represent emotional expression. Added to the idiosyncratic camera movements is the exchange of glances. With very little dialogue, the final scene reconciles the women and denounces the authoritarian father. The question of the marriage and the contest between the two sisters remains unresolved, although Kimiko's sudden final transformation obliquely suggests that she may be marriageable after all. The film ends with a scene in the local barbershop in which a number of men wonder what will become of the sake shop. Although the father is tough, he is not a villain, and Naruse cannot be said to be taking sides in his depiction of social change. Kunie blames the dead mother—who, she says, did not love her husband enough—for the presence of the mistress, and indeed a motherless home is often a dysfunctional one in melodramatic narrative. However, with the revelation of Kimiko's true parentage, Oya is installed as a new maternal figure. Thus, order is restored and life in the neighborhood continues, with a few economical cinematic strokes.

Tochuken Kumoemon
MAN OF THE HOUSE

The male protagonist of *Tochuken Kumoemon* (1936), played by Tsukigata Ryunosuke, is an egoistic performer of rokyuko drama who sports a flashy ponytail and is followed around by a coterie of flunkies and advisers (the main one played by Fujiwara). One critic said that the film should really have been called "the wife of Tochuken Kumoemon."[58] As played by Hosokawa Chikako, the wife is a long-suffering woman who accompanies Tochuken on the samisen, even after he has taken up with a geisha, played by Chiba Sachiko. When his wife gets TB, Tochuken refuses to see her in the hospital, as he cannot bear to think that she is "just a woman." He wants to think of her as a performer, an ideal; he excuses his own arrogance with the same argument, claiming that he doesn't care about being a good father, because his performance is the main thing in his life. His son, he says, "tries to make me a perfect person. He tries to separate me from my performance."

When the scandal of Tochuken's adulterous liaison with Chidori, the geisha, becomes public, his son Sentaro gets into a fight at school defending his father's name. Tochuken becomes extremely angry, threatening to kill his son for his bad behavior. At the point where his arrogant machismo threatens to go completely out of control, the phone call from the hospital comes informing him of his wife's death. In Taisho Japan, technologies of telephones, telegrams, and telephones become important narrative conveniences that are available within an otherwise traditional setting, effectively rendering the setting both modern and bourgeois. A large part of the film is set in Tochuken's spacious Japanese home, complete with courtyard garden. In Naruse's first foray into a Taisho setting, the move away from gendai geki is symptomatic of the times, and he would be obliged to set a number of subsequent "arts" films in the past in the years to come.

The depiction of Tochuken as an egoistic patriarch could also be described as the film's modern gesture. The scenes of Tochuken reciting *rokyuko* in the theater are very well done, composed of multiple tracking and panning shots dissolved into each other, including sweeping shots of audiences assembling and then listening attentively. This film is in many ways a prelude to *Tsuruhachi and Tsurujiro*, in which the female lead is much more developed. The centrality of such an obstinate and unlikable character as Tochuken may doom the film's success, but its contradictions indicate that Naruse's preoccupation with gender included this singular portrait of male arrogance.

The Road I Travel with You
FAMILY POLITICS

A number of Naruse's films from this period are set among the upper middle class, featuring families who live in Western-furnished homes, wear fashionable Western clothes, and seem to have a great deal of leisure time. On one level, a film like *The Road I Travel with You* (*Kimi to yuku michi*, 1936) is about this display of wealth, even if the characters are not particularly empowered by it. *The Road I Travel with You* concerns two brothers of marriageable age and their mother, a former geisha who has been set up by an absent patron in a spacious country home in Kamakura. The futures of the two boys, torn between love matches and arranged marriages, are inseparable from the loaded questions of family status, money, and decisions made by the heads of wealthy families. The mother, played by Kiyokawa Tamae, is anxious to please these other families and is somewhat insensitive to her sons' wishes. They boldly accuse her of caring more for money than for their happiness.

A typical shinpa-style melodrama, the film is somewhat stagy in its rhythms and is not redeemed by any noticeable acting talent. Although the two men are caught within conflicting social pressures (*giri*) and personal desires (*ninjo*), the film is oddly lacking in emotional depth. Even Kasumi (Yamagata Naoyo), the lover of one of the sons, whose family has promised her to another man (from a far more prestigious family) is simply mopey and pathetic. She ends up committing suicide soon after Asaji, the geisha's older son, drives his car off a cliff. The other couple are a bit more cheery, but their characters remain very two-dimensional. Yuji, the second son, has been asked to be adopted into another wealthy family, but he has fallen in love with Kasumi's friend Tsukiko (Tsutsumi Masako), who is the only remotely familiar Naruse character in the film.

Yuji and Tsukiko first see each other in a train, catching each other's eyes in one of the film's best sequences, in which Naruse uses montage and camera movement to express their flirtation. Like the scene of Asaji's crazed driving along a seaside highway (in a convertible sports car), these scenes supply a dynamic energy that is otherwise lacking from the setbound drama. Neither Asaji's car crash nor Kasumi's drowning (in her father's garden pond) are actually shown, although they are heavily foreshadowed. While the suicides smack of an earlier age, the younger couple is identified as being more modern. Tsukiko wears Western clothes, while all the other women are in kimono; Yuji is training for the Olympic trials (unfortunately, not depicted in the film either) and seems to assume he can disregard his mother's wishes without question. Although Tsukiko and Yuji don't end up together at the end of the film, there is a suggestion that they might—that the choices of death or obedience are not the only ones. It is Tsukiko who leaves, saying she has to wait for a day when she is stronger. Other Naruse heroines will demonstrate this strength, and indeed had done so before, in films such as *Every Night Dreams* and *Wife! Be Like a Rose!*

The Road I Travel with You thus ends somewhat inconclusively, the air rife with unresolved tensions. Yuji's last words are to tell his mother that she is stupid—for saying that Kasumi could have been a good wife if she had only listened to her parents. Her failure to understand this woman's death is, indeed, a rather obstinate response and typical of the curious way in which no one seems to connect in the film. Naruse was clearly not moved by the material that he adapted from an original story by Miyake Yukiko. Nevertheless, it is indicative of the way that social and literary conventions of aristocratic Japanese culture—the class hierarchies built upon and sustained by the exchange of children through marriage—were transposed into the modern idiom of film melodrama. In conjunc-

16. Heihachiro Okawa in *The Road I Travel with You* (*Kimi to yuku michi*, 1936), P.C.L.

tion with some of the film's other motifs—the chance encounter in the public space of the train, the speed and mobility of the driving scene—those conventions are perhaps rendered irrelevant and outmoded. As Yuji says to his mother so rudely, they are stupid. The contradictions that are so strongly articulated in this film further suggest that Naruse was more comfortable in the milieu of the working and lower middle classes, and the family politics of an anachronistic aristocracy provided little emotional grist for his expressive aesthetics.

Morning's Tree-Lined Street
ROMANTIC FANTASY

In 1936 Chiba Sachiko had her third starring role in a Naruse picture, in which he returns to the milieu of the shoshimin-eiga. In *Morning's Tree-Lined Street*, she plays a young woman, Chiyo, who travels from her hometown, or *furusato*, to Tokyo to find work. As suggested by the title, this film takes up the theme of the city, beginning with a series of traveling shots from Chiyo's point of view on a bus leaving the countryside and entering the metropolitan cityscape. After some fruitless job hunting in downtown Tokyo, Chiyo accepts a job as a bar hostess in Shiba ward. Well away from glamorous Asakusa and Ginza, this is a neighborhood bar where the women are dirt poor, each having only one kimono to their name. Contrary to the title, there are few trees to be seen, although a small stream crossed by a little bridge gives the setting some character. The film contains a surprising number of exterior scenes, including shots of canyonlike downtown streets strangely empty of traffic.

Although Hayashi Fumiko is not mentioned in the credits for *Morning's Tree-Lined Street*, the film is strongly reminiscent of her narratives of drinking, poverty, and the life of single women in the city. Chiyo lives with the other hostesses above the bar, which is run by a benevolent madam—one of the first "women's houses" in Naruse's oeuvre. The women often get as drunk as their customers, who are mainly salarymen on their way home. Chiyo falls in love with one of the patrons, a nondescript man named Ogawa (Okawa Heihachiro), and at about forty minutes into the fifty-nine-minute film, Chiyo and Ogawa appear together on a train. While Chiyo rattles on about their future together, Ogawa is clearly upset and worried. They book into a hotel but flee when Ogawa sees a newspaper headline saying that he has embezzled public funds. Their romantic getaway turns into a full-fledged car chase until they are cornered in the woods by the police. Ogawa asks Chiyo to die with him, but she refuses, begging him to turn himself in instead. At this point Chiyo wakes up in her bed above the bar with a terrible hangover, and the whole romantic thriller narrative is revealed to have been a dream. Ogawa comes to say good-bye, as he is being transferred away from Tokyo. Chiyo sits by the reflecting stream outside the bar, agreeing with her friend that it is a beautiful day to go job hunting.

The fantasy of a crime narrative, linked to the romance of travel, is clearly a movie-influenced dream, and *Morning's Tree-Lined Street* takes the spectator along on the protagonist's imaginary adventure. Naruse offers no clues as to the shift from "reality" to fantasy. Before they flee from the police, Chiyo is depicted in the fantasy sequence as deliriously happy, singing in the moonlight and reminiscing about her hometown. Shots of the ocean and the rural landscape complete the image of the pastoral romance, which is as generic as the crime fiction.

Based on Naruse's own script, *Morning's Tree-Lined Street* is one of the key P.C.L. films in which he carves out a space for female subjectivity in Japanese cinema. Everyday life in the city, contrasted with a fantasy of romantic escape, is, in the final moments of the film, transformed for Chiyo into a safe place. The dream sequence seems to purge her fears of the city, enabling her to find her place within it. The theme of life going on, with which so many of Naruse's films find closure, constitutes a kind of redemption of everyday life after the dramatic disruptions of the narrative. In *Morning's Tree-Lined Street*, in addition to the dream sequence, other scenes set in the night streets are edited to convey a sense of unease. For example, after Chiyo sees her friend Shigeyo on the street with a man who may be blackmailing her, or may be a pimp of some kind, the two girls walk together, past a backdrop of softly lit cafés and inns, with a light Japanese song in the background: everyday life in the neighborhood at night. But when they stop to talk, the editing becomes erratic, cutting across the axis and framing empty spaces into which the women's faces move. Shigeyo is vague about her relationship with the man, but Chiyo senses for the first time that there may be more than meets the eye in the hostessing business. The poetic atmosphere is suddenly charged with anxiety and fear. Chiyo's dream sequence will subsequently develop the duplicity of men, and after leaving Shigeyo, she is harassed by a couple of drunks.

Even in this brief sequence on the street, Naruse uses editing alongside lighting and music to convey something of the experience of life in the city. The scene has a sensuality to it that is indicative of how, on the one hand, he depicts the water trade as a form of everyday life in modern

17. Chiba Sachiko and Akagi Ranko in *Morning's Tree-Lined Street* (*Asa no namiki michi*, 1936), P.C.L.

Japan; and also how he exploits the vocabulary of film language—subverting the conventions of continuity editing—to depict the contradictory experience of that life.

Feminine Melancholy
THE DAUGHTER-IN-LAW

Naruse's next film, *Feminine Melancholy* (*Nyonin aishu*, 1937), returns to the image of cosmopolitan Tokyo, including not only the city, with its department stores, train stations, jazz music, and telephones, but the household of a wealthy family. Irie Takako stars in the film, and her production company coproduced it as a vehicle for her.[59] She plays Hiroko, a woman who marries into the family through an arranged marriage only to be treated as a maid or, as she says to a friend, "a doll." She patiently puts up with her husband's irresponsibility, her in-laws' condescending treatment, and the frivolous behavior of her two sisters-in-law, until she finally confronts them in the film's penultimate scene. On the roof of a department store overlooking the city, Hiroko meets her handsome cousin Ryosuke—who is clearly the right man for her—but instead of running into his arms, she talks about finding herself and exploring her newfound independence.

Feminine Melancholy is one of the most damning critiques of women's social roles to be found in prewar Japanese cinema. Insofar as Hiroko's family is evidently much poorer than her husband's, the arranged marriage is depicted as a form of servitude or slavery. Hiroko makes every effort to play the part of the good daughter-in-law, but the family continues to take advantage of her. Although the city is the setting of Hiroko's drama, and she is introduced as a salesgirl in a Ginza shop before her marriage, she herself is dressed in kimono throughout the film. In contrast, one of the sisters-in-law, Yoshiko (Tsutsumi Masako) is a clothes horse, sporting a variety of high-fashion outfits. The first shot of her in the film starts with her high heels, moving up her body, as if to introduce her character through her clothes. Yoshiko has become involved with a low-life character, Masuda, to whom she gives money borrowed from other family members, including Hiroko.

The climax of the film comes when Hiroko takes a phone call from Masuda, who has holed up in a hotel, having embezzled money from his company. Hiroko refuses to give him up to the authorities (including her husband) but persuades Yoko to go to him because he loves her. Not only does Hiroko choose the melodramatic "woman's story" solution to the crisis, by which she establishes a bond with the "bad girl," effectively reforming her; in the confrontation, Hiroko's husband physically pushes her around, proving himself to be the real villain of the story. In this scene, set in the spacious tatami sitting room of the family home, Naruse employs a series of slow camera movements tracking in to the key players and tracking out to reframe characters in two-shots and groups. It is a slightly more refined or restrained version of the rapid camera movements that accompany the emotional drama of some of his silent films. As Yamane Sadao has noted, Naruse also makes an innovative use of architecture in this scene. All the family members are assembled, but they are standing, which suggests a real disturbance of the household. The tatami rooms are designed for polite conversation, but here they become the setting of angry pushing and shoving.[60] Yamane also points out that throughout the film, the thin shoji walls allow the family members to summon Hiroko at all hours by yelling through the house. The dramatic confrontation involving husband, wife, sister-in-law, and parents-in-law is overheard by the two younger members of the family standing in the next room.[61] The dysfunctional family is depicted as a virtual insult to the harmonious structure of the Japanese home.

18. On the roof of the department store. Irie Takako and Saeki Hideo in *Feminine Melancholy* (*Nyonin aishu*, 1937), P.C.L.

In fact, this is one of the first films in which Naruse exploits the architecture of the Japanese home for the "home drama" aesthetic that will dominate his work of the 1950s. He positions his camera at 90 degrees to the *fusuma* walls, uses the *shoji* frames to frame the action within shots; employs low camera angles for sitting figures and for perspectives down corridors within the home; and uses 360 degree space for scenes set around tables. The spaciousness of the home is reminiscent of the mise-en-scène that became associated with Ozu's postwar filmmaking. Both Ozu and Naruse tended to set their prewar films in the more cramped quarters of the lower middle and working classes. Compared to Ozu's use of these minimalist, geometric sets, Naruse's characters can be found far more often standing than sitting. Nevertheless, for both directors, starting in the 1930s, the Japanese home served as a structural allegory for the harmony of the family, a harmony that is inevitably threatened by their narratives of family relationships.

The mansion, however, is not a completely traditional home. Some of the rooms are furnished in a Western style, and the family is very much a cosmopolitan example of the way that money could buy a kind of cultural diversity in the 1930s. *Feminine Melancholy* features two scenes in which girls dance to jazz music. In the first instance, Hiroko dances with her younger sister in their mother's home, to prove to her mother that she can survive in a "modern home." But she breaks off in the middle of the dance, crying that she is not "modern enough" for her promised husband. Yamane suggests that the scene also depicts a stark contrast between the small tatami room and the jazz dancing. Later in the film, in one of the Western rooms of Hiroko's new home, her husband's youngest sister dances with her schoolgirl friends. Hiroko serves them a meal, after which they dance amid the oversized furniture. The girls all agree that they would never agree to an arranged marriage, effectively confirming Hiroko's fear that she is not "modern enough."

Even though she's a perfectly good dancer, by wearing her hair in the "married woman's style," Hiroko effectively cuts herself off from these new women in her husband's family. *Feminine Melancholy* depicts a complex and contradictory world in which the wealthy family wants the best of both worlds, losing their dignity and moral authority in the process. As a melodramatic heroine, Hiroko clearly occupies the place of the virtuous moral occult, yet it is important to point out that modernity itself is not demonized. Hiroko's dilemma is precisely to be caught up in a changing world. Her final gesture, leaving the family and her husband in a bold gesture, is evidence of the New Woman who has been born, even without a change of clothes.

In his review of *Feminine Melancholy* in *Kinema Junpo*, critic Mizumachi Seiji praises Irie's performance as the best of her talkie career.[62] However, he is very critical of the film itself, which he sees as a typical story of a woman in an unhappy marriage. He is not sympathetic toward the heroine's patient suffering and describes the nagging mother-in-law as a "hackneyed theme." Naruse's detailed "documentation" of Hiroko's role in the household is dismissed as a "manneristic obsession," and Mizumachi suggests that the director is hiding behind "the shadow of the materials." Most severely, he criticizes Naruse for "abandoning his authority as an auteur" by resorting to "shinpa-tragedy," which is seen as a capitulation to a form that has "wielded a powerful hold over the imagination of the masses." Although Mizumachi notes that Naruse has probed into "the deepest recess of the female psyche," he doesn't recognize this as the film's achievement, perhaps because he is looking for something else from the director. His review reveals the difficulties Naruse faced in maintaining his "auteur status" while moving with the tides of popular culture. For Mizumachi, the character of Yoko is the more typical Naruse heroine, perhaps because she is dragged down by her delinquent lover; however, in retrospect, it is evident that Hiroko's tenacious survival of adverse circumstances looks forward to Naruse's postwar heroines.

Avalanche
NARUSE AND LITERARY MODERNISM

The production company of *Avalanche* (*Nadare*, 1937) is listed as P.C.L./Toho, the last time that P.C.L. is identified in Naruse's filmography. With this film, the director shifted gears yet again to make one of the most anomalous films in his oeuvre. He did not fare any better with the critics, and he himself declared it to be a failure,[63] yet, as a collaboration with a prominent intellectual of the period, Murayama Tomoyoshi, it is indicative of Naruse's participation in the construction of Japanese modernity. In this film, based on a popular serialized novel by the best-selling author Osaragi Jiro, Naruse and Murayama experimented with some innovative techniques to create subjective effects of interior consciousness. The film's protagonist, Goro (Saeki Hideo), periodically pauses while a dark filter drops like a screen over the image and he speaks his inner

19. The veil comes down. Saeki Hideo in *Avalanche* (*Nadare*, 1937), P.C.L.

thoughts in voice-over. In one instance it is used for Yayoi—the woman he loves but is not married to—to communicate her feelings directly to the audience. The device is not terribly effective, and its intrusive nature was harshly criticized by Mizumachi Seiji in *Kinema Junpo*.[64]

A bigger part of the problem with *Avalanche* is its speechiness. The voice-over monologues are only one element of a script that places an enormous emphasis on spoken language. Moreover, the editing style is, with a few exceptions, remarkably static, with few of the cuts on movements and glances that by this point Naruse had integrated into his usual decoupage. In one of the film's key scenes, Goro argues with his father, both of them articulating their positions while standing facing each other in a Western-furnished room. Using conventional reverse-angle cutting and a few camera movements as the men move around the room, this four-and-a-half-minute scene fails to convey the emotional tension of a conversation in which the son tells his father that he wants to end his marriage, and the father tells the son that he is a spoiled and arrogant young man who has no consideration for the feelings of his wife. The scene ends with Goro complaining in voice-over about his father's "old morality" and his own right to do as he pleases in these new times.

Avalanche is furthermore unusual in its use of luxurious Western-style homes. The only Japanese-style house in the film is that of Goro's wife Fukiko's family. When Goro meets his father for lunch, they dine in a Western restaurant in a downtown building overlooking the city. Yayoi (Edogawa Ranko) lives in a huge mansion herself and has an elegant cottage in Kamakura, also decorated in a lavish Western style. While Fukiko (Kiritachi Noboru) dresses in kimono with a wife's hairstyle, reprising the theme of the unhappy wife, Yayoi wears fashionable outfits with huge collars, pumps, and hats with veils. Yayoi is not Goro's mistress, but his true love whom, for unexplained reasons, he did not marry. She is a kind of existential heroine who lives with her bedridden brother. Without Goro, she says, her life has no purpose. She meets Goro in the woods and in nightclubs, where they discuss their complicated relationship.

Avalanche also reprises the theme of the fantasy escape when Goro takes Fukiko away to a hotel at the end of the film. What she thinks will be a romantic getaway turns ugly when Goro proposes double suicide, and then, in voice-over, decides that he won't die, but Fukiko will. On the verge of administering the dose of poison, he hears his father's voice berating him for being a shallow and superficial person. Telling himself that he is not giving in to his father, he simply changes his mind and lets Fukiko live. The film closes with Yayoi on the beach in high-heeled pumps, walking her dog, with her brother tagging behind.

The device of the lowered screen is certainly an unusual technique, and despite the awkwardness of the film, it points to the way that Naruse did not hesitate to continue experimenting with the possibilities of film language. Tsuneishi Fumiko has linked the "veil" in *Avalanche* to Naruse's career-long depiction of the distance between men and women: "Naruse was able to develop a method of expressing the unbridgeable gap between people within an elegant flow, but his most frank and matter-of-fact expression of the distance between human beings is the veil in *Avalanche*."[65] She also notes that Fukiko seems naive enough to "believe her husband's limpid eyes," whereas most of Naruse's strongest female characters "impatiently try to push aside the veil that hangs between them and their men." By the end of the film, though, it is evident that Fukiko has been watching the "ever-present veil between man and woman."[66] The veil in this reading is a literalization of the theme of emotional distance and the misunderstandings and miscommunication that persist between men and women in Naruse's cinema, by which he was able to bring the modernism of the novel into line with his own, more vernacular form of modernism.

An ironic critique of class is strongly implied by the decadence of the film's excessive decors and fashions, although it is an oblique critique to be sure. Certainly the father's moral authority is upheld, even though he is rich. Fukiko's father comments to a friend that Goro's father is "different than the common run of dirty moneymakers," agreeing that he displays "some good sides of the old feudal times." Clearly we are in a milieu of complicated ideological pressures and contradictory morality. Although it is hard to know how the film came into being, Murayama's Marxist views may well be responsible for the bourgeois setting, which Naruse characteristically elaborates in such meticulous detail that the narrative is virtually overwhelmed by stylish materialism. The emptiness of this decadent lifestyle is reinforced by the uncharacteristic lack of emotional depth.

Harootunian describes Murayama as an admirer of constructivism and futurism. He founded an avant-garde movement in the 1920s that was designed to challenge bourgeois notions of autonomous art and integrate the productivity of machines and industry into art making. His notion of subjectivity "seemed to hover somewhere between the social collectivity, represented by the indeterminate masses, and the machine."[67] Although Murayama's machine aesthetics are perhaps most indebted to Marinetti, he also echoes Benjamin's notion of "the artist as producer," insofar as he advocated a commitment of the artist to the public sphere. This would explain why his filmmaking endeavors included working with Naruse at P.C.L.[68] Mechanical reproduction, including printing, photography, and film, were the means by which artists could become producers. There is no reason to think that Naruse was necessarily familiar with Murayama's theories, but their collaboration suggests another way of reading Naruse's ambivalent status as a studio-based auteur in the mid-1930s. He was, much more than Murayama, an artist deeply immersed in an industrial mode of production. But as the contradictions of *Avalanche* make clear, he was not comfortable in the milieu of the modernist novel with its existential crises and tortured "new men." The film fails to convey the feelings described in its opening epigraph taken directly from the Osaragi novel: "Today we all live in such a precarious world that even a person of strong will like Goro can be carried away by an avalanche."

In Naruse's melodramatic imagination, moral crises and avalanches are deeply embedded in the everyday world of material culture. Individual crises are exteriorized in car accidents, camera movements, and musical scores. In this world, the psychological dilemmas of a man like Goro have no significance and no practical relevance to everyday life. There are no unknown forces that cause men to change their minds, as all events are materially anchored in social life. The character Yayoi says at one point that "conscience exists only in relation to society," and indeed the real drama of *Avalanche* is a society in transition.

Learn from Experience
DECADENCE AND EXCESS

Naruse made one more film in 1937, *Learn from Experience* (*Kafuku*) with Irie Takako, at P.C.L., although it was distributed by Toho.[69] Released in two parts, each running seventy-eight minutes, *Learn from Experience* was based on a novel by one of the most popular novelists of the time, Kikuchi Kan. Irie plays a long-suffering woman, Toyomi, whose lover, Shintaro, abandons her for another, richer woman (Yurie, played by Takehisa Chieko) when his father insists on an arranged marriage to save the family fortune. While Yurie is a headstrong modern woman, Toyomi is more refined and restrained, and indeed costume plays an important role in this film, part of which is set in a Ginza clothing shop. Toyomi bears a child out of wedlock, and in the second installment the two women become friends, although Yurie has married the erstwhile lover Shintaro. After many ups and downs, and mediation by Toyomi's friend Mitsuko, Yurie and Shintaro end up adopting the baby (which is Shintaro's), while Toyomi gets a job working in a nursery.

While the visual style of *Learn from Experience* is fairly pedantic, adopting the long shot of standing figures as its dominant compositional device, it is remarkable for the way it showcases modern life in Tokyo. In the first half of the film, the twenty-something-year-old characters are seen strolling in Ueno Park, dancing in Tokyo dancehalls, and shopping for Western clothes in Ginza. In part 2, the clothing shop becomes a key site where the women encounter one another, and the parade of latest fashions includes an excessive array of collars, belts, ribbons, hats, printed dresses, and wide-striped suit jackets. Indeed the shot scale may in fact be chosen precisely to display these fashions. The narrative meanders through an amusement park, complete with Ferris wheel, and a baseball game. The baby becomes a virtual trophy as the women pass it back and forth, shop for it, dress it, nurse it, and fight over it, before it ends up being held aloft by the father in the penultimate scene. His gesture is echoed by a last shot of Toyomi lifting a child in the nursery. For the first time, she is seen without her kimono, sporting a huge white bow at the collar of her dress; likewise, it is the first time that Shintaro appears to notice the baby.

Kikuchi Kan, the author of *Learn from Experience*, is said to be the Japanese writer whose novels have been most often adapted to film.[70] In the same year as Naruse's film was released, three different versions of Kikuchi's novel *A Beautiful Hawk* (*Utsukushiki taka*) were produced.[71] The restoration of the patriarchy at the end of *Learn from Experience* indicates the author's political orientation. Kikuchi was an influential film critic, whose column in *Nihon Eiga* in the late 1930s became a catalyst for the conceptualization of a nationalist cinema inspired by Nazi aesthetics and ideology.[72] While Naruse may not have been parodying this material, there is a sense in which the excessive discourse of fashion intrudes on the melodramatic narrative. The director was clearly uninspired by the story and its bourgeois characters, yet the virtuous character Toyomi does seem somewhat lost in this world. Her hard-won happiness is not fully convincing at the end of the film, which is not to say that *Learn from Experience* is in any way subversive or critical, but simply to note that it partakes of a melodramatic mode of representation and all that that entails.

Melodrama and Japanese Classical Cinema

Throughout this critical period of the mid-1930s Naruse's characters are embattled by moral choices thrown up at them by the contradictions of everyday life. Often these choices are the result of conflicting priorities in the melodrama of social change, when virtue is "occulted" within what Peter Brooks calls the "surface of reality." Indeed, even if Naruse's cinema of this period is far less excessive than his silent films, it is very much a cinema of expression, grounded in a detailed realism of everyday life. Like the melodramatic theater of the nineteenth-century French stage, Japanese classical cinema was in many ways developing a language for a new, bourgeois social formation. In the 1930s the Japanese middle class was still immersed in consumer capitalism, yet becoming more and more distanced culturally from the epicenter of mass culture. Thus, this new language, a dramaturgy founded on a "new lyricism of gesture," circulates around the recognition of virtue, which is typically embodied in the female protagonist.

Brooks's definition of melodrama as "a drama of articulation, a drama that has as its true stakes the recognition and triumph of the sign of virtue,"[73] is true not only of the woman's film genre or josei eiga that Naruse explored in films such as *Morning's Tree-Lined Street* and *Feminine Melancholy*, but equally in some of his male-centered films, such as *Tochuken* and *Avalanche*. In each instance, however, the psychological drama is played out against a mise-en-scène of visual detail, and accompanied by soundtracks of musical accents. The strength of the woman's films is often bound up with the "sensual" quality of this expressionistic detail, which accentuates the stakes of the characters' dilemmas. As a classical cinema, Naruse and his contemporaries were forging an audiovisual language for a society undergoing rapid and often contradictory cultural shifts. In many ways, the cinema provides a continuity, even a stable discourse, throughout thirty years of social upheaval.

In 1937, 562 films were produced in Japan, marking the industry's peak year of production.[74] Naruse's three titles of that year represent only a small fraction of this output, which also includes key films by Ozu, Mizoguchi, Gosho, Shimazu, Itami, Yamada, and many others. Period films continued to be made throughout the 1930s, although the jidai geki was a genre in decline throughout most of the decade.[75] In the sheer volume of films produced, it is evident that motion pictures had become a huge business and a fundamental component of national culture, which by this time had become an important cultural export to Japan's Asian colonies. Naruse's cinema may not necessarily be representative of all the generic and stylistic diversity of the period, yet it does point to the ways that studio film production became more conservative.

Naruse's filmmaking style began to partake more of the conventions of the Hollywood system, but it remained very much embedded in Japanese culture throughout his P.C.L. films. We can certainly see a continued use of 360-degree space, especially in scenes set in tatami rooms, and other occasional violations of the "codes" of narrative realism. These deviations may not be necessarily Japanese, but they are frequently linked to the spaces of domestic architecture and are also apparent in the films of some of Naruse's contemporaries, especially Ozu. Moreover, one can identify a systematic use of Japanese iconography and aesthetic conventions through the films, including cutaways to poetic compositions of nature and landscapes to punctuate transitions, along the lines of Ozu's famous "pillow shots." In *Learn from Experience* there is even a pan over a display of cherry blossoms, and a glimpse of the river flowing by. A more conventional repertoire of iconography is hard to imagine. In 1937, a critic in *Eiga Hyoron* wrote that even though "there is a certain excitement" generated by the familiarity of Naruse's films, as "the biggest victim of the rationalization of film represented by P.C.L." Naruse was a "tragic figure."[76]

Within Naruse's fall from critical grace are some valuable clues as to the role of cinema in the continuing construction of cultural life in a Japan anxious to "overcome modernity." For example, we need to recognize the importance of costume as a cultural discourse in these films. The kimono-clad Toyomi in *Learn from Experience* embodies that unevenness referred to by Harootunian that is constitutive of Japanese modernity. Played by Irie Takako, who was a notorious moga actress in the late 1920s and early 1930s, this character is in some ways emblematic of the ideological shifts that had taken place by 1937. In the world of Kikuchi Kan, everyone lives and dresses in decadent Western style, and Naruse complies by decorating his sets with huge bouquets of blossoms—no ikebana to be seen. While this image of Japan is not the one typically associated with Japan after the China Incident, it is indicative of the new contours of "modernity" of popular culture. Toyomi and the serving girls in their kimonos might as well be stranded in a "white telephone" film of prewar Italy. This dream world of ostentatious luxury would shortly be curtailed, and even in 1937, the dominant female image on the Japanese screen was the self-sacrificing mother.[77]

To describe this cinema as a "classical cinema" is a means of acknowledging, in part, its role in the formation of a modern national culture. Like the Hollywood classical cinema of the 1930s, which was forced to conform to the mandate of the Hays code, the Japanese cinema was increasingly bound to project a "clean" image of the nation. But like the American cinema, too, contradictions and fissures within such a censored mandate were bound to appear. Rethinking classical cinema as a form of vernacular modernism is a means of recognizing the detail and sensuality of material culture and the emergence of new subjectivities within the homogeneity of a visual style associated with cinematic classicism. In its Hollywood incarnation, this classicism has been theorized both as an effect of industry standardization and as an ideological form associated with bourgeois realism,[78] although neither conception can fully account for the modernity of the cinema as a social practice and popular entertainment form.

It may seem ironic to be proposing a Japanese classical cinema at precisely the moment when film studies scholars are beginning to question the legitimacy of that term in the American context.[79] However, classical

Japanese cinema conforms to neither the "classic realist text" of the apparatus theorists nor the normative style described by David Bordwell. The classical cinema that I see emerging in Naruse's films of the 1930s is predicated on melodrama as the popular form specific to the experience of modern life. As Linda Williams explains, many critics who have challenged the hegemony of the notion of classical cinema have nevertheless retained it as a means of referring to the mass-cultural "mainstream" aspect of moving pictures, with the important caveat that it be reconfigured as a modality of melodrama.[80] Comedy, romance, realism, and the infinity of genres that are subsumed within the rubric of the classical can also be understood as varieties of melodrama.[81]

Why should this not also be the case with the Japanese cinema? Like the American cinema, it evolved to meet the needs of what Williams describes as a "modern, rationalist, democratic, capitalist, industrial, and now postindustrial society seeking moral legibility under new conditions of moral ambiguity."[82] Film scholars' preoccupation with the realist novel has downplayed the equally important role of theatrical melodrama as a nineteenth-century antecedent of the cinema. Recognition of this dimension of classical cinema also enables us to locate Japanese cinema in relation to popular Japanese theatrical forms such as shinpa and *chanbara*. In conjunction with the realist impulse of cinematic representation, these melodramatic forms are put into the service of "moral legibility,"[83] which in both the American and Japanese classical cinemas frequently concerns the plight of women in patriarchy.

It should be evident that as an industrial product, from the 1930s until the early 1960s, certain continuities remained in place that allowed Japanese cinema to play a vital role in nation building, even while the nation endured a dramatic series of ideological upheavals. Naruse's contribution to this classicism, while marginal, is nevertheless valuable, and not only as a heuristic tool with which we can observe the ingredients of Japanese modernity on the screen. For audiences at the time, he arguably provided a rare set of texts in which questions of women's roles in family and public life were scrutinized. No other director provided as complex figures of modern women in this decade as did Naruse with his films about "new women," professional women, café waitresses, wives, and daughters-in-law. Not only are these fascinating portraits produced in collaboration with key actresses, they are situated within a detailed cultural landscape of class differences, popular culture, and rituals of social practices such as drinking, traveling, spectating, shopping, and other activities of everyday life.

While Anderson and Richie claim that in the 1930s Naruse moved from melodrama to the shoshimin-eiga,[84] I think it is more the case that he refined the melodramatic excesses of his silent films into a realist style that was grounded in a social realism of the lower middle class. Melodrama remained a cornerstone of his cinematic style as a mode of expression appropriate to a representation of emotions, cathartic climactic scenes, and depictions of the "moral occult" of virtuous characters. If many of these conventions are similar to those found in Hollywood films, many are also to be found in the Japanese theatrical tradition of shinpa, and in the popular novels and plays that Naruse adapted, and they should not be simply dismissed as American imitations. To the extent that Naruse was undoubtedly influenced by the Hollywood of Lubitsch and von Stroheim, and the gangster films and comedy films of the American studios, he recognized this cinema as the language of modernity. In his films of the 1930s, we can see him incorporating this cinematic language—including its dimensions of fantastical escape—into the realm of everyday life in modern Japan.

In this formulation of classical cinema, it is not "opposed" to other practices, whether they be art cinemas, cinemas of excess, or from other cultures, but it is a classicism that points to the flexibility of a narrative form that crosses linguistic and other boundaries. It is in this sense that in 1930s Japan, while harnessed to a national culture, a "classical cinema" could also, at the same time, undermine that nationalism by implicitly alluding to a global modern culture of "the movies." While this cinema was to have a very different historical trajectory than its American counterpart, by 1937, with the establishment and full institutionalization of the studio system of production, a base had been established for what can only be described, in retrospect, as a Japanese classical cinema.

3

Not a Monumental Cinema

WARTIME VERNACULAR, 1938–1945

The chronicler who narrates events without distinguishing between major and minor ones acts in accord with the following truth: nothing that has ever happened should be regarded as lost to history. —WALTER BENJAMIN

Naruse made thirteen films between 1938 and 1945, during the height of the China and Pacific wars, a period in which the government held strict control of all film production. Although none of these titles are usually counted among his best works, they are nevertheless key titles in Naruse's construction of a modern idiom that remained more or less in keeping with the ideological mandates of the period. During these years, he worked with period settings in films such as *Tsuruhachi and Tsurujiro* (1938) and *The Song Lantern* (*Uta Andon*, 1943) without completely forsaking modern characters for a mythical treatment of the Japanese past. He also made a number of important films with contemporary settings, such as *The Whole Family Works* (*Hataraku ikka*, 1939) and *Hideko the Bus Conductor* (*Hideko no shasho-san*, 1941), that feature the emergence of young people as new subjectivities in a changing world. He did not overtly challenge the mandates of national policy during the war years but he was able to develop the terms of a vernacular modernism specific to Japanese popular culture that ran parallel to the regime of *kokusaku eiga*, or "national policy films."

The ideology of *kokutai* dictated by the Ministry of Education stipulated that all cultural production must conform to the twin principles of "a return to Japan" and an embrace of the emperor system and its hierarchical structure of Japanese society. The mandate to relinquish all attachment to Western iconography, materialism, and individualism was designed to provide a "ritual basis for the modern national state."[1] Although the kokutai decree was first issued in 1937, a specific Film Law was not passed until 1939. However, an effective system of self-censorship was in place after the 1937 decree, and the shift in Naruse's style and subject matter from his last P.C.L. film, *Learn from Experience*, to his first official Toho film, *Tsuruhachi and Tsurujiro* (1938), reflects more than a change in studios. In fact P.C.L. was simply absorbed by Toho, and one unit of it was renamed the Toho Culture Film Section, dedicated to documentary production.[2] In 1938 the film industry agreed to observe a rigorous set of principles designed to "elevate" Japanese film culture above the decadent tendencies it had ostensibly sunk to under the influence of foreign movie cultures.[3]

Kokutai no hongi, or "the cardinal principles of our national polity," entailed a revival of Japanese cultural practices that had long since been forgotten in the popular imagination and had to be reinvented for the purposes of cultural uplift. The underlying principle was to construct, through the edifice of historical authenticity, a spiritual unification of the nation in the war effort. The "Japanese fighting spirit" or *seishinshugi* that inspired so many Japanese men to sacrifice themselves for the invincible cause of total victory was linked to a larger home-front propaganda campaign. The legitimacy of Japanese occupation of Asia entailed a denunciation of "Western modernization" and its corrupting influence on social customs.

With the film law of 1939, all members of the film industry, including actors, technicians, directors, and distributors, had to be licensed, which usually entailed being tested for their political commitment to the war effort.[4] Scripts were censored for traces of decadent behavior and materialism, including such things as women smoking; and the shoshimin-eiga genre was ostensibly banned,[5] presumably because it had become too deeply engaged with the materialism of modern life. The first directives issued by the Home Ministry in August 1937 included proscriptions against: "1) subjecting the army to ridicule, 2) excessively bloody depictions of the cruelties of war, 3) depictions of family pathos when a man is called into the army, and 4) depictions of pleasure-seeking and degenerate life-styles."[6] After 1940, the regulations included the promotion of national policy themes alongside the prohibition of inappropriate subjects, and the restrictions got progressively stricter as the war went on. With increasing scarcity of resources, by 1940, the use of electricity and the construction of theaters and equipment were seriously curtailed, while slogans such as "luxury is the enemy" entailed a rigorous elimination of any of the stylish depictions of modernity that Naruse had included in films such as *Avalanche* and *Learn from Experience* in 1937. Needless to say, heavy Japanese losses and the real conditions at the front were kept secret from the Japanese public, who were told only about glorious victories and the triumphant spread of Japanese culture across the Pacific and the Asian continent.

On the face of it, Naruse, along with the rest of the film industry, complied with these regulations. To continue working, there was little choice, and as Darrell Davis argues, it is a mistake to dismiss the work of individual directors because of their capitulation to the demands of the state.[7] Anderson and Richie point out that "no genre escaped being used for ultranationalistic propaganda, nor did any director."[8] Davis has further discussed in some detail the aesthetics of the "monumental style" that emerged under this regime as a group of films that "complement their indigenous subject matter with a unique style."[9] Films such as Mizoguchi's *Story of the Last Chrysanthemums* (1939) and *The Loyal 47 Ronin I–II* (*Genroku Chushingura I–II*, 1941–42), he argues, dispense with conventional narrative techniques in the aspiration of formal means of articulating a distinctive style and feeling of Japanese heritage.[10] Monumental films, while set in the Japanese past, dispense with the generic characteristics of the jidai geki and Japanese melodrama that had been developed over the previous two decades for a more ponderous and "magisterial" aesthetic. For Davis, the edicts of national policy films provided filmmakers such as Mizoguchi with the opportunity to depart from the "classical" Hollywood style that had largely infiltrated the Japanese industry by the late 1930s. In his analysis, the films function as propaganda not through didactic "messages," but through the production of a "cultural sacrament offered to the Japanese people," offering "a sense of belonging to a living entity much larger than the lone, often alienated self."[11]

Davis interprets the political implications of the monumental style as a form of national spirituality linked to Japanese identity in order to establish its credentials as an art cinema. I would argue that this national spirit was constructed, not revived, through the monumental style, along with its implications of authoritarian and imperialist culture. The difficulty of accounting for Japanese auteurs' participation in a repressive regime is an ongoing theme in Japanese film studies, of which Davis's attempt to redeem Mizoguchi on aesthetic grounds is only one example. Many filmmakers, critics, and intellectuals underwent a process referred to as *tenko*, an ideological reorientation or conversion to the principles of the militarist state. This usually meant the renunciation of the Marxist and liberal formations that had been developed in the 1920s by many artists, intellectuals, and writers.

Although Naruse was never articulate as an ideologue, and thus was never officially subjected to any form of tenko, his filmmaking reflects a certain backing off from the individualism of some of his P.C.L. and Shochiku features. Moreover, the strictures against bourgeois decadence, along with the reinvention of tradition, might be seen as assets to his filmmaking, in the sense that they enabled him to hone a style appropriate to the lower middle classes and to explore some of the aesthetic styles of traditional Japanese arts. By respecting the regulations of the period, he was able to continue working, and he was forced to shed some of the more obvious foreign influences, even if, formally and stylistically, his filmmaking became even more conventionally classical in the Hollywood sense. It also appears that he did not always respect these regulations as rigorously as one might expect, and in the subsequent analyses, I will argue that he did so only circumspectly and unconvincingly.

Naruse's wartime cinema is not monumental, and cannot be accommodated within the transcendental values of an art cinema. On the contrary, close analysis of his films indicates that the aesthetics of Japanese classical cinema that were in place by 1937 could not be and were not eradicated by the national policy mandates. While he conformed to the proscriptions against mogas and decadent consumerist behavior and stayed away from his favored urban contemporary settings, traces of modernity continue to inform Naruse's cinema. To the extent that he focuses on the experience of everyday life, and that he continues to make entertaining melodramas with modern characters—even, as we shall see, in period settings—Naruse's wartime cinema constitutes not only a counterpoint to the monumental style, but also a subtle undermining of the ostensible principles of national policy propaganda. This does not make him a radical, because the true radicals were either reprimanded and cut off, or prevented from making films at all.[12]

In his impressive study of Japanese film culture in the Fifteen Years' War, Peter High explains how government officials connected to the Information Bureau and the Home Ministry handed down a constantly changing series of demands that were often contradictory, making it more and more difficult for filmmakers to know how to stay in line. For example, the Film Law proscribed against "slice-of-life" films, essentially shoshimin-eiga, yet in 1941 they demanded that filmmakers provide a "People's Cinema" according to the following criteria: "With its roots thrust deep in the life of the people, it will realize the lofty ideals of our nation. Arising from a deep artistic sense, People's Cinema will loyally serve national policy as the organ of enlightenment and propaganda."[13] Filmmakers were also told not to be "arty," which was considered to be both elitist and individualist and thus potentially disconnected from the people. In this climate, High notes, "control bred bewilderment, bewilderment bred anxiety, and anxiety bred pleas for even more exacting control. This was the psychological vicious circle that finally subjugated the Japanese filmmaker."[14] He quotes Iijima Takashi, complaining in 1942 that with a system that "depresses the creative spirits in the film world . . . a general falling off in quality will result."[15]

While the received opinion seems to be that Naruse experienced a "slump" from the mid-1930s to the early 1950s, it is clear that the entire industry was negatively affected by the lack of resources and restrictions on freedom of expression throughout this period.[16] It is true that Naruse won no *Kinema Junpo* prizes between 1935 and 1951, but neither did he toe the line quite as carefully as some of his colleagues. The ways that he adapted to the national policy mandates in order to continue producing popular cultural texts during these years provide a fascinating insight into the everydayness of Japanese culture during the war. As a vernacular modernism, his films are indicative of a level of experience that is not recognized in most histories of the war. Moreover, his films remain extraordinarily well crafted.

Of the thirteen films that Naruse made during this period, eleven are extant. The two missing films, *Shanghai Moon* (*Shanhai no tsuki*, 1941)[17] and *Until Victory Day* (*Shori no hi made*, 1945), sound like they are set on the military front, or at least outside the Japanese homeland, and they are probably his most overt examples of kokusaku eiga, or national policy films. Naruse continued working when production was dramatically limited, from 1943 to 1945, with a diminishing availability of resources and increasingly difficult conditions of production. In the last year of the war, when he produced two titles, the total national output was only twenty-six,[18] which suggests Naruse's role as a stalwart member of the industry.

Naruse's films may have been officially sanctioned, but for the most part they remain outside the official culture of the period, which, along with the monumental films discussed by Davis, includes a series of "culture films"—documentaries designed to educate the public. Peter High points out that although the filmmakers involved with the culture film navigated a perilous route through the inconsistent and ambiguous dictums of official censorship during the Fifteen Years' War, in the 1930s, "the Japanese were the only advanced nation fighting a major war and making films using modern talkie film technology."[19] Indeed, Japanese officials were very conscious of the importance of cinema as a means of uniting the populace and distracting them from the increasingly bleak state of the national emergency. Throughout this period, dramas and entertainment films, including both gendai geki and jidai geki, were considered to be important to the public, even if they were always accompanied by newsreels. By 1944, when the Pacific War had turned against Japan, and the home front was threatened, officials declared an urgent need for uplifting, cheery films, even though by this point many theaters had been converted to factories, and vital raw materials were diverted to military functions.

Naruse's two lost kokusaku eiga are not necessarily representative of the dominant mode of propaganda, but they do indicate that the Home Ministry understood the feature film industry as cooperating with the war effort through the provision of entertainment. *Shanghai Moon* is set in Shanghai in 1937. Yamada Isuzu plays a terrorist who infiltrates a radio station broadcasting pro-Japanese programs. She becomes involved in a love triangle with two patriots, a woman singer and a soldier, but she cannot follow her orders to kill them and is killed herself instead by her fellow terrorists. Naruse traveled to Shanghai to make *Shanghai Moon*, but as Peter High notes, he distanced himself from the militarist fervor implied by the film. Instead, he spoke about the wonderful American films that he saw overseas and, contra kokutai orthodoxy, lamented the absence of foreign films from Japanese screens.[20]

Until Victory Day was probably made for the troops abroad. It features an "entertainment rocket" out of which Takamine Hideko, Yamada Isuzu, and the popular comedian Furukawa Roppa pop to entertain soldiers at the front.[21] High quotes Tokugawa Musei, who also acted in the film, remarking after the war that, "you could actually feel the approach of inevitable defeat in the utter imbecility of its storyline. The fact that it had been directly commissioned by the navy made it all the more pathetic."[22] High suggests that it was made "so late in the war that very few actually saw it."[23] These two films are evidence enough that, even if some of Naruse's other titles depart somewhat from the national policy mandate, he was by no means outside the sphere of the militarist ideology. The melodramatic premise of *Shanghai Moon* shows how he was able to adapt conventions of Hollywood cinema to the war effort, in which he was not alone. Other directors made similar "spy pictures,"[24] clearly influenced by American and European examples that had been in circulation since the 1920s.

It is also worth noting that both of these war films, *Shanghai Moon* and *Until Victory Day*, are concerned with performances of popular culture. This theme runs throughout Naruse's wartime films, as he repeatedly returns to variations on the role of performance and the production of popular culture. Without making any claims about modernist reflexivity, this ongoing preoccupation with cultural performances and texts is constitutive of Naruse's modernity, which was not overcome but merely disguised during this period.

Back to Japan
ARTS AND HISTORY FILMS

Four of Naruse's wartime films may be said to approximate the monumental style, or at least to work with similar materials of traditional Japanese culture. *A Tale of Archers at the Sanjusangendo* (*Sanjusangendo toshiya monogatari*, 1945) is a samurai film of sorts, while *Tsuruhachi and Tsurujiro* (1939), *The Song Lantern* (1943), and *The Way of Drama* (*Shibaido*, 1944) are all about performers trained in the techniques of the arts and explore the challenges involved in remaining true to these practices. Insofar as they are about the "way of the artist," they can be described as *geido* films. While they all include extended sequences of performances, they also involve a lot of backstage melodrama involving psychological distress, romantic longing, paternalistic fathers, heavy drinking, and financial woes. These scenes tend to be shot in fairly conventional ways, with the exception of Naruse's continued use of 360-degree shooting space for both interior and exterior sets. He uses the elegant tatami rooms of the Meiji period to excellent effect, but it cannot be said that the settings are endowed with the kind of national spirit that Davis attributes to the monumental style. If the ideal of that aesthetic is "the balance of behavior, the perfection of design, and the contemplation of space,"[25] Naruse continually disturbs this perfection by cutting between characters discussing the ups and downs of their messy lives.

Naruse had already worked in this genre with *Tochuken Kumoemon* in 1936, but the three later films mark a refinement, both in his use of architectural space and in his depiction of the psychologically complex performer. *Tsuruhachi and Tsurujiro*, *The Song Lantern*, and *The Way of Drama* are all set in late Meiji Japan, and they all feature female performers as well as male, even if the men tend to be the central figures. Yamada Isuzu appears in all three titles, and Hasegawa Kazuo appears in the first and third, both of them major Toho stars. The critic Iijima Tadashi categorizes all three geido films as *shinpa-geki* or "new-style dramas" in his 1953 classification of Naruse's oeuvre,[26] and indeed the settings and the melodramatic storylines are consistent with shinpa drama.

Tsuruhachi and Tsurujiro is named for a duo who perform ballads in a style called *shinnai* or *gidayu*, in variety show formats. Tsurujiro (Hasegawa) sings, while Tsuruhachi (Yamada) accompanies him on the shamisen. He constantly criticizes her playing until she can't take it any more and marries a rich man. Tsurujiro is not nearly as successful without her, but when their former manager successfully reunites them, Tsurujiro insists that Tsuruhachi deserves better than the inconstant life of a performer, so he sends her back to her husband and her elegant lifestyle. The film is rife with condescending attitudes toward women, and Tsuruhachi is faced with a choice between marriage and performing, as if the options were irreconcilable. Although it was her mother who taught the pair their successful technique, Jiro (Tsurujiro) insists that Toyo (Tsuruhachi) keeps making mistakes. "A wife must follow her husband," he says. She argues with him, and the so-called mistakes do indeed seem to be minor differences of style. When the pair are briefly reunited at the end of the film, she confesses that music is her true calling and she will be fulfilled only by being able to perform. The film upholds Jiro's cruelty by refusing Toyo this opportunity, but it is such an absurd ending that its effect is principally to foreground Toyo's utter disempowerment as a female musician.

A critical discussion in the pages of *Kinema Junpo* concerning *Tsuruhachi and Tsurujiro* is revealing of the disjunction between film culture and national policy in 1938. The critics find the ending dissatisfying and unconvincing, and while one participant suggests that "we could critically reflect on the fact that in the past such sentiments were still alive in the life of Japanese people," critic Shimizu Chiyota retorts, "I don't have any patience for a film like this."[27] Although the critics seem to like aspects of the film, particularly Yamada's performance as Toyo, they are critical of Naruse's inability to distance himself from the material or to put his stamp on it. They complain that the film is not "attuned to the zeitgeist of our time," which is an interesting comment, given the cultural politics of the period. *Tsuruhachi and Tsurujiro* was adapted from a prizewinning

20. Camera pan from audience to stage. Hasegawa Kazuo and Yamada Isuzu in *Tsuruhachi and Tsurujiro* (*Tsuruhachi Tsurujiro*, 1938), Toho.

novel by Kawaguchi Matsutaro, which was in turn adapted from a 1934 Paramount film called *Bolero* starring George Raft and Carole Lombard. Shimizu Chiyota says the ending of the Hollywood original, in which the Raft character dies, is much more satisfying. The Hollywood version, he says, has a much more "straightforward beauty" than the Edo aesthetic of human emotions. Tomodo Junichiro responds that "by basing its story on a foreign film, *Tsuruhachi* fails to represent the genuine spirit of Edo."[28]

Evidently, although *Tsuruhachi and Tsurujiro* is respected as one of the top Toho films by these critics, for whom it is Naruse's best since *Every Night Dreams* (*Yogoto no yume*, 1933), it does not follow through on its kokutai premises. This is not only because of the contradictions that surface around a strong female protagonist who is not given her due by the narrative. It is also because Naruse is exceedingly vague about the film's historical setting and the details of the performance style that the film is about. The critics are uncertain about the songs' significance and are unable to appreciate the aesthetics of shinnai, complaining that the film lacks "interest as a historical record of popular culture of the time." In a letter published in *Kinema Junpo*, Mita Ikumi describes the film as being about *yose* artists at the beginning of the Taisho period, and while he appreciates the formal beauty of the film, it lacks the realism that Naruse is most comfortable with.[29] For Mita, the director should have focused on the social forces that stood in the way of the couple's success. Indeed, in each of his wartime geido films, Naruse shows more concern for the unfolding of complicated plots involving the characters' identities as performers, than for the historical accuracy of the period and the performing arts in question. Most audiences of the time would have needed as much contextual information as those of today to appreciate the finer points of those traditional arts.

For its part, *The Song Lantern* is about no theater, although except for the opening scene, none of the performances are set on a stage. More often they concern individuals or small groups singing, dancing, and playing shamisen or percussion instruments in tatami rooms. The plot hinges on the specialized techniques involved in these performances, requiring precise training. While there are references to *nogaku*—a singing style—and *matsuzake*—a dance—no real explanation or context is offered. The plot, moreover, follows a classic melodramatic formula of mistaken identity and recognition of virtue, centered on a central character who, contra kokutai policy, is a very individualistic hero. The film stars Hanayagi Shotaro, a popular theater and film star who had recently starred in Mizoguchi's *Story of the Last Chrysanthemum* (*Zangiku monogatari*, 1939).

The Song Lantern is based on a novel by Izumi Kyoka (1873–1939), a Taisho-era writer whose plays were neither strictly shinpa nor shingeki in style, although many of his novels were adapted for the shinpa stage.[30] Although it is said that he did not achieve real recognition for his writing until the 1950s, Mizoguchi adapted one of his works in 1933 with *The Water Magician* (*Taki no shiraito*), and several other films were made during the interwar period from his stories. As a playwright and novelist, Izumi Kyoka is best known for the supernatural and occult elements in his stories (e.g., Shinoda's adaptation of one of his plays in *Demon Pond* [*Yasha ga ike*, 1979]), although he is also described as a melodramatist, and Naruse certainly tempered any mystical elements that might have been in the original into a more romantic, realist, drama.

In his production notes for *The Song Lantern*, Naruse stresses the fact that he was concerned to capture the "taste" of Izumi Kyoka.[31] He also reports that the changes he made to the script that he was given by the producer were not appreciated by the shinshei-shinpa school collaborators with whom he worked on the production. Nevertheless, his realist aesthetic seems to have prevailed. His preparations for shooting the script consisted mainly of traveling to the towns where the original story was set: Yamada, Furuichi, Toba, and Kuwana. Finding little of the Meiji-era features remaining in these places, he finally settled on a town farther along the eastern coast, Numazu, and for the Toba area coast, Enoshima Island. Naruse also took the time to go to a no play and consulted with a no theater expert. Working with the theater company, who helped coach the actors in the performance style appropriate to Izumi Kyoka, Naruse was concerned to preserve the tone and atmosphere of the original within the very different aesthetics of cinema. Thus, *The Song Lantern* involves a confluence of three dramatic forms — no, shinpa, and film — and shows how the "back to Japan" edict of the times actually helped cineastes like Naruse to think through the formal and aesthetic issues involved in adapting traditional arts to the screen. The mediating role of shinpa in the move from no theater to cinema should not be underestimated.

If Kyoka often wrote about active heroines,[32] they are missing from Naruse's version of *The Song Lantern*, which is essentially a story about the patriarchal lineage of the performing arts. Kitahachi (Hanayagi Shotaro) plays a no theater actor who humiliates an old man named Sozan, a master of nogaku in a rural area. Kitahachi upstages him in his own

21. Isuzu Yamada, Hanayagi Shotaro, and Oya Ichijiro in *The Song Lantern* (*Uta andon*, 1943), Toho.

home, causing the man to commit suicide. For his hubris and disrespect, Kitahachi's own master (his adoptive father) disowns him, barring him from ever performing again. As a down-and-out street singer, Kitahachi meets Sozan's daughter Osode (Yamada Isuzu) and teaches her a special dance that will enable her to make a living as a geisha. He does this out of remorse for his role in her father's death, without revealing his identity. When Osode performs this dance for Kitahachi's father and uncle, they immediately recognize it and realize that she could have learned it only from Kitahachi. This leads to a reconciliation of father and son, who, together with the uncle and Osode, perform a song together in a room opening onto a moonlit garden to close the film.

As Osode, Yamada Isuzu plays a much more submissive woman in this film, one who is not well developed as a character. She does perform an excellent dance, however, chanting in a surprisingly deep voice. There is no question that all of these geido films contain excellent records of traditional performance styles, in which actors were evidently trained by real masters. The world of the arts, as an extension of the water trade, was one of the few areas where women held any kind of social power in the Edo and Meiji periods. Naruse explored women's central roles in this milieu somewhat in the 1950s and 1960s, but neither he nor anyone else, as far as I know, featured women protagonists in the water trade during the "return to Japan" mandate of the late 1930s and early 1940s. The male hero of *The Song Lantern* is in many ways a modern hero who challenges authority, although he is reformed by the end of the film. To the extent that he learns the lesson of filial piety, the film falls into line with kokutai ideology. The idealism of the narrative is, however, far more romantic than spiritual, including the closing scene with the tatami room opening onto the Japanese garden.

Naruse said of *The Song Lantern* that "the Department of the Interior was very intrusive," while of *Tsuruhachi and Tsurujiro* he said that the picture "suited his tastes" and he thoroughly enjoyed working on *The Way of Drama*.[33] Pleased with all three pictures, despite the pressures of the period, there is a sense that the wartime ethos provided Naruse with the opportunity to explore what might be called "classical Japanese" aesthetics. His pace slows and he more consistently uses interior architecture as framing elements within his shot compositions, a strategy that will continue to inform his postwar films as a sign of Japaneseness. Throughout all three of these films, there are some remarkable shots and sequences that may not be "monumental" but are nevertheless elegant, controlled, and formally stylized.

The Way of Drama is set in the Osaka world of *kabuki*, once again in the late Meiji period, although it also deals with the politics of popular culture and competing theatrical styles such as those that employ amateur actors to dramatize contemporary events. The film opens with a histrionic scene of a battle fought in Western-style uniforms, probably the Russian-Japanese War of 1904–5. Shinzo (Hasegawa) is a mediocre actor in a troupe under the direction of Yamatoya, for whom theater is more than entertainment but is an educational tool, and for that reason he lowers his prices to make it more accessible to the general public. Not coincidentally, these were also key features of the kokusaku mandate. Interestingly, Yamatoya also warns other theater owners not to be "too optimistic" about the war and not to give people false expectations about the final outcome. Shinzo is sent under false pretenses to Tokyo, where he learns to be humble and to train in the actor's craft. Yamatoya also manipulates Shinzo's lover, Omitsu (Yamada), to leave him for the sake of his art. A performer in her own right, Omitsu nevertheless sacrifices her art and her lover until Shinzo returns as an accomplished actor. In keeping with Yamatoya's aim of presenting "historical heroes"

22. The final shots of
The Way of Drama
(*Shibaido*, 1944), Toho.

for the edification of the public, Shinzo plays a samurai warrior in full kabuki costume—a great change from his first appearance as a shinpa soldier.

Once again, although ostensibly returning to the (not too distant) Japanese past, Naruse has produced a very modern story, with great allegorical significance to his own situation as a producer of popular culture. To be sure, the actor's training, for which Shinzo must forsake all worldly attachments and learn humility, is in keeping with a nationalist sentiment of promoting traditional Japanese culture. "The way of drama" is, of course, not unlike *bushido*, "the way of the warrior," but as a character, Shinzo acts more like the modern individualist hero, who ends up saving his master's theater and winning the girl.

The male protagonists of all three of Naruse's geido films resort to drinking when they are down and out. Tsurujiro gets the most irresponsible, creating havoc in an inn, but Shinzo in *The Way of Drama* and Kitahachi in *The Song Lantern* also have their dark moments in their cups. The two male actors Hasegawa and Hanayagi are both accomplished in the classical arts that their characters perform, and they are able to move between two quite different performance styles in each of these films. Hasegawa was a top star of the period who had made a name for himself—as Hayashi Chojiro—in Shochiku swordplay films in the 1920s and 1930s. Shortly after Toho lured him away and changed his name, he was attacked by Shochiku-hired thugs who slashed his face.[34] By 1939, he was starring in a series of Toho national policy films set in China and had become a major figure in kokusaku culture.[35]

The roles of Yamada Isuzu, on the other hand, get progressively more submissive and sidelined in each film. This may be symptomatic of the era, as many of the advances in gender politics made during the previous two decades were reversed. It is significant that Naruse's signature treatment of women's stories and female protagonists was downplayed during the war years where we find most of his films centered around male protagonists. Of all thirteen wartime films, only one—*Hideko the Bus Conductor* (*Hideko no shasho-san*, 1941)—includes a fully developed female character who, unlike Yamada's character in *Tsuruhachi and Tsurujiro*, is able to stand up for herself.

Two scenes in these geido films are, however, exceptional love scenes, played between Yamada and Hasegawa in *Tsuruhachi and Tsurujiro* and between Yamada and Hanayagi in *The Song Lantern*. In both instances they are set in pastoral forest locations, where the play of light and shadow is evocative of the famous forest scenes of *Rashomon*, made almost ten years later. Naruse uses 360-degree space to move around the characters. In *The Song Lantern*, he uses crane positions high above the ground for a scene in which the man teaches the woman a dance from the Noh repertoire. Hasumi Shigehiko has discussed these two scenes as examples of Naruse's modern signature "engraved on top of the movie." For Hasumi, this signature, which usually involves the encounter of a man and a woman, involves Naruse's use of light as the primordial material of cinema. His treatment of couples, as in these two scenes, is often extraordinarily delicate, suggesting to Hasumi Naruse's profound understanding of love—and the heterosexual couple—as the archetypal cinematic subject.[36]

Lighting is also an important aspect of Naruse's street scenes in these films. Set in the downtown entertainment districts of Osaka and Tokyo, many scenes take place in bars and on night streets, where lanterns mark the entrances to inns and theaters and soft lights glow through paper walls. These studio sets, while more or less authentic to period and city, look forward to the narrow streets of bars made famous in Ozu's films of the 1950s and 1960s. In Naruse's geido films, however, as in his prewar and postwar films, the street is not simply atmospheric but is an important site for encounters, for key conversations, and for a constant transit between private and public spaces. (In contrast, Ozu's streets are usually empty.) The soft lighting also gives the streets a rare warmth and beauty, as Naruse takes the urban cityscape and transforms it into a passage through another era.

Except for the two pastoral woods scenes, these are city films, and both *Tsuruhachi and Tsurujiro* and *The Way of Drama* concern the economics of theater ownership and management. All three *geido* films include shots of audiences at the various performances, almost always respectfully attentive. In the ups and downs of Tsuruhachi's and Tsurujiro's careers, a variety of classes of theater are depicted, including huge high-end venues with theater seating, and smaller, cheaper venues with audiences seated on tatami. Conversations between anonymous audience members serve to indicate the show's popularity and reception. Panning shots over rows of faces, cut with profile shots of the performers, have the effect of linking performers and audiences in such a way as to underline their mutual involvement in the events. In these scenes of spectatorship, the films effectively represent the public to themselves—the film's own audience. In this repeated motif of the people as a crowd, or as a mass, Naruse articulates his own modernity within the context of the genre.

A Tale of Archers at the Sanjusangendo shares with the geido genre the historical impulse of a return to Japan, although it is not about the arts. This time Naruse goes back to the Tokugawa era to make one of the two samurai films in his career.[37] The story is about an archery competition, and a young archer named Daihachiro (Ichikawa Sensho) who tries to win back the title to redeem his family's name after his father committed suicide for losing the title to a rival family. Daihachiro, who is not only young, but insecure and effeminate, is persecuted by members of the rival archery family until a mysterious samurai (Hasegawa Kazuo) steps in to protect him. Tanaka Kinuyo plays Daihachiro's guardian, a madam who took him in after his father's death. She is clearly attracted to the mysterious samurai staying at her inn, although nothing ever happens between them. Eventually, the identity of the protector is revealed to be the archrival himself, whose archery record Daihachiro has committed himself to beat.

For the sake of the art of archery (*kyudo*), Hoshino (Hasegawa) breaks rank with his own family to teach Daihachiro the true meaning of the game, which is "not to compete with the number of arrows, but to dedicate one's life and to show what one can do." Kyudo is about discipline and dedication, principles familiar from the geido films, bushido, and kokutai policy. The dialogue is full of men vowing to die for each other and for their causes. Daihachiro wins the competition when Hoshino gives Okinu (Tanaka) a secret potion to rub into the young archer's shoulder, thereby adding a spiritual or supernatural element to the "way of kyudo." Complete with a few well-choreographed samurai skirmishes and spacious elegant sets, *A Tale of Archers* is perhaps the closest Naruse came to approximating the monumental style. Shot on location in Kyoto, his use of the Sanjusangendo temple's long gallery is quite spectacular and impressed Tokyo viewers who were subjected to perpetual air raids. One critic noted, "We the survivors live amid the gnarled ruins of a blasted landscape. With what longing do our eyes behold the sublime beauty of that temple! Beyond that, we desire nothing more. Nothing."[38]

Even here, there are important ways in which the "monumental" style is undermined by traces of modernity. Even though the archery is played only by aristocrats, Naruse includes an ongoing commentary by the townspeople who gather to watch the competition. Their gossip about the players is very similar to equivalent scenes in the geido films, so that archery becomes another instance of a public sphere being created around the event. Moreover, the film opens with a series of speechy voice-over passages in which a tour guide sets up the background to

23. Ichikawa Sensho and Tanaka Kinuyo in *A Tale of Archers at the Sanjusangendo* (*Sanjusangendo toshiya monogatari*, 1945), Toho.

the story for tourists visiting the temple after which the film is named. Although they are Edo-era tourists, a relay of spectatorship is established linking the film's spectators to the eager crowds awaiting the big competition. A panel commemorating Daihachiro's father's achievement is enshrined in the temple, a monument that could conceivably still be intact. The informality and familiarity of the spectators create a kind of temporal ambiguity: the film is ever so slightly framed as a flashback, as if Naruse was ultimately incapable of setting the story entirely in the distant past. It is not only the dramatization of a legendary story; it is also about the consumption of that story as a national pastime.

One of the samurai skirmishes is set in a wide tree-lined street, where the play of light and shadow provides an extraordinary setting for the action, which is cut in 180-reversed long shots. But perhaps most unusual about this samurai film is Tanaka's character, Okinu. Her desire for the mysterious Hoshino is conveyed almost entirely by subtle eye movements and gestures. This is the second collaboration between Naruse and Tanaka, who first appeared in *Two Eyes* (*Sobo*, 1933). In one short, quick montage sequence, close-ups of Daihachiro's arrows hitting their targets are intercut with Okinu fixing her hair and kimono in a small mirror. In the end, Okinu's unrequited yet inarticulate passion is the more moving narrative trajectory, essentially upstaging the tale of the archery competition that plays itself out so nobly.

The samurai's solitary departure at the end of the film, while a predictable generic requirement, strikes a more powerful note of disappointment for the failure of the understated romantic subplot. In June 1945, when the film was released, it would have been precisely this sense of loss that had to remain unrepresented for the sake of national unity and the fighting spirit (*seishinshugi*). No doubt the many women deprived of their loved ones would have found Okinu's sadness—inarticulate, yet melodramatically legible—to be deeply moving.

Slices of Life
WARTIME HOME DRAMAS

Between 1939 and 1942, Naruse made four shoshimin-eiga set in wartime conditions. Despite the proscription against "slice-of-life films,"[39] these titles deal with the everyday lives of families coping with the effects of the war—and of course the usual melodramatic conflicts of financial crisis, paternity, and romantic liaisons. They represent a return on Naruse's part to the realism of everyday life that he explored in the mid-1930s. *The Whole Family Works* (1939) and *Sincerity* (*Magokoro*, 1939) are the two key surviving films of this period that make the link between Naruse's prewar and postwar shoshimin-eiga. Both are very strong films about parent-child relations. Although Naruse complained that the censors were becoming "intrusive" on the latter, he describes the former as one of his "all-time favorites."[40]

Sincerity ends with a lot of flag-waving as the father boards a train that will take him to the front, and it deals with the war far more directly than *The Whole Family Works*, a film in which the war is reduced to a menacing nightmare that haunts its narrative about the future occupations of a family of teenage boys. Both films emphasize impoverished living conditions and the hard work of day-to-day survival, although only in *Sincerity* is there a specific discourse on class difference. Both films are also extraordinarily beautiful, although in very different ways. While *The Whole Family Works* is darkly lit, set in a poor quarter of the city, mostly at night, *Sincerity* is set in the sun-drenched countryside with a fast-running river and shaded country lanes.

The Whole Family Works is about a family of eleven, most of whom have to work to keep food on the table, including the grandparents and the teenage boys. The eldest son, Kichi, wants to go to college to become an electrician, but it would mean losing a major breadwinner in the family. He consults with his teacher and discusses the situation with the family and his girlfriend; he gets drunk and is genuinely torn about the right decision. In the end, Kichi may decide not to go to school, but it is a reluctant decision and an irresolute ending to a narrative in which very little happens. In a *Kinema Junpo* collective critique, the critics are enthusiastic about the film's dark, brooding realism.[41] They find it moving and more hopeful than the novel on which it was based. They see a turn-

24. Ubukata Akira, Tokugawa Musei, and Honma Noriko in *The Whole Family Works* (*Hataraku ikka*, 1939), Toho.

ing point in Naruse's career, due largely to his relegation of women to the sidelines—a revealing comment about the tastes of the critical establishment—although they also point out that his depiction of women is the weakest aspect of the film. Indeed, Kichi's father is far more sympathetic than his mother, who is depicted as a selfish nag. Although there are no big stars in the picture, and the grandparents at least are played by nonprofessionals, the drama is very well executed.

One of the roundtable critics, Mizumachi Seiji, suggests that Naruse had changed with *The Whole Family Works*, but not toward the ideological imperatives of the day. Other critics have suggested that this may be the place to find Naruse's resistant gesture, or the place where an antiwar message might be found. Audie Bock, for example, points out that he challenged the proscription against "slice-of-life" films with *The Whole Family Works* and renders the wartime slogans on the walls ironically irrelevant to the issues of poverty and sheer survival faced by the family. I would argue that *The Whole Family Works* cannot be described as an antiwar film, especially given Naruse's aversion to "messages," and insofar as the dominant theme picked up by the *Kinema Junpo* critics is filial piety, it falls very much within kokutai policy. Yet the film can be said to undermine that policy through its aesthetic and ironic overtones, and through its implicit social criticism.

Most ironic are the closing shots in which the group of young brothers playfully perform somersaults in a fairly complex acrobatic choreography on the second floor of the house while the parents look up from below. The carefree attitude is reminiscent of the nansensu comedies of the early 1930s, but in this context it serves as a counterpoint to the looming scenario of war. Earlier in the film, the boys play a war game that Naruse cuts with a "dream sequence" of real war scenes, and other magazine images clearly inscribe the ongoing conflict into the film. The boys read their homework in a cacophony of voices which, like the acrobatics, tends to mock the regimen of drills and recitation one expects from a war film. Each boy dreams of a professional vocation, only one of which is to join the armed forces. In 1939, with international tensions escalating, it is inevitable that all the boys would simply be conscripted and probably killed. Maybe this is a retrospective reading, but it is nevertheless a powerful one, given the openness of this final scene, which is a performance as much as a game.

The penultimate scene, in which the family gathers for a conference mediated by a teacher from the local school, is extraordinarily solemn. Preceded by a two-minute sequence of shots in silence, punctuated by rain dripping and a clock ticking, the family is seated in a group patiently waiting for the teacher to open the discussion. Kichii's articulate explanation that his dead-end job may provide food for the family but limits his own future is very moving. His aim to study to be an electrician to put food on the table renders his brothers' ambitions to be lawyers and navy officers fanciful and unrealistic. Finally, although the dilemma is not resolved, the twenty-two-year-old son has convinced the teacher—and the viewer—that he has the wisdom required for social change, a wisdom grounded in the harsh realities of everyday life, and in filial duty. Although his girlfriend the café waitress is completely marginal to this scene, and to the family, her role as an independent woman who befriends the boys makes an important link between Kichii's resolve and the new gender roles of the next generation.

Peter High singles out *The Whole Family Works* as one of the few films that slipped by the censors. He points out that the script was based on a novel by Tokunaga Sunao, who was strongly identified with leftist "proletarian" literature before the war.[42] High suggests that Naruse employed a "sleight of hand" to solve the dilemma of closing a narrative that deals so thoroughly with the blind alley of poverty. He quotes Naruse himself confessing to be "in despair" over the ending, as he could neither embrace the individualism of Kichii breaking away from the family, nor depict self-sacrifice with the doom and gloom implied in his social-realist aesthetic. Instead, as High points out, Kichii's final decision, as vague as it is, is couched within the rhetoric of spiritist group solidarity. While the teacher commends Kichii for "doing his best" (*ganbaru*), the phrase is echoed by the brothers, who declaim their ambitions—while doing somersaults—in the same charged rhetoric of patriotic ambition.[43]

Through techniques of lighting and framing, the picture of poverty in *The Whole Family Works* is endowed with a certain nobility and grace, which culminates in the final scene of somersaults. One shot of a boy at the window with the whole family spread out behind him on the tatami, under a single hanging bulb, uses the architectural framing for an image of family unity in bleak conditions. The dim light from overhead bulbs is soft and shadowed; night scenes with rain are pierced with streetlights; and the darkness creates a strong sense of the burden of poverty, along with other unnamed threats. No money is seen to change hands, although there is much talk of low wages and high prices. The city itself is depicted as dark, with deep narrow streets and dangerous traffic.

The Whole Family Works also features an amazingly experimental soundtrack, including periodic trumpet lines (one of the sons plays a trumpet), clappers at night in the empty streets, and a lively mix of themes and instruments at dramatic points in the narrative, frequently moving into minor keys. The music is credited to Ota Takashi, with whom Naruse worked on only one other film (*A Fond Face from the Past* [*Natsukashi no kao*, 1941]), but it is indicative of the modernity underscoring his wartime film practice. Far from a monumental film, *The Whole Family Works* obliquely criticizes a nation that would force families into such irresolvable conflicts as the one facing this family, doomed to an interminable life of poverty.

The *Kinema Junpo* critics were, of course, mistaken to think that Naruse had abandoned his emphasis on women. His next film, *Sincerity*, features two strong female characters, played by Irie Takako and Murase Sachiko, each of whom have a daughter. The girls are schoolmates, but one (Nobuko) is from a middle-class home and the other (Tomiko) is from a poor family. Tomiko's mother Tsutako (Irie) is a single mother who works from home as a seamstress, while Nobuko's mother lives in an elegant home with her husband, Kei. Eventually, it is revealed that

25. The final departure scene of *Sincerity* (*Magokoro*, 1939), Toho.

Kei had a romantic relationship with Tsutako, and may be Tomiko's father as well, but he is conscripted shortly after this revelation and goes off to war.

This is very much a home front film, in which the women are involved in supporting activities, and the whole town cheers on the new recruits. As Kei is a banker, he is conscripted as an officer. He is introduced brandishing a magnificent sword, indicating his readiness for his call-up, for which everyone congratulates him when it comes. The wartime context is little more than a backdrop to the story of paternity and former love. The complex emotions among the women are conveyed through cutting on eye movements and eye lines, and through the use of the pastoral location.

Sincerity contains many scenes of quiet pastoral beauty. Even the scenes played between the two young girls are intensely moving, and Yamane has indicated how the effects are produced largely through the unorthodox reverse-field cutting.[44] Several scenes are set on a rocky riverbed where the girls play, and where Kei goes fishing. The girls and women are often seen running to or from this river along country lanes in kimono and clogs, making the constricting effect of these clothes on women's movements particularly evident. The rural setting in the film tends to foreground entrenched gender disparities. Kei is extremely condescending to his wife, whom he blames for their daughter Nobu's poor grades at school. Both he and the teacher claim it is a wife's responsibility for a child to do well, and he berates her for being unsophisticated. Tomiko's mother, on the other hand, while poor, is cultured, and her daughter does much better at school. Kei's condescension is so brutal that one can only have sympathy for these women, one of whom he has abandoned and the other one he scorns.

At the center of *Sincerity* appears an exceedingly strange object: a huge French doll resting in a large cardboard box. Kei gives it to Tomiko after she and her mother rescue Nobu from an accident at the river, but Tomiko returns it, and Nobu brings it back to Tomiko. Of all the toys that appear in Naruse's films, this is the most excessive. Only one close-up of the toy is included, but it is evident that it is a blond, blue-eyed doll. It takes on the symbolic burden of the father's inability to manage these families of women and also points outside the film to European culture as a source of luxury goods. The doll is not a plaything, but an iconic artifact in a symbolic economy, and it is not an object that would be condoned by the Home Ministry, even if in 1939 Japan was not yet at war with the Euro-American powers.[45]

The language of modernity in *Sincerity* consists of a discourse of class and cosmopolitanism that contradicts the quiet harmony of village life. It upsets the relations between the women in Tomioka's home, where she lives with her mother and grandmother. The doll also disrupts Nobuko's home, provoking her mother to trot after her in kimono when she returns the doll to Tomiko. Finally, it is Tomiko who holds the doll in her arms in the final scene at the train station where all the women go to see Kei off to war. Everyday life is transformed by this object, which seems to possess some kind of magical properties, effectively displacing the anxiety of the war, which could only be depicted in the most celebratory manner. Once again, Naruse subtly undermines the national policy mandates of the time by highlighting the unevenness of modernity and its thorough penetration of everyday life.

A Fond Face from the Past is also set in a rural community, specifically a village outside Kameoka, near Kyoto. In some ways this short, thirty-six-minute film is Naruse's most moving negotiation of the militarist restrictions of the time, perhaps because it is also his most direct engagement with the culture of war. When a newsreel comes to Kameoka featuring a local man named Yoichi, it causes some excitement in the community and, of course, in Yoichi's own family. First of all his mother makes the long trek from the village to see the film, and Naruse obligingly shows the newsreel (*Nippon News*, no. 14), which begins with the same marching music that opens his own film, followed by a curious baby judging contest in Los Angeles featuring two hundred Japanese babies. Released in January 1941, almost a year before the Pacific war begins, this "found footage" is indicative of Japanese imperialist ambitions beyond Asia long before Pearl Harbor.

We actually see clips from the battlefield newsreel twice. The first time, the mother is crying so much that she misses the shot of her son. The second time, when some neighbors make the trip to the theater, a medium close-up of a soldier in profile is identified as Yoichi. The main storyline, however, involves Yoichi's wife Sumi (Hanai Ranko), who lives with his mother and young brother Koichi. She pretends to see the film, walking all the way to Kameoka with a baby on her back, but buys a toy plane for Koichi instead. Koichi finally compares all the contradictory versions of the film that are reported to him and confronts Sumi, who confesses that she couldn't see the film because she would have cried and that would have been unpatriotic. In other words, she vows to be tougher than the mother by denying herself the glimpse of her husband. While some wartime films featured "defeminized" women who demonstrated stereotypically masculine traits of fortitude and determination,[46] this is not the case with Sumi. Instead, she is depicted as a woman whose concern for her husband is repressed by the obligation not to show grief or fear for men at the front.

The title itself, *A Fond Face from the Past*, is suggestive of the tensions and contradictions embedded in this short film. While the newsreel, by definition, would be of current events, Naruse's title renders it nostalgic, as if Yoichi were already dead. The ideal militarist mother, according to High, was one whose greatest happiness came with her son's death. Such modeling of exemplary emotions necessarily entailed "the expunging of all hint of independent thought or individual psychology."[47] In fact, the scene of the mother crying at the movies is curiously lacking in emotion. Mano Tsuruko, who plays the mother, dabs at her eyes with a handkerchief but shows little expression. Her daughter-in-law's refusal to see the film spares her from this contradictory subject position, because the only acceptable emotion would be pride in Yoichi's death.

The nostalgia is reinforced by the pastoral imagery of the film. In some respects, with its shots of women working in the fields, reflecting streams and mountainous landscapes, this is one of Naruse's more beautiful treatments of the Japanese countryside. It is not completely idyllic, though, as soldiers performing training maneuvers and planes flying overhead constantly cross the paths of the main characters. Koichi and his friends, a gang of ten-year-old boys who are wildly enthusiastic about all the military activities, lend the film a dynamism and energy that offsets the pathos of the women's struggles with tears. In this film, the toy airplanes are clearly means for the children to emulate adult activities, and in doing so they enable Naruse to enact another subtle "sleight of hand" by providing uplift where none in fact is warranted.

Iijima Tadashi actually classifies *Fond Face* and *Mother Never Dies* as "contemporary issue" films, along with *Shanghai Moon* and *Until Victory Day*. Writing in the postwar period, he may have wanted to separate these titles from Naruse's family dramas, which by 1953 had become his signature style. However, I think it is important to recognize how Naruse used the katei mono or home drama in the context of the woman-centered home front during the Pacific war. As a melodramatist, the domestic realm was an important site for Naruse in his exploration of social relationships. If the family is the model for the hierarchical structure of the Japanese nation, it would necessarily be an emblematic format for kokusaku eiga, regardless of the ostensible ban of shoshimin-eiga.

26. Mother at the movies. Mano Tsuruko in *A Fond Face from the Past* (*Natsukashi no kao*, 1941), Toho.

27. Irie Takako in *Mother Never Dies* (*Haha wa shinazu*, 1942), Toho.

The fourth shoshimin-eiga that Naruse made during the war, *Mother Never Dies* (*Haha wa shinazu*, 1942), demonstrates this propaganda potential of the home drama, but not coincidentally, this film is infused with a maudlin sentimentality that the director is usually able to temper with a more subtle, understated, style. Despite its title, the mother, played by Irie Takako, dies 40 minutes into the 103-minute film. Dying of cancer, she kills herself to spare her family the expense of a long illness, although only her long suicide note is offered as explanation of her death, which occurs offscreen. The daughter of a samurai, the mother even prepares a kind of ritual meal before she dies. Her spirit enables her husband Sugai (Sugai Ichiro) and son Shugo (Saito Hideo) to "do their best" (*ganbaru*) to recover from the impoverishment that afflicts the family. The story begins in 1929 with Sugai losing his job in the stock-market crash. He works his way up, over the course of the narrative, from mirror-cleaner in a barber shop, to cleaning product salesman, to mechanic (he studies at night), to inventor, to company president. At this second-to-last stage, when his boss offers him money for his patent, he declines, saying that he did it for the good of the country and for his wife's memory. He receives enough money for her gravestone but eventually is given a factory to run, and eventually a whole company.

In this world where everyone is kind and benevolent, the mother's spirit casts a kind of spell over everyone. Her son Shugo graduates from college just as war breaks out with the China Incident of July 1937, which is illustrated by a montage of battle scenes. His father notes that "this might be the big one . . . it's time you got serious." To put him on the right path, his father reads him his mother's suicide note in which she begs her husband to make Shugo into a "fine Japanese man." Although Shugo does not get conscripted, he does vow to "do his best" by abandoning his decadent and lazy habits and dedicating himself to learn how to be a good vice-president in his father's company.

Most spiritist films, according to High, were set in military settings, involving young men in training or in munitions factories, who go through a kind of spiritual struggle in order to find the "true Japanese spirit" within themselves.[48] Often these seishinshugi films entailed a renunciation of familial affections for the sake of national service. The spiritist films that emerged after 1940 thus represent a certain departure from the humanist films such as *The Whole Family Works* and *Sincerity*. In *Fond Face*, one can see the two tendencies in conflict with one another, but in *Mother Never Dies*, it is evident that Naruse cannot entirely give up the humanist strain in his work, although he is fully capable of using the humanist home drama as the basis of a spiritist film. *Mother Never Dies* offers a neat ideological harmonization of family, capitalism, and country in which the patriarchy is consolidated around the national spirit through the memory of a self-sacrificing mother.

Hideko the Bus Conductor and the Wartime Comedies

Of the three comedies that Naruse made during the war, only one can be described as a real kokusaku film: *This Happy Life* (*Tanoshiki kana jinsei*, 1944). The other two, *Traveling Actors* (*Tabi yakusha*, 1940) and *Hideko the Bus Conductor* are certainly in keeping with kokutai policy but manage to avoid direct references to the war, even though they are clearly set within that context. All three suggest an interesting twist on national policy principles in that they point to a certain sacred character of everyday life. While this is most explicit in *This Happy Life*, the other two can also be described that way. These are all stories in which "nothing happens," or very little happens other than life going on, and characters gaining some kind of insight into the value of everyday life. They are also slices of life, but rather than being home dramas, they are set among communities and travelers.

Traveling Actors is a kind of parody of the geido films. Fujiwara Kamatari, who changed his name to Fujiwara Keita in 1946, so as not to be confused with a historical figure,[49] plays the front legs of a horse in a traveling troupe. Under the stewardship of a pseudo-kabuki actor Kikugoro, these itinerant actors perform a kind of country kabuki, or *taishu engeki*, in small rural towns. Hyoroku (Fujiwara) boasts about his craft to his novice sidekick (who plays the back legs of the horse) as if it were an art of great refinement. When the horse's head is accidentally damaged, the fake horse is replaced by a real horse and the actors are demoted to stable boys. Trying to impress some local ladies, the actors, dressed in their horse costume, finally chase the real horse out of town, cantering down a country lane.

Naruse claims that, although *Traveling Actors* was heavily edited by the censors, it is one of his own favorites.[50] It is full of gags, and more show business politics, as the actors have to negotiate with the local patron. At one point they notice a young man in uniform passing by. "That could be us," they agree somberly, and continue on their business of literally "horsing around." The actors sleep in the theater, and as itinerant performers, they exhibit a kind of homelessness that is at once a long-standing convention of the Japanese performing arts and in keeping with the wartime experience of mobility. *Traveling Actors* is set mainly in one small town, where the traveling theater is a main source of entertainment. *Traveling Actors* was a staple of Japanese popular culture specific to post-Meiji Japan that peaked in the 1930s, after which it gradually gave way to cinema and television as mass-cultural forms. However, in *Traveling Actors*, except for the singular reference to the passing soldier, the setting is more or less outside of time.

This Happy Life is about another small community, this time centered around a main street where all the characters have small shops. Each is identified with a profession, including bookselling, clock repair, tobacconist, and barber. Introduced by a patriotic poem recited in voice-over, a new family arrives in the community and teaches the town how to derive small pleasures from everyday life. In a regime of scarcity, their lives are enriched by making toys out of leaves, crafts out of household junk, and gourmet food from table scraps. Soma (Yanagiya Kingoro) and his two daughters have a kind of magical capacity to endow everyday life with spirituality, although the Germanic menu they serve to guests is a good clue as to the sources of their inspiration. Especially after 1941 and the advent of the Pacific War, the Japanese industry was greatly inspired — if not aesthetically influenced — by the Nazis' use of popular culture for propaganda purposes.[51]

When Soma's youngest daughter visits a sick child, she encourages him to see raindrops dancing, and sure enough, the children — and the viewer — see a choreographed fairy dance emerge from the puddles outside the window. This film is like a musical in its attempts to give a utopian character to desperate living conditions. The elder daughter sings as she does housework, finding an intriguing rhythm in the barrel maker's hammering. The family hosts a theatrical evening in which the children perform traditional songs and dances, including a sword routine by a young boy. Explicit and direct references are made to the war in this film, as one woman's husband is at the front, and one of the young boys is preparing to go. Soma is benevolent and mysterious but nevertheless paternalistic. His authority is unquestioned despite the townspeople's initial bewilderment, and the film is ultimately a didactic lesson in how to make the most of very little. Despite this propaganda aspect, it is indicative of Naruse's overall strategy during these years to concentrate on the detail of everyday life, rather than the "monumental" aspects of an imperialist culture. The antimaterialist thrust of kokutai policy fed into his expertise in the "home drama" aesthetics of simplicity. Although the didacticism of *This Happy Life* is not his usual style, the dispersal of activity over a collection of characters, and the ongoing issues of economic survival are familiar tropes.

Embedded within this narrative is a small triumph for a young woman whose mother has allowed her to work at a local cooperative before she gets married. Every little miracle in the town is attributed to Soma and his family, and even if this accomplishment is likely intended to promote female labor in munitions factories, it is significantly pitched as a victory over an "old-fashioned" mother. In the end, the family leaves as mysteriously and suddenly as they arrived, with all their belongings loaded onto a cart, presumably off to inspire some other community to reap the benefits of a deteriorating wartime economy. They carry with them a "spiritism" similar to that of *Mother Never Dies*, although in this film it is less connected to nobility than to the natural world and the routines of everyday life. Like the 1942 film, the drama is too contrived to be convincing, and where it succeeds at propaganda it fails as quality filmmaking.

Hideko the Bus Conductor, named for its star actress, the seventeen-year-old Takamine Hideko, is actually a remarkable film about a young woman "coming out" as a professional, articulate, speaking subject. Featuring Naruse's strongest female character during this period, it marks the beginning of one of Japanese cinema's most successful director-actor collaborations. Having recently starred in Yamamoto Kajiro's *Horse* (*Uma*, 1941) to great acclaim, Takamine was heralded as a rising star.[52] She had been acting since she was six years old, so although she had no formal training, by 1941 she was a veteran of the industry. *Hideko the Bus Conductor* is not only named for her, it marks her transition from child actor to actress. Okoma (Takamine) dresses plainly, in the white blouse and knee-length dark skirt that she and many other actresses would don

28. Takamine Hideko and Fujiwara Keita (Kamatari), in *Hideko the Bus Conductor* (*Hideko no shasho-san*, 1941), Nanyo Toho Eiga.

as the "uniform" of the postwar unmarried woman. The slippage between actor name and character name reflected in the title of this film is indicative of a larger tendency in Japanese film criticism and film culture to refer to characters by the names of the actors portraying them.

Her hair pulled back in a ponytail, Okoma/Hideko works as a bus conductor in the small rural community of Kofu in Yamanashi prefecture. She and the driver Sonoda (Fujiwara) are employees of a very small company owned by a lazy and corrupt boss who sits around drinking cool drinks all day in his office. It is insinuated that the one-bus company is probably a facade for some illegal activity, but Hideko and Sonoda try their best to make it turn a profit. They describe themselves as "loyal retainers" of the bus company.

Inspired by a radio broadcast of a tourist spiel from Tokyo, Hideko proposes a similar scheme for their village service. She and Sonoda persuade a writer staying at a local inn to write a narration to be read along the bus route. The narration refers to the sights of the famous highways of the Edo era and indicates how the local landscape is linked to various well-known tales. The tours will ostensibly "help people imagine how people traveled in the old days," and the film is thus in line with national policy; but what really brings this slight narrative to life is the traveling shots from inside the bus. The camera jiggles along with the bumpy country roads, framing the landscape through the bus windows. In fact, it is a very modern mode of transport and a very modern story of exploitation, popular culture, and entrepreneurship.

The writer also teaches Okoma the appropriate gestures for pointing out the window, as she learns the rituals of public performance. On one level, the film is about the construction of historical narrative and the disjunction of everyday life from the sacred past, as the banal rural landscape fails to look any different than it did before; but on another level, it is about the coming out of Hideko Takamine as a woman and as an actress. The absurdity of the conductor offering such tours to the local children and villagers is finally abated in the very last scene, in which three young men in hiking gear board the bus. Okoma/Hideko bravely overcomes her shyness and launches into her spiel, clearly having become a professional young woman who commands authority. The spark of desire between her and the appreciative male audience further inscribes her personhood within a regime of sexuality, performance, and subjectivity, even if it is abruptly curtailed with the end credits. In this film, the sense of movement and transience is explicitly associated with social change. However small their accomplishment, Okoma and Sonoda have triumphed over their indolent, corrupt boss to save the company.

Wartime Vernacular

Naruse's emphasis during the war years on scarcity, impoverishment, and frugality in all of his gendai geki was not only in conformity with regulations against representing luxury, it was also the reality of many people's lives during this period. Kurosawa describes the difficulties of shooting at Toho in 1945 when his actors were too hungry to stand for long periods.[53] The fact that films continued to be made at all is quite astonishing in light of the severe effects of the war on everyday life in Japan. Naruse's wartime films no doubt served a key role in keeping the population entertained and somewhat confident in the survival of the industry. The recurring theme of the production of popular culture—from *Tsuruhachi and Tsurujiro* to *Hideko*, creeping into even his final production of the war years, *Tale of the Archers*—indicates a self-consciousness on both Naruse's part and the studio's regarding their roles as producers of popular culture during the war.

The modernity of Naruse's wartime cinema is definitely inflected with a discourse of nationalism as each of his wartime films clearly incorporates key principles of kokutai principles. His shift away from female to male protagonists is indubitably linked to this ideological program—even if it is not, as we have seen, a complete shift. Yamada Isuzu's performance in *Tsuruhachi and Tsurujiro* and Takamine Hideko's first appearance in a Naruse film are important roles and strong characters. Above all, it is evident that Naruse was an extraordinarily versatile filmmaker, whose mastery of film language enabled him to work in a number of different genres. Melodramatic plot lines and the detail of everyday life continue to inform these films, and these techniques may ultimately be how we can identify Naruse's variant of vernacular modernism.

Rather than trying to position Naruse as a collaborator or as a resister—ultimately a fruitless task—we would do better to consider the implications of his wartime work to the ongoing construction of Japanese modernity. The continuities that are evident with his prewar and postwar films impel us to account for the nationalist elements of his cinematic enterprise. As Harootunian points out, modernism and fascism in Japan were in the end two sides of the same problem of capitalism and representation. In the national fantasy, he argues "the folk was employed as a stand-in for the artwork . . . modernism and fascism sought the impossible task of re-enchanting the world and thereby restoring the auratic to a life where only its dimmest and fading traces still managed to survive for the moment."[54] Like European modernity, the mass culture of cinema lent itself exceedingly well to the nationalist-imperialist cause.

The fine line between the right and the left with respect to the modernity of the cinema is emblematically noted by Walter Benjamin: "The violation of the masses, whom fascism, with its *Fuhrer* cult, forces to their knees, has its counterpart in the violation of an apparatus which is pressed into serving the production of ritual values."[55] In the Japanese instance it is evident that a similar cult of nationalist spirit was harnessed to the cinema and, through the films of studio-based directors such as Naruse, integrated into the language of classical cinema. Susan Buck-Morss has taken up Benjamin's concerns at the end of the artwork essay to conclude that if cinema caused a "crisis in perception," fascist aesthetics succeeded by creating the fantasy of a reconstituted mass body. Her remarks on the dialectic of individualism and the social body shed light not only on the question of Naruse, but also on the wartime viewers of his films, represented perhaps by the mother in *Fond Face from the Past* watching but not seeing her son in a newsreel; weeping, but not feeling: "If the individual does find a point of view from which it can see itself as whole, the social techno-body disappears from view. In fascism (and this is key to fascist aesthetics), this dilemma of perception is surmounted by a phantasmagoria of the individual as part of the crowd that itself forms an integral whole—a 'mass ornament' to use Siegfried Kracauer's term that pleases as an aesthetics of the surface, a deindividualized, formal, and regular pattern."[56]

In her discussion of vernacular modernism, Hansen argues that only by thinking through the relation between classical cinema and modernism can we fully grasp the effects of film as a mass medium. Rather than thinking of classical cinema as being opposed to the modern, she urges us to conceptualize it as "part of the historical formation of modernity."[57] In the Japanese case especially, this has to include the technologies of mass culture deployed through the Fifteen Years' War and the monumental cinema described by Davis. In Naruse's oeuvre we can see a very clear movement from a cinema of fragmentation, speed, and discontinuity in the early 1930s to one that incorporates the harmonies and elegance of the traditional arts. Despite these profound stylistic shifts, the films continue to be preoccupied with the emergence of new subjectivities, with women, and with sensual, emotional states of being.

Particularly in comparison with the monumental style of some of his contemporaries, Naruse's modernity remains resolutely vernacular, attached to the everyday life of modern Japan. Whereas the monumental style "resisted classical Hollywood technique at the level of form for the crucial wartime purpose of renewing the audience's perception of the Japanese cultural heritage,"[58] Naruse tended to retain his quick cutting style that was based on the relations between characters. Period settings may provide background and atmosphere, but they do not in themselves take on the sacred or "mythic" character that Davis ascribes to the "ultranationalistic" films of the period. This is not to say that they do not have a Japaneseness. However, the national culture that Naruse seems to be closest to is that of the popular arts. The literary man who provides Hideko's narration is an outsider to Naruse's world. He lends the film and its protagonist an aura of respectability, but he is also gently mocked as a skirt-chasing drunk. Okoma/Hideko, like many of Naruse's wartime protagonists, has holes in her shoes, but she manages to smile. Only in Naruse's *The Whole Family Works*, the darkest film of these years, is there a sense of despair. Its critical success shows how film culture could, despite the censorship and harsh working conditions, survive as a mode of critical social realism despite the ideological imperatives of the day.

4

The Occupation Years

CINEMA, DEMOCRACY, AND JAPANESE

KITSCH, 1945–1952

For developing, living forms, what matters is that they have within them something stirring, useful, ultimately heartening—that they take "kitsch" dialectically up into themselves, and hence bring themselves near to the masses while yet surmounting the kitsch. . . . Only film can detonate the explosive stuff which the nineteenth century has accumulated in that strange and perhaps formerly unknown material which is kitsch.—WALTER BENJAMIN

By all accounts, and from every perspective, the ideological turnaround of August 15, 1945, the day Emperor Hirohito publicly surrendered Japan and "came down from the clouds," was abrupt and effective. The film industry, along with every other sector of society, entered the postwar period with the mission of creating a "new Japan" under the guidance of the former enemy embodied in General MacArthur and his occupation authority, SCAP (Supreme Commander of Allied Powers). Former "collaborators" with the imperial war mandate turned quickly to fulfill the agenda of a renewed "democratic" nation, and Naruse was as eager as his colleagues to provide new cultural forms for a population hungry for entertainment. As with the war years, this was the only way to continue working as a film director, and Naruse once again demonstrated his flexibility and accommodating sensibility. Needless to say, it was a difficult period, not only because of the ideological confusion implicit in the directive to forget the past and invent a whole new culture, but also due to the scarcity of materials that continued into 1947 and the labor strikes that brought the film industry to its knees in 1947 and 1948.

Aesthetically, this is probably the weakest phase of Naruse's career, partly because — for reasons that remain obscure — he did not work with the best actresses or writers until 1951. In that year, toward the very end of the occupation, he directed Tanaka Kinuyo in *Ginza Cosmetics* (*Ginza Gesho*), Takamine Mieko in *Dancing Girl* (*Maihime*, 1951) and Hara Setsuko in *Meshi* (*Repast*). In 1951 and 1952 he adapted works by Kawabata Yasunari, Tanizaki Junichiro, and Hayashi Fumiko. His first adaptation of a Hayashi Fumiko story, *Meshi*, became the first of a series of "marriage films" and set the tone for the films that constitute the peak of his career in the mid-1950s. It attracted rave reviews and declarations that he had finally recovered his past form. The films he made from 1946 to 1950 may have been hampered by mediocre acting talent and weak scripts, but they constitute a fascinating series of experiments with new styles and new themes. Even if the occupation films tend to be kitschy, their mix of competing discourses is indicative of the changing times and the difficulties confronting the rebuilding of a national culture.

The American censors, under the auspices of the Civil Information and Education Section (CIE), supervised and vetted all scripts and finished films until June 1949, at which point the task was taken over by a Japanese-run agency called EIRIN (Film Ethics Regulation Control Committee).[1] As early as November 1945, the CIE supplied lists of prohibited and recommended subjects, and as Kyoko Hirano notes in her study of the period, the Americans were particularly hypocritical in their censoring of evidence of their own censorship. Although openness and transparency were part of the democratic ethos, the occupation government could not lead by example. Moreover, their policies were inconsistent and shifted quite dramatically over the course of the seven-year occupation, from a socialist-oriented notion of democracy, to a fully cold war implementation of bourgeois capitalism.

On the list of CIE's prohibited subjects, alongside the well-known prohibition of "feudalistic" or militaristic subjects, was "the subjugation or degradation of women."[2] Indeed, the equality of women was high on the occupation agenda, and at least one historian has argued that the women's rights that were enshrined in the new constitution of 1947 were the most progressive the world had ever seen.[3] Despite the idealism of the new constitution, however, systematic discrimination remained in place, both in the workplace and in the home. Women voted for the first time in 1946, and thirty-nine women were elected to the Diet, although by 1955 the number of female politicians had dropped to nine.[4] Kathleen Uno points out that "the term *ryosai kenbo* ('good wife wise mother') fell into disuse after 1945, but the conservative ruling party (the Liberal Democratic Party [LDP]) and private companies continued to formulate policies which assumed that wifehood and motherhood came first for women."[5] In other words, while some rights were gained, due not only to the American legislators, but also to the lobbying of an emergent array of women's groups, entrenched gender codes were hardly overcome overnight.

In Naruse's *The Battle of Roses* (*Bara Gassen*, 1950), one can see evidence of the backlash that was inevitably produced as a corollary to the new legislation of women's rights. A woman who becomes president of a large cosmetics company is depicted as being not only manipulative and calculating but also vulnerable and ignorant of the ways of the world. Nevertheless, in Naruse's cinema of the occupation, he is clearly inspired by the CIE directive: "Do not confine women to roles consisting only of childbearing and housework, considering their newly upgraded social status."[6] *White Beast* (*Shiroi yaju*, 1950) features a woman doctor; *Dancing Girl* features a woman who runs her own ballet school; *A Descendant of Taro Urashima* (*Urashima Taro no koei*, 1946) features a woman reporter and a women's rights activist; and *The Angry Street* (*Ikari no machi*, 1950) features a woman dentist. Nevertheless, in *Even Parting Is Enjoyable* (*Wakare mo tanoshi*, 1947) and *Ginza Cosmetics* we find women on the margins of society, working as entertainers and waitresses. This may be a more familiar terrain for Naruse, but they are not exactly "liberated women."

One of the other CIE directives, the demonstration of "individual initiative and enterprise in solving the postwar problems of Japan,"[7] is perhaps the more appropriate framework for considering Naruse's cinema during this period, as the emphasis on individualism enabled him to develop psychologically complex characters. While these include both male and female characters, there is no question that he contributed to the ongoing discussion of what Sandra Buckley describes as "being-woman."[8] Because it constitutes an intersection of many discursive practices, "being-woman" is a contradictory and unresolved subject-position through which the woman's body is aligned and misaligned with the state. In the sprawl of Naruse's film practice across so many domains of everyday life, his cinema enables us to map the cultural and historical inscription of gender in postwar Japan. Moreover, we can also understand how these discursive practices are vitally linked to those of the prewar period, as Naruse's investigation of female subjectivity begins, as we have seen, in the early 1930s.

Naruse referred to the occupation period as a "noisy age."[9] Emiko Yamanashi notes that the immediate postwar period was not referred to by the Japanese as the "occupation era" until foreign scholars began bandying about the term. It was more often thought of simply as a time of confusion.[10] Having lost the war, Japan was obliged to reinvent itself as a modern nation that was completely cut off from its own past—despite the enshrinement of the emperor within the new constitution. Mitsuhiro Yoshimoto has argued that postwar Japanese film embraced a "victim consciousness" in which the psychic disavowal of the wartime period and its implications took the form of a conversion narrative in which "nostalgia for the prewar and celebration of the postwar as a radical new beginning simultaneously coexist."[11] Yoshimoto suggests that the fetishization of August 1945 as a "nodal point of fantasy" is the focal point of postwar film melodrama. I would like to look at Yoshimoto's argument a little bit more closely in order to clarify his methodological approach and to develop a slightly different method of relating film to national culture that I believe is more appropriate to Naruse's cinema.

For Yoshimoto, melodrama functions as a narrative means of negotiating the ideological contradictions of postwar Japan. It is the "bad conscience of bourgeois intellectuals" insofar as it foregrounds the contradictions of capitalism and modernization. In his analyses of several films by Mizoguchi, Yoshimoto shows how melodrama functions as a "subversive ideologeme" (39). In the case of Kurosawa, he suggests that individualist characters like Gondo in *High and Low* (*Tengoku to jigoku*, 1960) and Murakami in *Stray Dog* (*Nora inu*, 1949)—both played by Mifune Toshiro—resist melodramatic "sentimentality," which nevertheless persists in the narratives as the return of the repressed. Yoshimoto argues that Naruse's *Floating Clouds* (*Ukigumo*, 1955) is one of the few postwar melodramas to "indict Japanese imperialism and . . . the responsibilities of ordinary people who benefited from Japanese colonial enterprise" (47). He points out that in this film it is evident that "issues of gender and nation converge into each other" and that it is indicative of how the sense of nationhood in Japan "is often reconstructed only at the expense of women" (48).

The melodramatic mode enables Yoshimoto to read postwar Japanese films as allegories for the nation, and while his analyses may be convincing and useful, it is a methodology that will apply only to a handful of films. *Floating Clouds* is Naruse's only film to deal directly with the war and its aftermath, and the political implications noted by Yoshimoto are not readily apparent in any other of his films, even those that are easily categorized as melodramas. Conceptualizing melodrama as a subversive strategy is a valuable means of theorizing the relation of a film text to cultural history and a longstanding film studies tradition. However, it tends to imply a melodramatic theory of history itself. Thus, for Yoshimoto, postwar Japanese melodrama is intrinsically bound with the relation to the West. The inferiority felt by the Japanese people after the war, he claims, is manifest in melodramatic narrative in its sublimation of the active subject of history. "To the extent that it feeds on their awareness of the lack of a Western style of subjectivity in Japan, the melodramatic constantly reminds the Japanese that Japan is trapped in the geopolitical space of Western hegemony" (41). He further describes this *ressentiment* as a persistent colonial mentality. The continuity of the prewar and postwar periods is disavowed as "the problematic of colonialism and imperialism is carefully erased from the postwar discursive space" (43).

Yoshimoto's reading of Japanese melodrama is informed in part by Jameson's *Political Unconscious*, but he does not refer to the Jameson text that would seem to be more relevant, "Third World Literature in the Era of Multinational Capitalism." Yoshimoto certainly does not claim that Japan is a third world country, yet his argument runs parallel to Jameson's contention that third world literatures are necessarily allegories of their national struggle for autonomy. Yoshimoto's readings exemplify Jameson's claim that, in third world literatures, "the story of the private individual destiny is always an allegory of the embattled situation of the public third-world culture and society."[12] In Yoshimoto's isolation of an art cinema as representative of the national psyche, he follows Jameson's implied category of "literature" and leaves himself open to some of the criticisms that have been leveled at Jameson.

Aijaz Ahmad has challenged Jameson's theory on a number of points, most of which can also be applied to Yoshimoto, who, like Jameson, tends to frame Japanese culture primarily in terms of "colonialism" and "imperialism." In totalizing historical phenomena in terms of binary oppositions, the differences within different forms of colonialism and nationalism tend to be elided, as are the class and gender divides within different national formations. Ahmad proposes that a cultural theory of world literature begin with the proposition "that we live not in three worlds but in one; that this world include the experience of colonialism and imperialism on both sides of Jameson's colonial divide."[13] Such a perspective is especially appropriate to Japan, which is historically both colonizer and colonized (although the American occupation might be better named neocolonialism). Moreover, as Ahmad points out, the world is united not by liberalist ideology but by global capitalism.

From this perspective, we can return to the idea of a Japanese classical cinema that was barely interrupted by the war. Indeed, as Marilyn Ivy has noted, "there is no doubt that the centralized wartime appropriation and consolidation of the machinery of the media formed the structure on which nationwide postwar mass cultural formations were built."[14] In other words, while Yoshimoto is correct to identify melodrama as the dominant mode of postwar Japanese cinema, we need to find a theory of melodrama that would account not only for the art cinema, but for the "everyday" cinema of an industrial practice. As Ahmad asks of Jameson, "are only those texts which give us national allegories . . . admitted as authentic texts of Third World literature, while the rest are by definition excluded?"[15] We need to consider the films of Mizoguchi and Kurosawa—and those of many other directors—as part of a film culture that carried on the project of articulating the sensorial experience of modernity, a project that was first adapted to the interests of military imperialism and then refashioned to meet the needs of the occupation authorities.

If Naruse's output during the American occupation is not his best effort, neither can it be interpreted as a national allegory of "victim consciousness" in the sense developed by Yoshimoto. Neither Naruse nor his characters can (or should) be considered to be "representative" of the nation. But his films are interesting precisely because of what they can tell us about Japanese culture during this contradictory and confusing era. They point to the ways in which the ideological discontinuity between prewar and postwar culture was mapped onto a continuity of Japanese cinema. As melodrama, Naruse's cinema straddles the often arbitrary distinction between mass culture and art cinema and can thereby help to point to a different conceptualization of cultural history than that proposed by Yoshimoto. However, I do want to maintain the methodology implicit in Yoshimoto's recognition of the melodramatic aspects of postwar Japanese cinema and to follow him in reading the films "against the grain."

The phrase "brushing history against the grain" evokes the symptomatic reading of melodrama as a modernist form, but it is also a phrase used by Walter Benjamin in his essay "On the Concept of History." In fact, it is fundamental to Benjamin's notion of cultural history, which he elaborates in more methodological detail in his 1937 essay on Edward Fuchs. Benjamin distinguishes in this essay between the historical materialist, for whom the past coheres as a series of narratives, separated according to discipline and object of study, and the cultural historian for whom the work of the past "could, even in part, drop conveniently, thinglike, into mankind's lap."[16] For Benjamin, Fuchs, a nineteenth-century German collector, writer, and cultural critic, serves as a model of the cultural historian not only because of his own practice and art criticism, but also because Benjamin is compelled to develop a new methodology in order to write about him. Neither an intellectual per se nor a writer of fiction, Fuchs, like Naruse in another culture and another century, seems to have been deeply implicated in the production of mass culture. In keeping with his well-known work on film, Benjamin is interested in Fuchs because of his revision of the concept of art. He notes, "The consideration of mass art leads to a revision of the concept of genius; it reminds us to avoid giving priority to inspiration, which contributes to the genesis of the work of art, over and against its material character, which is what allows inspiration to come to fruition" (269).

In Fuchs, Benjamin recognizes the appreciation of "anonymous artists," and the mass arts that refute the cult of the leader embodied in the fetish of "the master's name." Writing in 1937, Benjamin imputed a certain urgency to a critical methodology that would "blast apart" the historicist's method of studying cultural history as an "inventory which humanity has preserved to the present day" (267). This leads him to his famous epitaph, "there is no document of culture which is not at the same time a document of barbarism." He follows this with the remark, "No cultural history has yet done justice to this fundamental state of affairs, and it can hardly hope to do so" (267). Despite his pessimism, Benjamin does articulate the terms of a cultural history that is always incomplete. The past offers us a glimpse of the incompleteness of the present, and in its material excess it threatens to unsettle the conceptual frameworks of historical materialism. Applying this to auteurist methodology, a developmental history of Naruse's career—which will always be implicit in this narrative—is an example of the kind of historicism Benjamin criticizes; if we try to look at the films as a series of cultural accidents, we would be closer to the kind of dialectical cultural materialism that Benjamin advocates.

In Naruse's cinema of the 1940s, the war and the occupation are little more than shadows over the films, yet they are films in which context is everything. Naruse's own "genius" is practically obscured by these shadows, to the extent that this cinema may typify the kind of cultural material that Benjamin and Fuchs are concerned with. If for Benjamin "the continuum of history—once blasted apart by dialectic—is never dissipated so widely as it is in the realm known as culture," the collection of titles assembled under the name Naruse may serve as a dialectical method for challenging the fetish of August 1945. This moment of radical historical discontinuity needs to be reinserted into Japanese modernity as a shift in the terms of everyday life. While the occupation entailed on some levels a forcible "Americanization" of Japanese culture, we have seen how Naruse had already integrated many features of American cinema into his filmmaking in the 1930s. If he had to back away from some of those features during the war years, he was now free to return to the metropolitan sphere of the shoshimin-eiga that he had only briefly abandoned. The awkwardness of his embrace of so-called democratic subjects is counterbalanced by the persistence of tropes of his prewar cinema and stylistics.

At the heart of the ideological swing provoked by the surrender in August 1945 was the dilemma of the Japanese subject. Having lost the war by participating in a national collective blindly following an irresponsible leadership, the "democratic revolution" insisted on the creation of a new Japanese subject of agency, self-determination, and autonomy. At the same time, as Eric Cazdyn notes, "One must submit to the occupation and reconstruction project. . . . Japan lost the war, and the citizens had to pay by mortgaging their individuality. But how can one be free to act on one's own, to resist a militaristic oligarchy, if from the other side of the state's mouth comes the order radically to sacrifice one's individuality?"[17] Indeed, the issue of war responsibility, with which the film industry grappled during the first years of the occupation, revolves around this very issue of self-determination. The most effective defense against accusations of collaboration, that "I was deceived"—which the director Itami Mansaku argued in one of the more reflective commentaries on the period—was to admit that one had relinquished all thought, spirit, and will.[18]

For Cazdyn, this dilemma of individual responsibility is the constitutive problematic of the "second moment" of Japanese film history, the first being Japan's status as a colonizing nation. Naruse had already begun to grapple with this issue of self-determination in films such as *Feminine Melancholy* (*Nyonin Aishu*, 1937) and *The Whole Family Works* (*Hataraku ikka*, 1939), and it is in fact a thematic that predates postwar culture, even if it was given a new twist under the occupation mandate. In the films of the late 1940s, Naruse often provides caricatures of the new individualism, but he also begins to explore more complex psychological portraits. It is above all the unevenness and contradictoriness of these films that I want to focus on, and to see them as a kind of random sampling of occupation culture. If the cinema was well situated to articulate the terms of democratic subjectivity in occupied Japan, it also serves as an ideal site to explore the contradictions implicit in this new subjectivity.

In her study of occupation cinema, Joanne Izbicki lists the competing pressures on the new Japanese subject as including not only the regulating influences of SCAP and Japanese governmental bureaucracy, but also the economic and physical devastation and the social and sexual dynamics of a massive influx of American popular culture.[19] The mixing of American GIs with Japanese women may have been the most dramatic transformation of everyday life on the streets of the cities, but it was also a strictly prohibited topic for filmmakers and is thus invisible in occupation cinema. Nevertheless, sexual expression was a recommended subject, and Naruse tackled it head-on in his 1947 film *Spring Awakens* (*Haru no mezame*, 1947), one of his most beautiful films of the period. As Izbicki notes, the primacy given to sexuality and the emancipation of women suggests the melodramatic nature of occupation policy itself. She points to MacArthur's status as benevolent patriarch and sentimental hero, and to the rhetoric of salvation within the SCAP apparatus as further evidence of the structures of family and desire that shaped occupation culture.[20]

For the occupation government, "democracy" necessarily entailed the consolidation of a strong middle class, especially in the anticommunist discourse that held sway after 1947. As Izbicki notes, theorists of melodrama, including Peter Brooks, Thomas Elsaesser, and Chuck Kleinhans, have argued convincingly for the alignment of melodrama with the ascendancy of a middle class.[21] Thus, the melodramatic mode of postwar Japanese cinema is not simply a dramatization of victimhood, although that paradigm is certainly present. It is also a discourse of class and family, instrumental to the construction of a "good citizen" who would also at the same time be a subject of individual responsibility, with freedom of choice and rights to happiness. Izbicki notes that in the cinema, issues of democratic rights during this period were not nearly as prevalent as issues of happiness and personal freedom. In the early years of the occupation, Naruse's characters tend to achieve this happiness, but by 1950, it is achieved only at a price, and at this point the melodrama of suffering can serve as a form of social indictment.

Within Yoshimoto's discussion of melodrama, as in many commonsense views of the genre, sentimentalism is associated with a closed-down system complicit with dominant ideology, whereas melodrama, as a modernist discourse, potentially subverts that ideology. When we are dealing with a period of such cultural complexity as that of occupied Japan, it is evident that neither *melodrama* nor *ideology* has fixed definitions. Izbicki suggests that the distinction between sentimentality and melodrama will vary according to the cultural norms and tastes of the viewer. She also suggests that "sentiment" arises when a film's style is clichéd or conventional, and that sentimentality obscures class and gender inequalities, lending itself to a "pretense" of democracy.[22]

Naruse himself describes one of his best pictures of this period, *Ginza Cosmetics*, as one in which he tried to avoid sentimentality,[23] but rather than deciding which of the films are more sentimental than others, and thus which ones may be ideologically subversive and which ones may be more "on message," my analyses will explore the terms of subjectivity and style that are articulated within them. It is evident from these pictures that subjectivity cannot be separated from the material culture in which it is constructed, including not only the abstractions of economic relations but also the styles and fashions, architecture and music—the "sensuous" contours of everyday life. That people continued to go to movies despite the economic hardships of the immediate postwar period shows the role that cinema played in producing the terms of desire appropriate to the era.[24]

The thirteen films that Naruse made during the occupation years can be divided into four groups. The first two films he made in 1946 and 1947 might be described as "democratization films" that deal directly with issues of political corruption (*A Descendant of Taro Urashima*) and exploitation of labor (*Both You and I* [*Ore mo omae mo*, 1946]). His next two films feature women protagonists and explore the conditions of "being woman" in the new Japan. *Spring Awakens* promotes sex education and features Naruse's first "kissing scene," while *Even Parting Is Enjoyable* (1937) is a short that was made as part of a Toho omnibus production and represents a new focus for Naruse on psychological drama. Naruse made no films at all in 1948, and the single 1949 film, *Delinquent Girl* (*Furyo shojo*, 1949), is not extant. The third group of films consists of the four titles he released in 1950, some of which he began production on during the previous two years: *Conduct Report on Professor Ishi-*

naka (*Ishinaka sensei gyojoki*, 1950), *The Angry Street* (*Ikari no machi*, 1950), *White Beast*, and *The Battle of Roses*. These are all multicharacter films, set in very different but highly specific settings and constellations of Japanese society. They might be thought of as "sentimental ethnographies" in which Naruse works through the implications of the profound social changes of the postwar period. In the last four films that he made during the occupation, Naruse collaborated with three of the top actresses of the period, working from scripts based on books by major novelists. *Ginza Cosmetics*, *Dancing Girl*, and *Meshi* were followed by his only postwar period film, *Okuni and Gohei* (*Okuni to Gohei*, 1952), based on a play by Tanizaki Junichiro.

A Descendant of Urashima Taro
DEMOCRATIC REVOLUTION

Naruse's first two films after the war were made in a brief window of time when the CIE actively encouraged filmmakers to revolutionize Japanese society and politics. The goal of transforming Japan into a peaceful nation free of aggressive military tendencies entailed a complete overhaul of the corporate capital establishment on which Japan's political and industrial institutions were established. Because many of the occupation staff were New Dealers, they saw an opportunity to promote an array of socialist reforms without the opposition that such policies were meeting, by the 1940s, in the United States.[25] SCAP recognized the close collaboration of the *zaibatsu* (family-centered concentrations of wealth) with the military imperialists, and the reforms of the early occupation included a dismantling and deconcentration of capital.[26] With the resurrection of the Communist Party and the legislation of trade union law in 1945, the labor movement caught on quickly. Feeling the pains of postwar economic collapse, the film industry, along with many other sectors, saw the emergence of labor unions in many of the big companies, Toho prominent among them.

In February 1947, however, General MacArthur banned a general strike that had been called for by union leaders, initiating a "reverse course" of occupation policy. As American cold war politics increasingly came to affect the fate of postwar Japan, even the dismantling of the zaibatsu was scaled down in 1948.[27] Thus Naruse's first two postwar features, released in 1946, belong to a very specific, fleeting moment in Japanese history. Hirano describes the first film, *A Descendant of Urashima Taro* (*Urashima Taro no koei*, 1946) as a "crudely propagandistic

... exposure of wartime profiteers," which it is. Its didactic agenda is not only an anomaly within Naruse's career, it is embedded in an unusually surrealist narrative. In *Urashima Taro* and his subsequent film, *Both You and I*, Naruse displays a surprising knack for political satire inspired by the "democratic revolution" of the early occupation.

Reputedly based on Frank Capra's 1939 film *Mr. Smith Goes to Washington*, *A Descendant of Urashima Taro* is about a repatriated soldier (Fujita Susumu) who becomes a populist politician in the Japanese Happiness Party. Urashima's single accomplishment is a particular yell, a three-note musical pattern that he bellows over the radio, and from the top of the Diet building, as an expression of his unhappiness with the state of the nation. He explains his position to Akako, a young reporter played by Takamine Hideko, in one of the film's ideological speeches: "I'm an unhappy person. But I don't yell just for myself. All the Japanese people were victims of militarism and despotism. . . . I'll keep fighting until a truly democratic Japan can be born anew." Sporting a beard as signifier of his status as a repatriated soldier, Urashima has taken the name of a mythological figure who was seduced by a spirit princess disguised as a sea turtle. Although he claims at first to have been stranded on a South Seas island since the end of the war, he later denies it. Neither he nor his story is entirely credible, and the whole film takes on the aspect of a fable, in which Naruse largely abandons his realist aesthetic for a tale that combines the supernatural with political satire.

Akako "discovers" Urashima and quickly sells him to her editor, who in turn sells him to a new political party that badly needs a populist figurehead to obscure their connections to war crimes, the black market, and the zaibatsu. The Japanese Happiness Party is thoroughly corrupt, and Urashima serves as a valuable puppet for them. This may be the basis of the Capra movie as well, but there is an important difference: in the American film, the Jimmy Stewart character challenges the corrupt political establishment through his championing of American constitutional rhetoric and the heroism of legislators such as Abraham Lincoln. *A Descendant of Urashima Taro* makes a mockery of such populist posturing in the empty rhetoric of Urashima's repeated wordless yell. Throughout the film, this yell is echoed by crowds of people on streets, in factories, in fishing villages, and on farms. It also becomes a musical motif, first taken up by an operatic chorus, then integrated into an instrumental background score. When he is remade as a politician, Urashima tries to teach his fellow party members to make the cry, but they need a lot of coaching to produce the proper sound.

29. Fujita Susumu and Takamine Hideko in *A Descendant of Urashima Taro* (*Urashima Taro no koei*, 1946), Toho.

The capitalist backer of the Happiness Party has a daughter, Otoko (Yamane Hisako) who appoints herself as Urashima's personal assistant, stealing him away from Akako. Urashima refuses to fall in love with her, but when he is feted by the politicians in a fanciful party scene complete with tacky floor show and lavish decor, Otoko claims to be the undersea princess of the myth. Part femme fatale and part demon-woman, Otoko represents the seduction of power and wealth that Urashima ultimately resists. The film also includes a scene in which two "spirit" versions of Urashima fight over his soul. As he sits in a large boardroom with a Greco-Roman winged hero statue behind him, one spirit tries to persuade him to "spread his wings and fly above the people." The other spirit version of himself, hovering over the table in superimposition, reminds him that he is human and cannot fly. He should remember his mother's face, which is the moral of the Urashima myth, that the spirit world and the human world are separate. Urashima has lost his family in the war, but he ultimately chooses the human path rather than that of divine glory. In this he of course follows the lead of Emperor Hirohito, who "came down from the clouds" in August 1945.

The voice of reason in *Urashima Taro*, the person who convinces Akako that her hero has become a mere puppet for a corrupt organization, is Akako's aunt, Joshi Senkyoku, played by Sugimura Haruko. Clearly modeled on the emergent rash of women politicians, Joshi runs some kind of women's political organization and articulates the film's second message on behalf of SCAP: "The people are becoming acutely aware that good politics is a part of a good life. What politics are good politics? What sort of politics are really good for people? The people are beginning to understand these things. It's a mistake to take the people for the ignorant mass they used to be."

The story concludes when Akako persuades Urashima to "be human" and stand up for himself. He shaves off his beard, rendering himself useless as a recognizable poster boy. The politicians try to bribe him to perform his distinctive yell, but instead he comes clean, announcing at a political rally that the Japan Happiness Party is "wearing a democratic mask, but they are trying to preserve the old political system. . . . They are a minority that wants to rule over the majority." At this point Joshi addresses the crowd, convincing them to accept Urashima's apology: "Urashima, will you swear to regain your soul?" she asks. He swears he will, and the crowd cheers, supporting his commitment to "fight against the enemies of the people for all of Japan."

We may ask why Naruse was so willing to work with this kind of didactic script when he managed to get through the entire war without resorting to such bald-faced propaganda. The scriptwriter Yagi Ryuichiro had worked on pictures like *Suicide Troops of the Watchtower* (*Boro no kesshitai*, 1943) and seems to have been unfazed by the switch of allegiance and ideology. The answer may lie simply in the fact that within, or behind, the political discourse and mystical mumbo jumbo, Naruse was able to incorporate his own humble realist figure in the persona of Takamine Hideko as Akako. Her character in this film is closely related to that of Hideko the bus conductor in the 1941 film of that name. Although she is a bit more grown-up, she has a similar naïveté, and the narrative involves her coming to recognize her vulnerability and overcome it. Compared to the Jean Arthur character in *Mr. Smith Goes to Washington*, Akako is quiet and restrained, and the whole romance plot is reduced to a brief trace of disappointment when Urashima is stolen from her by Otoko.

Akako first finds Urashima wandering in Ueno Park, and the film features several scenes in which she walks down the streets of the ruined city with only the flattened landscape and the walls of burned-out homes behind her. In her tasteful short-skirted reporter's outfit, she looks slightly out of place but very much the image of the new woman for a new Japan in these scenes. Naruse also makes use of a theatrical set of ruins (Greco-Roman in design) for several scenes, including the last one in which Akako, Urashima, and his companion Torimaru (who accompanies him throughout the film as a shadowy voice of reason), discuss their hope for the new Japan. The suppression of the romance plot is significant, as it not only leaves the two protagonists, Urashima and Akako, as independent subjects, but it likewise leaves the emphasis on the collective fate of the reborn nation—as opposed to the romantic coupling that concludes the American original.

Stylistically, *Urashima Taro* is most interesting for its kitschy set pieces and excessive score. The theatricality of the film is linked in part to the superficiality and artifice of the corrupt politicians, but in the context of this particular moment of political awakening, it brings to mind some of Benjamin's remarks on kitsch in *The Arcades Project*. For Benjamin, kitsch is at once the mixing of styles and the excess of commodity culture and can be read as a signal of bourgeois class guilt. It is the allegorical form of the dreaming collective that can also be the key to its awakening. Thus his historiography is stimulated by the surrealist project: "We construct here an alarm clock that rouses the kitsch of the previous century to 'assembly' and thus operates totally with cunning."[28] As Susan

Buck-Morss notes, Benjamin's dialectical fairy tale sees history in terms of a "phantasmagoria" of wish-images that the collective has more or less slept through. But, she adds, "the commodity form of the dream generated the expectation that the international, socialist goal of mass affluence could be delivered by national, capital means, and that expectation was a fatal blow to revolutionary-class politics."[29]

To apply this model of kitsch to a Japanese film from 1946 is to suggest that *A Descendant of Urashima Taro* constitutes a kind of phantasmagoria of the lost opportunities of a revolutionary democracy based in the collective aspiration for national renewal. As a studio product made under fairly strict terms of censorship, it is a film that does not take itself entirely seriously. The kitschy mise-en-scène and narrative, drawing on sources as diverse as *Mr. Smith Goes to Washington* and an ancient Japanese fable, might be interpreted as a kind of "awakening" from the dream of empty platitudes and political posturing. If the overt ideology of the film is not quite prepared to separate political freedom or liberal democracy from capitalism, the stylistic cacophony essentially dismantles the realist phantasmagoria. The instability of the nation is unambiguously conveyed in this most "surreal" film of Naruse's oeuvre.

The many shots of crowds in the film's opening scenes clearly register "the collective" as a Japanese public eager for clues to future happiness. Urashima and his supporters, including the film's only true political leader, Joshi, do not offer any political platform. Their message ends up being simply a matter of truth against lies, in which the mortality of the emperor is cleverly linked to a critique of the corrupt zaibatsu. To say that the film is a potential awakening from the dreaming collective is not to suggest that it was or could be a revolutionary film; it is rather to recognize the failure of revolutionary consciousness within the wishes of the phantasmagoria. If for Benjamin the culture of nineteenth-century Paris marks the residue of failed revolutionary energies, we could say the same thing of this brief foray into anticapitalist social democracy of the early occupation. Naruse recognizes only the enfranchisement of women, reinforced in the characters played by Takamine and Sugimura, yet the melodramatic utterance of Urashima is an expressive gesture of the inarticulate desires of an entire populace.

Urashima Taro offers only one moment of visual flourish. When Urashima appears, late, in the lobby of the hall where he is to address a political rally, with his beard shaved, he is suddenly recognizable as the actor Fujita Susumu, one of Toho's big stars of the time.[30] From a long shot of him entering the lobby, Naruse cuts to close-ups of two of the politicians and one of Otoko, each time moving laterally toward Urashima with the separate figures. The abrupt cutting style and camera movements fragment the space and delay the close-up of the clean-shaven Fujita. By this time, Naruse's melodramatic stylistics, announcing the emotional climax of the narrative, have become kitsch in themselves. Given all the discursive borrowing and intertextuality of the film, there is an immediacy of representation in this sequence that we might point to as the film's own awakening. Unlike the banal "special effects" superimpositions of Urashima's split selves, here the montage and camera movement recall the energies of interwar modernity. The flourish is deployed briefly, retrospectively recalling the moment when the promise of Japanese modernity was last seen in the early 1930s. It reminds us to scan the phantasmagoria of mass media for the wish-image of the dreaming collective.

Both You and I
THE SALARYMAN'S REVENGE

Naruse's second "political" film, *Both You and I* (*Ore mo omae mo*, 1946), is a revisiting of the salaryman genre of *Flunky, Work Hard* but this time the two salarymen, after being thoroughly humiliated and exploited by their boss, finally confront him and accuse him of wartime profiteering. They threaten to "stick together" and "fight for our rights" in the face of a threatened, but unspecified, reorganization of the company. Ooki (Hanabishi Achako) and Aono (Yokoyama Entatsu) are comic characters, very much along the lines of the duo of *Traveling Actors*. Hanabishi and Yokoyama were a well-known *manzai* act and thus appear in the film as characters familiar to audiences of the time.[31] Until the penultimate scene, they are estranged from their fellow workers, sucking up to the boss by performing at drinking parties. When they are asked to help prepare for a party at the boss's home, they find themselves doing sweaty yard work. Their reward is a trip to a spa, but they are simply tricked into carrying back loads of black-market supplies for the party. Aono is persuaded to send one of his daughters to help serve food at the party, but she is so shocked at how her father is humiliated that she insists he go home so as not to discourage a potential suitor of her sister's who is a guest at the party.

The comedic aspects of the film are balanced by the home settings of the two salarymen, and it is in the shoshimin-eiga aspects of the film that the moral truths reside. Aono is a widower with four children, including two marriage-age daughters. Ooki lives with his wife and son, and both homes are Japanese-style dwellings in which Naruse situates his camera at tatami level for characters seated on the floor. The boss's home, of course, is furnished in lavish, luxurious Western style, while the office features unusual Bauhaus-style modern architecture, which is accentuated by a crane shot at one point. Thus the class conflict is dramatized in terms of visual style. The ideological discourse of the film is introduced through Ooki's college-age son rehearsing a play at home with his friends about striking workers. Ooki and his wife listen to them singing a May Day song and rehearsing a script in which a labor leader challenges his boss by accusing him of collaborating with militarists and exploiting his workers. Concerned that the neighbors might overhear them, Ooki argues with his son, insisting that he is "too indebted" to his boss to say such things. The son, Sadao, accuses him of outmoded thinking. However, by the end of the film, Ooki summons the courage, and when he and his buddy Aono finally stage their confrontation, their coworkers applaud them enthusiastically.

In Naruse's first sound film, *Three Sisters with Maiden Hearts*, a broken sandal constitutes a narrative catalyst, and it is this *geta*, or Japanese sandal, that returns in *Both You and I* as a central motif. Shoes often figure as signs of home, and shots of shoes at a doorway will indicate who is home; but shoes for Naruse are usually broken, or lost, or damaged, indicating the owner's poverty or misfortune. In this film, when Ooki first comes home, he sees the array of shoes belonging to his son's friends, but a dog has run off with one of his own sandals. Meanwhile, a parallel situation develops in Aono's home when his sandal breaks and he asks his daughter in jest if that is his "ration" sandal. The single-sandal theme comes back to haunt the two men when Aono leaves the party saying he is sick to save face in front of his daughter and the suitor. The boss insults the pair by saying that Ooki might as well leave too, since without Aono, he is as boring and useless as a single sandal. In fact, the two are a great comedy team, and their performances of kabuki and geisha routines, in which Aono usually dons a woman's garb, are very good. The opening scene of the film, set in an inn with the drinking party seen in silhouette through the lighted fusuma showcases their talents as performers. Despite the truth of the boss's comment regarding their performance, Aono and Ooki interpret the dismissive comment to mean that together they are only as good as one person. This is what finally makes the two men angry and, spurred on by Ooki's son, they are moved to confront the boss the next day at the office.

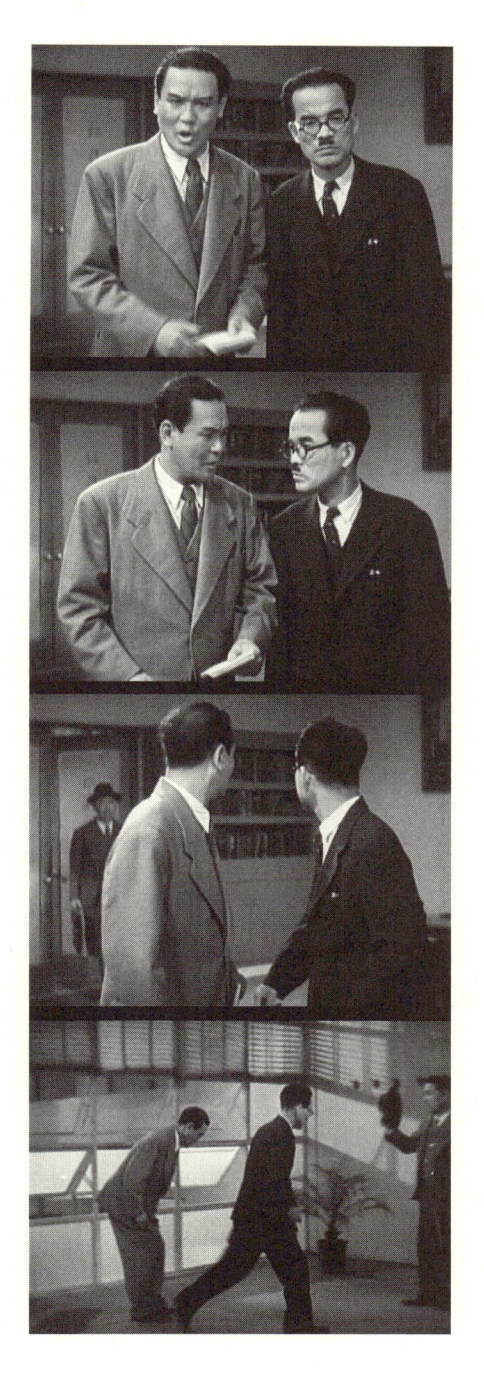

30. The salarymen practice confronting their boss before he arrives. Hanabishi Achako and Yokoyama Entatsu in *Both You and I* (*Ore mo omae mo*, 1946), Toho.

Part nansensu comedy, part shoshimin-eiga, the salarymen's revenge is only partially convincing. Aono and Ooki are last seen walking home from work through the grid of suburban Tokyo doing their same old slapstick routine in which Ooki searches his pockets for ideas for suitors for Aono's daughter. They compare their triumph to the feeling of having taken something for an upset stomach, something, they decide, like a new drink that goes *fizz*, something like a soda! In other words, not much is actually going to change. Nevertheless, if we compare the outcome of this story to the sense of resignation and powerlessness in a film such as Ozu's *I Was Born But . . .* (*Umarete wa mita keredo*, 1932), something must have changed. No longer powerless, the salarymen have at least glimpsed something of the truth of what the scholar Aono Suekichi realized in 1930, that the tragedy of the salaryman is the perpetuation of feudal customs within the structures and institutions of modern capitalism. In Harootunian's account of Aono's theory, he says:

> Society, he observed, was producing new forms of knowledge and new skills that were being mastered by the salaryman class. But capitalism, he noted, had made no attempt to distinguish among commodities. In the calculations of the market, there was no real distinction between "shoes" and "knowledge," but only among units of quantity. To maintain price levels, it was often necessary to "burn" great quantities of commodities. When knowledge and skills become commodified, the difficulty was compounded because the salarymen who had mastered these skills were not commodities that could easily be discarded or destroyed to maintain market price. But they could always be fired from their jobs.[32]

Naruse's parable, which he scripted himself, is essentially an illustration of Aono's argument, complete with shoes. However, given the endurance of the salaryman character in popular culture, Aono and Ooki are familiar caricatures, and their enlightenment is but a fleeting moment in classical Japanese cinema. The indictment of capitalist corruption is thoroughly infused with the accusations of militarist collaboration and black-market profiteering, which may have been the stimulus for such a story under SCAP regulations, but it also tends to qualify the labor politics as symptomatic of that particular context. Like *A Descendant of Taro Urashima*, the film has its moments of kitsch—including the nansensu renditions of kabuki and geisha routines, and the recitals of Western music at the boss's party—and we could point to them as points of "awakening" of the dreaming collective, interruptions of the narrative with discursive excess and contradiction.

Spring Awakens
SEX EDUCATION

The two films that Naruse made in 1947, while very different stylistically, both deal with female protagonists and their different struggles with the expression of sexual desire. While the short film *Even Parting Is Enjoyable* is about a "kept woman" being dumped by her boyfriend, the feature film *Spring Awakens* (*Haru no mezame*, 1947) deals with the more banal question, "Where do babies come from?" Very much a "democratization picture," this story of young teenagers in a small town is a surprisingly strong film in which Naruse explores the psychological and social issues of adolescence with a great deal of sensitivity. Although clearly intended to promote the importance of sex education, *Spring Awakens* doesn't answer its own question in the end and ironically falls prey to its own critique of the repression of sexual knowledge. In its contradictoriness, however, it demonstrates the tensions that were felt within the film industry and the public regarding the CIE's demand that Japanese films include more "kissing scenes" and expressions of physical love.

The young people in *Spring Awakens*, three girls and three boys, find themselves surrounded by traces and hints of sex, but no one will explain it to them. Most of the adults simply say that babies come with marriage, but when one of their school friends becomes pregnant and one of their maids is fired for having an affair, they become more curious. Of the six kids, Kumiko (Kuga Yoshiko) emerges as the protagonist. She has an affinity for Heine's poetry, which she admits to not completely understanding, and her romantic sensibility makes her particularly vulnerable to the strictures of the repressive culture. The extent of this repression is depicted at the school where one of the teachers claims to have found a "very suggestive" picture on the school premises, although the picture itself is never shown or identified. In another instance, a student gets in trouble for drawing an anatomically correct figure on the blackboard. Kumiko is found to have a snapshot taken of her with a boy, which gets her into trouble. Through a discourse of visual culture, the "unspeakable" becomes linked to the adolescents' romantic ideals and flirtations, but they still can't figure out what the connection is.

Fortunately, there is a doctor in the town, played by Shimura Takashi, in the paternalistic role he would come to be famous for in Kurosawa's films *Drunken Angel* (1948), *The Quiet Duel* (1949), and *Stray Dog* (1949). Here he plays Dr. Ogura, a benevolent father who hands his son a book on "sexual science," which he says, will answer all the boy's questions.

When Kumiko's parents call him in to help them with their daughter, Dr. Ogura offers the film's final didactic message: "There comes a time when as a parent you have to stop thinking of your kids as little children. It's the responsibility of parents to make kids feel the things that develop within them the right way. It's a dangerous thing to let adolescence run its course without any guidance." Kumiko's parents are obliged to consult the doctor only after Kumiko's first kiss, which scares her so badly that she finally angrily confronts her mother, demanding that she explain the facts of life.

The kissing scene, Naruse's first, is a remarkable scene in itself. Much of the film is set among the woods, rivers, and pathways around the town, and as the title suggests, it is the "awakening" of springtime that stirs the passions of the young teenagers. Kumiko goes to the grounds of a temple where Noshiro, one of her classmates, has just finished a painting. He is so excited he grabs her and they run down to a meadow, rolling on the sensuous, warm grass. Exploiting the 360-degree space of the open countryside, Naruse shoots this 108-second sequence in a montage of twenty-two shots from every conceivable angle and distance as the two kids roll away from each other and toward each other, finally awkwardly falling together. When Noshiro finally sits up and leans over Kumiko, his shadow falls over her face. They both look worried. He grabs her and kisses her quite roughly, and the movement is quickly followed by a close-up of the grass into which a geta is thrown. The romantic music that has been building throughout the sequence suddenly stops and Kumiko stands up and runs off into the distance, followed by Noshiro shouting apologies. What happens between the kiss and the tossed geta is left entirely to the imagination, and the construction of the sequence renders the kiss much more than the conventional romantic soft-focus cliché that CIE might have anticipated.

As Kyoko Hirano explains, many Japanese actors, directors, and viewers had trouble with the inclusion of kissing on screen because it was traditionally done in private, not in public. Some of the opponents of kissing on screen argued that it would encourage kissing in public; others argued that it would be sensationalistic; and others felt that, since it did not come "naturally" to Japanese, it would be poorly acted.[33] Uehara Ken and Hara Setsuko were among the actors who refused to do it, and indeed with only one significant exception,[34] neither of them engage in any physical contact with each other or anyone else in the films they made with Naruse. Hirano explains that the Americans linked the sexual

31. The first kiss. Kuga Yoshiko and Sugi Hiroyuki in *Spring Awakens* (*Haru no mezame*, 1947), Toho.

openness of kissing to a culture of honesty and transparency that they associated with the democratic ideals they were trying to instill in the Japanese consciousness. Hirano suggests, "They felt uneasy when they perceived that the Japanese were not expressing themselves openly."[35] Despite the initial resistance and controversy, sexual liberation caught on pretty quickly and kissing became a mainstay of Japanese film, starting with *Twenty-Year-Old Youth* (*Hatachi no seishun*, dir. Sasaki Yasuchi, 1946). It was not long before striptease and girlie magazines spawned a whole new set of gender issues for Japanese women.

What is especially interesting about *Spring Awakens* is the way that it isolates a moment before sexuality was "known," before it entered the sphere of visual culture on the massive level that it soon came to occupy in Japan. While Naruse convincingly "argues" in this film for sexual education, he does so from a perspective of innocence on the threshold of disappearing. At the same time he points to other discourses of pleasure and sexual ambiguity that have longstanding roles in Japanese culture. The setting of the film in the Japanese homes of a sun-drenched town includes an inn called the Akebono, where one of the mothers runs a small "entertainment" business. Her daughter, Kumiko's friend Hanae, is often called away to help entertain clients, although this girl is as ignorant as her friends about sex. The maids at the Akebono tease the young boys, while Hanae's mother is depicted as laid-back and friendly with the kids, who study together at her home despite the din of partying from downstairs. The coexistence of this ongoing culture of gender-based entertainment with Dr. Ogura's book on "sexual science" is symptomatic of the unevenness of Japanese modernity. The young people are caught up within a complex and contradictory network of forces. Kumiko wants to study for exams, but her mother needs her to help around the house; on the sidelines of the school playing field, Kumiko overhears some classmates discuss the new rights of women, and the injustice of being sidelined for having their periods (for which they use the euphemism *gobyoki*, or "sickness").

This is a new generation, but the film situates their struggle for autonomy and knowledge within the framework of the shoshimin-eiga. The confrontation between Kumiko and her mother is among the most moving in Naruse's oeuvre. As the girl moves into close-up, begging her mother to tell her the secret of sex, the mother (Sugimura Haruko) whimpers and dissembles, finally complaining that it is unfair to be put on the spot. Modernity in this film is very clearly linked to knowledge, but it is the beauty of the mise-en-scène, with its use of nature, weather, and the framing architecture of the Japanese home opening onto lush sunny landscapes, that stimulates the quest for knowledge.

The sensuality of the climactic kissing scene is provided by the warm grass and beautiful vista. Naruse's violent, dramatic cutting of the scene takes up the energy that is provided by the young people throughout the film as they run around and play sports. Thus, despite the banality of its ostensible subject matter, this "idea picture" enables Naruse to return to the domain of the home drama as it is inhabited by a passionate new subjectivity, the sexually aware teenager of the new Japan. At the same time, he retains a sense of decorum regarding the issue of sexuality, precisely by withholding the details that the kids are so eager to learn. These are secrets better kept inside the pages of the manual, or within the walls of the pleasure house, and he convincingly demonstrates that there can be openness without vulgarity, that cinema need not show everything just because it can.

In *Spring Awakens*, melodrama functions as an expressive discourse. In the final scenes, after Kumiko's parents receive their lecture from the doctor, we see Kumiko laughing on her bed, brightly lit, as she jokes with her little sister. Then she is waving to her friends swimming in the lake. This final image, of Kumiko standing on the shore in a straw hat, conveys that the end of the story is simply that she has grown up; but now that it is summer and the kids are out of their school uniforms, she has acquired some independence from this group. The conjunction of gender knowledge and autonomy makes this psychological portrait Naruse's most successful "democracy picture." The didactic message is embedded in a visual discourse in which natural beauty plays more than a supporting role; it allegorizes the moral discourse of truth and transparency and helps Naruse avoid the sentimentality that such a story might have acquired.

Even Parting Is Enjoyable
BEING WOMAN IN THE NEW JAPAN

Even Parting Is Enjoyable is in some respects the polar opposite of *Spring Awakens*. Released in March 1947, it is a twenty-five-minute episode of a four-part omnibus feature that was intended to showcase the postwar revival of Toho studio, and it placed eighth in *Kinema Junpo*'s top films of the year. The other episodes were directed by Toyoda Shiro, Yamamoto Kajiro, and Kinugasa Teinosuke, and according to Bock, Naruse's segment was originally intended for Abe Yutaka.[36] Using only two sets, a bar and an apartment, the short film is about a dancer named Mitsuko (Kogure Michiyo) whose younger lover leaves her. Although there is no kissing involved, the couple dances closely together in the apartment, and there is a certain sensationalism implied in the characterization of Michiyo as a kept woman. She has been warned that Arita (Numazaki Isao) has another lover, but when he visits she pretends not to be attached, then seduces him with tango music, only to finally let him go by pretending to have another lover herself. The bartender and his wife across the street are meanwhile entertaining an older man named Yoshioka, whom they are trying to set up with Mitsuko. When Yoshioka phones her from the bar, she pretends to make a date with him. Arita leaves, Yoshioka drunkenly tells his friends that he doesn't know what happened, and Mitsuko is last seen alone in her apartment with the phone ringing.

The simplicity of this film is its biggest asset, and if the performances were stronger, it would have lived up to its potential as melodrama. The psychological portrait of a woman pretending not to be hurt, trying to use her "talents" as a seductress and failing, is a challenge for a performer, demanding an ability to "put on" a series of different faces. Naruse uses lighting and music effectively, and together with the use of the telephone, there is a noir element to this very urban story. Mitsuko's act is, however, upstaged by Arita's new woman, whom Mitsuko derides as a lowly news vendor. Quietly waiting for Arita in the bar, knitting, this "other woman," dressed in a simple kimono, is obviously a morally superior woman to the notorious dancer. For her part, dressed in a checked blazer with permed hair and a glittery broach, Mitsuko is the essence of kitsch. In other words, the stylistics of the film tend to work against any sympathy we might have for Mitsuko, although she does seem, in the end, to have lost.

An interesting comparison to make with this film is the short *The Human Voice* (*Una voce umana*) that Rossellini made with Anna Magnani in 1948. Based on Cocteau's play *La Voix humaine* and released as part one of *L'Amore* (the second part being *Il miracolo*), Rossellini's film also features a woman in an apartment with a telephone. The films have in common a dramatic intensity based in a woman's psychological state upon being left by a man. Magnani's tour-de-force acting may be on a level of hysteria and emotional outletting that was unheard of in Japanese cinema of the late 1940s, but like the dancer in Naruse's film, Magnani is all about pretense, disguise, and equivocation. Where Rossellini draws on the resources of operatic performance, Naruse and his actress draw on the aesthetics of controlled restraint more typical of Japanese drama. Both women are clearly implicated in a network of social forces over which they have no control. These two boudoir dramas, equally kitschy in their interior decor and materialism, become the settings for deep existential crises as the two women find themselves wholly cut off from society. Mitsuko's trick on the drunk in the bar and Magnani's duplicity are manipulative actions that the narratives demonstrate to be acts of desperation.

Naruse and Rossellini are both more typically realist filmmakers, and other parallels between their projects will emerge—parallels not of influence but of coincidence. Postwar Italian cinema was far less constrained and much more ready to articulate the awakening from fascism than was the Japanese. It would take another study to more thoroughly compare the two national cinemas, and these two directors more specifically. But both directors had a focus on female protagonists and developed some strong women characters in the postwar era. That they both produced these studies of romantic psychology using the telephone as an instrument of duplicity shows their parallel experiments with melodramatic representation.

If *Spring Awakens* constitutes a vision of the awakening of Japan within the terms of everyday life, *Even Parting Is Enjoyable* offers only the tacky accoutrements of the kept woman as its dialectical form of "awakening." Here the permed hair is the wish-image of a dreaming collective, seduced by the glamour of Hollywood. Taken together, though, the two films point toward the conditions of the "being woman" of the New Japan. At once armed with knowledge, sexuality, and independence, she is nevertheless caught up within an image-sphere of melancholia, exploitation, and sensationalism. In Naruse's lost film of 1949, *Delinquent Girl*, the two trajectories appear to converge; the synopsis suggests a story about schoolgirls who get mixed up with a bad crowd.

Professor Ishinaka
SENTIMENTAL ETHNOGRAPHY

Labor unrest began at Toho studio as early as March 1946, when a strike won workers a salary increase and union rights. As the most "modern" studio, with streamlined production methods of production, Toho was the studio most closely aligned with the government during the war, and it specialized intensively in war films. Its streamlined organization also made it very ready to adopt the democratic principles advocated by the early directives from SCAP and CIE, which linked war responsibility to the upper echelons of studio management. Among the first tasks of the All Japan Film and Theater Employee Union Association was to compile a list of war criminals, made up of top executives from all the major studios.[37] The remaining Toho executives and management were, however, intent on increasing the profitability of the company and, in a climate of exponential inflation and rising admission prices, turned huge profits.[38] The Japan Motion Picture and Drama Employees Union, seeking wage increases to keep up with the rate of inflation, held a series of strikes at Toho, bringing production to a halt in May 1948. Toho made only four films in 1948, and Naruse made none.[39]

Where was Naruse during this period, and did he support the Toho strike? The evidence suggests that he basically kept a low profile and worked where and when he could. Hirano says that he joined an "Artists Group" in August 1948 that demanded the resignation of Toho executives Watanabe and Mabuchi.[40] The incident sparked the lockdown and occupation of the studio by workers for 134 days, ending in a confrontation with Japanese police forces, who were backed up by American troops and tanks. As a director with some seniority in this very hierarchically organized company, Naruse's name no doubt carried some weight needed by the more activist members of the studio, but while many of his favorite actresses were very visible during the strike, he himself kept well out of the spotlight.[41]

Hirano claims that Naruse directed theater pieces while Toho was shut down, although she offers no further details.[42] He did join the Film Art Association, along with Kurosawa and a number of other directors, producing films jointly with other companies.[43] Bock says that *Spring Awakens*, *Delinquent Girl*, and *Conduct Report on Professor Ishinaka* were planned as a series that was interrupted by the war. *Delinquent Girl* is credited as a Toyoko Eiga production, and *Conduct Report on Professor Ishinaka* and *Ginza Cosmetics* were produced by Shin Toho, a Toho subsidiary. *White Beast* was started while Naruse was freelancing, but completion was delayed because the star, Miura Mitsuko, left for the United States before shooting was finished.[44] This was clearly a turbulent period, and the four films that Naruse made in 1950 are very much the products of an unstable industrial context. *The Battle of Roses*, which was produced by the Film Art Association in conjunction with Shochiku, seems to have been hastily put together, with some surprisingly abrupt editing and a rather poor script.

All four films made in 1950 feature performances that can be most kindly described as "under-rehearsed," although both *Conduct Report on Professor Ishinaka* and *White Beast* are well-made films with remarkably different visual styles. Along with *The Battle of Roses*, these 1950 films are all about distinctive communities and constellations of characters. Key protagonists certainly center each film, but the narratives are more about the social dynamics among the groups than about character or psychology. While this is a longstanding feature of Naruse's film practice, it takes on an anthropological aspect in these films, as if the narratives were ethnographic studies of the specific communities in question, each one based in a distinctive locale or social sphere. The other thing these films have in common, besides featuring a series of strong-minded female characters, is an emphasis on romance as a storytelling device. These are very much "sentimental" melodramas, and we could even describe *Conduct Report on Professor Ishinaka* as a trilogy of short romantic comedies. Set against the backdrop of the social upheaval of current events, these three films are narratives of hope and optimism, as new couples are formed to carry on the work of the New Japan.

In *Conduct Report on Professor Ishinaka* (*Ishinaka sensei gyojoki*, 1950), the professor (Miyata Shigeo) is a novelist living in Aomori prefecture, the northernmost tip of Honshu, just south of Hokkaido, but the professor has only a minor role in the film named for his character. He appears in each of the three short vignettes that make up the film as a local authority who is consulted by the townspeople. Each story features the courtship of a young man and woman, and in each instance it is suggested that the professor will undoubtedly write a novel about the events that have transpired. Based on an original story by Ishizaka Yojiro, the film has a reflexive element by which it comments on its own process of taking the materials of everyday life and transforming them into narrative. This realist conceit is enhanced by the rural setting, which is photographed with some care, including the mountainous landscapes and the farmhouse interiors. Many of the actors have strong Aomori accents, and Naruse even includes footage of several local festivals, complete with lanterns, banners, dances, and songs. The film is in some respects a sequel to *Hideko the Bus Conductor*, taking up both its rural setting and its writer character, although the women have grown up a little since 1941.

Against this ethnographic context, or within it, are interruptions of the world outside. In the first episode, "A Story of Buried Gasoline," a young man believes that drums of gasoline were buried in a certain orchard during the war and asks the professor to help him negotiate access in return for a share of the profits. Kawai (Hori Yuji) was a soldier posted in the area, but his memory is poor. After some fruitless digging and copious drinking, it turns out that the young man was really interested in the farmer's daughter Moyoko (Mokusho Kumiko), and the buried gasoline was simply a ploy. The highlight of this episode is the girl's performance in samurai costume for the men in her father's home. After a few minutes, Moyoko takes her *taishu engeki* act outside, and Kawai chases her around the apple orchard playing mock *kendo*. Their kiss is offscreen but signaled by two apple cores dropping together from the tree branch on which they are perched. Professor Ishinaka blesses their union and forgives Kawai for misleading him and his friends.

In the second episode, "A Story of an Argument," a burlesque show comes to town. Two men, Kihara (Nakamura Tadayoshi) and Yamada (Fujiwara Kamatari), are scandalized by the poster of a scantily dressed blonde woman, but Yamada has been given two free tickets, so they decide to go for educational purposes. To help reconstruct Japan, they decide, they must not waste the tickets but use them as "examiners" to improve public morals. Yamada's daughter Mariko (Sugi Yoko) finds out and gets together with Kihara's son, hoping to blackmail their fathers when they leave the theater. Mariko plans to ask for a dress, and she convinces Hidekazu (Ikebe Ryo) to ask for a suit. Their plan doesn't quite work out, though, and the four of them get into an argument that is partly a flirtation between the two young people. Professor Ishinaka eventually sorts it all out by pointing out to the two fathers, each of whom insists it was the other's idea, that burlesque shows aren't inherently evil. He also talks Mariko and Hidekaza into confessing their attraction to one another.

The burlesque show itself is, not surprisingly, the highlight of this episode of *Professor Ishinaka*. A troupe of ten Japanese dancers do can-can chorus-line dances for an entirely male audience. Although it is billed as a "nude show," the women are dressed in tights and vests and are mainly showing a lot of leg. Naruse includes the compulsory "between the legs" and profile shots of the dancers, but the bulk of the show is seen in long shot. The girlie show was very much a phenomenon of the immediate postwar era and is featured in other films, most notoriously Kinoshita's *Carmen Comes Home* (1951) and Kurosawa's *Ikiru* (1952). Izbicki notes that in many instances, within the context of the occupation's destruction and democratization, "the viewing of such performances is discussed by characters within the story as a liberating experience of some sort."[45] Democratic freedoms, in other words, included the freedom to

32. Fujiwara Kamatari at a burlesque show in *Conduct Report on Professor Ishinaka* (*Ishinaka sensei gyojoki*, 1950), Shin Toho.

see women's bodies, and for women, new forms of objectification and subjugation. The so-called nudie show was rarely actually nude but featured far more exposed flesh than Japanese men had ever seen outside the public bath or the brothel.

In *Professor Ishinaka* the spectacle of the female body produces guilt rather than liberation, as the men have to be instructed by the wise man that they should not be ashamed. The "liberating" aspect of the film is more subtly articulated and is in fact an important link between the three segments of the film. The Sugi Yoko character, like the farmer's daughter in "the buried gasoline" episode and the young farm girl Yoshiko in the last episode, is a very forthright young lady. These three women may live in a small town in northern Japan, but they aren't afraid to say what they think, get what they want, and go where they want to go. Neither shy nor particularly feminine, they are very modern heroines who are nevertheless thoroughly integrated into the rural community.

In the final episode of *Professor Ishinaka*, "Story of a Haywagon," Yoshiko (Wakayama Setsuko) walks to town to visit her sister in the hospital, taking her some fresh vegetables from the farm. She sees a movie and the next day heads back to her village. A farmer gives her a lift in his hay wagon, but after stopping for a break, she accidentally climbs onto the wrong wagon and falls asleep, only to wake up in a strange village with a strange young man. Fortunately, Teisaku (Mifune Toshiro) has a friendly family with whom the girl eats and spends the night. Yoshiko is very talkative and laughs a lot with Teisaku's mother, but the Mifune character, Teisaku, is extremely shy. Mifune plays up the strong silent type, protecting Yoshiko from local boys when they go out to see a local festival. Before she continues on her way home, the mother asks the local policeman to certify that Yoshiko's virginity was not compromised during her stay. The policeman brings along Professor Ishinaka to help him with this task, and after Yoshiko leaves, the professor convinces Teisaku to follow and court the girl, as they are clearly attracted to each other.

"Story of a Haywagon" is a kind of fairytale, as Yoshiko meets a palm reader in the opening scenes who tells her that she will meet her future husband very soon. Naruse takes the opportunity to showcase the quaint customs of the rural community, where old-fashioned virtues still hold sway. The certification of Yoshiko's virginity is somewhat at odds with her bold mannerisms. Teisaku is so shy that she accuses him of being mute, and as she tells the policeman, it is she who grabbed him when she was frightened in the dark. As with the other two episodes, Aomori is depicted as a place where social change is taking place, including a shift in gender roles, but life goes on nevertheless, with many customs and rituals intact. Professor Ishinaka's presence in the town is a kind of proof of enlightenment as he is able to interpret these changes in a positive light. Although the film is about the emerging generation gap, the potential conflict between the parents and their young-adult children is held in check, mainly by the harmony implicit in the rural atmosphere.

The Angry Street
THE DANGEROUS POSTWAR CITY

Immediately following *Professor Ishinaka*, Naruse returned to Tokyo for a very different film, depicting the moral decadence of postwar Tokyo. Strongly influenced by the street realism of film noir, *The Angry Street* (*Ikari no machi*, 1950) includes a great deal of location shooting in the rebuilt city, including downtown streets, residential neighborhoods, the campus of the University of Tokyo, and the high life of jazzy dance halls. Sudo (Hara Yasumi) and Mori (Uno Jukichi) are two university students who make money by picking up rich girls in dance clubs and conning them into giving them cash. Mori is the brains of the operation, and Sudo is the suave dancer who picks up the girls. Over the course of the film, Sudo becomes involved with three different girls and is drawn into the gangster milieu, which he seems unable to resist even though he is responsible for his mother, grandmother, and sister, Masako (Wakayama Setsuko). In this world of bad boys and girls, Masako is the pillar of strength and moral virtue who finally enables Mori to straighten out. The film ends in the hospital, after Sudo has been slashed across the face by a hoodlum and refuses to repent or change his ways. Mori asks her, "If I can't save him, how can I be saved?" She responds, "To live honestly, to save my brother, we have to work together," and they clasp hands in the dark corridor of the hospital.

The students' involvement in crime is grounded in the historical context of postwar Japan and contrasted to the means by which some of their fellow students support themselves. Many are selling lottery tickets and cheap dishes and toys on the street, and others are delivering inventory to a factory. Sudo and Mori mock their colleagues who stoop to such menial tasks, and they scorn the student government leaders who are addressing the problem of student employment. Neither their families nor their fellow students know their real source of income, and when Sudo's grandmother finds out what he has been doing, she promptly dies. Because they have no visible means of support, their fellow students assume they are rich, and Sudo and Mori refer to themselves as "intellectual athletes," following the example of Yamazaki Koji, a Tokyo University student who set up an underground money-lending business called the Hikari Club. Toward the end of the film, Mori tells Sudo that they were wrong about Yamazaki, who in fact killed himself in 1949 after running out of cash.

Against the poverty of the students and their families, one of the boys' targets, Kimiko (Kisho Kumiko), comes from a rich family who has connections with the gangster world. Her parents eventually send the hoodlum to injure Sudo, as they are concerned about his liaison with their daughter. Kimiko herself is more than willing to hand over thousands of yen to Sudo and move in with him. Another girl, Fusako (Kuga Yoshiko), is more genuinely exploited by Sudo, to whom she gives her watch, and she is eager to give more money, although she is of more modest means than Kimiko. At first Sudo is reluctant to "go all the way" with these girls, but by the end of the film, he seems to have overcome his inhibitions and practically rapes Fusako. Although the narrative is not entirely forthcoming about the actual substance of his relations with the different women, as Naruse insists on discreetly cutting away from any kind of romantic liaison, one of Sudo's conquests, Tagami (Hamada Yuriko), is definitely a new kind of woman. Like the other girls, Sudo meets her at one of the dance halls, but she is a bit older than the others and claims to work as a dentist. When Sudo visits Tagami, several gangsters show up at her office to show her stolen goods that she seems to fence for them. Tagami is essentially a femme fatale, and Mori suspects that it is she who is conning Sudo rather than the other way around. Unfortunately, Tagami is not particularly well developed as a character and quickly disappears after luring Sudo into her world of crime.

While the characters in *The Angry Street* are not quite as "bad" as those in American film noir, Naruse has mastered the lighting and urban style of the postwar cycle of crime films. The opening credits are superimposed on a series of shots of the city, moving in from high angles of intersections to street-level views of department stores and pedestrians. The crisscrossing streams of traffic, trains, and crowds depict a bustling, fast-moving urban scene, which is also glimpsed from under a dark shadowed underpass. The sequence ends with two shots of narrower streets from a closer view, leading into the opening scene in a dance hall. The clubs themselves feature modern architecture, lots of dancers, drinks, and jazz music. Naruse had visited this terrain in some of his 1930s films, although the gangster world that was in the background of those films has moved into the foreground. The low-key lighting and gangsters wearing fedoras and slicked-back hair are more specifically postwar, but the culture of the dance hall, where young men and women mix outside the milieu of the family, is a modern institution of the prewar years.

The style of the film may be influenced somewhat by the success of Kurosawa's *Drunken Angel*, which won the first place *Kinema Junpo* award in 1948. Although the film features two male protagonists, Naruse's view is still that of the woman's film. Sudo's mother is forced to sell socks in the street, but Sudo tells all his rich girlfriends that he is from an aristocratic family. Indeed it is the mother's sorrows and Masako's sincerity that finally win. Nobody dies in the end — except the grandmother — and the only violence is quickly accomplished. The rhetoric of salvation with which the film concludes is announced in an opening title as well, which explains that "the expression 'angry streets' refers to a situation in which the love of justice and trust in others is trampled." This is a debased world in which the struggle for survival has led many people down the wrong path, and evidently the city is to blame.

Naruse represents life in the metropolis not only through location shooting, but also through a detailed depiction of the material culture of everyday life in the city. Specifically, several scenes actually open with close-ups of objects from which the camera either tracks back or cuts abruptly away. Functioning almost like inverted establishing shots, these "still-life" images set the scene from the inside out. In one instance, it is an open can of fish and a beer in Mori's apartment, and a wad of money is tossed onto the table before cutting away to a medium shot of Mori;

33. Transitional montage sequence in *The Angry Street* (*Ikari no machi*, 1950), Toho.

in another, a steak on a plate opens a scene of the two students in a restaurant, evidently having moved up in the world. A tray of drinks in a hotel introduces the scene in which Sudo wakes to find Tagami gone; a shot of flowers and a clock, followed by a wallet and a scarf on the tatami floor introduces a scene with Kimiko and Sudo. Finally, a shot of a purse opens a scene with Fukuda and Sudo in Mori's apartment, suggesting obliquely that it is Fukuda's money that Sudo is interested in despite his words of seduction. Other close-ups of objects are inserted into scenes, including a vase of flowers that is knocked over while Sudo roughly embraces Fukuda, suggesting a possible rape. All of these shots are offered to the viewer as symbols and as literal signs as well as props in the drama. They are never linked to a character's direct point of view, and in several instances they are beside the characters rather than in front of them.

In this way, Naruse puts his own stamp on a rather predictable genre picture, linking the immoral behavior to a very materialist discourse on class. As in the American crime melodrama, crime does not pay, and the hubris of the criminal is a futile attempt at social mobility. However, set against the desperate conditions of postwar Tokyo, in which housewives and students are obliged to sell trinkets on the street, this gangster picture ends up being a lesson in humility. It is only in the city where the rich and poor are found in such close proximity, and the democratizing space of the dance hall is a unique public space where the classes potentially mix. For the grandmother, who is scandalized at the thought of Sudo receiving a letter from a girl (Fukuda, asking about her watch) to whom he hasn't been properly introduced, the dance hall is also dangerous because, for men, it is "effeminate." The city is evidently a space where even gender norms are inverted. Tagami, the seductress, is proof of Sudo's fall into the trap of the urban jungle.

With the close-up inserts of objects in this world, Naruse's city is not a psychological space but a materialist one. The subjective dimensions of women's experience that were developed in *Spring Awakens* and *Even Parting* are not evident in *The Angry Street*. Uno Jukichi turns in a good performance as Mori, who undergoes a kind of epiphany in the film, but the other characters are little more than pawns in a game of genre. The family melodrama finally trumps the gangster narrative, which turns out to have been principally a drama about the emergence of juvenile delinquency and the shattering of the family. Naruse's 1949 film *Delinquent Girl* is described as a similar story of youth gone astray in the big city. While the Tokyo locations ground *Angry Street* in the lived history of the postwar city, the discourse on objects, on food and drink, jewelry and purses, constitutes an environment not of space but of things—the things that are coveted, the things that bring pleasure, and the things that signify the economic and sensual construction of everyday life in the modern metropolis.

White Beast
FEMALE PSYCHOSIS

The third film that Naruse made in 1950, *White Beast* (*Shiroi yaju*, 1950), was described by *Kinema Junpo* critic Tsumura Hideo three years later as "so indescribably miserable as to haunt me even today." Tsumura represents the bulk of Japanese critics of the time, who felt that Naruse experienced a terrible slump throughout the 1940s and this film seemed to be "the bottom of the ocean."[46] The critical establishment was clearly not prepared to accept a woman's prison film featuring former prostitutes recovering from venereal diseases, unwanted pregnancies, and estranged lovers. With its catfights, hysterical tantrums, film noir lighting, and dramatic music, *White Beast* is indicative of the new influences of the Hollywood psychological thriller on Naruse. *Caged* (John Cromwell, 1950) initiated a cycle of women's prison movies in the United States that may or may not have been shown in Japan, but the stylistics of *White Beast* draw on the same paranoid woman's films and film noir conventions that preceded the American cycle.

In conjunction with these "thriller" elements, Naruse also returns in this film to some of the educational principles of the "democracy pictures" advocated by SCAP. The film is unambiguous in its platform of reform for prostitution, although it also makes very clear that many women had no choice during the war but to sell their bodies. The White Lily Institution, in which the story is set, is less a prison than a boarding house, located outside the city. Among the staff is a woman doctor, Nakahara (Iino Kimiko), who examines and treats the inmates. Yamamura So plays the institution's director, Izumi, a benevolent father figure to all the wayward young ladies, and a love interest for Nakahara. While American women's prison movies usually feature monstrous female wardens and authoritarian disciplinary male figures,[47] the White Lily offers a more nurturing environment. The inmates are not "masculinized," as they so often are in the Hollywood versions, but feminized through the redemptive model of love represented by the coupling of Nakahara and Izumi.

The title, *White Beast*, refers to the Miura Mitsuko character (Yukawa), who is "tamed" by the institution. (The word *shiroi*, "white," connotes prostitution, and the word *yaju*, "wild beast," is not as masculine as it is in English.) Yukawa defends her activities as a prostitute and is unrepentant and angry about being detained. Prostitution was made illegal in 1946, although the postwar economic collapse, along with the huge influx of American GIs, ensured that the sex industry flourished unabated throughout the occupation. It wasn't until 1956 that the more effective Prostitution Prevention Law was passed, due mainly to the efforts of women's lobby groups.[48] While this law shut down the 340-year-old Yoshiwara district, it also put 260,000 women out of work, forcing them into the unregulated black market of the underground economy. At one point in *White Beast*, a bureaucrat or politician visits the facility and gives a condescending speech to the women, accusing them of being selfish and greedy and "dragging down the whole of Japanese womanhood," to which Yukawa heckles back, "Who are our customers?" It is to Naruse's credit that he tackles issues of the sex trade that "polite society" did not want to address. The film may not take a stand, finally, on the feminist issues that it raises, and it may cloak them in the exaggerated designs of Hollywood-style paranoia, but it nevertheless acknowledges the complexity of the shifting norms regarding women and their bodies in postwar Japan. Although the bureaucrat represents the state, his speech is clearly out of sync with the more sympathetic approach of the White Lily staff.

The ideological project of the film is thus to negotiate between the ethos of democratic "liberation" and freedom of choice, and the dangers of the sex trade. The main path of reform is hard work, and the women spend their days at sewing machines, while in the evenings they dance to jazz music. Yukawa is a hysterical heroine who manages to retain her high kitschy fashions and permed hair throughout her stay at the White Lily. She is also a kleptomaniac who develops a crush on Izumi. Yukawa insists that she is "not dirty," but that she has simply followed her own free will, yet, in 1950, the reform of prostitution was evidently linked to a medical discourse. She finally acknowledges that she has syphilis, and Izumi tries to convince her that the treatment for the disease will also cure her bad attitude. She tries and fails to seduce him, and finally trips and falls down the stairs (a classic device of American melodrama of the 1940s), and she confesses to her thievery. Yukawa is last seen in silhouette as a solitary figure against the sunrise, while Izumi shares a romantic cigarette with Dr. Nakahara.

Yukawa's rather dramatic experiences are paralleled by several other

34. Transitional montage sequence in *White Beast* (*Shiroi yaju*, 1950), Toho.

stories involving other inmates/patients at the White Lily. The community of women gives the film its anthropological character, despite the highly stylized mise-en-scène and Miura's histrionic performance. Yukawa's sister Sayama is discovered to be pregnant, and she decides to keep the child despite the absence of a father. Another girl, Ono (Nakakita Chieko), is reunited with her lover from before the war, but he has a hard time accepting that she has not been faithful. Ono is ashamed of herself, although she was driven to prostitution out of hunger and has recovered from her venereal disease. However, after this repatriated so-called lover rapes her, Izumi convinces Ono that it means he really loves her, and they are eventually reunited. Yet another resident, Masuda, with whom Yukawa has a jealous fight on the all-ladies dance floor, ends up going completely mad and dies from her advanced case of syphilis. Finally, an undeveloped subplot concerns Izumi's accountant who is embezzling money from the institution, linking the White Lily to the larger scourge of postwar corruption.

Stylistically, *White Beast* marks a significant departure for Naruse, and it demonstrates his flexibility and versatility as a director. This is Naruse's third film with cinematographer Tamai Masao, who is responsible for the director's most popular films of the 1950s.[49] The photography of the institution, a large rambling house with long corridors, dormitories, and offices, lends the narrative a sense of psychological complexity that is somewhat lacking from the script itself. The staircase is singled out several times with close-up shots of feet on the stairs to emphasize urgency and suspense. Naruse's favorite "shoe" motif appears in a clever cut from a foot tapping on the evening dance floor to a shoe pumping the pedal of a sewing machine the next morning, effectively linking the routines of daily life at the White Lily.

Despite its cinematographic achievements, *White Beast* is above all a social issue film. In the implied sensationalism of the topic of women's sexual hygiene, its ethnographic aspect borders on exploitation. Naruse's next film follows in this pattern, this time taking the scandalous lives of high-flying businesswomen as its titillating topic.

The Battle of Roses
WOMEN IN CHARGE

The Battle of Roses (*Barra gassen*, 1950) is based on a newspaper serial about a woman-owned cosmetic company. The rather convoluted story, involving three sisters and their various trials and tribulations, unfolds in a narrative made up of many short scenes. The average length of a scene is eighty-two seconds, for a total running time of ninety-seven minutes. Many shots end abruptly,[50] crudely cutting off with clipped dialogue, and until the very last scene, there are few of the scene-setting atmospheric effects that so often distinguish Naruse's cinema. The quick pace of the film creates the sense of fast-paced city life, as the sets and locations include offices, homes and apartments, bars, cafés, restaurants and inns, movie theaters, trains, cars and streets, a golf course, an employee exercise room, a rooftop, and a hospital. Moreover, the successes and scandals of the company are reported in various newspapers and magazines, which together with the moviegoing and the advertising—and the cosmetic business itself—situate the story within a discursive network of mass media and urban culture.

In some respects, *The Battle of Roses* is a caution against the dangers implicit in giving women new privileges and powers. Masako (Miyake Kuniko), the eldest daughter who takes over the company after the eldest brother dies, marries off her sister Hinako (Wakayama Setsuko) to a company employee whom she refuses to promote. Instead, Masako names her own inexperienced boyfriend as vice president. Hinako's hus-

35. Wakayama Setsuko, Miyake Kuniko, and Katsuragi Yoko in *The Battle of Roses* (*Bara gassen*, 1950), Shochiku and Film Art Association.

band tries to kill her (by boiling her alive in her bath), has an affair, and is finally transferred to Hokkaido. The third sister, Chisuzu (Katsuragi Yoko), moves into her own apartment and is seeing a man without marrying him, just to try it out, for "practical freedoms" and "experience," refusing any arranged marriage her elder sister might plan for her. Of course her lover turns out to be married and destitute, and his poor wife confronts Chisuzu to extort money. Of the three women, Hinako, the good, suffering sister, ends up most likely to marry the film's single attractive, honest man, but she has yet to get her divorce from the husband in Hokkaido by film's end. Immersed in the world of popular culture, the cosmetics industry stands in the film as "women's business," but the women themselves seem unable to manage it without falling prey to the manipulative corruption of consumer capitalism. Various platitudes about women's biological need to be helped and their softness indicate the women's insecurity and vulnerability, as if they had been thrown into a man's world without adequate preparation.

Although the setting is dynamically opposed to that of a film like *Conduct Report on Professor Ishinaka*, there is nevertheless an ethnographic dimension to *The Battle of Roses*, even if it is represented in the terms of an exploitation film, drawing on the sensationalism of the "liberated" woman. The exaggerated costumes of haute couture, flowery kimonos, and argyle sweaters, often clashing together, make this in some respects Naruse's most kitsch-laden film, as he uses visual style to maintain the sensationalism of the original newspaper serial. The pettiness of the narrative conflicts is a far cry from the dramatic intensities of other occupation films such as *Spring Awakens*, *Taro Urashima*, and *White Beast*. The whole film is almost like a bad dream from which the characters awaken in the last scene. On a rainy afternoon, Masako and Chisuzu are reconciled and as they look out into the garden, the rain suddenly stops and they decide to start over.

Ginza Cosmetics
RETURN TO THE WATER TRADE

With the three films released in 1951, Naruse's career began to revive. All three titles—*Ginza Cosmetics, Dancing Girl*, and *Meshi*—feature female protagonists in urban settings, and especially in the first and last of these films, the atmosphere and ambiance of the particular urban neighborhoods are developed in some detail, so that they become constitutive elements of the story. This realism, combined with finely drawn psychological portraits of women in tenuous romantic and family relationships, becomes the foundation of his best films of the 1950s and 1960s. References to the war and occupation continue to be made, but there is little trace of the democratic imperatives of CIE censorship. Whether Naruse finally felt more free to follow his instincts, or whether the right material just happened to come his way, it is hard to tell. Naruse himself admitted in a 1960 interview that starting with *Ginza Cosmetics* (*Ginza gesho*, 1951), "I seemed to have relaxed."[51]

The screenwriter for *Ginza Cosmetics*, Kishi Matsuo, had written several critical essays on Naruse in the 1930s and clearly understood the director's strengths and potential.[52] Naruse was inspired by his script, which was based on an original story by Inoue Tomoichiro, but insisted that it be made more realistic. According to Audie Bock, "Kishi rewrote, embellishing with locations, characters and conversations he and Naruse knew from their own Ginza back-street bar-hopping."[53] Naruse himself notes that for *Ginza Cosmetics*, he took a "hint" from the Hayashi Fumiko story "Fallen Women," which he had left behind at Shochiku in the early 1930s. Indeed, there is much foreshadowing of subsequent Hayashi-based films to be found in *Ginza Cosmetics*. As a few days in the life of a bar hostess, this film is above all a forerunner of the 1960 film *When a Woman Ascends the Stairs* (*Onna ga kaidan o agaru toki*), although Tanaka Kinuyo's character Yukiko is much farther down the ladder of hostess "society" than the sophisticated Takamine Hideko character of the 1960 film. One of Yukiko's friends, Shizue (Hanai Ranko), is an early version of Kin in *Late Chrysanthemums* (*Bangiku*, 1954), a hardnosed survivor who "makes all the right moves." As she explains to

36. Yukiko loses a customer. Tanaka Kinuyo in *Ginza Cosmetics* (*Ginza gesho*, 1951), Shin Toho.

Yukiko, she takes care of the money angle first so that she can always do what she wants.

Among the accomplishments of *Ginza Cosmetics* is a dedramatization of narrative as the film follows Yukiko through a series of events that serve mainly to display the difficulties of her life and her strength of character in the face of the hardships facing a bar hostess. Tanaka's character is partially a reprise of streetwalking characters she had recently played in films by other directors, such as Mizoguchi's *Women of the Night* (*Yoru no onnatachi*, 1948). Reviewing *Ginza Cosmetics* in *Eiga Hyoron*, Fujii Shigeo says that although he thought he had seen enough of Kinuyo—and he had written off Naruse as a poor, B-movie director—he was pleasantly surprised by this film. He points out that Naruse does an excellent job with the child, Yukiko's son, Haruo: "the child, who could be such a burden to Kinuyo, is not used as a means of drawing sympathy from the audience, as the typical cheap tearjerker would do."[54] Left on his own while his mother is working, Haruo is a self-sufficient child, but when he gets lost one day, Yukiko runs off to find him. She is obliged to leave the nice young man she is with, Ishikawa, who is visiting Tokyo, with her sister Kyoko (Kagawa Kyoko), who wastes no time falling in love and marrying him.

The relationship between the sisters is very close, and it is this sympathetic relationship among women that Naruse may have gotten from Hayashi, and which he develops in a number of later films. Yukiko is disappointed about losing Ishikawa, but does not begrudge her sister for making a successful match. The two women have a number of conversations about how hard it is to find nice, reliable male companions. At the end of the film, Yukiko is left alone with her child, vowing to work hard for his sake. Nothing has changed, although over the course of the film, Yukiko has been shortchanged by one customer and nearly raped by a wealthy patron whom she had approached for a loan. Her vulnerability and good nature are contrasted to some of the women with whom she works, who consort with gangsters or, like Shizue, are selfish and manipulative. Ishikawa is originally Shizue's date, and she asks Yukiko to "take care of him" while she is busy with another boyfriend; then Yukiko loses him to Kyoko when she has to search for her son. Yukiko smokes and drinks heavily, at one point staggering home after a long night; but with Ishikawa she becomes a polite, demure lady, suggesting briefly that she is not dissembling for him, but that she has some other "proper" personality from which she has "fallen" to her role as single mother and bar hostess.

Fujii complains that aside from some landmark sites such as the Hattori building and the covered-over Sanjukanbori, the "smell" of the Ginza is missing from Naruse's treatment of the famous district. He finds it less satisfying than the treatment of Asakusa in Naruse's 1935 film *Three Sisters with Maiden Hearts*.[55] In fact, Naruse seems to have used sets for many of the Ginza exteriors, which become deeply shadowed corridors between closely built houses. The crowded streets of bars are lit with a panoply of neon signs in English as well as Japanese (Yukiko works at a bar called the Bel Amie, which Ishikawa recognizes from a Maupassant story). Locations are used extensively as well, though, and in her tour of the area, Yukiko points out to Ishikawa the changes that have taken place since the war. There may be no American GIs to be seen (in keeping with the CIE policy), but the sense of postwar transition is strongly felt.

Naruse also throws in his trademark street musicians, itinerant children's storytellers, and vagrants, which give the district the feel of the folk subsisting on the margins of the commodity capitalism suggested by the neon display. Yukiko's own home in the Ginza, situated above a music teacher, is a neighborly place where everyone helps look out for her son Haruo. With the combination of location shooting and sets, Naruse blends the prewar shoshimin-eiga into the setting of the postwar city, effectively incorporating the prewar culture of the ruined city into the narrow alleys running behind the new facade.

Yukiko herself is something of a prewar relic, slightly out of sync with the new gaudy culture, and the film leaves her forging ahead, walking over a bridge with her son, into a future that seems to hold no place for her noble character. This is perhaps the point where Naruse's modernity becomes recognizable as a discourse of ressentiment. Melodramatic loss and nostalgia take on the symbolic weight of social allegory, and *Ginza Cosmetics* may be seen within the framework of victim consciousness that Yoshimoto has identified in postwar Japanese cinema. Yukiko is like a Hayashi character, a survivor despite all odds, and her trials and tribulations need to be recognized in terms of cultural critique and the realist depiction of the life of a bar hostess as a new tendency of postwar Japan, marking Naruse's ongoing reworking of the tendency film genre of the early 1930s.

Dancing Girl
THE CURSE OF FREEDOM

Dancing Girl (*Maihime*, 1951) may not be as successful a picture as *Ginza Cosmetics* or *Meshi*, but it is an important transitional film, as Naruse deploys some of the flamboyant melodramatic devices that he used in the 1930s in the context of a story that is very much a postwar narrative. Elaborate, distinctive camera movements at moments of high dramatic tension tend to displace acting technique in the representation of psychological states. Used only in conjunction with the two main women characters, Namiko (Takamine Mieko) and her daughter Shinako (Okada Mariko), the camera movements now seem to detract from the emotional weight of the drama. From the failure of this film, we can glimpse something of the change in the aesthetics of realism implicit in the representation of the democratic self of postwar Japan.

Writing about the "discovery of interiority" in the Meiji period, Karatani Kojin notes that "interiority is not something that had always existed, but only appeared as the result of the inversion of a semiotic constellation." He links the rise of *genbun itchi*, the vernacular writing system that was both less stylized and less formal than the dominant Chinese-based system, with a new dramatic performance style in which meaning was constituted "as an inner voice recorded and expressed by the face."[56] The expressive face replaces the decorated doll-faces and masks of *bunraku*, no, and kabuki. Karatani's thesis on interiority effectively challenges Roland Barthes's essentialist argument that such interiority is unknown in Japan.[57] Karatani demonstrates how it was incorporated into Japanese culture during the Meiji period. Moreover, he indicates how closely bound were the developments in writing and performance, and how these in turn are linked to landscape painting. He effectively presents a theory of early Japanese modernity within the terms of visual

37. Takamine Mieko and Yamamura So in *Dancing Girl* (*Maihime*, 1951), Toho.

culture. Over a hundred years later, in postwar Japan, we can see how this "semiotic inversion" is recapitulated in the cinema.

Within the dictates of occupation policy, and within a cultural milieu determined to recover from a decade of self-deceit and governmental deception, a new realism demanded a new cinematic language. Western criticism has tended to label this postwar realism as a form of humanism, mainly because it was eminently "legible" to foreigners who therefore championed it as "universal." By looking more closely at Naruse's cinema and the contradictions that are apparent in it, we can perhaps better identify this humanist realism as a depiction of interiority.

Set in Kamakura, *Dancing Girl* is in some respects an important precursor to Naruse's 1954 masterpiece *Sound of the Mountain* (*Yama no oto*), which is also based on a Kawabata novel. The problem with *Dancing Girl* is that Shindo Kaneto's script remains bound to a novelistic structure with multiple characters and storylines, and the main plotline of a disintegrating marriage gets lost in the mix. Also, unlike the 1954 film, Naruse turns it into a bourgeois drama, treating the upper-middle-class lifestyle somewhat histrionically, along the lines of his 1937 film *Learn from Experience*, indulging in the decadence of fashion and architectural kitsch. The clutter of bulky Western furniture in small Japanese homes is awkward, and the characters seem uncomfortable. One of the key scenes in *Dancing Girl* is the one in which Yagi (Yamamura So), Namiko's husband, confronts her at the dinner table in front of their two teenage children. He rudely states that he knows about Namiko's affair, an unspoken truth that the family has long known but never acknowledged. The awkwardness of the scene is enhanced by the tightness of the furniture in the room, and it is difficult to feel sympathy for any of the characters.

Takamine Mieko was at the time one of the top movie stars, renowned for her beauty and glamour, and the film was likely designed as a vehicle for her. Frequently dressed in a tailored white suit, she seems to glow, and her impassive face is in fact as inexpressive as that of a doll. When someone compliments her on an elegant kimono, her husband notes that during the war, such luxury goods were considered to be vulgar. As a former ballerina and now the owner of a ballet school, Namiko indulges in such luxuries, but the film is ambivalent in its treatment of such things. Namiko's daughter Shinako (Okada) is an aspiring dancer, and the penultimate scene features her prima donna performance in *Swan Lake*. Although she is of marriageable age, Shinako rebuffs a potential suitor by saying that she is frightened of marriage because she might end up like her mother, caught up in an adulterous affair and a loveless marriage.

All the characters in *Dancing Girl* seem perpetually unhappy. Namiko's affair with Takehara (Nihonyanagi Hiroshi) has been going on for twenty years and tortures them both. One of the dancers in Namiko's school has left to become a stripper. The plague that affects all these characters so deeply is the curse of freedom. Indeed, the film is littered with platitudes of Kawabata's nostalgia such as: "When Japan lost the war it lost its spiritual beauty. . . . freedom has been haunting Japan for quite some time." While the topic of adultery was previously prohibited,[58] here it is treated as symptomatic of a society obsessed with debilitating freedoms. Within the nostalgic longing for an irretrievable past is a subtle critique of occupation ideology and the social instability that has accompanied the "democratic revolution."

The film ends with Namiko finally choosing her estranged husband over her lover. Although the decision is sudden and fairly arbitrary, Naruse films it with a huge sweeping crane shot accompanied by romantic ballet music bleeding in from the previous scene. Namiko enters the garden of the Kamakura home, where Yagi is pacing restlessly, and the camera follows her movement until Yagi catches sight of her. After a series of reverse shots, their eyes finally meet and the camera moves up and back into the overhanging pines, leaving the couple facing each other on the threshold of the lighted house. If *Dancing Girl* can be considered in terms of the negotiation of a woman's rights and responsibilities within the new context of personal freedoms, it also confirms David Pollack's assessment of Kawabata's aesthetics of resignation.

Pollack says of Kawabata's literature that his male characters are gods, "inactive centers of narrative galaxies around which starry females eternally revolve in fulfillment of their fated destinies. Threatened male authority is undoubtedly the dominant theme of Kawabata's novels, but that authority emerges relatively unscathed, thanks to the active intervention of women—whose very existence, after all, depends on keeping it propped up."[59]

In *Dancing Girl* Yamamura So's character of Yagi is eminently respectable, a university professor who wrote a book that is said to be slightly critical of conservative Japanese historiography and thus potentially consistent with the new regime. While neither he nor Namiko are fully fleshed out as characters in the film version, it is very much the woman who is the unstable element in the edifice of the family, whose happiness is sacrificed for the upholding of the system. Likewise, Naruse's stylized treatment of Namiko's capitulation tends to cancel her interiority and displace it onto a transcendental gesture in keeping with the deus ex machina ending.

Meshi
THE SALARYMAN'S WIFE

In his first adaptation of a Hayashi Fumiko novel, Naruse produced his first strong postwar female protagonist, the housewife Michiyo played by Hara Setsuko. *Meshi* (*Repast*, 1951) opens with an epigraph attributed directly to the author: "How could I love the pitiful human lives more than I do, the pitiful human lives, which survive in this infinitely wide universe?" The film version of *Meshi* was made in the same year that Hayashi died, 1951, and was based on a serialized story that she left incomplete. Often translated simply as "food," *meshi* also refers to "cooked rice" and to the simple tastes of ordinary people. It also has implications of a useless life, or the unglamorous necessities of life.[60] In adapting Hayashi's novel, Naruse uses the device of voice-over, through which the literary voice of first-person narration so crucial to the modern Japanese novel is used to develop an "interiority" and sense of self.

Hayashi's story was about a marriage, but Naruse's film places the emphasis more directly on the housewife, played by Hara Setsuko. In voice-over she describes her neighborhood in Osaka, where the film is set, then continues to describe her life there over the film's opening shots: "My husband is sitting at the dining table. I go to the kitchen to cook the miso soup. Yesterdays and tomorrows, 365 days a year, we have the same mornings and nights. I wonder if the lives of women are simply to get older and will end in the kitchen and the table." The tedium of everyday life is broken by the arrival of her husband's niece, Satoko (Shimazaki Yukiko), who has run away from her home in Tokyo. Her flirtation with Michiyo's husband, Hatsunosuke (Uehara Ken), disturbs the household, and Michiyo decides to visit her own family in Tokyo to think things over. She meets an old boyfriend, Kazuo (Nihonyanagi Hiroshi) but then learns that Satoko is also interested in him and has even gone to a hot-springs resort with him. Michiyo meets up with her husband in Tokyo and she decides to return to Osaka with him. On the train going back, she says in voice-over: "My husband is sitting beside me. His eyes are closed. His usual profile. A man who is floating in the river called life, he is tired, still fighting. Living with this man, I am seeking happiness for us together. Could it be my true happiness? Maybe this is what a woman's happiness is."

This ambivalent return to the role of housewife is not in Hayashi's original. She left the novel unfinished, just as the husband and wife were establishing their lives apart. While Keiko McDonald describes Naruse's ending as a happy one, I'm not so sure.[61] Michiyo may be ready to resign herself to her role as a good wife, but there is nothing in the film to suggest that this might bring happiness. The contradictions of the ending of *Meshi* are very much in keeping with Hollywood melodrama, in which, as Laura Mulvey has pointed out, more is stirred up than can possibly be settled. If no closure is possible, any reconciliation speaks of "mute surrender to society's overt pressures [and] defeat by its unconscious laws."[62] Michiyo's decision to return to her humdrum life is motivated only by the lack of options available to her. According to Ide Toshiro, who cowrote the screenplay with Tanaka Sumie, he and Tanaka thought the film should end with a divorce, but Toho (presumably producer Fujimoto Sanezumi) insisted that a film that was sympathetic to the wife could not possibly end in divorce. Ide says that rather than fight for her version, Tanaka walked away from the project.[63] In any case, as one of the contemporary critics, Toda Takao, notes, the final voice-over narration does not sound much like Hayashi; he suggests it was added for "mass appeal."[64]

Meshi works principally because of the intensity of Michiyo's inchoate desires. She herself seems uncertain of what she wants, and Hara's performance is central to the film's ambivalence and contradictoriness. Although she is attracted to Kazuo, she reminds him that she is still married and is unable to act on her desires. Satoko, the upstart niece, acts on all her impulses, and while she may be depicted as unvirtuous and unwise, there is no question that her influence is deeply unsettling

38. Hara Setsuko and Uehara Ken in *Repast* (*Meshi*, 1951), Toho.

to the marriage. Michiyo is very critical of this modern young woman, yet Satoko's presence enables her to question her life as a housewife. Uehara Ken plays the husband, Hatsunosuke, as the epitome of the lazy, bored salaryman. The tedium of housework is matched only by the lack of passion in their marriage. If the niece Satoko is "a strange product of postwar Japan" (and Shimizu notes that in old-fashioned melodramas she would be something of a sorceress), the film is definitely "something that connects directly to contemporary life," as another critic put it.[65]

Like the Hollywood melodrama, in *Meshi* there are strong undercurrents of sexuality, of repressions and unspeakable desires that underscore the narrative. There are also brief explosions of music, bad weather, and hysterical laughter that point to these tensions. As Mulvey suggests of director Douglas Sirk's women's films, "it is as though the fact of having a female point of view dominating the narrative produces an excess which precludes satisfaction."[66] Despite Hayashi's epigraph that opens the film, it is clear that we are not, after all, being asked simply to pity "*human* lives in this infinitely wide universe," but specifically women's lives in postwar Japan. From Hayashi, Naruse takes the settings of the Osaka and Tokyo neighborhoods and downtown streets. It may be a film about housework, but Michiyo's unsettledness is not unrelated to her adventures outside the house.

One critic compares *Meshi* to Ozu's *Early Summer* (*Bakushun*, 1951), pointing out that where "Ozu's world is closed, the world depicted in *Meshi* is an open one."[67] Futaba Juzaburo describes *Meshi* as "a much broader and social work." As a drama of manners (*fuzokugeki*), he says the film is lively, and he admires Naruse's ability to sustain the emotional tension. The comparison with *Early Summer* is significant here, as it indicates how the directors' styles were significantly diverging in the postwar era. For Futaba, Naruse's film is more directly connected to contemporary life, whereas he sees Ozu as being preoccupied with the feelings of the older generation in *Early Summer*. *Meshi*, he says, is "not an old curio sitting on a shelf," and indeed Naruse's narrative is far more grounded in the actions and motivations of the characters, whereas by 1951, Ozu had settled into the stately rhythms of static compositions that mark his mature period.

The Osaka neighborhood where Michiyo and Hatsunosuke live is an extraordinarily detailed set, including a narrow street leading onto a cross street. Many of the neighbors are introduced as secondary characters, providing a flavor that led critic Shimizu Chiyota to say that "the Osaka white-collar worker is shown with a documentary precision and flavor."⁶⁸ Michiyo's family house in a Tokyo suburb near Yano Station is likewise handled with care. When Hatsunosuke takes his niece sightseeing through Osaka, leaving Michiyo at home scrubbing floors, the crosscutting establishes a discrepancy of space and mobility that threatens the marriage. However, Michiyo's day with her old school friends and her walks through Tokyo are important scenes that place her in public spaces.

Outside the home, there is nothing for Michiyo except women envying her marriage, and by taking us through these spaces, Naruse situates his story in the historically specific setting of the postwar city. The final reconciliation of the couple is essentially a deus ex machina, one very reminiscent of Rossellini's *Voyage to Italy*, in which George Sanders and Ingrid Bergman, on the verge of a divorce, are miraculously reunited by being swept into a Saint's Day parade in southern Italy. Michiyo and Hatsunosuke are likewise briefly swamped by a crowd of street musicians in Tokyo, and it may be the spirit of the *shitamachi* by which they are able to redeem their lives in Osaka, but it lacks the miraculousness of Rossellini. This is not to critique Naruse, but to suggest that the contradictions and pitifulness of the lives depicted in *Meshi* are not so easily redeemed. They are far too embedded in the fabric of postwar Japanese society.

Meshi is Naruse's first collaboration with scriptwriters Tanaka Sumie and Ide Toshiro, who continued to provide scripts for him throughout the decade, and they do a good job of reducing the dialogue and narrative material so as to avoid the problems of *Dancing Girl*. One might argue that Naruse's adaptation of Hayashi transforms her work into melodrama, simply by virtue of the structures of cinematic language and its privileging of the facial close-up. Hara's acting is singled out by many of the contemporary critics, and it is indeed one of her most nuanced performances. When Michiyo learns that Satoko has not only been flirting with her husband, but has also gone out with a man who Michiyo herself has become attracted to since learning of her husband's disloyalties, she says nothing to the girl. Instead she turns away and, sitting on the step to the garden, breaks out into laughter. Fade out to a new scene. Hara relies on gesture and facial expressions to convey her disappointment with her husband and her inarticulate desire for some kind of change in her life, and her performance here goes well beyond the masklike smile that she is most known for in her films with Ozu.

As a melodramatist, Naruse does not aestheticize suffering in the ways that a director like Mizoguchi does but remains grounded in the familiar setting of the lower-middle-class home and the shitamachi. Inserted close-ups of objects pictured from a high angle that flatten them against the tatami floor—an ashtray, coffee cups, shoes—help to establish the detail of material culture that constitute the rituals of everyday life. An ashtray out of place tells a story; shoes turned the wrong way around tell another. A neighbor runs after her husband every morning with the lunch that he repeatedly forgets. As several contemporary reviewers pointed out, Naruse proved with *Meshi* and *Ginza Cosmetics* that he excelled in the portrayal of emotion (*shinkyo sakuhin*)—and not only the emotions of the central Michiyo character, but the whole constellation of characters in which she moves.[69]

In adapting Hayashi's literature to the screen, there is no question that Naruse was responsible for taming it for public consumption. As Toda Takao noted in a review that carefully compares the film with Hayashi's unfinished novel, Naruse's Osaka is a picture-postcard view of the city, and the film for this critic is "the polar opposite of the semi-documentary form which Hayashi Fumiko was trying to work out in her novel." Where she left her characters to wander through the novel without any obvious direction, Naruse's film jettisons the realism of incompletion with the structure of closure. As we shall see in subsequent adaptations, he smoothes out Hayashi's rough edges; but even so, he brought her work to a wider audience and, with actors like Hara Setsuko, brought her characters to life.

From her earliest autobiographical, confessional pieces published in some of the first women's literary journals in the 1920s, to her recognition as a novelist in the 1950s, Hayashi's writing was consistently stigmatized by the diminutive label of women's writing. In the 1920s, "women's style" referred to a specific set of conventions that Joan Ericson describes as "attributes presumed to be natural in a woman's voice": "sentimental lyricism and impressionistic, non-intellectual, detailed observations of daily life."[70] The conundrum of women's writing is, as Ericson notes, resolved only by finding a means of preserving the specificity of female experience without reducing the work to the gendered identity of the author,[71] which suggests the importance of Naruse's contribution. His interest in women's writing and a woman's genre seems to come not from an interest in women or feminism, but from the emotionalism and narrative possibilities that he brings out in Hayashi's work.

If several critics accuse him of catering to a mass audience, we need to ask what the gender of that mass audience might be, and to recognize Naruse's accomplishment in bringing this work into the public sphere.

Meshi was originally scheduled to be directed by Chiba Yasuki and was offered to Naruse only when Chiba became ill. Ide Toshiro says that it was unusual for Naruse to be asked to substitute for a younger and less established director, and moreover, because he had not made a successful film since the 1930s, some Toho executives were reluctant to give him such a valuable star-studded property to direct.[72] Ever the company man, Naruse humbly accepted the project, and its huge success propelled him into the next decade with a string of critical and commercial hits.

Okuni and Gohei
BACK TO JAPAN AGAIN

Naruse's last film of the occupation period is a surprising return to jidai geki. Just as he was establishing himself as a master of the postwar shoshimin-eiga, he took on an adaptation of a Tanizaki play set in the Edo period. *Okuni and Gohei* (*Okuni to Gohei*, 1952) may well have been Toho's attempt to match the international success of *Rashomon*, which won the top prize at the Venice Film Festival in 1951. Certainly the success of *Rashomon* in Japan and abroad spawned a rash of spectacular period films, briefly reviving the "back to Japan" movement as the occupation prohibitions against representing the feudal past were gradually relaxed. Naruse's film concludes with a brief critique of the samurai code of bushido, anticipating the more critical manifestations of the genre of the late 1950s and 1960s.

Okuni and Gohei is about a high-born woman, Okuni (Kogure Michiyo), who travels around the country with Gohei (Otani Tomoemon), a samurai retainer who is in service to her. They are in search of Tomonojo (Yamamura So), who has killed the man who was Okuni's husband and Gohei's master, and they cannot return to their lord's home until they have fulfilled their duty of hunting down and killing Tomonojo. Although Okuni pays lip service to this task, a flashback indicates that Tomonojo was her first love. Her family arranged her marriage with Iori, a brutal, unloving man, forcing her to break up with the gentle, flute-playing Tomonojo. In some respects this is an extremely simple, almost minimalist film that centers on Okuni and Gohei's complicated relationship. When Okuni comes down with a fever, Gohei attends to her, and the two are drawn closer together despite their relationship of mistress and vassal.

In the climactic, penultimate scene, Tomonojo confronts the two travelers with the knowledge of their relationship. He has been following

39. Kogure Michiyo and Otani Tomoemon in *Okuni and Gohei* (*Okuni to Gohei*, 1952), Toho.

them, haunting Okuni with his flute, which she recognizes. He begs them not to kill him but to abandon their quest and the samurai codes to which they are bound, encouraging them to realize their love outside the closed society to which they plan to return. However, Okuni orders Gohei to kill Tomonojo, who defends himself with only a piece of bamboo. Before his last breath, the dying man confesses to Gohei that he and Okuni were once lovers. She denies it, although as viewers, we have been offered the truth of Tomonojo's version of events. As the couple head back home, the sound of the flute follows them, suggesting that Tomonojo's death will destroy their attempts at future happiness.

Tanizaki's original play, written in 1921, has been described as "a modest and ironic parody of a traditional *kabuki* vendetta play."[73] Naruse and scriptwriter Yasumi Toshio have added a lengthy prologue to the short one-act play, extending the aimless wandering of Okuni and Gohei and delaying the appearance of Tomonojo. While Tanizaki has more than half the drama devoted to the confrontation between the samurai and the lady with her retainer, Naruse waits until the last half hour of the ninety-minute film before Tomonojo speaks in the present (although he is seen in flashback and in disguise, following the couple). Yamamura So's language and performance are extremely unusual for a jidai geki. His language is modern and not the faux-Edo dialogue that is conventionally used. Perhaps because of this shift in emphasis, Tanizaki's parody is somewhat overshadowed by the love story, so that the critique of the samurai code, articulated by Tomonojo, seems abruptly tacked onto a film that otherwise indulges in the mannered depiction of aristocratic Edo-era aesthetics.

With its final scenes set amid a meadow of tall grasses dotted with stone lanterns, and hills rising in the background, Naruse emulates some of the nature motifs of *ukiyo-e*. The interior sets are all elegantly decorated inns where Okuni and Gohei stop on their travels. Their journey takes them through small towns where they see a Chikamatsu puppet play, a community dance with music and singing, and the various signs of the seasons changing. Okuni is always dressed in fine kimonos, although Kogure's makeup looks more 1950s than Edo-era. The film is indeed a beautiful one, if somewhat clichéd in its visual style, as Naruse indulges in the orientalism of Japanese kitsch. The eroticism of Tanizaki's story is conveyed with a subtlety of restrained passion. The flute music with which Tomonojo teases the couple creates a sensuous tension that is furthered by Naruse's use of dolly shots at moments of dramatic intensity.

Given the aesthetic treatment of the relationship between Okuni and Gohei, Tomonojo's critique of the samurai way and his plea for a life outside its mores is not terribly convincing, either to the couple who kill him, or to the viewer who has been indulged with the intensities of their illicit relationship. In 1921, Tanizaki's parody of bunraku puppet theater may well have been a radical gesture, but thirty years later, at the end of the American occupation, Naruse's romantic treatment of classical Japanese aesthetics is produced within a very different cultural economy.

Hasumi Shigehiko has suggested that *Okuni and Gohei* is best regarded as an experimental film in which Naruse plays out some of his favorite themes in a context that is practically abstract.[74] He completely sheds the details of everyday urban life in which most of his characters are so deeply immersed. This film is about a man and a woman who struggle with their relationship across the lines of class. The two adjacent rooms, which so often comprise the living space of Naruse's sets, appear repeatedly in this film as the two rooms of an inn. In the scene where Okuni finally says to Gohei that he should no longer address her as "madam," they are seated on opposite sides of the threshold between the two rooms, with the shoji open, but the tatami border between them. For Hasumi, the essence of Naruse's cinema lies in the man and woman theme, especially when one of the partners tends to the other's illness. In *Okuni and Gohei*, the narrative is stripped down to the point where this event is sufficient for what Hasumi calls a "movie-like" scheme.[75]

Especially compared to *Ginza Cosmetics* and *Meshi*, the character of Okuni is less consistent and less grounded than many of Naruse's female characters. Cut off from her "home," abandoned to the trials and tribulations of the journey, she is without direction. She herself seems unsure of which man she loves. The narrative suggests that she is searching for Tomonojo to be reunited with him, not to kill him, but when they finally meet, she is full of vengeance for her unloved dead husband. She even grabs a knife and is prepared to fight him herself. Although she has begged Gohei to abandon the search, he insists on repaying his debt by carrying out the revenge, and she finally capitulates without explanation. Given the romantic themes of the jidai geki films that Naruse made during the war, it does seem as though the stylistics of the period film offer him a melodramatic language, as Hasumi implies. In fact, he continues to use the architectural space of the traditional Japanese home and inn throughout the rest of the decade, virtually abandoning Western furnishings except for offices and public spaces. However, the female subjectivity that he began to explore in the late years of the occupation is a very modern persona that is not sustained in this jidai geki, the last one of his career.

Although Tanizaki's play was published long before the war, at the end of the occupation it may be possible to read it as a parable of misplaced trust and lost opportunity. Okuni and Gohei kill their chance at freedom and are left to face an unchanged world, much as the Japanese found themselves at the end of the American occupation, left at the end of a long journey with only a vague—and dangerous—memory of "home" before the war and defeat. Yamamura So's Tomonojo is a seductive character, and Okuni's attraction to him is palpable despite her final change of heart. If the film is a parable, warning not to let go of democratic reforms, it is admittedly oblique; and it is above all the atmospheric abstraction and haunted ending that lends it the tone of allegory. Naruse's return to jidai geki is symptomatic of the times, inspired primarily by the high returns the genre was garnering in the early 1950s.

The open, unsettled ending of *Okuni and Gohei* is nevertheless a key feature of Naruse's best postwar work, as he develops a modernist style premised on ambivalence and uncertainty. The recurring theme of a man and a woman is also a recurring story of tensions between men and women, of relationships that are doomed to fail and women who are left to fend for themselves. Naruse's characters rarely finish their journeys at the end of the film, as romance never leads them out of this world into another. In this sense, his modernism remains vernacular, in a language of material culture, rather than style, language, and form. His is a "woman's cinema" in its melodramatic treatment of romance as a narrative of desires, of subjectivities on the brink of something new that is perpetually just out of sight. Turning to jidai geki, he is unable to rise above the fossilized language of a stylized repertoire of landscape, gesture, and abstract space, precisely because it evacuates the detritus of everyday life.

Most astonishing about the thirteen films that Naruse made during the American occupation is the wide-ranging discursive repertoire that he explored. During this "noisy period," the director tried out an eclectic series of scripts, from the nascent "democracy pictures" to ambitious literary adaptations, and developed a range of new techniques. Considering the range of uneven material with which he worked, his so-called slump provides considerable insight into occupation culture. Not only did he try out new genres, his films became highly intertextual, as he frequently works against genre conventions. The kissing scene in *Spring*

Awakens, like his "revision" of *Mr. Smith Goes to Washington* and even his rewriting of Hayashi's *Meshi*, are unexpected turns, as these genres provided him with new narrative forms and new types of characters, rather than simply new formulas.

Despite the critical consensus that this period constituted a slump, it is evident that Naruse was working through fundamental issues of visual representation that any cultural renewal necessarily demands. After his initial embrace of democratic ideals and cultural kitsch, we can see how he gradually tempered didacticism into a melodrama of the new Japanese woman. Her biggest tragedy is the failure of the new democracy to provide full emancipation from the constrictions of a society that remained all too familiar at the end of the "confusion era."

5

The Japanese Woman's Film of the 1950s, 1952–1958

> Mount Fuji!
> Here stands a lone woman who does not lower her head to you
> Here is a woman laughing scornfully at you.
> —HAYASHI FUMIKO

Between 1952 and 1958, Naruse directed fourteen feature films, half of which placed in the *Kinema Junpo* top-ten lists. This is the body of work that has confirmed his place among the pantheon of great directors, not only nationally, but internationally. While the films of this period have obvious continuities with those that came before and after, I have chosen to bracket the period with *Mother* (*Okaasan*, 1952) and *Anzukko* (1958) for historical reasons that may be fairly arbitrary but are nevertheless useful means of demarcating this phase of Naruse's career. *Mother* is the director's first film after the end of the occupation, and although occupation censorship had more or less relaxed by 1951 and *Meshi* is really the film that initiated Naruse's postwar comeback, *Mother* belongs to the new era of the film industry in which studios and directors had a freedom of expression that had long been denied. At the other end of the decade, *Anzukko* is the last film that he made in academy aspect ratio, the single exception being *The Stranger within a Woman* (*Onna no naka ni iru tanin*, 1966), and he otherwise permanently shifted from the 1.33:1 academy ratio to the wide Tohoscope format of 2.66:1 after *Anzukko*. These arbitrary bookmarks allow us to look at some of the commonalities within the 1950s films and to better understand how Naruse adapted his particular version of "the woman's film" into a modernist idiom.

An editorial error in a 1993 issue of *Cahiers du cinéma* shows how auteurist film criticism has tended to misread the context of Naruse's filmmaking. In an introduction to two excellent articles by Joel Magny and André Scala, the editors introduce Naruse as the director of a film based on the novel called *Mother* by Maxim Gorky.[1] In fact, Naruse's film of that name is based on a children's essay and its narrative couldn't be more different than Gorky's. Throughout the decade, his films remain grounded not only in a realist aesthetic but in the issues and concerns of Japanese audiences living through a period of profound social upheaval. Far from the "socialist realism" of Gorky, Naruse's realism remains within a humanist vein of Japanese literature. Most of the films are based in literary sources published within twenty years of the films, and many of those novels, including those of Hayashi Fumiko, were originally published in serial form in magazines and newspapers. In other words, despite the formal innovation and emotional poetry of these works that admitted them into the canon of cinematic modernism, they were key contributions to the popular culture of postwar Japan.

Based on these literary sources, Naruse developed the distinctive style for which he is best known. What Yamane Sadao describes as a "rhythm of emotions"[2] is constructed through subtle patterns of editing, lighting, performance style, and set design. The sense of rhythm is created through a fairly regular shot length of eight to ten seconds, for both shot-reverse-shot dialogue scenes, and for the series of shots that make up the transitions between scenes. Nonverbal forms of expression, including the actors' abilities to communicate without words; balanced shot compositions; and the cycling of days, nights, weather, and seasons, are key also to the sense of timing. The flow of the narrative, aided by extradiegetic soundtrack music that is rarely overwrought and frequently silenced, creates an effect of passive contemplation for the viewer. Naruse's realist style is instilled with a poetry of awakening, recognition, and the beauty of small things, and to this extent it partakes of the aesthetics of haiku. In fact, I will suggest that Naruse's cinema enables us to perceive the possible affinities between Benjamin's dialectical image and the awakening associated with haiku poetry.

One of the reasons Naruse was able to develop a distinctive style and aesthetic throughout the decade was that although Toho had structured itself in the 1930s as a "producer system" of production, by the 1950s, Naruse was allowed to assemble his own staff, or *kumi*, with which to work. Tamai Masao shot ten of the fourteen films; Saito Ichiro wrote the scores for all of them; Chuko Satoshi was the art director on seven titles. Of the three scriptwriters (who occasionally worked on the same script), Ide Toshiro gets six credits during these years, Tanaka Sumie receives five, and Mizuki Yoko seven. Equally important are the cast members, especially those who appear frequently in supporting roles: Kato Daisuke (seven credits), Nakakita Chieko (nine), and Kobayashi Keiju (five). Naruse's box office success during the 1950s was also closely tied to the star system, as he worked with many of the top figures of the period, including Mifune Toshiro, Kyo Machiko, and Mori Masayuki, as well as Hara Setsuko, Uehara Ken, and Takamine Hideko. Veteran actors Yamamura So and Sugimura Haruko play leading roles in a number of key titles from the period, and Naruse also helped launch careers for several younger actresses including Kagawa Kyoko, Sugi Yoko, and Okada Mariko.

The "conditions of possibility" within the Japanese studio system as it reestablished itself after the occupation are described by Hasumi Shigehiko as the "miracle" of the "everyday" of Japanese cinema.[3] Hasumi points out that this rebirth coincided with the return of those industry personnel who had been purged during the occupation for their roles in producing propaganda during the war. Fujimoto Sanezumi, who produced nine of Naruse's films during this mid-1950s period, also produced three of the director's films during the war and three during the occupation. According to Nogami Teruyo, he was blacklisted and subsequently depurged in 1952, although her dates are not consistent with other reports.[4] Thus, while the model of the director system established by Kido Shiro at Shochiku prevailed as the most successful system in postwar Japan, and both Kurosawa and Naruse were established as the heads of production units at Toho, Naruse's kumi also included a powerful producer whose role in the stability and success of the director's career through the 1950s should not be underestimated. Even within this system, Naruse made two films during the 1950s at Daei studio, taking at least a few key cast and crew members with him each time, cementing his status as a powerful auteur.

Naruse's style during this period has a certain look, with recurring features, including fairly quick editing, low camera angles for tatami-seated figures, use of 360-degree space, match cutting, and a fairly conventional use of "movie music" soundtracks to emphasize moments of melodramatic emotion. However, despite the stability of his technical crew and the recurring faces of a stable of actors, the films of the 1950s also vary quite a bit aesthetically. The triumvirate Tamai-Chuko-Saito, who were responsible as a team for camera, art direction, and music on seven titles, did not achieve identical results each time. To be sure, they learned to execute some of Naruse's favorite techniques, such as traveling shots of pairs of actors walking and talking, soft-lit night scenes punctuating the narrative with a quiet peacefulness, and the incidental music of street vendors, or *chindonya*. But while many of the films are shot with a shallow depth of field, emphasizing close-ups and tight domestic spaces, others are more expansive with more depth and movement. Stylistically, they share a commitment to domestic space and to the quiet street life of neighbourhoods in urban spaces that range from the shitamachi to suburban developments, back alleys, and more spacious country avenues. During these years, Naruse moves among a range of class settings—from a shack in the Ikebukuro black market in *Floating Clouds* (*Ukigumo*, 1955) to the elegant country residence of a writer and his family in *Anzukko*.

Naruse was evidently recognized as a reliable director and associated with the shoshimin-eiga, and because he remained more or less within the generic structure of the home drama, his cinema of the mid-1950s provides something of a map of the changes taking place within the family and within the class structure of Japanese society. This is of course a highly mediated map, drawn by the authors whose work he adapted to film, as much as by the film industry. A recurring theme is the emergence of a new generation. Many of the films concern the relations between parents and adult children, especially mothers and marriage-age daughters (e.g., *Mother*, *Lightning* [*Inazuma*, 1953], *Late Chrysanthemums* [*Bangiku*, 1954], and *Flowing* [*Nagareru*, 1956]). As the young people of the new generation struggle to find their way out of constricting social norms, their parents are at once the guardians of prewar cultural memory and increasingly redundant in a "reformed" society. The coexistence of the new and the old, the modern and the premodern, extends to all levels of these films, including not only characterization but also mise-en-scène, music, and the detail of everyday life. If the social alienation of the rebuilt city is the biggest threat to happiness, the city also offers a range of new opportunities and social practices to this new generation.

Equally prominent within this group of fourteen films is the childless couple. *Meshi* initiated a cycle of marriage films in which Naruse revisits the salaryman and his wife, who find themselves stranded in their own homes, with little purpose to their lives other than holding on to a piece of real estate. Many of the films pose serious existential questions about modern life, especially for women. In these films we see how the promise of Japanese modernity has failed both men and women, and how psychological stress has affected the stability of the family system. Melodrama is frequently linked to states of mind that are clearly recognizable as depression. Despite the illegality of abortion, it is a recurring theme as women exercise their choice not to be burdened with a child they cannot raise themselves or will not raise in an unloving relationship. Unlike the professional women of the occupation films, the 1950s heroines are either housewives or they work in the water trade (*Late Chrysanthemums* and *Flowing*). The housewives may be able to make some money from working at home, but the few entrepreneurial successes—Kin in *Late Chrysanthemums* and Oshima in *Untamed* (*Arakure*, 1958)—are virtual social outcasts.

While I will not deny Naruse's "honesty" in depicting a world of hardship, the realism of this cinema harbors within it a persistent sense of possibility. The characters may frequently bemoan "this world" as if everything were stacked against them, yet their world is a very particular time and place in which everything is also possible. Through detailed readings of the individual films, I hope to underscore the contemporaneity and novelty of the narratives, starting with the observation that they are not without humor. If they were really as dismal as is sometimes implied, they would not likely have been as popular as they were.

The strength of these films lies also in the performances, particularly those of the female leads, especially Takamine Hideko, Hara Setsuko, Tanaka Kinuyo, and Sugimura Haruko. These women were at the peak of their careers, and their work with Naruse is especially nuanced. Within the context of his shooting style, which relies less on dialogue than on nonverbal expression, these actors are able to convey complicated and deep-seated emotions through their facial expressions, eye movements, and body language. Naruse tends to construct his scenes from many short shots, which can make it difficult for performers to fill out their characters, but many actors—both men and women—delivered some remarkable performances in this group of films. The writer Kawabata Yasunari commented that "Japanese actresses are always expert at playing *mizu-shobai* roles [geisha, prostitutes, professional entertainers, etc.] but their playing of wives and young women is usually bad. It is because in real life, wives and young women hold back something in their emotions while mizu-shobai women show all."[5] Kawabata highlights a certain prejudice in Japanese culture against female expressivity, which is associated with immoral behavior. Thus, the strongest performances by women in Japanese cinema consist of a subtlety, containment, and "holding back." One way of appreciating the performance styles of Hara, Takamine, and Tanaka is to look at the way they exercise restraint even while communicating emotional depths and complexity. Although Takamine can certainly let loose, and does so in *Untamed* and *A Wanderer's Notebook* (*Horoki*, 1962) especially, in most of her films with Naruse, she uses facial expressions and posture rather than dialogue and action to great effect. All of these actresses perfect the "dropped eyes" technique as a means of demonstrating politeness and sorrow; but they also have a good stare, often directed straight at the camera, that indicates a level of resistance within their troubled characters.

Naruse's reliance on actors is underlined by the roles of Takamine Hideko and Uehara Ken in a short film that Naruse made in 1955 as part of a Toho omnibus called *The Kiss* (*Kuchizuke*). The other two shorts in the compilation are by Suzuki Hideo and Kakehi Masanori. Naruse's half-hour segment is called "Women's Ways," and it is interesting to see how he turns his marriage theme into a light comedy within which Takamine manages to add a level of melancholy through her performance. Uehara plays a doctor, and Takamine plays his wife, Tomoko; Nakamura Meiko is a nurse who lives with them as Uehara's assistant. Tomoko accidentally reads the nurse's private diary, discovering that the woman has a crush on her husband. She curbs her jealousy by finding a suitable husband for the young nurse, enticing the local greengrocer (Kobayashi Keiju, in a particularly comic turn) to propose to the girl. Everything goes as planned, Tomoko tells her husband what has happened, and she confesses to the nurse that she read her diary. Once everyone is friends again, the film ends with a coda in which Tomoko is introduced to her husband's new twenty-two-year-old nurse. The woman is strikingly beautiful, and Tomoko realizes that these nurses are infinitely replaceable and she is doomed to a lifetime of jealousy. Takamine's final scene alone in the kitchen is entirely wordless, with only her heavy sigh and a suddenly bleak piano score indicating the darker underside of an otherwise happy ending.

The reprisal of the childless marriage theme in "Women's Ways" is indicative of how Naruse became linked to certain recurring narrative tropes within the industrial mode of production. The short film is also bookended by itinerant musicians passing by the home/clinic—another familiar conceit of Naruse's—and the comic romance between the nurse and the grocer is set against a nighttime festival in the neighborhood. None of these themes or devices is to be found in the other two-thirds of the omnibus, which features other stories about young women facing marriage questions. But perhaps the real significance of this short film is in its signposting of Takamine Hideko's maturation into a wife. Although she would briefly return to the unmarried daughter role in *Flowing* (1956) in the company of a number of older actresses, Takamine was otherwise committed to roles as a married woman or widow in her remaining ten films with Naruse.

In 1955, Takamine married assistant director and screenwriter Matsuyama Zenzo, who was responsible for the script of "Women's Ways," and her own career illustrates some of the contradictions facing women in postwar Japan. Although it was common for actresses to retire as homemakers once they were married, Takamine continued working, she claims, for the sake of the studio. After the success of *Floating Clouds*, she was a lucrative Toho property, and she couldn't let down her fans. She was only thirty-one, and she boldly stated that she wanted to "create a new style of wife who has a job."[6] Very outspoken about the difficulties of her career (which is also in the interests of preserving a certain modesty and humility regarding her talents), Takamine describes her first twenty years as being a "money-making machine" for her family.[7] In 1955, when she became the top star in the country, Takamine published a confessional accounting of her reported salary of ¥500,000 per month. At a time when 48 percent of salaries were less than ¥8,000 per month, it was necessary to assure her fans that there were many expenses associated with her profession, including American cigarettes and a private secretary.[8] It is true that studios did not cover these expenses for their stars,[9] but her "confession" is indicative of her need to bridge the class gap that was widening between her screen persona and her offscreen status as a rich woman.

In many of her roles, Takamine displays the seriousness associated with her hardworking star image; but she also maintains a certain independence and autonomy from the other characters. Naruse's films are by no means humorless, and Takamine—along with Uehara and many of the other stars and character actors—is also capable of smiling. Naruse's contribution to *The Kiss* shows how close his marriage films are to domestic comedy. In addition to the moments of humor, we can point to several recurring structural devices that indicate a level of resistance that challenges the reputation that Naruse has gained as a dark filmmaker. Many of the films of the period end with one or two women walking down a street, over a bridge, or down a path. This is a form of closure that leaves something open, some possibility for hope that lies within the companionship of women, the openness of space, and the directionality of movement. The stories themselves are littered with the signs of social and historical transformation, and Naruse frequently leaves his characters on the threshold of history. Moreover, the sense of hope implied in these endings is not a mere afterthought. It is generated throughout the narratives, through the stubborn willfulness of the characters, and through more subtle techniques of editing and lighting.

The flashes of recognition indicated in the titles of *Lightning* and *Sudden Rain* also occur in other films—moments that pass quickly, almost unnoticed, but moments in which a great deal is immanent. Naruse systematically sidesteps big narrative events such as weddings and funerals, which take place exclusively offscreen. Instead, it is the rare exchange of looks, or a peculiar ellipsis, or even a broken filmstrip (in *Untamed*) that constitutes an event in the film. As the last example suggests, these moments interrupt the realism and are almost reflexive without fully becoming obvious or avant-garde. Indeed, a formal analysis cannot account for their full impact. The simplicity of everyday life, conveyed in the details of architecture, cats, shoes, and costumes, and the rituals and routines of drinking, eating, and smoking, become a discursive counterpoint to the speed and complexity of modernity. The old subsists within the new, but money and the constant exchange of cash keeps everything down to earth. If, as I will suggest, a utopian modernism is articulated within the interstices of Naruse's women's films, it is predicated on the memory of past forms of collectivity embedded in the shitamachi and in Japanese domestic architecture.

Given his predilection for women's stories, the utopian sense of the possible is grounded in the real changes in gender roles that postwar democracy made possible. However, Naruse's ambivalent and ambiguous endings, in which his female characters are poised on the brink of history, confirm the ideological entrapment of women within social structures that continue to restrict their roles as agents of history. In this sense, the utopianism of these narratives is firmly embedded within the ideological. Only through the dialectics of interpretation can their potential be realized, and my method in this chapter is informed by Fredric Jameson's approach to such texts: "to project an imperative to thought in which the ideological would be grasped as somehow at one with the Utopian and the Utopian at one with the ideological ... to formulate a question to which a collective dialectic is the only conceivable answer."[10]

For Jameson, ideology functions within mass culture only by harboring a utopian impulse within it. In the context of the women's film, we can identify this utopian impulse as a form of desire. Romantic longing and repressed sexuality become allegories for the category of the subject who, in Naruse's cinema, is almost always a woman. Actresses supply voices and bodies to women whose literary forms are far more sketchy. "The collective" is not only the Japanese but also the community of women to whom the films were originally marketed, and it might also include contemporary audiences willing to read the films against their ideological grain. The question, quite simply, is that of female subjectivity in postwar Japan.

As I have suggested, the films contain within them moments of immanence that function as clues to the dialectical inversion that they harbor within the context of mass culture. Indeed, the modernist impulse of this cinema consists in its deep ambivalence. In the 1920s and 1930s, the modern came from elsewhere, and as Harootunian explains, Japanese modernity involved "the formation of new subject positions, and gender and sexual identities that actualized the conditions for configuring a distinctive ideology and its numerous variations called modernism."[11] After the war and occupation, the category of the modern had been tested and found wanting, and a new era of economic prosperity had opened up. "Postwar modernism" was the terrain of a new generation, for whom the war and occupation were their parents' problem, placing the question of identity at center stage. For this generation, it was imperative to be both Japanese and modern, but the historical footing for such identity was extremely shaky. In the mass culture of this period we can see how these new identities were formed, and Naruse's cinema provides a special insight into the construction of female subjectivity within the context of postwar modernism.

Naruse's depiction of modernity becomes a modernist modality with the increased alienation and fragmentation of the built environment, the crisis of national identity, and the dissolution of families torn apart by generational rifts. If his films bridge the classical and the modern, it is because the cultural specificity of the Japanese vernacular—the details and rhythms of everyday life—accommodated him to the mainstream of Japanese cinema. The architectural components of empty space—regularly shaped rooms, thresholds, attached rooms with shoji panels, tatami seating arrangements, and cramped entryways—are features that might be read as a kind of vernacular language of space that is fully integrated into Naruse's narrative style.

Throughout the following analyses of the films of the mid-1950s, I will suggest how the architecture functions as a framing device and as a means of inverting and disrupting point-of-view editing patterns. Often the frames of windows and doorways set up objective or pictorial views of the characters that oscillate with the more subjective dimensions of performance. These framing devices are often thresholds and openings, but they also function as symbols of entrapment and containment. The systematic use of frames within frames is thus part and parcel of Naruse's modernism and his affinity with traditional Japanese forms, and at the same time a key to his engagement with women's fiction.

Miriam Hansen's phrase "vernacular modernism" was designed precisely to challenge the distinctions between modernism and classical Hollywood cinema that film theorists have conventionally assumed. If classical Japanese cinema as it evolved in the postoccupation period is exemplified by Naruse's practice, it is a classical cinema without classical editing, and thus an excellent example of what Hansen is pointing toward. When Japanese films began to be distributed abroad in the 1950s, they were viewed as an "art cinema" outside Japan. In the domestic market, however, they tended to be viewed simply as popular culture, albeit in a hierarchical system predicated on auteurism. As Naruse was considered a prestige director, his films were credited with a certain status, especially when he adapted literary texts by notable authors such as Kawabata, Koda Aya (*Flowing*), Tokuda Shusei (*Untamed*), and Hayashi Fumiko.

Walter Benjamin proposes the concept of technique as a means of identifying the formal properties of the artwork and its position in the mode of production.[12] This is especially important to an understanding of how a director like Naruse uses cinematic devices in the context of specific genres, transforming literary material and the materiality of everyday life into the technologies and practices of the mass media. Within the commodification of culture in postwar Japan, Naruse was a major player. He established himself as an important filmmaker during the 1950s by working consistently with a set of generic principles that centered around women and the home. The various generic labels of wife films, mother films, shoshimin-eiga, and home drama sometimes obscure the consistency with which the woman and the home were the formal principles of a product that he produced for a growing industry. More than ever before, women were being targeted by the studios as a major market, and Naruse had the goods.

In my reading of the films of this high point of Naruse's career, it will become evident that the preceding remarks are not equally applicable to all of the films. His most famous title of the era (famous in Japan at least),

Floating Clouds is in some respects anomalous, both in its homelessness and in its different approach to narrative structure than the other titles of the period. Its tragic ending is not matched until *Yearning* (*Midareru*, 1964). Even so, homelessness is the dialectical counterpart of the home drama and is an important means by which Naruse interrogates and challenges the conventions of the genre. Moreover, in my analyses of *A Wife's Heart* (*Tsuma no kokoro*, 1956) and *Anzukko*, I will suggest that these films are not as strong as many of the others, and that they lack that utopian impulse that I have identified above. However, I do not believe this entails that they are "fully ideological," upholding a status quo in which women are perpetually subjugated. The disappointments and defeats registered in these films may still serve a dialectical function for viewers who, even at the time of their original release, regarded them as anthropological "essays" on the practices of everyday life in postwar Japan.

The films of the mid-1950s throw into relief the particular social practices that lie at the basis of so many of the narratives. These practices are consolidated in restrictive family structures, corporate culture, and urban planning. The narratives thus provide "lessons" or demonstrations of a system that holds back the potential of modernity for women without being overtly political or didactic. Significantly, toward the end of the decade, the revolutionary promise of democracy seems to be fading from sight. As traditional cultural forms were appropriated by the conventions of middle-class taste, the promises of democratic reform can be seen to dissolve into consumer capitalism. As the women's movements fostered in the occupation collapsed toward the end of the 1950s, Naruse's cinema also loses its edge. His final depiction of modernity as a vehicle for female subjectivity is set in the Taisho period in *Arakure* (*Untamed*, 1957), in which the energy of a willful woman is displaced onto a fantasy of modernity long past.

Mother and Genre Revisionism

Naruse's 1952 film *Mother* (*Okaasan*) ranked seventh in the 1952 *Kinema Junpo* poll and helped the director establish the "comeback" that was initiated by *Meshi* the year before. The film is perhaps more sentimental than some of the other films from this period of Naruse's career, yet the sentimentality is couched within a distinctive treatment of the home drama, in which the home itself plays a vital role. Based on a story that won a composition contest sponsored by a candy company's "Mother

Glorification Society," Mizuki Yoko's script retains the sweetness of the original by opening and closing the film with voice-over narration spoken in a childish voice by Toshiko, the family's teenage daughter (Kagawa Kyoko). She introduces her mother as someone used to bending while sweeping. Seeing Tanaka Kinuyo, one of the top actresses of the time, coming off a string of feminisuto pictures with Mizoguchi[13] and recently back from a trip to the United States, in this stereotypical role of the prematurely aged housewife triggers the central contradiction of the film.[14] Tsuboi Sakae, author of the novel *Twenty-Four Eyes*, was critical of *Mother* in her review in *Eiga Hyoron*, saying that she found such a bleak picture of motherhood unacceptable. She underlines the film's ambivalence when she says that although she cried along with everyone else at the press screening, she found the stereotypes to be too heavy-handed.[15] The crux of the story involves the question of the mother's remarriage after her husband dies, a possibility that the daughter cannot tolerate. In the end, the mother (who is never actually named in the film) sacrifices her own desires, which makes the daughter happy, but the lingering sense of dissatisfaction and longing is palpable.

The unsettledness of the film's ending refers back to the postwar context, which is introduced at the beginning of the film in no uncertain terms. Before Toshiko's narration even begins, titles introduce the film's setting: "A suburb of Tokyo, 1950. Where humble people live a hard working life." In Toshiko's introduction, she tells us that the family's laundry business was destroyed "when Tokyo burned," and that her small cousin Tetsuo has been living with them since he and his mother were repatriated from Manchuria. Later in the film, after the father dies from cancer, a friend of the family comes to help teach Mother and Toshiko how to run the laundry business that the father had just begun to rebuild before he died. The kids refer to Kimura (Kato Daisuke) as Mr. P.O.W., as he arrives freshly released from a Siberian prison camp.

Thus, the family's story is clearly set in a moment of change and transition, when the city is slowly being rebuilt, and the scars of the war are still fresh. Other key characters include a local baker (Shinjiro [Okada Eiji]) who courts Toshiko by baking "Picasso bread." He also sings Italian opera, and it is he who suggests to Toshiko that her mother might marry Kimura, which Toshiko finds shocking. Shinjiro tells her that it is a new age, and she has no right to restrict her mother's freedom. Another peripheral character is the mother's sister Noriko (Nakakita Chieko), who is studying to become a beautician, using Toshiko and her little sister Chako as models. Noriko and Shinjiro are forward-looking young professional characters, but the Tokyo suburb is also depicted as a community with ritual events, including street musicians advertising traveling shows and a festival at which the young people perform traditional songs and dances in amateur fashion.

Naruse tells the story of the family in a series of sketchlike episodes. Before the father dies, the elder son Susumu dies of tuberculosis. The boy's death is treated elliptically, with no drama except for Toshiko's minimal voice-over: "What is a human being born for?" Naruse cuts from a scene of Susumu lying on the tatami at home (he has escaped from the sanatorium to be near his mother) to Toshiko taking flowers to his grave. The father's death is treated somewhat more dramatically, with a musical crescendo and Toshiko running for a doctor; but again, Naruse cuts directly from her running to the family receiving guests after the funeral. Life goes on after these deaths, and as the family is plunged into deeper misery, Mother is increasingly deified. To make ends meet, she agrees to let her younger daughter Chako be adopted by relatives who lost their only son in the war and can afford to educate the girl. Meanwhile Mother continues to care for Noriko's child. The sentimentality of the film is thus grounded in the detail of everyday life in postwar Japan, including the ways that children are caught up in the economics of survival. Chako is miserable in her new home but is conscious of the sacrifice that she has to make for her family.

The detailed depiction of everyday life extends to the laundry business and the various practices of dyeing and ironing that the family members learn. The simplicity of the film is one of its greatest assets, and the performances of Tanaka, Kagawa, and Kato are all remarkably understated. This is the first of Kato Daisuke's thirteen roles in Naruse's films, and the director exploits his jovial, perpetually upbeat character as a foil for women characters caught up in emotional turmoil. Not that Tanaka displays any distress as the mother. Mother's only symptom is displaced onto an upset stomach that afflicts her when she takes the children to an amusement park for Chako's farewell. The little boy, Tetsuo, mistakenly eats the dried prunes that she had intended to take against the nausea that she is prone to while traveling. While the outing itself is a dynamically edited kinetic frenzy, with roller coasters and water slides, Mother's illness makes it, for her, another endurance test that she bravely survives.

The trip to the amusement park is one of several scenes set outside the home, yet the home is the centerpiece of the film. The set is virtually transparent and reversible: two adjoining rooms with a dirt-floored

40. Kogawa Kyoko, Tanaka Kinuyo, and Kato Daisuke in *Mother* (*Okaasan*, 1952), Shin Toho.

laundry, kitchen, and entryway facing onto the street. From the tatami rooms one can see through the entryway to the street, and in the other direction, the ruins of the neighborhood houses are a constant presence in the background. The only furniture is a round table brought out for meals, and when Susumu and his father are successively ill, their prone bodies are stretched out under quilts in one of the rooms. In Naruse's framing, there are frequently two or three planes of action, with either a body in the foreground or someone working in the background—or both—setting off the middle-ground action. The threshold ledge between the tatami rooms and the laundry area becomes a kind of liminal space that Kimura never crosses.

The relationship between Mother and Kimura is conveyed entirely without dialogue. Their affection for each other is communicated only by smiles, and when he leaves (only because she is able to run the business without him), she simply says that she will be lonely. She rests momentarily at the laundry counter while a melancholy wood-flute theme punctuates the silence before the final soundtrack of heavy strings and soaring vocals closes out the film, accompanied by Toshiko's childish voice-over praising her mother's virtues. The sense of despair and missed opportunity is principally created by the rituals that Kimura has enjoyed with Mother. The turning point of the film comes with a cut to a small tray on which Mother serves Kimura a glass of sake and a snack of parched beans, Kimura seated on the ledge of the tatami room. In the scene before, the baker and Toshiko are having a picnic with the "Picasso bread" (the younger children are playing nearby) and he has just asked her if her mother will marry Kimura. Her expression of shock is followed by this quiet scene of everyday ritual.

THE JAPANESE WOMAN'S FILM OF THE 1950S

Naruse's directorial gesture is contained in the cut to the tray in Mother's hands, as he links two scenes set in disparate places and very subtly indicates the flaw in the perfect family that Toshiko believes in. This failure of understanding is the slippage of generations, and it is the point at which Naruse undermines the trivial generic story that the film is based on. The full impact of the brief scene of Mother and Kimura is achieved by the meanings attached to that particular snack, and the architecture of the home. Previous scenes have established that parched beans were a favorite of the deceased father. The positioning of Kimura in the liminal space means that the reverse shots are always in 180-degree reversal, emphasizing the spatial discontinuity underlying the ostensible integrity of the home.

The close-up of the tray in Mother's hands, as she says "dozo" (please), is followed by a two-shot of Mother and Kimura, so although it is Kimura's point of view, it is not followed by the expected reverse shot. In the two-shot setup, with the camera in the laundry/entrance area, Mother and Kimura have a conversation and she slips some money onto the tray. This is followed by a long shot of Toshiko, Chako, and Tetsuo on the street. They are then seen entering the home behind Kimura, as the camera is now positioned inside the tatami room in a 180-degree reversal of the previous two-shot. Naruse has cleverly elided the time of the children's return journey while continuing the undercurrent of Toshiko's concern. After entering the home, she glances at Kimura, followed by a shot of him eating, obliviously, after which she glares and drops her gaze. This short sequence indicates how the realism of detail—including the Picasso bread and the parched beans—and the impression of temporal continuity harbors a network of emotional tensions belied only by the close-ups of Toshiko, who says nothing.

Toward the end of the film, shortly before his departure, Mother serves Kimura a dish of *tsukemono* (pickled vegetables), which he savors and of which she is evidently proud. Their relationship is one of companionship, and it is doomed for no reason other than the daughter's distaste. Toshiko's voice-over closes the film by anxiously wondering about her mother's happiness. It is thus deeply ironic, but the sadness is mainly generated by the failure of communication and understanding, the irrevocable power of social conventions, and the growing gap between generations. The daughter's denial of her mother's happiness implies a rejection of her mother's entire generation as the bearers of misery and despair, but Naruse's treatment of the story suggests that this is unfair and cruel. The generic mother is revealed to be an individual with real feelings and desires, but she is unable to change her role in a system that she also upholds.

As genre revision, *Mother* takes the formal properties of the haha-mono genre—the home, the children, the details of everyday life—and renders them an impossible ideal. As Hollywood classical cinema was undergoing the same kind of genre revision in the 1950s, we can perhaps see Naruse's classicism in terms of a similar postwar turn. Indeed the deaths of the son and the father early in the film set the tone of a necessary reconfiguration of family life after the war. In this light, Naruse's discontinuous editing style serves to highlight the cinematic space of the home. He isolates objects, such as the tray with the beans, as story elements; he uses 360-degree space to reconfigure characters in significant compositions; he cuts between discrete temporalities and spaces for rhetorical effect. These devices are not necessarily "reflexive" in that they are embedded within an otherwise "invisible" editing system, but they are nevertheless techniques through which the generic traits of the film are inverted and unsettled.

Critics of the time appreciated that Naruse had broken with the "lurid vulgarity" of the haha-mono, although they did not recognize the social criticism that Naruse's revisionism implies. Indeed, this may be a reading available only from the critical distance of our present perspective. Tsuboi notes that the mother is deeply unhappy, despite her deification, and she criticizes Naruse for suppressing the possible relationship with Kimura, saying, "isn't this like throwing cold water on the hopes of so many people who are widows and mothers?"[16] The sadness conveyed by Tanaka is the sadness of someone caught in a social trap, which is embodied in the home and in the national character to which the home and family system are inextricably linked. To follow her own heart would be to break her children's faith in the system that she has come to embody. The key contradiction of the film is that she does have a body. While a children's story can conveniently overlook that fact, in the cinema, in the person of Tanaka Kinuyo, this body belongs to a desiring subject.

Lightning
HAYASHI FUMIKO AND THE *SHITAMACHI*

Naruse's second adaptation of a Hayashi novel, *Lightning* (*Inazuma*, 1952), depicts a much rougher image of postwar Tokyo than the humble families of *Meshi* and *Mother*. Equally poor, the fatherless family in *Lightning* consists of a mother (Urabe Kumeko) of four adult children, each from a different father. One brother is a war-ravaged unemployed bum; one sister Nuiko (Murata Chieko) is a selfish, brash, and manipulative woman; and another, Mitsuko (Miura Mitsuko), loses her husband, only to be sucked into a world of debt, extortion, and the *mizu shobai* (water trade). Rumors of insurance money coming to Mitsuko after her husband's death provoke everyone, including the mother, to squabble over the nonexistent proceeds. The fourth child, Kiyoko (Takamine Hideko), finds the whole lot of them disgusting, although she tries her best to help Mitsuko and ends up reconciling with her mother. Her sisters try to set her up with an uncouth money-lending man named Goto, whom the sister Nuiko ends up stealing for herself, dropping her deadbeat alcoholic husband to do so. The drunken fight that follows between Goto and Nuiko's husband is what finally drives Kiyoko out of the home, to her own apartment in the suburbs.

This film was made at Daiei studio, with Tanaka Sumie, who also worked on *Meshi*, as scriptwriter. Although it is not clear why Naruse went to Daiei for this picture, the fact that he was able to work with Takamine and Tanaka indicates the extent of the "borrowing" practices that went on within the industry. Naruse's success with *Lightning* (which won second place in the *Kinema Junpo*'s 1952 rankings) and *Meshi* encouraged Toho executives to pair Naruse again with Hayashi, and in the seven films that he ended up making from her stories, she arguably had a postwar revival, despite her untimely death in 1951. The themes of women's struggles in a changing urban landscape were equally pressing in the postwar setting, even though Naruse's depiction of the shitamachi was often that of the prewar city of pedestrian alleys and backstreet communities.

Hayashi Fumiko was most prolific as a writer during the interwar period, and the original story *Inazuma* was published in 1935. Some of her books, such as *Horoki* (*Diary of a Vagabond*), were best sellers, and her work challenged many of the literary categories and distinctions of the time. Hayashi's writing tends to mix literary genres of prose and poetry, and she consistently blurred the boundaries between autobiography and fiction, experience and narrative storytelling. As Seiji M. Lippit notes, Hayashi brings into relief a certain limit of writing. For Lippit, Hayashi is an exemplary modernist, not only because of the heterogeneity of her writing, but also because of her use of urban space and the way that she worked with and against the concept of "home." Her narrator-character in *Horoki* resists the institutions of family, marriage, and the sexual economy of prostitution, and as Lippit points out, "the text also registers the impossibility of simply going outside this ideological system. Instead, it is in the marginal, in-between spaces of the city and the culture that Hayashi's heroine negotiates her own subjectivity."[17] While Lippit discusses only *Horoki*, much the same can be said of the other female protagonists in Naruse's adaptations of her work, including *Lightning*.

Positioning Hayashi as a modernist writer who inverts the gender paradigms of the I-novel or *shishosetsu* is perhaps a more useful approach than the pejorative categories of women's writing. As Lippit points out, Hayashi's narrator in *Horoki* is "both subject and object of desire."[18] Her heroines enact their multiple subjectivities through the negotiation of urban space; the fragmentation of city life is the means by which their own ambivalent relations to the home, the family, and institutions of power are articulated. In adapting her work, Naruse transposes the dual focus of her autoethnography to cinematic form, oscillating from subjective to objective, even anthropological perspectives.

Lightning is punctuated throughout with passing peddlers hawking their wares, itinerant musicians (*chindonya*), and children playing in the street. People live close together in two-storied homes, often fronted by a small shop or café adjoined to the living space. The hand-to-mouth existence is one of harsh survival, and for critic Iida Shinbi, the film's achievement is in capturing Hayashi's characters, drawn from the shitamachi.[19] For Nobugawa Naoki, however, this was the prewar shitamachi, and he was not convinced by Naruse's updating of the story, finding it to be still a prewar tale with only cursory references to the postwar climate—such as the details of pachinko and a motorbike. Although he applauds Takamine's performance, he points out that she is not a true postwar character. "She doesn't yet have the severe view of human life that postwar people have."[20]

Issues of real estate and the urban landscape are central to the film. The would-be suitor Goto owns a bakery in Ryogoku and an inn in Shibuya, and he eventually sets up Mitsuko as a bar hostess in yet another part of town. Kiyoko and Mitsuko travel across a bridge to a run-down part of town (Koto-ku) to visit a woman who claims to have been the lover of Mitsuko's deceased husband, and who has been left with a child and no support. Played by Nakakita Chieko, this woman is treated very sympathetically even though she tries to extort money from Mitsuko. In the family's shitamachi home, Kiyoko gazes wistfully at a poster depicting a suburban landscape. When she finally moves to Setagaya to escape her chaotic family, she rents a room from a lonely old woman. With several scenes of Mitsuko and Kiyoko carrying bags across the city, the film moves through a variety of different neighborhoods, suggesting a city of movement, flexibility and transience.

Kiyoko herself is a tour guide on a bus, reviving the role that Takamine played in her first film with Naruse in 1941, although now she is a far more sophisticated city girl. The film opens with her giving her spiel on a shaky bus traveling down Ginza Dori. Dressed throughout the film in a clean white blouse and a dark skirt, Kiyoko easily finds friends among the smart young people she meets—her mother's boarder, who works as a tutor, and a brother and sister in the suburbs who play Chopin piano music next door. As Iida noted at the time, these neighbors are a bit too perfect and seem like "residents of heaven" compared to the other characters.[21] Kiyoko is left somewhat stranded between the ideal represented by these Musashino neighbors and her crude shitamachi family.

In adapting Hayashi's work, Naruse replaces her first-person narrative with the persona of Takamine Hideko, for whom dialogue is far less important than posture and facial expression. In *Lightning* she exhibits a maturity that distinguishes her from the rest of the squabbling family. Not only does Kiyoko walk away from her family, she blatantly refuses the marriage they have attempted to arrange, and she seems to have no need for a husband. In Hayashi's novel, the family still pressures Kiyoko to marry the disagreeable man whom she has quite firmly rejected, even after she moves out.[22] In the film, however, the issue of the arranged marriage is more or less dropped, and instead, Kiyoko meets the handsome next-door neighbor, who kindly carries her bags for her and looks a little like a magazine model. Although Hayashi's writing can often be quite erotic, Takamine and Naruse tame it considerably, as Takamine remains a shy and proper young lady.

In both book and film, the dysfunctionalism of Kiyoko's family is attributed to the illegitimacy of the four children. As Susanna Fessler has argued about the theme of illegitimacy in Hayashi's writing, it causes characters not so much psychological distress as social problems of fitting into a society that is so bound to a family system.[23] When Kiyoko asks her mother whether marriage ever made her happy, her mother responds, "Happiness is a concept that was invented in the modern world." However, Kiyoko clearly thinks she deserves it, and on the basis of her sisters' marriages, she does not think happiness is achieved through marriage. Her job as a tour guide gives her not only some economic independence, but also mobility, and the passage through public space seems to be a catalyst in the heroine's awakening.

The final scene of the film, in which Kiyoko's mother comes to visit her in her new second-story room in the suburbs, is one of the finest in Naruse's oeuvre. Running ten minutes, the scene depicts both mother and daughter breaking into tears as they express their disappointment with each other and their family. At one point Kiyoko moves to the window ledge and gazes out at the lush landscape of homes and hills. Piano music rises from the neighbors' lighted home below. While her mother cries, a lightning flash seems to crystallize the break Kiyoko has made with her past. Two shots of the cracks of light across the sky are intercut with her profile, as Naruse cuts across the axis to position Takamine perfectly in profile watching the sky, followed by her other profile framed in the window of her new home. Mother and daughter quickly reconcile and the film ends with them walking together along a softly lit quiet street to the station.

In this scene, the home becomes a cinematic space where the woman's subjectivity and desire are rendered visible in the dynamics of looking. The flash of lightning, accompanied by the neighbor's piano, is not only a moment of visual and audio excess, it is linked directly to Kiyoko's gaze and therefore signifies her interiority, her subjectivity, and her desire for happiness. Naruse's use of 360-degree shooting space often frames his characters against all four walls and open windows of the rooms they occupy. The home is like a stage on which the women perform their roles; but the home often opens onto a garden, or a view of the city, as it does here, offering a constant reminder of the world that lies outside the home. The image of Takamine Hideko looking out over a railing, poised on a kind of threshold of domestic space, is emblematic of the emergence of female subjectivity inscribed within Naruse's cinema.

The end of *Lightning* is ambivalent. There is still something wrong with the picture, something unsettling that points to the contradictoriness of the female protagonist's desires. A clue comes from Hayashi's own remarks on the novel, which she found to be unspeakably lonely.[24] We know that in the suburbs life may be quiet and peaceful, but also that there will be none of the street vendors and itinerant musicians who link every change of scene in Naruse's shitamachi. Although Kiyoko has escaped her family and the arranged marriage, the alternative of a rented room in a middle-class home is not exactly paradise. What remains is Kiyoko's search for happiness. This deep ambivalence marks Naruse's modernism, an ambivalence around the woman and her place in the social structure. He borrows this from Hayashi and translates it into the audiovisual language of cinema. In *Lightning*, the food that

41. Takamine Hideko in *Lightning* (*Inazuma*, 1952), Daiei.

everyone eats is soba noodles, a delicacy that the shitamachi family buys from street stalls, but which the suburban landlady cooks herself from scratch. On this level of detail, Naruse's modernism remains couched in the vernacular.

By linking his name with one of postwar Japan's most popular woman writers, Naruse might have helped women of the time imagine the terms of a more gender-equitable society. Hayashi herself was known as an unconventional, freewheeling, and outspoken literary figure who refused to be bound by conventions of polite behavior. If one of the effects of cinematic adaptation of literature is to transform it into melodrama, Naruse is able to enhance and develop the discourse of female subjectivity that Hayashi had already mapped out against the realism of Japanese society. The harshness of Hayashi's Japan is undoubtedly tempered by Naruse's studio sets and movie stars, but the ongoing commentary on women's lives and the unrelenting and unrequited desire for happiness becomes a harsh critique of modern Japan and the false promises of "democratization." Moreover, as Nobugawa Naoki noted, compared to the sentimentality of *Mother*, this time Naruse was better able to "control the emotions."[25]

Husband and Wife
MARRIAGE AND ITS DISCONTENTS

Meshi, *Husband and Wife* (*Fufu*, 1953), and *Tsuma* (*Wife*, 1953) are sometimes referred to as Naruse's "marriage trilogy." They constitute a remarkable set of variations on the theme of marriage, although the theme arguably continues through several other films of the 1950s, in particular *Yama no oto* (*Sound of the Mountain*, 1954) and *Shuu* (*Sudden Rain*, 1956). All five films were produced by Fujimoto Sanezumi, who by this time was becoming an important figure in Naruse's career. Although he had been working on and off with Naruse since 1941, after *Meshi*, he was able to arrange for the director to work consistently with the trio of screenwriters Mizuki Yoko, Tanaka Sumie, and Ide Toshiro, and with stars Hara Setsuko, Uehara Ken, and Sugi Yoko, who form the backbone of the marriage films and help give the Naruse pictures of the 1950s a trademark style.

Appearing in four of the five marriage films (all except *Sudden Rain*), Uehara Ken is partially responsible for setting a consistent tone of middle-class boredom and despondency, portraying a series of apathetic

42. Husband, wife, and roommate watching a show. Uehara Ken, Mikuni Rentaro, and Sugi Yoko in *Husband and Wife* (*Fufu*, 1953), Toho.

salarymen: irresponsible, unfaithful, and often disrespectful of long-suffering, hardworking wives. He also reprises the role in *Late Chrysanthemums*, which is not a marriage film but shares the setting of the lower-middle-class shitamachi home. In *Husband and Wife*, he lazily reads the newspaper, smokes cigarettes, and is perpetually glum except when drinking; in scenes at the office, he is doing much the same thing, as well as going to movies with the young office ladies. While his disinterest in his wife and home are perhaps excessive, his performance of boredom is in many ways the basis of these films' loosely structured, eventless narratives.

Sugi Yoko appears opposite Uehara in *Husband and Wife* in a role that was supposed to go to Hara Setsuko but went to the novice actress when the great star was taken ill. Ide Toshiro claims that he wrote the original screenplay with Sugi in mind—an actress whom he regarded as a new type of woman. He thought that she would be able to say the word *abortion*, which, in his opinion, neither Hara nor Takamine would have been able to utter. However, in the final film, the word is never actually spoken (Ide claims that Naruse couldn't have Sugi say the word either).[26] In the penultimate scene of the film, Nakahara (Uehara) tells his wife that they can't afford to have a baby now. She simply says "I don't want to do that," but Naruse cuts to the next scene where the couple go together to an abortion clinic, stopping awhile in a park nearby before entering. Moments after entering the building, though, Kikuko (Sugi) comes running out, passing her husband and returning to the park bench, unable to go through with the operation. He suggests that they get something to eat and says that they will be able to find a way to raise the child after all. The scene is quite beautifully staged, with the mottled light of the sunlight in the trees dancing over the couple standing in a long shot.

It is a rather sudden change of heart on the part of Nakahara, but also in keeping with the weakness of his character. According to Ide, this ending was the idea of Mizuki, who was brought in as a cowriter. Interviewed in 1987, Ide's somewhat egotistical view of his work with Naruse reveals the gender dynamics involved in the scriptwriting process. He says that Mizuki's contribution to the script was the provision of a "woman's point of view," even though she was a well-respected playwright and screenwriter at the time.[27] In any event, despite the contributions of his screenwriters, Naruse usually cut out large amounts of dialogue when it came to actually shooting the scenes. Sugi observed that "he cut out the unnatural parts" and created "an environment in which the things he was aiming for came out naturally. He'd set up your lines and the filming so that a kind of naturalistic acting would come out once you started."[28] Like Takamine Hideko and other actors who worked with Naruse, Sugi claims that he never gave her any direction. "He never said 'do this' or 'do that' or 'try to portray this.' He never even got angry with me."[29]

The effect of naturalness is in fact carefully constructed through the use of architecture, lighting, dialogue, and props. Within an "environment" designed to inspire a certain mood and way of living, actors use posture, gesture, and facial expressions to convey a great deal, relying less on "technique" than on responding to their situation, lending the films a certain ethnographic or documentary feel. In *Husband and Wife*, Mikuni Rentaro plays Nakahara's coworker Takemura, with whom the couple move in and to whom Sugi's character Kikuko is dangerously attracted. Mikuni is a much more expressive actor, with a large body and large movements. According to Sugi, he tended to overact in rehearsal, but on camera he became tense and thus appropriately subdued for Naruse's style. In any event, Mikuni conveys a level of personality and charm that is completely lacking in Uehara's character. The emotional tension of the narrative is produced through the contrast between the two men and the very different ways that they treat Kikuko. Kobayashi Keiju, who plays Kikuko's brother, appears in seven of Naruse's postwar films, often in a secondary role. He claims that he worked well with Naruse, because of his body type and his relaxed manner. Interviewer Murakawa suggests that "Naruse didn't treat actors as performers, but as objects, and he made his films as if he were observing objects. That's why he might have preferred an actor who didn't act like an actor," to which Kobayashi responds that of course he was acting but also admits that he consistently provided a bright and cheery personality to the films he was in, suggesting that on some level Naruse was treating his actors as documentary subjects.[30]

Because the newly married couple in *Husband and Wife* have to move out of Kikuko's parents' home and have been unable to find affordable housing — due mainly to Nakahara's indolence — they decide to move into the first floor of Takemura's home. He has recently become a widower, so Kikuko does his cooking and cleaning for him, becoming a wife with two husbands, as one of her friends points out. While Nakahara is unappreciative of her work, Takemura thanks her and treats her with respect. The beauty of the film lies in the way their relationship is handled, as a flirtation that Kikuko desperately resists, despite Takemura's obvious appeal. Finally, toward the end of the film, the couple finds a new home in a quiet suburb, but with the proviso that children are not allowed. Kikuko waits until they are installed in the new home before telling her husband that she is pregnant, implying that she had to get out of Takemura's home to save the marriage.

At one point Nakahara and Kikuko offer advice to Kikuko's brother and his new wife, but they clearly disagree on the principle of marriage and the expectations each places on the other. Nakahara describes marriage as a pair of scissors then quickly digresses to his wife's perceived failings. The film is full of the details of everyday humiliations and crises — a ripped overcoat, spilled soup, and the inability of the two "husbands" to cook themselves a meal when Kikuko leaves them on their own. Marriage in *Husband and Wife* is the sum of all these things — the routines and materials of everyday life, the exchange of labor, the sexual needs, and the cost of having children. Nakahara's sudden reversal and apparent willingness to respect his wife in the last moment of the film may save the marriage in a deus ex machina resolution, but the arbitrariness of this reversal contains a kind of spark of realization and revelation that is comparable to the flash of lightning at the end of *Lightning*. It's almost a satori experience, especially in the setting of the urban park, outside the walls of the home, where the idea of marriage finally crystallizes in an image that is more metaphysical than sentimental.

Homelessness and transience are again prominent themes in *Husband and Wife*. In the opening scene, Kikuko climbs the stairs to view the city from the top of a department store, waving to her friends below. From this lofty position, she finds herself brought down to Takemura's broken-down house in the shitamachi, where the neighbors are never too far away, and the cold weather penetrates the thin walls. But the real contrast in this film is between the alienating urban life of the salaryman and the communal life of the shopkeeper. Kikuko's family runs a busy shop selling grilled eel in a neighborhood with festivals and street life. Nakahara works for an electric company and is at the mercy of his bosses, who move him from one place to another. After they move in with Takemura, Nakahara is sent away again on a business trip, during which his wife becomes close to Takemura. Both Nakahara and Takemura flirt with girls from the office, indicating another community from which Kikuko is excluded. Thus the notion of marriage is drawn across the changing contours of everyday life in postwar Tokyo. A good marriage in this life can only be a happy accident; while the film may uphold the ideal of a happy marriage, it also systematically represents the obstacles to achieving such an ideal within the fragmenting social fabric of urban sprawl. As in *Meshi*, it is the housewife who pays the price of loneliness and isolation in the new domestic configurations of the postwar city.

Wife
WHAT IS IT TO BE A WOMAN OR A WIFE?

In the third film of Naruse's cycle of marriage films, based on the Hayashi story *Brown Eyes* (*Chairo no me*, 1948), the optimistic turnarounds of the first two films are forsaken for a much more bleak view of married life. In *Wife* (*Tsuma*, 1953), the couple, played by Takamine Mieko and Uehara Ken, cannot resolve their differences, even though their dissatisfactions amount to little more than ennui. The film ends with the same morning ritual with which it begins: Juichi (Uehara) leaves for work, while Mineko (Takamine) cleans the house. Over both scenes, husband and wife each complain in voice-over about their empty marriage. Juichi's last thoughts are that a divorce may allow them to live again, while Mineko wonders where she would go if she were to leave. "What is it to be a woman or a wife?" she asks herself. She has managed to put an end to her husband's affair, but now that they are back where they started, life goes on with the couple trapped in a marriage that the film has proven to be little more than a social institution.

With *Wife*, Naruse shifts the modality slightly away from the ethnographic realism of *Meshi* and *Fufu*, toward a more melodramatic intensity. He admitted as much to a reviewer who claimed that Takamine Mieko was too sophisticated for a middle-class housewife. Naruse noted that the stylization was necessary for a "melodramatic film of feelings." Most striking about *Wife* is that Uehara's character Juichi is the most emotionally tortured. He is just as depressed and listless as his characters in *Meshi* and *Fufu*, but this time the husband becomes involved with a widowed single mother from the office. Sawara (Tanami Yatsuko) seems to initiate the affair by inviting Juichi to an art exhibit. Shortly thereafter, she moves to Osaka where he visits and spends the night with her. They meet in cafés and parks, and Juichi plays with Sawara's little boy, but the relationship is doomed to failure due to Juichi's status as a married man. His wife, Mineko, eventually confronts the mistress, Sawara, and threatens to kill herself rather than grant a divorce.

Juichi is genuinely heartbroken, clearly in love with Sawara, and somewhat browbeaten by his wife, a woman who takes things into her own hands. Frustrated with her husband's inability to get promoted, Mineko runs the boarding house where the couple live in order to augment their income. When she finds out about the affair, she sends a lawyer to Juichi's office, who demands that he visit her family to explain his behavior. Finally, Mineko goes to find Sawara where she is staying with a friend in Tokyo, and the two of them walk to a café where they can talk. The scene of the women's confrontation is quite remarkable. Mineko wears a kimono, while Sawara wears a tailored skirt with a pencil skirt, and the two women walk in lock step, the camera moving with them, even in reverse-shot patterns as they converse while walking. Their confrontation is surprisingly businesslike, as Mineko aggressively demands that Sawara back off from the affair, which she agrees to do, stating simply that Mineko is "very old-fashioned." Seeing her with the professional-looking Sawara walking rhythmically together, their parallel situations are underlined. Sawara is able to support herself and her child, but she is lonely.

What makes *Wife* such a strong melodrama is the way that both husband and wife are depicted as sympathetic characters. While Mineko is always busy dealing with her tenants or housecleaning, Juichi is frequently seen sitting down and looking despondent, perched on the

43. Tanami Yatsuko and Takamine Mieko in *Wife* (*Tsuma*, 1953), Toho.

threshold of the garden, or framed through the shoji panels. This insight into a male character's romantic woes is rare in Naruse's oeuvre, but it is achieved partly at the expense of Mineko's character, who is depicted as a bad housewife. Juichi finds a hair in his lunchbox at work; when a friend comes over to help the couple, she is shocked at the messy, badly equipped kitchen. Indeed, for at least one female critic, Mineko was seen to be responsible for the failure of her marriage because she did not give enough affection to her husband.[31] Another woman writer, however, suggests that it is the husband's fault, and points out that he has choices, whereas the housewife has none.[32]

These critics point to the ways that in challenging social norms and interrogating prescribed gender roles, a film like *Wife* provided a forum for public debate. It is at once a comedy of manners and a melodrama, in which the blend of realism and emotional intensity brings issues of class and gender into the cultural sphere. In fact Mineko is not a hysterical woman at all, and like *Meshi*, this film seemed to touch a nerve in contemporary society, sparking a public debate in the form of film criticism on the question of marriage roles. According to Ide Toshiro, Hayashi's original story was about a woman whose eyes turn brown when she gets hysterical—a pretty woman who turns bad. Takamine Hideko was unwilling to play such a woman and turned down the role.[33] Ide also notes that Hayashi had been commissioned to write *Meshi* after *Brown Eyes*, although the latter had less "mass appeal" as a serial. In any case, both films did very well at the box office.

The boarding-house context of *Wife* provides a constellation of characters whose stories parallel and mirror the situation of the main couple. One woman surprises everyone by taking a job in a Ginza bar and leaving her unemployed husband to fend for himself. She tells Mineko that she can't depend on men and she wants to live life freely, in her own way. Another woman commits suicide when she discovers that her husband is having an affair. Mineko may threaten to kill herself, but she clearly isn't the type. She is a real Hayashi character, a stubborn survivor who doesn't fit into the prescribed role of wife and mother. In Susanna Fessler's account, Hayashi's serialized novel depicts an escalating tension between husband and wife, who take turns escaping the home.[34] The need to guard the house against theft is a recurring theme in these marriage films, as the housewife's opportunities to go out are severely limited by the flimsiness of the papered doors and windows of Japanese architecture.

Naruse includes one scene from the novel in which both husband and wife want to go out on a Saturday. Although we know that Juichi has a date with Sawara, he tells his wife only that he has "important business." She has been waiting all week to have a chance to go and visit a friend, to whom she says she "had to get out of there," when she finally does get out. Her friend notes drily that a man loses his dignity when he is asked to mind the house. (Naruse elides the solution and simply shows the two of them out at their separate appointments. In the novel, one of the tenants is asked to watch the house.) The scene in which Mineko walks with Sawara is the only time she is fully mobile in the entire film. It is Juichi who really escapes, though, going to art galleries and movies with Sawara, who is closely associated with public space. At one point, Juichi sips sake on a train with his boss headed for Osaka. The boss asks him if he feels the freedom of escape while together they ogle a young woman traveling alone.

Mineko's neglect of her husband may be what drives him to another woman, but the film still asks us to be sympathetic to the wife's plight. In a conversation with her unmarried younger sister, Mineko insists that it is not too much to ask for love from a marriage, and that it must be more than an institution and a formality for there to be happiness. Once again, the problem that the film poses is that of a woman's happiness. Even if the world is liberated, Juichi is told by the lawyer, it does not mean that he can have a happy life while causing his wife pain and suffering. Hayashi's writing is full of characters who keep living despite life's interminable trials and tribulations. The specter of suicide is often lurking in the background as a road not taken, and in this clinging to life, her stories contain a grain of hope for the future. Mineko may threaten to kill herself, but when she hears about another woman in her situation committing suicide, she is shocked, and says, "She didn't have to die!" This is in fact her last line before the closing scene of the couple going through their morning routine in silence.

As melodrama, *Wife* depicts a world in which private and public space circumscribes the emotional life of a couple who become representative of marriage itself. By situating a childless couple at the center of these marriage films, Naruse is able to focus on the emotional states of husband and wife as individuals — or perhaps as "man" and "woman." From Hayashi's writing Naruse borrows an ongoing discourse on men and women as essential categories doomed to be in perpetual opposition. Mineko tells her mother that things went wrong because if he has "a man's will," she has "a woman's will." When Juichi plays with a toy car with Sawara's young son, he says he could stay that way forever. This is the idea of a modern family fully implicated in commodity capitalism, but it is only an ideal, to which reality will never measure up. Juichi doesn't have the will, in the end, to leave his wife, and he ends up back in the boarding house, where the couple's two attached rooms open onto the garden like a stage on which they are doomed to perform their monotonous routines.

The question of a woman's happiness, posed in the existential final phrase, "What is it to be a woman and a wife?" is in fact the question of being a salaryman's wife. If one chooses not to conflate one's identity and raison d'être with motherhood and children, what else is there? How can picking up one's husband's discarded suit and tie and helping him change into kimono at the end of every day be rewarding? In *Wife*, it becomes clear that the existential quest for meaning in life is also a question for men in postwar urban culture; the salaryman who is sent hither and thither by philandering bosses is equally stuck in an unforgiving system.

Older Brother, Younger Sister
A TALE OF SOUND AND FURY

In 1953 Naruse made his second film at Daiei, and while there are some parallels with *Lightning*, which he had made there the year before, *Older Brother, Younger Sister* (*Ani imoto*) exhibits a style very different from that of his Toho features. Although it placed fifth in the annual *Kinema Junpo* roundup, it lacks the subtlety of the marriage films and Hayashi adaptations, and it ventures into a terrain of melodramatic excess and theatricality that the director had more or less abandoned since the 1950 film *White Beast*. The script is more verbose, the performances are more exaggerated, the shooting style uses more deep space and high contrast lighting, and metaphorical shots of a turbulent river punctuate the narrative. These are all conventions of film melodrama that Naruse had managed to circumvent in his understated shoshimin-eiga, and there is no explanation for their return here, other than Ide Toshiro's observation that Naruse had trouble refusing projects.[35] The film's overblown qualities enable a comparison with the American film melodrama that was emerging in the United States in the early 1950s, and it throws into relief the more restrained melodramatic language of Naruse's other films of the period.

Older Brother, Younger Sister is based on a short story of the same name (*Ani imoto*) by Muro Saisei that was originally published in 1934. As with *Lightning*, Naruse switches the setting to the period of the film's production, highlighting the social transformation of postwar Japan and its effects on a dysfunctional family. Naruse's major alterations of the literary original include an elevation of the social status of the family from impoverishment to lower-middle class, and a much more developed characterization of San, the "good" sister in the family.[36] Played by Kuga Yoshiko, the adolescent heroine of *Spring Awakens*, San is a familiar Naruse protagonist, but this time it is almost as if she has been dropped into another movie. San attends a nursing school in sensible shoes, white blouse, and calf-length skirt, commuting to Tokyo from the family home in a village outside the city. The brother and sister of the film's title are San's sister Mon (Kyo Machiko), a "fallen woman," and her brother Ino (Mori Masayuki), a rough and angry workingman who rarely seems to work. The father, Akaza, played by Yamamoto Reizaburo, is an extremely unhappy man who slaps his son around every time they meet. The mother, Riki, is played by Urabe Kumeko, reprising her role from *Lightning* as the mother struggling helplessly with her wayward adult children.

Where Muro's original novel focused on the father of the family, Naruse's film pays more attention to the two sisters and their mother, with San emerging as the strongest subjective presence in the film. Again, we could compare her character to Takamine's in *Lightning* as the sibling who observes the degradation of her own family and plots her way out. However, where the earlier film used urban space as a key formal and narrative trope to give the girl's escape topographic shape, in *Older Brother*, San and Mon leave the family and their village only to repeatedly return, and the film is set entirely in the countryside. In the film's final scenes, the two girls walk together through a sunny meadow under Mon's parasol, heading for the bus that will take them back to the city. Even though Mon has just had an all-out violent fight with her brother, she says she will return to see him along with the mother and father who are thoroughly disappointed with her allegedly degenerate lifestyle in the big city.

Kyo and Mori were big stars of the time, and this film was released very close to the release of Mizoguchi's international hit *Ugetsu* (1953) in which they star. (Kyo and Mori are also paired together in *Rashomon* [1950].) Naruse seems to have given them free rein in *Older Brother* to act out the drama of a brother who despises his sister's wanton ways. Ino beats up a young student who comes to visit the family to take responsibility for Mon's pregnancy. Like his father, Ino is a macho figure, swag-

44. Kyo Machiko in *Older Brother, Younger Sister* (*Ani imoto*, 1953), Daiei.

gering and loud; the student Obata (Funakoshi Eiji) is comparatively meek and mild. (Even when he learns that the baby was stillborn, Obata insists on leaving a packet of money.) When Mon learns of the beating, she becomes angry, and in the ensuing physical fight with Ino, she taunts him, he slaps her, and furniture is turned over.

Mon visits the village wearing a gaudy kimono and permed hair, turning heads and generally embarrassing the family. She confesses to her sister that although she has come to know men very well, no man would have her, and she has no need for them anyway. Although it is never entirely clear what she does for a living in Tokyo, her dress and her manner suggest that she works as an entertainer or bar hostess. Her outrage at Ino betrays her affection for the poor student, whom she has otherwise dismissed as beneath her. For her part, San's relationship with a noodle maker from the village is ruined by her sister's reputation, and he is married off to another woman by his family. San scorns his weakness of character but is visibly upset by the betrayal. She claims that her work is more important than marriage, and she is committed to her education and career, although silent reaction shots at any mention or sight of her former lover indicates that she has been deeply hurt.

The film is thus a family drama in which sexuality lies just beneath the surface of everyday life. While Muro's original suggested an animality within the dynamics of a poor family unable to articulate their needs and anxieties,[37] Naruse's adaptation brings the film more in line with American family melodrama, in which class and sexual difference constitute a discourse of hysteria and repression. Thomas Elsaesser's observations on the American family melodrama are suited to *Older Brother* more than to any other title in Naruse's oeuvre. Writing about key films of the 1950s by directors Douglas Sirk, Vincente Minnelli, and Nicholas Ray in his essay "Tales of Sounds and Fury," Elsaesser describes the aesthetic effects of mise-en-scène, music, and stylistic excess as expressions of social and sexual conflict: "The social pressures are such, the frame of respectability so sharply defined that the range of 'strong' actions is limited. The tellingly impotent gesture, the social gaffe, the hysterical outburst replaces any more directly liberating or self-annihilating action, and the cathartic violence of a shoot-out or a chase becomes an inner violence, often one in which the characters turn against themselves."[38]

In *Older Brother*, physical violence becomes the means by which the family members express themselves, and the incestuous relationship between brother and sister is only thinly disguised (Ino tells Obata that he used to sleep with Mon when they were children). Moreover, the patriarchal dynamics of family life are directly linked to the social pressures of a changing economy. The father, Akaza, was once in charge of a huge damming operation on the river, managing thousands of workers and boats, and an important enough figure in the village to be responsible for local festivals. Since concrete has replaced stone masonry, he is now unemployed and the family lives off the proceeds of his wife's ice cream stand. Once the "lord of the river," he has become a counter clerk who serves up ice cream with a nasty snarl.

Like the American family melodrama, *Older Brother* is characterized by dramatic discontinuities, with action rising to hysterically pitched battles and falling to pastoral landscapes and quiet country roads. The family home is a farmhouse structure with a brazier in the middle of one large room. As it is a hot summer season, the shoji are all open, creating a stage-like space open on three sides to a surrounding unkempt garden. At one point during a meal in which Ino and Mon are arguing, the mother asks for an intermission so that they can all eat—a sly reflexive gesture in an otherwise deadly serious drama.

Despite the openness of the space, Naruse renders it claustrophobic by his shooting style, which moves around the characters sitting, lying, and standing in the big open room. Continually crossing and recrossing the axis, the editing is guided by character movement and dialogue rather than by spatial framing. A lantern festival at night constitutes a beautiful interruption of the action and demonstrates Naruse's flair for night scenes, but the lanterns jostling each other as they float down the river is also an expression of the crowdedness of the film's mise-en-scène. Indeed, San sees her former lover there with his new wife. Mon's kimonos, with large patterns, along with her fans, popsicles, and parasols, constitute a discourse of excess and sensuality that seems to overwhelm the family, and indeed the whole village. In the first shot of Kyo, she is bathing by the family well, dressed only in a slip. Thus the film exhibits classic symptoms of feminine sexuality that are dramatically linked to changes in the social formation that have undermined the authority of the father.

As Elsaesser notes of American family melodrama, pathos is used "to explore psychological and sexual repression, usually in conjunction with the theme of inferiority." This inadequacy of response often has "a sexual code: male impotence and female frigidity," which gives rise, in his view, to "a tragic self-awareness" that is "called upon to compensate for lost spontaneity and energy."[39] These remarks certainly resonate with *Older Brother*, especially with Kyo's character, who argues to her mother that she is not a bad woman, although she is certainly a ruined one. San's character, however, remains somewhat outside the dynamics of the family melodrama. She is a survivor who promises to make the move into the next phase of the national imaginary. Without forsaking her family, she will become a professional woman in the big city. She may lack the dramatic and sexual intensity of her sister Mon, but she cannot be described as "frigid." She pines for her lost lover, but it is evident that she is much better without him.

The landscape in *Older Brother* is unremarkable, and the dammed river displaying the labor of stone masonry is even a bit ugly. Naruse redeems it only by staging some children splashing periodically, and the surrounding farmland is principally a space of encounters, a social space rather than a natural one. The final scene of the two sisters walking along a path through a meadow is by now a familiar ending for Naruse, closing the film on a note of passage as the two women walk away from the camera. As a film about the transformation of family and landscape, the country lane at the end is the symbolic route to Tokyo. Although they are leaving their home behind, the sisters' intimacy signifies the repressed discourse of the shoshimin-eiga that this "tale of sound and fury" has so brashly subverted. As the film's figure of virtue, San may be a survivor, but she is so because of her complicity with the past and the family. Her sister has become the symptomatic victim of the failure of the family, but the violence that she and her brother have displayed is in turn linked to a discourse of individualism and desire. By bringing the two sisters together in the end, Naruse manages to bridge the stereotypical dichotomy between good girl and bad girl, rendering San as the vanishing aura of the family. The diminished authority of the father has given rise to an Oedipal violence that only the melodrama of the woman's film can overcome.

Sound of the Mountain
NARUSE AS MODERNIST

Naruse describes his third adaptation of a Kawabata novel as one of his personal favorites. *Sound of the Mountain* (*Yama no oto*, 1954) was a project that the director himself proposed to Toho,[40] and it stands out as one of his most powerful films. Not only does he replicate the subtlety of the marriage films, casting Hara Setsuko and Uehara Ken as the central childless couple, but the story of a marriage also takes on existential dimensions in his approach to Kawabata's narrative. The dramatic intensities of a failing marriage are intersected by the desires and anxieties of the film's protagonist Shingo (Yamamura So), the father of Uehara's character, Shuichi. Shingo's relationship with his daughter-in-law Kikuko (Hara) is one of deep affection and sympathy, and the more Shuichi screws up the marriage, the closer Shingo and Kikuko become. In a film in which husband and wife never meet each other's gazes, the exchanges of looks between father and daughter-in-law signify a level of understanding and completion that is the film's most striking feature. In true melodramatic fashion, theirs is a doomed relationship, and yet the tenderness and affection between the older man and the younger woman is one of the most passionate relationships in Naruse's oeuvre.

Given Kikuko's status in the household (she calls Shingo "Father"), *Sound of the Mountain* flirts precariously with incest, taking up a theme from *Older Brother*, but in this instance turning it into an existential dilemma. Moving back and forth between the family home in Kamakura and various locations in Tokyo, the film maps the troubled relationships onto the postwar context. Space, freedom, and female subjectivity are the terms with which a melodrama of profound suffering becomes a modernist treatment of postwar Japanese society. The family this time are upper middle class, and their home is a beautiful sprawling traditional style building surrounded by a carefully maintained garden. Shingo is something of an aesthete, and the home in Kamakura is virtually cut off from the outside world. Shuichi and Shingo take the train back and forth to work every day, but Kikuko is kept in Kamakura like a hothouse flower.

Although Mizuki Yoko's script is faithful to the Kawabata novel in many respects, she and Naruse once again shift the emphasis from the male perspective to that of a woman's film. The film's poster features Hara Setsuko most prominently, followed by Uehara, with Yamamura So reduced to a much smaller figure, suggesting that the studio wanted to capitalize on the success of *Meshi*, produced just two years previously. The script also necessarily eliminates a great deal of Shingo's interior monologue, including his ongoing commentary on the physical attributes of the women in his life. Kawabata's protagonist is a man of the old world, and his sexist worldview may be accounted for as a character trait, yet the novel offers little insight into the minds of any of the other characters. Shingo has a series of erotic dreams that are obliquely linked to the women in his life and to the deaths of his friends, who die throughout the novel from various causes. In the novel, the old man's mortality underscores all the relationships and the novel's overall worldview.[41] Naruse's version of the story may eliminate the eroticism of Kawabata's prose, but it enables a much fuller depiction of the female characters, especially Kikuko, as desiring subjects.

The family has recently lost their maid, so Kikuko is burdened with an endless series of household chores, which she performs cheerfully even though her husband sometimes doesn't come home at night, and when he does, he is dead drunk. The woman critic Mikawa Kiyo noted that female audiences would be bound to sympathize with this depiction of the role of a daughter-in-law—although she also accuses the Kikuko character of being too weak.[42] Indeed Kikuko is extraordinarily passive, in keeping with the typical Kawabata heroine—although in the last scene of the film, as we shall see, Naruse suggests that there is potential for change. Another critic, Takami Jun, offers a somewhat different perspective, saying that he liked the fact that Shingo's point of view is privileged, but younger audiences might be more interested in the younger characters whom he could not appreciate.[43] These critics indicate how this very "literary" film was apprehended in terms of contemporary social issues, no doubt because of Naruse's continued emphasis on the everyday rituals of domestic life.

The final scene of *Sound of the Mountain* has been discussed by many critics as a remarkable commentary on cinematic space. Kikuko calls Shingo at his office and asks to meet him in Shinjuku Garden. She has been away for a few days visiting her own family. As they walk through the park, she says she has decided to break up with Shuichi. Shingo tells her that Kinu, Shuichi's mistress, is having a child. He also tells her that she should take her freedom for the sake of her own happiness, and they agree to a parting. After reluctantly accepting the freedom that has been granted her, Kikuko looks out at the expanse of meadow and says, "a great deal of attention has been paid to the vista . . . you are able to see to

45. The vista. Yamamura So and Hara Setsuko in *Sound of the Mountain* (*Yama no oto*, 1954), Toho.

great depths." Shingo asks what a "vista" is, and she answers, "It means the line of an outlook."

Combining elements of French and English garden styles with traditional Japanese, Shinjuku Gyoen was a novelty of Meiji Japan. It opened in 1906 as an imperial garden and was largely destroyed during the war, reopening in 1949 as a national garden open to the public. Shingo and Kikuko walk along tree-lined paths, pausing on a bench with a view of a meadow modeled on an English landscape, designed around a perspectival view. After Kikuko's comment on the vista, Naruse does not follow with her point-of-view shot as might be anticipated, but rests on Hara's close-up as she dabs the tears from her eyes with a faint smile. Shingo looks back at her and then turns to walk away from the camera. She walks into the shot to join him, and the film ends with the two figures walking into the distance framed by a large tree in the foreground. Naruse and cameraman Tamai Masao shoot the Shinjuku Garden vista with the same lens that they use in Kamakura, flattening the landscape and focusing on characters in the middle distance and the tree in the foreground. Nature in *Sound of the Mountain* exists primarily in the characters' ongoing commentary on seasonal changes and rare species of flowers. On a few occasions shots of the rooftops and distant hills surrounding the Kamakura home are inserted, but they are little more than stock shots. In Shinjuku Garden, Kikuko and Shingo walk along a receding avenue of leafless trees before reaching the open field, but the final "vista" is dominated by the foreground tree framing the view, effectively inverting the depth of field.

Naruse and Mizuki have altered Kawabata's original story by taking the lines about the vista away from Shingo and giving them to Kikuko. Significantly, it is the first time that she says something that is not a response to someone else, or the expression of an emotion. To this extent it suggests that she has finally emerged from her suffocating role as daughter-in-law, and the complex feelings she holds for her father-in-law will be resolved into a new perspective on life. Furthermore, this is not the last scene in the novel, but occurs about three-quarters of the way through the book, at the end of which the family has been reunited, Shuichi has left his mistress, and they all plan an outing together to the old family home. In Naruse's version, with the Shinjuku Garden scene closing the film, it is far more likely that Kikuko will make a clean break with the family she has married into. As the narrative conclusion, the scene becomes emblematic and suggestive with its implicit reference to cinematic space.

The French critic Andre Scala places this final scene of *Sound of the Mountain* centrally in his discussion of Naruse's cinema in relation to Dutch genre painting of the seventeenth century. For Scala, Naruse's cinema and the art of Vermeer, Pieter de Hooch, Hals, and Rembrandt von Rijin, work "in their own way among three elements: the everyday, the relationship between the looks and the acts of the protagonists, and composition."[44] While he is making a general argument about Naruse's mature style, Scala finds this Shinjuku Garden scene emblematic because it expresses "a tension between the fullness of the visual perceptions and the inner concentration emphasized by the dialogue." However, in his analysis, "the vista that Naruse has chosen is not the dimension of the possible; it is without a future." Indeed, if the cinematography of this scene fails to exploit the potential depth of field, the "vista" remains little more than a background to the action, and the "inner concentration" seems to take precedence over the vista. As I have suggested, the articulation of the words *vista* and *perspective* by Kikuko indicates a shift and an opening up of possibility, and the term is rich in metaphorical meaning. It is as if she has been inspired by the landscape, even if she remains very much part of it, the object of the gaze rather than its subjective origin.

Another reading of this Shinjuku Garden scene is provided by Hasumi Shigehiko, who links it to several other scenes in Naruse films in which a man and a woman walk together through trees, leaves, and shadows. The camera moves with the characters, cutting between them as they converse, and within this large spatial expanse, the only orientation is the relationship itself. Given the absence of fixed points of reference, the man and the woman are virtually alone, despite the intercut shots of other couples and families in the park. For Hasumi, "Yamamura So and Hara Setsuko, as they walk side by side, thus seem to slowly step into endless expansion as the movie meets the movie in its true sense."[45] This reading of Naruse's modernism recognizes the lack of perspective in the mise-en-scène, and links it to the romantic aesthetic with which Naruse has replaced Kawabata's eroticism. For Hasumi, "the void" is held off by the virtues of simplicity; but I think it is equally important to recognize the contours of this "void," the depth of space with its implications of ocular perspective, and the subjective centering of vision, an aesthetic that Naruse carefully invokes without fully adopting in his own mise-en-scène.

Scala and Hasumi both provide important keys to Naruse's modernism, noting the ways that he uses space and a discourse on looking to represent the complexities of the relationship between the man and the woman. Their formal analyses can (and should) be further amplified by a reading of the modernity of this scene implicit in the public "democratized" status of Shinjuku Garden. Shingo notes that it is amazing that "such a park could exist in the middle of Tokyo." Given the love of nature that has been one of the primary bonds between him and his daughter-in-law, the garden envelops them in a utopian discourse of the possible. In the novel, Shingo wonders, "Did the scene tell one that the youth of the land had been liberated?" and while Naruse's script omits these words, I would argue that the sense of possibility is nevertheless registered in the location itself, and in Hara's final smile.

As usual, it is an ambivalent ending, and not only because Naruse's style remains tied to a very different aesthetic than that implied by the reference to perspective and depth. Kikuko is a character drawn to the old ways, and her affection for Shingo is bound up with the wifely duties that she performs for him—bringing him tea, picking up his clothes, and so on—but she is also of the postwar generation. She has an abortion on her own initiative, telling the family about it only afterward. Moreover, Naruse's style remains one of observation. While Hara's performance of misery, especially after she has had the abortion and cries uncontrollably at home with Shingo and his wife, is extremely powerful, she is very guarded, much like her persona in Ozu's films of the same period. Kikuko's troubles are highlighted and amplified by Hara's performance, but she never fully escapes the circumscribed roles of wife and daughter-in-law. As a home drama and a woman's film, the existential dilemma is not of Shingo's mortality, but of Kikuko's freedom.

The other women in the film are far more outspoken and articulate their troubles much more directly than does Kikuko. Nakakita Chieko has one of her best supporting roles as Shuichi's sister, Fusako. Her husband has left her with two children. She accuses her father of having married her to an unreliable mate, and points out how much kinder he is to his daughter-in-law than to her. Kinu, Shuichi's mistress, is a war widow with her own dressmaking business. She believes that she deserves to have another woman's husband as her lover, and to have his child, because of her loss. She can do without Shuichi, whom she says beats her violently. A fourth young woman, Eiko (Sugi Yoko), frequents dance halls with both Shingo and Shuichi, but eventually takes Shingo to Kinu's home out of sympathy for Kikuko. Together with Kinu's roommate, Ikeda (Tanami Yatsuko), the film features four young single women, all trying to make their way in a world in which men like Shuichi have been psychologically destroyed by the war. Mizuki has added several remarks in the script alluding to the trials and tribulations of women, comments that are more typical of Hayashi Fumiko than of Kawabata. Yasuko, Shingo's wife, accuses her husband of not understanding how women feel: "The sadness of a woman is very different from the sadness of a man."

From Kawabata, Naruse has developed an aesthetic vocabulary with which to explore the contradictions of Japanese modernity. The simplicity and harmony of the garden, the no mask that Shingo acquires from a deceased friend, the architecture of the house—all these things can't stop the dissolution of Shingo's family. His affection for Kikuko is a blind against the failed marriages of his children and a foil for his own mortality. Naruse also counters the individualism of Kawabata's psychological narration by placing Shingo within a constellation of characters whose relationships are articulated through composition and framing, very much along the lines of the Dutch masters of the seventeenth century. Within the terms of the observational style of the shoshimin-eiga, the aesthetics of the old world are incompatible with love, romance, and the escape from restrictive social roles. Shuichi himself, while on one level another of Uehara's despondent salarymen, seems driven to adultery by the stasis and formality of his father's home.

At one point in the film, Shingo places a no mask on the face of his secretary Eiko (Sugi Yoko). The gesture affects Shingo as an erotic display, but it is also a gesture of repression and subjugation in which Sugi Yoko is turned briefly into a doll. Chuko Satoshi describes a scene that does not appear in the film, but may well have been shot, in which Shuichi asks Kikuko to put on the mask. As Chuko describes it, the mask of a young boy "had an aspect that reminded one of young female sexuality," and on Hara, it revealed the sensuality of her character.[46] We can only speculate that either the scene was cut because it revealed too much, ironically by masking the woman's face, or that Chuko is misremembering the film. In fact, when Eiko dons the mask, she seems to suddenly look like Kikuko, an impression heightened by Shuichi's awestruck gaze. In fact, the mask theme of *Sound of the Mountain* complements Hara's distinctive star image and performance style. It is easy to assume, as Chuko does, that Hara puts on the mask because she is an actress who is always somewhat masked.

Hara's performance, in which gesture, facial expression, and glances say far more than her words, has a masklike aura. The mask for Hara constitutes a kind of doubleness, as if her "well-proportioned beauty" were only one layer, the public one, of a more complex personality that remains hidden beneath it. By 1954 Hara had acquired the iconic power of Japan's "eternal virgin," having starred in a long series of war films, followed by Kurosawa's "democracy" picture *No Regrets for Our Youth* (*Waga seishun ni kui nashi*, 1946) and a string of Ozu home dramas, including *Late Spring* (*Banshun*, 1949), *Tokyo Story* (*Tokyo monogatari*, 1950), and *Early Summer* (*Bakushu*, 1951). Her star image was thus closely bound to the national imaginary, in which the ideology of the virgin harbored an ideal of cultural purity. Hara Setsuko's screen persona is one of tight control, under which a current of strong emotion can often be detected. Part of her popular appeal was due to a certain honesty and integrity of character, enhanced by the home drama genre that kept her in extremely plain costumes. However, she also excelled in expressing highly contradictory and conflicted emotions. She can be at once hopeful and doubtful at marriage proposals; she laughs when she is most sad and cries when she is most happy. The contradictions and tensions within Hara's star image are very much bound up with a nativist sensibility, a longing for the past combined with a recognition of the impossibility of such a return. Among her secrets is her reputed quarter-German heritage that may account for her slightly Caucasian look.

Several theorists have argued that traditional Japanese culture lacks the duality of exterior and interior—body and soul—that is such a cornerstone of melodramatic acting styles in the West as well as a key component of Method acting.[47] The introduction of realist acting styles to Japanese theater and cinema thus entailed a shift in the very conception of the subject. In Japanese, the same word, *omote*, refers to both mask and face, and the meaning of an actor's expression is ostensibly legible on its surface.[48] Roland Barthes has even argued that there is no "inwardness" in classical Japanese theater.[49] There is something called *netsuen*, or intense display of emotion, derived from kabuki, which refers to excessive performance and is typically the province of male actors. However, the privacy of intimate emotions is traditionally absent, like women, from public view. On the few occasions in which Hara "acted out" in *No Regrets for Our Youth* and *The Idiot* (*Hakuchi*, 1951), for example, critics found it repugnant and even monstrous.[50]

The production of an inwardness of subjective expression is implicitly linked to modern acting techniques. The withholding of inwardness, however, in the context of cinematic narrative, can also signify a morality linked to a national culture that protects a certain reading of the body. Hara's sexuality is in the end her biggest secret: she retired after her last film with Ozu, and according to Donald Richie, her disappearance at age forty-three was the cause of great resentment, especially as she has remained a recluse ever since, closely protecting her privacy. She refused to grow old in public. The spectacle of the woman's body may have been a key ingredient of Japanese modernity, but it also tended to repress the emergence of female subjectivity. In the 1950s, the construction of femininity remained precariously balanced between subjectivity and a protection of traditional gender roles, and Hara Setsuko arguably played a crucial role in the display of this balance.

In *Sound of the Mountain*, Shingo is a guardian of traditional cultural forms, and his attraction to Kikuko is inseparable from her aura of refinement and traditional femininity. His particular obsession with the mask might be read as a modernist gesture (on the part of Kawabata and Naruse), a recognition that the old man is imposing a form of character onto the young woman that is somewhat idealistic and irresponsible. He wants to double her beauty by masking it with an image of beauty. Hara herself gives an especially expressive performance, and despite Kikuko's affection for Shingo, she seems to understand what is going on. In her films with Naruse (in addition to this one, she plays lead roles in *Meshi* and *Sudden Rain* and a smaller role in *Daughters, Wives, and a Mother* [*Musuma, tsuma, haha*, 1960]), Hara is far more expressive than in some of her other roles with other directors, but her expressions are always deeply ambivalent. Through her performance, and the changes made to Kawabata's story, *Sound of the Mountain* most eloquently details the difficulties of female emancipation and the contradictions of female subjectivity within Japanese modernity. The price of freedom for Kikuko is the loss of her father-in-law and the aesthetics of nature, simplicity, and the old world with which he is identified.

Late Chrysanthemums
WOMEN'S STORIES IN POSTWAR JAPAN

The title of *Late Chrysanthemums* (*Bangiku*, 1954) evokes a familiar trope of Japanese poetics: the equation of women with flowers, whose beauty peaks and fades. There is beauty to be sure in the fading, as the flower and the woman become symbolic of the mortality of all things. But this iconography seems inadequate, if not inappropriate, to the representation of women in 1950s Tokyo. Indeed, Naruse's film challenges the paradigm of the title by situating his fading flowers—four middle-aged women who were geisha together before the war—in the midst of the complex social and economic landscape of postwar Tokyo. Their

46. Sugimura Haruko in *Late Chrysanthemums* (*Bangiku*, 1954), Toho.

struggle for survival and self-esteem cannot be aestheticized in nature imagery; they are not objects for the poet's gaze, but subjects with their own stories to tell about modern Tokyo.

Late Chrysanthemums is based on three Hayashi short stories written in the late 1940s, two of them among her most well known works. "Bangiku" won the women's literary prize *Joryu bungakushu* in 1949,[51] and "Suisen" ("Narcissus") was acclaimed by such literature authorities as Edward Seidensticker and Mishima Yukio.[52] Screenwriters Tanaka Sumie and Ide Toshiro linked these two stories with a third, "Shirasagi" ("White Heron") for the script of *Late Chrysanthemums*. In this film, set within a studio version of the prewar shitamachi, Naruse indulges in a nostalgic fantasy of the old city subsisting within the heart of the metropolis. Sugimura Haruko, who plays the lead in *Late Chrysanthemums*, was a stage-trained actress, although she was usually cast in supporting roles, perhaps the best known of which is as Shige, the older sister, in *Tokyo Story*.[53] Her starring role in this film is one of the rare occasions that she was given to develop a complex character on the screen, and she is very much responsible for the success of this film, which Naruse admits is so simple that he was allowed to make it only because of the success of his other Hayashi adaptations.[54]

The narrative of *Late Chrysanthemums* comprises four days, over which period several storylines unfold around the character of Kin (Sugimura), who exchanges visits with three of her old geisha colleagues. The film begins and ends at 11:25 a.m., indicated by a shot of a clock on Kin's wall, and the narrative closely observes the rhythms and cycles of everyday life in the city, such as meals, sunlight and shadows, newspaper and milk deliveries. While Kin lives in a well-appointed home with a small garden, a maid, and a small dog, her friends have fallen on harder times. Her

47. The "Monroe person" passes. Mochizuki Yuko and Hosokawa Chikako in *Late Chrysanthemums* (*Bangiku*, 1954), Toho.

occupation as a moneylender and real estate speculator is frowned on by her friends, who are nevertheless dependent on her resources. Kin has helped finance a small bar that Nobu (Sawamura Sadako) runs with the assistance of her husband. When Kin tries to find her friend Tamae at the hotel where she works, a woman throws a bucket of water after her as she leaves, a gesture of distaste directed at the moneylender.

Kin's third friend, Tomi (Mochizuki Yuko), works as a janitor in an office building where she also deals in black market cigarettes. Tomi's character is as intriguing as Kin's; a typical Hayashi woman, she is hard drinking and very practical. She won't pay Kin anything but comes home to Tamae, her housemate, with pork cutlets procured with pachinko winnings. Tamae (Hosokawa Chikako) is the most classically beautiful of the four women, and, being rather sickly, comes closest to embodying the fading flower of the film's title. If there is a narrative trajectory to this film, it is Tamae's emergence from her dark home into the sunlight of metropolitan Tokyo where, in the last scene, she affects a certain gesture, a casual flip of the hand practiced by both Kin and Tomi, that indicates nothing and everything. It suggests an ability to be ironic, an ability to see oneself as a modern subject, in step with a world that is changing so quickly that one has to live in the moment to survive.

If there is a moral trajectory to the film, it is, however, oblique. This is a narrative in which nothing happens beyond the day-to-day banalities of life in the city. Over the course of the film, Tamae and Tomi both see their grown children leave them; Kin receives disappointing visits from two former lovers, but the women all survive these setbacks and emerge renewed and ready to face whatever the city should throw up against them next.

THE JAPANESE WOMAN'S FILM OF THE 1950S

Through a scattering of gossip dropped over the course of the film, we know that after a failed suicide attempt before the war, Kin had her former lover Seki arrested for attempted murder, and he was jailed and then sent to Manchuria. When he comes to see her, Kin is extremely rude and refuses to loan him money. In the transition from the night of the second day to the morning of Seki's visit, a musical theme of clacking sticks is resumed, a gentle rhythmic motif that suggests an offscreen source of an itinerant musician that is never revealed. This musical motif is first introduced during Kin's passage through the city collecting money in the first day of the narrative. As she turns into her own street, she glimpses Seki at the far end of the road. With the rhythmic tapping of the sticks, the two play hide-and-seek within the labyrinth of small passages, hidden stairways, and shadowed lanes. Kin finally manages to get home without him seeing her. This short sequence, occurring early in the film, is at once ominous—as Seki has not yet been introduced as a character—and strangely peaceful, as the quiet city with deep shadows absorbs a lingering sense of unease.

The fluidity of the montage as the film cuts between various spaces and characters is enhanced by various visual motifs. For example, after Seki's visit on day three, the scene closes with Kin drinking tea alone in her pristine tatami room while her maid sweeps and the soft rhythmic clacking resumes. Cut to Tamae sweeping in a very similar composition, picking up the rhythm of the maid's broom. Kin arrives at Tamae's home to collect money. The graphic matching of domestic activity has effectively covered an ellipsis in which Kin has traveled from her home to her friend's. Through these techniques of sound effects and montage, *Late Chrysanthemums* is embedded in the rhythms and patterns of everyday life of women in the city.

More than an hour into the one-hundred-minute film, Kin's former lover Tabe (Uehara Ken) arrives. The scenes that follow constitute the film's emotional climax, as Kin flirts with him, prepares herself behind closed doors, and they settle in for an evening of drinking, music, and talk. However, after a few moments, Kin reveals in voice-over her disappointment with the man, who, it turns out, has come to see her for the same reason as everyone else: to borrow money. In fact, Uehara's character is yet another disaffected salaryman cheating on his wife. As he gets drunker and drunker, Tabe makes a futile pass at Kin's deaf maid, while Kin goes to the other room and burns his photograph. It starts to rain, and Kin opens the doors to the garden, allowing the sensual softness of the night air into the room that is drained of passion.

This long scene is interrupted three times with another scene played out at Tomi and Tamae's home, which is much more darkly lit. The two women get drunk together, reciting classical poetry about wayward children and unreliable men.⁵⁵ Finally, they fall into a futon together but are too worried about their children to fall asleep. Tomi does Tamae's hair and flatters her about her former elegance. The crosscutting concludes with shots of Tamae sleeping and Tomi stumbling around drunkenly, Tabe sleeping alone, and Kin sleeping beside the maid, with the sound of rain linking Tomi and Tamae's melancholy space with the quiet rooms in Kin's home. While the scene with Kin and Tabe reveals the vulnerability of Kin's character beneath her hard-hearted appearance, the other scene offers a vision of women's camaraderie and spirited resistance to the cruelties of everyday life. The careful crosscutting of the two scenes thus produces a contrast, and at the same time, a pattern of emotional tension and release, integrated in the end, into the rhythms of drinking, sleep, and rain.

The last day begins with the soft clacking of sticks. Kin says goodbye to Tabe, and at 11:25, she is with her real estate partner Itaya (Kato Daisuke), counting money, at exactly the same time they met on the first day shown in the film. Nobu arrives to tell Kin that Seki has been arrested, but Kin refuses to bail him out. She says, coldly, "'Eat or be eaten' isn't just for men." Meanwhile, Tamae and Tomi are seeing Tamae's son Kiyoshi off at the train station, where he is leaving for a coal-mining job in northern Hokkaido. At the station they see two geisha in full regalia. They may look like dolls, out of place in the bustle of the station, but Tomi stares at them enviously, recalling past pleasures that are no longer available to her. She guesses they are off to a hot-springs resort. But then, on a bridge overlooking the railway tracks and the sprawl of the city, a young woman in a tight skirt and heels passes Tomi and Tamae with a swaying step. Tomi exclaims that she is "imitating that Monroe person" and promptly does her own imitation, which is what finally makes Tamae laugh and gesture with a bent wrist.

This concluding scene is followed by a last glimpse of Kin and Itaya out in the city on their way to see a property. Kin briefly searches for her ticket to exit a subway station, finds it in her purse, and proceeds down a long flight of steps with Itaya beside her. As the music rises, they move into extreme long shot, descending down to an unremarkable urban square. As an ending, this shot strongly suggests continuity and, like the women's laughter in the previous scene, a sense of change and transformation. The iconography of trains, bridges, and stairs is not only symbolic but also locates the fiction within the documentary frame of location shooting. Significantly, both these final scenes are set in metropolitan Tokyo, outside the narrow streets and nostalgic space of the studio-created shitamachi labyrinth where the women's homes are located. Despite the suffering they have endured, they are ready and willing to make their way in the modern world in which they have come to know themselves.

Late Chrysanthemums was described by a *Kinema Junpo* critic as a josei eiga, a woman's film. This critic, Sugimoto Heiichi, appreciated the characterizations of women that went "beyond the stereotypes" and noted how different these mothers were from the more typical depictions of motherhood in the haha-mono (mother film), including Naruse's own *Mother* (1952).[56] Despite his ultimate endorsement of the film as a "tour de force," Sugimoto is critical of a perceived lack of psychological depth in *Late Chrysanthemums*. A similar critique was articulated by Iida Shinbi in the film journal *Eiga Hyoron*. This critic praises Naruse's choice of subject matter in *Late Chrysanthemums*, as well as his "unparalleled skills in mise-en-scène." However, he is critical of Naruse's adaptation of the Hayashi stories because of the way that the characters' different backgrounds are elided. He notes that in the original stories, each of the women's "drifting sex life" is provoked by some incident such as a rape or an abandonment. For Iida, Naruse's depiction of the four women lacks not only the depth of Hayashi's writing, but also her strong authorial point of view.[57]

Both Iida and Sugimoto describe *Late Chrysanthemums* as a *seitai-eiga*, or ecological film, recognizing its sociological view of characters deeply immersed in their urban setting of postwar Tokyo. However, Naruse's lack of moral assessment of his characters clearly challenged the norms of humanist criticism of the period. Iida indicates how the dispersed, multifocal narrative of *Late Chrysanthemums* is linked to an authorial modesty, as if Naruse were surrendering himself, in a sense, to his subject matter. Although Sugimoto acknowledges the strong performances of the principal actors, he is distressed by the cold-heartedness of the Sugimura character, who is "not hurt." The attitude of "eat or be eaten" (a phrase that Naruse takes directly from Hayashi) seems not to be appreciated by these critics.

In fact, what Naruse has done with the Hayashi material is more anthropological than psychological. Despite the characters' romantic longings and memories of the war and prewar times, their activities and their movements through the city are governed mainly by the circulation of money. The itinerant beggars and salespeople who periodically interrupt the narrative, or are glimpsed in the street or heard hawking their wares, further sustain the rhythms and patterns of commerce as the substance of everyday life in the city. They also inscribe a current of desperation and poverty within the cycles of everyday life, a tension that appears to be eased only by excessive drinking. As former geisha, Nobu and Tamae work in peripheral water-trade establishments—the hotel and the bar—and Tomi is a regular at Nobu's bar, where she reminisces about her alcoholic adventures in Manchuria before the war.

Among the beggars who appear in the film is a nun who knocks at Tomi's door asking for alms, and there are other ritualistic practices represented in the film, including Naruse's signature brand of street musicians promoting a theatrical performance. Kin is observed praying to a small shrine in her home, and while these may be small details with no direct relevance to the narrative, they indicate the ways in which Japanese modernity has absorbed and incorporated elements of an older way of life. Naruse's use of domestic architecture in his framing and cutting of interior scenes is itself emblematic of the balance and harmony of traditional Japanese aesthetics, and it conveys the sense that the four main characters are rooted in the past. However, given the references to Manchuria and the war, it is a complicated past, profoundly implicated in the failures of the nation. The photo of Tabe that Kin burns in disgust is a picture of him in uniform; her hopes for a rekindled love affair are dashed along with the pride that she—and he—once had in their country.

The coexistence of different values and practices is most clearly underlined by the late encounter with the woman whom the ladies dub "that Monroe person," after Marilyn; but it is also implied in the two narrative lines concerning Tomi's daughter Sachiko (Arima Ineko) and Tamae's son Kiyoshi (Koizumi Hiroshi). Sachiko, who works in a restaurant, is a practical girl, much better equipped than her mother for the modern world. When Tomi comes looking for a loan, Sachiko tells her mother that she is getting married the next day. Tomi sacrifices her kimono to pay for the wedding but appears to drink most of the proceeds. Sachiko boldly asks Kin for a wedding gift of cash, meeting the moneylender on her own terms. She and her fiancé are moving to a rented room that they will have to share with other tenants in Tokyo's real estate crunch—precisely the development that Kin seeks to get a piece of with her partner Itaya.

Kiyoshi is not quite as practical or hard-nosed as Sachiko, although he confesses to his mother that he is seeing a woman who is another man's mistress. Tamae raised him alone, telling people he was her brother, but when he gives her money from this woman, they argue about who has subjected whom to a life of hardship and ill-gotten gains. Kiyoshi's mistress wears a kimono, as do the older women, whereas Sachiko wears the sensible skirt and blouse of the young modern woman. These fashion indices suggest that Kiyoshi is being drawn into his mother's anachronistic way of life. Kiyoshi eventually leaves his mistress and his mother for a paying job in the mines of Hokkaido, a familiar theme of 1950s shoshimin-eiga—the relocation of men and women around the country by corporate culture. The question of children and the ostensible rewards of motherhood is a key theme of the film. Visiting Kin, Tomi says, "Money is everything. You must be happy in your nice house." Kin replies: "But you have a child. You are more fortunate than I." Then she adds, "Money moves around me, but nothing is really mine." Later, when Tomi and Tamae are drunkenly assessing their losses in life, they decide that "a woman's happiness shouldn't lie in her children."

The twenty-year-old children in *Late Chrysanthemums* seem to know their places, or at least are able to find their way within the new demands of "democratic" Japan. If the older women are left in midstride, they are nevertheless on their way to finding their own paths. It should be noted that their survival in the modern world is to some extent at the expense of others. Both Kin and Nobu are able to run their small businesses on the basis of small domestic hierarchies: Kin's deaf maid, who can't eavesdrop on her financial conversations, is a childlike companion to the moneylender; Nobu's husband, of Asian descent but clearly not Japanese, takes orders from his wife in a way no Japanese man would do. Nobu asks Kin for a loan so she can have a baby, and it is Nobu who runs the bar, indicating an inverted social hierarchy within her family. Neither of these women are depicted as authoritarian employers or household tyrants, so Naruse cannot be accused of any matriarchal fantasies of feminist social inversion. Instead, these relationships are symptomatic alternatives to the dominant model of the Japanese family system in which women's place is tightly circumscribed.

While *Late Chrysanthemums* cannot be described as a feminist film, it should be recognized as engaging with questions of female subjectivity in the metropolitan culture of postwar Tokyo. The promises of democracy may have rewarded Kin's character, but at the expense of her sexuality, along with any conventional form of "femininity," as the critical discourse on the film indicates. These promises have clearly failed the other characters, including the men, who are all deeply in debt. The final encounter with "that Monroe person" is emblematic of the iconography of a vernacular modernism that the older women in the film learn to read and understand. As a home drama without a conventional family, set outside the Japanese family system, *Late Chrysanthemums* poses the question of a woman's self-determination within the terms of popular culture. Naruse's attachment to the life style and design of the prewar shitamachi does not preclude the women's integration into the modern city. Their eventual emergence in the film's final scene represents the subjective experience of historical transformation in modern Japan.

Floating Clouds
NARRATIVE AND MEMORY

Floating Clouds (*Ukigumo*, 1955) is a film with an epic span. Due to its engagement with the geopolitical history of the immediate postwar period, it has found a special place in the national imaginary and tends to be Naruse's best-known film in Japan. In the opening shots of the film, Takamine Hideko as Yukiko emerges from a series of stock shots of repatriated Japanese civilians trudging home after the war. Because Yukiko's story includes flashbacks to her wartime posting in Indochina and her liaison with an American GI in Tokyo, it intersects with controversial social issues that by 1955 were rapidly becoming a history at risk of being forgotten. The story of *Floating Clouds* is focused on a love affair between Yukiko and another repatriated civilian, but their romance cannot be disentangled from the postwar conditions that the lovers confront on their return to Japan, and the trajectory of their affair is an expression of the state of the defeated nation as a society adrift. Based on Hayashi Fumiko's last completed novel (1949–51), the title *Ukigumo* (frequently translated as "Drifting Clouds") is a common metaphor for an aimless life. Hayashi borrowed the title from Futabatei Shimei's "first modern novel" (1887–89), shifting the emphasis from the male to the female protagonist.[58]

Takamine's character Yukiko is a typically stubborn and resilient Hayashi heroine, although not without a sense of humor when she witnesses her relative (and occasional lover) Iba perpetuate a fraudulent religious cult for profit (she eventually manages to steal most of his proceeds from him).[59] Her lover Tomioka (Mori Masayuki), although largely unemployed, is in some respects similar to Uehara's salarymen: a despondent and irresponsible man, prone to drinking and womanizing and not in control of his own life, shuffled around the country by the powers that be. Despite the familiarity of these characters, *Floating Clouds* is an anomalous film and represents a significant departure for Naruse. It was not the first time he had used stock shots or flashbacks, but they participate here in a complex narrative structure in which memory and time become much more prominent features than in the spatialized narratives—the home dramas—with which he had become identified. As Hasumi Shigehiko notes, with no "two adjacent rooms" (Naruse's favored domestic set), the characters and the film lack stability.[60] The couple pass through one or two homes, but they never stay. They are constantly on the move, through Tokyo, to a hot-springs resort (Ikaho), and finally to Kagoshima and the island of Yakushima in Kyushu in southern Japan. They meet in inns and bars; they stroll together through the ruined streets of the city, through parks and through the forests of Indochina. Yukiko lives briefly in a small "storage house" as the companion of an American GI (who is merely glimpsed and overheard in passing), and briefly as Iba's mistress in an elegant, well-appointed home; Tomioka lives in a suburban home until he sells it and sends his wife to the countryside. He rents a room in a tenement surrounded by children playing in the corridors.

Despite their repeated attempts to rekindle the love they experienced in Dalat during the war, Yukiko and Tomioka cannot find happiness in postwar Japan. She is especially persistent in seeking him out, but he is ambivalent, unwilling to commit to her, until the final scenes in which she accompanies him to Yakushima, contracts TB, and dies alone in the mountains in a thunderstorm. Only as she becomes ill and finally dies does Tomioka display any real affection for Yukiko. Until that point, he seems drawn to her almost helplessly, but at the same time he is attracted to other women as well. Because of his womanizing, Yukiko becomes the sympathetic focal point of the narrative. It is her story and her death to which the meandering narrative finally leads.

Hayashi's narration actually shifts between the two protagonists' inner thoughts,[61] whereas in the film Yukiko's perspective is unambiguously privileged. While she suffers, Tomioka is cold-hearted, apparently taking advantage of her affections. Jean Douchet points out that as a "ladies' man," Tomioka "likes his ladies dead."[62] Indeed, Yukiko's death is preceded by those of Tomioka's wife (of natural causes) and a woman named Osei (Okada Mariko), with whom he had an affair while visiting Ikaho with Yukiko (Osei is killed by her husband, possibly out of jealousy). Douchet's ironic comment points to the way that while Yukiko is hopelessly stuck on one man, Tomioka moves carelessly through a

48. The Ikebukuro storehouse home. Takamine Hideko and Mori Masayuki in *Floating Clouds* (*Ukigumo*, 1955), Toho.

series of women. Yukiko's last words to her lover accuse him of being a womanizer, causing her undue stress in her weakened condition. Indeed, the novel ends with Tomioka leaving Yakushima to meet up with a woman he met on the way there.[63] Hayashi depicts the inner thoughts of a man who is so affected by the defeat of Japan that his life has lost its meaning; his despair is the main obstacle to the realization of their love affair. Whereas the novel can be described as an "anti-love story that from the beginning destroys and negates the pattern of the *Bildungsroman*,"[64] Naruse's film is very much a love story, with all the pathos and melodrama that the genre entails.

Mitsuhiro Yoshimoto has offered a provocative reading of *Floating Clouds* in terms of national allegory. In his view, the suffering of the couple "is in some sense a form of punishment for their complicit relationship with Japanese imperialism." He explains: "The ultimate death of the woman in Yakushima, which resembles the jungle of Southeast Asia, seems to confirm this reading of the film. Naruse's seemingly apolitical melodrama is in fact one of the most subtle yet severe indictments of Japanese imperialism and of the responsibilities of ordinary people who

THE JAPANESE WOMAN'S FILM OF THE 1950S

benefited from Japanese colonial enterprise."[65] For Yoshimoto, the film stands out for its refusal to follow through on the "conversion narrative" of postwar Japanese melodrama in which prewar Japan is "converted" seamlessly into the new postwar society, a conversion that depends on the denial of the war and its emergence from prewar modernity. In his reading of *Floating Clouds*, the Takamine character "refuses to convert . . . to a comfortable ordinary life in postwar Japan," and the film demonstrates that "Japan as an imagined community is often reconstructed only at the expense of women."[66]

While Yoshimoto's interpretation accounts for the woman's sacrifice and points to the ways that *Floating Clouds* departs from contemporary narrative treatments of the war, the characters cannot be said to feel responsible for their role in the war. On the contrary, the flashbacks of Dalat constitute a dreamlike fantasy. Tomioka served as an official in the Imperial Forestry Ministry, and Yukiko was posted there as a typist, but the imagery is more that of a country retreat than a workplace. They meet in an elegant colonial mansion, where they are served by local servants (one of whom Tomioka flirts with), and they stroll together through a pastoral landscape of babbling brooks, leafy forests, and flowery meadows. Dalat is a virtual escape from Japanese social conventions, an escape that they hope to recapitulate in their journey to Yakushima, where Tomioka finally finds a new posting. The final flashback, inserted as Tomioka weeps over the body of Yukiko, features Takamine dressed in white skipping (in white platform shoes) down a forest path in Dalat.

As Susanna Fessler notes of Hayashi's novel, "there is an overall sense of loss: loss of innocence, loss of love, and loss of experience."[67] Hayashi herself traveled through China and Southeast Asia during the war, writing reports from the front that were nothing if not consistent with kokutai policy. Her failure to apologize for these activities was criticized after the war,[68] and there is little evidence that *Floating Clouds* constituted any kind of remorse on her part. I would argue that, contrary to Yoshimoto's interpretation, the deep ambivalence of both novel and film lies in the implicit memory of wartime as a kind of utopian paradise.

The romantic memory of Dalat propels the film to its final tragic conclusion. The destiny of the lovers is precisely the failure to recover their experience as colonial expatriates. When they finally arrive in Yakushima in a torrential downpour, Yukiko needs to be carried on a stretcher from the boat. In some respects, this is Takamine's most glamorous role in a Naruse film, and she is frequently lit with a soft light in which she positively glows. Her hair is worn loose, and in a number of instances she is dressed in the flashy outfits of a mistress or prostitute. Her death scene, in which she crawls across the floor to close a banging shutter, coughing and crying all the way, is high melodrama. The woman nursing her enters the house, and Tomioka, far away in a hill station, suddenly turns to the camera intuitively sensing Yukiko's death (an image that would be recapitulated by Oshima Nagisa in *Cruel Story of Youth* in 1960). Several times they have contemplated double suicide, using it as an excuse to travel to remote inns, where they inevitably call it off due to lack of will or inspiration and some obscure desire to live.

By the time they go to Yakushima, Tomioka has finally found a job and Yukiko has successfully stolen ¥300,000 from Iba, who took advantage of her before the war. In the inn in Kagoshima, where the lovers wait to travel to the island, the staff refer to Yukiko as "madam," and they are finally recognized as husband and wife. But in true melodramatic fashion, it is too late. Yukiko has already fallen ill, and their happiness will forever elude them. As Douchet notes, this is a film with no future, a film in which people are doomed to live in a perpetual present tense, "a time of love, not a time of desire."[69] Perhaps this is a kind of punishment; perhaps their desire is too closely tied to an experience deemed in the postwar period to be invalid and unacceptable to be reawakened after the war. Yukiko may be a thief, but that is her only crime. She went to Dalat to escape the dismal domestic situation that she endured with her sister's family and in-laws. The war offered her an opportunity to escape the Japanese institutions of womanhood, even if it turned out to be a false hope. Yukiko and Tomioka are not characters who have committed a crime; they are characters caught up in the sweep of history over which they have no control, as the deus ex machina of Yukiko's death insists.

The sense of a perpetual present tense, cut off from future and past, is precisely the achievement of Naruse's film, which once again transposes a melodramatic woman's film into a modernist idiom. The narrative transitions from one space to another, moving abruptly from mansion, to family home, to black market storage shed, from public park to hot-springs resort, are always abrupt. Indefinite amounts of time pass between sequences, and the transitions are rarely established or prepared for. In one two-minute scene demonstrating Naruse's narrative economy, Yukiko has an abortion and reads of Osei's death in the hospital. In many much longer scenes, Yukiko and Tomioka sit by a table in a sparsely furnished inn or restaurant, drinking, smoking, recounting their last parting, or planning their next ill-fated encounter. At one point they pass a crowd of striking workers singing "The Internationale" (in another scene that Oshima would revisit in the opening scenes of *Cruel Story of Youth*). The lovers are sidelined by history, on the margins of postwar society.

From interviews with some of the crew on this film, it seems as if Naruse's idiosyncratic shooting methods affected the outcome of *Floating Clouds* perhaps more than any other of his films and are partially responsible for the sense of a perpetual present tense. He shot the scenes out of order, so the actors lacked a sense of momentum or continuity from one scene to the next. As art director Chuko Satoshi points out, he and his team were required to build more than twenty different sets for this film, as well as work on locations in Kyushu, Ikaho, and Izu (where they put up fake palm trees to masquerade as Indochina).[70] Mizuki Yoko suggests that *Floating Clouds* was a particularly frustrating shoot for her, because as she was revising her screenplay to eliminate scenes set on location, according to Naruse's orders, he had already left Tokyo and started shooting on the locations she had been asked to take out.[71]

Takamine at least had access to the script beforehand, but when it came to the big picture, she was at the mercy of the director's inclinations. She says, "He'd have an image of the movie inside his head so he could shoot any part of it. Preparing yourself so you could follow along was the responsibility of the actors."[72] For her first "romantic" role with Naruse, Takamine reportedly spoke all her lines into a tape recorder to give to the producer Fujimoto Sanezumi to prove that she was not suitable for the part, although it is not clear whether this was before or after Mizuki's script had been hacked away at.[73] Takamine praises Mori Masayuki for his work in *Floating Clouds*, saying that it was "his film." In fact, they both give superlative performances, embodying the characters as truly desperate lovers whose fate seems always out of their control.

In her obsessive passion for Tomioka, Yukiko comes to resemble a heroine like those of nineteenth-century Victorian literature, focusing her entire being on a man who is clearly undeserving of her affections. For his part, Tomioka is not unlike Heathcliff in *Wuthering Heights* (1847): charming and rugged, associated with the outdoors, a man who women seem to continually throw themselves at. Yukiko is forced into other liaisons for the sake of survival and stoops even to thievery to seduce Tomioka (she calls him to join her after she robs Iba), yet she is wholly defined by a single-minded passion. The excessiveness of her relentless pursuit of Tomioka may be seen as an expression of female desire that cannot be contained by a repressive society. Postwar Japan, like Victorian England, offered women education but little opportunity for career advancement or professional status. Yuikiko's skills as a typist and an accountant are not enough for her to support herself, so she is compelled to use her body for profit. Through the late 1950s and 1960s, as Takamine played more romantic roles, Naruse's cinema would more and more resemble the tragic fatalism of Victorian literature, in which women's suffering is expressed in endlessly frustrated romantic relationships.

The mobility and meandering narrative of *Floating Clouds* follows the two protagonists through a series of iconic locations, including ruined sections of Tokyo (which Fujimoto notes were hard to find in 1954),[74] the forested woodlands of the Izu Peninsula, the wharf in Kagoshima where Mori looks for a boat, the crowded Ikebukuro marketplace, and the hot-springs town of Ikaho, for which Naruse used a rare crane shot to film the lovers walking up and down the steep shadowed stairs of the village. The film includes many emblematic shots of the lovers: in the bath, in the rain, on a boat, among the ruins, and so on. As Hasumi remarks, the image of "a man and a woman" is most powerful in this film, as they alone anchor and connect these disparate public and private spaces.[75] Often their despair is registered only in sorrowful looks and dejected poses, huddled around a brazier to keep warm or walking together through desolate landscapes.

As Douchet notes, the relentless flow of the narration creates the sense of a void: "Life, a constant presence, flows incessantly, simply because this kind of life is unstoppable. But it has no meaning in it, it is empty."[76] He further accounts for Naruse's occasional disruptions of continuity editing in this film as an inversion of space that "jolts the senses." Indeed, *Floating Clouds* is Naruse's most formally ambitious film, in its elliptical narrative structure and deep ambivalence regarding the memory of war. It was a rare film in 1955 that dealt so squarely with the sorrow of a defeated nation, and a reactionary reading in which Yukiko's death is symbolic of a national death is as valid as Yoshimoto's more progressive interpretation of it as an indictment of imperialism.

Noriko Mizuta's assessment of Hayashi's novel is true of the film as well: "Through her depiction of Yuikiko's wandering amid the emptiness and desolation of the defeat that marked the end of modernity in Japan," Hayashi presents "an impossibility of development." The parallels with *Rashomon* may go further than their shared borrowing of Ravel's "Bolero" for their soundtracks. Like Kurosawa's film, *Floating Clouds* conveys a depth of uncertainty and instability, although in this case it is more intricately linked to postwar Japanese society and significantly lacks the optimistic finale of *Rashomon*. There is no social rebirth on the horizon at the end of *Floating Clouds*. The paradise that the lovers dream of and remember becomes Yukiko's graveyard, and Tomioka is doomed to drift aimlessly after she dies.

Sudden Rain
SUBURBAN ETHNOGRAPHY

Although *Sudden Rain* (*Shuu*, 1956) might be thought of as Naruse's fourth "marriage film," the depiction of the city and postwar society is far colder than the neighborly communities of *Meshi*, *Husband and Wife*, and *Wife*. In *Sudden Rain*, the couple's marital difficulties are inseparable from the urban alienation of suburban Tokyo. The neighbors in this unnamed residential area are, for the most part, selfish, nosy, and rude. The salaryman Ryotaro (Sano Shuji) and his wife Fumiko (Hara Setsuko), another childless couple, are so bored with each other they can't think of anything to do on a Sunday but sit around and mope. *Sudden Rain* is an extraordinarily bleak film, with little narrative resolution to the couple's difficulties. Yet in its detailed depiction of everyday life in postwar Tokyo, and in Hara Setsuko's exceptional performance, the film, as the title suggests, offers a poetic treatment of a dismal situation.

Weather and weather imagery play an important role in Naruse's cinema. Heavy rain in *Okuni and Gohei* and *Floating Clouds*; extreme heat in *Older Brother Younger Sister*; extreme cold in *Husband and Wife*; thunderstorms in *Meshi* and *Sound of the Mountain*—all help to create sensual atmospheric conditions and dramatic contexts for the narrative action (or nonaction, as the case may be). Titles referring to cloud patterns (*Floating Clouds*, *Summer Clouds* [*Iwashigumo*, aka *Herringbone Clouds*, 1958], *Scattered Clouds*, [*Midaregumo*, 1967]), flowers (*Late Chrysanthemums*), and even natural processes (*Flowing*), provide symbolic frameworks for elliptical stories. In *Sudden Rain*, these two principles of atmosphere and symbolism converge. A sudden shower occurs during a scene in which Fumiko and Ryotaro are at home with Aya (Kagawa Kyoko), Fumiko's niece, arguing about what she should do about her husband's bad behavior on their honeymoon. Ryotaro defends the man, who has gone drinking all night leaving his new wife in the hotel alone, while Fumiko is shocked. In the midst of the argument, the next-door neighbor Nenkichi (Kobayashi Keiju) runs to their back door to tell them it's raining. He helps Fumiko bring in her laundry, but his wife

49. Sano Shuji and Hara Setsuko in *Sudden Rain* (*Shuu*, 1956), Toho.

Hinako (Negishi Akemi) angrily berates him for leaving bags out in the rain on their front porch.

The only other narrative reference to sudden rain in the film is Fumiko's habit of meeting her husband at the station with an umbrella and rain boots if he has not taken them with him in the morning. Hinako does not do this for Nenkichi, who envies Ryotaro for his "perfect wife." The one time we see Fumiko performing this task, Ryotaro doesn't come home all night. Within the banality of existence in this gender-based domestic setting, rain showers are little more than interruptions in the routines of everyday life, moments that bring out the tensions and contradictions that underscore the deadly boredom and continuity of life in the suburbs. By giving the film the title "Sudden Rain," Naruse implies that there may be some beauty to be seen in these interruptions. Like the lightning flash in the film named after it, the implication, derived from Japanese poetic form, is that a sudden insight might be gleaned from a provocative image of nature. It could be the beauty of decay, as in the image of late chrysanthemums, or simply transience as in the cliché of cherry blossoms (which Naruse manages to avoid using, more or less, throughout his career). One interpretation of *Sudden Rain* would be that the idea of a passing shower or unexpected rain points to the possibility of social transformation—that the unfairness and discrimination that Fumiko, as a bored housewife, experiences, will not persist forever.

Like the "dialectical image" in Benjamin's materialist historiography, the flash of recognition that is implied in the Zen notion of *satori* is precisely the "now" of present time that interrupts the continuity of a historiography invested in the concept of progress. Within the context of postwar Japanese consumer culture and the depression of suburban life, Benjamin's thoughts regarding the status quo as the catastrophe are very relevant. He argues, "If the object of history is to be blasted out of the continuum of historical succession, that is because its monadological structure demands it."[77] The past has truly been forgotten in *Sudden Rain*. There are no references to the war, and the culture of flower arranging and kimono are the province of rich housewives, who flaunt it as a sign of social status. If my interpretation seems forced, it is in turn informed by Benjamin's principle of historiography: "Historical 'understanding' is to be grasped, in principle, as an afterlife of that which is understood."[78] In any case, the strength of *Sudden Rain* lies in the evocative tension between the alienating effects of consumer society (and its related gender-based discrimination) and the "beauty of small things," or principle of *wabi*, which is conveyed in the title. Benjamin's theory of the dialectical image suggests a reading of this tension as a form of rescuing critique.

Cinematographer Tamai Masao has offered an interesting anecdote about shooting *Sudden Rain*. The home consists of two adjoining rooms opening onto a garden, and the lighting throughout the film is generally bright with sunlight (the single night scene features Fumiko walking back from the station through wet, glowing streets). Tamai and Naruse argued intently about how far they could push the lighting for the scene in which the sudden rain shower occurs, but there are two different versions of the anecdote. In one place, Tamai says they used artificial lighting and that Naruse let it get darker and darker before "he let the rain fall," asking the crew to keep shooting even after the light meter failed to respond.[79] In another interview, Tamai implies that they used natural light, saying that the daylight became darker and darker. Tamai wanted to wait until the rain passed before shooting the scene, but Naruse insisted that they push the lighting to its limits in order to stay on schedule and within the budget.[80] In fact, the light does drop dramatically throughout the scene preceding the rain shower, and it looks more like natural than artificial light to my eye. For Tamai, this is evidence of Naruse's stubbornness and shows how little the director communicated his ideas to his crew. Whether the dimmed lighting was intended or accidental, the effect of the sudden shower erupting from a situation that is both narratively bleak and visually dark is at once very subtle and extremely powerful.

Although the film is very cogent on the plight of the salaryman, it is the wife who is most in need of redemption. Fumiko's troubles are not limited to her inconsiderate husband, who is depicted as being utterly helpless around the house, demanding constant service and attention. She has befriended a stray dog, who destroys the belongings of all the neighbors, including a chicken. She is called to a community meeting where everyone complains about everyone else (the meeting is held in a kindergarten and is not without irony, as everyone perches on tiny chairs). Although she is a careful shopper, Fumiko is the target of a pickpocket when she watches an entertaining sandal vendor. The festive atmosphere of the local shops turns out to be merely a trap, including the displays of toasters and blenders that she can't afford. Hinako, the young wife next door, wears her hair long and her skirts short, and even goes to the movies with Ryotaro when Fumiko is too depressed. When Ryotaro's salaryman friends come to visit and Fumiko serves them chicken and sake, they discuss a scheme in which they could take a severance package offered by their boss (which, as Fumiko points out, is insultingly small) to start a restaurant. They propose that Fumiko work in it due to her good looks and elegance. Kato Daisuke, playing one of Ryotaro's colleagues, says to Fumiko: "It's a woman's era. As you are so beautiful, you should take advantage of it. You don't have to stay at home." Fumiko is amused and kind of likes the idea, but Ryotaro is scandalized and angry with her for even considering the proposal.

The film ends shortly after an argument in which the couple talk about separating. Fumiko says she wants to work, and seems finally ready to express her pent-up feelings. A child's paper balloon is thrown accidentally into their yard and Ryotaro goes out to toss it back to the two little girls next door. Fumiko follows him and they hit the ball back and forth between them, yelling "harder, harder." Nenkichi and Hinako come out and watch, and the camera pulls back to frame the two children in the foreground (with an old lady who enters the yard to watch this strange behavior), Ryotaro and Fumiko in the middle ground, and the neighbor couple in the background. The yards and houses are identical suburban units. If for Benjamin, "surrealism is the death of the nineteenth century in comedy,"⁸¹ the absurd ending of *Sudden Rain* evokes an equally comic death to the promises of democracy.

The presence of children may suggest, however crudely, that the marriage will be saved when the couple has a family; it is nevertheless an ambivalent ending to a film that has gone to some lengths to suggest that this life is miserable and hopeless. Ryotaro takes medicine for his stomach, can't eat anything, and constantly taps his foot, suggesting a nervous, stressful psychological malady aggravated by riding the packed commuter train every day (although he blames it on Fumiko's "hard rice"). All he wants to do is return to his hometown. In the last scene, they receive a note and a new honeymoon picture from Aya, saying she has made up with her husband, but Fumiko sneers, unimpressed. She has finally come around to agreeing with her niece, who earlier shocked her with her critique of men and marriage.

Based on a story by Kishida Kunio, *Sudden Rain* is full of witty insights into contemporary life, such that the shoshimin-eiga becomes a vehicle for an ethnographic treatment of the postwar middle class. When Aya complains about how her husband left her alone on their honeymoon, Ryotaro mocks her by implying that she has unrealistic expectations based on the polite behavior of foreign men. His own macho behavior may be justified as the rights of a Japanese man, but the film makes it very clear that his wife is losing her patience with it. This is the new panic time of the salaryman. The gossipy women neighbors discuss a movie that made them cry and comment on its parallels with their own lives and friends. This may be a comedy of manners on one level, but it focuses on the most insidious elements of social behavior. The community meeting is especially harsh. Fumiko apologizes for being too self-absorbed and failing to appropriately greet everyone on the street when she passes.

When Fumiko goes to meet her husband on the roof of a department store, she briefly catches the eye of another woman (the wife of one of Ryotaro's old schoolmates), who is dressed in an elegant kimono. Fumiko clutches her humble jacket to her throat and drops her eyes. The exchange of glances between the two women is their only encounter in the film, but it says a great deal about Fumiko's self-image. In a film in which people rarely meet each other's eyes, this fleeting moment of recognition seems to seal Fumiko's impoverished fate, but as a dialectical flash, it also offers hope for change. Without cutting back to a reverse shot of Ryotaro, Fumiko apologizes for being late, speaking to the camera, as if to the lady whose eye she has just met. But when the reverse shot is finally offered of Ryotaro—over Fumiko's shoulder—Fumiko's gaze is angled differently. This technique in which characters seem to speak directly to the camera, looking just to the side of the lens, with the reverse shot delayed and either mismatched or withheld altogether, is a familiar device of Ozu's, and one which Naruse begins exploiting more often in the late 1950s. The effect is to have the characters address the camera as if it were judging them. As Naruse explores themes of social injustice, prejudice, and humility, speeches delivered in direct address take on the aspect of an appeal.

Indeed, all of *Sudden Rain* is incredibly open, inviting the spectator to judge these characters who represent a plethora of competing behaviors. Nenkichi, the neighbor who appreciates Fumiko's wifely ways, is the only real note of stability in the film, but he is himself caught up in a culture of repetition and conformity, brushing his teeth side by side with Ryotaro in their suburban patches of lawn and offering Fumiko a gift of coupons for soba noodles in lieu of the traditional new neighbor gift of actual soba. With *Sudden Rain*, Naruse pushes the marriage film to its limits, dissecting the minutiae of the domestic hell of a salaryman and his wife, doomed to perform rituals that consumer culture has rendered redundant. Hara's enigmatic smile, like the sudden showers of the film's title, are all there is to suggest that this is not the end of history, but an incentive for change.

A Wife's Heart
A FILM IN WHICH NOTHING HAPPENS

Like many directors of world cinema, Naruse's films are often narratives in which nothing happens. Rather than dramatic action, the emphasis is on the poetic and emotional ups and downs of everyday life. A familiar realist style, the narrative in which nothing happens has become established as a classic modality of art cinema. Small events take on greater significance, and emotional turmoil is expressed through performance and subtle effects of cinematography, mise-en-scène, and montage. Many of Naruse's marriage films and "home dramas" might be described this way, but *A Wife's Heart* (*Tsuma no kokoro*, 1956) pushes this aesthetic to a certain limit. It is not so much that nothing happens, so much as nothing is seen to happen. In fact, it is in many ways a deeply melancholy film, but part of its sadness is precisely the lack of expression of sadness.

Generically speaking, *A Wife's Heart* is another marriage film or tsuma-mono (wife film), featuring another young, disaffected, childless couple. However, it is also a family film along the lines of *Sound of the Mountain*, *Lightning*, and *Older Brother*—without the hysterics of the latter two titles, or the poetry of the former. Audie Bock says that "the film is said to show a total rigidity of the family system,"[82] and indeed it is a stultifying situation that Kiyoko (Takamine Hideko) finds herself in as the daughter-in-law of a middle-class, shop-owning family in a small town. Bock claims that Naruse "wanted to show stronger women" after the passive Yukiko of *Floating Clouds*, but Takamine's Kiyoko is not strong enough to change the system. Nor is she strong enough to follow her heart, which, the film suggests ever so obliquely, does not belong to her husband.

The eventlessness of *A Wife's Heart* is epitomized by an empty center, a hole in the middle of the narrative. Kiyoko goes for a stroll in a temple grounds with the unmarried brother of her friend Yumiko (Sugi Yoko). The brother, Takemura Kenkichi, is played by Mifune Toshiro, whose strong masculine persona (bolstered by his star image) is in striking contrast to Kiyoko's husband Shinji, played by Kobayashi Keiju (who lacks even the delinquent apathy of Uehara Ken's useless husbands). Kiyoko has approached Kenkichi to borrow money for a café that she and Shinji are hoping to open, as he works for a bank. He agrees to lend them ¥300,000 with no collateral, but Kiyoko is persuaded to give that money to Shinji's older brother Zenichi (Chiaki Minoru), who has lost his salaried job and has returned home to open a restaurant himself. Kenkichi continues to see Yukiko at a restaurant where she is apprenticing and he is a customer. They go to a movie together, although that outing is not depicted (nor is the movie title indicated), and toward the end of the film, Yukiko and Kenkichi are seen walking in some temple grounds.

Yukiko and Kenkichi are in a café on the temple grounds, waiting out a sudden rain shower. They talk a bit about the past, when they came to this place with Yumiko just after the war, and then, after Kenkichi notices some children playing in the rain, they talk about kids and marriage. Kiyoko says, "If you marry without thinking about it, though, it can be a big headache later." Realizing what she has implied, she drops her eyes. A few shots of the rain in the garden are intercut in the pregnant pause that follows. Mifune leans forward a little and says "Kiyoko-san," followed by a quick cut to Takamine, who drops her eyes. The scene cuts back and forth between the two, inserting a shot of a woman slipping behind the bar in the background. The screen fades to black and comes up on the couple still seated at the same table, but from a new

50. Mifune Toshiro and Takamine Hideko in *A Wife's Heart* (*Tsuma no kokoro*, 1956), Toho.

angle—a 180-degree reversal—framed by the door of the café. The rain has stopped and they agree to go. The shot of them standing dissolves to a close-up of Kiyoko looking in a mirror in her bedroom and the beginning of a new scene.

A fade to black normally indicates a temporal ellipsis, or at least a change of location, but in this instance it signifies nothing but an absence or lack. Nothing happens in that blackout, and yet it is the emotional heart of the film. It effectively inscribes a form of longing that is otherwise imperceptible except for Kiyoko's sorrowful face in the mirror. The momentary blackness is all that is offered to indicate what might have been, what is desired, and what has been lost. The dramatic climax of the film consists of nothing more than romantic music, rain, a garden, "a man and a woman," to use Hasumi's expression, and a blacked-out screen. The incidental interruption of the café proprietor singled out by the camera is all that is needed to signify the social barriers inhibiting the romance signaled by the couple's exchanges of looks.

Back home, in Kiyoko and Shinji's bedroom, husband and wife confront each other's indiscretions. Shinji tells Kiyoko about an unfortunate incident that he has been mixed up in: a local geisha, Fuku, has killed herself after spending the night with him at a hot-springs resort. Fortunately, everyone agrees that it was not his fault (she had marital problems of her own), and his name is not reported in the papers. Fuku's death is not seen; neither is Shinji's little fling with her. However, gossip about Kiyoko and Kenkichi has reached Shinji, and he tells her she can do what she wants. Kiyoko doesn't answer, but it shortly becomes clear that she has chosen her husband and his demanding family over her heart.

Ide Toshiro wrote the original screenplay for *A Wife's Heart*, but Naruse eliminated one of Ide's central characters—a friend of the Mifune character and a series of violent attacks between the two men and Shinji vying for Kiyoko's attention. Ide says that "Japanese people don't go for things like that and Naruse couldn't make a film like that anyway."[83] In fact, Ide's screenplay sounds a bit like the style of the *taiyozoku* (sun tribe) films that hit the scene in 1956, spawning a youth film culture that would soon eclipse Naruse's ponderous aesthetics. Ide describes the final version of *A Wife's Heart* as "boring," and even though he made seven more films with Naruse, says he began to think after this that he could not work with the director. Despite Ide's somewhat self-centered account, it is worth noting that this is the only title from this period that is not based on a literary original, and it shows in the weakness of the script.

The film is more distinctive for its cinematographic features than for its screenplay. Set in a spacious middle-class home, *A Wife's Heart* is shot somewhat differently than Naruse's previous home dramas. Using the complexity of a sprawling house adjoined to a dry-goods shop staffed by unnamed employees, a garden, and an empty lot (where Kiyoko and Shinji plan to build their café), the film is full of shots of characters passing each other in corridors, exchanging quick glances that convey the household tension. The home is ruled over by the matriarchal Ko (Miyoshi Eiko), an expressionless woman who arranges marriages (and flowers) and prefers to have her daughters-in-law do the housework than to hire a maid. The family business is floundering, but she seems unconcerned, even in denial about the changing economic climate. She has spent the family savings (¥300,000) on a dowry for the youngest daughter Sumiko (Negishi Akemi), who subsequently hints that she might move back home as she has more courage than other wives who put up with bad marriages.

When the wife of the elder son, Kaharu (Nakakita Chieko), arrives with her daughter, it gives Kiyoko the time to apprentice as a cook (and go out with Kenkichi), but Kaharu annoyingly rearranges things. Misplaced nail clippers in this film are a big event. Indeed, the materialism of the constant talk of huge sums of money is inscribed in the paraphernalia of the bourgeois establishment: dishes, cushions, mirrors, and cabinets. It may not be a cluttered home (except for the storeroom), and it maintains the traditional sparse aesthetics of Japanese domestic architecture, but it is far more full of things than previous Naruse sets have been. The detail of objects is partially a function of the choice of lenses: whereas in *Sudden Rain* the background is blurry and the characters are usually in close and medium shots, in *A Wife's Heart* a wider angle includes more in the frame, with more of the background in focus.

The interior sets of *A Wife's Heart* are just a little bit too perfect, leading the critic Sugiyama Heiichi to note that not only is he growing tired of Naruse's films about soured married life, this film is not sufficiently embedded in "the actuality of life."[84] In some ways this film is indicative of the ways that Naruse's cinema struggled to adjust to the new values of postwar Japan. While in the 1930s the traditional home bore the signs of poverty, modesty, and the virtues of small things, Naruse was able to carry that aesthetic into the postwar period through his shitamachi sets—a technique that is revisited in his very next film, *Nagareru* (*Flowing*, 1956). Here, though, as in *Sound of the Mountain* and many of the subsequent films of the later 1950s and 1960s, the traditional home signifies the luxury of open space and the expense of craftsmanship. The furnishings, the dishes, and the detail of the architecture—including the wooden floors and frames that are polished by dutiful daughters-in-law—have become iconographic of bourgeois taste and old-world values. The family system, of which Ko, as a semiprofessional matchmaker, is a principal caretaker, is visually fortified by the precision of the domestic interiors. Kaoru's daughter Rumi is always dressed like a little princess, and she bounces her ball alone on the polished floors while her errant father disappears and reappears only to drink and claim his rights as the eldest son, rights that Ko happily endorses.

The film ends with a closing shot that matches the film's opening establishing shots of the family shop sign and an aerial view of the town with the mountains in the background. Kiyoko efficiently squashes the rumors about Kenkichi and herself, and she returns to the plans for the café, performing her housewifely duties with a smile on her face. In the final scene, Ko is trying to arrange a marriage for Yumiko. Life goes on, and all is returned to normal as if nothing has happened—and indeed, except for the death of a local geisha, nothing has. One woman critic of the time, Abe Tsuyako, admired Kiyoko's ability to overcome her feelings, noting that she is motivated not by "old morals," but by her business sense.[85] However, two women writers, Enchi Fumiko and Yuki Shigeko, noted the double standard that the film leaves unquestioned: that the husband's affair is a passing fancy, while the wife risks everything by going for a walk with another man. For these critics, the film does not seriously question the family system, and they find the "calm and sensible" tone rather conservative.[86]

Although these women's views differ, they nevertheless confirm that the film upholds the status quo and is a more closed narrative than many of Naruse's titles from this period. It lacks the radical ambivalence that informs the melodramatic narratives of those films that endorse and uphold the woman's subjective desires; and it is oddly lacking in humor. The irony of a household seemingly dependent on a daughter-in-law's liaisons with a local banker to survive goes unnoticed, as invisible a ploy as the casual event of a dead geisha, and as empty as the black hole in the middle of the film. *A Wife's Heart* is a film without a spark of life, a film that blackens its own gesture of romance, and in this respect it inadvertently points to something dead.

Flowing
HOUSE OF WOMEN

The third film that Naruse released in 1956 is, strikingly, the most complex of the three. *Flowing* (*Nagareru*) is based on a novel by the woman writer Koda Aya. The script by Tanaka Sumie and Ide Toshiro is a tour de force of screenwriting, involving an astonishing number of sub-plotlines associated with the women of a geisha house facing imminent extinction. Cutting between the various characters, the film is nevertheless firmly centered in the Tsuta house in the old "pleasure quarters" of Tokyo near the Sumida River. It is one of the few Japanese films to penetrate the walls of this women's world without sensationalism or titillation. The ensemble acting of a roster of top actresses with only a few very minor male roles makes this one of the key woman's films in Naruse's oeuvre, and despite the narrative complexity, the film's production design adheres to the director's signature use of Japanese domestic architecture for a simplicity and formality of style. Indeed, in the face of all the social changes that the women of the Tsuta house encounter, the film ends with a reaffirmation of the traditional arts of music and dance on which the geisha world is founded.

The Tsuta house consists of two adjoining rooms, a kitchen, a maid's room, an entryway, and a corridor on the ground floor, and a second floor where the madam, Tsutayako (Yamada Isuzu) lives with her daughter Katsuyo (Takamine Hideko). The house is an *okiya*, where geisha check in before and after appointments; they pay the madam a percentage for brokering the engagements and for the prestige of the house. The downstairs area is fairly cramped, and the women are always overhearing each other's conversations, including those on the telephone prominently located in the corridor. A constant flow of traffic moves through the house as deliverymen, family members, doctors, and moneylenders are constantly coming and going, as are the women of the house. Above this hive of activity, Tsutayako occasionally receives visitors in her spacious quarters. She also dresses there and displays the elegant paraphernalia of the accomplished geisha that she is. Abandoned by her husband and unlucky in love, she owes money to her elder sister Otoyo (Kahara Natsuko) and has taken in her niece Yoneko (Nakakita Chieko), along with Yoneko's daughter Fujiko (Matsuyama Natsuko). The six-year-old is training to be a geisha, and the film opens and closes with her performing a dance to the strains of the samisen. In the ways of the geisha world, the future of the house more or less depends on this child, as

Tsutayako's own daughter has chosen not to follow in her mother's footsteps.

The larger storyline of the film involves the fate of the okiya itself, instigated by an incident in the opening scenes in which a young geisha from the country, Namie, accuses Tsutayako of cheating her. Katsuyo defends her mother, even though she later admits that there are ambiguities about the house's accounting procedures. Indeed, it is not sex but money that is the primary currency of *Flowing*. Namie's uncle arrives and demands ¥300,000 compensation, invading the house with his loud and drunken manner, and Tsutayako is compelled to borrow money from Mizuno Ohama (or "Mrs. Mizuno," as Donald Richie's subtitles refer to her). Played by the veteran actress Kurishima Sumiko, who starred in Naruse's 1933 film *Every Night Dreams*, Mrs. Mizuno is an officer in the geisha guild and the madam of her own house. An imposing figure, she wields an authority that is hitherto unknown in Japanese cinema for a woman to carry.

Mrs. Mizuno bails out the Tsuta house by providing money from a male patron, Mr. Hanayama, through his assistant Seki (Mizoguchi Seiji). Hanayama himself never actually appears in the film but functions as a kind of invisible power behind Mizuno. She tries to set up a date with him and Tsutayako, but only Seki arrives at the restaurant, with apologies from his boss (Seki and Mizuno may well be in collusion to dupe Tsutayako, although that aspect of the plot is never completely resolved). Later in the film Mizuno announces that Hanayama would not provide any more support, but that she would be willing to buy the Tsuta house to help Tsutayako pay off her debt to her sister. That Mizuno is not to be trusted becomes abundantly clear when she tries to persuade Oharu, the maid (Tanaka Kinuyo), to leave the Tsuta house and work for her when she takes over the okiya and makes it a branch of her own business. Oharu asks what will become of her present employers, and Mizuno replies: "If they want to continue, let them go across the river and work. Those new girls are not much. . . . You have to work hard to be a geisha."

Oharu turns down Mizuno's offer and, being the paragon of virtue that she is, she remains silent about her experience. Her loyalty to the Tsuta house secures the idea of the geisha business as a viable cultural establishment, despite its evident failings on the economic front. Oharu arrives early in the film to apply for employment and quickly ingratiates herself among the women for her maternal manner, her trustworthiness, politeness, generosity, and level-headedness. It is she who cares for Fujiko when the child is sick, and it is she who calls Mrs. Mizuno when Tsutayako and Katsuyo are taken to the police station to resolve their dispute with Namie's uncle. A widow who has recently lost her son, she brings to the Tsuta house, and to the film itself, the values and virtues of the home drama ideology of ascetic simplicity. Tanaka's character could have walked directly out of Naruse's *Mother*, but while her humble manner is in direct contrast to the geisha, her role is fundamental to the film's project of bridging the two worlds of quotidian domesticity and exotic demimonde.

Takamine's character Katsuyo provides yet another dimension to the house of women. While she respects her mother's profession, she is a pragmatic modern woman and can see that she will have to support her mother eventually, given the probable destiny of the anachronistic enterprise in which she has grown up. Her mother tries to set her up with Seki, and they do eventually take a walk together along the Sumida River. Shot in Naruse's favorite perambulating man-and-woman-traveling composition, their conversation quickly goes to the question of Katsuyo's future. "Who would marry me?" she asks, assuming that the daughter of a geisha would not appeal to anyone. She ignores Seki's hesitant reply, "I don't know about that." Katsuyo sees herself as half geisha and half not. Framed against the cityscape across the river, in a tight sweater, she is clearly ready to move on to a new life. By the end of the film, she has installed a sewing machine on the upper story of the house and is attempting to learn a new trade to support herself.

Rounding out the cast of characters are Someko (Sugimura Haruko) and Nanako (Okada Mariko), who provide the film with an important element of humor that helps to create the sense of community among the women of the Tsuta house. Nanako is evidently of the postwar generation, a new-style geisha or *ima noko* ("today's girl") of the kind that Mrs. Mizuno dismisses as unworthy of the title. Like Katsuyo, she occasionally wears stylish Western clothes, and her mannerisms lack the refinement associated with the geisha world. Both Nanako and Someko are constantly plagued by errant and irresponsible lovers, and they seem to be the only two women in the film who actually go out to entertain customers. In one scene, they come home quite drunk and prance around as if they can't stop partying. But in a subsequent scene, Someko accuses Tsutayako of cheating them and completely breaks down, crying, "Is it true that women don't need men?" She subsequently reconciles

51. The upstairs room. Yamada Isuzu, Takamine Hideko, and Tanaka Kinuyo in *Flowing* (*Nagareru*, 1956), Toho.

with Tsutayako, and in the final scenes she plays the samisen with the madam, demonstrating her proficiency and dedication to the rigors of the profession.

Sugimura's performance is especially comic. Someko is obsessed with a repertoire of superstitious folklore, and her love of cheap street food helps to ground her character, and by extension the okiya, in the everyday life of the shitamachi. Like *Late Chrysanthemums*, *Flowing* is shot in a studio version of the prewar shitamachi that has miraculously survived the war. Some location shots of the elevated subway line and neighboring streets circa 1956 are incorporated, but the small street on which the house fronts is clearly a set. The integration of the house into the city is accentuated by the views from the windows of the second story. From the front window, where Takamine frequently lingers, a cityscape of roofs and chimneys stretches into the distance. Through the back, overlooking a tiny garden, one can glimpse neighboring houses with women occasionally doing housework.

Koda Aya's novel was serialized in the journal *Shincho* only one year before the film's release. Koda herself worked as a maid in a geisha house in the winter of 1951–52 in order to escape the pressures of her life, and she based her novel on that experience.[87] For contemporary Japanese audiences, the insight and originality of both novel and film was the relationship between "professional women" (*kuroto*) and "amateur women" (*shiroto*), and the access provided to the world of the geisha by Koda through her protagonist Rika, the maid. (In both novel and film, the geisha arbitrarily change the woman's name when she arrives, from Rika to Oharu.) In Koda's novel, Rika is an educated woman not unlike herself, in keeping with the autobiographical element of the story, but in the film she is not only a less prominent protagonist, her background is somewhat more humble. In both versions, however, she is a recently widowed, middle-aged homemaker, through whose eyes the demimonde of the pleasure quarters is perceived. Ann Sherif notes that Koda was very much aware of the vast literature on the geisha world and set out to develop a new perspective that might depart from the two typical male approaches of voyeuristic fascination and the portrayal of women's suffering.[88]

Sherif also notes that Koda's novel was criticized for the complexity of the plot and the multiplicity of characters and subplots. She claims that what holds the whole narrative together is Koda's attention to detail and her sensuous descriptions of the everyday life of the okiya—precisely the realist sensibility that underscores Naruse's film. The okiya in the novel is described as being somewhat squalid and surprisingly messy, although in the film it is predictably pristine, if somewhat cramped. But the major changes that Tanaka and Ide made in their script concern the ending and the expanded role of Takamine's character. In Sherif's discussion of the novel (which has not been translated), she doesn't even mention a counterpart to Katsuyo, who, in the film, has been given some of the lines that Sherif indicates were originally those of the maid. In Naruse's version, Katsuyo shares with Rika/Oharu the perspective of an amateur observing the goings on of the closed world of the pleasure quarters. Moreover, while the film concludes with Oharu remaining loyal to Tsutayako and her "family," in the novel she accepts the offer to manage the house after the Tsuta women have been removed (hardly a realistic proposition for the uneducated Oharu of the film).

In her discussion of the novel, Sherif also suggests that there is an eroticism in the deployment of the gaze. As in the film, Koda avoids any representation of sex or sexuality, but according to Sherif, "Eroticism in *Flowing* takes on the particular form of the desiring gaze—specifically the gaze of woman taking pleasure in looking at woman."[89] The Rika/

Oharu character in the novel is attracted to the inherent eroticism and sensuality of the geisha life; she is "dazzled" and entranced by what she sees. In the film, the gaze is much more dispersed and de-eroticized. Oharu is certainly singled out as an observer, and in one instance she is seen among rows of hanging kimono, full of awe. In another scene, Oharu helps Tsutayako with her hair as she prepares to go out, and the two women are framed together in the mirror. Oharu admires the madam's fine skin, but the effect is more one of worship, and the desiring gaze is as much a narcissistic desire on Tsutayako's part as she sees herself framed with her maid's adoring gaze. It is a passing moment, linked to the architecture of the room with the rails of the window overlooking the garden. The shot presents a formal aesthetic of beauty, underscoring the role of the geisha as guardians of traditional culture.

By adding the Takamine character as another "observer," the film develops a strikingly passive view of the geisha milieu. Katsuyo and Oharu are often glimpsed in the background or on the sidelines, but the cutting in the film is quite erratic and certainly doesn't privilege any point of view. Some critics at the time noticed Naruse's elimination of a strong perspective, describing the film as "*zuihitsu*-like" or "essay-like."[90] *Zuihitsu* refers to a genre of writing in which the author expresses his or her impressions and thoughts without thesis or conclusion.[91] I would argue that *Flowing* does have a conclusion, even if it is typically ambivalent. But thinking of the film as a kind of essay can in fact be a productive approach, because Naruse is working on many levels of mise-en-scène and performance. For example, within and behind the paraphernalia of the geisha world—the kimonos and the obis, the hairdos and music lessons—is a background display of electrical appliances. While only the telephone is regularly used, the sets include things like TVs, radios, and fans. Tsutayako uses an electric massager, and at the end of the street on which the Tsuta house is situated, one can glimpse a constant stream of cars and trucks. These details indicate how the modern world is closing in on the geisha world, in which the customs and rituals of Edo period life are just barely surviving. Many of the actresses, moreover, actually went and met with the women on whom Koda based her novel and tried to base their gestures and behavior as well as their characters on these living models.[92]

In addition to these "ethnographic" elements, Naruse's essaylike approach is developed through his editing strategies, which move smoothly through quite a number of locations and spaces. In the smaller rooms downstairs and the larger space upstairs, and at Mrs. Mizuno's spacious home, the axis is regularly broken, as the principle of framing is much more governed by the lines of the architecture than by "correct" angles of point of view. In a couple of instances, the characters are situated on the diagonal of the room with the reverse-shot editing moving around them to frame all four walls of the room. The central corridor of the Tsuta house is shot from both ends, placing the phone arbitrarily on the right- or left-hand side of the frame. The street outside that runs at right angles to the corridor is likewise shot from both ends, placing the house on either the left or right of the frame. Characters are frequently centered in the corridor-like street as they leave or approach the house, and figures occasionally rush into a shot when moving quickly in the narrow corridor. The effect of this spatialization is to insist on a kind of formality in a world that otherwise seems to be slipping away from the regularity of form.

Only in the final sequences in which the women are gathered together to teach new pupils do they seem to be in harmony with their surroundings. This last scene, which lasts seven minutes, crosscuts between Katsuyo upstairs sewing and the geisha downstairs giving a lesson to some young pupils. Oharu serves everyone rice cakes, linking the two spaces. Someko and Tustayako play a samisen duet, observed by Oharu in the kitchen, the new pupils, and Yoneko and her daughter, who opens the scene by performing a dance for the assembled women. It is an extremely formal scene in which time seems to stop. Once again, the space is reversed when shot from both ends of the room. At first, the samisen playing is accompanied by the whirring of Katsuyo's sewing machine above them. Then Saito Ichiro's soundtrack segues into a swelling conclusion of strings and harp, and it becomes evident that the musical theme is based on the samisen melody that the women are playing. The final shots move out of the house to a shot of kimono-clad women walking past the house on the street, and finally to boats on the river spanned by a bridge. Time does not stop after all, as the women are being swept into a future in which they have become the guardians of the past.

Shortly after *Flowing* was released, the women's magazine *Fujin Koron* published a roundtable discussion with six of the actresses from the film along with the novelist Koda Aya and scriptwriter Tanaka Sumie. The principal theme of their discussion is the way amateurs and professionals are brought together in the film, and the roundtable highlights the different perceptions of geisha that were held by women in postwar Japan.[93] Tanaka Sumie says that a woman from "a certain woman's organization" was shocked that she had worked on such a film, because it is about an "unhealthy lifestyle" and "prevents emancipation." Indeed, in the mid-1950s women's groups had successfully brought about legislation against prostitution and continued to campaign against "immoral" practices that threatened the sanctity of the family.[94] Takamine Hideko replies that she thinks those women will nevertheless want to see the film because it is so rare to see a geisha film that includes amateurs who are not simply competing for men. Koda suggests that geisha treat men better than wives do, and have better manners, so amateurs might learn something from *Flowing*. For her, more interaction between amateurs and professionals would help smooth out social and domestic relations. She notes that geisha with an amateurish style (the *ima noko*, such as Okada in the film) are becoming more popular because of the way they implicitly bridge the two worlds, behaving spontaneously rather than with the strict formality of a "really professional geisha."

The merits of *Flowing* are discussed in this roundtable in terms of the information that it might provide about "the enemies of ordinary wives and daughters," and Tanaka Sumie adds that these "ordinary women"—who would of course be the readers of *Fujin Koron*—have long felt inferior to geisha because since the early Meiji period, "the only women who could talk to men on equal terms have been geisha in good districts." Kurishima notes that her character was based on "an admirable woman of authority." Even Tanaka Sumie, who is otherwise surprisingly critical of the demimonde, recognizes the empowerment and social mobility that is available to women in that world and jokingly asks if she should enter it herself. Besides Koda, only Sugimura and Yamada seem entirely comfortable with the milieu; indeed, both provide remarkable musical performances within the film that would have been possible only through training similar to that of the geisha. Sugimura says, "I just think it's a way of life for women." In bringing Koda's novel to the screen, Naruse takes her project of bridging the two worlds that much further, providing a film essay on the merging of the two worlds of Japanese women.

Toward the end of the roundtable, Tanaka Sumie asks Koda about the title. "Does it refer to the unrootedness of the characters, or to the river?" Koda replies that she had wanted to call her story "Hashi temae," which means "This Side of the Bridge," but because it's an "old word" she looked for something newer, and came up with "Flowing." She adds: "The bridge is over the river, providing a broad view, and across it there is something different. No one crosses the bridge without hesitation. We stop to look around. There is a moment of hesitation. Those who cross to the other side do so" (197). If Koda's explanation seems (in translation at least) to mean the opposite of "flowing," she nevertheless points to the way that the film depicts historical transformation not as a process of inevitability, decline, and loss, but more as a dialectical process in which choices are made, opportunities are recognized or declined, and changes are offered and received. Within the constellation of characters in *Flowing*, different women take different paths. Some will seize the opportunities of the postwar milieu, Mrs. Mizuno by adopting the conniving ways of big business, and Katsuyo by asserting her identity and autonomy. Others, such as Tsutayako, Someka, and Oharu, will persist in the old ways with pride. By expanding the role of Katsuyo and giving it to Takamine Hideko, Naruse's film adds to Koda's novel a sense of the emerging generational rift of postwar Japan. But within the genre of the women's film, mother and daughter remain close, and there is a sense that a changing world does not necessarily entail a total break with the past.

Flowing flows in other ways as well. The title could well refer to the film's narrative structure, comprised of many short three- to four-minute scenes, constantly moving between characters and spaces. Short scenes of a kimono salesman displaying his wares to the women, a policeman visiting and being served soba delivered over the back fence, and a geisha being presented by another house suggest how the Tsuta house is linked to a larger circuit of enterprises and services, both geographically and economically. The narrative momentum is also occasionally punctuated by meditative moments of the street at night, or the emblematic river, or the cat Ponko slithering along the roof shingles, brief shots that slow down the rhythm of the film's "action" with reminders of the passing of time.

The "flow" of the title might also refer to the flow of money that circulates among the characters, money that is frequently isolated in close-up either as a stack of bills on a table, or in a discretely passed envelope. The decline of the geisha house is unquestionably an economic issue, and the film does not hide from the hard facts of running such a business. The materialism of Naruse's mise-en-scène indicates that these "professionals" are after all not so far removed from the everyday world of the ordinary "amateur" women who would have constituted the film's original audience. Whether the geisha can sustain this middle-class lifestyle without men is the question that the film poses — without, in the end, admitting that the answer is, most definitely, no. The unspoken truth of this house of women is that despite the apparently utopian space of community, art, and domestic harmony, the women's business is to serve men. If Naruse has successfully circumvented the male gaze through which this world is conventionally seen, he has also cleverly hidden the source of the women's income. Without a patron, the house is ultimately doomed to extinction, as women's access to capital was still extremely limited in 1956.

Untamed and *Anzukko*
WHITHER THE NEW WOMAN?

By the late 1950s, much of the energy and optimism of the women's movements spawned in the occupation years had dissipated. A good indicator of the shifts that took place during the postwar years can be found in *Fujin Koron*, one of the leading women's magazines of the postwar era. In the immediate postwar period, *Fujin Koron* published articles on all aspects of women's lives, including the politics of domestic labor and the peace movement, but by 1957 the magazine began to concentrate more exclusively on fashion and homemaking issues.[95] Beauty contests, celebrity gossip, and discussions of correct styles of "femininity" were the dominant concerns of *Fujin Koron*'s many competitors. By 1958, progressive ideas were no longer selling magazines, and the editorial policy accordingly shifted away from the intellectual approach it had fostered in the earlier part of the decade. Beth Katzoff points out that even in the resurgence of the women's movement in the 1970s, feminists were largely cut off from the domain of popular culture, and the women's magazines of that era were equally apolitical.[96]

In Naruse's films of the late 1950s, we can perhaps see how the dynamics of the New Woman, which had underscored his 1930s films and informed many of the 1950s characters, were fading from sight. Takamine Hideko's performance in *Untamed* (*Arakure*, 1957) is among her most active and energetic, and her character is one of the most liberated in Naruse's oeuvre, but the film is set in the Taisho period, effectively displacing her feminist energy onto a dated depiction of modernity. Naruse's subsequent film *Anzukko* (1958) is a marriage film in which the wife, played by Kagawa Kyoko, becomes trapped in a hopeless relationship with a violent drunk, but unlike her predecessors in Naruse's previous marriage films, she is unable to resist him, largely because she is so enthralled by her patronizing father.

Untamed is based on a novel that was originally serialized in 1915 by Tokuda Shusei, whom some Japanese literary critics regard as one of the nation's first great novelists.⁹⁷ His naturalist style was grounded in a populist milieu and vernacular use of language. *Arakure* was his most popular novel and gained critical recognition as the top book of the year in 1915. The book, with a title that has been variously translated as *Rough Living* and *The Wild One*, features a heroine who is exceptionally independent and indomitable. Although she is based on a real woman of Shusei's acquaintance, she is hardly representative of Taisho-era gender norms.⁹⁸ As one man after another disappoints her, Oshima casts them aside and moves on, working hard to move from a life of servitude, to become a seamstress running her own business with a lot of ups and downs along the way. She makes Western fashions and wears them, rides a bicycle, and is always ready to swing her fists when angered.

Critic Richard Torrance suggests that even though Oshima was not Shusei's only "new woman" protagonist, the author was not necessarily an advocate for women's rights, but was "attracted to a new kind of human being he perceived in his contemporary society . . . someone who paid no heed to social conventions" (107). Although Naruse's adaptation, scripted by Mizuki Yoko, necessarily condenses the novel, the character of Oshima survives intact, and the period detail conveys the sense in the novel that, in Torrance's words: "Modern capitalism seems invigorated, enormously liberating, enriching people more than it impoverishes, and creating the tragic denouements of a lifetime every week and a half or so" (9). Indeed, the film moves so abruptly from one phase of Oshima's life to the next that the speed of modernization is very literally enacted. Torrance suggests that Oshima's character is someone who "is still with us," in her embodiment of an entrepreneurial spirit and the way that she "has no place in the traditional order" (13). But of course this is precisely the contradiction of women in Japanese modernity: to succeed as an independent subject, a woman must step outside the boundaries of social norms and practices.

In 1958, Takamine Hideko was more than ready to meet the challenge of portraying this woman on screen. Her sneering attitude and physical technique render Oshima as a stubborn survivor who is able to use men but also able to fall in love and have her heart broken. Although it is hard to say exactly which American films she and Naruse might have been watching, it is highly probable that her performance was inflected by some of the postwar roles of Joan Crawford and Bette Davis, and the 1940s screwball comedy performances of actresses like Rosalind Russell and Katharine Hepburn. Oshima has no-holds-barred fistfights with her first husband, Tsuru (Uehara Ken), her second husband, Onoda

52. Takamine Hideko in *Untamed* (*Arakure*, 1957), Toho.

(Kato Daisuke)—whom she also turns a hose onto—and with Onoda's mistress, Oyuri (Miura Mitsuko). Even with the man she really loves, Hamaya (Mori Masayuki)—who is married and ends up dying of consumption—she gets drunk during an argument and accidentally breaks a fancy screen in an inn. The film ends shortly after Oshima's fight with Oyuri. She leaves the woman's smashed-up house and phones the young tailor that she and her husband have recently hired, suggesting that he leave with her to start up a new business. He agrees to meet her at a hot-spring resort and will bring along the top apprentice, which will effectively cripple Onoda's business. The new young man, Kimura, is played by Nakadai Tatsuya, who even in this small role exudes the spirit of the next generation of Japanese actors.

One can almost detect the contemporaneous taiyozoku ("sun-tribe") films in Takamine's energetic performance, and the references to sexuality would hardly have been possible on the screen a few years earlier, even if the novel is far more explicit than the film about such things as the state of the heroine's genitals after bike riding. Of course, none of the taiyozoku films featured a female protagonist as progressive as Oshima. Naruse claims that the theme of the "strong-willed independent female lead character wasn't too popular at the box office" at the time *Untamed* was made, which may be why he chose a period setting for this character that, to him, is "the opposite of Yukiko in *Floating Clouds*." Nevertheless, in adapting the novel, he "tried to put more modern female attributes into Oshima's character,"[99] attributes that, despite being contemporary to the late 1950s, were not popular.

Although the novel covers the years 1884 to 1910, the film begins with a title setting the date as "the beginning of Taisho," which is 1914, closer to the date of the original publication of the novel. From Shusei, Naruse includes a great deal of period detail, including both city life and the rural setting of an inn in the mountains. With her second husband, Oshima exploits the market for ready-to-wear fashion, which was inaugurated by the Russo-Japanese war and would have been rejuvenated in World War I. One of the new Taisho-era entertainments featured in the film is the electrical light display in the Tokyo exhibition of commerce and industry. Oshima and Hamaya view the display from a Western-style restaurant.

Oshima also goes to a movie with her lover Hamaya, and *Untamed* actually includes an authentic-looking clip from a Taisho-era film, complete with a *benshi* providing narration and an onnagata in the woman's role. While movie dates were common practice in the 1950s and a familiar activity from Naruse's films of the period, it is unlikely that a man of Hamaya's class would have taken his mistress to the movies in the 1910s.[100] When the film breaks abruptly, during a romantic beach scene, the strip of broken film is briefly glimpsed before the screen goes to white as Naruse interrupts the narrative realism with a clever reflexive device. *Untamed* treads a careful line as it imposes behaviors from the 1950s onto the nascent modernity of early Taisho; historical authenticity takes second place to the depiction of an independent woman. As the filmgoing scene is not in the original novel, it suggests how Naruse might have seen his own role in the construction of a feminist public sphere.

The novel includes a great deal of movement, as Oshima travels from one town to another and between neighborhoods in Tokyo. In the first scenes of the film, she is the second wife of a rich man (Tsuru) in Tokyo, but when the marriage collapses, she travels to a town in the mountains where she works at an inn to pay off her brother's debts. When her affair with Hamaya becomes evident to the madam who runs the inn where she works (and which Hamaya owns), she is banished even further, to a hot-spring resort where she washes laundry in the river. Concerned that she is working as a prostitute, her father comes to take her home, forcing a separation from her lover, but back in Tokyo, she soon takes up with Onoda. As she falls and rises and falls in social status, her hairstyles reflect her variously married and unmarried status. Almost every change of scene finds her in a new setting, sporting a new style of clothing, from flashy kimono to conservative kimono, to Western frills, to a poor woman's rags. As a "period" film, *Untamed* covers a lot of ground, displaying the diversity of everyday life in Taisho Japan. The extensive use of the telephone is a modern device that enables the scriptwriters to move between diverse spaces and accelerate the narration.

The image of society in *Untamed* is one of social upheaval and possibility in which Naruse goes back to the dynamics of everyday life that he exploited in the 1930s, but this time with a much more active protagonist than was found on the screen at that time. As Torrance writes of the novel: "The everyday in *Arakure* is always on the verge of disintegration: families break up, businesses fail, social mobility is the rule. But somehow people 'get by.' *Arakure* is a celebration of the ambiguity and mystery of the everyday."[101] The real irony of *Untamed* is that Takamine's Oshima is a woman of the 1950s, but she is unleashed on the Japan of forty years earlier, a Japan that by the 1950s was "ancient history" and virtually unrecognizable in the present. In this displacement there is a certain refusal of the possibilities of the everyday that existed in the 1950s no less than they did in the 1910s. Naruse's representation of his contemporary Japan was becoming increasingly melancholy and bleak, as if he could not find Oshima within his own world. As in his occupation cinema, one senses in a film like *Untamed* the unrealized possibilities of modern Japan. The snapped film in the Taisho theater provides one clue to the dialectical form of the image in *Arakure*, but the potential of modernity can also be located in the detail of fashion, and in this sense it is significant that fashion plays such a crucial role in this film.

For Walter Benjamin, women's fashion exemplified the cult of the "new" within modernity and demonstrated the transformation of revolutionary energies into the image culture of consumer society. His most cryptic remark on fashion, that "the eternal is more the ruffle on a dress than some idea" is in fact a basic definition of the dialectical image, the material embodiment of revolutionary historiography glimpsed within the phantasmagoria of modernity.[102] It constitutes his refusal of the concept of "timeless truth" and proof of the transience of historical knowledge. Insofar as fashion is always on the cusp of the new, it is the signal for "new legal codes, wars and revolutions" (64). Adorno reportedly scribbled "counterrevolutions" in the margins of that last remark in Benjamin's manuscript of the *Arcades Project* (959), indicating his dismay at the linkage of fashion to revolution. One would not want to argue that women's apparel, or in this case, Edwardian costume in Taisho Japan, constitutes a revolutionary moment in women's history. Nevertheless, because the dialectical power of fashion is that "it emerges in the medium of the oldest, the longest past, the most ingrained" (64), the spectacle of Oshima in *Untamed* announces the end of an era.

Nowhere does the ruffle of a dress speak more clearly than on Takamine, riding boldly through Tokyo on her bicycle, sporting the latest in Western excess. She is at once a surreal and revolutionary figure. Her energies are, however, directed toward the past rather than the future. Perhaps the brief moment in which the film-within-the-film breaks might be perceived as a clue to the releasing of the revolutionary energies of *Untamed*, but Naruse's nod to the avant-garde is merely that, a gesture rather than an action, and Oshima is left to pursue her desires in a time and place other than 1950s Tokyo.

Naruse's next film, *Anzukko* (1958), marks the further foreshortening of the utopian vision of the future that lies within the contradictions and ambiguities of so many of his films detailing women's trials and tribulations in postwar Japan. Making another marriage film, Naruse was in danger of recycling a familiar story in which he was no longer invested. Because the first third of *Anzukko* is set in a rural community surrounded by hills, lakes, and mountains, a widescreen format would have enhanced the landscape photography, which is in fact the film's chief asset. As his last title in academy aspect ratio when the industry had more or less moved into widescreen formats, it was likely produced as a B picture, with reduced resources. Based on another novel by Muro Saisei (author of *Older Brother, Younger Sister*) the writing is not as strong as many of the other films of the previous six years. Compared to the other marriage films, the couple's difficulties are more directly caused by the psychological distress of the husband, Ryokichi (Kimura Isao), than by the socioeconomic circumstances so evidently at play in films such as *Meshi*, *Wife*, *Husband and Wife*, and *Sudden Rain*.

The wife, played by Kagawa Kyoko, is named Kiyoko, and although her nickname is Anzukko (apricot child), after that fact is established no one refers to her as anything but Kiyoko. Kagawa's performance is competent, but she doesn't have any of those melancholy expressions with which Hara Setsuko reveals her sadness, and the character lacks the depth of some of the other "wife" roles of previous years. She is a stubborn and resilient heroine, but Kiyoko is so close to her father (with no edgy hints of incest whatsoever) that she lacks independence and autonomy. The father, Heishiro (Yamamura So), is a successful writer, while Kiyoko's husband is obsessed with the idea that he too is a writer, even though he never sells a story, and Heishiro's publisher friend declares him to be completely without talent. Ryokichi predictably turns to drink, and Kiyoko attempts to support them by taking in piecework at home. When it becomes clear that they can't maintain the lifestyle to which she is accustomed, the couple leave Tokyo and move in with Kiyoko's family. Ryokichi resents being supported, and in a drunken rage he destroys Heishiro's beautiful garden.

Anzukko spans a ten-year period, beginning in 1947. The shortage of men after the war has made it difficult for Kiyoko to find a husband, and the war figures in the film as a metaphor for survival and struggle. Heishiro sees his daughter as a soldier in the battle of life. Kiyoko's brother becomes successfully married and employed, while she sinks into an increasingly desperate situation. She and Ryokichi live in a poor district of Tokyo with friendly neighbors, and the only indication that anything might have changed in the city over the decade is the presence of a truck selling sweets and gifts. Unlike the dancing and singing of Naruse's usual street venders and promoters, here the neighborhood is abused by the repetitive squawking of a loudspeaker blaring its promotion of "Maruniya's canned happiness . . . deliciousness in a can." More than anything in the film, this small detail (unnoticed by the characters) underlines the profound change in everyday life that has taken place. Kiyoko's inability to determine her own destiny is implicitly linked to the erasure of older forms of popular culture and entertainment that had hitherto persisted within Naruse's depiction of modern Tokyo. The styles and traditions of prewar Japan seem now to be the province of the rich, while the poor are doomed to the superficial detritus of the new Japan.

Anzukko is essentially an oedipal drama about male anxiety and insecurity in which women are mere pawns. The hysteria is too predictable, and even if the dramatics are less excessive in this film, neither are they particularly well staged. Most disappointing is the ending, in which Kiyoko ends up going back to her husband even though there is no indication that he will ever change his ways. Her father actually encourages her to stick with the doomed relationship. After she leaves, he says to his wife that "when she comes home exhausted, when she can't go on any more, then we'll talk about them splitting up." The wife, who has offered nothing but a few lines of polite conversation throughout the entire film, says, "But that's the way women lose out," to which Heishiro replies, "Men lose too. But women lose their whole lives, and men lose in one moment. That's a big difference."

How can we interpret these final lines? Heishiro seems to suggest that his daughter is doomed to unhappiness regardless of the outcome of her marriage, while her husband still has a chance for happiness if he doesn't lose his wife. In the film's opening scenes, Kiyoko's parents are looking for a husband for her and seem to be very progressive in their willingness to let her choose from among the potential suitors. Why she settles on Ryokichi is not clear, except that he is from her hometown and not a stranger from Tokyo. It can hardly be described as a love match. Ryokichi rather insidiously gossips about one of his rivals in order to win Kiyoko's hand. However, there seemed to be a spark of attraction between Kiyoko and the suitor who Ryokichi maligns (he claims the man did something "bad" in the war), so it may in fact be she who has lost everything by choosing the wrong man.

Ryokichi cannot hold down a job, but this is a question less of the economy than of his own refusal to be anything less than a writer like Kiyoko's father. He thinks himself to be above the station of a salaryman. Yamamura So gives a fine performance, although his gentleness is merely a mask for a patronizing patriarch, and the character lacks the introspective dimension of Yamamura's comparable role in *Sound of the Mountain*. At one point, feeling sorry for his daughter, Heishiro takes her on a shopping spree in Tokyo, and the accumulation of packages they come home with is testimony to the middle-class lifestyle that he represents. The only critique of the consumerism is voiced by Ryokichi, whose perspective is so clouded by jealousy and guilt that it can hardly be taken seriously as class consciousness. He, too, longs to be bourgeois, and the "writing" that he, and his father-in-law are preoccupied with is not intellectual production, but a metaphor for bourgeois leisure.

The elegant family home with its papered walls that frame Ryokichi anxiously writing is, like the landscape, among the visual highlights of the film, although it too would have lent itself well to a more rectangular frame. The visual style of *Anzukko* is otherwise fairly static, without any revealing lacunae, like that of *A Wife's Heart* or spatial configurations like those of *Nagareru*. Supporting roles by Naruse's team of character actors, including Kato Daisuke, Kobayashi Keiju, and Nakakita Chieko, offer some brief moments of humor, but the film is otherwise unrelentingly bleak. That Naruse could produce such a mediocre film within a string of titles that have been described as masterpieces — or at the very least, ambitious and unusual — is testimony to his continued status as a studio director who could simply "go through the motions" on projects to which he was assigned.

Critic Morita Tama noted in his review of *Anzukko* that the cause of Kiyoko's unhappy marriage is actually her father,[103] which, while perceptive, is more of a social observation than an interpretation of the film.

As one sees so often in the contemporary writing on Naruse's cinema, his family dramas are treated as lessons and models for behavior. In this instance, Morita warns women not to be envious of the heroine's relationship with her father. However, the film itself inscribes no distance from its characters, no place from which to judge anyone but the tortured would-be writer Ryokichi, and Naruse himself may have missed this dimension or interpretation of the story.

Muro Saisei was a well-respected author of the time,, and his tale of a failed marriage may have seemed to be appropriate for Naruse to direct; but the director clearly lacked sympathy for the middle-class sensibility that Muro embodies. In Japan, no less than in Hollywood, the male melodrama of class anxiety was ripe for cinematic treatment in the 1950s. For whatever reason, Naruse was unable to see through the predictability of the story or to write in a more enlightened female role (he coscripted the film with Tanaka Sumie). Like many of his films of the period, *Anzukko* ends with a woman walking down a road, but in this case we know exactly where she is headed—into the abyss of marital collapse, with no relief in sight.

Naruse, Cinema, and Haiku

In the films of the 1950s, Naruse's vernacular modernism is evidently tempered into a more formal aesthetic, yet he never loses touch with the experiential aspects of everyday life. Within the highly controlled mise-en-scène and shooting style is a sense of contingency and surprise. The sudden insight sparked by a rain shower or flash of lightning might be related to the poetic principle of haiku poetry in which brief lines describe a set of images. While the poetic principle of satori, or awakening, is derived from and refers back to Zen Buddhism, it is fair to say that as a principle of Japanese aesthetics, by the 1950s the technique of haiku was not necessarily religious or philosophical but had become an aesthetic convention. Haiku poetry originated as a Zen practice designed to provoke an experience of transcendent enlightenment. The awakening is typically produced by images of nature, often marking a moment of time—a cuckoo's cry, a frog jumping into the water—or a disjunction of visual or aural contrast.[104]

Noël Burch has identified a similar principle of Japanese poetry in Ozu's cinema, which he calls the "pillow shot": the moments when diegetic space is interrupted or suspended,[105] highlighting the intrinsic parallels in the montage structure of haiku and cinema. Although Burch suggests that similar effects are to be found in Naruse's films, I have already indicated that Naruse's inserts of still shots of objects and spaces are used quite differently. They are almost always linked, however tangentially, to the diegesis of the film, and have a more materialist functionality about them. He frequently includes a shot of a kettle on a brazier, but like the timeless stillness of the quiet nighttime shots in which the home is seen from outside with softly lit paper windows, these shots are types of establishing shots and not pillow shots at all.

However, we can identify a very different poetic technique that is less of a formal device. It is more experiential and is linked to the eye lines and emotions of characters—the sudden recognition or insight inspired by sensual (audiovisual) pleasure: the view of Shinjuku Garden in *Sound of the Mountain*, or the flash of lightning described above in *Lightning*. These moments are made possible in part by the ambivalent depiction of subjectivity achieved in the cinema, where we look at and with the characters. That haiku poetry still survives in postwar Japan is amply demonstrated by a recent anthology of haiku poetry by Japanese women. According to the editor of the collection of English translations, Makoto Ueda, more women than men now write haiku in Japan. Moreover, the magazines that were founded in the 1930s by women poets have thrived and expanded to 150 magazines (in 2003), and the culture has rendered the discriminatory phrase "women's haiku" (*josei haiku*) redundant as women authors have moved into the forefront of the practice.[106]

A few examples from women poets who were contemporaries of Naruse are indicative of the form and substance of this poetic style as it was transformed by women poets.

The baby carriage
And the wild waves
Side by side in summer
—Hashimoto Takako (1899–1963)[107]

The fierce snowfall—
I'll die, having known no hands
Other than my husband's
—Hashimoto Takako[108]

A woman stands
All alone, ready to wade
Across the Milky Way
—Mishuhashi Takajo (1899–1972)[109]

On the scale
My bathed and steaming body
This night of snow
—Katsura Nobuko (b. 1914)[110]

Loosely dressed
I meet with somebody
This night of fireflies
—Katsura Nobuko[111]

As these examples illustrate, haiku poetry is grounded in the detail of everyday life. If for the Zen monks of an older time it was a means of freeing themselves from the constraints of rational thought, for modern women poets, the fragmentary structure provides a vehicle for emotional expression. Naruse's cinema may not have an explicitly spiritual dimension, but its emotional expressiveness often takes the form of intellectual knowledge or intuitive awakening from the unrelenting disappointments of life. To better recognize the materialist dimension of Naruse's poetics of montage, we could do worse than underscore the parallels between the awakening techniques of haiku poetry and Walter Benjamin's monadological dialectics of revolutionary consciousness.

6

Naruse in the 1960s

STRANDED IN MODERNITY, 1958–1967

Melodrama addresses us within the limitations of the status quo, of the ideologically permissible. It acknowledges demands inadmissible in the codes of social, psychological or political discourse. If melodrama can only end in the place where it began, not having a programmatic analysis for the future, its possibilities lie in this double acknowledgement of how things are in a given historical conjuncture and of the primary desire and resistances contained within it.
—CHRISTINE GLEDHILL

In the last decade of his career, from 1958 to 1967, Naruse continued to turn out a steady stream of pictures for Toho, releasing fourteen titles that spanned a variety of genres and styles. During these years, the industry went through a number of major transitions, finding its audience increasingly drawn to the new medium of television, even while a new generation of directors invigorated the cinema with new energy, ideas, and images. By 1965, half of all film production was devoted to *roman porno*, or "pink movies," the soft-core porn product with which the industry was best able to compete with television.[1] Throughout these cataclysmic changes, Naruse appeared to be out of sync with the zeitgeist, and many critics have conveniently dismissed this last period of his career as a kind of decline, in parallel with the fortunes of the industry of which he was such a stalwart member.[2] However, a close look at the films themselves indicates that he remained very much connected to the new social fabric and its fashions. Not surprisingly, Naruse's cinema offers a privileged view of the transformations affecting so many facets of everyday life. The sense of loss that pervades these last fourteen films is produced within an ongoing recognition of the new subjectivities and psychological effects of this latest national renovation.

The Japanese film industry actually reached its highest postwar peak in 1960 in terms of total films produced (548) and active theaters (7,457). Audience numbers peaked in 1958 with 1.1 billion, but by 1965 they had dropped to 373 million.³ None of the major film studios managed to capitalize on the television market, and Toho survived the crisis of the 1960s only through its substantial land holdings.⁴ Although many of the directors associated with the Japanese new wave made their first films at Shochiku and Nikkatsu, they soon broke with the assembly-line production methods of the studios to form independent companies. Art Theatre Guild (ATG) was founded in 1962, at first as an exhibitor of foreign independents, screening films by the French Nouvelle Vague, American independents such as Cassavetes, and other international auteurs such as Satyajit Ray and Glauber Rocha.⁵ By 1967, ATG also began coproducing films, and in the 1970s it became the most important sponsor of independent cinema in Japan. Roland Domenig argues that ATG was not in direct competition with the major studios but complemented their drastically reduced production schedules, helping them survive the marketing shifts of the era, as independently produced films continued to be distributed by the studios and screened at their theaters. However, for the first time in Japanese film history, a distinction between art cinema and commercial cinema emerged with the rise of the independently produced feature.⁶

With his longstanding affiliation with Toho, Naruse became increasingly identified with the old guard. He continued to work in the home drama genre, even while that genre quickly found its niche in television programming, becoming a mainstay of the new medium. Naruse's home dramas of the 1960s, especially *Daughters, Wives, and a Mother* (*Musume, tsuma, haha*, 1960), *As a Wife, as a Woman* (*Tsuma toshite, onna toshite*, 1961), *Woman's Status* (*Onna no za*, 1961), and to a certain extent *Yearning* (*Midareru*, 1964), are increasingly bleak. The genre may have always, on some level, been about the disintegration of the family, but these films paint an especially dismal picture, bringing into play new concerns about the support of the elderly and the status of widowed daughters and daughters-in-law within a system that no longer needs them. During this decade Naruse also made several romantic melodramas in which his female protagonists endure the pangs of unrequited and/or impossible desires: *Summer Clouds* (*Iwashigumo*, 1958), *When a Woman Ascends the Stairs* (*Onna ga kaidan o agaru toki*, 1960), *Yearning* and *Scattered Clouds* (*Midaregumo*, 1967). While images of sexuality proliferated all around him, Naruse resisted the lure of the erotic, even if his heroines occasionally succumbed. He remained, throughout his career, a paragon of discretion, preferring the lyricism of suggestion and evocation to the directness of the naked human body.

While Naruse may not have entered the polemical realms of sexual politics or antigovernment protest, his filmmaking became increasingly preoccupied with an analysis and critique of social institutions. The terms and conditions of divorce and separation agreements, the state of the Ainu people in northern Japan, the corporate takeover of family businesses, legislation of inheritance, and land distribution—all these practices and regulations affecting everyday life are taken up and scrutinized in Naruse's last decade. Women are frequently seen to be losers in the new social formation, and as the rich get richer and the poor get poorer, Naruse's cinema maintained its class consciousness and acquired a new educational function. He may have tended to focus on women attached to "old world" values, but without becoming didactic, he nevertheless shared a critical stance with his new wave contemporaries that it is important not to overlook. Some of his protagonists, like Yae (Awashima Chikage) in *Summer Clouds* and Yumiko (Tsukasa Yoko) in *Scattered Clouds*, are new New Women, but their options remain limited. They have the education and the will to break out of old patterns of behavior, but neither woman has a place or a role to play in the new Japan.

Despite the progressive, liberal politics of his late films, Naruse's reluctance to fully embrace the new attitudes and directness of the new generation effectively set him apart from the new formation of modernity. As early as 1958, Oshima championed the new taiyozoku ("sun tribe") films of Nakahira Ko (*Crazed Fruit*, 1956) and Masumura Yasuzo (*Giants and Toys*, 1968), who, he says, "naturally rebelled against the traditional forms, injecting their films with the new forms that arose from their commitment to their own perceptions. Moreover, to make their work easier, they dared to ignore the old premodern side of their audience. This is their chief characteristic, and they are thus inevitably called modernists. These men therefore occupy positions as innovators in Japanese film today."[7]

In Oshima's critical writings, he charged the "premodern" cinema with a static homogeneous conservatism depicting a society of passive victims. The "modern" cinema, of which he became an exemplary figure after

1959, was predicated on an articulation and expression of the director's own will and subjectivity. Inspired and influenced by the emergent independent foreign cinema, and the literary and cinematic youth culture represented in the "sun tribe films," the new wave directors intended to shock their audiences with avant-garde aesthetics, sensory excess, and radical politics.

With the incredible mobilization of student activists contesting the Anpo Treaty of 1960, the U.S.-Japan security treaty that effectively brought Japan into line with American cold war policy, the new wave cinema was strongly identified with a new generation desperate to make a break with the past. At age fifty-five in 1960, Naruse was part of that past. However, as Hasumi and Yamane point out, he was particularly valuable to the struggling Toho studio because of his "directorial precision and care in strictly adhering to the budget and shooting schedule."[8] He was responsible for two "anniversary" Toho pictures in 1962 and 1967, commemorating the thirtieth and thirty-fifth years of the studio's history. Given his notorious self-effacing privacy and his refusal to offer narrative endings with strong messages, Naruse represented everything that Oshima and his cohorts were opposed to.

Even if Oshima does not appear to be aware of Naruse's contribution to film culture through the 1960s, it is significant that he does not dismiss Naruse completely. Oshima suggests that Nakahira's "critical spirit" owes something to the "psychology of human physiology," a realm in which he says Naruse excels.[9] Implicit here is a recognition of the way that Naruse developed keen psychological portraits throughout his woman's films of the 1950s. He would go on, in the 1960s, to further explore psychological states of being in the modern world. Two of his late films, *The Stranger within a Woman* (*Onna no naka ni iru tanin*, 1966) and *Hit and Run* (*Hikinige*, 1966), could be described as psychological thrillers. In the second film, Takamine Hideko plays a character who becomes seriously unhinged, while Tsukasa Yoko's character in the same film—a rich housewife—is driven to suicide through guilt and despair. Other characters wrestle with wayward sons, irresponsible lovers, and unkind families, and throughout the 1960s Naruse creates a series of complex portraits of women (and some men) grappling with modern life. The new wave filmmakers were in fact indebted to their predecessors in multiple ways. Not only Naruse but also directors such as Toyoda, Kurosawa, Kobayashi, and Ichikawa had already laid the groundwork for the representation of subjectivity in postwar Japan. As we have seen, Naruse's protagonists in the 1950s are not all victims, but are more often survivors of an increasingly dysfunctional society, and the same can be said of his characters in the 1960s.

Oshima wants to describe his generation of cineastes as the modernists of Japanese cinema, yet, as I have argued, Naruse was at the forefront of a modernist movement that exploded in the cinema in the late 1920s and early 1930s and managed to sustain its potential through the war and occupation. For Oshima, "modernization is, at the same time, internationalization,"[10] and this was precisely the accomplishment of Naruse's prewar career: to incorporate modern methods of representation and production into a Japanese idiom of popular culture. The modernity of Japanese cinema had become unrecognizable to the postwar generation precisely because it had become a form of classicism. Corporate corruption and immoral behavior were not new in the 1930s, and they were not new in the 1960s. Since the Meiji period, Japanese modernity has been in a continual process of reinvention, which tends to perpetuate an amnesia about previous stages of modernity, of which the new wave filmmakers' rejection of their cinematic forebears is only one example. By dint of the continuity and stability of a "classical" system of representation that relied on a fairly limited repertoire of genres and a constantly recycled set of personnel, this classicism had by 1960 reified a notion of the national that had become extremely conservative.

The studio system was Naruse's only creative framework, and he never strayed from its production methods. Nevertheless, working at Toho throughout his last decade, he also collaborated with a number of writers, technicians, and actors who were part of the new cinema, including writers Hashimoto Shinobu and Yamada Nobuo and composers Takemitsu Toru and Mayazumi Toshiro. Actors Dan Reiko, Nakadai Tatsuya, Takarada Akira, and Kayama Yuzo were responsible for "new generation" characters with new sets of values and attitudes. Meanwhile, Naruse maintained his usual stable of actors, including Takamine Hideko, who appears in eight of his last fourteen films, and the character actors Kato Diasuke, Nakakita Chieko, and Urabe Kumeko. Kusabue Mitsuko appears in eight films in strong supporting roles, playing no-nonsense sisters or independent professional women. Tsukasa Yoko is introduced in a small part in *Summer Clouds*, and she reappears in four additional titles, to emerge as Naruse's final emblematic actress of the 1960s.

The last stage of Naruse's career might be described as a type of "late cinema." Joe McElhaney has written about the late cinemas of Fritz Lang, Alfred Hitchcock, and Vincente Minnelli from this period of the early 1960s. Like Naruse, these directors found themselves somewhat adrift on the tides of a cinematic modernism that was constituted in part against the classicism that they had come to represent. In order to be relevant in the renovated cultural landscape of new wave experimentation, they were compelled to try to reinvent themselves, only to produce films that "failed" both as modernist and classical texts. McElhaney argues that auteurist methodology that incorporates the late films from directors' alleged declines in the 1960s provides a valuable means of "tracing out the development and subsequent decline of classical narrative filmmaking in the 1960s."[11] Like the directors in McElhaney's study, in his late films Naruse is particularly preoccupied with vision, and the expressive discourse of melodrama. One can see a kind of struggle with an experimental style of film language that had emerged to depict an unstable moral universe on the one hand, and a lingering attachment to the coherence of a moral integrity and set of cultural values on the other. McElhaney argues that "The filmmakers seem to be desperately attempting to maintain a coherent vision of cinema and of the worlds which they are filming. But the narrative worlds which are being depicted, the ideological and moral issues at stake here, continually run the risk of outstripping the film language being employed, so that a sense of failure and inadequacy is always closely following on the success the films seem to achieve."[12]

In these late films, Naruse does not stop experimenting and does not shy away from new modes of narrative. He indulges, very successfully, in the new technical possibilities of widescreen and color, and he introduces a repertoire of "special effects" in *Hit and Run*. Two films—*As a Wife, as a Woman* and *A Woman's Story* (*Onna no rekishi*, 1963)—incorporate complex flashback structures, and in both *Stranger within a Woman* and *Scattered Clouds*, flashbacks become important markers of subjectivity. The stylistic excesses that come along with these new techniques and narrative strategies are inseparable from a world in which no one can be trusted. Here again, Naruse shares with his American colleagues a moral vision that seems increasingly difficult to sustain. In my analyses, I find that time after time, Naruse leaves his protagonists "stranded in modernity," and in this sense they may stand in for the director himself.

Glimpses of the new youth culture can frequently be seen in the background of Naruse's films of the 1960s, occasionally moving into the foreground in films such as *Approach of Autumn* (*Aki tachinu*, 1960) and *Flow of Evening* (*Yoru no nagare*, 1960), even while the titles of these films clearly situate them within an aesthetics of mono no aware. Fast cars and motorcycles, miniskirts, new sexual mores and behaviors, jazz music, and yakuza gangsters are seen to be part of everyday life in rural and urban Japan. If Naruse's cinema is somewhat out of sync with this new generation, he cannot be accused of ignoring it. Within this accelerated culture of modernity, he returns to a theme that dominated his very first films: the car accident. Not unlike Godard, Naruse finds in the car accident an emblematic sign of modernity out of control. Unlike Godard—and more, perhaps, like the directors of his own generation—his melodramatic sensibility turns increasingly toward the aesthetics of loss.

Naruse's aesthetics of melancholia do not constitute a form of nostalgia, however; and this is what seals his status as a modernist in my view. His characters always look forward, toward a future that can only be better than the past. The flashback episodes of *As a Wife* and *A Woman's Story* go back to the war, depicted as a time of danger, scarcity, and confusion. The only film of this last period to be set entirely in the past is *A Wanderer's Notebook* (*Horoki*, 1962), which depicts the life of Hayashi Fumiko in the terms that she herself provides in her autobiographical novel of the same name: a life of severe deprivation, hunger, and exploitation, which she overcomes through hard work and literary ambition. In contrast, the world of the 1960s that dominates these late films is one of bourgeois creature comforts. Modernity has brought economic prosperity, symbolized in shiny new cars, and Naruse never pretends there is anything in the past to go back to.

Symptomatic of the cultural crisis that these films map out is the fact that the families are overwhelmingly lacking in paternal authority. Male heads of households may appear, but they are either incompetent (Mori Masayuki in *As a Wife* and *Daughters, Wives and a Mother*), ignorant (Nakamura Ganjiro in *Summer Clouds*), corrupt (Ozawa Eitaro in *Hit and Run*), or completely nuts (Kato Daisuke in *When a Woman Ascends the Stairs* and Kobayashi Keiju in *Stranger within a Woman*). The new young men with whom the women keep falling in love are transferred out of the country. As melodramas, Naruse's late films depict the disintegration of the social fabric, but the image of dissolution is always a dialectical one. Even in Tohoscope (Toho studio's widescreen format), Naruse remained a *montagiste*, refusing the conventions of continuity editing and the reality effect of long takes.[13] In this sense, his films retain the sense of construction, dialectical effects, and techniques that culminate in the car accidents that dominate his last two films.

The notion of dialectical history produced in Naruse's last decade is best expressed by Walter Benjamin, who claims that "the concept of progress must be grounded in the idea of catastrophe. That things are 'status quo' is the catastrophe."[14] To return to these largely forgotten films now, with the hindsight of history and the insight of transnational global feminism, is thus a means of rescuing those characters who Naruse left stranded in modernity, on the brink of history. Here Benjamin's remarks on dialectical cultural history may also be eminently applicable to Naruse as a classicist who was dismissed along with a set of traditions that he helped to reify as a form of national cinema. Benjamin asks, "What are phenomena to be rescued from?" He answers: "Not only, and not in the main, from the discredit and neglect into which they have fallen, but from the catastrophe represented very often by a certain strain in their dissemination, their 'enshrinement as heritage.' — They are saved through the exhibition of the fissure within them. — There is a tradition that is catastrophe."[15]

The fissures and contradictions in the films of Naruse's last decade are frequently the result of production pressures, and in some cases it is evident that the director was not fully in control of the productions. But the decade also saw some of his finest filmmaking. In particular, those titles that really succeeded are built around the romance theme, which emerges as the director's final means of constructing female subjectivity in film narrative. Before 1958 he had explored this theme in only a few films, most notably in *Floating Clouds*, but also in *Even Parting Is Enjoyable* (1947), and *A Wife's Heart*. The spectacular possibilities of widescreen color photography bring new sensual qualities to his melodramatic mode in *Summer Clouds* and *Scattered Clouds*. His use of black-and-white Tohoscope for *When a Woman Ascends the Stairs* and *Yearning* is equally powerful. Naruse never broke entirely with the realist flavor of his prewar cinema, and although the expressive elements of music, color, and movement become linked to women's perpetually unsatisfied desires, the women are inevitably constrained by the crude realities of everyday life.

Summer Clouds
THE WOMAN IN THE GARDEN

Summer Clouds (*Iwashigumo*; aka *Herringbone Clouds*, 1958) heralded a new phase of Naruse's career. His first widescreen film is also his first color film. Shot by his longtime cinematographer Tamai Masao, the spectacular possibilities of the new format are announced in the title sequence of sunset-tinted clouds. The opening shots of an expanse of rice paddies receding into a mountainous landscape set the epic tone of this family drama. The political terms of confrontation are themselves established in the first conversation between Yae (Awashima Chikage) and Ogawa (Kimura Isao) discussing the terms of the new constitution, the civil code, and the land reforms that have brought great change to the rural community of Atsugi, a town near Yokohama. In this film about generational conflict and momentous social change, Yae plays a pivotal role as a mediator between generations. She carries the whole film in a quite remarkable performance as a single-mother war widow with one foot in the future as a journalist, and the other quite firmly planted in the rice paddy.

The family relationships in *Summer Clouds* are complicated. Yae's brother Wasuke (Nakamura Ganjiro) is the film's stubborn patriarch who holds onto the old ways, while two of his sons and one of his nieces are determined to leave the farming life. The narrative involves a number of interlinked subplots, involving the dissolution of the family and the land that once held it together. Implicit in the old system was the subjugation of women as daughters-in-law who marry into families to work the land and maintain the household. Yae, who arranges a marriage for Wasuke's oldest son, Hatsuji (Kobayashi Keiju), insists that the new bride not move in with Wasuke's family to become a laborer for the family. She refuses to allow her brother to throw a big wedding in the traditional style, as if he were buying a daughter-in-law. Because Yae seems closer in age to Hatsuji than to her older brother, she is well positioned to negotiate this new arrangement. The woman in question, Michiko (Tsukasa Yoko), is in fact a docile wife with much less personality than Yae or Hamako, Wasuke's niece, and she ends up happily working in the fields beside her husband.

Yae is an exceptionally progressive character. She smokes, and she is learning to drive a car, following the lead of her friend Chie (Aratama Michiyo), who owns a restaurant. She is highly respected by her nephews and nieces, whom she encourages in their various careers. They refer to the fact that she writes for a magazine, although she is never seen writing. She works the land that belongs to her late husband's family more or less alone, also taking care of her mother-in-law, who is largely preoccupied with a daughter in Tokyo. Using a powered hand-guided tiller, Yae is also associated in the film with progressive agricultural techniques. One character suggests that she will likely be one of the first in the village to own a truck.

Yae is also a woman with a sexual identity, and she has an affair with Ogawa, the journalist, even though he is married. This is not the first instance of an adulterous affair in Naruse's oeuvre, and of course he remains exquisitely discreet, but the depiction of desire and sexuality is more keenly suggested here than in any of the previous films. The couple get together to arrange Hatsuji's marriage and find themselves at an inn where they spend the night together. Naruse cuts from Yae nervously waiting for Ogawa to arrange for the beds to be prepared, to an image of a gurgling stream in the woods, to an exterior shot of the inn the next day with Yae opening the shoji windows. This subtle, yet powerful sequence is in contrast to their second meeting in which, with equally minimal means, Naruse indicates the urgency of Yae's desire. The couple go upstairs to a suite above Chie's restaurant. Yae closes two sets of interior shoji behind them, Ogawa slides open the exterior windows, and Yae abruptly closes them. A glimpse of the couple embracing is caught through a transparent panel in the door, followed by a shot of them inside, embracing. Cut to the fields the following day with a surge of music, and the romantic scene is over. Ogawa is inevitably transferred to Tokyo, and he leaves with little sense of remorse or regret. The affair was a casual liaison for him, while it was evidently much more than that for her. As Yae, Awashima conveys the woman's deep sense of loss in the final shots of her tilling the land—a lonely figure in a lush, fertile landscape.

The script by Hashimoto Shinobu, based on a story by Wada Den, is in some respects extremely progressive for 1958. Hashimoto had been working with Kurosawa since 1952, writing scripts for *Ikiru* (1952) and *Seven Samurai* (1954). He would subsequently write the scripts for Kobayashi Masaki's two radical samurai films, *Hara-kiri* (1962) and *Rebellion* (1967), as well as Kurosawa's *The Bad Sleep Well* (1960), among other titles. Significantly, his script for *Summer Clouds* incorporates key elements of the woman's film. It is through the discourse of Yae that the film's social critique is articulated, even if "the feminine" ends up being implicitly linked to the land, and Yae's own ambitions seem drastically limited. However, as we have seen, the drama of frustrated and unrequited desire functions as an implicit challenge to the social norms that often prevent women from realizing their full potential as social subjects.

In *Summer Clouds*, the rights of the individual embraced in the postwar constitution are defended against the "feudal" ways of the family system, and the film specifically articulates the hardship and social in-

53. Awashima Chikage in *Summer Clouds* (*Iwashigumo*, 1958), Toho.

equality for women that the old system perpetuated. As late as 1974 Gail Bernstein observed that young farm women were still responsible for many of the chores on the farm, as well as household responsibilities, and many women also earned extra income outside the home and the farm (not unlike Yae with her journalism). Bernstein also points out that the educated postwar generation find themselves "witnesses to the declining rural population and sensitive to their children's aspirations."[16] Already in 1958, *Summer Clouds* depicts a last generation of farmers. Perhaps because Atsugi is not far from Yokohama and Tokyo, the family faces its devolution sooner than the more remote communities in Bernstein's study. However, the parallels between *Summer Clouds* and Bernstein's text, based on the testimonies of farm women on the island of Shikoku in Ehime prefecture, indicate the keen sociological bent of Naruse's film.

Naruse had been down this road before, with the 1953 film *Older Brother, Younger Sister*, which also deals with the implications of a changing rural economy to the family system of Japanese society. In *Summer Clouds*, the lush textures of widescreen color bring out a new value in the land itself: the sky, mountains, fields, and rivers are all shot so as to accentuate their pastoral beauty. Many scenes are also set in Chie's restaurant and other "urban" sites, including the bare-bones home of Wasuke's son Shinji, who has taken a salaried job at a bank. In comparison to Shinji's hovel, and the declining state of affairs in the 1953 film, the homes in *Summer Clouds* are almost luxurious. Not only are they wide and spacious, with minimal furnishings, the shoji are punctuated with hand-painted panels, lending them an air of sophistication. Yae herself does not dress like a peasant, and she frequently wears expensive kimono when she goes into town.

Yae's brother Wasuke is upset that his niece Hamako intends to go to university, claiming that if she becomes educated and marries a salaried man, she will no longer be a peasant. He hopes that she will marry his son Junzo so that his brother's land will stay in the family, although Junzo wants to train to be an auto mechanic, and Hamako has struck up a relationship with the other son, Shinji. There is a contrast between Wasuke's insistence on his family's identity as a peasant family and the apparent middle-class settings of the homes. In fact, Wasuke is the head of a land-owning family, who would have purchased the land from indebted samurai in the Meiji period, only to see their acreage drastically reduced in the land reform legislation of 1946. Under SCAP directives, landlords were entitled to retain a maximum of only seven and a half acres, and the rest of their land was turned over to their former tenants.[17]

The "traditions" to which Wasuke clings are thus only one hundred years old, and Wasuke's "feudalistic" values are tied more closely to his own diminished authority within a fragmenting social formation, than to the economics of agriculture. Although it is becoming increasingly difficult to make a good living from farming, Wasuke's blustering behavior pertains more to the changes in gender roles than to the realities of the new economy. He is finally convinced by Yae to sell some land in order to support Junzo's education, conceding that the rights of individuals enshrined in the new civil code may ultimately be the only means of maintaining the family's declining fortunes. The film may not put it in these terms literally, but such is the implication of Wasuke's ultimate reliance on Yae's council and support. Among the real strengths of *Summer Clouds* is Nakamura Ganjiro's performance as Wasuke. A former kabuki actor who uses large gestures and a wide range of expressions, he turns what might have been an aggressively macho role into a portrait of a man who is very much out of step with the times.

While the relationship between Yae and Wasuke is the main site where the political tensions are negotiated, Wasuke's eldest son, Hatsuji, represents the continuation of the family's attachment to the land. The final scenes include shots of the house-raising ceremony for him and his new wife, Michiko. The couple is also linked to another festive community parade that includes ritual song and costume. Michiko's foster mother, Toyo (Sugimura Haruko) — who is a former wife of Wasuke, just to complicate the entanglement of family relations — owns land that the couple build on. Because the woodlands were not affected by the land reform legislation, she is effectively more land-wealthy than Wasuke. Meanwhile, Hatsuji's brother Shinji, the banker, has begun dating Hamako, the university-bound niece, who gets pregnant, scandalizing everyone and filling out the scope of the new and old social behaviors represented in the extended family.

With a running length of 128 minutes, *Summer Clouds* has the aspect of an epic drama, and the spectacle of the Tohoscope wide landscape accompanied by an orchestral score certainly enhances the sense of historical import. The score, by Naruse's longtime collaborator Saito Ichiro, is used sporadically, mainly for transitional shots of the landscape, and is dominated by a melancholy theme heavy on the cello and bass. Shots of the verdant green fields are inserted periodically throughout the film, framed by the mountains and patterned by the regular rectangular divisions of the rice paddies. In one instance, two transitional shots of the fields are followed by an interior view of a garden, and indeed the film's aesthetics render the landscape of Atsugi as a kind of Japanese garden, subtly blending the economic and social issues with an aesthetic of cultivated beauty.

This may be Naruse's most successful "rural" film, in which he indicates the inevitability of change while not letting go entirely of community ritual and the sense of social cohesion. Yae, the widowed daughter-in-law, is abandoned by her lover and effectively left out of the reformed society, even if she is the catalyst of change. Her pride and identity remain intact, primarily in the contours of her bold image. In his first foray into the new technologies of color and widescreen, Naruse maintains the formal principles of the shoshimin-eiga, maintaining a very centered framing style, especially for groupings of figures seated at low, central tables. Thus, while the spectacular effects of the new technologies point toward a new Japan, the familiar settings of the home drama embody the rituals of family and home. With her worldly ways, Yae is slightly out of keeping with the domestic aesthetic of the home drama, but it is precisely the contradiction between her independence and the social structure implicit in a farming economy that the film illustrates in so striking a fashion. Her frustrated desires symbolize the lost potential of the rich farmland and the fertile landscape.

Whistling in Kotan
NARUSE'S POSTCOLONIAL MOMENT

Naruse's second film based on a script by Hashimoto Shinobu is a remarkable treatment of racial discrimination against the Ainu, the indigenous people of Hokkaido in northern Japan. Although it is unremarkable stylistically, and the melodramatic narrative has a few too many plot twists, *Whistling in Kotan* (*Kotan no kuchibue*, 1959) is very much in keeping with the humanist strain of postwar Japanese cinema. Hashimoto's script is based on a novel by Ishimori Nobuo, which won an award for children's books in 1958.[18] As the first book and film about the Ainu to reach the mainstream, *Whistling* was a landmark in Japanese cultural history.[19] Although the Ainu had been the subject of a few ethnographic films, *Whistling* remains one of the only feature films in which they appear.[20] It suggests how Naruse's affinity for women's social subordination could be adapted to other oppressed groups, and how he remained flexible and open to the winds of change. Compared to his woman's films, though, *Whistling* is a far more didactic and programmatic narrative. Its gesture of resistance is, in the end, finally defeated, and the film lacks the spirit of defiance within despair that we find in *Summer Clouds*, along with so many of the other films of the 1950s.

Perhaps because of its casting, *Whistling* lacks the strength of personality that Naruse achieves in so many of his woman's films. With stars Mori Masayuki and Shimura Takashi in supporting roles, most of the cast, including the leads, are played by low-profile actors who may well be of Ainu descent. The two principle characters are teenagers who live with their father Iyon (Mori). Both the girl, Masa (Koda Ryoko), and her younger brother, Yutaka (Kubo Takeshi), encounter undisguised racism at school. They are accused of stealing and cheating, against all evidence, and Yutaka finds a note pinned to his back saying "This boy is to be sold to tourists." Within their circle of Ainu friends and relatives, they are advised to put up with this abuse as generations have before them. Only one cousin, Koji, is identified as an activist, and when Yutaka visits him in Shiroai, he ridicules the Ainu whom they pass on the beachfront performing ritual dances and selling artifacts to tourists. "They are playing at being Ainu," he says. He tells Yutaka not to trust the Japanese, even those who appear to be sympathetic and supportive of Ainu.

Koji's words are proven right in a subplot concerning the children's grandmother and her adoptive daughter Fue, who has fallen in love with the son of the school principal, Tazawa (Shimura Takashi). Although Yutaka held up Tazawa as exemplary of an Ainu-friendly Japanese, the man balks at the grandmother's request to condone the marriage of his son to an Ainu woman. He sends the old woman home in despair, the girl runs off, and the grandmother dies of grief. Yutaka takes Koji's advice to heart, and shortly after the old woman's death, he challenges the school bully to a fight in the schoolyard, only to be cruelly outnumbered and attacked by the Japanese boy and his friends (Naruse avoids depicting any violence, but the term "juvenile delinquency" is used by the boy's elders). In yet another subplot, Iyon, the children's father, loses his job at the American air base, turns to drink for a while, and then lands a job as a forester. The first day on the job, he is killed by a falling tree, leaving his orphaned children at the mercy of a mean uncle (Koji's father). The uncle evicts Masa and Yutaka from their home, and the film concludes with Koji explaining to Yutaka that even among the Ainu there are untrustworthy people like his father, and ethnicity really doesn't matter after all. "We all have to carry on, with strength. That's the only way." The film thus recants its own activist precepts and falls back on a humanist sentimentality in which the children are left as submissive subjects within the family of Japan.

Ainu activism dates back to the Meiji period, with the establishment of the Hokkaido Former Aborigines Act, revised after another decade of activism in the 1930s to give Ainu full citizenship and access to education and other institutions.[21] It was not until the 1970s that Ainu activists began challenging assimilation policies and to articulate the terms of cultural and social identity, motivated in part by global aboriginal movements. In the 1950s, at the time this film was produced, Ainu identity was defined in terms of "blood,"[22] and indeed, in one key scene in the school science lab, Yutaka challenges the school bully to a blood test to prove that their blood is not so different after all. Ainu identity was also articulated in terms of the tourist industry, and it is this discourse with which the film engages most directly. At the same time, the film itself, and the book on which it was based, helped to stimulate the postwar tourist industry in Hokkaido. As Lisa Hiwasaki argues, Ainu tourism is a double-edged sword, because while it helps to promote cultural preservation, it is also a form of exploitation, fetishizing premodern identities and keeping Ainu craftspeople in low-paying jobs producing souvenirs.[23]

Despite cousin Koji's disdain for those who produce tourist art, the only value of which, he says, is that it is "disappearing," Yutaka sees the carving of souvenir bears as a lucrative profession. He apprentices with two middle-aged men, who warn him that even if he's good at it, if he starts carving, "you'll never get yourself out of the misery of Ainu existence." Nevertheless, by the end of the film the boy seems to have few alternatives. His sister, Masa, also becomes implicated in the world of visual culture when she is chosen as a model for the high school art teacher Taniguchi. The teacher eventually moves to Tokyo to pursue a career as an artist, and his portrait of Masa seems to jump-start his career. Although the portrait itself is barely glimpsed, the implication of this subplot is that the artist has captured the "otherness" of the Ainu by painting Masa's portrait against a pastoral scene. The other schoolgirls are intensely jealous, and the only explanation in the narrative for why Taniguchi picked Masa as his model is her Ainu identity.

Taniguchi sends Masa a postcard from Tokyo, describing the rat race of the metropolis as a "Darwinian jungle." He says that when he gets depressed, he thinks of Masa and her brother, who "never give in even in the worst of circumstances." His words are repeated in voice-over at the end of the film as the two kids leave their home. The plight of the Ainu is essentially championed as a model for survival in Japanese modernity, even while the film allows little room for the two teenagers to challenge the forces stacked against them. One of the Ainu bear carvers says to Yutaka, "Let's be the last generation of Ainu to have given up," a statement that further compounds the narrative trajectory of cultural loss, disappearance, and subjugation. In a film that features very few camera movements, the closing scene includes a couple of jarring backward

54. Romantic pastoralism in *Whistling in Kotan* (*Kotan no kuchibue*, 1959), Toho.

tracking shots, emulating Masa's point of view as she turns to see her home receding in the distance.

In Naruse's cinematic adaptation of *Whistling*, the pastoral setting of the Ainu is reproduced in lush widescreen landscapes, emphasizing their proximity to nature. No doubt this further contributed to the development of Hokkaido tourism, which combines natural scenery with the mystique of a vanishing culture. The family home is located beside the Chitose River, some distance from the town of Chitose. While the domestic interiors are a slightly rustic version of typical Japanese architecture, the exteriors are in the style of Ainu villages. On the level of mise-en-scène, the film depicts a very well-assimilated family who conduct their day-to-day lives as any other poor modern family would. The proximity to nature is, however, somewhat forced. One scene of Yutaka fishing with a spear on the river is a romantic cliché of pastoral solitude, and its main purpose is to point out the illegality of such activity. A local elder chastises the boy for catching a salmon, a deliberate nod to the fact that since the late nineteenth century, Ainu have been prohibited from fishing. (Because Ainu life was largely organized around salmon fishing, this was a major factor in their colonization. Japanese commercial fishermen are the only ones allowed to catch salmon, and Ainu need to apply for special licenses for ritual "First Salmon" ceremonies.)[24]

This minor fishing episode in *Whistling* shows how the narrative attempts to cover a lot of ground, encompassing a range of issues and characters representing different points on the scale of Japanese-Ainu relations. The original novel is very long, with two parts, which partially explains the number of storylines and subplots that are condensed in the film.²⁵ The pastoral landscape provides an important visual unity to the film, and yet the views tend to be fairly conventional and Tamai Masao's use of the scope frame and color is less exciting than either *Summer Clouds* or *When a Woman Ascends the Stairs*, films that display creative uses of the new formats. It is possible that Naruse might have been aware of the emerging trend of pro-Indian Westerns coming out of Hollywood (e.g., *Broken Arrow* [1950] and *The Searchers* [1956]), although the contemporary setting of *Whistling* distinguishes it from any other treatments of indigenous peoples internationally in the 1950s.

Whistling is progressive in its attempt to bring the issues of Japan's indigenous people into the public sphere. The whistling of the film's title is evoked during Koji's activist speech on the beach at Shiroai and comes to be associated with his critique of Japanese society. In typical Narusian fashion, the film ends up having it both ways—articulating the terms of resistance and colonial repression and ultimately giving into this repression with little hope for social change. In this instance, there is a certain irony insofar as the film helped to perpetuate the myth of a vanishing people even while helping to guarantee their "mythic" survival through the tourism industry. The Ainu, represented finally by two orphans, are dependent on the Japanese for their survival, even while they are made to be emblematic of survival itself.

The contradictions that inform Naruse's treatment of Ainu heritage and identity are in fact symptomatic of modern Japanese culture itself. The recognition of Ainu "difference" in conjunction with their access to a capitalist economy and the rights of modern subjects goes directly to the anxieties at the heart of Japanese modernity. As Marilyn Ivy argues in her book *Discourses of the Vanishing*, a certain unease persists in Japan regarding the loss of cultural autonomy and racial homogeneity within the "destabilizations of capitalist modernity."²⁶ She describes the fetishization of the past within a psychoanalytic framework of loss and disavowal: "Despite the labors to recover the past and deny the losses of 'tradition,' modernist nostalgia must preserve, in many senses, the sense of absence that motivates its desires."²⁷ The presence of the Ainu in Japan is a longstanding challenge to the racial purity of the nation, and their disappearance is thus at once necessary to the imagination of the nation and symbolic of the loss of Japanese cultural and racial autonomy in global modernity.

Like many of Naruse's films, *Whistling* ends with a road stretching into the distance. The deaths of their father and grandmother leave the children stranded in modernity, but it is a modern world that they have not yet entered, despite their school uniforms, and the ending remains somewhat unresolved. The receding tracking shots of the pastoral homestead or *kotan* (the Ainu term for "village") inscribes a sense of loss that is very much a modernist nostalgia, one that is produced ironically, through the twists and turns of a highly contrived narrative. The mantra of struggle and survival are keys to a future that in 1958 was still difficult to imagine. Within the ideological debates of the period, *Whistling* might be best read as an endorsement of the full assimilation and divestiture of Ainu identity, which was the position of the Ainu political leaders of the time.[28] The activist challenge constituted a humanist appeal to equality and fraternity, but the politics of indigenous nationhood within the modern state were still many years from being developed.[29] However, despite these contradictions, *Whistling* should be recognized as an important film in world film history for its recognition and humanist treatment of Japanese colonialism.

When a Woman Ascends the Stairs
A WORLD OF APPEARANCES

After three films with rural settings, and one set in the Taisho period, Naruse finally returned to the streets of Tokyo in 1960 with *When a Woman Ascends the Stairs* (*Onna ga Kaidan o agaru toki*). The Ginza setting, constructed from both locations and sets, is extremely contemporary, with bar signs, neon lights, and traffic indicating that this is very much a postwar shitamachi. The streets may still be narrow, but the competitive water trade (*mizu-shobai*) depicted in the film is closely tied to the corporate culture of high finance and expensive entertainment in downtown Tokyo. Keiko (Takamine Hideko) works as a bar hostess in this renovated "floating world," where she struggles to keep her head up and her integrity intact. This is one of Naruse's best-known films outside Japan, and it well deserves the attention it has received. Not only is it an emotionally sustained melodrama of unrequited love, it also has a strong documentary flavor, enhanced by Keiko's sporadic voice-over, which offers a commentary on the life of a Ginza bar hostess.

Shot in black-and-white Tohoscope by Tamai Masao, *When a Woman* is one of Naruse's most formally interesting films of the 1960s. The interiors are almost always framed in medium shot, both for Western-furnished rooms (which predominate) and for Japanese-style rooms. The consistency of the two-shot framing of characters seen from the waist up on the left and right sides of the frame is comically announced in an early scene in which two pairs of women gossiping about a bar hostess who has recently committed suicide are matched. The women may be different, but like their conversation, they are identical in their spatial position in the frame. (Keiko is in the background of both shots with two other people, suggesting that the two matched shots are separated by a 90-degree angle.) With this fairly tight framing, all the interior spaces appear cramped and small. Keiko's expensive apartment is tiny, yet quite a lot of activity takes place around her small dining table, which fills the foreground of most of the shots.

The detail within the mise-en-scène is especially pronounced in this framing, adding to the "documentary" aspect of the film. Critic Iijima Tadashi claimed that for him, *When a Woman* offered a rare insight into the world of Ginza hostess bars. He says that the bars looked nothing like any bars in other films, and he hardly ever went to bars himself.[30] Implicit in Iijima's review of the film is a thinly disguised disdain for the women who work in hostess bars. Foreign audiences who are unfamiliar with this very Japanese institution may assume that Japanese audiences would necessarily know all about them. In fact, the level on which Keiko works is a rarefied world accessible only to salarymen in the upper echelons of corporate culture. Even to Japanese audiences in 1960, and to contemporary audiences, the film provided a rare picture of a glamorous and slightly dirty world. In the early 1960s, the hostess clubs that had replaced the geisha business as the dominant form of the water trade in postwar Japan were at their most glamorous, flourishing in all the major cities. While some clubs employed thousands of girls, other, more elite clubs like the ones in the film were reserved for a high-end clientele.[31]

Keiko, however, doesn't really belong in this milieu, as several characters tell her, and the narrative really turns on the difference of her character. Like Naruse's two previous films about working women, *Late Chrysanthemums* and *Flowing*, this film bridges the social gap between the domestic world of married women and that of professional women working in the mizu shobai. As Iijima puts it in his review, the film is about "how the very intelligent and middle-aged widow or the unmarried woman who does not have any specific skills or talents, and is not part of the clerical workforce, makes a living in contemporary society."[32]

Keiko is a widow whose husband was hit by a truck some time after the war ended. When he died, she vowed never to love another man, and indeed she harbors a loyalty to the past that is also a sign of her moral integrity and virtue in a debased milieu. Over the course of the film she has no less than four suitors, three of whom are identified in an early bar scene. Her fellow hostess Junko (Dan Reiko) points them out to another woman: the richest man, Goda (Nakamura Ganjiro); the banker, Fujisaki (Mori Masayuki); and the fat man, Sekine (Kato Daisuke). Sekine doesn't have a chance with Keiko, says Junko, and besides, he's married. Unfortunately, Keiko doesn't know this and falls hard for Sekine when he proposes to her.

In a film that takes place almost all at night, the ups and downs of this particular upset are expressed through sunlight. After Sekine proposes, we see Keiko happily cleaning her apartment with sunlight streaming through the windows. The phone rings, and it is Sekine's wife looking for him. Dressed in her fancy kimono and cloak, Keiko goes out to the suburbs where she speaks to the wife in an empty lot with smokestacks behind them and children playing noisily around them. The space and the sunlight make a striking contrast to the rest of the film, even if it is a depressing sight. Sekine turns out to be a somewhat disturbed individual who plays at being someone he isn't. His psychosis is endemic to the modern metropolis, and the scene puts Keiko's thwarted desires in the clear light of day. She wasn't in love with him but fell for the lure of a home and a husband. The bright lighting of the scene underlines the fact that things are not always as they appear in Ginza.

The modernity of *When a Woman* lies in its treatment of the world of appearances that is the Ginza. In this respect, the film might be compared to Sirk's 1959 film *Imitation of Life*. Where the American film concerns an ensemble of women, Naruse's melodrama locates its tensions within a single character who struggles to remain true to herself within the deceptions and contradictions of her world. An ongoing commentary on fashion and the expenses that a woman like Keiko needs to incur includes the costs of kimonos, luxury apartments, and taxis. She often ends her day, slightly drunk, at home with her abacus, calculating the day's receipts. But despite all the time and money she spends on her appearance, Keiko is criticized by a bar proprietress for dressing too conservatively, and by her mother, who criticizes her for being too flashy. While most of her colleagues at the hostess bars wear dresses—usually with sparkles or frills and plunging necklines—Keiko sticks to kimonos and is never seen dressed otherwise. This is a sign less of tradition than of class. Keiko always looks more dignified than the other girls; indeed, her kimonos are likely to be far more expensive than their ready-to-wear

55. Awaji Keiko, Takamine Hideko, and Ozawa Eitaro in *When a Woman Ascends the Stairs* (*Onna ga kaidan o agaru toki*, 1960), Toho.

fashions. At the hairdresser, she tries to avoid a style that might make her appear "too matronly," as she is somewhat older than the other hostesses.

Keiko is, in fact, a *mama-san*, which means that she is the head hostess in a bar, responsible for cultivating personal relationships with the customers. Businessmen come with their employees and associates to a given club in order to visit the mama-san, who makes sure they are provided with the best service — that is, hostesses to chat with and drink with. The men may have their favorites among the girls, but the mama-san sets the tone and the standard for the club. While she may appear to hold power within her bar, in fact Keiko is caught within a complicated hierarchy of management. She does not own the bars she works in but is responsible for currying favor with the clients and making sure they pay. When business is bad, all the blame rests with her.

The plot of *When a Woman* interweaves Keiko's love life with her attempts to succeed in the dog-eat-dog world of the mizu shobai. Yuri starts her own bar with the supportive patronage of a certain businessman, and indeed Keiko receives a similar offer from Mr. Goda (Nakamura) from Osaka. He places a huge stack of cash on the table between them, but she refuses his terms, which include weekends with him when he visits Tokyo. Keiko's young protégé Junko is not so proud, and is quite happy to have Goda set her up in exchange for a bit of that which is never named (but is most definitely implied). Keiko's plan for her own bar is to collect subscriptions from her wealthy clients, enough to invest in her own establishment. She intends to run the bar with her manager, Komatsu (Nakadai Tatsuya), who works for her at the Lilac and at the Carton, where she moves shortly after the rebuke from the boss of the Lily. Komatsu may be Keiko's employee, but he keeps an eye on her working the bar, berating her for being rude, on occasion, to clients. Among Komatsu's jobs is the collecting of debts from the patrons, who seem to frequent the bars on credit. Keiko's plan to raise money from people who are already in debt to her seems somewhat far-fetched. Nevertheless, it is testimony to her persistence and tenacity, and this is what it takes to climb the stairs day after day.

Keiko's voice-over monologue, sporadic as it is, serves a number of functions in the film, providing narrative information and poetic reflection, often intermingling the two in a subjective commentary. At one point, she betrays the fact that business and pleasure cannot be so easily separated. Entering a tall office building, she says, "For women on this street, life is a battle I must not lose." She explains the objective of the subscription book, adding, "I hate discussing money with the man I love," as she enters Fujisaki's office. Fujisaki is a married man, but despite her own vow of chastity, she is hopelessly attracted to him. Mori Masayuki, naturally, plays the role of heartthrob exceedingly well. When they finally spend the night together, it comes very close to being romantic. A spilled glass beside the bed is the token signal of a consummated affair, but Fujisaki quickly proves himself to be a cad. Before he leaves her in the morning, he announces that he is being transferred to Osaka and that he hasn't the courage to break up his family by taking a mistress. He leaves her some valuable stocks, sealing her complicity with and dependency on the corporate world. In the final scene of the film, she sees him off at the train station, deeply embarrassing him by returning the stocks directly to his wife—and not forgetting a toy for the child. The wife is impressed, sensing Keiko's sophistication, and comments that she doesn't look like a bar hostess.

Keiko may get the last word in with Fujisaki, but we leave her climbing the stairs once again to the bar, saying, "Certain trees bloom no matter how cold the wind." Her monologue from the outset contains references to the changing seasons, in keeping with the poetry of the floating world. The discourse on appearances may be a modern gesture, but insofar as the film invokes the aesthetics of transience (mono no aware) in Keiko's voice-over, it links the glamour of the modern city to a much older discourse of everyday life in Tokyo's pleasure quarters. Keiko's opening lines indicate this blending of the old and the new: "On late autumn afternoons, bars near the Ginza are like girls without makeup."

Night in the city in *When a Woman* is very much a display, and the film has many shots of the corridor-like streets stacked with lights receding into the distance. The stairs that Keiko repeatedly climbs lead to different bars, but they are always framed the same way—as a chute that seems to suck her up. Close-ups of her *tabi*-adorned feet (tabi are white socks that are worn with kimono and sandals) are inserted each time, making little visual haikus from the film's title. The lighting in these stairwells and in the bars themselves contains multiple discreet sources, creating textured chiaroscuro effects in which the white feet glow briefly. The overall aesthetic of the film is distinctly noir, even if it is not a film about a crime. The tight framing of interior spaces, along with the ongoing discussion of real estate and rent, make this an emblematic city film, but it is also very much a woman's film.

There may be no crime committed, but women are hurt, and their heartbreaks and their suicides are inseparable from the business in which they work. Yuri dies from an accidental suicide that she stages in order to deflect her creditors. Her benefactor—like all the men in Keiko's life—turns out to be a heartless exploiter who tries to collect Yuri's debts from her poor mother. Keiko's final slap in the face comes from her longtime friend and manager Komatsu. When he finds out about her liaison with Fujisaki, he hits her and calls her a tramp. He says he has loved her all along but respected her vow on her husband's grave. It's a rather hysterical moment in the film, with Keiko demanding that he leave before she screams, and Nakadai's extroverted performance style gets briefly out of Naruse's control. As the penultimate scene, it finally separates all the men from the women whose world they control. Keiko's chances for a fulfilling relationship seem to be as slim as her chances of owning her own bar one day.

The Ginza world is contrasted by the depiction of Keiko's home life. She retreats to recover from an ulcer at her mother's home in Tsukudajima, a waterfront neighborhood not far from Ginza. However, both her mother and her brother bleed her for money. Naruse refrains from his usual framing of Japanese domestic interiors, so that the home itself is devoid of the familiar aesthetic values of balance and spatial harmony that he often uses for these working-class settings. There is a realist element in Keiko's support of her poor family, but the contrast between the two worlds also feeds into Keiko's ambivalence toward marriage. She has no illusions about domestic life, spending so much of her time with married men, even if she occasionally fantasizes about it as an alternative to her own struggle for survival.

Like his other films set in the milieu of the demimonde, Naruse provides a glimpse into the everyday lives of so-called professionals, revealing the details and routines of their parallel world. This includes the detail of material culture—kimonos, perfumes, beauty parlor paraphernalia, and whiskey brands—and Keiko serves a Western breakfast in her apartment complete with toast and a coffee service. The film includes a brief lesson on the role of sex in the hostess bar business, when Keiko says in her voice-over: "Around midnight, Tokyo's 16,000 bar women go home. The best go home by car, second-rate ones by streetcar, and the worst go home with their customers." Shots of anonymous women on the night streets illustrate Keiko's words. Keiko would count herself as among "the best," yet she is not above taking a very special customer home with her. The night with Fujisaki includes a fair amount of drinking, as she is on the rebound from her disastrous liaison with Sekine, and by letting her guard down, she reveals, however briefly, that her vow to her dead husband is as much a survival tactic as anything else.

In an anthropological study of Tokyo hostess bars conducted in the early 1980s, Anne Allison interviewed women inside and outside the world of hostess clubs, which had changed very little since the 1960s, at least in terms of their social role. She found that most wives were unclear about what hostesses provide to men, but that they believed that "whatever a hostess does, she does because she's a woman." Allison's project is to explore the gender norms on which this social practice is predicated — and which it inevitably perpetuates: "The implication, in short, is that the service men require is a feminine one. Women serve, and receiving this service somehow bolsters the male relationships essential to work in Japan."[33] The hostess bars are thus condoned even by the wives who are excluded from them, because they are seen to be intrinsic to the business of doing business in Japan. Thus the wife that Keiko meets in the final scene of *When a Woman* does not blame her for her husband's errancy but respects her as a professional.

Allison also notes that in hostess bars, men often discuss women's bodies in their presence, assessing their various assets, and often touch women's breasts and bottoms. The women are not supposed to mind, but to play along with the game, and as Allison notes, the sex play is often for the benefit of the other men.[34] Naruse's depiction of hostess bars seriously undercuts the domination of the male gaze, rendering it a space where women are in control. His editing eschews conventional point-of-view structures, and the framing enhances the ensemble acting in which Keiko's perspective is the only privileged gaze. Nevertheless, Keiko is groped once by a drunken customer, and when she complains, she is quickly whisked away by some other women who apologize profusely to the customer. This milieu is very much an alternative universe, where men are able to express themselves without constraint, and where women can earn money in amounts far beyond those available to most other working women.

While Allison's study constitutes a feminist critique of this Japanese institution, Naruse's film stops short of such an intervention. Keiko, like many Narusian heroines before her, is caught within a fixed social system. If she tries hard, she can succeed in this world, but there is really no way out, except through marriage, should she be lucky enough to find a reliable man. The example of the proprietress who owns the second bar that she works at, who is reminiscent of the Kurishima character

(Mrs. Mizuno) in *Flowing*, is evidence that it is possible for women to move to the top in this business. The difficulty facing Keiko is how to satisfy her womanly desires to be loved in a world where no one can be trusted and romance and flirtation is the name of the game.

Far from being critical of the hostess bar scene, *When a Woman* depicts the epitome of modern, cosmopolitan Tokyo. The English-language bar signs, the foreign-looking and foreign-sounding men and women in the bars (accents and skin colors suggest other Asian ethnicities), the latest fashions and cars, all create a sensuous environment that seduces the viewer as much as it does the rich clients. Key to this sensuous appeal is the soundtrack by Mayuzumi Toshiro, which introduces a soft jazz theme over the opening credits. (Mayuzumi provided scores for most of Imamura's film of the 1960s, and this was his only collaboration with Naruse.) Although music is used only sporadically throughout the film, the background sounds of "lounge music" give the film a very contemporary feel. Even forty-five years later, the film can still be said to have captured something that persists in Tokyo nightlife. No doubt when Iijima claimed that he had never seen bars like those in the film, with their low tables and long, low vinyl banquettes, he also meant that he had never heard bars like this. The cosmopolitan veneer is, however, just another veil over a social institution that is thoroughly Japanese in its regulation of gender roles.

When a Woman is also one of Takamine's finest performances. Her character may be only thirty years old, but she is extraordinarily worldly and sophisticated. Takamine exposes her vulnerabilities while always maintaining a certain poise. Her characterization benefits from the contrast with Junko, the young hostess who moves in with her and steals the patron Goda from under her nose. Dan Reiko's performance is bubbly and girlish, as her clothes are frilly and loud. She is almost like a daughter figure in the film, representing a new generation of women. Keiko is her mentor and friend, and she forgives her for stealing Goda, but in their world, no one can be trusted. Yuri betrays Keiko early in the film by stealing her customers, but they make up shortly before she dies. This is a woman's world, despite its reliance on men, and Keiko's character is emotionally bonded not only to the other hostesses, but also to the various wives on the periphery of her world. *When a Woman Ascends the Stairs* is not only a beautifully crafted film, it remains one of the only Japanese films to explore a woman's view of the world of Tokyo hostess bars.

Daughters, Wives, and a Mother
DISINTEGRATION OF FAMILY AND GENRE

As part of a 1960 woman's study group, two women, Kiyokawa Mieko and Sekine Miwako, agree that Naruse's film *Daughters, Wives, and a Mother* (*Musume, tsuma, haha*, 1960) is not a "fun" film.[35] Indeed, it is among the more bleak of Naruse's pictures, depicting how a large Tokyo family splinters apart and loses its property. In a palette of browns, grays, and dark greens, the bulk of the film is shot in lifeless interiors with characters sipping tea and hashing out deals in which emotions and money are exchanged and expropriated. The women critics are critical of Naruse's "lack of passion" regarding the eleven family members and various assorted relatives and friends, and as usual, he is accused of not taking a position regarding the issues raised by the film. As a study of the disintegration of the family system, it is, however, a remarkable film, especially if we look at the way that a discourse on and about media technology runs as a kind of undercurrent through the film. All the passion and desire is sidelined into this parallel discourse, creating an unusually dialectical text. It is hard not to read this displacement as a commentary on the media and its role in the dissolution of the family system—a media industry in which Naruse himself is inevitably complicit.

Sixteen central characters is a lot for one narrative to sustain. Two separate critical essays from the period suggest that the scope of the film is too wide, and its depth too short.[36] They might be referring to the mise-en-scène as well as to the narrative, as the scope frame is always full of two or more characters, none of whom is fully fleshed out. Iida Shinbi suggests that there are too many stars in this film, and perhaps Naruse was constrained by the need to give them all adequate screen time.[37] Indeed, the film is somewhat top heavy with headline actors, pointing to cracks in the production apparatus and suggesting that the studio itself was struggling for survival if it needed to consolidate so much talent into one picture.

The extended family of the film is configured around Aki Sakanishi (Mimasu Aiko), the widowed mother of five children. She lives with her older son, Yuichiro (Mori Masayuki); daughter-in-law, Kazuko (Takamine Hideko); and their six-year-old son, Yoshiro, the only grandchild. The youngest daughter, Haruko (Dan Reiko), also lives with them, and the oldest daughter, Sanae (Hara Setsuko), moves into the large suburban home as well after her husband dies early in the film. Another daughter, Kaoru (Kusabue Mitsuko), lives with her husband (Koizumi

Hiroshi) and his mother, Kayo (Sugimura Haruko), in a small house. The youngest son, Reiji (Takarada Akira), lives in an apartment with his wife, Mie (Awaji Keiko). In addition to the family, Nakadai Tatsuya appears as a potential suitor for Sanae, as does Uehara Ken. Ryu Chishu has a walk-on part, and Naruse's regular character actors, Kato Daisuke and Nakakita Chieko, also have supporting roles.

The discussion of money is pervasive throughout the film. Everything has a price, from the cakes and wine that are consumed, to the gifts that the family bring for their mother on her sixtieth birthday. Sanae receives ¥1 million from her husband's life insurance, and everyone wants a piece of it (echoes of *Lightning* [1953]). Nakakita plays a moneylender who visits various family members to arrange or collect on loans (echoes of *Late Chrysanthemums* [1954]). But the most pressing monetary issue is real estate, especially after Yuichiro loses the family home in a bad business deal for which he has mortgaged the house and sunk half of Sanae's settlement. Over the latter half of the film, the problem of where Aki, the mother, will live is debated among her children and their spouses. Kaoru cannot stand living with her mother-in-law and is not afraid to say so, raising the question of Kayo's future as well if she were to be left alone by her son. Sugimura's performance as Kayo is a brilliant depiction of the domineering, manipulative mother-in-law who makes the life of a daughter-in-law a living hell. At one point Kayo and Aki go to visit an old folks' home, where they watch three elderly ladies perform a traditional dance. It seems like a cheery place, but Kayo is not impressed and says she'd rather die than go there. Toward the end of the film, Aki receives a letter from the residence, suggesting that she might have made inquiries, but her daughter-in-law, Kazuko, hides it from her. In Aki's family, it is the children who can't stand the thought of their mother in a residence, and so they fight over her, but Aki does not seem to be willing to decide her own destiny, so nothing is resolved.

The problem of the daughter-in-law is implicit in the dissolution of the family system. Kaoru works as a kindergarten teacher, and her mother-in-law constantly accuses her of spending too much time at the movies, spending her extra income. Kaoru and her husband eat out a lot, as they have no privacy at home, but as in the marriage films of the 1950s, it is the wife who is most unhappy with their living situation. Kazuko (Takamine), on the other hand, is a kind of perfect daughter-in-law, but her husband frequents hostess bars, comes home late, and is evidently a poor businessman. (No one questions Yuichiro's bad judgment in the film, and the blame for the financial loss is put on Kazuko's uncle, whose business her husband risked the family mortgage on.) Before her husband dies, Sanae (Hara) complains vigorously about her in-laws, who she says are arrogant. She says she is not strong enough to live with them, but she is shortly brought down to earth and confronted with her own dependency when her husband dies abruptly in a car accident. Haruko (Dan), the outspoken younger sister who works in an office, points out that Sanae is qualified to be nothing more than a tea server or the wife in a rich family.

The question of Sanae's remarriage becomes a key subplot of the film, but it is oddly contradicted by the star system. As Sanae, Hara Setsuko cannot quite escape her star image as the "eternal virgin." She cannot say no to anyone who asks her for money; neither can she say no to any potential suitor. She meets Kuroki (Nakadai) through her younger siblings Reiji and Haruko, whom he has hired to create publicity for his winery. These characters, along with Reiji's wife and Haruko's boyfriend, are all strongly identified with a new generation that enjoys Western material culture. Scenes with these characters either out in the country or in the photo studio are markedly brighter, with light-blue fashions and sky-blue backgrounds punctuating the film's otherwise drab mise-en-scène. For her part, Sanae is always dressed in an elegant kimono, even when she accompanies Kuroki to a dance hall.

After their date, Kuroki takes Sanae to her brother Reiji's apartment, where she has never been before. Reiji's wife, Mie, has gone off on a trip to protest Reiji's alleged infidelities (in fact, she has gone to visit friends in a hostess bar). Sanae's entry into this "other world" of the modern couple is perhaps the highlight of the film. She picks up a vacuum cleaner excitedly and drags it around the apartment. She is surprised to hear that even this kind of couple—living without parents—have arguments. The kiss between Kuroki and Sanae was evidently billed as one of the attractions of the movie,[38] but it is not very convincing. Hara seems as terrified as the young girl in Naruse's 1947 film *Spring Awakens*. Sanae finally decides that she will not marry Kuroki, although she thanks him for giving her energy. Instead, she will marry Gojo, a master of the tea ceremony, improbably played by Uehara Ken (whose image as the feckless salaryman is hopelessly at odds with this essentially walk-on role). She wants to take her mother to live in Kyoto and, in keeping with the idealism of Hara's star image, forsakes romance for family duty. Her mother, however, doesn't want to go, and the film ends without resolving the problem of Aki's future. Will she live with Haruko, to help raise future grandchildren? Will she live with Yuichiro and his family in a

56. Hara Setsuko and
Nakadai Tatsuya in *Daughters, Wives, and a Mother*
(*Musume, tsuma, haha,*
1960), Toho.

small apartment? Or will she respect her children's independence and go to an old-age home?

Several critics of *Daughters, Wives, and a Mother*, commenting on the fate of seniors in Japan, compare institutionalization to the practice of leaving elderly people in the mountains to die (*ubasute yama*), a ritual most famously depicted in the film *Ballad of Narayama* (*Narayama Bushiko* [Kinoshita, 1958], remade in 1983 by Imamura Shohei). Kiyokawa and Sekine say that this is the predominant image of the predicament of the elderly in Japan, but that Naruse's film helps to dispel it by providing a fair treatment of the social issues. They say it would be a novelty if the old woman chose to go to a senior's residence.[39] For critic Ohashi Yasuhiko, this is the main question of the film: how the elderly can take care of themselves. The financial problems that the two old ladies face are symptomatic of a poor country, he says,[40] and indeed, in 1963 social welfare programs were still at a very early stage of development in Japan.[41]

Naruse closes the film with an extraordinary scene that underscores the problems of the elderly without providing any resolution to the conflicts and contradictions that the film has set forth. Aki meets an elderly man (Ryu Chishu) in a neighborhood park where she often takes her grandson. This time she is alone, but the man has a baby carriage. They discuss the fact that the park will soon be closed to put up an apartment building, and the man explains that he is babysitting for his neighbors as he has no other source of income. The baby cries, and Aki calms it down. The man is clearly helpless when it comes to children. Is this Aki's future? With the hint of romance, Naruse suggests that Aki is a survivor, despite her children.

Ohashi quotes Naruse as saying that he did not want to be didactic but to offer choices of possible actions in *Daughters, Wives, and a Mother*.[42] The film is a fairly sophisticated treatment of the ethical questions raised in a changing society, but as I have suggested, it also incorporates a parallel discourse on media and representation that may not have been intended by the director, but instead could have resulted from some of the production pressures. One gets the sense that the shoshimin-eiga as a genre cannot be sustained, as it has become irrelevant in a media landscape of advertising, individualism, and immorality. In their discussion of the film, Kiyokawa and Sekine observe that Naruse is an "old-fashioned" director, and his female characters are too passive. Hara's character is declared to be too idealistic, although, compared to younger directors, they recognize and appreciate Naruse's realism as a means of addressing social issues. Ohashi's review suggests that Hara has become too big and too rich for her role as the self-effacing dutiful daughter. As he points out, her clothes are far too elegant for her social status.[43]

At one point in *Daughters, Wives, and a Mother*, Reiji and Haruko invite Sanae to join them on a hike through Kuroki's vineyard, where they shoot some home movie footage. Later, the family gathers to watch the movies, which include not only scenes from their day in the country, but also shots of Kazuko doing housework. The entire family laughs at the slightly sped-up images of Kazuko sweeping and hanging laundry. These are, however, canonical images of the shoshimin-eiga, which Naruse has frequently endowed with a poignant understanding. The significance of such everyday rituals is here subject to ridicule, and Takamine Hideko, as Kazuko, is visibly upset. There is something slightly sacrilegious about the scene, as if Naruse were laughing at his own trademark images.

Sanae is also "tricked" in the home movie footage, which Reiji has edited in such a way as to suggest that she and Kuroki disappear behind a tree for some kind of romantic liaison. Sanae is acutely embarrassed by the scene, and it underscores the ways in which she is out of sync with the new world of Kuroki, Haruko, and Reiji. In fact, Naruse's film also plays a kind of trick on her, setting up the romance with Kuroki and then inexplicably banishing her to Kyoto as the wife of a master of tea ceremony, a man whom she barely recognizes when she meets him in Ueno Park. Sanae's decision to do what is right for her mother is consistent with Hara's star image but flies in the face of the attractions set up by the film. When her mother refuses to go to Kyoto and be a burden on her daughter, Hara's character is left somewhat stranded. It is almost as if she is in another movie, a more conventional shoshimin-eiga, like the many films that she made with Ozu over the course of her career. Naruse refuses to embrace her conservatism, and her selflessness seems outdated in this brave new world of high-tech gadgets and independent living.

This was Hara's last film with Naruse, and it provides a valuable insight into her decision shortly thereafter to end her career and retire from public life. Donald Richie says that she was severely criticized for her abrupt disappearance, as if she had a duty to her fans and her studio to sustain her career indefinitely.[44] In fact, it was a brave move in which she seems to have finally taken her career into her own hands, perhaps because she was unwilling to endure the kind of narrative contradictions that are imposed on her in a film like *Daughters, Wives, and a Mother*. In some respects, Naruse's own sensibilities were becoming outdated as well, but in this film we can see him visibly struggling with the new forms and subjectivities that were dominating the media landscape, embodied here by actors Dan Reiko, Nakadai Tatsuya, and Takaruda Akira.

Tokyo in 1960: TWO FILMS

The year 1960 was a busy one for Naruse. He released *When a Woman Ascends the Stairs* in January; *Daughters, Wives, and a Mother* in May; and two more films in July and October. These last two titles are further evidence of the production constraints that were affecting Naruse's ability to turn out quality films. *The Flow of Evening* (*Yoru no nagare*, aka *Evening Stream*, 1960) was codirected with Kawashima Yuzo, and although it features a number of big stars, it almost seems like two separate films crudely tacked together. *The Approach of Autumn* (*Aki tachinu*, 1960), on the other hand, has no major stars, and the lead characters are both children. Although it is overly sentimental, it conveys the simplicity and humility of some of Naruse's earlier "slice-of-life" shitamachi films, and in this sense is something of a relief from the dramatic busyness of *The Flow of Evening*. Both films are set in Tokyo, and both feature groups of young people who remain peripheral, background characters but nevertheless personify the new generation that is transforming the city. The narratives of these two films unfold, as their titles suggest, as slices of life in the end times of Naruse's generation. The cycles of everyday life, the changing seasons, and the rhythms of night and day are violently disrupted by a new speed and energy that pulses within these two uneven, unbalanced films.

In *The Flow of Evening*, Kawashima is said to have directed the "younger generation scenes," while Naruse shot the "geisha house" scenes,[45] although the film does not break down quite that easily. Most of the young women in the film are in fact geisha, and there are only a couple of older characters, so it is hard to know exactly which director shot which scenes. Kawashima was born in 1918, and had been directing since 1944,[46] so at age forty-four, he was only slightly closer to the younger generation than the fifty-five-year-old Naruse. My guess is that Kawashima was responsible for the comic segments featuring a group of young geisha who misbehave and tend to chatter and giggle a lot, a gaggle of girls, led by one particularly outspoken young woman named Kintaro (Mizutani Yoshie), whereas Naruse may have shot the more restrained and melodramatic scenes in which one person speaks at a time.

The young geisha in *Flow of Evening* are exaggerated versions of the

57. Kusabue Mitsuko, Tsukasa Yoko, Mizutani Yoshie, and Shirakawa Yumi in *The Flow of Evening* (*Yoru no nagare*, 1960), Toho.

ima no ko ("today's geisha") that Naruse introduced in *Flowing* (1956). The girls in this film get drunk, tease the customers, pour beer on them when offended, repeatedly threaten suicide, and generally lack the refinement and grace traditionally associated with their profession. In fact, they are little more than bar hostesses in kimono, although they accompany their clients to inns and restaurants, rather than to modern bars. The film opens with the group of girls wearing bathing suits rather than kimonos, flirting with boys at a swimming pool. Later in the film, two girls go "parking" in a tail-finned convertible with two boys, just like American teenagers were doing in the movies of the period. One of the geisha is a little more serious than the others: Ichihana (Kusabue Michiko) is in the process of divorcing her husband and starting a new relationship with a kimono dealer named Takiguchi (Takarada Akira). They actually have a playful love scene, which may well have been shot by someone other than Naruse. Ichihana's husband, however, is jealous and slightly crazy. In a dramatic scene toward the end of the film, while Takiguchi is distracted buying cigarettes, the husband grabs Ichihana on a train platform and forces her to jump with him in front of an oncoming train. The scene is well executed, but the melodramatic, hysterical, and violent moment is but a blip in the "flow" of life in the fast lane in the big city, and the characters are barely missed.

The other narrative line in *Flow of Evening*, which Naruse may have been more responsible for, features Yamada Isuzu as a restaurant manger named Aya. The establishment is actually owned by a businessman named Sonoda (Shimura Takashi), and it is a classy place where patrons are treated to real geisha performances, while being served sake by the young girls from the local okiya (geisha house). Aya and Sonoda each has a daughter who, like Katsuyo (Takamine) in *Flowing*, is an ama-

STRANDED IN MODERNITY   349

teur in a world of professional geisha. These two girls, Miyako (Tsukasa Yoko) and Shinobu (Shirakawa Yumi), have some training in the arts, and Miyako performs a classical dance for guests at the inn, scandalizing some people because of her amateur status. The girls are all friends with each other and discuss the pros and cons of marriage, and the free-and-easy life of the party-loving geisha. In the end, Shinobu, Sonoda's daughter, chooses marriage, while Miyako, Aya's daughter, becomes a geisha. As Miyako, Tsukasa Yoko may have a small role in the film, but it is a central one, pointing to her emergence as Naruse's principal actress in the 1960s.

Miyako is actually forced into her decision to become a geisha, as she has to support her mother, who is fired by Sonoda after he finds out that she has been having an affair with the cook, Ita (Mihashi Tatsuya). This is the melodramatic centerpiece of the film, as Miyako has also fallen in love with Ita, not knowing about his relationship with her mother. A former prisoner of war with a bad leg from the war, Ita's victimhood seems to attract both mother and daughter, transgressing both generational and class boundaries. When Ita announces he is quitting the restaurant, Aya seizes a kitchen knife and begs him to die with her. It's another hysterical interruption of the film, and like the train-platform scene, an unlikely explosion of violence that is inserted into Naruse's restrained study of everyday life in the Ginza.

As a depiction of the Ginza, circa 1960, *Flow of Evening* heralds the decline of the institutions on which the district was founded. It can no longer be isolated from the intrusions of the contemporary world: English-speaking guests are among the patrons, and the girls learn English and mimic their clients from the defense ministry. The floating world is threatened by the speeding world of global culture imminent in the upcoming Olympics. Women are traded and violated at whim. When his daughter is presented to him in full geisha regalia, Sonoda remarks that such a woman is like a sheep among wolves. Although he profits from the water trade, he is evidently uncomfortable seeing his own daughter in the geisha role. Nevertheless, the film finally affirms the survival of the institution in the last shots of Miyako's triumphant debut. Tsukasa's regal manner as Miyako suggests a redemption of the degraded institution. However, because she has been driven to it by the heartbreak of losing Ita, becoming a geisha is rendered as something like joining a nunnery. Unknown to her, while she is being introduced to the Ginza neighbourhood, her mother is leaving to live in disgrace with Ita in Kobe. The life of a geisha may be glamorous, but it is also lonely, and

Miyako's choice is tinged with an aspect of doom. She is in a sense, the last geisha in Ginza.

Approach of Autumn is also set in Ginza. In the opening scenes, a young boy and his mother arrive from the country, awkwardly dodging the traffic in the city. Hideo (Osawa Kenzaburo) is about ten years old, and his mother leaves him with her brother and his family, who run a grocery store, while she takes a job in a *ryokan*, or traditional inn. Like the similar establishment in *Flow of Evening*, this is a hotel-restaurant where male clients are served by women. Soon after she starts working there, Shigeko (Otawa Nobuko) strikes up a relationship with a patron (Kato Daisuke) and more or less abandons her son. Hideo is left to fend for himself, working in his uncle's grocery store. He proves to be a good worker, but he has to defend himself against the local bullies, who have him pegged as a country boy.

This slice-of-life film recalls the day-to-day struggles depicted in some of Naruse's prewar films like *The Whole Family Works* and *Sincerity*. Shooting in black and white, Naruse may well have been trying to recall the style of those films, as well as the shitamachi films such as *Ginza Cosmetics* and *Late Chrysanthemums*. As his first producing effort, and the only film for which he took sole production credit, *Approach of Autumn* was released as the B film on a double bill with Kurosawa's *The Bad Sleep Well*.[47] Although it is ultimately far more sentimental than the best of Naruse's slice-of-life films, and lacks the social critique implicit in so many of his depictions of family life, *Approach of Autumn* is interesting for its depiction of Tokyo. It shares with the Kurosawa film a view of the city as a sprawling, overdeveloped ugly metropolis breeding distrust and deceit, although Naruse is concerned less with corporate corruption than with the disintegration of family life.

As the central character, ten-year-old Hideo's experience of Tokyo is frightening and alienating, and he is left at the end of the film at the top of a department store, with the city spreading out into the distance behind him. In his hand is a beetle that he has retrieved from a box of apples sent from his hometown — a trace of the country that he treasures as the only sign of an identity within the menacing city. The department-store roof is a location that appears several times in the film. Hideo's friend Junko, a little girl who lives in the ryokan where his mother works, takes him up to the rooftop to see the ocean, which they can barely glimpse in the distance. Later, the two children take a taxi to the reclaimed land in Tokyo Harbor in another attempt to see the ocean. The city they explore is an ugly, sprawling wasteland with no place for children.

58. Night riding in
The Approach of Autumn
(*Aki tachinu*, 1960), Toho.

Teenagers, however, seem to have no trouble having fun in the city and its rural surroundings. Hideo's cousin Shotaru (Natsuki Yosuke) rides a motorcycle and takes the boy out at night to cruise the neon-lit highways around the city. Shotaru is a kind and surprisingly sympathetic character who plays the guitar and has a busy social life, taking girls to the beach on his bike or in his delivery van. Both he and his sister Harue (Hara Chisako) talk back to their hardworking father (Fujiwari Kamatari) in ways that would not have been acceptable in the past. The only reference in the film to contemporary events is a remark by Harue's boyfriend that he hopes to get a job in a large corporation despite his participation in the student demonstrations. He tells Harue that he did nothing to attract the attention of the police, so he's sure that they would not be able to identify him.

These young people appear in the film almost as outgrowths of the city, inseparable from its speed and its immensity. The drama of the film is the drama of growing up into a world that is so unlike the boy's hometown, not only in its physical geography but also in its new moral codes and social behaviors. *Approach of Autumn* leaves its protagonist on the threshold of adolescence, and on the threshold of a new city, but the freedom alluded to in the speeding motorcycle ride is eclipsed by the boy's palpable homesickness for the more familiar world of his childhood.

In both *Flow of Evening* and *Approach of Autumn*, people abruptly move and disappear. Tokyo is a city of transience and instability. The most drastic disappearance is the abrupt exodus of Hideo's friend Junko at the end of *Approach of Autumn*. She and her mother—who is a mistress of an Osaka businessman—pack up and leave without warning, leaving the ryokan stripped of its furnishings. In the final scene, Hideo goes to show Junko his beetle, only to find everyone gone, although a maid tells him that his mother has returned. He chooses not to see her but to go up to the rooftop. In *Flow of Evening*, Aya is also abruptly stripped of her duties in the restaurant and replaced with another woman. Typically, in the home drama, this is the fate of the salaryman, shuttled around by the arbitrary decisions of corporate managers. In these films, it is the women in the water trade who find themselves homeless, forced to move from one establishment to another, from one city to another, leaving behind their children. In Naruse's Tokyo of 1960, the city is a force that dismantles and disperses the Japanese family.

Three Woman's Films of the 1960s

Most of Naruse's films of this decade could be classified as woman's films, and many of the titles indicate as much. While they tend to have less stylistic and narrative integrity than the 1950s woman's films, several are nevertheless centered around a central protagonist, and in this respect have a strong psychological focus. Takamine Hideko stars in three relatively unknown films from this period: *As a Wife, as a Woman* (*Tsuma toshite, onna toshite*, aka *The Other Woman*, 1961), *Woman's Status* (*Onna no za*, 1962), and *A Woman's Story* (*Onna no rekishi*, 1962). The last two titles are dismissed by Audie Bock as being so "mediocre" and "negligible" that they have been omitted from film reference books—an ironic indication of women's status in Japanese film history.[48] While they may not be among Naruse's strongest films, these titles by no means deserve such caustic erasure, and they are notable and important films on several levels.

In the larger tapestry of Naruse's oeuvre, these three woman's films are constituent moments in the weave of thematics, visual style, and personnel. Although they are relatively "flat" and restrained, the narratives tend to foreground the social institutions implicated in women's unequal place in modern Japan. The women's trials and tribulations are caused in part by car accidents and unreliable men; but at the same time, their social roles are examined in terms of modern institutions and social change. All three films are based on original screenplays, the first two by the team of Ide Toshiro and Matsuyama Zenzo, and the third by Kasahara Ryozo. A recurring theme of all three films is the dependency of a woman on her son for her status in a family, although in each case the family relations are configured differently and the loss of the son has different results. The three films are all in Tohoscope, but only *As a Wife, as a Woman* is in color — and it is an extraordinarily muted palette of greens, browns, and beige. The very occasional touch of red — on a bar hostess's dress, or an obi, and in a flashing traffic light at the dramatic climax of the film — become dynamic accents in the practically monochromatic mise-en-scène. *Woman's Status* is shot in very flat lighting, stylistically and narratively anticipating the 1964 film *Yearning*, with which it shares many features. *A Woman's Story*, on the other hand, features a chiaroscuro lighting design with deep shadows. All three were shot by Yasumoto Jun, indicating that Naruse approached each narrative with very different visual ideas.

As a Wife, as a Woman was based on case studies from the domestic court and was discussed in a roundtable discussion in the journal *Screenplay* that accompanied the publication of the screenplay the same month as the release of the film (May 1961).[49] From this exchange between producer Fujimoto; screenwriter Ide; Ohama Hideko, from the domestic court; and three "ordinary women" — a housewife, a hostess club manager, and an office worker — it is apparent that the film was intended to have educational value. The film essentially poses an ethical dilemma and, in the words of Fujimoto, asks the audience to "figure it out themselves," a rather curious assertion for a studio producer to make. Indeed the film offers little "entertainment value," and Takamine barely even cracks a smile.

The story of *As a Wife* takes up where *When a Woman Ascends the Stairs* leaves off, with Takamine offering a parting gift to Mori Masayuki's wife. Takamine and Mori play different characters, of course, in a different narrative universe, yet the opening situation is as if they had continued their affair for ten years and now it is going sour. Takamine (Miho in this film) wants to break off with Keijiro (Mori's character) because he seems ashamed to be with her and has not spent one night at her home in the ten years of their affair. She has come to realize that, as his mistress, she cannot fall in love with anyone else. For fifteen years, Miho has been managing the Ginza bar that Keijiro owns. She thinks that she deserves some compensation for her investment, and she needs some security for her future if she breaks off the affair. The bar, however, is registered in the name of Keijiro's wife, Ayako (Awashima Chikage), who refuses to comply with Miho's demands.

The two women try to negotiate a settlement in a restaurant owned by one of Miho's friends deeded to her by her own patron. As a bar hostess,

59. Awashima Chikage and Takamine Hideko in *As a Wife, as a Woman* (*Tsuma toshite, onna toshite*, 1961), Toho.

Miho has a circle of friends who advise her that she has been exploited and deserves to be treated with respect. She demands ¥3,000,000, which Ayako blatantly refuses. The two women are both tough negotiators, but as the wife, Ayako has the upper hand. She has already mortgaged the Ginza bar to open a new one in the booming area of Shinjuku and will not offer Miho more than ¥500,000. Miho's friend and erstwhile suitor Minami (Nakadai Tatsuya) tells her that the average settlement for such cases is less than ¥100,000, a figure that is based on the court documents that the scriptwriters consulted. In the *Screenplay* discussion, Ms. Ohama from the court implores the producer not to include this information, as "it is nothing but contempt of women."[50]

Miho's trump card is revealed about halfway through the film in a flashback to the war, in which she is shown to be the mother of Keijiro's two children, who are now teenagers. Because Ayako was unable to bear children, she adopted Miho's two kids, who were raised believing Ayako to be their real mother. Miho's grandmother (a former geisha who lives with Miho) persuades her to reclaim her children in lieu of the monetary compensation that is being denied her, so Miho kidnaps her son Susumu for a day, treating him to dinner and amusement rides. When he finds out her secret (from the grandmother, as Miho is unable to confess), he runs home and tells his parents and his sister, Hiroko. The children are disgusted with all the adults, and in the ensuing climactic confrontation, it becomes apparent that Keijiro is largely to blame for maintaining such a duplicitous household, and that he has no idea how to resolve the situation. Ayako asks for a divorce, the children move out, and Miho leaves the bar to end up selling food from a street stall. She is not actually seen in her final lowly station, though. The film ends with Susumu visiting his sister at her university residence; they go to the movies for the afternoon.

The story of a man with two "wives" is one that recurs in Naruse's 1930s films *Not Blood Relations*, *Wife! Be Like a Rose!*, and *The Girl in the Rumor*. In the 1960s the focus has shifted from the melodramatic expressionism of those films to an examination of the systemic inequities of Japanese society. The institutions of the family and the water trade, and the legal systems of adoption and domestic courts, effectively support and enable a man to have both a wife and a mistress. The hierarchies of class and gender in which the wife's role is privileged over the mistress's are upheld by the unquestioned authority of the father and the male heir, although in a family such as Keijiro's in *As a Wife, as a Woman*, this is revealed to be an empty center. A bumbling university professor, Keijiro is not nearly as strong or intelligent as the two women in his life. Miho points out that she has worked hard for her entire life, living only for one man. She asks Ayako to return her son to her so that she will have something to live for, and Ayako replies that she is the one who deserves compensation for raising him. In an intermittent series of family flashbacks, the two children are constantly bickering with each other, perhaps to underline the challenges of child rearing—although in the present tense of the narrative, Ayako has a live-in nanny.

As a Wife, as a Woman poses some serious questions about women's work and social responsibility, and the gender inequities of a family system that more or less condones extramarital affairs for men. All these issues are taken up in the roundtable discussion, including the observation that typically such real-life situations continue under the surface of reality and rarely result in divorce. In a separate article in the same issue of *Screenplay*, Ide Toshiro notes that although he had submitted scripts ending in divorce for many previous wife films (tsuma-mono), including *Meshi*, *Wife*, and *A Wife's Heart*, these endings had always been changed by the producers. This is the first time such a conclusion had been accepted, and he wonders why the breakdown of the family has become such a welcome subject. "Is this progress?," he asks.[51]

I would argue that yes, this is progress. Insofar as Naruse includes the distressing figures of typical compensation for the "severance" of a mistress, the film goes some distance in articulating how the issue of women's rights is implicit in the breakdown of the family. The catch, however, is that the movies that the children are off to see to relieve their suffering are not likely to include *As a Wife, as a Woman*. The film is stately and elegant, and the flashbacks are cleverly integrated, linking past and present with visual cues; at the same time, its tensions are tautly held, unrelieved by anything more than a flashing red light. While some critics have endorsed the film,[52] in my view, the price of Naruse's politics in this case is his expressive use of cinematic form. The lack of expressionism carries over to *Woman's Status*, another examination of the institutions of family, inheritance, and social status.

In *Woman's Status*, Takamine plays a widowed daughter-in-law in a large family of five daughters and two sons. In many respects it is a typical home drama, revolving around the marriages of three of the daughters. One of them ends up being successfully "matched" with a promising young salaryman who will shortly be sent to Brazil. Another daughter, Umeko (Kasabue Mitsuko), is a little older and has a successful business teaching ikebana and tea ceremony. A younger daughter works in a movie theater box office and falls for a university student. The third-eldest daughter, Michiko, returns to Tokyo with her husband when the father (Ryu Chishu) falls ill. He recovers quickly, but the young couple won't leave, as they are unemployed and homeless. Two of the married children in the Ishikawa family have children, but they are girls, and Takamine's character, Yoshiko, has the only son in the family, a young teenager named Ken. The boy has trouble passing his entrance exams for high school and devastates the family when he commits suicide by jumping in front of a train. This incident, which occurs about 90 minutes into the 110-minute film, is not depicted but merely foreshadowed by a shot of Ken strolling sullenly near a train; the drama is focused on the family's telephone call from the police.

Following the theme exemplified in Ozu's *Tokyo Story* (1953), it is the widowed daughter-in-law who has the most moral integrity in the family. By 1962, however, it becomes apparent that Yoshiko's loyalty to her dead husband's parents is somewhat old-fashioned. She is a character stranded in modernity. While the other family members struggle to earn their livings by whatever means they can, running a noodle shop, a boarding house, or the family dry goods store, which is attached to the home, Yoshiko has placed her entire future in the success of her son. She suspects that the pressure she has put on him may have driven him to suicide, but when he dies, she loses all legal standing in the family. She has nowhere to go, no means of support, and has to watch as the other siblings squabble over who will inherit the family home that would have been hers.

Yoshiko's integrity is established through her relationship with Musumiya (Takarada Akira), a young car salesman who falls in love with her. She rejects him, and further tries to dissuade her sister-in-law Umeko from falling for him, as she has discovered he is a con artist (although

Umeko thinks she is simply jealous). The role of cars, car ownership, and car salesmanship is a recurring theme in these three woman's films; and along with the growing city of Tokyo, it is an index of modernity. Musumiya sells foreign imports, and his car is what gains him access to the boarding house and the family that owns it (Yoshiko's sister-in-law Matsuyo). The dispersal of the family throughout the city is finally underlined in the final scene, in which the father (Ryu Chishu) and mother (Sugimura Haruko) stroll through a suburb with Yoshiko, looking for a nice small house that they can buy to be free of their expanding family. Because of Ken's death, they too are displaced, as their oldest son is now in line to inherit the home and plans to move in with his wife and daughters. It isn't clear what Yoshiko's fate will be—whether she will remain with them, remarry, or be cast out. But she does seem to be left with her in-laws as some kind of relic of the past, stuck without a role in the changing world.

The third film in this trio, *A Woman's Story*, offers a more optimistic resolution to the ongoing examination of women's unequal (and unfortunate) place in the social fabric of early-1960s Tokyo. This film ends with a familiar image of two women walking together down a road, although the two women—Nobuko (Takamine) and her mother-in-law Kimiko (Kahara Natsuko)—have endured a great number of trials and tribulations to reach this point. The film begins and ends with scenes set among a company of women in Nobuko's successful hair salon, but the scope of the film is much more vast than this happy place. Flashbacks start filling in the details of Nobuko's marriage, her husband's death in the war, and her struggles to support her son and mother-in-law during the postwar period. Meanwhile, the story in the present tense involves her son Kohei (Yamazaki Tsutomu), a car salesman who moves in with a bar hostess against his mother's wishes. When Kohei is killed in a car accident, the bar hostess, Midori (Hoshi Yuriko), tells Nobuko that she is pregnant. At first Nobuko orders her to abort the child, offering her money for the operation, but Kimiko persuades her to relent, which she does. Midori ends up working in the hair salon, with Nobuko and Kimiko helping her to raise her son.

It is an episodic narrative, moving through many decades, as one tragedy after another besets these poor women. Shortly after she marries into the Shimizu family, Nobuko's father-in-law commits double suicide with a geisha after bankrupting the family business through poor investments in the transition to a wartime economy. After the war, Nobuko's benefits from her husband's company are cut off because of

60. Hoshi Yuriko and Takamine Hideko in *A Woman's Story* (*Onna no rekishi*, 1963), Toho.

the new occupation climate that has turned against war widows. She also discovers that her husband was having an affair with a loose woman until the day he left for the front. She rekindles a relationship with one of her husband's friends, Akimoto (played by Nakadai Tatsuya in his third film outing in a failed romance with Takamine), who miraculously survived the war, but his involvement with the postwar black market forces him to leave Tokyo.

A Woman's Story has a mobility and epic scope akin to *Floating Clouds* and *A Wanderer's Notebook*, which was released only two months earlier. In fact it spans a greater period than either of those films, as the earliest flashbacks announce the beginning of the China War, around 1937, while the scenes with Kohei and Midori include the cars speeding through the lit city that signify the changed pace of the 1960s. Within this historical span is a geographical range of locations, including the firebombed city, followed by a brief agricultural exodus when the women are relocated during the war, to a series of homes and neighborhoods charting the family's fall and rise. Nobuko and her son arrange to meet at one point by the Hachiko statue in Shibuya, a prominent sign of the new urban geography. The reconciliation between Nobuko and Midori takes place on a barren stretch of road where lonely high-rise apartment blocks loom in the rainy dusk. Except for the brightly lit hair salon, *A Woman's Story* is a fairly dark film.

The only explanation for Nobuko's change of heart regarding Midori is her mother-in-law's little speech about women that recapitulates the misfortune that they have experienced. Kimiko puts their story into a wider sociological frame of gender inequity in keeping with the ongoing refrains in Naruse's cinema about women's poor lot in life: "You know, thinking about the life of a woman, I realize that we have been taken advantage of. Men are selfish. A man lets a woman bear his children, then he does as he wishes and leaves the woman to survive him alone. My husband, Koichi, did this, and so did my son, Kohei. I think I'd like to be reincarnated as a man next time.... By the way, if Midori's child is really Kohei's, I'd like to keep it." Kimiko recognizes the problem but also understands that the boy is still the prize and the only key to social status. Like Yoshiko in *Woman's Status*, Nobuko and Kimiko's status in the family comes only through their sons. When Kohei dies, Kimiko says that she and Nobuko are no longer related, and she offers to move into a nursing home, to which Nobuko responds, "Don't talk like you've never met me. You can stay with me as long as you wish."

Nobuko emerges finally as a surprisingly modern and progressive woman, and like many of Naruse's heroines of the 1950s, she is a survivor. In the epic span of the narrative, it becomes further apparent that her hard work and ingenuity have virtually reinvented the family. Her antipathy toward women from the water trade who have lured away all the men in her life is finally tempered when she encounters Tamae (Awaji Keiko), who helps her get a start in the hairdressing business. When she first meets her, Tamae is fencing American products, from cigarettes to penicillin, earned by prostitutes during the occupation. Women's work is revealed to be the underpinning of the economy as well as the family, and the hair salon has replaced the hostess bar as a woman's business.

Like the other two woman's films *As a Wife, as a Woman* and *A Woman's Status*, the role of the child in *A Woman's Story* tends to underline the woman's social role and contribution and status, while the maternal role is deemphasized. The protagonists of these films are ultimately unloved, as their romantic relationships are always just out of reach and slip away before they can be consummated. In each instance, Takamine survives alone and childless, supporting parents and grandparents who have been left stranded by the modern world. In the disintegrating family system of 1960s Japan, it is the woman who loses, but these films also clearly point the way to a necessary reinvention of the woman's social role—even if they don't quite follow through on their own conclusions.

Horoki
THE COMMODIFICATION OF HAYASHI FUMIKO

Naruse's 1962 film *A Wanderer's Notebook* (*Horoki*, aka *Her Lonely Lane*) takes its title from an autobiographical novel by Hayashi Fumiko, yet it is not an adaptation of that work.[53] Fragments of Hayashi's text appear on screen in titles and are spoken in voice-over narration by Takamine Hideko, who plays Hayashi, yet the narrative is based on a play written by Kikuta Kazuo. The play, which has run continuously in Tokyo since 1961, is based on Hayashi's biography and differs substantially from Hayashi's autobiographical novel *Horoki*, based on events from the 1920s.[54] This film is not nearly as strong as Naruse's previous adaptations of Hayashi's stories, even if he was undoubtedly asked to direct it on the basis of the successes of *Meshi*, *Wife*, *Lightning*, *Late Chrysanthemums*, and *Floating Clouds*. According to Hasumi and Yamane, the film is regarded more as a Toho film than a Naruse film, as it was made to commemorate the thirtieth anniversary of Toho studio.[55] (In fact, it was Takarazuka Eiga that was founded in 1932, which then dissolved into Toho in 1937.)[56] The film was vigorously attacked at the time of its release for its conservatism.[57]

Hayashi's novel was originally published in installments in 1928 and 1929 in the journal *Nyonin geijutsu* (*Women's Arts*, one of the first women's literary journals). She revised and reissued the work in book form in 1930, adding a second volume in 1933. Two sequels were published in 1939 and 1949, which included revised versions of the original text. Joan Ericson points out that this mutable, ever-changing text was revised repeatedly to meet readers' changing expectations;[58] at the same time, by revisiting and rewriting various incidents and events, the multiple versions constitute a palimpsest of aesthetic and formal innovation. The work challenges the very notion of a stable, unique, and "original" text on many levels. The flexibility and inconsistency of the writing, which combines poetry and prose in an episodic diary format, gives rise to an extremely complex and innovative construction of subjectivity.

The slippage in Hayashi's text between first, second, and third person is constant. Poetry points to inner emotions, while quoted dialogue depicts the Fumiko character as seen, or heard, from "outside." *Horoki* includes references to other writers and historical figures and follows the ups and downs of Hayashi's personal and professional life. The work challenged many genre categories of its time, combining elements of "proletarian literature" and rumpen-mono (stories about the lumpenproletariat) with the I-novel and techniques of classical poetry.[59] Hayashi was mainly self-educated and well versed in Western literature, particularly Chekhov, Heinrich Heine, and the Norwegian writer Knut Hamsun—declared to be the most direct inspiration for *Horoki*.[60] In addition to being a huge commercial success, *Horoki* was also recognized and appreciated by the male literary establishment, even if it was marginalized within the terms of "women's writing." However, recent critics have recognized Hayashi's work as a major contribution to modern Japanese literature. Seiji M. Lippit includes her as a major figure in his study of Japanese modernism, arguing that the tropes of mobility and urban space developed in *Horoki* constitute an important mapping of the terrain of the gendered Japanese subject: "The nomadic movement that Hayashi's work describes is through [a] fluid and transitional landscape—across social categories such as domesticity, femininity, desire and class."[61]

From the various books and essays that have appeared in English, Hayashi Fumiko emerges as a heroic pioneer of Japanese women's literature. She was extraordinarily productive and she managed, through her writing, to escape from the poverty that inspired her first works to become a successful professional woman. This is essentially the story of Naruse's film version, yet where the literary emphasis is on her craft as a writer, the filmic emphasis is on the suffering that gave rise to her career. In many respects, Hayashi's own text does not lend itself to cinema, because it is essentially a performative text. The writer is produced by her own labor as a writer. *Horoki* is a diary of a woman who not only supports herself from her writing but literally feeds herself. Constant hunger and food fantasies are embedded in the texts that she sells in order to buy the food to satisfy the craving. Fumiko's romantic liaisons, mainly with unreliable, egotistical fellow writers, are likewise inseparable from the network of editors and publishers whom she relies on for cash. Hayashi's writing is unusually erotic and sensual, and she also writes candidly about working in cafés on the periphery of the sex industry, including small portraits of the many people she encounters in her nomadic movement through the city.

The time period covered by the novel is limited to the 1920s, the years that Hayashi struggled to establish herself as a writer, although the film extends beyond this period to include the publication of the novel itself and scenes from the beginning and end of Hayashi's life. Naruse's version of *Horoki* begins and ends with the author as a young girl traveling with her itinerant parents on a country road. The circularity of the narrative inscribes a fatalism of a very different order of writing than the disjunctive, open-ended novel. Scenes are added to illustrate the launch of the novel in 1930, and in the final scene, set some time close to the end of her life (she died of cancer in 1951) Hayashi is a wealthy gray-haired woman. The diary itself is thus framed by Hayashi's life story, in which the immediacy and spontaneity of the original are packaged into a closed system.

The difference between novel and film may be compared to Benjamin's distinction between the storyteller's craftsmanlike approach to narrative, and the novelistic preoccupation with death as "the meaning of life." For Benjamin, the two forms correspond to different modes of experience and memory: "The perpetuating remembrance of the novelist as contrasted with the short-lived reminiscences of the storyteller. The first is dedicated to *one* hero, *one* odyssey, or *one* battle; the second to *many* diffuse occurrences."[62] While the novel is individualistic, the storyteller's narrative is embedded in the collective. The novel provides the reader with "the hope of warming his [sic] shivering life with a death that he reads about," while the storyteller allows "the wick of his life to be consumed completely by the gentle flame of his story."[63] Hayashi's writing may have been autobiographical and confessional, yet it is also ethnographic; in its serialization, its rewriting, and its mass appeal, moreover, it cannot be accommodated into any singular or unified experience and is akin to the kind of narrative that Benjamin attributes to the storyteller.

In addition to the framing devices that are added in the film, a minor character from Hayashi's text has been developed into a larger and more developed character. Yasuoka Nobuo (Kato Daisuke) is a neighbor who lives in the same rooming house as Fumiko and her mother (Tanaka Kinuyo). He is a benevolent single gentleman who shares his food with the women, lends Fumiko money when she needs it, and offers to marry her. This character appears briefly in the novel as Matsuda, of whom the narrator says, "He epitomized all that I despised: a generous man to a fault."⁶⁴ She accepts a small loan from him, but their short-lived liaison is plagued by awkwardness and doubt. In the film, Yasuoka returns at various stages of Fumiko's life, witnessing her first husband hitting her and finally visiting her in her well-appointed home and garden in the film's penultimate scene. He functions as a kind of guardian or moral authority, witness to Fumiko's trajectory from abject poverty to nouveau riche.

In this closing scene, followed only by a flashback repetition of Fumiko as a girl with her parents, the writer is depicted as a heartless old woman who tells those who come to her for support that "poor people have to work. There's no other way." She refuses to finance an amateur magazine or to host a visiting relative. Yasuoka says she is entitled to be so harsh, as she has achieved her success through hard work, although he also notes that she looks tired. Sure enough, when he leaves, she puts down her head to sleep, and the final title quotes the phrase for which the author is best known in Japan: "Flowers are short-lived and have only troubles in abundance."⁶⁵ It is hard not to interpret this ending as a cruel joke on Hayashi, undermining her achievements by questioning her character — and not only her moral judgment but her aesthetic judgment as well. She has installed her aging mother in her large home and dresses her in a gaudy jacket that is uncomfortable and several centuries out of date. While these details may have some grounds in Hayashi's biography, it is an unusual way of ending a film that in so many other ways is a tribute to a woman's talent and success.

To be sure, Hayashi's own writing has a strong tone of fatalism, but it is couched in a social consciousness. Ericson translates one line from *Horoki* as "I feel like screaming, 'Motherfucking fate!'"⁶⁶ The strength of Hayashi's writing is her ability to triumph over her destiny through sheer will. She acknowledges that all around her "there was no shortage of suffering women,"⁶⁷ but when she herself is feeling down, she writes, "I was a shell of a woman. Without the means to go on living, there was no beauty in life. All I had left was my desire."⁶⁸ The novelistic framing story of the film, returning finally to the young Hayashi with her parents, effectively reduces her life to a narrative of unrewarded suffering and implicitly condemns her challenge to the conventions of polite society.

Aesthetically, Naruse's interpretation of *A Wanderer's Notebook* does not live up to the formal innovations he previously employed to capture the energy and drive of Hayashi's writing. It lacks the integrity of space of the home dramas *Meshi*, *Lightning*, *Wife*, and *Late Chrysanthemums*;

61. Takamine Hideko in *A Wanderer's Notebook* (*Horoki*, 1962), Takarazuka Eiga/Toho.

and it lacks the movement and dynamic temporality of *Floating Clouds*. The elliptical narrative is held together with fragments of Hayashi's text, most of which have been selected more for their narrative information than for their poetic commentary. Some scenes tend to collapse so much information that they fall flat as drama. For example, Fumiko moves in with a poor poet named Fukuchi, but in their first scene together he immediately displays his egotistical and patronizing character, leaving the viewer to wonder what she ever saw in him.

Takamine Hideko's performance as Fumiko is perhaps the most stylized of any role she played in Naruse's films. In the scenes set in cafés and teahouses where Fumiko works as a barmaid and hostess, she is wonderful as the hard-drinking, fun-loving woman depicted in Hayashi's novel. She sings and dances and wins a drinking competition, and she does not hesitate to criticize her customers' mistreatment of the women, which inevitably gets her in trouble with her women bosses. Despite these scenes, of which there are far too few, throughout most of the film Takamine assumes a slouching, despondent posture, registering a sullen disappointment in her body language and perpetual frown. This expression is rarely broken when Fumiko is sober, so although the film does showcase Takamine's "range of acting styles,"[69] in fact there are really only three positions: happy, sad, and drunk, of which the second occupies more than three-quarters of the film. When she smiles, it is like the sun coming out, but it happens only once in the film, after some poets visit the café where she works and compliment her on her poetry. Fumiko smiles, after which one of the poems from *Horoki* appears in titles over a scene of her writing at home: "I'm a red jasmine flower dug out of the field. When the wind blows strong, I fly up into the great blue sky like an eagle. Oh, wind! Blow your hot breath! Hurry! Blow this red jasmine!"

One explanation for Takamine's unusual acting in this film may be that Naruse was attempting to emulate the style of the silent cinema. Indeed, several scenes are performed entirely without dialogue, with Takamine reading passages from Hayashi's text in voice-over. The widescreen format tends to work against any such techniques, inscribing the formal and technological aesthetics of the 1960s onto the narrative. Moreover, the wide framing creates a sense of expansive space that does not sit well either with the story of poverty or with the "feel" of the 1920s. It could not be more different than the quick montage and exuberant camera movements of Naruse's own silent films.

Despite these criticisms, Naruse's *A Wanderer's Notebook* does capture some of the materialist aesthetic that is so distinctive of Hayashi's writing. Fumiko's struggles are set in a very detailed context of material scarcity, urban geography, and women's work. A constant itemization of the foods she desires and the food she is able to find punctuates the narrative: pickled radish, pork cutlet, noodles, Akita rice, egg, curry rice, and fantasies of steak and sushi. Fumiko prepares a meal for Fukuchi with money she has received for her writing. She lists the ingredients and their prices: "tofu for five sen, dried sardines cost three sen, and the pickled radish cost two sen," but Fukuchi rudely knocks the tray to the floor and takes money from her for cigarettes. Cash and coins are also featured in a constant exchange of small loans, usually laid carefully on the tatami. The jobs that Fumiko applies for and actually takes constitute a kind of inventory of employment opportunities available to women of the period: accounting (which she does very badly, not having the right training), factory work (making toys), waitressing (and hostessing in teahouses), and finally a potential job in the theater, which turns out to be a liaison with a shady theater director who, says Fumiko in voice-over, "needed my body more than my vita."

When Fumiko finally publishes *Horoki*, she is treated to a launch party where the poets and writers with whom she has become acquainted talk about her work. The scene is interesting in the way it includes the very commentary on women's writing that helped to keep Hayashi from being considered a serious writer during her lifetime. The men criticize her for capitalizing on her poverty, while the women wonder if she slept with the publishers. The frank discussion of her various romantic liaisons makes her seem promiscuous, while the chief critical attack is voiced by a fellow writer who says that her writing is like "garbage that had been stirred up with a stick." Her former lover (the man who beat her), Fukuchi, ultimately defends her at the launch in a surprising reversal of character. He confesses to be the "lowdown and gloomy" writer depicted in the novel and congratulates her on revealing "the beauty of the naked truth."

The discussion of literary values may be exceedingly simplified in the film, yet it resonates with Naruse's own career. Like Hayashi, his parents were part of the lumpenproletariat of Taisho Japan, surviving in the city through piecework and craftsmanship (his father was an embroiderer). Because he never drew directly on his own life story for scripts, nor was he ever very forthcoming about his own experiences, Hayashi serves as a kind of alter ego for him. His own open-ended narrative style, enmeshed in the "garbage"—the mundane detail of everyday life—in some respects parallels her unique approach, and indeed their careers were mutually enhanced through his adaptation of her work, even if she did not live to see it. Yet as a filmmaker in an industrial mode of production, he inevitably tempered her work.

The saddest thing about Naruse's version of *A Wanderer's Notebook* is that the "garbage" of Hayashi's life is not "stirred around with a stick" but commodified. Far from being "naked," the truth is fossilized, sentimentalized, and packaged as a tale of sorrow and moral censure. The film points to the many forms of exploitation that Hayashi and other women are subject to, but its potential as social critique is seriously undermined by its failure to endorse its central character's fundamental challenge to social norms of behavior. The stylistic edge of this challenge is in turn lost to the "packaging" impulse of commodity capitalism, in which

Hayashi's life story is no longer a performance of self but a sentimental tragedy. The great gap that the film exposes between the modernism of the 1920s and the crude sentimentality of the 1960s "tribute" is testimony to the decline of the studio system and its role in Japanese modernity.

Hayashi's life is finally encapsulated in a proverb (the troubled flower), invoking Benjamin's observation that a proverb is like "a ruin which stands on the site of an old story and in which a moral twines about a gesture like ivy around a wall."[70] Hayashi's storytelling held a special affection for the people of the shitamachi, on the peripheries of the modernizing nation; Naruse's cinema of the 1950s took up that affection for the collectivity of those on the margins of mainstream society. By the 1960s, when both Naruse and Hayashi had been rehabilitated into the center, "the raw material of experience" that formed the substance of Hayashi's writing was completely lost to what Benjamin names in "The Storyteller," as the age of information, a time when "no event comes to us without already being shot through with explanation."[71]

Yearning
A WOMAN'S DESIRE

The title of Naruse's 1964 film *Midereru* has been translated into English as *Yearning*, but its literal meaning is closer to "confusion."[72] Takamine Hideko's character Reiko is indeed confused and undecided about her love for a younger man, the brother of her deceased husband. Koji (Kayama Yuzo) refers to her as "sister" throughout the film, pushing their unconsummated relationship into the realm of incest. Reiko is strongly attached to the memory of her husband who died in the war, but despite her pledge not to remarry and her fear of scandal, it is evident that she is attracted to Koji. *Yearning* is a film about desire and the resistance to desire, but this melodramatic narrative is mapped onto another story of a family disintegrating under the pressure of economic development and a changing urban geography. The intensity of the potential love affair adds that expressionist element that was seen to be lacking in some of Naruse's related woman's films of the 1960s, particularly *Daughters, Wives, and a Mother* and *Woman's Status*.

Except the 1937 film *Feminine Melancholy*, this is the only title in Naruse's oeuvre to refer to a woman's state of mind (although the term *confusion* could be applied equally to the social context). Most striking about this film are the last twenty-four minutes (the last quarter of the ninety-seven-minute film), in which Reiko and Koji escape the claustrophobic cruelty of their family. The dynamic expressionism of their train journey bursts out of a stultifying environment of corporate and family pressures. Koji is initially introduced as a juvenile delinquent, but by the end of the film, the attraction between him and his widowed sister-in-law redeems him as a virtuous character. The two are drawn together largely through their outcast status. Koji's death finally puts an end to Reiko's confusion, but the film comes dangerously close to realizing the fundamental alliance between women's social oppression and rebellious youth. While Naruse may not have been able to follow through on the implications of the illicit relationship, the confusion of desire, yearning, and escape is sensuously inscribed. In true melodramatic fashion, the aesthetics of the characters' flight are balanced by those of the repressive social context from which they flee.

The first three-quarters of the film is set in a home attached to a shop, and most scenes are set in the compartmentalized rooms of this establishment. In addition to the usual "attached rooms" and kitchen of the ground floor, the set features an earthen floor corridor leading to the shop, bridged by a plank that allows the residents to move between rooms in their house slippers. The shop itself opens onto the street and is lined with rows and stacks of cans, bottles, and other dry goods. The detail of the mise-en-scène is like that of the shops in three previous Naruse films—*A Wife's Heart*, *Approach of Autumn*, and *Woman's Status*—and includes similarly detailed references to the store's inventory and the economics of a family-run retail business.

In this instance, the business is directly threatened by a new supermarket that has opened in the town (the town is not named in the film, but it seems to be not far from Tokyo). The film opens with a truck blaring announcements of the supermarket's first-anniversary specials. It quickly becomes apparent that the supermarket is driving the local shopkeepers out of business by selling everyday products like eggs at prices the shopkeepers can't possibly match. One of the neighbors is driven to suicide over the price of eggs, while in an unrelated scene, a group of young people compete in an egg-eating contest in a bar. Inscribed within the film is an insight into a culture of excess, corporate greed, and moral degradation. The supermarket owners are depicted as gangsters who taunt Koji about his inability to compete with their low prices.

The narrative turns on a proposition by Koji's brother-in-law to finance a supermarket on the land presently occupied by the family shop. Koji's two sisters, Hisako (Kusabue Mitsuko) and Takako (Shirakawa Yumi), persuade their mother to go along with the plan. The mother, played by

Mimasu Aiko, in a role very similar to her character in *Daughters, Wives, and a Mother*, is a passive woman unable to argue with her children, and she has let Reiko run her life and her business since her husband died. The only catch with the plan for a new supermarket is what to do with Reiko, who is the one who actually runs the shop. In fact, she rebuilt the establishment after it was destroyed in the war, and even though she was married only a few months before she lost her husband, she has remained with his family for the past eighteen years. Reiko's sister-in-law Hisako is eager for Reiko to remarry and even has a potential suitor lined up, valued at ¥70,000 per month (he is a department head in a company). The family's plan is that Koji should be the director of the supermarket, but Koji stands up for Reiko, insisting that she be the director.

The mother and sisters cannot deny that Reiko is more qualified than Koji, but they cannot imagine a scenario in which their brother, the family heir, would be subordinate to a widowed daughter-in-law. Reiko defers to them completely and, recognizing that she is an obstacle to the future success of the family, tells them that she has a secret lover and that she is ready to leave them. The mother and sisters are appropriately shocked and let her go. The two sisters are especially sinister in their conniving ways, and at the end of the final confrontation they scuttle away in a hurry that betrays their insincerity and confusion. Koji is as shocked as the others to hear about a fictional competitor for his affections. Although Reiko is lying when she says she has a secret lover, she has heard Koji's confession of love for her, which has thrown her into a state of confusion. She says very little, but shots of Reiko looking pensive, listening to Koji's footstep at night, and a game of glances and averted looks belie Reiko's disinterest. At one point, she tenderly helps him off with his raincoat, only to catch herself abruptly from endowing the routines of everyday life with the tinge of desire. For his part, Koji reforms his decadent habits and helps in the shop, mainly, it seems, to be closer to Reiko.

A number of scenes in the film exemplify Naruse's ability to exploit the aesthetic possibilities of black-and-white Tohoscope for strong effects of space, movement, and dynamic lighting design. One of these takes place at a temple grounds where Reiko invites Koji to meet her. In this short three-minute scene, the couple say very little, and she simply tells him that he will find out the next day what her plan is. However, the crosscutting between the two figures as Koji climbs the long flights of stairs leading to the temple site, while Reiko waits at the top, inscribes the tensions of their illicit romance. When they finally meet, Naruse's trademark technique of having one person walk out of frame and turn back to look at the other, is enacted as a kind of dance in 360-degree space involving the two actors, the camera, and the location. The temple grounds, from which a magnificent view is glimpsed in the background, is a simple site, such as one might find in many Japanese towns. The temple architecture is not extravagant, but set among pines, it provides an open space that is exploited by the spatial reversals, so that it makes a strong contrast to the compartmentalized space of the film's principle domestic setting.

The hint of romance in this scene is more fully developed in the remarkable train journey that takes Reiko and Koji away from their ungrateful family. After announcing her plan to return to her hometown, Reiko goes to the station, accompanied by her mother-in-law. After the train pulls out of the station, Koji unexpectedly appears from the adjoining car, bringing her magazines and fruit. He says that he will see her home. Shots of the train speeding through the landscape are intercut with shots of Reiko and Koji inside, and as the journey continues, Koji finds seats closer and closer to Reiko until finally they are seated together. Their exchanges of looks intercut with the forward momentum of the train and its distinctive sounds culminates in a scene at a station where Koji eats noodles on the platform and Reiko watches from inside. She signals to him to hurry, and the alarm bell rings until he joins her just as the train pulls out. The train ploughs through the night, and Reiko watches Koji sleep in the seat across from her. When dawn comes and the landscape glitters in the morning mist, she suggests they get off the train.

At the hot-springs resort to which they retreat, Reiko seems to lose her nerve, though. She admits that she is a woman with desires, but when Koji embraces her, she pushes him away. Koji leaves her in despair, and the sustained flirtation of the train journey is abruptly ended. Koji drowns his sorrows at a small inn, where an old lady (Urabe Kumeko) tells him she had a son his age who died in the war. He telephones Reiko to tell her that he will sleep with a girl he has found in a bar (a lie, of course) and is last seen disappearing into the darkness of the forest. The village the next morning is shot in a beautiful sparkling, slightly misty morning light, and from the fast-moving river running between the stacks of houses comes a constant sound of rushing water. After packing her dead husband's photo into her suitcase, Reiko looks out the window to see a body being carried into the village on a stretcher. In an

62. Takamine Hideko and Kayama Yuzo in *Yearning* (*Midareru*, 1964), Toho.

impossible close-up point-of-view shot, she sees the paper ring that she tied onto Koji's finger the night before. She is told that he fell off a cliff, and she runs down into the street, stumbling after the stretcher until she finally stops, caught in a close-up shot, while her face registers the crushing realization that she has lost exactly what she didn't know she wanted.

This is melodrama of the highest order, and it is accentuated by a soaring orchestral soundtrack highlighting the tragic event. But this music is quickly tempered by the more restrained lounge music with which the film opened. As Reiko runs helplessly after the vanishing body, she seems to be returned to the everyday, as she is indeed abandoned to herself. Edward Yang argues that with this ending, Naruse refuses to exploit our emotions but chooses instead to stop Takamine in her frantic chase: "She stands still. Her expression suddenly becomes calm as if she were saying to herself, 'This is life, and life must go on.' Quickly he cuts and the film ends there."[73] Like the long train journey that combines the time of waiting and boredom with the emergence of desire and yearning, this ending cuts across sentimentality with an ongoing inscription of the banality of everyday life.

Koji's accidental death is a contrived ending, and it is not at all clear whether it is an accident or a suicide. His conversation with the old woman, turning on the war, situates him as a member of a generation of guilty survivors, and thus as someone doomed to fail in his elder brother's footsteps. His love for his brother's widow may in fact be a love for his brother, even though it is his brother's ghost, captured in Reiko's closely held photograph, that stands firmly between the two ill-fated lovers. According to Takamine, Koji was supposed to have gotten drunk and to die in the snow, but no snow fell while they waited on location, so Naruse, ever the efficient film director, changed the ending. She says, "Naruse finally got tired of waiting for a snowstorm and had the brother-in-law kill himself."[74] This may explain the ambiguities surrounding the ending and the lack of signposts in Koji's character (who doesn't seem especially suicidal), but it also supports a reading of the scene as a suicide.

Viewing the film in 1989 with interviewer Phyllis Birnbaum, Takamine claims that it is the first time she saw the completed film, and it brings her to tears. "'But it's a Naruse film,' she said, wiping her yes, 'So it's too long, too slow. And all that hesitating.'"[75] Takamine puts her finger precisely on the film's unusual imbrication of melodramatic sensation and temporal distension. *Yearning* exemplifies the way that melodrama, far from being opposed to realism, is deeply embedded within an elaboration of social realism. This applies not only to the way that the love affair both is produced within and answers to a repressive social system, but also to the structures of temporality with which that system works. As a modernist idiom, the affective dimension of *Yearning* consists not only of the excesses of expressionist signification, but also of the representation of temporality, waiting, and boredom.

For Benjamin, boredom is the "index to participation in the sleep of the collective."[76] He sees it as the social experience of "eternal return," in which "the historicism of the nineteenth century capsizes.... The belief in progress—in an infinite perfectibility understood as an infinite ethical task—and the representation of eternal return are complementary. They are the indissoluble antinomies in the face of which the dialectical conception of historical time must be developed."[77] Benjamin is drawing on a vast literature on the aesthetics and politics of boredom as an experience of modernity in which the indeterminacy of desire, and of the void on which desire hinges, has been elaborated. Patrice Petro has taken up these arguments in the context of film studies to suggest that "an aesthetics of boredom retains the modernist impulse of provocation and calculated assault." While these aesthetics may be more readily identified in films such as *Jeanne Dielmann, 23 Quai du commerce* (Chantal Akerman, 1976), or in Warhol's cinema, it also pertains to a certain way of looking in which subjectivity is split.[78] Viewers see themselves viewing. Naruse's montage-based cinema can hardly be described as "boring," but his elaboration of the mise-en-scène and experience of everyday life participate in a similar experience of temporality. In the first half of *Yearning*, many scenes are staged around meals, in keeping with the rhythm of everyday life that underpins the home drama genre. The affect of desire is matched by an equally strong affect of feeling time pass.[79]

The *agnition* device of the "too late," on which the pathos of a film like *Yearning* is predicated, is produced through the splitting of knowledge and point of view.[80] But the tears that this device produces should not be dismissed as mere sentimentality. As Linda Williams argues, "Melodrama is structured upon the 'dual recognition' of how things are and how they should be."[81] Williams argues that melodrama is the "norm" of classical cinema, not its sentimental, feminized offshoot, as it is a central vehicle for the representation and negotiation of social justice. Christine Gledhill suggests that melodrama be considered as a modality rather than a genre, as it forms the basis for the negotiation of values of class and gender in mass culture. She argues that "melodramatic modality aims to render everyday life morally legible and its democratic morality is locked into an aesthetic of justice." Therefore, "it must, in order to command recognition, acknowledge the contested and changing signs of cultural verisimilitude, bringing radical as well as conservative voices into play."[82]

In *Yearning*, the audience knows that Reiko and Koji are in love, and the film demands that we recognize the obstacles that prevent them from realizing it themselves. Reiko is a woman clearly stuck in the past, adhering to conventions of behavior that no one around her seems to share. But the film also suggests that the past haunts the decadent present of the 1960s for a reason, holding open the memory of another social formation. The desire for escape, aestheticized in music, landscape, and movement—and in the romantic associations of the hot-springs resort and its traditional architecture—is in dynamic opposition to the decadent, dysfunctional society that Reiko has almost escaped.

If boredom is also a phenomenon of eternal return, we need to go back to the beginning of the film, to see how the final images correspond to those of the beginning. After an initial series of shots in which (bored) shopkeepers, including Reiko, wait for customers, watch the supermarket truck pass by, and learn about the low price of eggs, comes the scene in which four girls in a bar stuff their faces with eggs while the male customers "egg" them on. This grotesque image offends Koji, who gets into a barroom brawl over it. As an analysis of corporate capitalism, *Yearning* exemplifies Asada Akira's (admittedly ironic) notion of Japanese "infantile capitalism." Writing in 1987, Asada suggests that "in Japan, there are neither tradition-oriented old people adhering to transcendental values nor inner-oriented adults who have internalized their values; instead, the nearly purely other-oriented children provide the powerful driving force for capitalism. Let's call this infantile capitalism."[83]

Like many of Naruse's films, *Yearning* is about a family without a patriarchal center, which leaves it vulnerable to the authority of its own structure and systems, and to the vicissitudes of social change. A number of subplots and peripheral characters point to a generation gone astray, without direction. Koji himself is going down this road but is saved by his love for Reiko. The egg-eating scene is an especially strong sign of the pervasive delinquency, taking the mah-jongg and speeding that the young people do in other movies to a new level of depravity. It is like a hostess bar in which the infantile behavior of men is manifest in a new and cruel game (the girls look ill as they gorge themselves). Koji doesn't like the waste, but his only solution to these social ills and the survival of his own family in the new corporate culture of market surfeit is to make his sister-in-law company director, as he knows he is not able to fill that role himself. Although his character is not particularly well developed, Koji is an unusually generous and realistic male character, a rare entity in Naruse's cinema. Koji's family, however, cannot break out of the ascribed gender and inheritance roles of the "protected area" of the family system, which for Asada constitutes the "core of the Japanese ideological system." However stereotyped, he says, the family is a "soft" structure subsumed by a "seemingly horizontal, centerless, place."[84]

In *Yearning* the family is endangered by a culture of infantile capitalism—a culture that is driven by a pleasure-seeking, economy-boosting generation whose members have been cut off from their roots by the war. Koji escapes through death, but Reiko is left to face this new world alone. The melodrama of romance and unrequited desire may be idealistic and clichéd, but it points to the utopian possibilities latent within modernity. If only Reiko could see them, she could be free—to love a younger man, and to direct a company. The beauty of melodrama lies in the split subjectivity, leaving open the possibility that the viewer can see (and feel) precisely what Reiko does not quite apprehend; at the same time, the failure of the romance underlines the failure of society to allow these things to happen.

The Stranger within a Woman
PERFECT CRIME, PERFECT FAMILY

Naruse's turn to a film-noir thriller in 1966 is a surprising shift in style, indicating that even this late in his career, the director was amenable to new styles and stories. Returning to standard aspect ratio for the first time since *Anzukko* in 1958, the black-and-white cinematography of *Stranger within a Woman* (*Onna no naka ni iru tanin*, aka *The Thin Line*, 1966) builds on Naruse's long history of creative lighting design, exploiting its potential in this film for psychological effects. Cinematographer Fukuzawa Yasumichi achieves a more hard-edged, sharp image than the softer shades created by Tamai Masao in Naruse's previous noir film, *When a Woman Ascends the Stairs*,[85] and the soundtrack by Saito Akira is more discordant and experimental than the soft jazz of the 1960 film. *Stranger* marks the first and only time Naruse adapted a Western novel. The book, by the English writer (of Syrian descent) Edward Atiyah, called *The Thin Line*, was given to Naruse ostensibly to save him from the box-office slump that his string of woman's films had led him into.[86] According to Fujii Jinshi, the property was coveted by Ichikawa Kon, who had recently made *Kagi* (*Odd Obsession*, aka *The Key*), another psychological thriller, in 1959.[87]

Toho had produced a series of noir films between 1959 and 1961,[88] and Kurosawa's *High and Low* (*Tengoku to jigoku*), based on an American detective novel, placed second in the *Kinema Junpo* poll for 1963. *The Bad Sleep Well* (*Warui yatsu hodo yoku nemuru*) placed third in 1960; and in 1966, the same year as *Stranger* was released, Teshigahara Hiroshi made *Face of Another* (*Tanin no kao*), followed by *The Ruined Map* (*Moetsukita chizu*) in 1968—both based on Abe Kobo novels. Although Japanese noir first appeared after the war, with Kurosawa's *Drunken Angel* (*Yoidore tenshi*, 1948) and *Stray Dog* (*Nora inu*, 1949)—not to mention Naruse's *The Angry Street* (1950)—it had a revival in the 1960s. David Desser has suggested that the emerging culture of youth rebellion forced questions of identity and individualism into the cultural mainstream. "It took postwar prosperity to bring forward the latent ideological underpinnings of individualism."[89] Thus, alongside the open rebellion of some of the new wave films, with their spectacles of sex and violence, appeared a number of films exploring the psychological ambiguities of identity and morality set within the shadowed spaces of a city transformed yet again by the 1964 Olympics. As its title suggests, Naruse's version of noir remains linked to the woman's film. Set largely within the family home in Kamakura, at one point a teenage dance party with rock music can be glimpsed through the neighbor's window, an indication of the social upheaval of the era.

The storyline of *Stranger* is fairly simple: Tashiro (Kobayashi Keiju) strangles and kills the wife of his friend Sugimoto (Mihashi Tatsuya) before the opening scene, a scene in which he coincidentally meets Sugimoto in a bar in Akasaka very close to the apartment where the murder took place. Although Tashiro is not a suspect in the police investigation, he is racked with guilt and finally confesses to his wife, Masako (Aratama Michiyo). In an effort to further relieve his tortured sense of guilt, he then confesses to Sugimoto. Neither his wife nor his friend can believe that Tashiro actually did it, although flashbacks illustrate his version of events. In order to prevent him from turning himself in and disgracing the family, Masako finally poisons him. As Tashiro had bought the poison himself, with the intention of suicide, she is not suspected, so both husband and wife end up committing "perfect crimes."

In addition to the stylized lighting, the crime-centered narrative, and the flashback narrative structure, *Stranger* also features the familiar film-noir figure of the femme fatale. Played by Wakabayashi Eiko, Sugimoto's

63. Kobayashi Keiju and Aratama Michiyo in *The Stranger within a Woman* (*Onna no naka ni iru tanin*, 1966), Toho.

wife, Sayuri, appears in flashbacks as a seductive, sensuous woman of the 1960s, with long, loose hair and a miniskirt. Sugimoto knows that she has many male friends and is not terribly surprised to hear that she had a lover. Her death leaves him saddened, but he thinks she was probably partially responsible for her own death. Both men in the film are extraordinarily passive and inactive, doing little more than incessantly chain-smoking. Tashiro smokes nervously; Sugimoto smokes despondently. Sayuri smokes sexually. She is first seen in a flashback triggered by Tashiro's mother recalling her memory of Sayuri, who in her opinion, "was just too steamy." In the flashback, Tashiro lights Sayuri's cigarette. "She gave him a long, hard look," says the mother, while we see Sayuri catch Toshiro's eye provocatively over the flame of the lighter.

Tashiro confesses his crime to his wife as they enter a tunnel near a hot-springs resort where he has gone to recuperate from the nervous breakdown brought on by his guilt. The lighting in the tunnel provides a visual cue for the film's dominant metaphor of a "thin line." Tashiro's explanation shifts into a flashback depiction of the strangling scene in which Sayuri asks Tashiro to hold her neck harder and harder until she passes out. He says, "She passed out, but I didn't let go." He says that he felt as though he had crossed a thin line between dream and reality, "an invisible, thin line." As he describes crossing this line, we see Sayuri being strangled with an ecstatic look on her face, suggesting that the thin line for her lies between pleasure and pain. Finally, Tashiro says, "at one moment you're on one side, and the next you've crossed the line. But at that point she was already dead."

For Masako, this is not sufficient evidence that her husband really killed Sayuri. She thinks he has deluded himself, confusing dream and reality. When he seems determined to turn himself in, provoked by a colleague who embezzled money from his company and is caught by police, Masako takes the situation into her own hands. As she climbs the stairs to prepare the poison, she says, in voice-over, "As he tries to go out the front door with his head held high, I'll have to sneak him out the back. It's the only way." The mixing of poison and whiskey is interrupted by cutaways to spectacular fireworks going off at Yuigahama—a local Kamakura summer ritual—but Tashiro is not seen drinking the poison. In the subsequent scene, it is evident that he has died. Sugimoto prepares to leave for Osaka; Masako walks on the beach with her children.

In Fujii's analysis of *Stranger*, he argues that Naruse questions the veracity of the filmic image: "Made at a time when the studios were collapsing, and with its intricate architecture of vision, it challenges viewers by forcibly drawing them into a merciless critique of just what it means to watch a film."[90] Fujii's argument is bolstered by the unreliability of memory that is incorporated into the film through the character of Kato (Kusabue Mitsuko), Sayuri's friend who loaned her the apartment for her romantic trysts—the apartment where the murder took place. Kato recognizes Tashiro at the funeral. She has a flashback recollection of seeing him once outside her apartment building, but the figures in the flashback are in shadow and turned away from the camera. Shortly after she tells Sugimura this, Kato thinks she sees Tashiro on the street, but the man who passes is not him. In fact, a close viewing suggests that Naruse may have played a sleight-of-hand here, as the first sight of the passerby looks much more like Kobayashi Keiju than the second glimpse. In any case, this scene seriously undermines Kato's value as a witness, and it briefly places the film's own representations in question.

Fujii further suggests that the flashbacks themselves are unreliable, and that the film leaves open the possibility that Tashiro may actually be deluded in his guilt. Tashiro remembers taking a locket from around

STRANDED IN MODERNITY 379

Sayuri's neck, a gesture that is shown in the flashback episode of the strangling. Kato finds this locket exactly where Tashiro said it was, which would seem to confirm, through the logic of circumstantial evidence, that Tashiro was indeed the murderer. But Fujii claims that "there is no way to ascertain whether the contents of the *narratage* [flashbacks] are objective facts,"[91] basing this claim on the incident of Kato's faulty memory.

In my view, the flashbacks are more objective than subjective, and there is little reason to doubt their veracity, especially given that the first one is offered from the grandmother's point-of-view. Although Fujii may be correct in identifying the potential of the film's complex "architecture of vision," I don't find that the possibility of duplicity is really sustained. Noir narratives frequently turn on charmed objects, such as the locket in *Stranger*, but in this instance it is not even given a close-up, which is in itself unusual for Naruse, who loves the close-up view of things. Moreover, Kobayashi's performance of sustained melancholy leaves no room for doubt. Fujii argues that casting the more typically cheery actor as a murderer is like the casting of Jimmy Stewart in *Vertigo*,[92] but Kobayashi under Naruse's direction doesn't have the versatility of Stewart. In this film, he never puts on the happy face for which he is better known. Naruse, for all his technical skills, is neither a Lang nor a Hitchcock, and despite the single scene of misrecognition, noir is not his genre. Naruse is a director whose faith in the image is never shaken.

Kobayashi, who appears in at least eight Naruse films, describes his work with the director as highly controlled, a question of always underplaying and working against conventional expressions and reactions.[93] In *Stranger*, this underplaying masks the psychological complexity that is really needed to bring out the duplicity and ambiguity that Fujii sees in the film. As Tashiro, Kobayashi simply seems to give in to his guilt in the opening scene, and the film is little more than his getting to the point of confession. For a thriller, the film has little suspense. The tension lies in the emotional relations between the characters—the exchanges of glances and averted eyes. While Tashiro can't seem to look anyone in the eye, Masako is repeatedly framed in a wide-eyed glare, casting a corrective gaze on her husband, who simply shrivels before it. Moreover, the climactic scenes remain domestic, with dramatic effects of weather—sunlight, storms, and lightning—providing the film's most spectacular visual effects. The strength of the film lies in its engagement with the terms of the woman's film and domestic melodrama, and the more pressing question that the film raises is the significance of the title.

Naruse and screenwriter Ide Toshiro may have chosen to switch *The Thin Line* to *The Stranger within a Woman* (*Onna no naka ni iru tanin*) to link it with the director's signature genre.[94] But to which woman does the title refer? The seductive Sayuri, possibly the most sexualized woman in Naruse's oeuvre? Or the housewife who turns to murder to save her children from disgrace? In Atiyah's novel, it is more evidently the husband who harbors a stranger within himself, so although Ide's script adheres fairly closely to the original, the title shifts the focus from the husband to the wife. In the novel, it is the wife who hopes that her husband has confused reality with some kind of hallucination, but he himself has no doubt in his mind. The thin line for Atiyah is the one between respectable society and the criminal underworld, a theme that lends itself well to Japanese culture with its strong sense of propriety and correct behavior. However, the key scene that the script omits comes when the wife is first introduced in the novel. Her young teenage daughter breezily tells her father — coming home after just committing his horrible crime — that her mother gassed the cat in the oven after it had been hit by a car and injured. This casual remark plants the seed of recognition of the wife's stranger within. Because no such seed is planted in the film, Masako's final solution is completely unexpected, and the film lacks some of the psychological complexity underscoring the novel.

Stranger sets up a familiar opposition between the bad woman and the good one, and until the very last moments of the film, Masako is almost too good. This opposition is very much in keeping with the novel, in which the murderous husband is oppressed not only by his crime but also by the censorious atmosphere of his home life. The children in the film are terribly spoiled and among the most annoying in Naruse's oeuvre, constantly asking to be taken to Dreamworld or to go driving in the car. They play with noisy battery-operated toys, contributed by Sugimoto, who dotes on them far more than their father. If there is a discourse of excess in the film, it is the family unit, overseen by the benevolent grandmother. Masako's stranger within may be the force behind this idealized image. The final freeze-frame of the two children running toward their mother in sun-drenched white light is too perfect. Perhaps the narrative of adultery and guilt needs to be read as the unconscious truth behind an image that can no longer be taken at face value. In this film, the strong, survivalist woman — the Narusian heroine — surrounded by weak and feckless men finally goes too far, revealing the psychotic edge of a woman so devoted to respectability and the integrity of the family that she will murder her own husband to preserve that image of decorum.

Hit and Run
CARS AND CLASS

Car accidents play an important role in Naruse's cinema, especially in the early 1930s and in the 1960s. In the early films, such as *Not Blood Relations* and *Every Night Dreams*, collisions are highlighted and stylized by the director's dynamic editing techniques. In the 1960s, the accident more often occurs offscreen and is conveyed in a phone call. As a device of melodrama, the car accident thematizes the way characters are acted upon by forces outside their control, and in this sense it is emblematic of the modernity of this mode of representation. The gods of more classical forms of tragedy, both Japanese and Western, have been replaced by the accidental and coincidental effects of industrial modernity.

The car in Naruse's cinema is the embodiment of urban space characterized as a force of modernity in which speed, progress, and commodity capitalism take on an objective form. The violence of the accident is usually meted out against a child or husband, leaving women repeatedly widowed or childless. Trains are also part of the culture of danger, fear, and victimization implicit in modern methods of transportation, as parents lose their children to train accidents in *Flunky, Work Hard* (1931) and *Woman's Status* (1962). But the car, especially in the 1960s, also functions as a commodity, and thus plays a more complex role in Naruse's discourse of material culture. It is significant that the last two films of his career both feature car accidents as central events, occurring early in each film and setting the tone for two narratives that are otherwise very different from each other.

Hit and Run (*Hikinige*, 1966) is like *The Stranger within a Woman* in its depiction of a psychologically disturbed character, but it is much more of a woman's film than a thriller. In fact, it is the first time we find a mentally unhinged female protagonist in Naruse's cinema. Takamine Hideko plays a single mother (Kuniko), whose son is hit and killed by a woman driver, and the story follows her attempts to avenge her son's death. At first she wants justice to be served, but faced with the inequities of the legal system, she imagines killing the woman and her son, and she almost succeeds. However, the driver, Kinuko (Tsukasa Yoko), kills herself and her son before Kuniko can carry out her plan. In *White Beast* (1950), Naruse depicted mentally unstable women, but where those characters were deviants, produced within the postwar discourse of delinquency and twisted Freudian paradigms of hysterical femininity, the two women in *Hit and Run* are deeply disturbed. Moreover, their problems are not

64. Tsukasa Yoko in *Hit and Run* (*Hikinige*, 1966), Toho.

unrelated to the institutions of family, law, and corporate capitalism within which they live. In this film, the psychological distress of modernity that so afflicts male characters in modernist literature, including the men in *A Wanderer's Notebook*, *Yearning*, and *Stranger*, can finally be seen to be internalized by women. Thus women in Naruse's cinema have finally reached the limits of modern subjectivity, the point at which their individualism, agency, and interiority is broken and fragmented by the alienating pressures of urban modernity. To put this another way, in Takamine's last film with Naruse, she plays a character who goes insane.

Hit and Run is based on an original screenplay by Matsuyama Zenzo, and while both Takamine and Tsukasa rise to the challenge of portraying slightly unstable women, the story is somewhat forced, and Naruse's use of special effects pushes the story somewhat over the top.[95] Nevertheless, its excesses are produced within a narrative that also contains a critical view of corporate capitalism and its associated institutions of the family and the law. In her portrayal of the wife of a wealthy motor-company executive, Tsukasa conveys an elegant melancholy that she will carry into her leading role in *Scattered Clouds*. As Naruse's final leading lady, she conveys a certain grace in her expressions and posture, which is bolstered by her costuming. Her straight-lined skirts and dresses are evocative of Edith Head's choice of fashions for Tippi Hedren in Hitchcock's films of the early 1960s—*The Birds* (1963) and *Marnie* (1964)—and indeed *Hit and Run*, like *Stranger*, may well have been inspired on some level by Hitchcock's romantic thrillers.

STRANDED IN MODERNITY

Tsukasa's character Kinuko is having an affair with a young man, but from the outset of the film, the affair is on the rocks. Ogasawara (Nakayama Jin) wants to move to New York, and although Kinuko wants to go with him, she cannot leave her child. Their romantic liaisons are plagued by the desperate impossibility of the relationship. Kinuko is with Ogasawara when she accidentally hits Kuniko's child, and she doesn't stop for fear of being seen with him. When she gets home, she sees blood on her fender and confesses to her husband, Kakinuma (Ozawa Eitaro). However, he is afraid of a scandal affecting his business, so he asks his chauffer to confess to the hit-and-run. Both the chauffeur, a repatriated POW, and the family's housekeeper Fumie (whom Kinuko accuses of betraying her affair to her husband) are treated with condescension. They are conveniently blamed for other people's crimes, while they are completely dependent on the family for their livelihood and their anticipated retirements.

The discourse on class in *Hit and Run* is dramatized by the urban geography of Yokohama. Like Kurosawa's 1963 film *High and Low*, the wealthy couple live in a sprawling modern home at the top of a hill. Kuniko lives with her brother Koji, a yakuza gangster (Kurosawa Toshio), down the hill, and a recurring image in the film is of a gang of small boys scrambling up the cliff, which is how Kuniko's son is killed running out of the underbrush beside the steep and windy road. The chauffeur is charged and fined for the accident, but when Kuniko discovers from an eyewitness that it was a woman at the wheel, she quits her restaurant job and registers in a maid service, and is eventually assigned to work at the Kakinuma home. With her brother's help, she proves to her satisfaction that it was Kinuko who was responsible for her son's death, and thus her revenge is tinged with class antagonism. Kuniko decides that the best punishment would be for Kinuko to lose her son as well.

Kuniko's imaginary attempts to kill the little boy, Kenichi, whom she becomes responsible for, are depicted in bleached-out sequences marked by suspenseful music cues. She imagines throwing the child off a bridge onto a highway, and off a rollercoaster. Although she almost manages to gas the child in his bed, Fumie, the housekeeper, catches her,[96] and reaction shots of Takamine in all these events indicate that she is deeply conflicted by her murderous impulses. Toward the end of the film, a couple of sequences are enacted twice: once in an overexposed version of what Kuniko possibly wants to do, and a second version in normal lighting of what actually happens. In the first instance, Kuniko serves some food to Kakinuma, who is brooding over his scotch. She has just told him about his wife's affair. In the first, imaginary version of the scene, she lies down with Kakinuma, submitting to his embrace. In the repetition of the scene, she sits down and tells him about her ex-husband, who abused her.[97] This is the only indication in the film that Kuniko has any kind of sexuality, and the effect underlines her affinities with and possible jealousy of Kakinuma's wife.

The second and last imaginary scene underscores the two women's tragic affinities. In the overlit version of the scene, Kuniko sneaks into Kinuko's bedroom while the woman is asleep with her son and turns on the gas. In the dark, low-lit version of the scene that immediately follows, she discovers that Kinuko and Kenichi are already dead. Kuniko is immediately arrested and suspected of poisoning Kinuko and strangling Kenichi, and although she denies it at first, she eventually confesses to the crime. The police have discovered her identity and motive, and she is presumably plagued by her intention to have done it sufficiently to believe that she actually carried out the crime. However, in a final turn of fortune, Kakinuma reveals his wife's suicide note, and Kuniko is released. She remains a prisoner of her bad conscience, though, and is last seen compulsively helping people cross the streets of Yokohama waving a flag signaling PEDESTRIAN CROSSING (the flags are apparently provided by the city, available in stands at busy intersections). The film ends with a sign noting the daily toll of traffic accidents (seventeen), deaths (three), and injuries (eight).

The cinematography of *Hit and Run*, in widescreen black and white, combines documentary-like location shooting with fantasy sequences and special effects. In addition to Kuniko's imaginary activities, Kinuko (Tsukasa) has a nightmare after the accident that is illustrated with graphically displayed chalk figures. Cinematographer Nishigaki Rokuro's framing of the streets and alleys of downtown Yokohama, and the corridors of the Kakinuma home, creates a vortex effect with the space organized around central figures, but the detail of the sets and the fairly even lighting constitute an overall realism that is punctuated by a variety of stylized visual effects. The home itself features the latest modern conveniences and designs, laid out horizontally in the scope frame, echoing the architecture and decor of Kurosawa's *High and Low*, although on a somewhat smaller scale. The film also borrows the hard-edged wipe from Kurosawa's signature style, suggesting that Toho was possibly trying to replicate the success of *High and Low*.

The special effects that Naruse uses in *Hit and Run* point to the way that he was once again trying out new techniques and visual styles. For example, shortly after the chauffeur's trial, Kuniko is in a bar with her brother, getting drunk on the small compensation she has won from the court. Takamine's performance of an angry young woman is wonderful, and her drunken singing recalls similar scenes in *A Wanderer's Notebook*. However, where that film had her in a traditional hairstyle and kimono, here her hair is loose and her manner rough. The camera jerks and wavers with her erratic movements, as if it is handheld, although it is hard to imagine how the Tohoscope camera could have been handled that way. In any case, the scene takes on a documentary feel, pointing to the influence of the new techniques used by contemporary directors such as Oshima Nagisa and Hani Susumu.

The most visually striking shots of the film are set in the busy Yokohama streets, where Kuniko tries to tempt Kenichi to run into the stream of two-way traffic. The camera is set at the boy's eye level, and the cars speeding by tend to flatten the image, visually capturing the sense of speed and danger amplified by the overwhelming sound of the traffic. The visceral sense of this sequence is accentuated by editing with reversed screen direction, in keeping with the dynamic techniques of Naruse's 1930s accident scenes. When the boy finally dashes across, Kuniko loses her nerve and runs out to save him. At the end of the film she returns to the blur of traffic, accompanying pedestrians across the flow of moving vehicles, as if she has finally found her destined role in life. In its use of stylized special effects, *Hit and Run* may be the closest Naruse came in his postwar career to emulating the avant-garde cinema of his contemporaries. Max Tessier has pointed to the role of imaginary and fantasy episodes in the new wave and ATG films of the 1960s, arguing that for a number of directors, they provide means of pushing the boundaries of the real, and interrupting the narrative flow.[98] In *Hit and Run*, we find both the documentary impulse of the new wave and the destabilized sense of the real, as the psychological dimensions of the two women's desires, fears, and anxieties are given visual form.

Also in keeping with the political stance of some of Naruse's younger contemporaries, *Hit and Run* offers a critique of car culture. Kakinuma's company is advertising its new product—a new high-powered engine called the Blue Star—with the slogan "gamble your life on the moment," which has been criticized by the police. Kakinuma instructs his assistant not to change the slogan, as the controversy will create publicity. For this reason, he is especially concerned that his wife's hit-and-run accident be kept from the public. Caught between her husband's refusal to let her

65. Takamine Hideko in *Hit and Run* (*Hikinige*, 1966), Toho.

confess and her lover's insistence that she do so, Kinuko is finally driven to suicide. Moreover, the critique of car culture does not fail to incorporate the spectacle of speed and automobile design. Kakinuma meets with other executives at the beginning of the film, proudly displaying a motorcycle speeding around a track. But the real star of the film is the Renault Caravelle that Kinuko is driving when she hits Kuniko's child.

The light-colored Caravelle is a sporty two-seater with a stylized body design typical of the period. It is first associated with Kinuko's affair, as she and Ogasawara drive to the beach in it. Just before the accident, a shot through the front windshield creates the sense of speed that the two passengers seated close together might feel. In subsequent scenes, the Caravelle sits in the garage, abandoned but still glowing, as if it were eager to be once again unleashed on the streets of Yokohama. The Caravelle is feminine and ultramodern, not unlike Kinuko herself. It comes to symbolize everything that lies between the two women, Kinuko and Kuniko, over and above its narrative function as the thing that brings the two women together.

In her study of French film and culture in the 1950s and 1960s, Kristin Ross argues that the automobile is the commodity that became emblematic of modernity, mass culture, and American cinema during this period, and significantly, she points to the Renault as the company most central to this phenomenon.[99] The car became the fetishized consumer object of choice, holding out the promise of a utopian society of equality, and indeed Naruse offers such an image of the middle-class family symbolized by their purchase of a new car in his 1961 film *As a Wife, as a Woman*. Ross points out that cars were idealized in cinema some time before they became a normalized feature of everyday life in France,[100] and we could say the same thing about Japan. *Hit and Run* takes up several themes of French cinema of the era noted by Ross: the preoccupation with traffic (which Ross describes as exemplary of the "constrained time" of everyday life), on the one hand, and the blurred perception of a driver's vision, on the other.[101] Ross argues that the fetishized image of the car masks the unevenness and inequality of modern society, and indeed *Hit and Run* is concerned with a challenge to the ideology of car culture. Naruse depicts the automobile as a demonic machine of modernity, grinding the bodies of women, children, and the serving class in its gears and spitting them out as dead and damaged.

Scattered Clouds
DESIRE AND COSMOPOLITANISM

In the last film of his career, Naruse brought together many themes that had preoccupied him over the course of his career. In *Scattered Clouds* (*Midaregumo*, 1967), we find the car accident, the widow, the unrequited love affair, the business of the geisha and professional entertainer, the transferred salaryman, the traditional architectural sets, the city, and finally, a return to the Aomori countryside. All of these things are endowed with a new beauty in the director's finest use of color Tohoscope. From the high-rise apartments of the first part of the film, to the lush landscapes of Lake Towada, the use of color and space are particularly striking. The film also features a musical score by Takemitsu Toru—the only time that Naruse worked with the composer responsible for some of the best soundtracks for Oshima, Teshigahara, Shinoda, Hani, Kobayashi, and Kurosawa. The film arguably achieves a kind of melancholia that makes it one of the director's most powerful melodramas. An ill-timed love affair, with its sense of missed opportunity and loss, takes on epic proportions through its implication in social institutions and global mobility and cosmopolitanism.

Like *Hit and Run*, the story begins with a car accident, although in this film it takes place offscreen. Yumiko (Tsukasa Yoko) learns that her husband has been hit by a car while walking on the road in Hakone, a resort area where he has gone to do business. There is a suggestion that he had been drinking. A phone call comes to her sister's home, after which she is seen crying over a bandaged corpse in the hospital. The conflation of business and pleasure that pervades the film's depiction of corporate culture applies also to the driver of the car, Mishima (Kayama Yuzo), who gradually becomes Yumiko's love interest. Although an investigation into the accident finds that it was caused by mechanical failure, Mishima is transferred to Aomori by his company as punishment because there was a prostitute in the car, along with a client from Bangkok. Mishima is blamed for the negative publicity created by the accident, as the company would prefer to keep their entertaining practices confidential. When Mishima is transferred, his work appears to be more of the same: providing clients—both Japanese and foreign—with a good time, but after the accident and the move, he becomes more and more disaffected, drinking heavily to drown his sorrows.

Yumiko is a typical Naruse heroine in that she is a strong-willed survivor, but she is unusual in her elegance and sophistication. Takamine's character in *When a Woman Ascends the Stairs* has some of this poise, but Yumiko is even further removed from the corruption and sleaziness that is all around her. She begins the film as a pregnant young bride, learning English in order to accompany her husband to New York, where he is imminently to be transferred. After his untimely death, she aborts the child, having no means of financial support. Her entitlement to her husband's pension is contingent on her remaining part of his family, but her three-month pregnancy is too short for any support designated for the child; just to rub it in, the company representative adds that funds have been further deducted for the funeral wreath provided by the company. As her practical sister, Fumiko (Kusabue Mitsuko), predicts, the husband's family wastes little time in removing Yumiko from the family registry, leaving her with no income at all. Although she has studied English literature at college, she is qualified only for the most menial office and cashier jobs, and she is eventually persuaded to go to Aomori to work as a hostess in a ryokan that is owned by her sister-in-law Katsuko (Mori Mitsuko).

That both Yumiko and Mishima end up in Aomori is entirely coincidental. Although they each know the other is headed there before committing to the move themselves, Yumiko has given her husband's killer only the meanest of glares on their first few meetings. In each case, he meets her eyes asking for forgiveness, which she repeatedly refuses to grant. Brought together by the accident, they are bound together by the memory of it. Of his own will, Mishima sends Yumiko monthly envelopes of money through her sister, which she accepts reluctantly until she is officially cut off from her husband's family, after which she feels ineligible even for Mishima's support. In order to return his money, she visits him in Aomori on her way to the Lake Towada ryokan, and they have coffee together. Mishima notices that the waitress has spilled some of Yumiko's coffee into the saucer, and he switches cups. This small gesture is key to the budding romance between the two exiles from Tokyo. Mishima is a gentleman, and his manner toward Yumiko is very much in the style of a foreigner, a man who has shed the stereotypically rough, macho tendencies of the Japanese man.

Yumiko insists that she cannot possibly love the man who killed her husband, yet the two continue to be drawn together. Where Mishima is a gentleman, Yumiko is a lady. She is dressed throughout the film in tailored dresses and suits made from silk or cashmere. The solid pastel colors, discrete jewelry, and straight lines convey an elegance that becomes especially out of place in Aomori; even in trousers, picking herbs,

Yumiko is larger than life. The uniform kimono of the ryokan looks terribly wrong with her Jackie Kennedy haircut. She looks so much better in the fashions popularized by the American "queen." The film was scripted by Yamada Nobuo, who provided scripts for several yakuza and new wave films throughout the 1960s. He may have been one of the "powerful male scriptwriters" who Hasumi and Yamane claim bullied Naruse at this point in his career,[102] yet the film also clearly rises above its script through its stylish mise-en-scène.

Partly because they are in the same business of entertaining at hotels, Mishima and Yumiko continue to meet accidentally, and each time the desire and anguish that lies between them seems to escalate. She begs him to leave, so he applies for a transfer, only to be sent to Lahore, Pakistan, which seems to be considered by everyone who mentions it as a kind of purgatory, infested with poverty and disease—although Mishima tries to reassure himself that they have modern buildings there. Before he leaves, he and Yumiko arrange to go boating together on Lake Towada, but in the middle of the lake Mishima becomes feverish. As they pause in the rowboat, a cloud passing over the lake casts a shadow and a sprinkle of rain that gives the film its title. A camera movement following Yumiko's head turning toward shore captures her anxiety and dread, and her desire, as she realizes in the instant that Mishima is ill that she will lose him—even though she has not yet admitted to herself that she loves him. This gesture, in which music, camera, weather, and actor are united in one moment of longing, anticipates nothing so much as the romantic melodramas of Wong-Kar Wai that would follow some forty years later.

They decide to retire to a local inn, as Mishima is shivering with cold. Nursing him through a night of thunder and lightning, Yumiko finally relents and takes Mishima's hand. The scene recalls the tragic finale of *Floating Clouds* in the constellation of weather, illness, and desire, although the technical effects of color and sound take the drama up a notch in *Scattered Clouds*, even if it is more artifice than realism that is amplified in the blue lighting and elegant setting. Mishima survives the illness in this case, and the couple meet two more times before they finally part, presumably forever. They meet in the woods, first of all, where they kiss and act like lovers until Mishima asks Yumiko to go to Lahore with him. She cannot imagine a relationship with "an open wound at its heart," so she sends him away. But then, in the very next scene, Yumiko is so shaken she breaks a plate in the kitchen of the ryokan where she works. She watches rescue boats converge on the lake,

66. Kayama Yuzo and Tsukasa Yoko in *Scattered Clouds* (*Midaregumo*, 1967), Toho.

and overheard dialogue indicates that a double suicide has just occurred. Katsuko is having a stormy fight with the married man with whom she has been having an affair, in the midst of which Yumiko calls Mishima at his boarding house and catches him just before he leaves.

There follows a remarkable final scene, one that Naruse may well have designed as the final episode of his career, given its tone of finality. It is practically wordless, and like the train scene in *Yearning*, the lovers are brought closer together through travel, mobility, and time. Yumiko and Mishima sit in a taxi, going back to the inn where they spent their tumultuous night not long before. Perhaps they are going to consummate their ill-begotten affair, although in keeping with Naruse's career-long propriety, that part of the trip is left to our imagination. Perhaps they have intentions of double suicide, but no words pass between them. The taxi driver's eyes in the rearview mirror are all that is needed to suggest the illicit character of their mission. Flashing red signal lights and a caution sign precipitate their nervous wait at a railway crossing. Mishima lights a cigarette while the train clatters past. Three minutes is a long time in Naruse's quick-paced films, but it takes that long for the taxi to reach its destination. On the way to the inn they pass an accident: two cars smashed up on the side of the road, splattered with blood. Their first embrace in their room in the inn is interrupted when Yumiko has a flashback vision of the accident they just passed, a scene not unlike the still-life accident scenes that punctuate Godard's filmmaking of the late 1960s. Indeed, this whole sequence, in which time is curiously distended and the couple's fate seems uncannily intertwined with those of other couples' destinies, constitutes a sudden shift of pace, a movement into some other kind of cinema.

Finally Yumiko and Mishima sit down to eat a meal in their room. He apologizes to her for being "a barbarian" destined for Lahore rather than Europe, and he sings her a folk song in a lovely tenor voice about the bounties of the land while she stares down at her lap. The scene is dissolved into shots of Mishima alone on a train, and Yumiko alone by the lake, with Takemitsu's score taking up the folk-song theme. The musical theme, played by an accordion, has been introduced earlier, first over Yumiko's memories of her honeymoon at Lake Towada with her husband, and later over the scene in the rowboat. *Scattered Clouds* may be inconclusive, but the couple evidently refuse the option of double suicide. Instead, they have chosen to live with their memory of an accident and its duplication in another accident, which is finally given visual representation. The uncanny repetition of the accident ensures that it will be memorialized as the absence, the open wound that stands between them.

Scattered Clouds is very much a film for cinephiles, organized as it is around these moments in which time, space, and performance are crystallized in small details. Hasumi notes the moment when the lightning illuminates the two figures in the inn when Yumiko sits beside Mishima's futon all night. "What emerges then is 'a man and a woman' who are isolated from the rest of the world under special light, the definition of a movie by Naruse himself."[103] We could also point to more banal moments, such as the scene in Mishima's high-rise apartment when he breaks up with his boss's daughter. As Chris Fujiwara points out, Naruse's cutting and staging patterns in the scope frame are as dynamic and unconventional as those he uses in standard format.[104] The characters open and close the curtains of the sliding doors as if they were shoji panels, and the scene is completed with a close-up of the girl's patent-leather purse, which she snatches up before she leaves. Rather than dialogue, the breakdown of the relationship is conveyed through props, movements, glances, and abrupt shifts in angle and spatial orientation.

Other instances of melodramatic discursive representation include Yumiko's pale orange-and-green outfit that she wears when she reads her letter of excommunication from her late husband's family. Her dreary apartment is suffused with a bottle-green light, against which her outfit, along with the discordant strings, creates a mood of deep melancholy. Despite the suggestions that Naruse "did not like color film,"[105] he understood only too well how to exploit its potential for expressive effects. Shortly before this scene in her apartment, Yumiko passes a busy Tokyo intersection moments before Mishima passes it. Here the city becomes a site of paths not crossing, of missed opportunity and unfulfilled destiny, which will become the dominant theme of their relationship.

Above and beyond the technical achievements of *Scattered Clouds* is the use of landscape, reminiscent of Naruse's previous color films with rural settings: *Summer Clouds* and *Whistling in Kotan*. Not only does he indulge more deeply in the pastoral beauty, this film seems to acknowledge its status as a picture-postcard view of rural Japan. Lake Towada has now become a premier tourist destination, especially for Japanese, and even in 1967, the characters are more or less employed by the resort industry and its commodification of traditional pastimes. The unspoken alliance between Yumiko and Mishima is arguably linked to their unspoken disdain for the entertainment and tourism industry, although the film also clearly capitalizes on the location for the representation of their romantic liaisons in natural settings and inns. Nevertheless, if the central obstacle to their future happiness is the memory of the fatal car accident, the film itself is infused with the sense of loss.

We can perhaps attribute the profound melancholia of *Scattered Clouds* to Naruse's premonitions of mortality. However, the film once again embraces the future as inevitable and predicts the changes in the social fabric that will affect men and women, both as gains and as losses.

The multiple references to foreigners, foreign languages and customs, international travel, and displacement cannot be ignored. While there is no question that Yumiko is the essence of refined Japanese femininity, both she and Mishima are somewhat cosmopolitan. As I have suggested above, Mishima is a gentleman, subscribing to the ethos of "ladies first," a concept introduced to Japan by foreigners in the Meiji period and reinforced during the American occupation.[106]

In her book about Japanese women's attraction to Western men and Western culture, Karen Kelsky argues that alongside the social policies concerning women that were introduced during the occupation emerged a new erotic discourse favoring the Western "gentleman" over the paternalistic Japanese man. Although Kelsky is principally concerned with the internationalization of Japanese women in the 1980s and 1990s, when they became increasingly drawn to the opportunities for self-fulfillment offered outside Japan, we can perhaps situate Yumiko on the verge of this recognition. She is disgusted with the business-related liaisons that her sister Katsuko tries to arrange for her, and is evidently cut off from all other social institutions. Historically speaking, in 1966, she is fully aware of the alternative social configurations of gender that exist internationally (she has majored in English literature, after all), but she is not yet able to act on that awareness.

The irreconcilable love affair at the center of *Scattered Clouds* might thus be read in terms of what Kelsky refers to as *akogare*, which, she says, "translated variously as longing, desire, or idealization, is the word most often used both among and about women to describe women's feelings about the West."[107] This is not to suggest that Yumiko sees Mishima as if he were not Japanese, but to underline the ways that the film's engagement with the foreign points to a global elsewhere. Yumiko may be left at film's end alone, with no future, but it is only because she is preoccupied with memory and loss. She has essentially disgraced herself in the community by spending two nights alone with Mishima, yet she cannot follow him. Kelsky says of akogare: "If denial is where most internationalist narratives end, it follows that *akogare*, acknowledged or not, is where they begin."[108] Yumiko is bound for New York, but when she is diverted from that path and cast back into the institutionalized gender inequities of Japanese society, her longing for another identity is displaced onto the impossible lover and killer Mishima.

At the end of his last film, Naruse leaves his heroine alone, longing for that which is beyond her reach. The discourse of desire is produced within one of the director's most spectacular melodramas, provoking comparisons to Sirk's melodramas of the 1950s, in which stylistic excess may be said to constitute a form of ideological critique. Tsukasa Yoko's character is simply too stylish for a society that cannot contain her desire. Her longing opens onto an elsewhere beyond the parameters of Naruse's own cinema.

Thirty-four years later, Tsukasa appeared in the pages of *Cahiers du cinéma* wearing an elegant purple jacket cut something like her costumes in *Scattered Clouds*. Her description of the shooting of the film indicates that Naruse was as incommunicative as ever. He gave her no help in understanding the character of Yumiko and held no rehearsals. Most scenes were shot in short takes according to a preconceived plan that suggested to the actress that editing was more important than performance for the director.[109] If this is the case, then we must credit Tsukasa for much of the emotional drama of the film. She is extraordinarily expressive and demure, embodying precisely that duality of desire and its disavowal that the notion of akogare conveys.

A Late Cinema

Throughout the last decade of his career, Naruse remained concerned with the subjective dimensions and psychological states of women in modern Japan. His heroines are still survivors, even if they sometimes appear to be swimming against the tide of the new Japan. Social change in the 1960s had many dynamics, including a new cosmopolitanism, new anxieties brought about by increased importation of foreign customs and products, and new institutional restrictions. For the first time, in *Scattered Clouds* we see the new generation in leading roles, and they can't wait to get away from a Japan that is becoming unrecognizable. Society seems to have closed in on them, even if it is the car accident that becomes emblematic of accelerated modernity crashing into the wall of ethical and moral integrity.

Naruse was not the only director who worked from the 1920s into the 1960s. Gosho Heinosuke, Kinugasa Teinosuke, Ito Daisuke, and Yamamoto Kajiro all began their careers when Naruse was a mere prop man at Shochiku, and they all released films in the 1960s. While Ito survived by specializing in period films, Yamamoto in comedies, and Kinugasa in coproductions, Gosho seems closest to Naruse's strategies of aesthetic survival. As Arthur Nolletti argues, Gosho also turned to romantic melodrama for the most impressive films of his final decade,[110] although unlike Naruse, Gosho worked for both Shochiku and Toho in the 1960s, as well as several independents.

From 1958, in the face of large-scale changes in the industry and the social formation, Naruse did not shy away from trying out new genres and themes, as evidenced in *Hit and Run* and *Stranger within a Woman*. Nor did he shy away from addressing social issues concerning marginalized people such as the elderly and the Ainu. However, projects such as *Horoki*; *Flow of Evening*; *As a Wife, as a Woman*; and *Daughters, Wives, and a Mother* demonstrate his ongoing commitment and virtual indenturedness to Toho studio. Even in the less successful films, his ongoing preoccupation with the woman's film entailed a renewed recognition of the marginalization of women, especially widows, mistresses, and daughters-in-law, in the accelerated modernity of 1960s Japan. With his characteristic eye for detail, he zeroed in on the social facts, the new social practices and tendencies, and the new geographies of urban alienation and touristic exploitation that had so altered the fabric of everyday life.

Perhaps most exciting about this last decade is the director's ability to harness the discourse of desire implicit in romantic melodrama in the full technical spectrum of sound, color, widescreen, and music. *Summer Clouds*, *When a Woman Ascends the Stairs*, and *Scattered Clouds* exploit the full potential of cinematic expression to push the tensions and contradictions of Japanese modernity into critical perspective. His heroines' unrequited desires seem to infuse the sensuous fabric of everyday life as a challenge to the repressive structures of social protocol. As a last gasp of the studio system of which he was a central figure, these films are texts of longing, loss, and survival. The critical neglect of these late films can by explained only by the shift in critical priorities to the more radical cinema of the new wave, a cinema that actually shared a great deal with Naruse in the 1960s in its challenge to the status quo. However, his name belonged to a generation that was abruptly rendered anachronistic within a new formation and definition of Japanese modernity.

CONCLUSION

Placing in fourth position in the *Kinema Junpo* poll for 1967, *Scattered Clouds* was the biggest critical success of the last decade of Naruse's career. Shortly after it was completed, he was hospitalized with cancer. (Ill health had forced Naruse off work for most of 1964.)[1] Tsukasa Yoko and Takamine Hideko both report visiting the director during the last two years of his life, when he seems to have become more forthcoming and talkative than he ever was on set with his actors. Takamine says that, shortly before his death, in 1969, he reminded her of an idea he had hatched a few years earlier, of a film in which she would perform against a white curtain, with "no sets, no color . . . nothing but the drama itself, unfolding before a white backdrop with no impediments." On his deathbed, Naruse asked Takamine if she would act in this film for him.[2]

How can we account for this imaginary final film that seems to imply the essence of Naruse's ambitions as a filmmaker? It sounds like a strange combination of Warhol's minimalism and Karsh's celebrity photography, perhaps even with some of the documentary, improvisational aesthetics of Cassavetes mixed in. It is, in a word, far more avant-garde and experimental than any film that Naruse ever completed. While it suggests, on the one hand, that he may have been aware of the new photographic and cinematic aesthetics of the 1960s, it also points to the way that his filmmaking was focused, throughout his career, on the interface between the cinematic machine and the human face and body. Here we may return to Benjamin's remarks on the modernity of the cinema as an apparatus of representation. Remarking on the way that screen performance is a kind of "testing," he claims that the social significance of the cinema lies in the way it brings the relationship between technology and humanity into the public sphere. The film actor "takes revenge" on behalf of the city dwellers who lose their humanity daily in the face of an apparatus of standardized, mechanized testing and measuring. The film actor takes revenge "not only by asserting his [or her] humanity (or what appears to them as such) against the apparatus, but by placing that apparatus in the service of his [or her] triumph."[3]

Naruse avoided long-take aesthetics throughout his career, so his imaginary film can be envisioned only as a montage of shots, like the "tests" of a rapid-fire photo shoot, moments caught from the temporal continuum, frozen in time like a car accident. The actress and the camera would engage in a dialogue or contest over that moment, and the actress would inevitably win over the machine with the smallest expressive movement of her face. She would also of course risk becoming even further enmeshed in the cult of celebrity, through which the cinema is ever in danger of resorting to the ritualistic "cult" practices of corporate capitalism and authoritarian society. However, shedding the accoutrements of narrative cinema, Naruse would finally be free of what Benjamin describes as the "fetters of capitalist exploitation."[4] The actress would be responding to "the masses" directly, controlled through the invisible power of women's unarticulated desires, disappointments, and longings. This is the film, riddled with contradictions, that Naruse was never able to make.

The length of Naruse's career and the stylistic diversity of four decades make any summation of his style impossibly reductive. Nevertheless, from his earliest silent Shochiku features to his final Tohoscope melodramas, certain themes recur. As I have suggested, the edict that evicted him from Shochiku in 1934, that he was one Ozu too many, obscures the fundamental differences between the directors that became so much more evident in their later careers. Where Ozu is sunny, Naruse is dark; where Ozu is transcendental, Naruse is materialist. In the silent films, Naruse began to insert shots of objects—props, body parts, location details—that helped to ground his storytelling in the detritus of everyday life. His obsession with feet, floors, and shoes became linked to the exchange of cash, indicating a materialist sensibility borne not from ideological commitment but from a realist aesthetic devoted to those on the lower rungs of the modern social formation.

Naruse's preoccupation with women's stories originated in the generic formulas of shinpa drama, shoshimin-eiga, and the home drama, but he distinguished himself by the techniques he developed to depict female subjectivity in the cinema. From the expressive track-in dollies of his silent films, to his use of voice-over narration and the narratives of fantasy escape in the 1930s, he endowed the New Woman with a personality and desire that could nevertheless be accommodated within an increasingly conservative nationalist imaginary. Within the ideological constraints of the wartime and occupation administrations, he nevertheless continued to create strong portraits of women literally coming into being in films such as *Hideko the Bus Conductor* and *Spring Awakens*. In the 1950s, his woman's films rendered the institution of marriage an existential problematic. He may not have questioned it directly, but he repeatedly underscored the inequities, disappointments, and outright despair of an institution thoroughly enmeshed in corporate hierarchies and real estate topographies.

Naruse likewise approached women of the water trade as people in a business that was particularly vulnerable to the changes of modernity. In his late films, his heroines display the full symptoms of the modern subject, some of them psychologically damaged and destabilized, and others, like Takamine's Keiko in *When a Woman Ascends the Stairs*, and Tsukasa Yoko's Yumiko in *Scattered Clouds*, fully conscious of their marginalization and alienation. While his female characters suffer multiple crises and calamities, he refused to elevate their oppression as anything more than modern women facing problems endemic to human nature and modern society. The darkness of his films, often literally achieved through exquisite lighting designs, should not be interpreted as sorrowful. Nor are they open-ended; they are in fact carefully structured narratives that tend to bring his women protagonists to cumulative points of self-realization and actualization. Neither conventionally happy nor sad, closure for Naruse is terminally ambiguous, marking completion without total resignation, and almost always leaving open the possibility of awakening and change.

One of the recurring figures over the course of his long career is the choreography of a camera, a woman, and a man, usually in an exterior location. Cinematographer Tamai Masao describes it as a "looking-back" position, in which the movement of the scene is created through a rhythmic pattern of fixed shots in which one [actor] would take a step ahead and look back, then the other would take a step and go further."[5] Variations on this system appear throughout Naruse's career, with some of the most elaborate in *Feminine Melancholy* (1937) on the rooftop of a department store, *The Song Lantern* (1943) in a forest, *Sound of the Mountain* (1954) in a park, and *Yearning* (1964) outside a temple on a hill. In each of these scenes, the relationship between the man and the woman is steeped in ambiguity and uncertainty. The figure is emblematic of the ways that men and women in Naruse's cinema struggle to communicate, to bridge the gender divide that perpetually defers the happiness they seek. As a vernacular expression of Japanese modernity, Naruse suggests that the ideals of romantic love are incommensurable with the realities of the social formation.

The looking-back position demonstrates the crucial role of rhythmic pacing in Naruse's editing. His piecemeal style evolves in the postwar films into a rhythmic flow that embeds the emotional tensions of the narratives in the regularity of eventless routines. So much of the dramatic content is produced through the play of glances, dropped eyes, and guarded smiles, so much of the emotion in charged with rain, yet the rivers flowing by ensure that despair and regret will evolve into new chances for happiness. Indeed, the narratives of loveless marriages, failed romances, and broken families are never without elements of humor, hope, and humility. This is a melodrama not of peaks and valleys, as Naruse's longtime producer Fujimoto Sanezumi complained,[6] but of winding roads that take the viewer, along with the characters, through city streets and rural paths, apparently without direction, but not without destination.

The blank white sets of Naruse's final unmade film are profoundly antithetical to the rich "documentary" feel of his realist style and indicate how differently he may have understood his own filmmaking from the way that I have represented it in this book. I have suggested that his body of work serves as a kind of ethnographic portrait of modern Japan insofar as his home dramas depict the changing dynamics of everyday life. His filmmaking style retains a kind of doubleness, remaining constantly aloof and outside the characters and their homes. This attitude is literally enacted in the many shots of homes lit at night that register not only an observational distance but a sense of duration and distended temporality that is curiously sustained despite the relatively fast pace of the editing. Especially within the international context of contemporary film distribution, and with a growing historical distance, we tend to look *at* Naruse's characters as well as *with* them. Thus, because Naruse excelled in creating women characters who were able to recognize themselves as modern subjects, his oeuvre, as a series, provides a privileged view of the trajectory of the female Japanese subject over the thirty-seven years of his career. Naruse was "a very ordinary person"[7] who created an extraordinary body of work. Only an auteur fully inscribed within a studio system of film production could achieve such a contradictory postmortem commendation.

In her study of the internationalization of Japanese women, Karen Kelsky asks, "How, then, do we write an ethnography of desire as a 'social practice,' of the lived enactments of imagination?" She admits that her study of Japanese women's attraction to the West may not represent all women in contemporary Japan.[8] However, as a form of critical ethnography, it is an invaluable method of countering the notions of hegemony, normativity, and national identity that are so pervasive in the study of Japan. In this sense, Kelsky's study helps to bring this examination of Naruse's cinema full circle, back to the premises with which it began. Transnational global feminism may not be represented in the films themselves, but I hope to have shown how, as a methodology, it is a means of situating Naruse's filmmaking within a framework of critical ethnography. Aesthetics and film style in this analysis have been read as discourses of representation, expression, and sensual affect that bring the "other culture" closer in such a way that the otherness of both Japan and the West are dissolved in Naruse's evolving forms of vernacular modernism.

Naruse's cinema may not be a representative cinema, given all the surrounding cultural crosscurrents that continued to change over the thirty-seven years of his career. But it is a symptomatic cinema, pointing to the ongoing negotiation of women's subjectivity within the terms of Japanese modernity. Naruse himself probably never left Japan, except for his brief sojourn in Shanghai during the war. Remaining embedded within the vernacular of Japanese culture, he helped to shape that vernacular into the global forms of mass media. Nevertheless, insofar as his storytelling remained open, inconclusive, and intertextual, and that he continued to experiment with an ever-changing repertoire of techniques, styles, and genres throughout his career, he was also a key contributor to cinematic modernism.

After this tour through the body of Naruse's extensive oeuvre, we can return to Bock's provocative claim that Naruse is not, after all, a humanist. She describes his severe realism as lacking compensation.[9] However, against a vanishing humanism, this cinema retains a strong utopian impulse in its sustained orchestration of the desires of women to rise above the institutional and social forces that keep them down. Perhaps this is the tension between the director and his actresses; perhaps it is a reading produced within "eroticized agendas of modernity and universalism."[10] In such a context, contemporary cinephiles are rediscovering Naruse and he communicates to new, cosmopolitan audiences long after his death. As a form of critical anthropology, I have situated Naruse's rich and provocative body of work within an international framework, as it is only from such a perspective that the patriarchal nationalism of Japanese institutions can be challenged. If this book has intentionally displaced his cinema into the context of "a global cosmopolitan class that contains its own hierarchies of race, gender and capital," then so be it.[11] The unfulfilled promises of modernity are inevitably bound to disappoint, but Naruse enables us to share the pleasures and pain of the contradictory experience of women in Japanese modernity of the mid-twentieth century.

NOTES

Preface

1 The two films that remain "lost" as of this writing are *Until Victory Day* (*Shori no hi made*, 1945) and *Delinquent Girl* (*Furyo shojo*, 1949); the title rumored to be incomplete is *Shanghai Moon* (*Shanhai no tsuki*, 1941), which may be at the National Film Centre in Tokyo, although it was not made accessible to me to view.
2 *Even Parting Is Enjoyable* (*Wakare mo tanoshi*, 1947) is part of *Four Love Stories* (*Yottsu no koi no monogatari*); and *The Kiss* (*Kuchizuke*, 1955) is part of *Women's Ways* (*Onna doshi*). Some of the discrepancies in the available filmographies may be due to the inclusion or exclusion of these two short films, which I am including in the eighty-nine-film total.
3 Elsaesser, "Cinephilia."
4 Hansen, "Fallen Women, Rising Stars" and "The Mass Production of the Senses."
5 Singer, *Melodrama and Modernity*.
6 Hansen, "Fallen Women, Rising Stars," 13.
7 Benjamin, "On the Concept of History" (1940), in *Walter Benjamin: Selected Writings, Vol. 4*, 391.
8 See Miyoshi and Harootunian, *Postmodernism and Japan*, for a more extensive discussion of Japanese modernity and postmodernity.
9 Harootunian, *History's Disquiet*, 111.
10 Yoshimoto, "The Difficulty of Being Radical."

Introduction: The Auteur as Salaryman

1. The lack of critical attention Naruse has received in Japan is endemic to film studies in general, which has developed very slowly as an academic discipline in Japanese universities. See Yoshimoto, "The University, Disciplines, National Identity," 698.
2. Hasumi and Yamane, *Mikio Naruse*, 18.
3. Bock makes this point in "The Essential Naruse," 105.
4. Hasumi and Yamane, *Mikio Naruse*, 19.
5. Doniol-Valcroze, "Ma mère, je la vois," 50. The year of its release in Paris, *Mother* was placed on the "top ten" lists of Alain Resnais, Jacques Audiberti, Pierre Kast, Henri Angel, and Pierre Braunberger. See Jean Narboni, *Mikio Naruse*, 25.
6. Hasumi and Yamane, *Mikio Naruse*, 19–20.
7. Ibid., 24.
8. *Memories of Mikio Naruse*.
9. Ibid.
10. Interview with Takamine Hideko in Murakawa, *Naruse Mikio Enshutsujutsu*, 37.
11. Anderson and Richie, *The Japanese Film*, 364.
12. Okamoto, "What the Master Mikio Naruse Taught Me," 13.
13. Interview with Ide Toshiro in Murakawa, *Naruse Mikio Enshutsujutsu*, 160.
14. Burch, *To the Distant Observer*, 187.
15. Although the critique of Burch has been extensive, and a de rigueur component of Japanese film studies, two of the first articles to initiate the critique are Lehman, "The Mysterious Orient," and Kirihara, "Critical Polarities and the Study of Japanese Film Style."
16. Murakami Tadahisa, review of *Tsuma yo bara no yo ni*, *Kinema Junpo*, September 1, 1935, trans. Chika Kinoshita.
17. Bock, *Mikio Naruse* (Locarno) and *Mikio Naruse* (Chicago). The Chicago catalog contains an essay by Bock, "The Essential Naruse," which has been reprinted in the San Sebastian catalog. It is a much shorter version than the long essay in the Locarno catalog, which was (inexplicably) published only in French.
18. Bock, *Mikio Naruse* (Locarno), 39.
19. Yoshimoto, *Kurosawa*, 18.
20. Lopate, "A Taste for Naruse," 12.
21. Narboni, *Mikio Naruse*.
22. In comparing Naruse to Schubert and to Chekhov, Narboni fails to recognize the profound influence these two Western artists had on Japanese theater and cinema.
23. Narboni, *Mikio Naruse*, 83, my translation.
24. Schermann, *Naruse Mikio*.
25. Ibid., 8.
26. Bock, *Mikio Naruse* (Locarno), 15.

27 Throughout this book I will be using the term *shoshimin-eiga* to refer to what Anderson and Richie refer to as *shomin-geki* in their influential history of Japanese cinema, as the former seems to be the term used more commonly by Japanese critics.
28 Hasumi and Yamane, *Mikio Naruse*, 17. Bock says that Kido criticized Naruse's films for having "no ups and downs; the tone is too flat," while Hasumi and Yamane claim that Kido's complaint was that the films were too "pathetic."
29 Harootunian, *Overcome by Modernity*, xxiii.
30 Shimizu Chiyota said of *Repast* (*Meshi*, 1951), "This is an expression of Japan and Japanese life created by Japanese cinema in it its own manner, as brilliant as [that of Italy by] Italian neorealism." Review of *Meshi*, *Kinema Junpo*, December 1, 1951, 43.
31 Douchet, "About Naruse."
32 Yoshimoto, "Logic of Sentiment," 39–48.
33 Kurosawa Akira, "Preface," extract from *Something Like an Autobiography* [1984], in Hasumi and Yamane, *Mikio Naruse*, 13.
34 Brooks, *The Melodramatic Imagination*; Landy, *Imitations of Life*.
35 Thompson and Bordwell, "Space and Narrative in the Films of Ozu"; Burch, *To the Distant Observer*, 154–86.
36 Yoshide, "Reversing Light and Shadow," 162.
37 Ibid., 159.
38 Quoted in Takamine, "About Mikio Naruse," 10.
39 Yoshida, *Ozu's Anti-Cinema*, 13.
40 Narboni, *Mikio Naruse*, 148–49. Narboni bases his analysis in part on Ozu's diaries, in which he wrote at length about *Floating Clouds*.
41 Bordwell, *Ozu and the Poetics of Cinema*, 339.
42 Sato, *Currents in Japanese Cinema*, 195.
43 Ibid., 78.
44 Tsuneishi, "The Veil Comes Down," 180–81.
45 Takamine, "About Mikio Naruse," 9.
46 Ibid.
47 Okamoto, "What the Master Mikio Naruse Taught Me," 12.
48 Tatsuya Nakadai interview (2005), *When a Woman Ascends the Stairs*, Criterion Collection DVD, 2007.
49 Nakadai explains that he was usually given a point to focus on, and that Naruse knew exactly how the character to whom he would be talking would move during the scene, pointing out that Naruse could only shoot in such a way because he had such confidence in himself as a director.
50 Okamoto, "What the Master Mikio Naruse Taught Me," 12.
51 Mizuki, "Scriptwriter Yoko Mizuki," 188.
52 Hasumi, "Mikio Naruse or Double Signature," 87.
53 Naruse Mikio, "Works of Fumiko Hayashi and I," 170.
54 Bock, "The Essential Naruse," 105.

55 Interview with Takamine in Murakawa, *Naruse Mikio Enshutsujutsu*, 16.
56 "Le Témoignage de l'Actrice Yoko Tsukasa" and "Ume Takeda, Monteuse." Both interviews were recorded by Charles Tesson on November 29, 2000.
57 Takamine claims that Naruse did not like color film, which he began using in 1959, because it was a distraction from the drama. ("About Mikio Naruse," 9).
58 Murphy, "Approaching Japanese Melodrama," 31. The term *nimaime* refers to actors with second billing in Edo-era theater. Sato describes the role as a man who is "kind and gentle toward the heroine," giving the impression of a "frail helpless fellow who would fall over if nudged" (17).
59 Hasumi and Yamane, *Mikio Naruse*, 269.
60 Polan, "Auteur Desire," 1.
61 Benjamin, *The Arcades Project*, 460.
62 See Kerr, *Dogs and Demons*, for an account of the failures of contemporary Japan on the levels of environmentalism, finance, information, and so on.
63 Bordwell, *Ozu*, 42.
64 Ibid., 47.
65 Wada-Marciano, *The Production of Modernity*, 12.
66 Richie, *Ozu*.
67 Benjamin, *The Arcades Project*, 865.
68 Ibid., 64.
69 Habermas, "Walter Benjamin," 98. While Habermas draws mainly on Benjamin's later works, including *The Arcades Project* and the essays on Baudelaire and cinema, he also crucially relates these works to Benjamin's earlier writing on language.
70 Harootunian, *History's Disquiet*, 123.
71 Hansen, "The Mass Production of the Senses," 333.
72 Ibid.
73 Ibid., 341.
74 Mellen, *The Waves at Genji's Door*, 289.
75 Wada-Marciano, "Imaging Modern Girls."
76 High, *The Imperial Screen*, 252.
77 Miyoshi, *Off-Center*, 13.
78 Dussel, "Beyond Eurocentrism," 4.
79 Scott Nygren has made this point, but as Mitsuhiro Yoshimoto has pointed out, Nygren's discussion of Japanese modernity remains bound up in paradigms of otherness. See Nygren, "Reconsidering Modernism," and Yoshimoto, "The Difficulty of Being Radical."
80 Buckley, "A Short History of the Women's Movement," 153.
81 Pharr, "The Politics of Women's Rights," 222.
82 Ibid., 245.
83 Ueno Chizuko interviewed in Buckley, *Broken Silence*, 280.
84 Anderson and Richie, *The Japanese Film*, 320.
85 Gledhill, *Home Is Where the Heart Is*, 36.

86 Suzuki Juzaburo, Tomoda Junichiro, Mizumachi Seiji, and Shimizu Chiyota, "*Hataraku ikka* gappyo" ("Collective Critique of *The Whole Family Works*"), *Kinema Junpo*, March 11, 1939, 14–17, translation by Brian Reyes, Shirata Masumi, and Guy Yasko.
87 Tsuboi Sakae, "*Okaasan no waku*" ("The Framework/Limitation of *Mother*"), *Eiga Hyoron*, August 1952), trans. D. R. Lindberg.
88 Audrey, "Les Femmes et le Cinéma au Japon."
89 Doane, *The Desire to Desire*, 9.
90 Friedman, *Mappings*, 134.
91 Sato, *Currents in Japanese Cinema*, 139.
92 Bernardi, *Writing in Light*, 51.
93 Aoki, "Feminism and Imperialism," 28.
94 Miyoshi, *Off-Center*, 196.
95 Ibid., 196.
96 This phrase is borrowed from Minh-ha, *Reassemblage*, 96.
97 Chow, "Digging an Old Well," 410.
98 Friedman, *Mappings*, 137.
99 See Silverman, *The Subject of Semiotics*.
100 For a discussion of the applicability of psychoanalysis to Japanese culture, see Allison, *Permitted and Prohibited Desires*. Allison argues that insofar as psychoanalytic categories of fantasy, desire, and gender identification remain grounded in the family in Japan, psychoanalytic categories are eminently applicable to patterns of pleasure and taboo, even if the "grammar of desire" is located primarily in the materiality of Japanese culture—which includes the culturally specific domestic space of the home.
101 Doane, "The Woman's Film," 296.
102 Miyoshi, "Against the Narrative Grain," 153–54.
103 For a discussion of the parallels between Japanese and Western melodramatic traditions, see essays by Yoshimoto, Nygren, Russell, and Turim in Dissanayake, *Melodrama and Asian Cinema*.
104 Murphy, "Approaching Japanese Melodrama."
105 Singer, *Melodrama and Modernity*.
106 Brooks, *The Melodramatic Imagination*; Elsaesser, "Tales of Sound and Fury."
107 Ericson, *Be a Woman*, 19.
108 Gledhill, "Rethinking Genre"; Williams, *Playing the Race Card*.
109 Miyoshi, *Off-Center*, 212, emphasis original.
110 Miyoshi, "Against the Narrative Grain," 155.
111 My reading of Ozu has been partially developed in "Three Japanese Actresses of the 1950s" and in my review of *Late Spring* in *Cineaste* 32, no.2, (2007): 65–67. In these articles, I argue that Hara Setsuko's characters tend to refuse expressions of desire and disappointment. Yoshimoto implies a similar reading in his claim that the melodramatic elements in Ozu's films don't "cohere" as melodrama. See Yoshimoto, "Logic of Sentiment," 142.

112 Sakai, *Translation and Subjectivity*, 119–24.
113 Bruno, "Site-Seeing," 10.
114 Crary, "Modernizing Vision."
115 "*Shutai* itself is of hybridity that is inevitable in the *process* in which the subject is constituted, but erased and disavowed in the subject thus constituted" (Sakai, *Translation and Subjectivity*, 119).
116 Kaplan and Grewal, "Transnational Feminist Cultural Studies," 358.
117 This is not to say that there is no feminist movement in Japan. Sandra Buckley's anthology *Broken Silence* demonstrates that there is indeed a strong current of intellectual and activist feminism. However, a recurring theme in the book is the lack of cohesion of the various voices and activities associated with Japanese feminism.
118 Nornes, "The Postwar Documentary Trace."

1 Women in the City

1 Hasumi and Yamane, *Mikio Naruse*, 221.
2 Wada-Marciano, *The Production of Modernity in Japanese Cinema*.
3 Ibid., 16–47.
4 Kido Shiro, *Nihon Eigaden: Eiga Seisakusha no Kiroku* (Tokyo: Bungei Shunjusha, 1956), 52–56. Quoted and translated by Wada-Marciano in ibid., 177.
5 Wada-Marciano, "Imaging Modern Girls," 16.
6 Wada-Marciano, *The Production of Modernity*, 76.
7 Ortolani, *The Japanese Theatre*, 233.
8 Wada-Marciano, *The Production of Modernity*, 81.
9 Ibid., 83.
10 Tsuneishi Fumiko, program notes for Le Giornato Del Cinema Muto, 2005. Available at www.cinetecadelfriuli.org/gcm/edizione2005/edizione2005_frameset.html (accessed June 5, 2006).
11 Standish, *A New History of Japanese Cinema*, 54. Standish cites Kobayashi Kyuzo, *Nihon Eiga o Hajimetta Otoko: Kido Shiro Den* (Tokyo: Shinjinbutsu Oraisha, 1999), 66.
12 Bordwell, *Ozu and the Poetics of Cinema*, 24.
13 Ibid., 23.
14 Bordwell, "Visual Style in Japanese Cinema," 16.
15 Ibid., 17.
16 Naruse et al., "The Naruse Mikio Roundtable."
17 Tsuneishi, "The Veil Comes Down," 173–74.
18 Donald Richie, foreword to Kawabata, *The Scarlet Gang of Asakusa*, xxv.
19 Wada-Marciano, *The Production of Modernity*, 202–3.
20 Bordwell, *Ozu and the Poetics of Cinema*, 24.

21 Naruse et al., "The Naruse Mikio Roundtable," 518.
22 Bock, *Japanese Film Directors*, 121–22.
23 Anderson and Richie, 69–70. For more on Prokino, see Markus Abe Nornes, *Japanese Documentary Film: The Meiji Era Through Hiroshima* (Minneapolis: Minnesota University Press, 2003), 30–47.
24 Anderson and Richie, *The Japanese Film*, 64.
25 For a discussion of the relationship between melodramatic modernism and Japanese theater, see my "Insides and Outsides."
26 B. Sato, *The New Japanese Woman*, 77.
27 Wada-Marciano, "Imaging Modern Girls," 23.
28 Silverberg, "The Café Waitress," 217.
29 Ibid., 224.
30 Vertov, *Kino-Eye*, 17.
31 Harootunian, *History's Disquiet*, 156.
32 Penelope Houston, *Keepers of the Frame: The Film Archives* (London: BFI Publishing, 1994), 69; cited by Bernardi, *Writing in Light*, 17.
33 Gerow, "One Print in the Age of Mechanical Reproduction."
34 Benjamin, *The Arcades Project*, 456–88.
35 Harootunian, *History's Disquiet*, 141–50. The key Tosaka text is "Essays on the Japanese Ideology" (1935).
36 Harootunian, *History's Disquiet*, 150.
37 Ibid., 143.
38 Ibid., 133–40. Harootunian also discusses this work in *Overcome by Modernity*, 202–7.
39 Tomonori, *Twentieth Pordenone Silent Film Festival Catalogue*, 32.
40 Harootunian, *History's Disquiet*, 151–54.
41 Ibid., 155.
42 Ericson, *Be a Woman*, 27.
43 Karatani, *Origins of Modern Japanese Literature*, 45–75.
44 Ericson, *Be a Woman*, 30.
45 Harootunian, *History's Disquiet*, 116.
46 Ibid., 153.
47 Silverberg, "Constructing the Japanese Ethnography of Modernity," 30–54.
48 Silverberg's article includes reproductions of some of Kon's illustrations.
49 Harootunian, *History's Disquiet*, 132. He quotes Kon Wajiro from "Gendai fuzoku."
50 Silverberg, "Constructing the Japanese Ethnography of Modernity," 31.
51 The only real model for Tamae's character is Tsuru Aoki, the wife of Hayakawa Sessue. See Sara Ross, "The Americanization of Tsuru Aoki."
52 Tsuneishi, "The Veil Comes Down," 167.
53 Tokata Sachio, review of *Tsuma yo bara no yo ni* (*Wife! Be Like a Rose!*), *Eiga Hyoron*, August 1935, 119–23, trans. Chika Kinoshita.

54 Kitagawa Fuyuhiko, review of *Kimi to wakarete* (*Apart from You*), *Kinema Junpo*, April 11, 1933, 70, trans. Chika Kinoshita.
55 Elsaesser, "Tales of Sound and Fury," 79.
56 Ibid., 77.
57 Kitagawa, review of *Kimi to wakarete*, 70.
58 Tsuneishi Fumiko, program notes.
59 Wada-Marciano, "Construction of Modern Space," 168–71.
60 Ibid., 170.
61 Kitagawa Fuyuhiko, review of *Yogoto no yume* (*Every Night Dreams*), *Kinema Junpo*, July 1, 1933, 475, trans. Chika Kinoshita.
62 Eguchi Mitsuo, review of *Yogoto no yume* (*Every Night Dreams*), *Kinema Junpo*, July 21, 1933, 52–53, trans. Chika Kinoshita.
63 Matsui Hiro, review of *Yogoto no yume* (*Every Night Dreams*), *Eiga Hyoron*, July 1933, 145–47, trans. Chika Kinoshita.
64 Anderson and Richie, *The Japanese Film*, 69. There is very little information available in English on prewar censorship. Kyoko Hirano has only this to say about 1925 legislation regulating moving pictures: "It required film producers to submit completed films along with 'explanatory scripts' for government approval. The government reserved the right to cut films or ban their distribution altogether" (*Mr. Smith Goes to Tokyo*, 15). However, according to the Film Censorship Record, vol. 16, *Yogoto no yume* was not censored (Schermann, *Naruse Mikio*, 57). I'd like to thank Mitsuyo Wada-Marciano for pointing this out to me.
65 Singer, *Melodrama and Modernity*, 130.
66 Harootunian, *History's Disquiet*, 122.
67 Wada-Marciano, "Construction of Modern Space," 170.
68 Kitagawa, review of *Yogoto no yume*.
69 Wada-Marciano notes that Tokyo's two entertainment districts, Ginza and Asakusa, featured as very different cultural venues in SKS films (*Production of Modernity*, 125).
70 Harootunian, *History's Disquiet*, 126–27. He is quoting from Kon Wajiro, "Gendai fuzoku," in Nakamura Koya, *Nihon fuzokushi koza* (Tokyo: Yusankaku, 1929), 3:4.
71 Tom Gunning, "From the Kaleidoscope to the X-Ray."
72 Ibid., 52.
73 The notion of the viewer as voyageur is taken from Bruno, "Site-Seeing," 10.
74 The notion of the mobile gaze is from Friedberg, *Window Shopping*.
75 Karatani, *Origins of Modern Japanese Literature*, 107, 110.
76 Silverberg, "Remembering Pearl Harbor," 37.
77 Harootunian, *Overcome by Modernity*, 23.
78 Ibid., 25.

2 Toward a Japanese Classical Cinema

1. Naruse et al., "The Naruse Mikio Roundtable."
2. Narboni, *Mikio Naruse*, 114.
3. Naruse et al., "The Naruse Mikio Roundtable," 100.
4. "Hobe," *Variety*, April 14, 1937, 12, 33.
5. Smith, "Critical Reception of *Rashomon* in the West," 116.
6. The reviews that denounced the film as technically poor, dreary, and "no threat" to the American industry include "Hobe"; *Motion Picture Herald*, April 24, 1937; Frank S. Nugent, *New York Times*, April 13, 1937; and *Time*, April 26, 1937, 42–44. Those that praised the picture as a humanist drama providing insight into Japanese social customs include *National Board of Review Magazine*, April 1937, 16–17; *Film Daily*, April 16, 1937; John Mosher, *New Yorker*, April 10, 1937, 69–70; Mark van Doren, "Japanese Triangle," *Nation*, April 10, 1937, 419. Two magazines erroneously declare that Naruse was the leader of a theater troupe called Tsukiji, and is now the director of P.C.L. studios: "U.S. Sees First Japanese Movie; French Russian Influences Predominate in Screen Efforts," *Literary Digest*, April 10, 1937; Elsie Weil, "Kimiko," *Asia*, June 1937, 463.
7. Okubo, "Kimiko in New York," 183–97. Okubo's research on the background for the screening of Kimiko in New York is partly based on a roundtable discussion titled "Talking about Tourist and Export Films," *Eiga Hyoron*, August 1939.
8. Okubo, "Kimiko in New York," 184.
9. Anderson and Richie, *The Japanese Film*, 81–83.
10. The J.O. Company was created by Osawa Yoshio. The *J* of the title referred to the American Jenkins recording system that Osawa held the rights to; and the *O* for Osawa's name. Ibid., 82.
11. Anderson and Richie, *The Japanese Film*, 83.
12. Hansen, "The Mass Production of the Senses," 335.
13. Ibid., 338.
14. Burch, *To the Distant Observer*, 191.
15. Hansen, "The Mass Production of the Senses," 341.
16. Harootunian, *Overcome by Modernity*, 25.
17. See Gerow, "The Word before the Image."
18. Hasumi and Yamane, *Mikio Naruse*, 34.
19. Hansen, "Mass Production of the Senses," 339.
20. Bordwell, Thompson, and Staiger, *The Classical Hollywood Cinema*, 4. It might also be noted that the first use of the term *classical cinema* is attributed to André Bazin in "La politique des auteurs," *Cahiers du Cinéma* 70 (April 1957).
21. For a good discussion of the vicissitudes of classical cinema arguments, see Ray, "The Bordwell Regime and the Stakes of Knowledge."
22. Harootunian, "'Detour to the East,'" 7–8.
23. High, *The Imperial Screen*, 151.
24. Hasumi and Yamane, *Mikio Naruse*, 238–39.

25 Hansen, "Fallen Women, Rising Stars," 19.
26 Kishi Matsuo, review of *Tsuma yo bara no yo ni* (*Wife! Be Like a Rose!*), *Kinema Junpo*, August 1, 1935, 62, trans. Daichi Saito.
27 Murakami Tadahisa, review of *Tsuma you bara no yo ni* (*Wife! Be Like a Rose!*) *Kinema Junpo*, September 1, 1935, 118, trans. Chika Kinoshita.
28 Iida Shinbi, Tomoda Junichiro, Kitagawa Fuyuhiko, and Kishi Matsuo, "*Sannin shimai gappyo* (Collective Critique of *Three Sisters*)," *Kinema Junpo*, March 1, 1935, 122, trans. Chika Kinoshita.
29 High, *The Imperial Screen*, 26–29.
30 Tsuneishi, "The Veil Comes Down," 173–74.
31 Kawabata, *The Scarlet Gang of Asakusa*, 35.
32 Ibid., glossary, compiled by Alisa Freedman, 216.
33 Ibid., 129.
34 Iida Shinbi et al., "Collective Critique of *Three Sisters*" 121–24.
35 Ibid. The reference to neorealism (written in *katakana*) suggests that the Italian literary movement had been introduced to Japan by 1935.
36 Ibid.,124.
37 Bock, *Japanese Film Directors*, 107. Yamane says they divorced in 1940 ("Rhythm of Emotions," 45).
38 According to *Time* (April 26, 1937), Chiba was rated by U.S. critics as a "Nipponese Sylvia Sidney" in 1937.
39 Bock, *Japanese Film Directors*, 107.
40 Kano, *Acting Like a Woman in Modern Japan*, 183–217.
41 Burch, *To the Distant Observer*, 191.
42 Mark van Doren, "Japanese Triangle," *Nation*, April 10, 1937, 419.
43 Burch, *To the Distant Observer*, 190–191.
44 Okubo, "Kimiko in New York," 189.
45 "U.S. Sees First Japanese Movie: French, Russian Influences Predominate in Screen Efforts," *Literary Digest*, April 10, 1937, 28.
46 Weil, "Kimiko," 463.
47 Kishi Matsuo, review of *Tsuma yo bara no yo ni* (*Wife! Be Like a Rose!*), *Kinema Junpo*, August 1, 1935, 62, trans. Daichi Saito.
48 Tokata Sachio, "*Tsuma yo bara no yoni*: Beauty of Human Feelings (*ninjo*), the Order of the Form," *Eiga Hyoron*, August 1935, 119–23, trans. Chika Kinoshita.
49 Bock, "Japanese Film Directors," 110.
50 Barbara Sato, *The New Japanese Woman*, 128.
51 Weil, "Kimiko," 463.
52 Silverberg, "Remembering Pearl Harbor," 31.
53 Harootunian, *Overcome by Modernity*, 213.
54 Ibid., 214.
55 Tokata, "Beauty of Human Feelings," 123.
56 Bock, *Japanese Film Directors*, 125.
57 Shinojima Makoto, "*Uwasa no musume* dansho futatsu" ("Two fragments on *The*

Girl on Everyone's Lips"), *Kinema Junpo*, April 21, 1936, 90, trans. Ichiro Takayoshi.

58 Naruse attributes this remark to Mori Iwao. See Hasumi and Yamane, *Mikio Naruse*, 236.
59 For more on Irie Productions, which was started in 1932, see Kinoshita, "In the Twilight of Modernity," 91–127.
60 Yamane, "Rhythm of Emotions," 51.
61 Ibid., 50.
62 Mizumachi Seiji, review of *Nyonin aishu (Feminine Melancholy)*, *Kinema Junpo*, February 1, 1937, 114, trans. Ichiro Takayoshi.
63 Hasumi and Yamane, *Mikio Naruse*, 239.
64 Mizumachi Seiji, review of *Nadare (Avalanche)*, *Kinema Junpo*, July 1, 1937, 183, translation by Guy Yasko.
65 Tsuneishi, "The Veil Comes Down," 181.
66 Ibid., 180.
67 Harootunian, *Overcome by Modernity*, 103.
68 Harootunian describes Murayama as a filmmaker but does not give any details about any other productions he was involved with.
69 Both the San Sebastian catalog and Audie Bock's *Japanese Film Directors* credit the film as a Toho production, but the credits on the film itself indicate that it was produced by P.C.L.
70 McDonald, *From Book to Screen*, 313.
71 Ibid., 30.
72 High, *The Imperial Screen*, 62.
73 Brooks, *The Melodramatic Imagination*, 49.
74 Yamane, "Rhythm of Emotions," 44. This was higher even than the postwar high of 547 films produced in 1960.
75 Anderson and Richie, *The Japanese Film*, 90.
76 Yoshioka Toshio, "Shisei ni tsuite: Naruse Mikio no hoko," *Eiga Shudan*, October 1937, cited in Tsuneishi, "The Veil Comes Down," 177–78.
77 High, *The Imperial Screen*, 253.
78 While the "standardization" argument is developed by Bordwell, Staiger, and Thompson, the theorization of classical realism, inspired by Roland Barthes's notion of the readerly text, was developed by theorists such as Stephen Heath and Colin McCabe in the pages of *Screen* magazine in the 1970s and is also referred to as "apparatus theory" because of the theory of the ideological state apparatus that these theorists borrowed from Louis Althusser to apply to the classical realist film text.
79 See, for example, Singer, *Melodrama and Modernity*; Hansen, "The Mass Production of the Senses"; and Williams, "Discipline and Fun."
80 Williams, *Playing the Race Card*, 22.
81 Gledhill, "Rethinking Genre," 221–43.
82 Williams, *Playing the Race Card*, 23.

83 The phrase "moral legibility" is taken from Peter Brooks's influential theory of melodrama, *The Melodramatic Imagination*. In her discussion of melodrama as the dominant mode of American cinema in *Playing the Race Card*, Linda Williams uses this term extensively. She argues that it is more appropriate than Brooks's more commonly cited phrase "moral occult" to use in "the face of an increasingly secular, atomized and commodified culture" (25, 315).

84 Anderson and Richie, *The Japanese Film*, 96. Anderson and Richie use the term *shomin geki* to refer to what others call *shoshimin-eiga*.

3 Wartime Vernacular

1 Jansen, *The Making of Modern Japan*, 601.
2 High, *The Imperial Screen*, 101.
3 Davis, *Picturing Japaneseness*, 65.
4 Ibid., 66.
5 Anderson and Richie, *The Japanese Film*, 129.
6 High, *The Imperial Screen*, 292.
7 Davis, *Picturing Japaneseness*, 71.
8 Anderson and Richie, *The Japanese Film*, 135.
9 Davis, *Picturing Japaneseness*, 5.
10 Ibid., 2.
11 Ibid., 249.
12 According to Sato Tadao, Kamei Fumio's *Fighting Soldiers* (1940) was found to be unacceptable, and he was prevented from making any more films until the war was over. Many scripts were rejected, of course, by the censors, including at least one by Ozu Yasujiro (*Currents in Japanese Cinema*, 100–101).
13 High, *The Imperial Screen*, 339, quoting from "Kokumin Eiga no Juritsu," *Nihon Eiga*, May 1941, 57.
14 High, *The Imperial Screen*, 339.
15 Ibid., 377, quoting Iijima Takashi, "Shin taisei sonogo," *Shicho*, April 1942, 34.
16 Yamane Sadao is the only critic who challenges the notion that Naruse went into a "slump" during this period. See "Rhythm of Emotions," 38–39.
17 This film is rumored to be in incomplete form at the National Film Center in Tokyo.
18 Yamane, "Rhythm of Emotions," 44.
19 High, *The Imperial Screen*, 301.
20 Ibid., 187.
21 Hasumi and Yamane, *Mikio Naruse*, 248.
22 High, *The Imperial Screen*, 494, citing Tokugawa Musei, *Akarumi 15-nen* (Tokyo: Sekaisha, 1948), 250.
23 High, *The Imperial Screen*, 87.
24 Anderson and Richie, *The Japanese Film*, 133.

25 Davis, *Picturing Japaneseness*, 248.
26 Iijima Tadashi, "Naruse Mikio-ron" ("A Study on Naruse Mikio"), *Kinema Junpo*, July 15, 1953, 28–31, trans. Guy Yasko.
27 Iida Shinbi, Tomoda Junichiro, Shigeno Tatsuhiko, and Shimizu Chiyota, "'Tsuruhachi Tsurujiro' gappyo" ("Collective Critique of *Tsuruhachi and Tsurujiro*"), *Kinema Junpo*, October 1, 1938, 99–102, trans. Daichi Saito.
28 Ibid., 100.
29 Mita Ikumi, "Naruse Mikio to *Tsuruhachi Tsurujiro*" ("Naruse Mikio and *Tsuruhachi and Tsurujiro*"), *Kinema Junpo*, December 1, 1938, 58, trans. Daichi Saito.
30 Poulton, *Spirits of Another Sort*.
31 Naruse Mikio, "The Song Lantern," in Hasumi and Yamane, *Mikio Naruse*, 173–78. From *Shin-Eiga*, December 1942, trans. Language House Inc.
32 Freiberg, "Comprehensive Connections," 9.
33 Hasumi and Yamane, *Mikio Naruse*, 246, 240, 248.
34 Anderson and Richie, *The Japanese Film*, 86–87.
35 Ibid., 154.
36 Hasumi, "Mikio Naruse or Double Signature," 85.
37 The other samurai film is *Okuni and Gohei* (*Okuni to Gohei*, 1952).
38 *Asahi Shinbun*, July 5, 1945. Quoted in High, *The Imperial Screen*, 498.
39 Kyoko Hirano, *Mr. Smith Goes to Tokyo*, 17.
40 Naruse Mikio, "The Whole Family Works," in Hasumi and Yamane, *Mikio Naruse*, 241.
41 Suzuki Juzaburo, Tomoda Junichiro, Mizumachi Seiji, and Shimizu Chiyota, "'Hataraku ikka gappyo'" ("Collective Critique of *The Whole Family Works*"), *Kinema Junpo*, March 11, 1939, 14–17, trans. Brian Reyes, Shirata Masumi, and Guy Yasko.
42 High, *The Imperial Screen*, 174.
43 Ibid., 178.
44 Yamane, "Rhythm of Emotions," 40.
45 The doll bears a strong resemblance to the "Friendship Dolls" that were exchanged in 1927 as a gesture of goodwill between Japan and the United States during the interwar period. However, it is much bigger and more expensive than the friendship dolls. See wgordon.web.wesleyan.edu/dolls, accessed June 24, 2006.
46 High, *The Imperial Screen*, 257.
47 Ibid., 253.
48 Ibid., 223.
49 Yamane, "Rhythm of Emotions," 45.
50 Hasumi and Yamane, *Mikio Naruse*, 243.
51 High, *The Imperial Screen*, 297.
52 Galbraith, *The Emperor and the Wolf*, 35.
53 Kurosawa, *Something Like an Autobiography*, 140.

54 Harootunian, *Overcome by Modernity*, 414.
55 Walter Benjamin, "The Work of Art in the Age of Its Reproducibility," trans. Harry Zohn and Edmund Jephcott, *Walter Benjamin: Selected Writings*, Vol. 4, 269.
56 Buck-Morss, "Aesthetics and Anaesthetics," 140.
57 Hansen, "The Mass Production of the Senses," 335.
58 Davis, *Picturing Japaneseness*, 76.

4 Cinema, Democracy, and Japanese Kitsch

1 Kyoko Hirano, *Mr. Smith Goes to Tokyo*, 97.
2 Ibid., 44.
3 Pharr, "The Politics of Women's Rights," 221–52.
4 Buckley, "Altered States," 366.
5 Uno, "The Death of 'Good Wife Wise Mother'?," 303.
6 Hirano, *Mr. Smith Goes to Tokyo*, 149.
7 Ibid., 38.
8 Buckley, "Altered States," 350, 372.
9 Bock, *Japanese Film Directors*, 107.
10 Emiko Yamanashi, "Painting in the Time of 'Heavy Hands,'" 23.
11 Yoshimoto, *Logic of Sentiment*, 42.
12 Jameson, "Third World Literature in the Era of Multinational Capitalism," 69.
13 Ahmad, "Jameson's Rhetoric of Otherness and the 'National Allegory,'" 80.
14 Ivy, "Formations of Mass Culture," 244.
15 Ahmad, "Jameson's Rhetoric of Otherness and the 'National Allegory,'" 82.
16 Benjamin, "Eduard Fuchs, Collector and Historian," *Selected Writings*, Vol. 3, 267.
17 Cazdyn, *The Flash of Capital*, 6–7.
18 Itami Mansaku, "Senso sekininsha no mondai" ("The Problem of People Responsible for the War"), *Eiga Shunju*, August 1946, quoted and trans. Joanne Izbicki, *Scorched Cityscapes and Silver Screens*, 59, 62.
19 Izbicki, *Scorched Cityscapes and Silver Screens*, 36.
20 Ibid., 130.
21 Ibid., 133. See Peter Brooks, *The Melodramatic Imagination*; and see essays by Thomas Elsaesser ("Tales of Sound and Fury"); and Chuck Kleinhans ("Notes on the Family and Melodrama under Capitalism"), in Landy, *Imitations of Life*.
22 Izbicki, *Scorched Cityscapes and Silver Screens*, 119.
23 Hasumi and Yamane, *Mikio Naruse*, 255.
24 Izbicki notes that movie attendance increased by 34 percent from 1945 to 1946 despite increased admission rates and taxes. Industry profits increased throughout the occupation period, with the biggest jumps in 1947 and 1951 (*Scorched Cityscapes and Silver Screens*, 46).

25 Hirano, *Mr. Smith Goes to Tokyo*, 4.
26 Jansen, *The Making of Modern Japan*, 689.
27 Ibid., 689.
28 Benjamin, *The Arcades Project*, 205. I have used Susan Buck-Morss's translation of the phrase, which differs somewhat from that in the English edition. See Buck-Morss, *The Dialectics of Seeing: Walter Benjamin and the Arcades Project* (Cambridge: MIT Press, 1989), 272.
29 Buck-Morss, *The Dialectics of Seeing*, 284.
30 Fujita Susumu's career began in 1939, and he made his name in Kurosawa's *Sugata Sanchiro*, after which he starred in a number of Toho war films as well as Kurosawa's *No Regrets for Our Youth*, which was released in October 1946.
31 Yokoyama and Hanabishi were responsible for moving manzai comedy closer to stand-up, and are central figures in the development of contemporary manzai/stand-up in Japan. Thanks to Guy Yasko for this insight.
32 Harootunian, *History's Disquiet*, 137. Harootunian cites Aono Suekichi, *Sarariman kyofu jidai* (Tokyo: Senshinsha, 1930).
33 Hirano, *Mr. Smith Goes to Tokyo*, 155.
34 The exception is Hara Setsuko in *Daughters, Wives, and a Mother* (*Musuma, tsuma, haha*, 1960) in which Hara visibly cringes when Nakadai Tatsuya kisses her.
35 Hirano, *Mr. Smith Goes to Tokyo*, 161.
36 Bock, *Japanese Film Directors*, 129.
37 Hirano, *Mr. Smith Goes to Tokyo*, 214.
38 Ibid., 215.
39 Anderson and Richie, *The Japanese Film*, 165–74.
40 Hirano, *Mr. Smith Goes to Tokyo*, 227.
41 Hirano mentions Nakakita Chieko, Kuga Yoshiko and Wakayama Setsuko as prominent members of the procession that finally conceded the strike. The actresses, she says, were seen in tears (229).
42 Ibid., 226.
43 Yoshimoto, *Kurosawa*, 140.
44 Bock, *Japanese Film Directors*, 129, 130.
45 Izbicki, *Scorched Cityscapes and Silver Screens* 303.
46 Tsumura Hideo, "Naruse Mikio," *Kinema Junpo*, July 15, 1953, 30–31, trans. Chika Kinoshita and Guy Yasko.
47 Morey, "The Judge Called Me an Accessory," 87.
48 Bornoff, *Pink Samurai*, 219.
49 The first two films Naruse made with Tamai are *Delinquent Girl* (1949) and *The Angry Street* (1950).
50 The VHS tape that I was working with was released by Shochiku, and its running time of ninety-seven minutes matches that of published filmographies, so we can only assume that the sloppy editing is in the original and not a result of later print damage.

51 Bock, *Japanese Film Directors*, 108, quoting Naruse from "Eiga sakka no peisu" ("A Filmmaker's Pace"), *Kinema Junpo* 273 (1960), 58–59.
52 Kishi Matsuo, "Naruse Mikio ron" ("A Study on Naruse Mikio"), *Kinema Junpo*, December 1, 1936, 74–75, trans. Chika Kinoshita.
53 Bock, *Japanese Film Directors*, 108, based on an interview with Kishi.
54 Fujii Shigeo, review of *Ginza gesho* (*Ginza Cosmetics*), *Eiga Hyoron*, June 1951, 54, trans. Guy Yasko.
55 Ibid., 54.
56 Karatani, *Origins of Modern Japanese Literature*, 57.
57 Barthes, *Empire of Signs*, 61–62.
58 Hirano, *Mr. Smith Goes to Tokyo*, 16.
59 Pollack, *Reading against Culture*, 120.
60 Ericson, *Be a Woman*, 85.
61 McDonald, *From Book to Screen*, 61.
62 Mulvey, "Notes on Sirk and Melodrama," 79.
63 Interview with Ide Toshiro, Murakawa, *Naruse Mikio Enshutsujutsu*, 164.
64 Toda Takao, review of *Meshi* (*A Married Life*, aka *Repast*), *Eiga Hyoron*, January 1952, 85–86, trans. Guy Yasko.
65 Futaba Juzaburo, review of *Meshi*, *Kinema Junpo*, January 1, 1952, 116, trans. Guy Yasko.
66 Mulvey, "Notes on Sirk and Melodrama," 79.
67 Futaba, review of *Meshi*, 116.
68 Shimizu Chiyota, review of *Meshi*, *Kinema Junpo*, December 1, 1951, 43, trans. Guy Yasko.
69 Futaba, review of *Meshi*, 116; Fujji, 53.
70 Ericson, *Be a Woman*, 103.
71 Ibid., 103–6.
72 Interview with Ide Toshiro, Murakawa, *Naruse Mikio Enshutsujutsu*, 164.
73 Rimer and Gessel, *The Columbia Anthology of Modern Japanese Literature*, Vol. 1, 627. This volume includes a translation of *Okuni and Gohei* by John K. Gillespi (627–39).
74 Hasumi, "Mikio Naruse or Double Signature," 75.
75 Ibid., 75–78.

5 The Japanese Woman's Film of the 1950s

1 *Cahiers du cinéma*, April 1993, 47. No author is credited.
2 Yamane, "Rhythm of Emotions."
3 Hasumi, "On the Everydayness of a Miracle."
4 According to Nogami—whose writing is strictly from memory—Fujimoto's first Toho film after the war was *Wedding March* (1952), directed by Ichikawa Kon, and she claims that Ichikawa was responsible for rehabilitating the producer as

a condition of his return to Toho (*Waiting on the Weather*, 102). *Wedding March* also includes two key Naruse figures, Uehara Ken and Ide Toshiro. However, in addition to the occupation films that Fujimoto produced for Naruse, Kyoko Hirano reports that he was also responsible for the Toho anti-*zaibatsu* film *People's Enemy* in 1946, directed by Imai Tadashi (*Mr. Smith Goes to Tokyo*, 151). Whether he was blacklisted for his labor sympathies during the Toho strikes or for his production of wartime propaganda is hard to say, although my guess is that it is the former. Compounding the problem of reconstructing Fujimoto's career from English language documents is the fact that Nogami transliterates his given name as Masazumi, and Hirano as Naozumi.

5 Anderson and Richie, *The Japanese Film*, 396.
6 "Visiting Takamine Hideko, Who Got Engaged," *Shufu no tomo*, April 1955.
7 Birnbaum, *Modern Girls*, 213.
8 Giuglaris, *Le cinèma japonais*, 56.
9 Anderson and Richie, *The Japanese Film*, 394.
10 Jameson, *The Political Unconscious*, 286–87.
11 Harootunian, *History's Disquiet*, 66.
12 Benjamin, "The Author as Producer," *Selected Writings*, Vol. 2, 768–82.
13 By 1952, Tanaka had made eight postwar films with Mizoguchi, including *The Life of Oharu*, which was released the same year as *Mother*. Other "feminisuto" roles include *The Victory of Women* (1946), *The Love of Sumako the Actress* (1947), *Women of the Night* (1948), and *My Love Burns* (1949). Audiences might also have recalled her role as the tough bar hostess in Naruse's *Ginza Cosmetics* (1951).
14 Futaba Juzaburo, review of *Okaasan* (*Mother*), *Kinema Junpo*, July 1, 1952, 141, trans. Chika Kinoshita. Futaba says that Tanaka's mother is the first role really fit for her since her return from the United States, but he is worried that this success might turn Tanaka into another haha-mono actress.
15 Tsuboi Sakae, "*Okaasan* no waku" ("The Framework/Limitation of *Mother*"), *Eiga Hyoron*, August 1952, trans. D. R. Lindberg, 66.
16 Ibid., 67.
17 Lippit, *Topographies of Japanese Modernism*, 193.
18 Ibid., 177.
19 Iida Shinbi, review of *Inazuma* (*Lightning*), *Eiga Hyoron*, November 1952, trans. D. R. Lindberg.
20 Nogawa Naoki, "*Inazuma*: Naruse Mikio no mochiaji" ("*Lightning*: Naruse Mikio's Characteristics"), *Kinema Junpo*, October 15, 1952, 40, 62, trans. Guy Yasko.
21 Iida, review of *Inazuma*, 63.
22 Fessler, *Wandering Heart*, 106–7.
23 Ibid., 126.
24 Hayashi, "My Work," 168.
25 Nogawa, "*Inazuma*," 62.
26 Interview with Ide Toshiro, in Murakawa, *Naruse Mikio Enshutsujutsu*, 173.

27 Ibid., 174. See also Ozaki Hirotsugu, "Mizuki Yoko no koto" ("On Mizuki Yoko"), *Eiga Hyoron*, January 1956, 24–26, trans. Ayano Nishikai.
28 Interview with Sugi Yoko in Murakawa, *Naruse Mikio Enshutsujutsu*, 71.
29 Ibid., 74.
30 Interview with Kobayashi Keiju in Murakawa, *Naruse Mikio Enshutsujutsu*, 124.
31 Mikawa Kiyo, "*Tsuma*: Aijo ni mo kechi na tsuma" ("*Wife*: A Wife Stingy Even with Affection"), *Yomuri Shinbun*, May 3, 1953, 5, trans. D. R. Lindberg.
32 Ishigaki Ayako, "*Tsuma* to otto" ("*Wife* and Husband"), *Eiga Hyoron*, July 1953, 62–63, trans. Chika Kinoshita.
33 Interview with Ide in Murakawa, *Naruse Mikio Enshutsujutsu*, 168.
34 Fessler, *Wandering Heart*, 97–99.
35 Interview with Ide in Murakawa, *Naruse Mikio Enshutsujutsu*, 159.
36 McDonald, *From Book to Screen*, 221–36. Muro's *Ani imoto* has not been translated, and all references to the story and Naruse's changes are based on McDonald's analysis.
37 Ibid., 224. From McDonald's description, Muro's writing seems closer to the sensibility of Imamura in films such as the *Insect Woman* and *The Pornographers*, than to Naruse's.
38 Elsaesser, "Tales of Sound and Fury," 79.
39 Ibid., 88–89.
40 Hasumi and Yamane, *Mikio Naruse*, 263.
41 Kawabata, *The Sound of the Mountain*, 234.
42 Mikawa Kiyo, "*Yama no oto*: Kyokan sasou yome no tachiba" ("*Sound of the Mountain*: Sympathy for the Status of a Daughter-in-Law"), *Yomiuri Shinbun*, January 31, 1954, 5, trans. Chika Kinoshita.
43 Takami Jun, "Kanso" ("Impressions"), *Fujin Koron*, March 1954, 222, trans. Chika Kinoshita.
44 Scala, "Naruse and Some Dutch Painters," 47.
45 Hasumi, "Mikio Naruse or Double Signature," 84.
46 Chuko Satoshi, "Art Director Chuko Satoshi," in Hasumi and Yamane, *Mikio Naruse*, 206.
47 Sakabe, "Mask and Shadow in Japanese Culture," 247; Barthes, *Empire of Signs*, 62.
48 Sakabe, "Mask and Shadow in Japanese Culture," 244.
49 Barthes, *Empire of Signs*, 62.
50 Yoshimoto, *Kurosawa*, 116; Galbraith, *The Emperor and the Wolf*, 146.
51 Ericson, *Be a Woman*, 75.
52 Both *Bangiku* and *Narcissus* are available in English translation. See Hayashi, "A Late Chrysanthemum" and "Narcissus."
53 For a more detailed discussion of Sugimura, please see my "Three Japanese Actresses of the 1950s."
54 Hasume and Yamane, *Mikio Naruse*, 263.
55 Tamae quotes from the Islamic classic *The Rubiyat*; Tomi from haiku by the poet

Ikkyu (1394–1481). Sugimoto Heiichi notes that while the latter is an appropriate reference for a "simple" person such as Tomi, the former suggests more education than Tamae appears to have (Sugimoto Heiichi, review of *Bangiku*, *Kinema Junpo*, July 15, 1954, trans. Chika Kinoshita, 51).

56 Ibid., 51.
57 Iida Shinbi, review of *Bangiku* (*Late Chrysanthemums*), *Eiga Hyoron*, August 1954, 71–73, trans. Chika Kinoshita.
58 Ericson, *Be a Woman*, 78.
59 Different accounts of the novel and the film identify Iba as Yuikiko's uncle or as her brother-in-law, but it is clear from the novel and the film that he is the brother of Yukiko's sister's husband. Hayashi provides more details of their relationship than does Naruse, who offers only one ambiguous flashback of Iba assaulting Yukiko. In the novel it is clear that Iba is Yukiko's only relative in Tokyo after the war, and before she went to Dalat they both lived with her sister's family. Her status in that household was little more than a maid, and although Iba was married, he slept with Yukiko regularly after raping her. Nevertheless, after the war, Yukiko ends up borrowing money from him for her abortion, after which she becomes his mistress and accountant for his religious cult scam.
60 Hasumi, "Mikio Naruse or Double Signature," 70.
61 Hayashi, *Floating Clouds*.
62 Douchet, "About Naruse," 98.
63 In her discussion of the novel, Noriko Mizuta says that Tomioka encounters a local woman when he climbs the mountain, leaving Yukiko sick in bed. After she dies, he goes to Kagoshima, "gets drunk, buys a prostitute and abandons himself to his feelings of loneliness" ("In Search of a Lost Paradise," 343–44).
64 Ibid., 335.
65 Yoshimoto, *Logic of Sentiment*, 47.
66 Ibid., 48.
67 Fessler, *Wandering Heart*, 95.
68 Ericson, *Be a Woman*, 82.
69 Douchet, "About Naruse," 97.
70 Chuko, "Art Director Chuko Satoshi," in Hasumi and Yamane, *Mikio Naruse*, 206.
71 Mizuki, "Memories," 188–89.
72 Interview with Takamine in Murakawa, *Naruse Mikio Enshutsujutsu*, 6.
73 Ibid. Fujimoto recounts the same anecdote, although he credits Takamine with a zealousness toward the role ("Producer Sanezumi Fujimoto," in Hasumi and Yamane, *Mikio Naruse*, 181).
74 Ibid., 183.
75 Hasumi, "Mikio Naruse or Double Signature," 64.
76 Douchet, "About Naruse," 99.
77 Benjamin, *The Arcades Project*, 475.
78 Ibid., 460.

79 Tamai Masao, "The Essence of Mikio Naruse Lies in a Looking-Back Position: Testimony," extract from interview with Hasumi Shigehiko, Hasumi and Yamane, *Mikio Naruse*, 194.
80 *Memories of Naruse Mikio*.
81 Benjamin, *The Arcades Project*, 467.
82 Audie Bock, *Japanese Film Directors*, 133. Bock does not attribute the remark to anyone in particular.
83 Interview with Ide in Murakawa, *Naruse Mikio Enshutsujutsu*, 10.
84 Sugiyama Heiichi, review of *Tsuma no kokoro* [*A Wife's Heart*], *Eiga Hyoron*, June 1956, 54–55, trans. Kinoshita.
85 Abe Tsuyako, "Tsuma no kokoro: Kibo o shigoto e" ("*A Wife's Heart*: Turning Her Hopes to Work"), *Yomiuri Shinbun*, May 13, 1956, 12, trans. Chika Kinoshita.
86 Enchi Fumiko and Yuki Shigeko, "*Tsuma no kokoro* taidan: 'Otto no uwaki,' 'tsuma no uwaki'" ("Conversation about *A Wife's Heart*: 'Husband's Affair,' 'Wife's Affair'") *Sankei Jiji*, May 2, 1956, 4, trans. Chika Kinoshita.
87 Sherif, *Mirror*, 17.
88 Sherif also suggests that the main precedent for Koda's approach would have been *ninjobon*, a genre of Edo period literature that portrayed the women of the demimonde as "possessing great emotional freedom." Marketed to a female audience, "the *ninjobon* developed the women of the licensed quarter more fully as fictional characters" (78).
89 Ibid., 74.
90 Sugiyama Heiichi, review of *Nagareru*, *Eiga Hyoron*, January 1957, 90–91; Shiga Naoya, and Takehara Han, "*Nagareru* o mite kataru" ("Speaking about *Flowing*"), *Sankei Jiji*, November 21, 1956, 3, trans. Chika Kinoshita.
91 Thanks to Chika Kinoshita for this explanation of the term *zuihitsu*.
92 Koda Aya, Tanaka Kinuyo, Yamada Isuzu, Kurishima Sumiko, Takamine Hideko, Sugimura Haruko, Okada Mariko, and Tanaka Sumie, "Zadankai geisha to jochu to tsuma no ikikata: *Nagareru* no eigaka o megutte" ("Roundtable on the Ways of Life of Geishas, Maids, and Wives: On the Film Adaptation of *Flowing*"), *Fujin Koron*, December 1956, 188–97, trans. Chika Kinoshita.
93 Ibid.
94 Buckley, "A Short History of the Feminist Movement in Japan," 153.
95 Katzoff, "From Feminisms to Femininities," 10–12.
96 Ibid., 12.
97 Richard Torrance names Kawabata and Murao Nakamura, along with a long list of writers and critics who endorsed Shusei's status as a key "pinnacle" in the history of the Japanese novel (*Rough Living*, 1).
98 The model for Oshima was Suzuki Chiyo, the common-law wife of Shusei's brother-in-law (ibid., 8).
99 Hasumi and Yamane, *Mikio Naruse*, 269.
100 Cinemas in the Taisho period were presided over from the rear by an inspector

who ensured that men and women respected the segregated seating regulations. The police officer, who sat in a special seat called a *rinken*, had the authority to stop the screening if the audience misbehaved (Matsuda DVD-ROM, "Masterpieces of Japanese Silent Cinema").

101 Torrance, *Rough Living*, 106.
102 Benjamin, *The Arcades Project*, 69, 463.
103 Morita Tama, "Anzukko: Oyako no aijo ni tokekomenu otto" ("*Anzukko*: A Husband Who Cannot Melt into the Affection Between Father and Daughter"), *Yomiuri Shinbun*, May 16, 1958, 9, trans. Chika Kinoshita.
104 One of the best discussions of haiku and its relation to Zen is Suzuki, *Zen and Japanese Culture*, 215–68.
105 Burch, *To the Distant Observer*, 160–61.
106 Ueda, *Far beyond the Field*, xxxix.
107 Ibid., 103.
108 Ibid., 105.
109 Ibid., 113.
110 Ibid., 139.
111 Ibid., 137.

6 Stranded in Modernity

1 Anderson, "Second and Third Thoughts about the Japanese Film," 455. By 1968, pink films outnumbered studio-produced films, and after 1971 Nikkatsu produced pink films exclusively. See Domenig, "A Brief History of Independent Cinema," 9–10.
2 Richie, "Terminal Essay," 459. The notion of decline is also implicit in Hasumi and Yamane's overview of Naruse's career, "Mikio Naruse in Japanese History," in *Mikio Naruse*, 34–35.
3 Anderson, "Second and Third Thoughts about the Japanese Film," 456. Five hundred and sixty-two films were produced in 1937.
4 Richie, "Terminal Essay," 457.
5 Domenig, "A Brief History of Independent Cinema," 12.
6 Ibid., 9.
7 Oshima, *Cinema, Censorship, and the State*, 29.
8 Hasumi and Yamane, *Mikio Naruse*, 33.
9 Oshima, *Cinema, Censorship, and the State*, 34.
10 Ibid., 11.
11 McElhaney, *Qualities of Imperfection*, 393.
12 Ibid., 13.
13 Tohoscope used an anamorphic lens and had an aspect ratio of 2.66:1. It was modeled on CinemaScope and introducted in the late 1950s.
14 Benjamin, *The Arcades Project*, 473.

15 Ibid., 473.
16 Bernstein, "Women in Rural Japan."
17 Hane, *Modern Japan*, 347.
18 Ishimori was a Japanese writer who grew up in Sapporo, alongside the Ainu. His book has been recognized as an important moment in postwar children's literature. It received the Mimei Award for Literature and the Sankei Award for Children's Books and Publications in 1958. In addition to Naruse's film, it was also adapted for television and radio. See "100 Books."
19 Hiwasaki, "Ethnic Tourism in Hokkaido and the Shaping of Ainu Identity," 399.
20 For a history of the representation of the Ainu in ethnographic film, see Okada, "The Ainu in Ethnographic Films."
21 Siddle, "From Assimilation to Indigenous Rights," 111.
22 Ibid.
23 Hiwasaki, "Ethnic Tourism in Hokkaido and the Shaping of Ainu Identity."
24 Ono, "Ainu Homelands," 36.
25 "100 Books."
26 Ivy, *Discourses of the Vanishing*, 9.
27 Ibid., 10.
28 Siddle, "From Assimilation to Indigenous Rights," 111.
29 The Ainu lobbied for recognition as an indigenous nation in Japan starting in the mid-1970s, with some success in the early 1980s (ibid., 114–15).
30 Iijima Tadashi, "Naruse Mikio to *Onna ga kaidan o agaru toki*" ("Naruse Mikio and *When a Woman Ascends the Stairs*"), *Eiga Hyoron*, February 1960, 38–39, trans. Kumi Hishikawa.
31 Bornoff, *Pink Samurai*, 254.
32 Iijima, "Naruse Mikio to *Onna ga kaidan o agaru toki*," 39.
33 Allison, *Nightwork*, 58.
34 Ibid., 71.
35 Kiyokawa Mieko and Sekine Miwako (Nihon Joshi Daigaku Eiga Kenkyu-kai [Japan Women's University Film Study Group]), "Kyodo kenkyu: *Musume, tsuma, haha o kataru*" ("Collective Study: Speaking about *Daughters, Wives, and a Mother*"), *Eiga Geijutsu*, August 1960, 60–61, trans. Kumi Hishikawa.
36 Ibid., 61; Iida Shinbi, review of *Musume, tsuma, haha o kataru* (*Daughters, Wives, and a Mother*), *Kinema Junpo*, June 1, 1960, 73, trans. Kumi Hishikawa.
37 Iida, review of *Daughters, Wives, and a Mother* 73.
38 Kiyokawa and Sekine, "Kyodo kenkyu," 60.
39 Ibid.
40 Ohashi Yasuhiko, "Ie no nai onna: *Musume, tsuma, haha no Sakanishi Aki*" ("A Woman without Home: Sakanishi Aki in *Daughters, Wives, and a Mother*"), *Eiga geijutsu*, July 1960, special issue, *Nihon Eiga no Jyosei Zo* (Representations of Women in Japanese Films), 68–69, trans. Kumi Hishikawa.

41 Hane, *Modern Japan*, 368.
42 Ohashi, "Ie no nai onna," 69.
43 Ibid., 68.
44 Richie, *Different People*, 14.
45 Bock, *Japanese Film Directors*, 134–35; Gunji Yasuko, review of *Yoru no nagare (The Flow of Evening)*, *Eiga Hyoron*, August 1960, 79, trans. Chika Kinoshita.
46 "Yuzo Kawashima," Internet Movie Database, www.imdb.com/name/nm0442929, accessed February 9, 2006.
47 Bock, *Japanese Film Directors*, 135.
48 Ibid.
49 Fujimoto Sanezumi, Ide Toshiro, Ohama Hideko, Hasegawa Sachiko, Kamisaka Fuyuko, and Suzuki Kimie, "Zadankai: Eiga no naka no josei no ikikata" ("Roundtable: Women's Way of Life in Film"), "Tokushu: *Tsuma toshite, onna toshite* shinario bunseki" ("Featured Articles: Analyses of the Screenplay, *As a Wife, as a Woman*"), *Shinario (Screenplay)*, May 1961, 54–63, trans. Akira Takahashi.
50 Ibid., 59. This discussion took place before the film was actually shot and includes advice from the participants on what to include in the film, most of which seems to have been disregarded by Naruse and the production team.
51 Ide Toshiro, "*Tsuma toshite, onna toshite* no shinario raita toshite" ("As a Screenwriter of *As a Wife, as a Woman*"), "Tokushu: *Tsuma toshite, onna toshite* shinario bunseki" ("Featured Articles: Analyses of the Screenplay, *As a Wife, as a Woman*"), *Shinario (Screenplay)*, May 1961, 48–53.
52 Fujiwara, "Mikio Naruse," 1.
53 The English title of this film has been occasionally (and unfortunately) translated as "Her Lonely Lane," as well as "A Wanderer's Notebook." However, the translations of the literary original have been translated as "Vagabond's Song." See the fragments in Tanaka, *To Live and to Write*, 105–26, translated by Elizabeth Hanson; "Diary of a Vagabond," in Ericson, *Be a Woman*, 123–220, and in Brown, *I Saw a Pale Horse*, 89–114. I will refer to Hayashi's original as *Horoki* and Naruse's film as *A Wanderer's Notebook*.
54 Mori Mitsuko played Hayashi the first night in 1961 and continued to play the lead until at least 2005.
55 Hasumi and Yamane, *Mikio Naruse*, 17.
56 Film versions of Horoki were released in 1935 (P.C.L.) and 1954 (Toei). Fessler, *Wandering Heart*, 179.
57 Narboni, *Mikio Naruse*, 123. Unfortunately, Narboni does not cite any specific critics.
58 Ericson, *Be a Woman*, 69.
59 The best analyses of the novel are provided by Ericson (*Be a Woman*, 57–74) and Lippit (*Topographies of Japanese Modernism*, 159–96). Lippit makes the point about the multiple genres that the novel combines. Ericson develops the concept

and category of rumpen-mono and shows in some detail how Hayashi altered her text by adding figures and forms from classical poetry.

60 Hayashi invokes Hamsun herself in *Horoki* (Ericson, *Be a Woman*, 132); See also Fessler, *Wandering Heart*, 55.
61 Lippit, *Topographies of Japanese Modernism*, 167.
62 Benjamin, "The Storyteller: Observations on the Works of Nikolai Leskov" (1936), trans. Harry Zohn, in *Selected Writings, Vol. 3*, 154. Emphasis original.
63 Ibid., 162.
64 Hayashi quoted in Ericson, *Be a Woman*, 143.
65 Brown, *I Saw a Pale Horse*, 2.
66 Hayashi quoted in Ericson, *Be a Woman*, 163.
67 Ibid., 175.
68 Ibid., 190.
69 Marias, "Naruse's Serene Splendour," 123.
70 Benjamin, "The Storyteller," 162.
71 Ibid., 147.
72 Birnbaum, *Modern Girls*, 211.
73 Yang, "Generosity," 157. Yang says that this scene is "all in one shot," but in fact Takamine's run through the village consists of six shots, including two shots of the men carrying the stretcher. Yang's comment may be testimony to Naruse's invisible editing, but also evidence of the long-take realist aesthetic that cinephiles tend to subscribe to, and which Naruse never really uses.
74 Birnbaum, *Modern Girls*, 211.
75 Ibid., 211.
76 Benjamin, *The Arcades Project*, 108.
77 Ibid., 116, 119.
78 Petro, *Aftershocks of the New*, 64–68.
79 The relationship between affect and representations of temporality have been developed by Effie Rassos in "Everyday Narratives."
80 Neale, "Melodrama and Tears," 8. Agnition is "the mechanism of retraction and re-establishment of points of view," a term that Neal borrows from literary theorist Franco Moretti.
81 Williams, "Melodrama Revised," 48.
82 Gledhill, "Rethinking Genre," 236.
83 Asada, "Infantile Capitalism and Japan's Postmodernism," 275.
84 Ibid., 276. In making this argument about the family, Asada parodies Takeo Doi's notion of *amae*, developed in *The Anatomy of Dependence*.
85 Fujii Jinshi, "Shinema no naka no tanin," 147.
86 Ibid., 145.
87 Ibid., 146.
88 According to Fujii, "the directors who shaped this current of Japanese noir were Sugawa Eizo, who had made *The Beast Must Die* (*Yaju shisubeki*, 1959) and

Suzuki Hideo, who had made *Don't Let Them Get Away* (*Yatsura oo nigasuna!*, 1956) and *Black Pictures: A Cold Stream* (*Kuroi gasshu: Kanryu*, 1961). Sugawa Eizo had worked for Naruse as an assistant, and Suzuki had been one of the other directors in the omnibus film *The Kiss* (*Kuchizuke*, 1955)" (145).

89 Desser, *Eros Plus Massacre*, 77.
90 Fujii, "Shinema no naka no tanin," 165.
91 Ibid., 164.
92 Ibid., 150. Fujii could only really say this if he is unfamiliar with Stewart's roles in Anthony Mann's westerns.
93 Interview with Kobayashi Keiju, Murakawa, *Naruse Mikio Enshutsujutsu*, 5.
94 Claude Chabrol's 1971 adaptation of Atiyah's novel was called *Juste avant la nuit* (*Just Before Night*).
95 Donald Richie dismisses *Hit and Run* as "very bad," although he also misrepresents the film by saying that Takamine is the hit-and-run driver (Anderson and Richie, *The Japanese Film*, 459).
96 Fumie is played by Kahara Natsuko. The film also features several other of Naruse's stable of character actors, including Urabe Kumeko, Nakakita Chieko, and Kato Daisuke.
97 A couple of flashbacks earlier in the film have filled in some of the details of Kuniko's failed marriage, which don't exactly correspond to what she tells Kakinuma. Her husband, Bannai, is said to have been a good guy who was killed in an industrial accident. Kato Daisuke, who plays Kakinuma's business associate Kawashima, appears to have a double role in this film, appearing in heavy makeup in the flashbacks as Bannai as well.
98 Max Tessier, "The Power of the Imaginary in the Films of the Japanese New Wave in the 1960s and early 1970s," *Minikomi*, December 2005, 37–38.
99 Ross, *Fast Cars Clean Bodies*, 15–18. Among other cultural roles that it played, the Renault factory was a key site in the May 1968 demonstrations.
100 Ibid., 27.
101 Ibid., 21, 40.
102 Hasumi and Yamane, *Mikio Naruse*, 34.
103 Hasumi, "Mikio Naruse or Double Signature," 80.
104 Fujiwara, "Mikio Naruse," 4.
105 Takamine, "About Mikio Naruse," 9.
106 Kelsky, *Women on the Verge*, 35–84.
107 Ibid., 26.
108 Ibid.
109 Tsukasa Yoko, "Avec Naruse, on ne répétait presque jamais," *Cahiers du cinéma*, January 2001: 68–69.
110 Nolletti, *The Cinema of Gosho Heinosuke*, 214. Nolletti singles out *Hunting Rifle* (*Ryoju*, 1961) and *An Innocent Witch* (*Osorezan no onna*, 1965).

Conclusion

1 Fujii, "Shinema no naka no tanin," 143.
2 Takamine, "About Mikio Naruse," 8–9.
3 Benjamin, "The Work of Art in the Age of Its Technical Reproducibility" (1936), trans. Edmund Jephcott and Harry Zohn, *Selected Writings of Walter Benjamin, Vol. 3*, 111.
4 Ibid., 113.
5 Tamai, "Testimony," 197.
6 Bock, "A Gesture and a Pose," 240.
7 Tamai Masao in *Memories of Mikio Naruse*.
8 Kelsky, *Women on the Verge*, 27–28.
9 Bock, *Mikio Naruse* (Locarno), 39.
10 Kelsky, *Women on the Verge*, 25.
11 Ibid.

FILMOGRAPHY

Films of the 1930s

Mr. and Mrs. Swordplay (*Chanbara fufu*), 1930, 21 mins., Shochiku.
Pure Love (*Junjo*), 1930, 45 mins., Shochiku.
A Record of Shameless Newlyweds (*Oshikiri shinkonki*), 1930, 37 mins., Shochiku.
Hard Times (*Fukeiki jidai*), 1930, 26 min., Shochiku.
Love Is Strength (*Ai wa chikara da*), 1930, 65 mins., Shochiku.
Now Don't Get Excited (*Ne kofun shicha iya yo*), 1931, 15 mins., Shochiku.
Screams from the Second Floor (*Nikai no himei*), 1931, 30 mins., Shochiku.
Flunky, Work Hard, aka Little Man, Do Your Best (*Koshiben ganbare*), 1931, 28 mins., Shochiku.
Fickleness Gets on the Train (*Uwaki wa kisha ni notte*), 1931, 32 mins., Shochiku.
The Strength of a Mustache (*Hige no chikara*), 1931, 32 mins., Shochiku.
Under the Neighbour's Roof (*Tonari no yane no shita*), 1931, 34 mins., Shochiku.
Ladies, Be Careful of Your Sleeves (*Onna wa tamoto wo goyojin*), 1932, 28 mins., Shochiku.
Crying to the Blue Sky (*Aozora ni naku*), 1932, 53 mins., Shochiku.
Be Great! (*Eraku nare*), 1932, 39 mins., Shochiku.
Moth-Eaten Spring (*Mushibameru haru*), 1932, 103 mins., Shochiku.
Chocolate Girl (*Chokoreto garu*), 1932, 56 mins., Shochiku.
Not Blood Relations, aka The Stepchild (*Nasanu naka*), 1932, 78 mins., Shochiku.
Tokyo's Candy-Coated Landscape (*Kashi no aru Tokyo fukei*), 1933, length unknown, studio unknown.
Apart from You, aka Farewell to You (*Kimi to wakarete*), 1933, 60 mins., Shochiku.

Every Night Dreams, aka *Nightly Dreams* (*Yogoto no yume*), 1933, 64 mins., Shochiku.
My Bride's Coiffure (*Boku no marumage*), 1933, 75 mins., Shochiku.
Two Eyes (*Sobo*), 1933, 107 mins., Shochiku.
Happy New Year (*Kinga shin nen*), 1934, length unknown, studio unknown.
Street without End (*Kagiri naki hodo*), 1934, 87 mins., Shochiku.
Three Sisters with Maiden Hearts (*Otome-gokoro sannin shimai*), 1935, 74 mins., P.C.L.
The Actress and the Poet (*Joyu to shijin*), 1935, 72 mins., P.C.L.
Wife! Be Like a Rose! (*Tsuma yo bara no yo ni*), 1935, 73 mins., P.C.L.
Five Men in the Circus (*Saakasu gonin-gumi*), 1935, 64 mins., P.C.L.
The Girl in the Rumor, aka *The Girl on Everyone's Lips* (*Uwasa no musume*), 1935, 74 mins., P.C.L.
Tochuken Kumoemon (*Tochuken Kumoemon*), 1936, 73 mins., P.C.L.
The Road I Travel with You (*Kimi to yuku michi*), 1936, 69 mins., P.C.L.
Morning's Tree-lined Street (*Asa no namiki michi*), 1936, 59 mins., P.C.L.
Feminine Melancholy, aka *A Woman's Sorrows* (*Nyonin aishu*), 1937, 73 mins., P.C.L.
Avalanche (*Nadare*), 1937, 59 mins., P.C.L.
Learn from Experience, parts 1 and 2 (*Kafuku* I, II), 1937, 78 mins., Toho.
Tsuruhachi and Tsurujiro (*Tsuruhachi Tsurujiro*), 1938, 89 mins., Toho.
The Whole Family Works (*Hataraku ikka*), 1939, 65 mins., Toho.
Sincerity (*Magokoro*), 1939, 67 mins., Toho.

Films of the 1940s

Traveling Actors (*Tabi yakusha*), 1940, 70 mins., Toho.
A Fond Face from the Past (*Natsukashi no kao*), 1941, 36 mins., Toho.
Shanghai Moon (*Shanhai no tsuki*), 1941, 113 mins., Toho.
Hideko the Bus Conductor (*Hideko no shasho-san*), 1941, 54 mins., Nanyo Toho Eiga.
Mother Never Dies (*Haha wa shinazu*), 1942, 103 mins., Toho.
The Song Lantern (*Uta andon*), 1943, 93 mins., Toho.
This Happy Life (*Tanoshiki kana jinsei*), 1944, 79 mins., Toho.
The Way of Drama (*Shibaido*), 1944, 82 mins., Toho.
Until Victory Day (*Shori no hi made*), 1945, 59 mins., Toho.
A Tale of Archers at the Sanjusangendo (*Sanjusangendo toshiya monogatari*), 1945, 76 mins., Toho.
A Descendant of Urashima Taro (*Urashima Taro no koei*), 1946, 85 mins., Toho.
Both You and I (*Ore mo omae mo*), 1946, 70 mins., Toho.
Four Love Stories, Part II: Even Parting Is Enjoyable (*Yottsu no koi no monogatari, II: Wakare mo tanashii*), 1947, 124 mins., Toho.
Spring Awakens (*Haru no mezame*), 1947, 89 mins., Toho.
Delinquent Girl (*Furyo shojo*), 1949, 72 mins., Toyoko Kyoto.

Films of the 1950s

Conduct Report on Professor Ishinaka (*Ishinaka sensei gyojoki*), 1950, 95 mins., Shin Toho.
The Angry Street (*Ikari no machi*), 1950, 104 mins., Toho.
White Beast (*Shiroi yaju*), 1950, 92 mins., Toho.
The Battle of Roses (*Bara gassen*), 1950, 97 mins., Shochiku, Eiga Geijutsu Kyokai (Film Art Association).
Ginza Cosmetics (*Ginza gesho*), 1951, 87 mins., Shin Toho.
Dancing Girl (*Maihime*), 1951, 84 mins., Toho.
Repast, aka *A Married Life* (*Meshi*), 1951, 96 mins., Toho.
Okuni and Gohei (*Okuni to Gohei*), 1952, 90 mins., Toho.
Mother (*Okaasan*), 1952, 97 mins., Shin Toho.
Lightning (*Inazuma*), 1952, 87 mins., Daiei.
Husband and Wife (*Fufu*), 1953, 87 mins., Toho.
Wife (*Tsuma*), 1953, 95 mins., Toho.
Older Brother, Younger Sister, aka *Ino and Mon* (*Ani imoto*), 1953, 86 mins., Daiei.
Sound of the Mountain, aka *The Echo* (*Yama no oto*), 1954, 94 mins., Toho.
Late Chrysanthemums (*Bangiku*), 1954, 101 mins., Toho.
Floating Clouds, aka *Drifting Clouds* (*Ukigumo*), 1955, 123 mins., Toho.
The Kiss, Part III: Women's Ways (*Kuchizuke, III: Onna doshi*), 1955, 114 mins., Toho.
Sudden Rain (*Shuu*), 1956, 90 mins., Toho.
A Wife's Heart (*Tsuma no kokoro*), 1956, 97 mins., Toho.
Flowing (*Nagareru*), 1956, 116 mins., Toho.
Untamed (*Arakure*), 1957, 120 mins., Toho.
Anzukko (*Anzukko*), 1958, 108 mins., Toho.
Summer Clouds, aka *Herringbone Clouds* (*Iwashigumo*), 1958, 128 mins., Toho, Colour/Tohoscope.
Whistling in Kotan, aka *A Whistle in My Heart* (*Kotan no kuchibue*), 1959, 126 mins., Toho, Colour/Tohoscope.

Films of the 1960s

When a Woman Ascends the Stairs (*Onna ga kaidan o agaru toki*), 1960, 110 mins., Toho.
Daughters, Wives, and a Mother (*Musuma, tsuma, haha*), 1960, 121 mins., Toho.
The Flow of Evening (*Yoru no nagare*), 1960, 110 mins., Toho.
The Approach of Autumn (*Aki tachinu*), 1960, 78 mins., Toho.
As a Wife, as a Woman, aka *The Other Woman* (*Tsuma toshite, onna toshite*), 1961, 106 mins., Toho.
Woman's Status (*Onna no za*), 1962, 110 mins., Toho.

A Wanderer's Notebook, aka *Her Lonely Lane* (*Horoki*), 1962, 123 mins., Takarazuka Eiga/Toho.

A Woman's Story (*Onna no rekishi*), 1963, 125 mins., Toho.

Yearning (*Midareru*), 1964, 97 mins., Toho.

The Stranger within a Woman, aka *The Thin Line* (*Onna no naka ni iru tanin*), 1966, 101 mins., Toho.

Hit and Run (*Hikinige*), 1966, 94 mins., Toho.

Scattered Clouds, aka *Two in the Shadow* (*Midaregumo*), 1967, 107 mins., Toho.

BIBLIOGRAPHY

"100 Books." International Institute for Children's Literature, Osaka. www.iiclo.or.jp/100books/1946/htm-e/014main-e.htm. Accessed December 12, 2005.

Ahmad, Aijaz. "Jameson's Rhetoric of Otherness and the 'National Allegory.'" In *The Postcolonial Studies Reader*, ed. Bill Ashcroft, Gareth Griffiths, and Helen Tiffin, 77–82. London: Routledge, 1995.

Allison, Anne. *Nightwork: Sexuality, Pleasure, and Corporate Masculinity in a Tokyo Hostess Club*. Chicago: University of Chicago, 1994.

———. *Permitted and Prohibited Desires: Mothers, Comics, and Censorship in Japan*. Boulder, Colo.: Westview, 1996.

Anderson, Joseph L. "Second and Third Thoughts about the Japanese Film." In *The Japanese Film: Art and Industry*, expanded ed., ed. Joseph L. Anderson and Donald Richie, 439–56. Princeton, N.J.: Princeton University Press, 1982.

Anderson, Joseph L., and Donald Richie, eds. *The Japanese Film: Art and Industry*. Expanded ed. Princeton, N.J.: Princeton University Press, 1982.

Aoki Yayoi, "Feminism and Imperialism." In *Broken Silence: Voices of Japanese Feminism*, ed. Sandra Buckley, 17–31. Berkeley: University of California Press, 1997.

Asada Akira. "Infantile Capitalism and Japan's Postmodernism: A Fairy Tale." In *Postmodernism and Japan*, ed. Miyoshi Masao and H. D. Harootunian, 273–78. Durham, N.C.: Duke University Press, 1989.

Atiyah, Edward. *The Thin Line*. New York: Harper and Bros., 1951.

Audrey, Suzanne. "Les femmes et le cinéma au Japon." *Cahiers du cinéma* 30 (1953): 42–47.

Barthes, Roland. *Empire of Signs*. Translated by Richard Howard. New York: Hill and Wang, 1982.

Benjamin, Walter. *The Arcades Project*. Translated by Howard Eiland and Kevin McLaughlin. Cambridge, Mass.: Harvard University Press, 1999.

———. *Selected Writings, Vol. 2, 1927–1934*. Translated by Rodney Livingstone et al., edited by Michael W. Jennings, Howard Eiland, and Gary Smith. Cambridge, Mass.: Harvard University Press, 1999.

———. *Selected Writings, Vol. 3: 1935–1938*. Translated by Edmund Jephcott, Howard Eiland, et al., edited by Howard Eiland and Michael W. Jennings. Cambridge, Mass.: Harvard University Press, 2002.

———. *Walter Benjamin: Selected Writings, Vol. 4: 1938–1940*, edited by Michael W. Jennings. Cambridge, Mass.: Harvard University Press, 2003.

Bernardi, Joanne. *Writing in Light: The Silent Scenario and the Japanese Pure Film Movement*. Detroit: Wayne State University Press, 2001.

Bernstein, Gail Lee. "Women in Rural Japan." In *Women in Changing Japan*, edited by Joyce Lebra, Joy Paulson, and Elizabeth Powers, 25–49. Boulder, Colo: Westview, 1976.

Birnbaum, Phyllis. *Modern Girls, Shining Stars, the Skies of Tokyo: Five Japanese Women*. New York: Columbia University Press, 1999.

Bock, Audie. "The Essential Naruse." In *Mikio Naruse*, edited by Hasumi Shigehiko and Yamane Sadao, 103–16. San Sebastian: Festival Internacional de Cine de San Sebastian, 1998.

———. "A Gesture and a Pose: The Cinema of Mikio Naruse." *Artforum* 44 (2005): 238–41.

———. *Japanese Film Directors*. Tokyo: Kodansha, 1978.

———. *Mikio Naruse*. Translated by Roland Cosandey and André Kaenel. Locarno: Éditions du Festival International du Film de Locarno, 1983.

———, ed. *Mikio Naruse: A Master of the Japanese Cinema*. Chicago: The Film Center, School of the Art Institute of Chicago, 1984.

Bordwell, David. *Ozu and the Poetics of Cinema*. Princeton, N.J.: Princeton University Press, 1988.

———. "Visual Style in Japanese Cinema, 1925–1945." *Film History* 7, no. 1 (1995): 5–31.

Bordwell, David, Kristin Thompson, and Janet Staiger. *The Classical Hollywood Cinema: Film Style and Mode of Production to 1960*. New York: Columbia University Press, 1985.

Bornoff, Nicholas. *Pink Samurai: Love, Marriage, and Sex in Contemporary Japan*. New York: Pocket Books, 1991.

Brooks, Peter. *The Melodramatic Imagination: Balzac, Henry James, Melodrama, and the Mode of Excess*. New York: Columbia University Press, 1976.

Brown, Janice, trans. *I Saw a Pale Horse and Selected Poems from Diary of a Vagabond*. Ithaca, N.Y.: East Asia Program, Cornell University, 1997.

Bruno, Giuliana. "Site-Seeing: Architecture and Moving Image." *Wide Angle* 19, no. 4 (1997): 10.

Buckley, Sandra. "Altered States: The Body Politics of 'Being Woman.'" In *Postwar*

Japan as History, edited by Andrew Gordon, 347–72. Berkeley: University of California Press, 1993.

———. "A Short History of the Women's Movement in Japan." In *Women of Japan and Korea: Continuity and Change*, edited by Joyce Gelb and Marian Lief Palley, 150–86. Philadelphia: Temple University Press, 1994.

———, ed. *Broken Silence: Voices of Japanese Feminism*. Berkeley: University of California Press, 1997.

Buck-Morss, Susan. "Aesthetics and Anaesthetics: Walter Benjamin's Artwork Essay Reconsidered." *New Formations* 20 (1993): 120–44.

———. *The Dialectics of Seeing: Walter Benjamin and the Arcades Project*. Cambridge: MIT Press, 1989.

Burch, Noël. *To the Distant Observer: Form and Meaning in the Japanese Cinema*. Berkeley: California University Press, 1979.

Cazdyn, Eric. *The Flash of Capital: Film and Geopolitics in Japan*. Durham, N.C.: Duke University Press, 2002.

Chow, Rey. "Digging an Old Well: The Labour of Social Fantasy in a Contemporary Chinese Film." In *Reinventing Film Studies*, edited by Christine Gledhill and Linda Williams, 402–18. London: Arnold, 2000.

Chuko Satoshi. "Art Director Chuko Satoshi." In *Mikio Naruse*, edited by Hasumi Shigehiko and Yamane Sadao, 198–210. San Sebastian: Festival Internacional de Cine de San Sebastian, 1998.

Crary, Jonathan. "Modernizing Vision." In *Viewing Positions: Ways of Seeing Film*, edited by Linda Williams, 23–35. New Brunswick, N.J.: Rutgers University Press, 1994.

Davis, Darrell William. *Picturing Japaneseness: Monumental Style, National Identity, Japanese Film*. New York: Columbia University Press, 1996.

Desser, David. *Eros Plus Massacre: An Introduction to the Japanese New Wave Cinema*. Bloomington: Indiana University Press, 1988.

Dissanayaki, Wimal, ed. *Melodrama and Asian Cinema*. New York: Cambridge University Press, 1993.

Doane, Mary Ann. *The Desire to Desire: The Woman's Film of the 1940s*. Bloomington, Ill: Indiana University Press, 1987.

———. "The Woman's Film: Possession and Address." In *Home Is Where the Heart Is: Studies in Melodrama and the Women's Film*, edited by Christine Gledhill, 283–98. London: British Film Institute, 1987.

Doi Takeo. *The Anatomy of Dependence*, trans. John Bester. Tokyo: Kodansha, 1986.

Domenig, Roland. "A Brief History of Independent Cinema in Japan and the Role of the Art Theatre Guild." *Minikomi*, no. 70 (2005): 6–16.

Doniol-Valcroze, Jacques. "Ma mère, je la vois." *Cahiers du cinéma*, Janvier 1954, 50–51.

Douchet, Jean. "About Naruse." *Trafic*, no. 3 (1992). Reprinted in *Mikio Naruse*, edited by Hasumi Shigehiko and Yamane Sadao, 91–102. San Sebastian: Festival Internacional de Cine de San Sebastian, 1998.

Dunlop, Lane, trans. *A Late Chrysanthemum: Twenty-One Stories from the Japanese*. San Francisco: North Point, 1986.

Dussel, Enrique. "Beyond Eurocentrism: The World System and the Limits of Modernity." In *The Cultures of Globalization*, edited by Fredric Jameson and Masao Miyoshi. Durham, N.C.: Duke University Press, 1999.

Elsaesser, Thomas. "Cinephilia, or the Uses of Disenchantment." In *Cinephilia: Movies, Love, and Memory*, edited by Marijke De Valck and Malte Hagener, 27–44. Amsterdam: Amsterdam University Press, 2005.

———. "Tales of Sound and Fury." In *Imitations of Life: A Reader on Film and Television Melodrama*, ed. Marcia Landy, 68–91. Detroit: Wayne State University Press, 1991.

Ericson, Joan. *Be a Woman: Hayashi Fumiko and Modern Japanese Women's Literature*. Honolulu: University of Hawai'i Press, 1997.

Fessler, Susanna. *Wandering Heart: The Work and Method of Hayashi Fumiko*. Albany: State University of New York Press, 1998.

Fitzhugh, William W., and Chisato O. Dubreuil, eds. *Ainu: Spirit of a Northern People*. Washington: Smithsonian Institution with University of Washington Press, 1999.

Freiberg, Freda. "Comprehensive Connections: The Film Industry, the Theatre, and the State in the Early Japanese Cinema." *Screening the Past*, November 2000. www.latrobe.edu.au/www/screeningthepast/current/cc1100.html.

Friedberg, Anne. *Window Shopping: Cinema and the Postmodern*. Berkeley: University of California Press, 1993.

Friedman, Susan Stanford. *Mappings: Feminism and the Cultural Geographies of Encounter*. Princeton, N.J.: Princeton University Press, 1998.

Fujii Jinshi, "Shinema no naka no tanin: Saigo kara sanbanme no Naruse Mikio" ("The Stranger within the Cinema: Naruse Mikio's Third to Last Film"). In *Naruse Mikio no sekai he*, edited by Hasumi Shigehiko and Yamane Sadao, 144–66. Tokyo: Chikuma Shobo, 2005. Translated by Guy Yasko.

Fujiwara, Chris. "Mikio Naruse: The Other Women and the View from the Outside." *Film Comment*, September–October 2005. www.filmlinc.com/fcm/s005/naruse.html. Accessed May 9, 2006.

Galbraith, Stuart. *The Emperor and the Wolf: The Lives and Films of Akira Kurosawa and Toshiro Mifune*. London: Faber and Faber, 2001.

Gelb, Joyce, and Marian Lief Palley, eds. *Women of Japan and Korea: Continuity and Change*. Philadelphia: Temple University Press, 1994.

Gerow, Aaron. "One Print in the Age of Mechanical Reproduction: Film Industry and Culture in 1910s Japan." *Screening the Past*, November 2000. www.latrobe.edu.au/www/screeningthepast/htm.

———. "The Word Before the Image: Criticism, the Screenplay and the Regulation of Meaning in Prewar Japanese Film Culture." In *Word and Image in Japanese Cinema*, edited by Dennis Washburn and Carole Cavanaugh, 3–35. Cambridge, U.K.: Cambridge University Press, 2001.

Giuglaris, Marcel. *Le cinèma japonais (1896–1955)*. Paris: Éditions du Cerf, 1956.

Gledhill, Christine, ed. *Home Is Where the Heart Is: Studies in Melodrama and the Women's Film*. London: British Film Institute, 1987.

———. "Rethinking Genre." In *Reinventing Film Studies*, edited by Christine Gledhill and Linda Williams, 221–43. London: Arnold, 2000.

Gledhill, Christine, and Linda Williams, eds. *Reinventing Film Studies*. London: Arnold, 2000.

Gordon, Andrew, ed. *Postwar Japan as History*. Berkeley: University of California Press, 1993.

Gunning, Tom. "From the Kaleidoscope to the X-Ray: Urban Spectatorship, Poe, Benjamin, and *Traffic in Souls* (1913)." *Wide Angle* 19, no. 4 (1997): 25–61.

Habermas, Jürgen. "Walter Benjamin: Consciousness Raising or Rescuing Critique" (1972). In *On Walter Benjamin: Critical Essays and Recollections*, edited by Gary Smith, 90–128. Cambridge: MIT Press, 1988.

Hane, Mikiso. *Modern Japan: A Historical Survey*. 2nd ed. Boulder, Colo.: Westview, 1986.

Hansen, Miriam. "Fallen Women, Rising Stars, New Horizons: Shanghai Silent Film as Vernacular Modernism." *Film Quarterly* 54 (2000): 10–22.

———. "The Mass Production of the Senses: Classical Cinema as Vernacular Modernism." In *Reinventing Film Studies*, edited by Christine Gledhill and Linda Williams, 332–50. London: Arnold, 2000.

Harootunian, Harry. "'Detour to the East': Noël Burch and the Task of Japanese Film." Introduction to reprint of Noël Burch, *To the Distant Observer*, 7–8.

———. *History's Disquiet: Modernity, Cultural Practice, and the Question of Everyday Life*. New York: Columbia University Press, 2000.

———. *Overcome by Modernity: History, Culture, and Community in Interwar Japan*. Princeton, N.J.: Princeton University Press, 2000.

Hasumi Shigehiko, "The International Reputation of Naruse: In the Face of Misfortune, in the Age of Discovery." Eleventh Hong Kong International Film Festival Program, 1987.

———. "Mikio Naruse or Double Signature." In *Mikio Naruse*, edited by Hasumi Shigehiko and Yamane Sadao, 61–88. San Sebastian: Festival Internacional de Cine de San Sebastian, 1998.

———. "On the Everydayness of a Miracle: Ozu Yasujiro and Atsuta Yuharu." In *From Behind the Camera: A New Look at the Cinema of Yasujiro Ozu* (based on private materials of the late Atsuta Yuharu). Tokyo: Tokyo University Digital Museum, 2000.

Hasumi Shigehiko and Yamane Sadao, eds. *Mikio Naruse*. San Sebastian: Festival Internacional de Cine de San Sebastian, 1998.

———, eds. *Naruse Mikio no sekai he*. Tokyo: Chikuma Shobo, 2005.

Hayashi Fumiko. *Floating Clouds* (translation of first twenty-one chapters of *Ukigumo*). Translated by Y. Koitabashi and M. C. Collcutt. Tokyo: Hara, 1965.

———. "A Late Chrysanthemum." In *A Late Chrysanthemum: Twenty-One Stories from the Japanese*, ed. Lane Dunlop, 95–112. San Francisco: North Point, 1986.

———. "My Work." Translated by Susanna Fessler. In *Wandering Heart: The Work and Method of Hayashi Fumiko*, 168–170. Albany: State University of New York Press, 1998.

———. "Narcissus." Translated by Joan Ericson. In *Be a Woman: Hayashi Fumiko and Modern Japanese Women's Literature*, 221–235. Honolulu: University of Hawai'i Press, 1997.

High, Peter H. *The Imperial Screen: Japanese Cinema in the Fifteen Years' War, 1931–1945*. Madison: University of Wisconsin Press, 2003.

Hirano, Kyoko. *Mr. Smith Goes to Tokyo: Japanese Cinema under the American Occupation, 1945–1952*. Washington, D.C.: Smithsonian Institution, 1992.

Hiwasaki, Lisa. "Ethnic Tourism in Hokkaido and the Shaping of Ainu Identity." *Pacific Affairs* 73 (2000): 393–412.

Ivy, Marilyn. *Discourses of the Vanishing: Modernity, Phantasm, Japan*. Chicago: University of Chicago Press, 1995.

———. "Formations of Mass Culture." In *Postwar Japan as History*, edited by Andrew Gordon, 239–58. Berkeley: University of California Press, 1993.

Izbicki, Joanne. "The Shape of Freedom: The Female Body in Post-Surrender Japanese Cinema." *US-Japan Women's Journal English Supplement*, no. 12 (1996): 109–53.

———. *Scorched Cityscapes and Silver Screens: Negotiating Defeat and Democracy through Cinema in Occupied Japan*. PhD diss., Cornell University, 1997.

Jameson, Fredric. *The Political Unconscious: Narrative as a Socially Symbolic Act*. Ithaca, N.Y.: Cornell University Press, 1981.

———. "Third World Literature in the Era of Multinational Capitalism." *Social Text* 5, no. 3 (1986): 65–88.

Jansen, Marius B. *The Making of Modern Japan*. Cambridge, Mass.: Belknap, 2000.

Kano, Ayako. *Acting Like a Woman in Modern Japan: Theatre, Gender, and Nationalism*. New York: Palgrave, 2001.

Kaplan, Caren, and Inderpal Grewal. "Transnational Feminist Cultural Studies: Beyond the Marxism/Poststructuralism/Feminism Divides." In *Between Women and Nation: Nationalisms, Transnational Feminisms, and the State*, edited by Caren Kaplan, Norma Alarcón, and Minoo Moallem, 349–63. Durham, N.C.: Duke University Press, 1999.

Karatani Kojin. *Origins of Modern Japanese Literature*. Translated by Brett de Bary. Durham, N.C.: Duke University Press, 1993.

Katzoff, Beth. "From Feminisms to Femininities: *Fujin Koron* and the Fifties." *Social Science Japan*, no. 12 (1998): 10–12.

Kawabata Yasunari. *The Scarlet Gang of Asakusa*. Translated by Alisa Freedman. Berkeley: University of California Press, 2005.

———. *The Sound of the Mountain*. Translated by Edward G. Seidensticker. Tokyo: Charles E. Tuttle, 1970.

Kelsky, Karen. *Women on the Verge: Japanese Women, Western Dreams*. Durham, N.C.: Duke University Press, 2001.

Kerr, Alex. *Dogs and Demons: Tales of the Dark Side of Modern Japan*. New York: Hill & Wang, 2001.

Kinoshita, Chika. "In the Twilight of Modernity and the Silent Film: Irie Takako in *The Water Magician*." *Camera Obscura*, no. 60 (2005): 91–127.

Kirihara, Donald. "Critical Polarities and the Study of Japanese Film Style." *Journal of Film and Video* 39 (1987): 17–25.

Kurosawa, Akira. *Something Like an Autobiography*. New York: Random House, 1982.

Landy, Marcia, ed. *Imitations of Life: A Reader on Film and Television Melodrama*. Detroit: Wayne State University Press, 1991.

Lebra, Joyce, Joy Paulson, and Elizabeth Powers, eds. *Women in Changing Japan*. Boulder, Colo.: Westview, 1976.

Lehman, Peter. "The Mysterious Orient, the Crystal Clear Orient, the Non-Existent Orient: Dilemmas of Western Scholars of Japanese Film." *Journal of Film and Video* 39 (1987): 5–15.

Lippit, Seiji M. *Topographies of Japanese Modernism*. New York: Columbia University Press, 2002.

Lopate, Philip. "A Taste for Naruse." *Film Quarterly*, Summer 1986, 11–21.

———. *Totally Tenderly Tragically: Films and Filmmakers*. New York: Anchor Books, 1998.

Marias, Miguel. "Naruse's Serene Splendour." In *Mikio Naruse*, edited by Hasumi Shigehiko and Yamane Sadao, 117–23. San Sebastian: Festival Internacional de Cine de San Sebastian, 1998.

Marra, Michelle, ed. *Modern Japanese Aesthetics: A Reader*. Honolulu: University of Hawai'i Press, 1999.

McDonald, Keiko I. *From Book to Screen: Modern Japanese Literature in Film*. New York: M. E. Sharpe, 2000.

McElhaney, Joe. *The Death of Classical Cinema: Hitchcock, Lang, Minnelli*. Albany: State University of New York Press, 2006.

———. *Qualities of Imperfection: Melodrama and the Decline of Classical Cinema*. PhD diss., New York University, 1999.

Mellen, Joan. *The Waves at Genji's Door: Japan through Its Cinema*. New York: Pantheon Books, 1976.

Memories of Mikio Naruse (documentary film). The Silver Screen Society, 1997.

Minh-ha, Trinh. *Reassemblage* (film script). In *Framer Framed*, 95–105. New York: Routledge, 1992.

Miyoshi Masao. "Against the Narrative Grain." In *Postmodernism and Japan*, edited by Miyoshi Masao and H. D. Harootunian, 153–54. Durham, N.C.: Duke University Press, 1989.

———. *Off-Center: Power and Culture Relations between Japan and the United States*. Cambridge, Mass.: Harvard University Press, 1991.

Miyoshi Masao and H. D. Harootunian, eds. *Japan in the World*. Durham, N.C.: Duke University Press, 1993.

———, eds. *Postmodernism and Japan*. Durham, N.C.: Duke University Press, 1989.

Mizuki Yoko, "Scriptwriter Yoko Mizuki." In *Mikio Naruse*, edited by Hasumi Shigehiko and Yamane Sadao, 185–90. San Sebastian: Festival Internacional de Cine de San Sebastian, 1998.

———. "Memories." In *Mikio Naruse*, edited by Hasumi Shigehiko and Yamane Sadao, 188–89. San Sebastian: Festival Internacional de Cine de San Sebastian, 1998.

Mizuta, Noriko. "In Search of a Lost Paradise: The Wandering Woman in Hayashi Fumiko's *Drifting Clouds*." In *The Woman's Hand: Gender and Theory in Japanese Women's Writing*, ed. Paul Gordon Schalow and Janet A. Walker, 329–51. Stanford, Calif.: Stanford University Press, 1996.

Morey, Anne. "The Judge Called Me an Accessory." *Journal of Popular Film and Television* 23, no. 2 (1995): 80–87.

Mulvey, Laura. "Notes on Sirk and Melodrama." In *Home Is Where the Heart Is: Studies in Melodrama and the Women's Film*, edited by Christine Gledhill, 75–79. London: British Film Institute, 1987.

Murakawa Hide. *Naruse Mikio Enshutsujutsu: Yakusha Ga Kataru Engi no Genba. (Naruse Mikio's Directorial Technique: Actors Talk about Acting)*. Tokyo: Waizu Shuppan, 1997. Translated by Guy Yasko.

Murphy, Joseph A. "Approaching Japanese Melodrama." *East-West Film Journal* 7, no. 2 (1993): 1–38.

Narboni, Jean. *Mikio Naruse: Les temps incertains*. Paris: Cahiers du Cinéma, 2006.

Naruse Mikio. "Works of Fumiko Hayashi and I." In *Mikio Naruse*, edited by Hasumi Shigehiko and Yamane Sadao, 168–172. San Sebastian: Festival Internacional de Cine de San Sebastian, 1998.

Naruse Mikio, Hazumi Tsuneo, Futaba Juzaburo, Kishi Matsuo, Tomoda Jun'ichirô, Iida Shinbi, and Kojima Hiroshi. "Naruse Mikio zadankai" ("The Naruse Mikio Roundtable"). *Kinema Junpo*, September 21, 1934, 97–101. Translation by Chika Kinoshita.

Neale, Steve. "Melodrama and Tears." *Screen* 27, no. 6 (1986): 6–22.

Nogami Teruyo. *Waiting on the Weather: Making Movies with Akira Kurosawa*. Translated by Juliet Winters. Berkeley: Stone Bridge, 2006.

Nolletti, Arthur Jr. *The Cinema of Gosho Heinosuke*. Indianapolis: Indiana University Press, 2005.

Nornes, Markus Abe. "The Postwar Documentary Trace: Groping in the Dark." *Positions* 10, no. 1 (2000): 39–78.

Nygren, Scott. "Reconsidering Modernism: Japanese Film and the Postmodern Context." *Wide Angle* 11, no. 3 (1989): 6–15.

Okada Kazuo. "The Ainu in Ethnographic Films." In *Ainu: Spirit of a Northern People*, edited by William W. Fitzhugh and Chisato O. Dubreuil, 187–92. Washington: Smithsonian Institution with University of Washington Press, 1999.

Okubo Kiyo. "Kimiko in New York." In *Naruse Mikio no Sekai he*, edited by Hasumi Shigehiko and Yamane Sadao, 183–98. Tokyo: Chikuma Shobo, 2005. Translated by Guy Yasko.

Okamoto Kihachi, "What the Master Mikio Naruse Taught Me: Spirit and Technique." In *Mikio Naruse: A Master of the Japanese Cinema*, 11–13. Chicago: The Film Center, School of the Art Institute of Chicago, 1984.

Ono Yugo. "Ainu Homelands: Natural History from Ice Age to Modern Times." In *Ainu: Spirit of a Northern People*, edited by William W. Fitzhugh and Chisato O. Dubreuil, 32–38. Washington: Smithsonian Institution with University of Washington Press, 1999.

Ortolani, Benito. *The Japanese Theatre: From Shamanistic Ritual to Contemporary Pluralism*. Princeton, N.J.: Princeton University Press, 1990.

Oshima Nagisa. *Cinema, Censorship, and the State: The Writings of Nagisa Oshima, 1956–1978*. Translated by Dawn Lawson. Cambridge, Mass: MIT Press, 1992.

Petro, Patrice. *Aftershocks of the New: Feminism and Film History*. New Brunswick, N.J.: Rutgers University Press, 2002.

Pharr, Susan J. "The Politics of Women's Rights." In *Democratizing Japan: The Allied Occupation*, edited by Robert E. Ward and Sakamoto Yoshikazu, 221–52. Honolulu: University of Hawai'i Press, 1987.

Polan, Dana, "Auteur Desire." *Screening the Past*, March 2001. www.latrobe.edu.au/screeningthepast/fr0301/dpfr12a.htm. Accessed June 6, 2006.

Pollack, David. *Reading against Culture: Ideology and Narrative in the Japanese Novel*. Ithaca N.Y.: Cornell University Press, 1992.

Poulton, Cody. *Spirits of Another Sort: The Plays of Izumi Kyoka*. Ann Arbor: Center for Japanese Studies, University of Michigan, 2001.

Rassos, Effie. "Everyday Narratives: Reconsidering Filmic Temporality and Spectatorial Affect through the Quotidian." PhD diss., University of New South Wales, 2005.

Ray, Robert B. "The Bordwell Regime and the Stakes of Knowledge." In *How a Film Theory Got Lost and Other Mysteries in Cultural Studies*. Bloomington: Indiana University Press, 2001.

Richie, Donald. *Different People: Pictures of Some Japanese*. Tokyo: Kodansha, 1987.

———. *Ozu*. Berkeley: University of California Press, 1974.

———. "Terminal Essay." In *The Japanese Film: Art and Industry*, expanded ed., edited by Joseph L. Anderson and Donald Richie, 457–77. Princeton, N.J.: Princeton University Press, 1982.

Rimer, J. Thomas, and Van C. Gessel, eds. *The Columbia Anthology of Modern Japanese Literature*. Vol. 1, *From Restoration to Occupation, 1868–1945*. New York: Columbia University Press, 2005.

Russell, Catherine. "Insides and Outsides: Cross-Cultural Criticism and Japanese Film Melodrama." In *Melodrama and Asian Cinema*, edited by Wimal Dissanayaki, 143–54. New York: Cambridge University Press, 1993.

———. "Three Japanese Actresses of the 1950s: Modernity, Femininity, and the Performance of Everyday Life." *CineAction!* 60 (2003): 34–44.

Ross, Kristin. *Fast Cars Clean Bodies: Decolonization and the Reordering of French Cinema*. Cambridge, Mass.: MIT Press, 1995.

Ross, Sara. "The Americanization of Tsuru Aoki: Orientalism, Melodrama, Star Image and the New Woman." *Camera Obscura*, no. 60 (2005): 129–57.

Sakabe Megumi. "Mask and Shadow in Japanese Culture: Implicit Ontology in Japanese Thought." In *Modern Japanese Aesthetics: A Reader*, edited by Michele Marra, 242–51. Honolulu: University of Hawai'i Press, 1999.

Sakai, Naoki. *Translation and Subjectivity: On "Japan" and Cultural Nationalism*. Minneapolis: Minnesota University Press, 1997.

Sandler, Mark, ed. *The Confusion Era: Art and Culture of Japan During the Allied Occupation, 1945–1952*. Washington, D.C.: Smithsonian Institute, 1997.

Sato, Barbara. *The New Japanese Woman: Modernity, Media and Women in Interwar Japan*. Durham, N.C.: Duke University Press, 2003.

Sato Tadao. *Currents in Japanese Cinema*. Translated by Gregory Barrett. Tokyo: Kodansha, 1982.

———. "The Multilayered Nature of the Tradition of Acting in Japanese Cinema." In *Cinema and Cultural Identity: Reflections on Films from Japan, India and China*, edited by Wimal Dissanayake, 45–52. Lanham, Md.: University Press of America, 1988.

Scala, Andre. "Naruse and Some Dutch Painters." Translated by Michèle Le Gault and Linda C. Ehrlich. *Cinemaya* 31 (1995–96): 4–10. Originally published in *Cahiers du Cinéma*, April 1993.

Schermann, Susanne. *Naruse Mikio: Nichijo no kirameki* (*Naruse Mikio: The Glitter in the Everyday*). Tokyo: Kinema Junpo-sha, 1997.

Sherif, Ann. *Mirror: The Fiction and Essays of Koda Aya*. Honolulu: University of Hawai'i Press, 1999.

Siddle, Richard. "From Assimilation to Indigenous Rights: Ainu Resistance since 1869." In *Ainu: Spirit of a Northern People*, edited by William W. Fitzhugh and Chisato O. Dubreuil, 108–15. Washington: Smithsonian Institution with University of Washington Press, 1999.

Silverberg, Miriam. "The Café Waitress Serving Modern Japan." In *Mirror of Modernity: Invented Traditions of Modern Japan*, edited by Stephen Vlastos, 208–25. Berkeley: University of California Press, 1998.

———. "Constructing the Japanese Ethnography of Modernity." *Journal of Asian Studies* 51, no. 1 (1992): 30–54.

———. "The Modern Girl as Militant." In *Recreating Japanese Women, 1600–1945*, edited by Gail Lee Bernstein, 239–66. Berkeley: University of California Press, 1991.

———. "Remembering Pearl Harbor, Forgetting Charlie Chaplin, and the Case of the Disappearing Western Woman: A Picture Story." *positions* 1, no. 1 (1993): 24–76.

Silverman, Kaja. *The Subject of Semiotics*. New York: Oxford University Press, 1983.

Singer, Ben. *Melodrama and Modernity.* New York: Columbia University Press, 2000.

Smith, Greg M. "Critical Reception of *Rashomon* in the West." *Asian Cinema* 13 (2002): 115–28.

Standish, Isolde. *A New History of Japanese Cinema: A Century of Narrative Film.* London: Continuum, 2005.

Suzuki, Daisetz T. *Zen and Japanese Culture.* Princeton, N.J.: Princeton University Press, 1959.

Takamine Hideko, "About Mikio Naruse." In *Mikio Naruse: A Master of the Japanese Cinema*, edited by Audie Bock, 8–10. Chicago: The Film Center, School of the Art Institute of Chicago, 1984.

Tamai Masao, "Testimony." In *Mikio Naruse*, edited by Hasumi Shigehiko and Yamane Sadao, 191–97. San Sebastian: Festival Internacional de Cine de San Sebastian, 1998.

Tanaka Yukiko, ed. *To Live and to Write: Selections by Japanese Women Writers, 1913–1938.* Seattle: Seal, 1987.

"Le Témoignage de l'Actrice Yoko Tsukasa: Avec Naruse, on ne répétait presque jamais" (Actress Yoko Tsukasa: With Naruse, we rarely rehearsed). *Cahiers du Cinéma*, January 2001, 68–69.

Thompson, Kristin, and David Bordwell. "Space and Narrative in the Films of Ozu." *Screen* 17, no. 2 (1976): 41–73.

Tokuda Shusei. *Rough Living.* Translated by Richard Torrance. Honolulu: University of Hawai'i Press, 2001.

Tomonori Saiki. *Twentieth Pordenone Silent Film Festival Catalogue.* Sacile, Italy: La Giornate del Cinema Muto, 2001.

Tosaka Jun. "Essays on the Japanese Ideology." In *Tosaka jun zenshu*, Vol. 44. Tokyo: Keikusa shobo, 1977.

Tsuneishi Fumiko. "The Veil Comes Down: Naruse Mikio's Centre." In *Naruse Mikio no sekai he*, edited by Hasumi Shigehiko and Yamane Sadao, 167–81. Tokyo: Chikuma Shobo, 2005. Translated by Guy Yasko.

———. Program notes for Le Giornate del Cinema Muto 2005. www.cinetecadelfriuli.org/gcm/edizione2005/edizione2005_frameset.html. Accessed June 13, 2006.

Ueda, Makoto. *Far beyond the Field: Haiku by Japanese Women.* New York: Columbia University Press, 2003.

"Ume Takeda, Monteuse: Naruse montait ses films avec ses yeux et son cœur" (Ume Takeda, Editor: Naruse edited his films with his eyes and his heart). *Cahiers du Cinéma*, January 2001, 65.

Uno, Kathleen. "The Death of 'Good Wife Wise Mother'?" In, *Postwar Japan as History*, edited by Andrew Gordon, 293–322. Berkeley: University of California Press, 1993.

Vertov, Dziga. *Kino-Eye: The Writings of Dziga Vertov.* Translated by Kevin O'Brien. Berkeley: University of California Press, 1984.

Wada-Marciano, Mitsuyo. "Construction of Modern Space: Tokyo and Shochiku Kamata Film Texts." In *In Praise of Film Studies: Essays in Honor of Makino Mamoru*, edited by Aaron Gerow and Abe Mark Nornes, 158–75. Ann Arbor: Kinema Club, 2001.

———. "Imaging Modern Girls in the Japanese Woman's Film." *Camera Obscura*, no. 60 (2005): 91–128.

———. *The Production of Modernity in Japanese Cinema: Shochiku Kamata Style in the 1920s and 1930s*. PhD diss., University of Iowa, 2000.

Washburn, Dennis, and Carole Cavanaugh. *Word and Image in Japanese Cinema*. Cambridge, U.K.: Cambridge University Press, 2001.

Weil, Elsie. "Kimiko," *Asia* 37 (June 1937): 463.

Williams, Linda. *Playing the Race Card: Melodramas of Black and White from Uncle Tom to O. J. Simpson*. Princeton, N.J.: Princeton University Press, 2001.

———."Discipline and Fun: *Psycho* and Postmodern Cinema." In *Reinventing Film Studies*, edited by Christine Gledhill and Linda Williams, 351–78. London: Arnold, 2000.

———. "Melodrama Revised." In *Refiguring American Film Genres: History and Theory*, edited by Nick Browne. Berkeley: University of California Press, 1998.

Yamanashi Emiko. "Painting in the Time of 'Heavy Hands.'" In *The Confusion Era: Art and Culture of Japan During the Allied Occupation, 1945–1952*, edited by Mark Sandler, 23–37. Washington, D.C.: Smithsonian Institute, 1997.

Yamane Sadao. "Rhythm of Emotions: Mikio Naruse during the Prewar to War Years." In *Mikio Naruse*, edited by Hasumi Shigehiko and Yamane Sadao. San Sebastian: Festival Internacional de Cine de San Sebastian, 1998.

Yang, Edward. "Generosity: The Invincible Invisible." In *Mikio Naruse*, edited by Hasumi Shigehiko and Yamane Sadao, 153–57. San Sebastian: Festival Internacional de Cine de San Sebastian, 1998.

Yoshida Kiju, *Ozu's Anti-Cinema*. Translated by Daisuke Miyao and Kyoko Hirano. Ann Arbor: University of Michigan, 2003.

Yoshide Yoshishige, "Reversing Light and Shadow, or People Parting from Each Other: Yasujiro Ozu and Mikio Naruse." In *Mikio Naruse*, edited by Hasumi Shigehiko and Yamane Sadao. San Sebastian: Festival Internacional de Cine de San Sebastian, 1998.

Yoshimoto Mitsuhiro. "The Difficulty of Being Radical: The Discipline of Film Studies and the Postcolonial World Order." In *Japan in the World*, edited by Miyoshi Masao and H. D. Harootunian, 338–53. Durham, N.C.: Duke University Press, 1993.

———. *Kurosawa: Film Studies and Japanese Cinema*. Durham, N.C.: Duke University Press, 2000.

———. "Logic of Sentiment: The Postwar Japanese Cinema and Questions of Modernity." PhD diss., University of California, San Diego, 1993.

———. "The University, Disciplines, National Identity: Why Is There No Film Studies in Japan?" *South Atlantic Quarterly* 99 (2000): 697–713.

INDEX

Abe Kobo, 377
Abe Tsuyako, 294
Abortion, 12, 230, 248–49, 266, 281, 358, 390
Academy aspect ratio, 226, 309
Acting techniques, 14, 249, 268; restraint and, 230–31
Actress and the Poet, The (*Joyu to shijin*, 1935), 96–99
Adorno, Theodor, 308
Ahmad, Aijaz, 171–72
Ainu people, 317, 328–33, 397
Akagi Ranko, 117
Akogare, 395–96
Allison, Anne, 340
American cinema, 9–10, 23, 78, 85–87, 174, 256; American family melodrama and, 258–60; American release and critique of *Wife! Be Like a Rose!*, 83, 100; Japanese cinema vs., 128–30; vernacular modernity and, 25
Anderson, Joseph, 28, 46, 86, 130
Angry Street, The (*Ikari no machi*, 1950), 169, 177, 198–203, 377; still from, 202
Anpo Treaty (1960), 318

Anthropology, 18, 32, 236, 243; ethnographies and, 207, 300, 401–2; hostess bars and, 340; *Late Chrysanthemums* and, 274; sentimental ethnographies in, 177, 195; spectatorship and, 35, 37; woman's film and, 30
Anzukko (1958), 226, 229, 236, 304, 309–12, 376
Aoki Yayoi, 31
Aomori prefecture, 195, 198, 389–90
Aono Suekichi, 53, 186
Apart from You (*Kimi to wakarete*, 1933), 8, 45, 48, 60–65; still from, 64
Approach of Autumn, The (*Aki tachinu*, 1960), 320, 348, 351, 353, 369; still from, 352
Arakure (Tokuda Shusei), 304–8
Arcades Project, The (Benjamin), 181, 308
Architecture and homes, 15, 22, 24, 30, 109, 127, 233, 298, 401; in *Both You and I*, 184; family and, 30; female subjectivity and, 33; in *Feminine Melancholy*, 118, 120; in *Flowing*, 295, 298; in home-drama, 33; intern-

Architecture and homes (*continued*)
tional audiences and, 35; in *Mother*, 239–40; in Naruse's films of mid-1950s, 234–35, 239–41, 245, 254, 267, 275, 293–95, 298; in Naruse's films of 1960s, 326, 331, 339, 369, 371, 389; in *Okuni and Gohei*, 223; in postwar film, 176; in *The Road I Travel with You*, 112; in *Scattered Clouds*, 389; spectatorship and, 37; in *Summer Clouds*, 326; as visual mode of Japaneseness, 37; western in *Avalanche*, 123; in *When a Woman Ascends the Stairs*, 339; in *Whistling in Kotan*, 331; in *Wife! Be Like a Rose!*, 99–100, 104; in *Yearning*, 369, 371

Art Theater Guild (ATG), 316, 386
Asada Akira, 374–75
As a Wife, as a Woman (*Tsuma toshite, onna toshite*, 1961), 316, 320–21, 353–54, 356, 388, 397; still from, 355
Atiyah, Edward, 376, 381
Audrey, Suzanne, 29
August 1945, 167, 170, 174, 180
Auteurism, 19–25, 27, 32, 121, 173
Avalanche (*Nadare*, 1937), 90, 121–25; still from, 122
Awashima Chikage, 14, 323–25; in *As a Wife, as a Woman*, 355

Bad Sleep Well, The (*Warui yatsu hodo yoku nemuru*, 1960), 351, 377
Bar hostesses, 13, 17, 47, 208–10, 258; anthropological study of, 340; in *As a Wife, as a Woman*, 354–55; in *Every Night Dreams*, 65; in *The Flow of Evening*, 349; in Naruse's films of 1960s, 340–41, 349, 354–55; in *When a Woman Ascends the Stairs*, 333–35, 337–39, 341
Barthes, Roland, 211, 268
Battle of Roses, The (*Bara gassen*, 1950), 23, 169, 177, 194–95, 206–8; still from, 207

Being-woman, 169, 176, 193
Benjamin, Walter, 20, 23–24, 51–53, 70, 124; on boredom, 374; "On the Concept of History," 172; on dialectical cultural history, 322; on dialectical image, 286, 314; on fascism and cinema, 165; on Fuchs, 173; on historiography, 286; on kitsch, 167, 181; on modernity of cinema, 398–99; Paris arcades, 21; on proverbs, 368; on technique, 235; "The Storyteller," 363, 368; on women's fashion and modernity, 308
Bernstein, Gail, 325–26
Birds, The (1963), 383
Birnbaum, Phyllis, 373
Bock, Audie, 5–7, 16, 46, 101–2, 150, 194, 208, 353, 402; on *A Wife's Heart*, 290
Bolero, 140
Bordwell, David, 12, 22, 42, 44, 86–87
Boredom, 248, 374–75
Both You and I (*Ore mo omae mo*, 1946), 176, 183–86; still from, 185
Box office success, 19, 25, 228, 254, 306, 376
Brecht, Bertolt, 4, 11
Brooks, Peter, 11, 34, 126–27
Brown Eyes (*Chairo mo me*, Hayashi Fumiko), 251, 254
Bruno, Giuliana, 37
Buckley, Sandra, 27, 169
Buck-Morss, Susan, 165, 182
Bullying, 49
Burch, Noel, 4–5, 38, 85, 87, 99, 312
Burlesque, 32, 92, 196

Café waitresses, 13, 43, 47–48, 74
Cahiers du cinéma, 2, 16, 227, 396
Calligraphic style, 42, 45
Car accidents and themes, 6, 113, 125, 353, 396; in *Every Night Dreams*, 65, 68–70; in films of 1960s, 321, 358–59; in *Hit and Run*, 382–88; modern

medicine and, 79; in *Not Blood Relations*, 58; in *Scattered Clouds*, 389–94; in *Street without End*, 74
Carmen Comes Home (1951), 196
Cassavetes, John, 316, 398
Cazdyn, Eric, 39, 174
Censorship, 9, 52, 87–88, 132, 136, 151, 168, 182, 208, 226; *Every Night Dreams* and, 66
Chasteness, 13, 63
Chekhov, Anton, 362
Chiba Sachiko, 2, 4, 89, 97–98, 110; in *The Girl in the Rumor*, 108; marriage to Naruse, 96; in *Morning's Tree-Lined Street*, 115, 117; in *Wife! Be Like a Rose!*, 99, 103–4
Chiba Yasuki, 220
Childless couples, 229–31, 255, 261, 290
Chinese cinema, 32
Chocolate Girl (*Chokoreto garu*, 1932), 45
Chow, Rey, 32
Chuko Satoshi, 16, 228–29, 267; on *Floating Clouds*, 282
Civil Information and Education Section (CIE), 168–69, 177, 187–88, 193, 208
Class, 108, 112, 114, 148; in *Avalanche*, 124; in *Every Night Dreams*, 66; in *Flunky, Work Hard*, 53; in *Hit and Run*, 384; Japanese classical cinema and, 126; male class anxiety in *Anzukko*, 310, 312; middle class and, 126, 288, 293–94; Naruse's exploration of upper classes, 84; in Naruse's films of 1950s, 229, 254, 257, 288, 293–94; in Naruse's films of 1960s, 317; in Naruse's silent films, 44–46; Naruse's social realism and, 130
Clifford, James, 20
Colonialism, 171–72, 332–33
Comedies, 183, 231; marriage films and, 231–32; wartime, 159–64
Commodity culture, 23, 39, 51, 97, 104, 126, 235, 289; cars and, 388; in *Every Night Dreams*, 70; *moga* (modern girl) and, 46; in Naruse's silent films, 45–46, 80; in *Not Blood Relations*, 57–58, 60; in postwar Japan, 235; in *Street without End*, 77; toys as motif of, 53, 70
Conduct Report on Professor Ishinaka (*Ishinaka sensei gyojoki*, 1950), 176–77, 194–98; still from, 197
Corporate culture, 17, 236, 399; in *Hit and Run*, 382–83; in films of 1960s, 333–34, 375, 382–83; in *When a Woman Ascends the Stairs*, 334; in *Yearning*, 375
Cosmetics companies, 207
Cosmopolitanism, 79, 155, 395–96, 403
Costumes and fashion, 3, 23–24, 118, 304, 335; in *Avalanche*, 123–24; in *Dancing Girl*, 21; in *Hit and Run*, 383, 391; Japanese modernity and, 47, 51, 53, 79, 128, 308; in *Late Chrysanthemums*, 276; in *Learn from Experience*, 125–26; in *Older Brother*, 258–59; in postwar film, 176; in *Scattered Clouds*, 390, 396; in *Street without End*, 78; in *Untamed*, 307–8; in *White Beast*, 204, in *Wife! Be Like a Rose!*, 102–3, 105
Crary, Jonathan, 37
Crying to the Blue Sky (*Aozora ni naku*, 1932), 68

Daiei studio, 228, 242, 256
Dancing Girl (*Maihime*, 1951), 168–69, 177, 208, 211–14, 218; still from, 212
Dan Reiko, 319, 341, 348
Daughters, Wives and a Mother (*Musume, tsuma, haha*, 1960), 316, 342–48, 368, 370, 397; still from, 345
Davis, Darrell, 133, 165
de Hooch, Pieter, 265
Delinquent Girl (*Furyo shojo*, 1949), 176, 193–94, 201

Democracy, 27; "broken promise" of, 22, 28, 247, 288; Japanese subject and, 174; Naruse's films of mid-1950s and, 236; *Sudden Rain* and, 288
Democratization films, 176, 187, 191, 225, 268
Descendant of Urashima Taro, A (*Urashima Taro no koei*, 1946), 23, 169, 176–83, 207; still from, 179
Desire, 16, 22, 32–33, 215, 217, 224, 233, 240, 245, 260, 281–82, 322, 324, 397; of the gaze in *Flowing*, 299–300; occupation culture and, 175–76; in *Scattered Clouds*, 395–96; in films of 1960s, 317, 324; in *shoshimin-eiga* films, 32; temporality and, 374; in *Yearning*, 368, 373–75
Desser, David, 377
Deus ex machina, 218
Dialectical history, 321–22
Dialectical image, 286
Doane, Mary Ann, 30, 33
Domenig, Roland, 316
Douchet, Jean, 10, 278
Drunken Angel (*Yoidore tenshi*, 1948), 187, 200, 377
Dussel, Enrique, 27
Dutch genre painting, 265, 267

Early Summer (*Bakushu*, 1951), 217, 268
Editing, 6–7, 11–12, 16, 116, 227–28, 235, 241, 321, 401; in *Apart from You*, 61–62; in *Avalanche*, 122; in *Flowing*, 300; in *Hit and Run*, 382, 386; in *Morning's Tree-Lined Street*, 116; in *Older Brother*, 259; in *Scattered Clouds*, 296; in *Woman Ascends the Stairs*, 340
Edo period films, 220, 222
Education, 317, 326–27; Ainu people and, 329
Eiga Hyoron, 26, 237, 274
EIRIN (Film Ethics Regulation Control Comitee), 168

Elsaesser, Thomas, 34, 63, 258, 260
Emiko Yamanashi, 170
Emperor Hirohito, 180
Enchi Fumiko, 294
Ericson, Joan, 219, 361, 364
Essentialism, 28, 31, 211
Ethnography, 55, 77, 207, 288, 300, 401–2; realism, 251–52; sentimental ethnographies, 177, 195
Evening Stream (*Yoru no nagare*, 1960), 320, 348, 352–53, 397; still from, 349
Even Parting Is Enjoyable (*Wakare mo tanoshi*, 1947), 169, 176, 187, 191–93, 322
Eventlessness, 289–90, 401
Everyday life, 5, 7, 23–24, 126, 129–30, 174, 203, 233, 399; in *The Actress and the Poet*, 97–98; of American GIs and Japanese women, 175; anthropological spectatorship and, 35; in *Arakure*, 308; in the city, 22, 40, 42, 46, 49, 52, 55, 71, 77–79, 92, 104–5, 116, 200–201, 251; of commerce, 274–75; female subjectivity and, 82; films in which "nothing happens" and, 289; in *Flunky, Work Hard*, 53; of geishas in *Apart from You*, 65; of geishas in *Flowing*, 299; haiku poetry and, 314; home-dramas and, 401; interwar Japanese modernity and, 79–80; Japanese modernity and, 51, 54–55, 58; *Jidai geki* and, 224; marriage in postwar Tokyo and, 250–51; material culture and, 65, 77, 104, 125, 176, 339; melodrama and, 374; military activities and, 88; in *Mother*, 238–39; in Naruse's films of mid-1950s, 10, 229, 238–39, 258, 262, 270–72, 299, 307–8; in Naruse's films of 1960s, 317, 338; in postwar film, 176, 234, 236; postwar Japanese modernity and, 234; in *Repast*, 219; rituals of domestic life, 262; sacredness in Naruse's wartime comedies of, 159–60, 163; in *Street*

without End, 77; in Tokyo's pleasure quarters, 338; in *Untamed*, 307–8; vernacular modernity and, 234; wartime films and, 135, 149, 164; in *The Whole Family Works*, 152; in *Wife! Be Like a Rose!*, 104–5; of women in the city, 270–75; women's writing and, 34

Every Night Dreams (*Yogoto no yume*, 1933), 8, 65–73, 97, 382; still from, 69, 72

Eye movements, 13–14, 22

Face of Another (*Tanin no kao*, 1966), 377

Family businesses, 109, 251, 293, 317, 358, 369

Fantasy escape, 116, 123, 130

Fascism, 9, 164–65

Fashion. *See* Costumes and fashion

Female subjectivity, 20, 22–23, 25, 116, 170, 224, 396, 400–401; in *Even Parting is Enjoyable*, 322; everyday life and, 82; in *Floating Clouds*, 322; Hara Setsuko and, 269; of Hayashi's heroines, 243; in *Hideko*, 163; home-drama and, 32; Japanese cinema and, 27; Japanese modernity and, 16, 54, 80, 233–34, 236, 261, 269, 402; in *Late Chrysanthemums*, 276–77; in *Lightning*, 245; melodrama of Naruse and, 44, 80, 247; in *Morning's Tree-Lined Street*, 116; mother as emblem of, 54; narrative and, 32; in Naruse's films of mid-1950s, 241, 245–47, 261, 269, 276–77; in Naruse's films of 1960s, 322; in Naruse's silent films, 80; negotiation of urban space and, 243–44; in postwar Japan, 233–34; setting and, 33; *shoshimin-eiga* genre and, 32; spatial tropes and, 37; spectatorship and, 32–38; wartime films and, 165; in *A Wife's Heart*, 322; woman's films and, 28

Feminine Melancholy (*Nyonin aishu*, 1937), 9, 90, 117–21, 368, 400; still from, 119

Feminisuto, 13

Femme fatale, 377

Fessler, Susan, 244, 254, 280

Fifteen Years' War, 9, 30, 136, 165

Film Art Association, 194

Film Law of 1939, 132–33, 135

Film noir, 17, 198, 200, 203, 338, 376; revival in 1960s of, 377; Toho studio and, 377; woman's films and, 380; youth culture and, 377

Five Men in the Circus (*Saakasu goningumi*, 1935), 106–7

Flamboyant style, 39, 42, 44, 48, 78, 86, 111, 211; in *Apart from You*, 43, 61; in *Every Night Dreams*, 43, 71; Japanese modernity and, 43

Flashbacks, 320–21, 356, 358; in *Floating Clouds*, 278; in *The Stranger within a Woman*, 377, 379–80

Floating Clouds (*Ukigumo*, 1955), 10–11, 15, 170–71, 229, 236, 277–84, 322, 359, 361, 365, 392

Flowing (*Nagareru*, 1956), 10, 22, 232, 295–304, 334, 341, 349

Flow of Evening, The (*Yoru no nagare*, 1960), 320, 348, 352–53, 397; still from, 349

Flunky, Work Hard (*Koshiben ganbare*, 1931), 48–51, 53, 68, 97, 183, 382; still from, 50

Fond Face from the Past, A, 155–59, 165; still from, 157

Friedman, Susan Stanford, 30, 32

Fuchs, Edward, 173

Fujii Jinshi, 376, 379–80

Fujii Shigeo, 209

Fujimoto Sanezumi, 228, 247, 282, 401

Fujin Koron, 55, 301–2, 304

Fujiwara, Chris, 394

Fujiwara Kamatari, 89, 97, 106, 111; as Fujiwara Keita, 159, 161

Fukuzawa Yasumichi, 376
Furukawa Roppa, 136
Futaba Juzaburo, 217
Futari zuma (Two Wives), 100–101

Geido films, 137–38, 140, 142, 145–47; parody of, 159
Geisha, 13, 48, 112–13, 269, 275; in *Apart from You*, 43, 60, 62–63, 65; in *Flowing*, 295–303; in *The Flow of Evening*, 348–51; in *Late Chrysanthemums*, 269–70; in *Scattered Clouds*, 389
Genbun itchi, 54, 211
Gendai geki genre (films with contemporary settings), 26, 40, 52–53
Gender, 23, 219, 243, 299, 401; alternative international configurations of, 395, 402; Being-woman and, 169, 176, 193; codes of during occupation, 169; codes of in Japanese modernity, 55, 305; depiction of in postwar society, 277–84; film production and, 16–17; hostess bars and, 340; Japanese cinema and, 31, 34, 37–38, 80, 118; postwar Japanese modernity and, 233–34, 245, 269; postwar nationhood and, 170; scriptwriting and, 249; in silent film, 80; in *Sincerity*, 154; in *Wife*, 254. *See also* Female subjectivity; Woman's film
Ginza, 210, 244, 332–34, 339; in *The Flow of Evening*, 350–51; in *Street without End*, 74, 78
Ginza Cosmetics (*Ginza Gesho*, 1951), 168–69, 177, 208–11, 223
Girl in the Rumor, The (*Uwase no musume*, 1935), 47, 90, 96, 108–11, 356; still from, 110
Gledhill, Christine, 315, 374
Gorky, Maxim, 227
Gosho Heinosuke, 396–97
Green, Herbert, 83
Grewal, Inderpal, 38
Gunning, Tom, 77–78

Habermas, Jürgen, 23–24
Haha-mono films. *See* Mother films
Hamsun, Knut, 362
Hanabishi Achako, 183, 185
Hanayagi Shotaro, 140
Hani Susumu, 386
Hansen, Miriam, 24–25, 84–85, 89, 165, 235
Happiness, 126, 215, 229, 247, 255–56, 262; in *Lightning*, 244–45; in *Mother*, 240; in Occupation films, 175; in *Sound of the Mountain*, 262
Hara Setsuko, 14, 168, 188, 214, 219, 228, 230, 247–48; in *Daughters, Wives and a Mother*, 344, 347; female subjectivity and, 269; retirement of, 268–69, 347; screen persona as the "eternal virgin" of, 268, 344; in *Sound of the Mountain*, 261, 263, 265, 267, 269; in *Sudden Rain*, 284–85, 289
Hard Times (*Fukeiki jidai*, 1930), 46
Harootunian, Harry, 24, 51, 53–54, 77, 79–81, 86–87, 105, 124; on modernism and fascism, 164; on salarymen, 186
Hasegawa Kazuo, 138, 143, 145, 147
Hashimoto Shinobu, 319, 324; *Whistling in Kotan* script of, 328
Hashimoto Takako, 313
Hasumi Shigehiko, 1, 15, 223, 228, 265, 278, 318, 361
Hayashi Fumiko, 15–16, 18, 54, 115, 208–9, 214–15, 218–19, 227, 235, 243–45, 247; adaption of *Lightning*, 241; "Bangiku," 270; *Brown Eyes*, 251, 254; commodification of, 361–68; *Diary of a Vagabond* (*Horoki*), 54, 242; *Floating Clouds* and, 277–80, 283; heroines of, 277; *Inazuma*, 242; *Late Chrysanthemums* and, 270, 274; *Meshi*, 168; "Shirasagi" ("White Heron"), 270; "Suisen," 270; *A Wanderer's Notebook* (*Horoki*), 47, 361–68,

452 INDEX

397; *Wife* and, 251, 254–55; women characters of, 271
Heihachiro Okawa, 92, 94–95, 108, 110–11, 114–15
Heine, Heinrich, 362
Herringbone Clouds (*Iwashigumo*, 1958), 17, 317, 319, 322–28, 397; still from, 325
Hideko the Bus Conductor (*Hideko no shasho-san*, 1941), 131, 159–64, 195, 400; still from, 161
High, Peter, 26, 87, 134, 136, 151–52
High and Low (*Tengoku to jigoku*, 1960), 170, 377, 384
Hit and Run (*Hikinige*, 1966), 17, 318, 320, 382–88, 397; still from, 383, 387
Hitchcock, Alfred, 17, 319, 383
Hiwasaki, Lisa, 330
Hokkaido Former Aborigines Act, 329
Hokkaido tourism, 329–31
Hollywood, 26, 33–34, 85; classicism, 86, 133, 240; influence on Naruse, 203; melodrama, 215; SKS and, 40–42; vernacular modernity and, 25; Naruse's style vs. visual style of, 88–89, 99–100, 127, 130, 134; woman's film and, 26, 28–30
Home-drama (*homu dorama*), 36, 120, 229, 235, 241, 278, 316, 364, 400; architecture in, 33; everyday life in, 401; female characters and, 30; female subjectivity and, 32; *Floating Clouds* as departure from, 278; homelessness and, 236; Japanese history and, 35; *katei shosetsu* (domestic novels) and, 30; *Mother* and, 236, 238; of Ozu, 268; propaganda and, 156, 158; *Sound of the Mountain* as, 266; *Summer Clouds* as, 328; during wartime, 148–59; in which "nothing happens," 289; *A Wife's Heart* as, 293; *A Woman's Status* as, 357
Hosokawa Chikako, 91, 93, 111; in *Late Chrysanthemums*, 271

Housewives and housework, 25, 230, 286, 294, 298, 318; in Daughters, Wives and a Mother, 347; in *Flunky, Work Hard*, 48; in *Meshi*, 214–17; in *Mother*, 237; in *Wife*, 251–52, 254
Humanism, 227, 402; of Naruse, 5–6
Humanist films, 159, 212, 274, 328–29
Human Voice, The (*Una voce umana*, 1948), 192–93
Husband and Wife (*Fufu*, 1953), 247–52, 284, 309; still from, 248

Ichikawa Kon, 376
Identity and individualism, 377
Ide Toshiro, 16, 215, 218, 220, 228, 247, 353–54, 356; on *Brown Eyes*, 254; *Flowing* and, 295; *Late Chrysanthemums* and, 270; on Sugi Yoko, 248; *A Wife's Heart* and, 292
Iida Shinbi, 243–44, 274; on *Daughters, Wives and a Mother*, 342
Iijama Tadashi, 138
Iijimi Takashi, 156; on *When a Woman Ascends the Stairs*, 334
Ikiru (1952), 196
Illness, 5–7, 160, 238–39, 278–81, 391; in Japanese literature, 79; in *Three Sisters*, 92
Imitation of Life (1959), 335
Incest, 259, 261
Independent film, 316, 318, 397
Inoue Tomoichiro, 208
I-novel (*Shishosetsu*), 27, 36, 243
Internationalization, of Japanese women, 395, 402
Irie Takako, 14, 117, 119, 121, 125; in *Mother Never Dies*, 158; in *Sincerity*, 152
Ishimori Nobuo, 328
Issono Akio, 64
Itami Mansaku, 174
Itinerancy, 106–7, 231, 245
Ito Daisuke, 396
Ivy, Marilyn, 172, 332
I Was Born But . . . (1932), 49, 186

Izbicki, Joanne, 175–76, 196
Izumi Kyoka, 141

Jameson, Fredric, 171, 233
Japanese cinema and film industry, 4–5, 18, 34, 296; as "art cinema," 235; ATG and, 316; audience numbers, 316; bombing of Tokyo and, 51–52; burlesque in, 196; censorship and, 87, 132, 151, 168, 182, 208, 226; CIE and, 168, 187; cosmopolitanism of, 79, 395–96, 403; critical neglect of Naruse and, 38; "culture films," 136; export of, 83, 127, 235; film-going of Japanese audiences, 40; Film Law of 1939 and, 132–33, 135; film studies and, 38; *gendai geki* genre and, 52–53; Italian cinema vs., 10, 192–93; kissing scenes and, 187–91; labor unions and, 177, 193–94; as mass medium, 25, 164–65, 235; *moga* (modern girls) in, 48, 80; output of in 1937, 127; rise of independent film and, 316; spectatorship and, 35; *taiyozoku* films (sun tribe films) and, 317–18; television and, 86, 315–16; Tohoscope format and, 226; *See also* Silent films
Japanese classical cinema, 84, 172; American cinema vs., 128–29; Bordwell-Staiger-Thompson model and, 86–87; bourgeois sensibility at P.C.L. and, 90–91, 126; class and, 126; melodrama and, 126–30; mode of production in, 86, 129–30; Naruse's contribution to, 129; Naruse's use of star system and, 89; national culture and, 130; as part of historical formation of modernity, 85, 165; unevenness of Japanese modernity and, 126–28; vernacular modernity and, 85, 89, 127–28; women in, 129
Japanese feminism, 13, 25, 28, 37–38
Japanese literature, 30, 34, 41, 90, 362; cinematic adaption of into melodrama, 247; haiku aesthetics and, 227, 312–14; everyday life and, 314; women and, 313; *Shishosetsu* (I-novel) and, 27, 36, 243; sickness in, 79; women's writing and, 54. *See also* Hayashi Fumiko; Literary adaptations
Japanese modernity, 19; ambivalence and, 245; amnesia about previous stages of, 319; architecture and, 33, 234–35; August 1945 and, 174; boredom and, 374; car themes and, 70, 358–59, 388, 396; in *Every Night Dreams*, 70; failure of, 230; family and, 230; fashion and, 47, 51, 53, 79, 308; female sexuality and, 32; female subjectivity and, 16, 32, 54, 80, 236, 261, 402; feminization of culture and, 54; flamboyant style and, 42–44; foreign films and, 51; gender codes and, 55, 80, 233–34, 245, 269; interwar cinema and, 79–80; Japanese cinema and, 18, 25, 36–37, 45, 128; Japanese nationalism and, 47; Japanese subjects and, 234; mass media and, 86; material culture and, 53, 70, 79; melodrama and, 34, 63; Naruse's techniques of production and, 17–18; *Not Blood Relations* and, 58, 60; P.C.L. and, 84; postwar, 234; ressentiment and, 211; salarymen and, 53; *shinpa* aesthetics and, 41; *shitamachi* settings and, 33; silent film and, 39, 79–80; in *Sincerity*, 155; SKS and, 48–55; unevenness of, 49, 84, 87, 105, 126–27, 155, 190, 388; urban space and, 70, 78–79; utopian sense of possible in, 233, 376; visual language of Naruse in, 37; in wartime, 152, 155, 164; Western modernism and, 26–27, 82; in *Wife! Be Like a Rose!*, 4, 84, 100–101, 105; woman's films and, 32–38, 47; woman's happiness and, 24; women and, 236, 305, 382–83, 403

Japanese nationhood, 277, 279, 283, 403
Japanese subject, 27, 191; American popular culture and, 175; August 1945, 174; democracy and, 174; *shukan* (the epistemic subject) and, 36–37; *shutai* (subject as practical agent) and, 36–37
Jidai-geki films, 220, 222–24
Josei-eiga. *See* Woman's film

Kabuki, 41, 143, 159, 211, 222
Kagawa Kyoko, 29, 228, 237, 239; in *Anzukko*, 304, 309
Kagi (*Odd Obsession*, 1959), 377
Kakehi Masanori, 231
Kano Riho, 83
Kaplan, Caren, 38
Karatani Kojin, 79, 211
Kasahara Ryozo, 353
Katei shosetsu (domestic novels), 30
Kato Daisuke, 228, 238–39, 287, 319
Katsura Nobuko, 314
Katzoff, Beth, 304
Kawabata Yasunari, 9, 44, 81–82, 168, 230, 235; aesthetics of resignation of, 213; and *Dancing Girl*, 211–14; and *Sound of the Mountain*, 261–69; Asakusa, 44, 74, 90–93, 210; heroines of, 262
Kawashima Yuzo, 348
Kayama Yuzo, 319; in *Yearning*, 368, 372
Kelsky, Karen, 395, 402
Kido Shiro, 8, 26, 40–42, 82, 228
Kikuchi Kan, 125–26
Kikuta Kazuo, 361
Kinema Junpo, 10, 26, 200; collective critique of *Three Sisters with Maiden Hearts* in, 95–96; critique of *The Whole Family Works* in, 149–51; critique of *Tsuruhachi and Tsurujiro* in, 138; on *Every Night Dreams*, 66; on *Late Chrysanthemums*, 274; *Mother* and, 236; roundtable discussion with Naruse and critics, 81–82; on *White Beast*, 203

Kinema Junpo annual top ten, 4, 65, 135, 226, 236, 256, 377, 398
Kinoshita, Chika, 38
Kinugasa Teinosuke, 396
Kishida Kunio, 288
Kishi Matsuo, 208
Kissing scenes, 187–91, 224, 344
Kiss, The (*Kuchizuke*, 1955), 231
Kitamura Komatsu, 74
Kitagawa Fuyuhiko, 60, 66
Kitsch, 23, 167, 182–83, 192, 222, 225; in *Battle of the Roses*, 207; in *Both You and I*, 186; in *A Descendant of Urashima Taro*, 181; in *Even Parting is Enjoyable*, 193
Kiyokawa Mieko, 342, 346
Kiyokawa Tamae, 112
Kobayashi Hideo, 53–54
Kobayashi Ichizo, 84–85
Kobayashi Keiju, 228, 250; in *The Stranger within a Woman*, 377–78, 380
Koda Aya, 295, 298–99, 301–3
Kojima Hiroshi, 82
Kokusaku eiga (national policy films), 131, 133, 143, 145; family and, 156; *This Happy Life* as, 159; undermining of national policy propaganda by Naruse, 134–36, 150, 155, 164–66
Kokutai policy, 131–32, 136, 147, 159, 162, 164; *The Song Lantern* and, 140, 143; *The Whole Family Works* and, 151
Kon Wajiro, 54–55, 77
Kracauer, Siegfried, 24, 51, 165
Kuga Yoshiko, 187, 189, 257–58, 260
Kumi (staff) of Naruse, 227–28
Kurishima Sumiko, 65, 73, 296
Kurosawa Akira, 11, 170, 172, 187, 196, 283, 324, 351, 377, 384
Kusabue Mitsuko, 319, 342, 349, 369, 379, 390
Kyoko Hirano, 168, 177, 188, 190, 194
Kyo Machiko, 228, 257–58

Labor unions, 177, 193–94
Land distribution, 317, 323, 327
Lang, Fritz, 77, 319
Late Chrysanthemums (*Bangiku*, 1954), 10, 208, 230, 248, 269–77, 298, 334, 351, 361, 364; still from, 270–71
Late cinemas, 319–20, 397
Late Spring (*Banshun*, 1949), 268
Learn from Experience (*Kafuku* I, II, 1937), 23, 90, 125–27, 212
Lightning (*Inazuma*, 1952), 226, 233, 241–47, 250, 256–57, 290, 313, 361; still from, 246
Lippit, Seiji M., 242–43, 362
Literary adaptations, 4, 81, 91, 121, 126, 141, 168, 214, 218–20, 227, 235; of Hayashi Fumiko, 15–16, 241–42, 251, 254–56, 270, 274, 277–78, 361; of Ishimori Nobuo, 328; of Kawabata, 9, 261–62, 264; of Koda Aya, 295, 298–99; melodrama and, 247; of Muro Saisei, 256–57, 309; in Naruse's films of mid-1950s, 229, 247; *Sudden Rain* and, 288; of *The Thin Line*, 376; of Tokuda Shusei, 304, 306–7; of Wada Den, 324
Little Man, Do Your Best (*Koshiben ganbare*, 1931), 48–51, 53, 68, 97, 183, 382; still from, 50
Lopate, Phillip, 6

MacArthur, Douglas (American General), 177
Magnani, Anna, 192
Magny, Joel, 227
Makoto Ueda, 313
Male characters, 18, 26, 29, 112, 145, 164, 252; in *Five Men in the Circus*, 107; in Kawabata, 213–14; in modernist literature, 383; in Naruse's films of 1960s, 374–75, 378; in *The Stranger within a Woman*, 378; in *Wife*, 254; in *Yearning*, 374–75. *See also* Gender; Salarymen
Male gaze, 65, 340

Man with a Movie Camera (1929), 49
Marnie (1964), 383
Marriage films, 168, 213, 229, 253; *Anzukko* as, 309–12; childless couples and, 255, 290; comedy and, 231–32; films in which "nothing happens" and, 289; in films of 1950s, 247–48, 250–52, 254–55, 261, 284, 288–90, 293, 304, 309–10, 312; *Sudden Rain* as, 284, 288–89; Uehara Ken, 247–48; *A Wife's Heart* as, 289–90, 293
Masao Miyoshi, 27, 31, 34
Masumura Yasuzo, 317
Matsui Sumako, 98
Matsuyama Zenzo, 232, 353, 383
Mayazumi Toshiro, 319
McDonald, Keiko, 215
McElhaney, Joe, 319–20
Meiji period; Naruse's films set in, 18, 22, 138; woman's status in, 30–31
Mellen, Joan, 25–26
Melodrama, 12–13, 45, 90, 280, 401; American cinema of 1950s and, 256, 258; American family melodrama, 258–60; in *Apart from You*, 63; "brushing history against the grain" and, 172; car accidents and, 382; depression, 230; expressive discourse of, 320; female subjectivity and, 44, 80; in *Floating Clouds*, 279; in *The Girl in the Rumor*, 109; Hollywood, 215; Japanese classical cinema and, 126–30; Japanese modernity and, 34, 63, 129; of Kurosawa, 170; in *Learn from Experience*, 126; literary adaptations and, 247; of Mizoguchi, 170; in Naruse's films of mid-1950s, 256, 258–61, 281; in Naruse's films of 1960s, 316–17, 368–69, 373, 389; nationhood and, 170–71; in *Not Blood Relations*, 56–58; occupation films and, 225; in *Older Brother, Younger Sister*, 256, 258, 260; postwar, 34, 170–72, 175; realism and, 34,

373–74; relation to the West and, 171; *Repast* and, 218; in *The Road I Travel with You*, 112–13; *Scattered Clouds* as, 389; sentimentality and, 176, 195; in *Sound of the Mountain*, 261; in *Spring Awakens*, 191; as subversive ideologeme, 170–71; *When a Woman Ascends the Stairs* as, 335; in *Wife*, 252, 254–55; women's culture and, 54; in *Yearning*, 368–69, 373
Mifune Toshiro, 228, 290–91
Mikawa Kiyo, 262
Mikuni Rentaro, 249
Mimasu Aiko, 370
Minnelli, Vicent, 258, 319
Mishima Yukio, 270
Mishuhashi Takajo, 313
Mistresses, 100, 107–8, 252, 338, 354, 356, 397
Mita Ikumi, 140
Mizoguchi, 133–34, 141, 170, 172, 209, 218, 237, 257
Mizuki Yoko, 16, 228, 237, 247, 249; *Untamed* and, 305
Mizukubo Sumiko, 64
Mizumachi Seiji, 121, 150
Mizu-shobai, 230. See also Water trade
Mizutani Yoshie, 349
Moba (modern boys), 39
Mochizuki Yuko, 271
Modern girls (*Moga*), 31, 39, 46–48, 80, 86, 108; in *Not Blood Relations*, 56; in *Street without End*, 78; vernacular modernity and, 47
Modernity, 4–5, 9–10, 17–18, 21, 23, 31; Brechtian, 4, 11; SKS and, 48. See also Japanese modernity
Moga (modern girls), 31, 39, 46–48, 80, 86, 108; in *Not Blood Relations*, 56; in *Street without End*, 78; vernacular modernity and, 47
Mono no aware (sympathetic sadness), 22, 320–21; in *When a Woman Ascends the Stairs*, 338

Monumental films, 133, 135, 137, 147, 161, 165–66
Mori Masayuki, 228, 257, 279, 282; in *When a Woman Ascends the Stairs*, 338; in *Whistling in Kotan*, 328; in *As a wife, as a Woman*, 354
Morita Tama, 311
Morning's Tree-Lined Street (*Asa no namiki michi*, 1936), 90, 115–16; still from, 117
Mother films, 25, 28, 30, 73, 235–39, 276; daughters and, 229; genre revision of, 240–41; *Late Chrysanthemums* and, 274; *Mother Never Dies* (*Haha wa shinazu*, 1942), 156, 158–59; still from, 158
Mother (*Okaasan*, 1952), 2, 16, 22, 226, 236–41; still from, 29, 239
Mr. and Mrs. Swordplay (*Chanbara Fufu*, 1930), 40
Mr. Smith Goes to Washington (1939), 178, 181–82, 224
Mulvey, Laura, 215, 217
Murase Sachiko, 152
Murayama Tomoyoshi, 121, 124
Muro Saisei, 256, 309, 312
Murphy, Joseph, 34
Musicians and music, 96, 178, 210, 217; in *Feminine Melancholy*, 120; in *Five Men in the Circus*, 106–7; in *Flowing*, 301–2; in Naruse's films of 1950s, 228–29, 271, 275, 283, 301–2; in *Okuni*, 222; in postwar film, 176; in *Scattered Clouds*, 389; in *The Song Lantern*, 140; in *Summer Clouds*, 327; in *When a Woman Ascends the Stairs*, 341; in *The Whole Family Works*, 152; in *Yearning*, 373

Nakadai Tatsuya, 14, 306, 319, 348; in *Daughters, Wives and a Mother*, 343, 345; in *When a Woman Ascends the Stairs*, 339
Nakahira Ko, 317

Nakakita Chieko, 29, 228, 243, 319
Nakamura Ganjiro, 321, 323, 327, 335
Nakano Minoru, 97, 100
Nansensu comedies, 8, 46, 53, 57, 90, 151, 186
Naoki Sakai, 36–37
Narboni, Jean, 6–7, 12
Naruse Mikio, 30; character of, 2–3; critical neglect of, 1–2, 6–7, 38; death of, 3, 398; imaginary final film of, 398–99, 401; kissing scenes, 189–91; missing films of, 135; photo of, 8; rank of as director in Japan, 1; retrospectives of, 34–35; in San Sebastian, 2
Naruse Tsumeko (wife of Naruse), 2
National imperialism, 51–52, 171–72, 279, 283, 332–33. See also *Kokutai* policy
Nationalist discourses, 52, 87, 127, 279; Japanese classical cinema and, 128–30; Japanese modernity and, 47; Naruse's undermining of propaganda of, 134–36, 150, 155, 164–66; in silent film, 46–48, 80; in *Wife! Be Like a Rose!*, 102. See also *Kokusaku eiga*; *Kokutai* policy
National policy films. See *Kokusaku eiga*
New wave cinema, 17–18, 317–20, 386
New Woman, 80, 90, 97–98, 129, 305, 400; in films of 1950s, 304, 306–7; in films of 1960s, 317
Nikkatsu studio, 42, 316
Nishigaki Rokuro, 385
Nobugawa Naoki, 243, 247
Nolletti, Arthur, 396
No Regrets for Our Youth (*Waga sishun ni kui nashi*, 1946), 268
Nornes, Marcus, 38
Not Blood Relations (*Nasanu naka*, 1932), 42, 55–60, 356, 382; still from, 59
No theater, 41, 140–41, 211

Now Don't Get Excited (*Nee kofun shicha iya yo*, 1931), 46
Nyonin geijutsu (*Women's Arts*, journal), 361

Office lady, 47, 99, 102, 248
Ohashi Yasuhiko, 346
Okada Mariko, 228, 278, 297, 302
Okada Yoshiko, 59
Okamoto Kihachi, 3, 14
Okubo Kiyo, 83
Okuni and Gohei (*Okuni to Gohei*, 1952), 177, 220–25, 284; still from, 221
Older Brother, Younger Sister (*Ani imoto*, 1953), 10, 256–61, 284, 290, 326; still from, 258
Orientalism, 4
Osaka, 217, 219
Oshima Nagisa, 281–82, 317–19, 386
Ota Takashi, 152
Ozu Yasujiro, 8, 218, 357; on *Floating Clouds*, 12; home-dramas of, 268; *I Was Born But . . .* , 49, 186; Japanese poetry and, 312; Naruse Mikio and, 11–12, 22, 45, 61–62, 120, 217; "pillow shots" of, 61, 127, 312; Shochiku Kamata studios and, 40; silent films of, 45

Parent-child relations, 149; in Naruse's films of mid-1950s, 229
P.C.L. (Photo Chemical Laboratories), 9, 44, 124; bourgeois sensibility of, 90–91, 126; founding of, 84; Japanese culture and, 127; Naruse at, 81–99, 106–7, 115–17, 126–27; Naruse's move to from Shochiku, 82, 84; national cultural mission of, 86–87; production at, 9, 88
Petro, Patrice, 374
Pharr, Susan, 28
Piecemeal style, 42, 45, 401
Polan, Dana, 20
Political corruption, 176, 181, 186
Political films, 178, 181, 183

Pollack, David, 213–14
Popular culture, 6, 90, 121, 160, 163, 166; narratives based in postwar, 15; Naruse's filmmaking style and, 127; production of during war and, 164; war films and, 137; Western influence on, 30–31; woman's films and, 23, 37
Postwar films, 10–11, 27–28, 217–18; Japanese society in, 277–84, 309
Prison films, 203
Prostitution, 63, 78, 203–4, 242; in *Apart from You*, 61; in *Three Sisters*, 95. See also Sexuality
Psychological drama, 4, 176, 187, 191–92, 208, 211, 381; in films of 1960s, 318, 353; in woman's film of 1950s, 318

Quiet Duel, The (1949), 187

Rashomon, 83, 145, 220, 283–84
Ray, Nicholas, 258
Real estate, 229, 243, 275; in *Daughters, Wives and a Mother*, 343
Realism, 5, 10, 399, 401; ethnographic, 252; in *Every Night Dreams*, 66; haiku and, 227; humanism and, 227; interiority in, 211–12; melodrama and, 34, 373–74; in Naruse's films of mid-1950s, 232–33, 299; Naruse's style of, 7, 11, 96, 130, 141, 227; occupation policy and, 212; postwar, 212; social, 130; western influence on Japanese, 41; in *The Whole Family Works*, 149
Rembrandt, 265
Repast (*Meshi*, 1951), 10, 168, 177, 208, 214–20, 223, 226, 229, 242, 247, 251–52, 254, 262, 284, 309, 361, 364; still from, 216
Repression, 258, 260, 267
Rescuing critique, xv, 23–24
Richie, Donald, 28, 44, 46, 86, 130
Road I Travel with You, The (*Kimi to yuku michi*, 1936), 9, 90, 112–15; still from, 114

Roman porno (pink movies), 315
Ross, Kristin, 388
Rossellini, Roberto, 10, 192–93, 218
Ruined Map, The (*Moetsukita chizu*, 1968), 377
Rural films, 106, 154–55, 327, 329, 333, 394

Saeki Hideo, 122
Saito Akira, 376
Saito Ichiro, 16, 229, 301
Sakei Hideo, 119
Salarymen, 13, 26, 30, 186, 256; in *Both You and I*, 183–84; in *Flunky, Work Hard*, 53; Naruse's silent films about, 46; in *Repast*, 216; in *Scattered Clouds*, 389; in *Sound of the Mountain*, 267; in *Sudden Rain*, 284, 287–89
Samurai films, 147–48, 220, 222–23, 324
Sano Shuji, 284–85
Sato, Barbara, 46, 102
Satori, 286, 312, 314
Sato Tadao, 12–13
Scala, André, 227, 265
SCAP (Supreme Commander of Allied Powers), 28, 167, 175, 177, 180, 186, 193, 203
Scattered Clouds (*Midaregumo*, 1967), 3, 17, 317, 320, 322, 383, 389–98; still from, 391
Schermann, Susanne, 7
Screenplay (journal), 354–56
Screenwriters, 16, 247–49, 292
Seidensticker, Edward, 270
Seitai-eiga (Ecological films), 274
Sekine Miwako, 342, 346
Sentimentality, 176, 236, 238; in *Mother*, 247
Sex education, 187–91
Sexuality, 13, 175, 187–91, 217, 276; in *Apart from You*, 63; in *Every Night Dreams*, 66; female, 32; in *Flowing*, 299–300; Naruse's resistance in films of 1960s to, 317; in *Older Brother*,

Sexuality (*continued*)
  Younger Sister, 258–60; in *Sound of the Mountain*, 267; in *Spring Awakens*, 176; in *The Stranger within a Woman*, 379, 381. *See also* Prostitution
Shanghai Moon (*Shanhai no tsuki*, 1941), 135–37
Sherif, Ann, 299
Shimizu Chiyota, 138, 140, 217
Shimura Takashi, 187; in *Whistling in Kotan*, 328
Shincho (journal), 298
Shinjuku Garden, 262, 264–66, 313
Shinojima Makoto, 108
Shinpa theater (new school drama), 8, 17, 26, 52, 63, 88, 90, 108, 112, 121, 130, 138, 145; domestic novels and, 30; female subjectivity and, 80; *geido* films and, 137; Japanese modernity and, 41; *katei shosetsu* (domestic novels) and, 30; Naruse Mikio films and, 39, 42; *Not Blood Relations* and, 56, 58; no theater and cinema and, 141; at Shochiku Kamata, 41–42, 46; *Street without End* and, 76; *Wife! Be Like a Rose!* and, 100–101, 106; woman's stories and, 400
Shirakawa Yumi, 349
Shishosetsu (I-novel), 27, 36, 243
Shitamachi (low city of Tokyo), 218–19, 248, 251, 293–94, 298; in *Flowing*, 298; Japanese modernity and, 33; in *Late Chrysanthemums*, 270, 274; in *Lightning*, 242–45; as setting, 33; slice of life films set in, 348, 351
Shochiku studio, 8–9, 40, 45, 51, 65, 228, 316, 399, 400; *Apart from You* and, 60; Naruse's move from to P.C.L., 82, 84
Shochiku Kamata style (SKS), 39, 61; geisha and, 65; Hollywood model and, 40–42; Japanese modernity and, 48–55; Ozu Yasujiro and, 40; *shinpa* and, 41–42; social inequity in films of, 46; woman's films of, 40–42
Shoe motifs, 62, 184, 186, 206, 233, 399
Shoshetsu (modern Japanese novel), 34
Shoshimin-eiga genre (films about ordinary people), 8, 12, 22, 30, 36, 46, 70, 115, 130, 186, 229, 400; ban of during wartime, 156; *Both You and I* as, 183, 186; departures from, 15, 84; *Every Night Dreams* as, 66; female subjectivity and, 32; Naruse's silent films and, 46; in films of 1960s, 346–47, 70; *Summer Clouds* as, 328; in wartime, 149; women's desires in, 32
Silent films, 7–9, 40–41, 49–77, 95, 126, 399; avant-garde and, 44–45; *benshi* narration and, 67; "calligraphic style" and, 42, 45; class distinctions in, 44–46, 53; close-ups in, 62; commodity culture in, 45; female subjectivity and, 80; flamboyant techniques, 39, 42–44, 78; gender and, 80; hospital scenes and sickbeds in, 79–80; Japanese modernity and, 39, 45, 80; Meiji chocolate in, 45; melodrama in, 63; *moga* (modern girls) in, 47, 56, 78, 80; nationalist discourse and, 46–48, 80; of Ozu, 45; "piecemeal style" and, 42, 45; prostitution in, 78; SKS and, 42; Western modernism and, 44; woman characters in, 43–44, 48; woman's film and, 45
Silverberg, Miriam, 47–48, 55, 79–80
Simmel, George, 51, 70
Sincerity (*Mogokoro*, 1939), 149, 152–55, 351; still from, 153
Singer, Ben, 34, 70
Sirk, Douglas, 217, 258, 335
SKS. *See* Shochiku Kamata style
Slice of life films, 348, 351
Social institutions, 13, 17–18, 77, 317, 340–41, 353, 389

Song Lantern, The (Uta Andon, 1943), 131, 137–38, 140–43, 145, 401; still from, 142
Sound film, 95–96
Sound of the Mountain (Yama no oto, 1954), 10, 15, 212, 247, 261–69, 284, 290, 294, 311, 313, 401; still from, 263
Special effects, 320; in Flunky, Work Hard, 49; in Hit and Run 383, 385–86
Spectatorship, 146, 148; female subjectivity and, 32–38; as mode of travel and dwelling, 37; retrospectives and, 34–35; women and, 29–30
Spiritist films, 158–59, 162
Spivak, Gayatri, 38
Spring Awakens (Haru no mezame, 1947), 175–76, 187–91, 194, 207, 224, 257, 344, 400; still from, 189
Stepchild, The (Nasanu naka, 1932), 42, 55–60, 356, 382; still from, 59
Story of the Last Chrysanthemum (Zangiku monogatari, 1939), 141
Stranger within a Woman, The (Onna no naka ni iru tanin, 1966), 17, 226, 318, 320, 376–83, 397; still from, 378
Stray Dog (Nora inu, 1949), 170, 187, 377
Street without End (Kagiri naki hodo, 1934), 48, 74–79; still from, 75
Suburban life, 285–89
Sudden Rain (Shuu, 1956), 233, 247, 284–89, 309; still from, 285
Sugimoto Heiichi, 274
Sugimura Haruko, 14, 180, 228, 230, 302; in Daughters, Wives and a Mother, 343; in Late Chrysanthemums, 270
Sugiyama Heiichi, 293
Sugi Yoko, 14, 228, 249, 290; in Husband and Wife, 247–48; in Professor Ishinaka, 196–97
Suicide, 12, 92, 97, 113, 123, 158, 254–55, 281, 397; in Hit and Run, 385, 388; in Scattered Clouds, 293

Summer Clouds (Iwashigumo, 1958), 17, 317, 319, 322–28, 397; still from, 325
Surrealism, 182
Suzuki Hideo, 231
Suzuki Hiroshi, 16

"Taisho democracy," 44, 46
Taisho era films, 306–7
Taiyozoku films (sun tribe films), 292, 306, 317–18
Takamine Hideko, 3, 16, 19, 22, 47, 228, 248; in Daughters, Wives and a Mother, 342–43; in A Descendant of Urashima Taro, 178–79, 181; facial expression and posture of, 230–31; in Floating Clouds, 277, 279–82; in Flowing, 295, 298, 303; in Hideko, 161–63; in Hit and Run, 318, 382, 386–87; in The Kiss, 231–32; in Lightning, 242–46, 257; in roundtable discussion on Flowing, 301–2; in films of 1960s, 319, 333, 341–43, 353–54, 357, 361, 368; turning down of role in Wife by, 254; in Untamed, 304–6; visit to Naruse in last years of life, 398; in A Wanderer's Notebook, 361, 365–66; in When a Woman Ascends the Stairs, 208, 333, 336, 341, 390, 400; in As a Wife, as a Woman, 354–55; in A Wife's Heart, 290–91; in A Woman's Status, 357; in A Woman's Story, 359; in Yearning, 368, 372–73
Takamine Mieko, 168, 213; in Wife, 251–53
Takarada Akira, 319, 348
Takeda Ume, 16–17
Takemitsu Toru, 319, 389
Tale of Archers at the Sanjusangendo, A (Sanjusangendo toshiya montogatari, 1945), 137, 146–49, 164; still from, 148
"Tales of Sound and Fury" (Elsaesser), 258
Tamai Masao, 3, 16, 205, 228–29, 286–87, 376, 400; Summer Clouds and,

Tamai Masao (*continued*)
    322; *When a Woman Ascends the Stairs* and, 333
Tanaka Kinuyo, 14, 168, 208, 230, 237, 239; in *Flowing*, 296, 298
Tanaka Sumie, 16, 215, 218, 228, 242, 247, 301–2; *Flowing* and, 295; *Late Chrysanthemums* and, 270
Tanami Yatsuko, 253
Tanizaki Junichiro, 168, 177, 224
Television, 86, 315–16
Tenko, 134
Teruyo Nogami, 228
Teshigahara Hiroshi, 377
Tessier, Max, 386
Thin Line, The (*Onna no naka ni iru tanin*, 1966), 17, 226, 318, 320, 376–83, 397; still from, 378
This Happy Life (*Tanoshiki kana jinsei*, 1944), 159–60, 162
Three Sisters with Maiden Hearts (*Otome-gokoro sannin shimai*, 1935), 9, 16, 44, 91–96, 184, 210; stills from, 94–95
Thrillers, 77, 203, 318, 376, 383; *The Stranger within a Woman* as, 380
Tochuken Kumoemon (1936), 111–12, 127, 137
Toda Takao, 219
Tohoscope format, 17, 226, 321–22, 327, 354, 370; in *Scattered Clouds*, 389; in *When a Woman Ascends the Stairs*, 333
Toho studio, 2, 9–10, 16, 121, 125, 132, 140, 176, 191, 220, 228, 242, 256, 397; absorption of P.C.L. of, 85; film noir of, 377; labor unions and, 177; labor unrest at, 193; Naruse's films from 1958–1967 in, 315–16, 318–19; Naruse's value to, 318; "producer system" of production, 227; *Sound of the Mountain* and, 261–62; strikes at, 194; *A Wanderer's Notebook* and, 361
Tokato Sachio, 101

Tokuda Shusei, 235, 304, 306–7
Tokunaga Sunao, 151
Tokyo, 30, 33, 201; in *The Angry Street*, 198; in *Approach of Autumn*, 351–52; bombing of, 51–52; in *Every Night Dreams*, 70; in *Feminine Melancholy*, 117; Hayashi Fumiko and, 16; in *Learn from Experience*, 125; in *Lightning*, 241; *Mother* and, 237; in Naruse's films of 1960s, 348, 351–53, 358; Shochiku Kamata studio in, 39–40; in *Sound of the Mountain*, 261; in *Sudden Rain*, 284; in *When a Woman Ascends the Stairs*, 333, 341; in *Wife! Be Like a Rose!*, 101; women in postwar, 269–77
Tokyo Story (*Tokyo Monogatari*, 1950), 268, 357
Tokyo Twilight (*Tokyo boshoku*, 1957), 12
Torrance, Richard, 305, 308
Tosaka Jun, 52–53
Tourism, 329–31, 397
Toys as motif, 53, 58, 60, 68, 70, 154–55, 255, 381
Traffic in Souls (1913), 77–78
Transnational feminism, 37, 322, 402
Transportation accidents, in *Flunky, Work Hard*, 49; in films of 1930s, 79; in films of 1960s, 321; in *Street without End*, 74. *See also* Car accidents and themes
Traveling Actors (*Tabi yakusha*, 1940), 159–60
Tsuboi Sakae, 237
Tsukigata Ryunosuke, 111
Tsukuba Yukiko, 59
Tsuma-mono (wife films), 28, 30, 56, 235, 247, 356
Tsumura Hideo, 203
Tsuneishi Fumiko, 13, 123
Tsuruhachi and Tsurujiro (1938), 131, 137–38; still from, 139
Tsukasa Yoko, 14, 16, 349–50; as em-

462   INDEX

blematic actress of 1960s, 319; in
  Hit and Run, 318, 383; in *Scattered
  Clouds*, 389, 392, 396, 400; visit to
  Naruse in last years of life, 398
Tsutsumi Masako, 44, 91, 93, 95
Twenty-Year-Old Youth (*Hatachi no
  seishun*, 1946), 190

Uehara Ken, 188, 228, 231, 249, 272,
  305; in *Daughters, Wives and a
  Mother*, 343–44; in marriage films,
  247, 261; in *Wife*, 251–52
Ugetsu (1953), 257
Umezono Ryuko, 89, 91, 93–95, 108, 110
Uno, Kathleen, 169
Uno Jukichi, 201
Untamed (*Arakure*, 1957), 19, 230, 236,
  304–9; still from, 306
Until Victory Day (*Shori no hi made*,
  1945), 135–37
Urabe Kumeko, 257, 319
Urban space and culture, 22, 35–36,
  44, 51, 65–67, 71, 146, 206, 208, 210,
  218, 382; in *Apart from You*, 60; city-
  country dichotomy, 101, 104–5, 155;
  in *Wife! Be Like a Rose!*, 101; class
  and, 66; in *Every Night Dreams*,
  66–67; female subjectivity and, 243;
  in *The Girl in the Rumor*, 109; in *Hit
  and Run*, 384, 386; in *Horoki*, 362;
  interwar Japanese modernity and,
  78–79; Japanese cinema and, 70;
  Japanese modernity and, 33, 70; in
  Lightning, 242–44; in Naruse's films
  of 1950s, 229, 236, 243–44, 257, 298,
  303; in Naruse's films of 1960s, 351,
  384, 386, 389; in *Not Blood Relations*,
  58; in *Scattered Clouds*, 389; in silent
  film, 39, 43; spectatorship and, 37; in
  Street without End, 77–78; in *When
  a Woman Ascends the Stairs*, 338. See
  also Ginza; Shitamachi; Tokyo

Vermeer, 265
Vernacular modernism, 24, 31–32, 43–
  44, 51, 79, 87–90, 131, 401–2; in *Avalanche*, 124; Hollywood cinema and,
  25; Japanese classical cinema and,
  85, 127–28; in *Lightning*, 247; *moga*
  (modern girl) and, 47; Naruse's films
  of mid-1950s and, 277, 312; Naruse's
  postwar films and, 224, 234; Naruse's
  wartime films and, 135, 164–66; in
  Okuni and Gohei, 224; in *Wife! Be
  Like a Rose!*, 105
Vertov, Dziga, 49
Voyage to Italy, 218

Wada Den, 324
Wada-Marciano, Mitsuyo, 40–41, 47–
  48, 65–66; on *Every Night Dreams*,
  70
Wakabayashi Eiko, 377
Wanderer's Notebook, A (*Horoki*, 1962),
  47, 321, 359, 361–68, 383, 386, 397; still
  from, 365
Warhol, Andy, 398
Wartime films (1938–1945), 131, 134–37,
  145, 148–59
Water trade (*mizu-shobai*), 13, 116, 208,
  230, 275, 350, 353, 360, 400; in *Apart
  from You*, 60; silent films set in,
  46; in *When a Woman Ascends the
  Stairs*, 333–34, 337
Way of Drama, The (*Shibaido*, 1944), 9,
  137–38, 143, 145; still from, 144
Weather and weather imagery, 6, 217,
  227, 284–86, 290, 312, 380, 392
Weil, Elsie, 104
Western literature, 362
Western men, Japanese women's attraction to, 395, 402
Western modernism, 27, 82; silent film
  and, 44; denunciation of during
  wartime, 132
When a Woman Ascends the Stairs
  (*Onna ga kaidan o agaru toki*, 1960),
  17, 208, 317, 322, 333–41, 348, 390,
  397; still from, 336

Whistling in Kotan (*Kotan no kuchibue*, 1959), 328–33
White Beast (*Shiroi yaju*, 1950), 169, 177, 194–95, 203–7, 382; still from, 205
White Woman (1933), 78
Whole Family Works, The (*Hataraku ikka*, 1939), 9, 131, 149–52, 166, 351; still from, 150
Widescreen, 17, 320, 322, 326, 328, 332, 354, 397
Wife! Be Like a Rose! (*Tsuma yo bara no yo ni*, 1935), 4–5, 9–10, 42, 82, 87, 89–90, 99–106, 356; still from, 103–4
Wife films (*tsuma-mono*), 28, 30, 56, 235, 247, 356
Wife's Heart, A (*Tsuma no kokoro*, 1956), 236, 289–95, 322, 369; still from, 291
Wife (*Tsuma*, 1953), 247, 251–56, 284, 364; still from, 253
Williams, Linda, 129, 374
Woman's film, 1–2, 17–18, 25, 118, 127, 145, 318, 328, 376; anthropology and, 30; depiction of postwar society and, 277–84; emotionalism in, 28; essentialism in, 31; female subjectivity and, 28; film noir and, 380; *Flowing* as, 295; freedom and, 262, 266; *haha-mono* (mother films), 28, 30; *Hit and Run* as, 382; Hollywood context and, 26, 28–30; home-dramas and, 37; Japanese modernity and, 32–38, 47; *Late Chrysanthemums* as, 274; melodrama and, 28, 260; modern girls (*moga*) and, 31; Naruse Mikio and, 31–32, 219, 224, 399; Naruse's from 1952–1958, 27, 226, 262, 266; in Naruse's films of 1960s, 353–54, 358–61, 368, 382, 397; popular culture and, 23, 37; in postwar Tokyo, 269; in prison, 203; *shinpa* drama and, 41–42, 400; silent films and, 45, 47; SKS and, 40–42; *Sound of the Mountain* as, 266; *Summer Clouds* as, 324; in Tokyo, 270, 274, 358; *tsuma-mono* (wife films), 28; utopian sense of possible in, 233–34, 236, 265, 280, 303, 308–9; *When a Woman Ascends the Stairs* as, 338
Woman's Sorrows, A (*Nyonin aishu*, 1937), 9, 90, 117–21, 368, 400; still from, 119
Woman's Status (*Onna no za*, 1961), 316, 353–54, 357, 360, 368–69
Woman's Story, A (*Onna no rekishi*, 1963), 320–21, 353–54, 358–60; still from, 359
Women of the Night (*Yoru no onnatachi*, 1948), 209
Women poets, 313–14
Women's movement, 27, 236, 304
Women's rights, 28, 31–32, 207; *Dancing Girl* and, 213; during occupation, 168–69; in 1950s, 27
Women's writing, 27, 34, 54, 219, 243, 362; Naruse's interest in, 219

Yagi Ryuichiro, 181
Yamada Isuzu, 14, 138, 142, 145, 164, 302; in *Flowing*, 295, 298
Yamada Nobuo, 319; *Scattered Clouds* and, 391
Yamamoto Kajiro, 396
Yamamoto Reizaburo, 257
Yamamura So, 203, 228, 261, 263, 265; in *Anzukko*, 311
Yamane Sadao, 1, 118, 227, 318; on *A Wanderer's Notebook*, 361
Yasuka, 321
Yasumi Toshio, 222
Yearning (*Midareru*, 1964), 16, 236, 316–17, 354, 368–76, 383, 392; still from, 372
Yokohama, 65–66, 70–71, 384–86, 388
Yokoyama Entatsu, 183, 185
Yoshida Yoshishige, 12
Yoshikawa Mitsuko, 64

Yoshimoto, Mitsuhiro, 6, 10–11, 170–72, 176, 211; on *Floating Clouds*, 279–80
Youth culture, 17, 320, 352; film noir and, 377
Yuki Shigeko, 294

Zaibatsu (family-centered wealth), 177, 182
Zen Buddhism, 286, 312, 314
Zuihitsu (essay-like), 300

CATHERINE RUSSELL
is a professor of film studies at Concordia University.
She is the author of *Narrative Mortality: Death, Closure, and New Wave
Cinemas* and *Experimental Ethnography: The Work of Film in the Age of Video*,
and editor of a special issue of *Camera Obscura*, "New Women
of the Silent Screen: China, Japan, Hollywood."

Library of Congress Cataloging-in-Publication Data
Russell, Catherine
The cinema of Naruse Mikio : women and Japanese modernity / Catherine Russell.
p. cm.
Includes bibliographical references and index.
ISBN *978-0-8223-4290-8 (cloth : alk. paper)* —ISBN *978-0-8223-4312-7 (pbk. : alk. paper)*
1. Naruse, Mikio, 1905–1969—Criticism and interpretation.
2. Women in motion pictures. I. Title.
PN1998.3.N37R87 2008
791.4302′33092—dc22
2008013488